Y0-DXF-217

__Author Index (Volumes I-II)

AUTHOR
PRICE GUIDES

AUTHOR PRICE GUIDES

Volume One
REVISED

Compiled
by

Allen *and* Patricia Ahearn

With the assistance
of
Carl Hahn

Q&B

Rockville, Maryland

ISBN: 1-883060-04-4

Q&B

Quill & Brush
Box 5365
Rockville, MD 20848

For
Our Grandchildren
(the collectors, dealers, librarians,
writers and publishers
of the future)

John
Justin
Jacqueline
Noelle
Kelley
Ariana
Matthew
Thomas
Michael
Stephanie
and
Bridgette

CONTENTS

ACKNOWLEDGMENTS

We wish to thank the dealers whose catalogs we have used not only in compiling these guides initially, but in improving them over the years. These dealers are listed in the last section of this book. We want to specifically thank those dealers, collectors, librarians and publishers who took the time to provide additional detailed information to us - Alan Andres, Allan Asselstine, David Axelrod, George Banister, Audrey Bell, Bill Berger, Seth Berner, Christiana Blake, Kay Bourne, Chris Bready, Matt Bruccoli, Jackson Bryer, Robert Crass, Randy Himmel, Robert Hittel, William Holland, Robert Kent, Jeff Klaess, John Knott, Frederick R. Longan, David MacLean, Phil McComish, Charles Michaud, Hans Petzoldt, Len Rzepczynski, Andre Rombs, Daren Salter, Clair Schulz, Jim Trepanier, Robert Van Norman, David Van Vactor, Jim Visbeck and Floyd Watkins.

A special thanks to all those cited in the preambles to the individual guides.

Without the help of all of these people, the guides would not be possible.

INTRODUCTION

We started the *Author Price Guides* (APGs) in 1985. The market has changed drastically since that time. Prices for highly collected books have soared. We had always thought that fine copies of first editions were undervalued in the 60's, 70's and early 80's. Now we see prices that astound us, but do not seem to be unrealistic for truly fine copies. We believe the guides have helped expand the interest in first edition collecting and hope all who use them find them useful.

The *Author Price Guides* are intended to provide sufficient information to identify the first edition (first printing) of particular books (in hand) and provide estimates for these books as of the date of this book.

The *Author Price Guides* are prepared based on available information in bibliographies, dealer catalogs, auction records and our personal experience buying and selling first editions through our store, the Quill & Brush.

The series was started because there are few price guides covering all of an individual author's books; and the basic information necessary to identify first editions is not always available, even when "complete" bibliographies have been published.

In order to arrive at the price estimates, we have used auction records and all catalogs received over the last five years, as well as our own experience of over 30 years in the market. We realize that it is possible that some of the estimates may be unrealistically low or high but we believe that the vast majority of the estimates are in the ball park, plus or minus 20%. Some of the prices may seem high in relation to a particular bookseller's personal experience, however, the estimated prices are for copies without defects, and unfortunately most copies do have some defects. Booksellers usually rationalize these defects as minimal, but collectors find any defect is a good excuse not to buy. This is the reason we have provided estimates with and without dustwrappers. The point is that a copy in a well worn and chipped dustwrapper may **not** be worth much more than the APG estimate for a very good to fine copy without dustwrapper. Conversely, a very fine to mint copy of a book may be worth considerably more than the APG estimate.

The price estimates included in the APG's reflect current estimates and not projections. As such the APG's price estimates are not intended to place an upper limit on what a collector or librarian should pay for a fine copy, the estimates are, after all, just a guide based on an informed opinion. We have published a price guide to the identification and price of first books (1975, 1978, 1982, 1985 1989 and 1995 {latter two published by Putnams}). An analysis of the prices in the last edition indicates only about one percent of the titles decreased in price over a ten year period while some increased 30 times in value. This is not a sales pitch for investing in first editions, (or perhaps it is if you are willing to wait ten years), but is only mentioned to make the point that historically the prices of first editions have risen and we do not believe it would be reasonable to expect the APG price estimates to hold steady when dealers find the demand for certain titles indicate higher prices. It should also be understood that in most cases these dealers have paid higher prices in order to purchase the books for resale.

Many, probably most books were preceded by proofs or advance copies in paperwraps and are only listed if we can identify something about them in detail. Therefore, we include uncorrected proofs or advance reading copies in the guides only when we can indicate the color of the cover.

"A" items are the primary works of an author and we include all books, pamphlets and broadsides. In addition, we might occasionally include books edited by the authors and books that include introductions or forewords by the author. We do not include anthologies which include the author's work or magazine appearances.

The number of copies in the first printing will be included if known. We are attempting to collect this information but must admit it is not easy. Our experience thus far indicates that the most effective way to obtain the quantities is to find someone who works for the publishing house and is willing to take the time to locate the records (if they still exist) or have them located. We have had some success with Delacorte, Knopf, Little Brown, Houghton Mifflin, New Directions, Norton, Putnams, Simon & Schuster, and Viking. Even these publishers have changed personnel and we find when we go back we are not successful in getting information; thus we would appreciate any assistance with publishers that you could provide. Our goal, over time, is to obtain the quantities, ascertain that publishers' records do not exist, or that the information will not be released by the publisher. We have recorded data from *Publishers Weekly* and put (PW) after the quantities derived from this source. We believe the users should be aware these quantities may be overstated in some cases. The differences in the initial quantity announced in *Publishers Weekly* and the actual production quantity, if reduced, reflects the fact that the advance orders from booksellers did not support the larger print run. We are keeping records of our sources for the quantities and would be happy to furnish this information to bibliographers who have legitimate need.

We regularly update the APG's and believe this will afford an opportunity not only to update price estimates but also increase the accuracy of the information contained in each APG.

We hope the guides prove useful and that their content and accuracy will improve over succeeding years.

INSTRUCTIONS FOR USE

NUMBER - The individual numbered entries are entered chronologically based on the information available to the compilers at the time of preparation. Within each individual numbered entry the various printings are also listed chronologically with the following arbitrary sequence given to books that were published *simultaneously*:

signed lettered copy
signed numbered copy

hardbound trade edition
trade edition in paperwraps

We try to ascertain the precedence of U.S. or U.K. editions but, if we have no publication information, we assume the country of origin of the author would be the first.

TITLE - The first entry after the number is the title of the book in capital letters. The titles of the individual books are shown as they appear on the title pages (some abbreviations were used in the titles).

PUBLISHER - The second entry is the name of the publisher as it appears on the title page. If the publisher's name does not appear on the title page, the publisher's entry is enclosed in parenthesis, e.g. (Viking).

PLACE OF PUBLICATION - The third entry is the city of publication as it appears on the title page. If the city does not actually appear on the title page this entry is included in parenthesis, e.g. (NY). If more than one place is listed on the title page only the primary location, usually New York or London will be shown.

DATE - The fourth entry is the year the book was published. If the date of publication is not actually printed on the title page, the year will appear in this entry in parenthesis, e.g. (1971). Dates in parenthesis will be the date the book was copyrighted unless other information is available. If the date of publication or copyright date do not appear in the book "no-date" or the abbreviation "n-d" will appear and the date will be in parenthesis if known.

EDITION - The fifth entry is a code number which provides information on how to identify the first printing (first edition) of the particular book:

[ ]   The open bracket after a title means the bibliography does not include enough information to identify the first edition; and we have not actually seen a copy. It will be noted that in many cases where there is an open bracket, the place or date may be in parenthesis on the title page. In these cases, we obtained this information from other

dealer catalogs, as most dealers are conscientious in putting the place and date in parenthesis if they do not appear on the title page. Specific information to fill in these blanks would, of course, be welcomed.

[0] The book contains *no* statement of printing or edition. Usually only the copyright information and publisher, and perhaps the printer.

[1] The copyright page actually states the edition -"First Printing," "First Edition," "First Impression," "Published 19--," "First Published in 19--," and *does not* indicate any later printing. The important thing is that it actually indicates it is a first and/or includes the date and **does not state** any later printing information.

[2] This entry is for limited editions. In addition to any of the other methods of indicating the edition, these books contain a separate page (although, occasionally it might be on the copyright page), which furnishes any or all of the following detailed information - publisher, printer, date of publication, type of paper used, number of copies, the number of the particular book and the author's signature. These separate pages are bound either in the front of the book preceding the text or immediately following the last page of text. The inclusion of this page in the book is the most important factor in identifying these particular editions.

[3] The copyright page may or may not state "First Edition." "First Printing," etc. (as in [1] above) but more importantly it has a series of numbers or letters containing either a "1" or an "A"; i.e., "1 2 3 4 5...," "1 3 5 7 9 11 10 8 6 4 2," or "A B C D E F.." etc. All books (with the exceptions noted in [4] below) containing a series of numbers or letters without the "1" or "A," are later printings, **even if the book states "First Edition."**

[4] This designation is for either Random House; and Harcourt up until 1984. Both state "First Edition" on the copyright page. Random House includes a series of numbers starting with "2" and Harcourt a series of letters starting with "B." Both publishers remove the statement

"First Edition" on the second printing of the book. Harcourt we believe in 1984 (based on Alice Walker's books) changed to using "A B C D ..." on their first editions. We assume they take both the "A" and the statement "First Edition" off on the second printing.

[5]   This designates methods used by the following publishers. The user will be able to tell which of the following is applicable for a particular book by checking under the publisher of the book in the second entry of the guide (publisher).

APPLETON - Used the numerical identification "(1)" at the foot of the last text page of the book. This was changed to a "(2)" on the second printing, "(3)" on the third printing, etc.

GEORGE H. DORAN - Placed a design "GHD" on the copyright page of the first printing and removed it on later printings.

FARRAR & RINEHART - Placed "FR" on the copyright page of the first printing and removed it on later printings.

FARRAR & STRAUS - Placed the letters "FS" on the copyright page of the first printing and removed it on later printings.

RINEHART & CO. - Placed an "R" in a circle on the copyright page of the first printing and removed it on later printings.

CHARLES SCRIBNER'S SONS - Placed the letter "A" on the copyright page of the first printing and removed it on later printings, starting in 1930. In the 1950's Scribner started using a letter and a series of numbers starting with an "A" on the First Printings [e.g. A-6.65(v)] and changing to a "B" on the Second Printings [e.g. B-8.66(v)]. This code, [5], applies to any book Scribner published using either the "A" alone or in a series.

PAPERWRAPS (wraps) - The inclusion of "wraps" indicates this edition of the book was not hardbound, but issued in paperwraps. Alternatively, if "wraps" does not appear, the book is hardbound and has a dustwrapper unless otherwise stated.

NUMBER OF COPIES - This entry indicates the total number of copies (cc) in the particular edition, if known. It also indicates if the book is a numbered (no) or lettered (ltr) copy and if it was signed (sgd) by the author. If the number includes (PW) it means the source was *Publishers Weekly*, which means the number is usually a maximum as there are many instances where lower first printings were actually ordered based on advance sales.

ISSUE POINTS | OTHER DETAILS - If there is more than one issue of a particular first edition, the points necessary to identify the issue are furnished. This entry may also include a comment or other information.

PAGE NUMBERS - If page and line numbers are necessary to identify issues they are shown as follows - page 87 line 13 = "p.87:13."

REFERENCE - Each APG will list the bibliographical source or sources for that guide. If a particular APG has more than one reference, it can be assumed the primary source, reference (a) has been used for those books covered and Ref.b thereafter. In other words, if Ref.a was published in 1975, it was used for books up to 1975 unless otherwise stated; and if Ref.b was published in 1990, it would have been used from 1975 to 1990 unless otherwise stated. If certain editions or issue points were obtained from specific dealer catalogs, the names of the firm and catalog date will be shown.

PRICES - The prices after each entry are the compiler's estimates of the retail prices current as of the date of the price guide. The *first* number is the estimated price for the book without its dustwrapper or without the original box or slipcase. The *second* number is the estimated price of the book in its original dustwrapper and/or box/slipcase on books published in 1920 or later. If only one price is shown, the particular book was issued in paperwraps, or was published before 1920.

The prices shown are estimates based on the compiler's knowledge of the current market and should be considered as such. The first edition marketplace is a volatile one, based on supply and demand. The prices for certain books have risen greatly over the last few years, while the majority of books have shown only modest price rises, usually keeping pace with inflation but not doubling or tripling in price annually as (relatively) few books have done. The compilers make no pretensions that these guides are perfectly accurate. In the final analysis each user will have to make their own judgment in evaluating the book-in-hand. The guide, hopefully, will prove useful in arriving at an informed judgment.

No value has been assigned (NVA) to a title if the quantity was so small that a copy is truly rare; if we have not seen a copy or a recorded price and are not sure if it is common or scarce; or if we know a title has been sold at what appears to us to be a relatively high price, and we do not feel comfortable with that price as an accurate estimate.

ABBREVIATIONS:

cc	copies
ltd	limited
no	numbered
NVA	No Value Assigned
PW	*Publishers Weekly*
sgd	signed
( )	indicates that information contained therein is not on the title page of the book; or miscellaneous information
+	used at the end of a title which includes the words "And Other Stories (Poems/Essays)"
...	indicates that the complete title or other information has been abbreviated

Note: We have abbreviated the places of publication using standard abbreviations, i.e. NY=New York

EXAMPLE:

013a: DANTE Faber & Faber L (1929) [1] 2,000 cc.
Gray dustwrapper printed in blue and black. Earliest
state of dustwrapper has no review excerpts on front
flap and back cover $50/250

Translation:

013a: {the author's 13th book in the price guide} DANTE {title}
Faber & Faber {publisher} L {London} (1929) {date not on title
page} [1] {states "First printing"/"First published..." etc.} 2,000 cc
{number of copies} Gray dustwrapper printed in blue... {issue
points} $50/250 {$50 without a dw | $250 with dw}

CONDITION:

1975 to 1995: These are really "modern" first editions. Ninety-
nine percent of these books are fiction or poetry. Because
they have been published so recently, the prices listed
herein would be for very fine copies in **DUST-
WRAPPERS** (unless in wraps or a limited edition in
slipcase) with *NO DEFECTS* (including such minor things
as price-clipped dustwrappers, former owners' names
written in, bookplates, remainder marks on bottom page
edges, closed tears or tape repairs in the dustwrappers--
even though there may be no actual loss of paper on the
dustwrappers).

1945 to 1974: These books are a little older, but still copies must
be in **ORIGINAL DUSTWRAPPERS** (unless in wraps or
a limited edition in slipcase) with no major defects. These
books do not have to look as new as the foregoing (1970-
90). Also, the price-clipped dustwrapper and closed tears
would be more acceptable, but the book has to be fine with
the dustwrapper showing only minor wear, fading, or
soiling.

1920 to 1944: The book must be very good to fine with only
minimal (if any) soiling, **IN A DUSTWRAPPER** (unless
in wraps or a limited edition in slipcase) that is clean with

only minimal soiling or fading and only a few small chips (1/8 inch or less) and closed tears.

1890 to 1919: The book must be clean and bright with no loss or tears on the edges. The estimated prices are for copies without dustwrappers. It should be noted that books published in multiple volumes (usually three volumes, but also two and four volume editions), are rare and prices here are for very good copies in matching condition. Fine to very fine copies would probably bring much more.

THE AUTHORS

James Agee

JAMES AGEE
1905 - 1955

James Agee was born in Knoxville, Tennessee. He wrote poetry all his life, but only had one book of poems (his first) published during his lifetime. His second book was finished and copyrighted in 1939 but not published until 1941. Most of the critical reviews were unfavorable. Perhaps due to Agee's claim of dealing with the subject "not as journalists, sociologists, politicians, entertainers, humanitarians, priests, or artists, but seriously."

Agee's attitude was summed up by Peter Ohlin in his book *Agee* (Juan Obolensky, New York, 1966). Agee's career was "unfashionable and in constant conflict with what the times demanded...he managed to find fault with all the movements that have shaped so much of twentieth-century art, politics, and life. As a result he seemed to produce very little of significance compared with the authors who embraced new movements and took their places in the vanguard of more or less popular opinions...though his talents were generally recognized [they] ...were regarded more as indication of future masterpieces than as achievements in their own right." He was posthumously awarded the Pulitzer Prize for literature in 1958 for *A Death In The Family*.

Agee also wrote the following film scripts which have not been published (ref.b):

> THE QUIET ONE (1948)
> IN THE STREET (1952)
> GENGHIS KHAN (1952)
> WHITE MANE (1953)
> ABRAHAM LINCOLN (1953)
> GREEN MAGIC (1955)
> WILLIAMSBURG (uncompleted) (1955)

REFERENCES:

(a) Bruccoli & Clark. FIRST PRINTINGS OF AMERICAN AUTHORS. Volume 1. Detroit: Gale Research (1977).

(b) Moreau, Genevieve. THE RESTLESS JOURNEY OF JAMES AGEE. New York: Wm. Morrow & Co., 1977.

001a: PERMIT ME VOYAGE   Yale University
New Haven 1934 [0] $150/650

002a: LET US NOW PRAISE FAMOUS MEN
Houghton Mifflin Boston 1941 [0] 2,416 cc
(Publisher's records indicate 25 additional bound
copies -proofs?). Photographs by Walker Evans $150/600

002b: LET US NOW PRAISE FAMOUS MEN
Houghton Mifflin Boston (1960) [0] 5,000 cc.
Includes a new foreword by Evans and additional
photographs not in the original edition $25/100

002c: LET US NOW PRAISE FAMOUS MEN
Peter Owen L 1965 [0] $25/100

003a: KNOXVILLE: SUMMER OF 1915...
Schirmer NY 1949 [0] Musical score - Samuel
Barber's music, Agee's words $350.

003b: KNOXVILLE: SUMMER   1915...
Aliquando (Toronto 1970) [] 100 cc. An excerpt
from his book *A Death in the Family* (Chloe's
Books 1/95). $250.

003c: KNOXVILLE: SUMMER 1915...   Caliban
Press (1986) [2] 125 cc. Leather spine and cloth,
portrait of Agee by Mark Summers (J.A. Dermont -
List A 1987) $150.

004a: THE MORNING WATCH   (Botteghe
Oscure) Rome 1950 [0] Wraps. An offprint with

the statement on the copyright page "For Private Circulation Only" (Joseph the Provider Books 10/95) $1,250.

004b: THE MORNING WATCH   Houghton Mifflin Boston 1951 [0] 4,000 cc $75/250

004c: THE MORNING WATCH   Secker & Warburg L 1952 [0] $40/175

005a: NOA NOA: A SCREENPLAY   Oceanic Productions No place 1953 [] Mimeographed sheets bound with metal fasteners (Joseph Dermont 7/90) $500.

006a: A DEATH IN THE FAMILY   McDowell NY (1957) [0] Wraps. Proof copy with cover of trade dustwrapper $350.

006b: A DEATH IN THE FAMILY   McDowell NY (1957) [0] First word on p.80 is "walking." Title page printed in blue. Top edge stained blue-gray. Awarded the 1958 Pulitzer Prize for Literature $100/175

006c: A DEATH IN THE FAMILY   McDowell NY (1957) [0] First word on p.80 is "waking." Title page printed in black. Top edge unstained $15/75

006d: A DEATH IN THE FAMILY   Gollancz L 1958 [0] $20/100

007a: AGEE ON FILM McDowell NY (1958) [] Uncorrected Proof spiral bound at top edge. Made up from actual trimmed galley sheets. The words "On Film" omitted from the title page (Joseph The Provider Books 12/94) $250.

007b: AGEE ON FILM McDowell (NY 1958) [0] $12/50

007c: AGEE ON FILM Peter Owen L 1963 [0] $12/50

008a: AGEE ON FILM - VOLUME TWO McDowell (NY 1960) [1] $12/50

008b: AGEE ON FILM - VOLUME TWO Peter
Owen L 1965 [0] $10/50

009a: LETTERS OF JAMES AGEE TO FATHER
FLYE Braziller NY 1962 [0] $10/40

009b: LETTERS OF JAMES AGEE TO FATHER
FLYE Peter Owen L (1964) [1] $10/40

009c: LETTERS OF JAMES AGEE TO FATHER
FLYE Houghton Mifflin B 1971 [] New preface
and previously unpublished letters (ref.b) $10/35

010a: FOUR EARLY STORIES Cummington
West Branch 1964 [2] 285 no. cc. Wraps.
Collected by Elena Harap, illustrated by Keith
Achepohl. Issued in handmade paper dustwrapper $350.

011a: A WAY OF SEEING Viking NY (1965) []
Advance unbound sheets stitched in drab wraps
(James Jaffe 2/92) $300.

011b: A WAY OF SEEING Viking NY (1965) []
Photographs by Helen Levitt $40/200

KNOXVILLE: SUMMER 1915 See 003

011c: A WAY OF SEEING Horizon NY 1981 [2]
250 sgd no cc. Enlarged edition with corrected text
and 24 additional photos. Folio in boards and
slipcase, signed by Levitt (Barry Scott #11) $150/250

012a: MANY ARE CALLED Houghton Mifflin B
1966 [1] 2,000 cc. Written by Walker Evans,
introduction by Agee $35/175

012b: MANY ARE CALLED Houghton Mifflin B
1966 [1] 2,500 cc. Wraps $40.

013a: A MOTHER'S TALE Paper Texts NY
1967 [] Wraps. First separate edition (Alphabet
Books 7/91) $40.

014a: THE COLLECTED POEMS OF JAMES
AGEE Houghton Mifflin B 1968 [1] 6,000 cc $10/50

014b: THE COLLECTED POEMS OF JAMES
AGEE Calder & Boyar L 1972 [0] $10/50

015a: ALL QUARTERS ON THE NORTH:
COLLECTED SHORT PROSE Houghton Mifflin
B 1968 [0] Uncorrected proof in spiral bound
wraps with a different title on cover $150.

015b: THE COLLECTED SHORT PROSE...
Houghton Mifflin B 1968 [1] 6,000 cc $12/60

015c: THE COLLECTED SHORT PROSE...
Calder & Boyer L (1972) [0] $10/50

016a: THE LAST LETTER OF JAMES AGEE TO
FATHER FLYE Godine B 1969 [2] 500 cc.
Wraps $75.

016b: THE LAST LETTER OF JAMES AGEE TO
FATHER FLYE Mandragora Press (Deo Laus,
1969) [] (Black Sun Books) $25

017a: JAMES AGEE - SELECTED JOURNALISM
University of Tennessee (Knoxville 1985) [0]
Edited and introduction by Paul Ashdown $7/35

(1980)

EDWARD ALBEE

Edward Albee was born in Washington, D.C., in 1928. He was adopted when he was two weeks old by the heirs to a vaudeville fortune. When he was thirty years old he wrote his first play, *The Zoo Story*, and it opened off-Broadway on the same bill as Samuel Beckett's *Krapp's Last Tape*. His first full-length play, *Who's Afraid of Virginia Woolf?* (1962), ran for nearly two years and won both the Drama Critics Circle Award and the Antoinette Perry Award. It was recommended for the Pulitzer Prize but the prize was not awarded. Henry Popkin (in ref.d) notes that:

> ... apparently the Pulitzer trustees had objected to the play's frank sexual references. *A Delicate Balance* (1966) ran a little more than four months in New York, but a subsequent tour made it a commercial success. When this play won the Pulitzer Prize, the Pulitzer Committee was widely assumed to be responding to feelings of guilt over its failure to honor *Who's Afraid of Virginia Woolf?*

REFERENCES:

(a) Bruccoli & Clark. FIRST PRINTINGS OF AMERICAN AUTHORS. Volume 3. Detroit: Gale Research (1977).

(b) CONTEMPORARY DRAMATISTS. James Vinson, editor. London/New York: St. James Press/St. Martin's Press (1973).

(c) BOOKS IN PRINT 1984-1985. New York/London: R.R. Bowker Company, 1985.

(d) THE READERS ENCYCLOPEDIA OF WORLD DRAMA. John Gassner and Edward Quinn, editors. New York (1969).

001a: THE ZOO STORY AND THE SANDBOX Dramatists Play Service (NY 1960) [0] Wraps $175.

001b: THE ZOO STORY | THE DEATH OF BESSIE SMITH | THE SANDBOX Coward-McCann NY (1960) [0] Original dustwrapper price was $2.75 $35/175

001c: THE ZOO STORY | THE DEATH OF BESSIE SMITH | THE SANDBOX Coward-McCann NY (1960) [0] Dustwrapper is price clipped with $3.50 added at bottom (Robert Dagg 6/91) $35/150

001d: THE ZOO STORY | THE DEATH OF BESSIE SMITH | THE SANDBOX Coward-McCann NY (1960) [0] Wraps (Phoenix #201) $40.

001e: THE ZOO STORY AND OTHER PLAYS Jonathan Cape L (1962) [0] New title. Adds *The American Dream* and new introduction $25/125

001f: THE DEATH OF BESSIE SMITH French L (1962) [0] Wraps. First separate publication (1961 noted in Sherington #21) $60.

002a: THE AMERICAN DREAM Coward-McCann NY (1961) [0] First separate publication $35/175

002b: THE AMERICAN DREAM Coward-McCann NY (1961) [0] Wraps. Simultaneous issue $40.

002c: THE AMERICAN DREAM French L (1962) [0] $35.

002d: THE AMERICAN DREAM | THE DEATH OF BESSIE SMITH | FAM AND YAM Dramatists Play Service (NY 1962) [0] Wraps $30.

003a: FAM AND YAM Dramatists Play Service (NY 1961) [0] First separate publication (ref.b) $40.

004a: WHO'S AFRAID OF VIRGINIA WOOLF? Atheneum NY 1962 [1] 4,000 cc $60/300

004b: WHO'S AFRAID OF VIRGINIA WOOLF? Atheneum NY 1962 [1] Wraps. Issued simultaneously $75.

004c: WHO'S AFRAID OF VIRGINIA WOOLF? Dramatists Play Service (NY 1962) [] Wraps $40.

004d: WHO'S AFRAID OF VIRGINIA WOOLF? Jonathan Cape L (1964) [] $25/125

004e: WHO'S AFRAID OF VIRGINIA WOOLF? Parchment Gallery Charlestown, WV (1980) [2] 100 sgd no cc (signed by Albee). Broadside with drawing by E.E. Cummings $125.

005a: THE PLAY THE BALLAD OF THE SAD CAFE *Carson McCullers' Novella adapted...* Houghton Mifflin/Atheneum B/NY 1963 [1] $25/75

005b: THE PLAY THE BALLAD OF THE SAD CAFE *Carson McCullers' Novella adapted...* Houghton Mifflin/Atheneum B/NY 1963 [1] Wraps. Issued simultaneously $35.

005c: THE PLAY THE BALLAD OF THE SAD CAFE Dramatists Play Service (NY 1963) [0] Wraps $25.

005d: THE PLAY THE BALLAD OF THE SAD CAFE Jonathan Cape L (1965) [0] $15/60

006a: TINY ALICE Atheneum NY 1965 [0] 4,000 cc $15/75

006b: TINY ALICE Dramatists Play Service (NY 1965) [0] Wraps $30.

006c: TINY ALICE Jonathan Cape L (1966) [0] $15/60

007a: MALCOLM *from the novel by James Purdy*
Atheneum NY 1966 [1] 4,000 cc $15/60

007b: MALCOLM *from the novel by James Purdy*
Dramatists Play Service (NY 1966) [0] Wraps $25.

007c: MALCOLM *from the novel by James Purdy*
Cape/Secker & Warburg (L 1967) [0] $15/60

008a: A DELICATE BALANCE Atheneum NY
1966 [1] 4,000 cc. Awarded the Pulitzer Prize for
1967 $15/75

008b: A DELICATE BALANCE French NY
(1967) [0] Wraps $25.

008c: A DELICATE BALANCE Jonathan Cape L
(1968) [0] $15/50

009a: EVERYTHING IN THE GARDEN *from the
play by Giles Cooper* Atheneum NY 1968 [1]
4,000 cc $15/50

009b: EVERYTHING IN THE GARDEN *from the
play by Giles Cooper* Dramatists Play Service (NY
1968) [0] Wraps $20.

010a: BOX and QUOTATIONS FROM CHAIR-
MAN MAO TSE-TUNG *Two Interrelated Plays*
Atheneum NY 1969 [1] 4,000 cc $15/50

010b: BOX and QUOTATIONS FROM CHAIR-
MAN MAO TSE-TUNG *Two Interrelated Plays*
Dramatists Play Service (NY 1969) [0] Wraps $20.

010c: BOX and QUOTATIONS FROM CHAIR-
MAN MAO TSE-TUNG *Two Interrelated Plays*
Jonathan Cape L (1970) [0] $10/40

011a: ALL OVER Atheneum NY 1971 [1] 4,000
cc $10/40

011b: ALL OVER Jonathan Cape L (1972) [0] $10/40

011c: ALL OVER French NY (1973) [] Wraps $15.

012a: SEASCAPE Atheneum NY 1975 [1] 4,000
cc $10/40

012b: SEASCAPE Dramatists Play Service (NY
1975) [0] Wraps $20.

012c: SEASCAPE Jonathan Cape L (1976) [0] $10/40

013a: COUNTING THE WAYS & LISTENING:
Two Plays Atheneum NY 1977 [1] 4,000 cc $10/40

014a: THE LADY FROM DUBUQUE: *A Play in
Two Acts* Atheneum NY 1980 [1] (Ref.c) $10/40

014b: THE LADY FROM DUBUQUE: *A Play in
Two Acts* Dramatists Play Service (NY 1980) [0]
Wraps (ref.c) $15.

015a: THE WOUNDING: *An Essay on Education*
Mountain State Press Charleston, W.Va. (1981) [2]
50 sgd no cc. Simulated leather in dustwrapper $75/125

015b: THE WOUNDING: *An Essay on Education*
Mountain State Press Charleston, W.Va. (1981) [2]
200 no. cc. Wraps $50.

016a: EDWARD ALBEE, AN INTERVIEW AND
ESSAYS Houston 1983 [] Edited by Julian
Wasserman (Phoenix #187) $30.

017a: THE PLAYS VOLUME ONE Coward-Mc-
Cann NY (1981) [0] Wraps. Introduction by
Albee $25.

018a: THE PLAYS VOLUME TWO Atheneum
NY 1981 [] Wraps $25.

019a: THE PLAYS VOLUME THREE Atheneum
NY 1982 [] Wraps $25.

020a: THE PLAYS VOLUME FOUR Atheneum
NY 1982 [] Wraps $25.

Note: THE MAN WHO HAD THREE ARMS was
announced in 1984 but never published.

021a: LOLITA: A PLAY Dramatist Play Service
(NY 1984) [] Wraps (No hardbound edition) $40.

022a: CONVERSATIONS WITH EDWARD AL-
BEE   University Press of Mississippi   Jackson
(1988) [] Collected interviews 1961-1986. Edited
by Philip C. Kolin (Ampersand Books) $15/40

022b: CONVERSATIONS WITH EDWARD AL-
BEE   University Press of Mississippi   Jackson
(1988) [] Wraps $15.

023a: FINDING THE SUN Dramatist Play Service
NY (1994) [0] Wraps $20.

024a: THREE TALL WOMEN Dutton NY (1995)
[3] Also states "First Printing, January 1995". We
assume this must have been preceded by a French or
Dramatist acting edition but we haven't seen $10/25

NELSON ALGREN
(1909-1983)

Nelson Algren was born in Detroit. He received a degree from the University of Illinois. An admitted expert on human unhappiness, he chronicled the underside of the American Dream using his experiences as a migrant worker, carnival shill, WPA worker and his four years with the Venereal Disease Program in Chicago. He seemed to believe "the only really ugly thing on earth is the death that comes before true death comes" (*Never Come Morning*). *The Man with the Golden Arm* won the National Book Award for 1950.

REFERENCES:

(a) Lepper, Gary M. A BIBLIOGRAPHICAL REFERENCE TO SEVENTY-FIVE MODERN AMERICAN AUTHORS. Berkeley: Serendipity Books, 1976.

(b) Bruccoli & Clark. FIRST PRINTINGS OF AMERICAN AUTHORS. Detroit: Gale Research (1977). Volume 1.

001a: SOMEBODY IN BOOTS Vanguard NY (1935) [0] $300/1,500

001b: SOMEBODY IN BOOTS Constable L (1937) [ ] (Ref.b) $100/750

001c: THE JUNGLE Avon NY (1957) [0] Wraps. Abridged version of *Somebody in Boots*. No. "T-185" (later reprinted as "T-324") $35.

001d: SOMEBODY IN BOOTS Berkley NY (1965) [0] Wraps. No. "S1125." Contains new preface by Algren $40.

002a: GALENA GUIDE Federal Writer's Project [WPA] (Chicago) 1937 [0] Wraps. Algren contribution (ref.b). Map tipped-in at rear (Beasley Books) $175.

003a: NEVER COME MORNING Harper NY (1942) [1] Introduction by Richard Wright $75/350

003b: NEVER COME MORNING Avon NY (1948) [0] Wraps. No. "185." "Specially revised by author" $35.

003c: NEVER COME MORNING Spearman L (1958) [0] Noted in black cloth with lettering in gilt and in dark blue cloth with lettering in gilt $25/100

003d: NEVER COME MORNING Harper & Row NY (1963) [0] Wraps. New preface by Algren $35.

004a: THE NEON WILDERNESS Doubleday Garden City 1947 [1] 24 stories. Ads for other books on back of dustwrapper $35/150

004b: THE NEON WILDERNESS Doubleday Garden City 1947 [1] 24 stories. Reviews of this book on back of dustwrapper $30/100

004c: THE NEON WILDERNESS Avon NY (1949) [0] Wraps. 18 stories. No. "222" (ref.b) $35.

004d: THE NEON WILDERNESS Hill & Wang NY (1960) [0] Wraps. New introduction by Algren. No. "AC27" (ref.b) $30.

004e: THE NEON WILDERNESS Deutsch L (1965) [ ] (Ref.b) $25/75

005a: THE MAN WITH THE GOLDEN ARM Doubleday Garden City 1949 [1] Signed on tipped-in sheets. 1950 National Book Award winner for 1950 $150/300

005b: THE MAN WITH THE GOLDEN ARM
Doubleday Garden City 1949 [1] Award sticker
on dustwrapper (added later) $40/200

005c: THE MAN WITH THE GOLDEN ARM
Spearman L 1959 [ ] (ref.b) $25/125

005d: THE MAN WITH THE GOLDEN ARM
Cardinal (Pocket Books) NY (no-date) [1] Wraps.
Issued in dustwrapper $15/75

006a: CHICAGO: CITY ON THE MAKE Doubleday Garden City 1951 [1] Wraps. "Uncorrected
Proof" $250.

006b: CHICAGO: CITY ON THE MAKE Double-
day Garden City 1951 [1] $25/75

006c: CHICAGO: CITY ON THE MAKE Contact
Sausalito 1961 [0] Wraps. New introduction by
Algren $25.

006d: CHICAGO: CITY ON THE MAKE Angel
Island Oakland (1961) [] Wraps. "Third edition."
Adds Algren's epilogue "Ode to Kissassville" $50.

006e: CHICAGO: CITY ON THE MAKE Angel
Island Oakland (1961) [] Wraps. "Third edition."
Adds Algren's epilogue "Ode to Lower Finksville" $25.

007a: A WALK ON THE WILD SIDE Farrar
Straus NY (1956) [1] $25/125

007b: A WALK ON THE WILD SIDE Spearman
L (1957) [ ] (Ref.b) $25/75

007c: A WALK ON THE WILD SIDE Fawcett
Garden City (1963) [0] Wraps. Crest no. "d 496."
Revised by Algren (ref.a & b) $30.

008a: NELSON ALGREN'S OWN BOOK OF
LONESOME MONSTERS Lancer NY (1962) [0]

Wraps. No. "73-409." 13 stories, edited and introduction by Algren (ref.b) $50.

008b: NELSON ALGREN'S OWN BOOK OF
LONESOME MONSTERS Geis (NY 1963) [1]
15 stories.   Edited and introduction by Algren
(ref.b) $10/50

008c: NELSON ALGREN'S BOOK OF LONE-
SOME MONSTERS Panther (L 1964) [0] Wraps.
No. "1627." 13 stories (ref.b) $25.

009a: WHO LOST AN AMERICAN? Deutsch (L
1963) [0] $25/75

009b: WHO LOST AN AMERICAN? Macmillan
NY (1963) [ ] Uncorrected proofs in spiral bound
wraps $125.

009c: WHO LOST AN AMERICAN? Macmillan
NY (1963) [1] (Ref.b) $10/40

010a: CONVERSATIONS WITH NELSON AL-
GREN Hill & Wang NY (1964) [0] Wraps.
Written by H.E.F. Donohue. 6 page promotional
pamphlet $75.

010b: CONVERSATIONS WITH NELSON AL-
GREN Hill & Wang NY (1964) [1] Written by
H.E.F. Donohue, although the bulk of text is Al-
gren's $10/40

011a: NOTES FROM A SEA DIARY... Putnam
NY (1965) [0] $10/50

011b: NOTES FROM A SEA DIARY... Deutsch L
(1966) [0] (Ref.b) $10/40

012a: THE LAST CAROUSEL Putnam NY
(1973) [0] Wraps. "Uncorrected proof." Pad
bound in printed wraps (Wm. Reese Co. 9/90) $125.

012b: THE LAST CAROUSEL   Putnam   NY
(1973) [0] $10/35

013a: THE DEVIL'S STOCKING   Arbor House
NY (1983) [3] "Uncorrected proof" in orange
printed wraps "to be published Sept. 1, 1983" $60.

013b: THE DEVIL'S STOCKING   Arbor House
NY (1983) [3] Dustwrapper flap lists "*Puss in
Boots*" as first book (all copies?). Includes last
interview by W.J. Weatherby (Publ 9/30/83 @
$16.95) $15/35

013c: THE DEVIL'S STOCKING   Arbor House
NY (1983) [3] Wraps. Issued simultaneously
(Published 9/30/83 @ $8.95) $15.

014a: AMERICA EATS University of Iowa Press
Iowa City 1992 [ ] A cookbook published as one
of the inaugural volumes in the Iowa Szathmary
Culinary Arts Series.   Edited by David E.
Schoonover, foreword by Louis I. Szathmary II.
(Published 5/92 @ $22.95) $15/35

015a: HE   SWUNG   AND   HE   MISSED
Minneapolis 1993 [] First separate edition. Assume
wraps $25.

ANN BEATTIE

Ann Beattie was born in Washington, D.C. in 1947. She earned her B.A. at American University and a M.A. at the University of Connecticut. Beattie is a frequent contributor to *The New Yorker*. She has taught creative writing at the University of Virginia and Harvard.

001a: CHILLY SCENES OF WINTER Doubleday
Garden City 1976 [1] $25/125

002a: DISTORTIONS   Doubleday   Garden City
1976 [1] $30/150

003a: SECRETS AND SURPRISES   Random
House NY (1978) [ ] Uncorrected proof in red
wraps (Waiting for Godot 10/90) $100.

003b: SECRETS AND SURPRISES   Random
House NY (1978) [4] $10/50

003c: SECRETS AND SURPRISES   Hamish
Hamilton L (1979) [ ] (Keane-Egan, List D) $10/40

004a: FALLING IN PLACE Random House NY
(1980) [4] Wraps. "Special Readers Edition... from
Uncorrected Proof." P.228 duplicated as p.238 and
crossed out by publisher (Waiting for Godot #9).
(Our copy has error but not crossed out) $60.

004b: FALLING IN PLACE Random House NY
(1980) [4] (Published 5/12/80 @ $10.95) $10/40

004c: FALLING IN PLACE Secker & Warburg L
(1981) [ ] $10/40

005a: JACKLIGHTING Metacom Press Worcester (Ma) 1981 [2] 26 sgd ltr cc. "Not For Sale." Issued in dustwrapper (Joseph Dermont #37) $100/150

005b: JACKLIGHTING Metacom Press Worcester (Ma) 1981 [2] 250 sgd no cc. Wraps sewn in dustwrapper $75.

006a: THE BURNING HOUSE Random House NY (1982) [ ] Uncorrected proofs in printed red wraps (Pharos 1/90) $50.

006b: THE BURNING HOUSE Random House NY (1982) [4] (Published 10/5/82 @ $12.95) $6/30

006c: THE BURNING HOUSE Secker & Warburg L (1983) $6/30

007a: LOVE ALWAYS Random House NY (1985) [ ] "First" proof from corrected typescript (Waverly 10/89) $60.

007b: LOVE ALWAYS Random House NY (1985) [ ] "Uncorrected Proof" in yellow wraps (H.E. Turlington #28) $40.

007c: LOVE ALWAYS Random House NY (1985) [0] 40,000 cc (PW). (Published 6/10/85 @ $16.95) $6/30

007d: LOVE ALWAYS Michael Joseph L 1985 [ ] $5/25

008a: SPECTACLES Workman NY (1985) [ ] Wraps. Advance promotional material. One sheet folded to make two leaves (Watermark West # 2) $30.

008b: SPECTACLES Workman NY (1985) [3] Also states "First Printing, Sept. 1985" $6/30

009a: WHERE YOU'LL FIND ME... Simon & Schuster NY 1986 [3] "Advance Uncorrected Proofs" in tan printed wraps $40.

009b: WHERE YOU'LL FIND ME... Simon & Schuster NY 1986 [3] 25,000 cc. (Published 10/86 @ $14.95) $6/30

009c: WHERE YOU'LL FIND ME... Macmillan L 1987 [ ] $6/30

010a: ALEX KATZ Abrams NY (1987) [0] Text by Beattie, illustrations by Katz. (Published 4/87 @ $27.50) $15/40

011a: PICTURING WILL Random House NY (1989) [] Uncorrected proofs in yellow wraps $40.

011b: PICTURING WILL Random House NY (1989) [] (Published 1/90 @ $18.95) $5/25

011c: PICTURING WILL Jonathan Cape L (1990) [] $6/30

012a: WHAT WAS MINE Random House NY 1991 [] "Advance uncorrected proof" in pictorial wraps (Monroe Stahr notes "bluish wraps) $35.

012b: WHAT WAS MINE (Random House NY 1991) [0] 14 page excerpt in stapled pictorial wraps $25.

012c: WHAT WAS MINE Random House NY 1991 [] (Published 5/91 @ $20) $5/25

013a: AMERICANA Scribner NY 1992 [] Photographs by Bob Adelman, text by Beattie. (Published 10/92 @ $42.50) $12/60

014a: ANOTHER YOU Knopf NY 1995 [] (Published September 1995 @ $24)

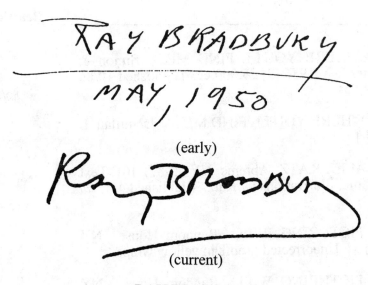

(early)

(current)

RAY BRADBURY

Bradbury was born in Waukegan, Illinois, in 1920. He was educated and has lived in Los Angeles since his early youth.

Although he has written the novels *Something Wicked This Way Comes* and *Fahrenheit 451*, Ray Bradbury is primarily a writer of short stories. Ever the storyteller, Bradbury aims in each story at producing the horror, the surprise, or the single dominant effect of Poe, one of his principal mentors. Nonetheless, his short story collections - notably *The Martian Chronicles* and *Dandelion Wine* - have an overall meaning which exceeds the meaning of the parts.

...Perhaps his greatest value is as a social critic and a commentator on technology.

...Bradbury suggests the unity of all technology: Ezekiel's wheel in the middle of the air, the wheeling space station and lawnmower, and the wheels in the man's watch...for distinguishing as almost no other writer (science fiction or otherwise) has distinguished between American expansionist technology and technology *per se*, Ray Bradbury deserves close attention and highest praise.

-Curtis C. Smith
Contemporary Novelists

Note: We have added a few of the unpublished playscripts but there are still a number not included in this guide.

REFERENCES:

(a) Nolan, William F. THE RAY BRADBURY COMPANION. Detroit: Bruccoli-Clark, Gale Research, 1975.

(b) Currey, L.W. SCIENCE FICTION AND FANTASY AUTHORS. Boston: G.K. Hall (1979).

(c) Inventory or private collections.

001a: DARK CARNIVAL Arkham House Sauk City 1947 [2] 3,000 copies stated but 3,112 copies per Derleth's *Thirty Years of Arkham House*, 1970 $200/1,000

001b: DARK CARNIVAL Hamish Hamilton L (1948) [1] Abridged, deletes 7 of the 27 stories $100/400

002a: THE MARTIAN CHRONICLES Doubleday Garden City 1950 [1] First state in green binding (ref.c) $250/850

002b: THE MARTIAN CHRONICLES Doubleday Garden City 1950 [1] Second state in blue binding (scarcer than green binding) (ref.c) $150/750

002c: THE MARTIAN CHRONICLES Bantam NY (1951) [1] Wraps. Adds prefatory quotes by author (ref.c) $50.

002d: THE SILVER LOCUSTS Rupert Hart-Davis L 1951 [0] New title. Proof in unprinted wraps with label on front cover. Same contents as in published book (Ferret Fantasy 6/93) $300.

002e: THE SILVER LOCUSTS Rupert Hart-Davis L 1951 [0] New title. Deletes "Usher II" and adds "The Fire Balloons" $60/250

002f: THE MARTIAN CHRONICLES Time Inc. NY (1963) [0] (One "X" on last page.) Wraps.First printing of complete text. Contains Doubleday edition plus "The Fire Balloons" and "The Wilderness" — $50.

002g: THE MARTIAN CHRONICLES Doubleday Garden City (1973) [0] First hardcover edition of complete text. Contains illustration from 1971 Italian edition and bibliography by William F. Nolan — $15/60

002h: THE MARTIAN CHRONICLES Limited Editions Club Avon, CT 1974 [2] 2,000 no cc. signed by Bradbury and illustrator Joseph Mugnaini. Issued in slipcase. (Complete text.) (Ref.c) — $150/250

002i: THE MARTIAN CHRONICLES Olivetti (Italy 1979) [2] With watercolors by Folon. (Original text) (ref.c) — $250.

002j: THE MARTIAN CHRONICLES Easton Press 1989 [2] "Collector's Edition." Signed by Bradbury. Issued in full leather — $100.

002k: THE MARTIAN CHRONICLES *The Fortieth Anniversary Edition* Doubleday New York (1990) [] Includes "The Fire Balloons" and new foreword — $6/30

003a: THE ILLUSTRATED MAN Doubleday Garden City 1951 [1] — $100/500

003b: THE ILLUSTRATED MAN Rupert Hart-Davis L 1952 [0] Deletes 4 stories and adds 2 stories — $60/300

004a: NO MAN IS AN ISLAND (National Women's Comm. L.A. Area Chapter Brandeis Univ. Beverly Hills 1952) [1] Wraps — $450.

004b: NO MAN IS AN ISLAND (National Women's Comm. Brandeis Univ. Westchester Chapter Hartsdale, NY circa 1956) [0] Wraps (ref.c) $350.

004c: NO MAN IS AN ISLAND (National. Women's Comm. Brandeis Univ. {No-place} Feb. 1964) [0] Wraps. 3 mimeographed pages (8 1/2" x 11") (ref.c) $175.

005a: THE GOLDEN APPLES OF THE SUN Doubleday Garden City 1953 [1] $60/300

005b: THE GOLDEN APPLES OF THE SUN Rupert Hart-Davis L 1953 [0] Deletes 2 stories $40/200

006a: FAHRENHEIT 451 Ballantine Books NY (1953) [0] Wraps. Contains title novel plus short stories "The Playground" and "And The Rock Cried Out." Precedes hardcover by 4 to 6 weeks (ref.c) $75.

006b: FAHRENHEIT 451 Ballantine Books NY (1953) [2] 50 copies for author bound in full red cloth with gold stamping (ref.b) $3,250.

006c: FAHRENHEIT 451 Ballantine Books NY (1953) [2] 200 sgd no cc. Bound in asbestos. Approximately 50 copies sold in trade dustwrapper though not called for (ref.c) $5,000/6,000

006d: FAHRENHEIT 451 Ballantine Books NY (1953) [0] 4,250 cc. Red boards lettered in gold or yellow (ref.b) $200/1,000

006e: FAHRENHEIT 451 Rupert Hart-Davis L 1954 [0] Contains title novel only $60/300

006f: FAHRENHEIT 451 Simon & Schuster NY (1967) [1] New introduction by author (full contents) $25/125

006g: FAHRENHEIT 451 Macmillan of Canada Toronto (1968) [0] Pictorial hardcover without dustwrapper (ref.c) $60.

006h: FAHRENHEIT 451 Del Rey/Ballantine NY (1979) [1] Wraps. Afterword by author. "47th printing August 1979." Original unedited text (see afterword) (ref.c) $30.

006i: FAHRENHEIT 451 Limited Editions Club NY 1982 [2] 2,000 no cc. Bound in aluminum in slipcase, signed by author and the illustrator, Joseph Mugnaini. New introduction by author (ref.c) $250/350

006j: FAHRENHEIT 451 *40th Anniversary Edition* Knopf NY 1993 [2] 500 sgd no cc. Issued in slipcase (Pepper & Stern 3/95) $100/175

006k: FAHRENHEIT 451 *40th Anniversary Edition* Knopf NY 1993 [] $7/25

007a: SWITCH ON THE NIGHT Pantheon Books (NY 1955) [0] Gray boards in dustwrapper (later printings have pictorial covers without dustwrapper, similar to library edition) (ref.c) $75/350

007b: SWITCH ON THE NIGHT Rupert Hart-Davis (L) 1955 [0] $50/250

007c: SWITCH ON THE NIGHT Pantheon Books (NY 1963) [0] Library edition with pictorial cover. First issue has definition of a library edition on rear cover (ref.c) $75.

008a: THE OCTOBER COUNTRY Ballantine Books NY (1955) [0] 50 copies for author. Bound in full red cloth with gold stamping (ref.b) $2,500.

008b: THE OCTOBER COUNTRY Ballantine Books NY (1955) [0] First state has Ballantine logo inverted on spine (ref.c) $200/500

008c: THE OCTOBER COUNTRY Ballantine Books NY (1955) [0] Second state with corrected logo (actually scarcer than first) (ref.b) $100/400

008d: THE OCTOBER COUNTRY Ballantine Books NY (1956) [0] Wraps. No. "F139." Adds prefatory note by author (ref.b) $40.

008e: THE OCTOBER COUNTRY Rupert Hart-Davis L 1956 [0] $50/200

008f: THE OCTOBER COUNTRY Ace Books L (1961) [1] Wraps. Abridged, deletes 7 of the 19 stories and adds 1 story $40.

009a: SUN AND SHADOW (The Quenian Press) Berkeley 1957 [2] 90 cc. Wraps. One copy (a printing error per publisher) has been seen with copyright notice on page [22] instead of page [20] (ref.c) $1,000.

010a: DANDELION WINE Doubleday Garden City 1957 [1] $50/250

010b: DANDELION WINE Rupert Hart-Davis L 1957 [0] $30/150

010c: DANDELION WINE *A Musical Book...* (Starlite Los Angeles 1973) [] Mimeographed sheets brad-bound in yellow printed wraps. Unpublished playscript. About 35 to 40 copies (L.W. Currey 8/92) $250.

010d: DANDELION WINE Knopf NY 1975 [1] New introduction by the author (ref.c) $10/50

011a: A MEDICINE FOR MELANCHOLY Doubleday Garden City 1959 [1] $50/250

011b: THE DAY IT RAINED FOREVER Rupert Hart-Davis L 1959 [0] New title. Deletes 4 stories and adds 5 stories. First state binding in medium blue boards (ref.c) $50/250

011c: THE DAY IT RAINED FOREVER Rupert Hart-Davis L 1959 [0] Second state binding in very dark blue boards (ref.c) $40/175

012a: THE MEADOW *A One-Act Play* (No publisher, place or date) [] Approximately 25 copies. Mimeographed sheets (20 leaves) on light green paper. Brad-bound in blue printed wraps. Unpublished playscript prepared by Bradbury in 1960 (L.W. Currey 8/92)　　　　　$200.

013a: THE ESSENCE OF CREATIVE WRITING (San Antonio Public Library San Antonio 1962) [0] Wraps　　　　　$75.

014a: THE SMALL ASSASSIN New English Library L (1962) [1] Wraps. Combination of stories from *Dark Carnival* and *October Country*; "Ace Book No. H521" (ref.b)　　　　　$75.

015a: SOMETHING WICKED THIS WAY COMES Simon & Schuster NY 1962 [1]　　　　　$75/350

015b: SOMETHING WICKED THIS WAY COMES Rupert Hart-Davis L 1963 [0] Joe Mugnaini dustwrapper from rough design by Bradbury　　　　　$50/250

016a: R IS FOR ROCKET Doubleday Garden City (1962) [1] Includes two previously uncollected stories　　　　　$35/175

016b: R IS FOR ROCKET Rupert Hart-Davis L 1968 [1]　　　　　$25/125

017a: THE ANTHEM SPRINTERS AND OTHER ANTICS The Dial Press NY 1963 [0] Wraps. No. "A75." Precedes hardcover by 4 to 6 weeks (ref.c)　　　　　$75.

017b: THE ANTHEM SPRINTERS AND OTHER ANTICS The Dial Press NY 1963 [0]　　　　　$50/250

017c: THE ANTHEM SPRINTERS AND OTHER ANTICS *A Comedy in Three Acts* (Alert Duplicating L.A. 1966) [0] 107 leaves mimeographed on

one side only. Text differs. Less than 25 copies
(Lloyd Currey 8/92) $250.

018a: THE MACHINERIES OF JOY Simon &
Schuster NY 1964 [1] $40/200

018b: THE MACHINERIES OF JOY Rupert Hart-
Davis L 1964 [0] Deletes 1 story $25/125

019a: THE PEDESTRIAN (Roy A. Squires Glendale, CA 1964) [2] Approximately 300 copies (per
publisher). Wraps in plain envelope (ref.c) $150.

020a: A DEVICE OUT OF TIME *A One Act play...*
(No publisher, place or date.) (Opened at the
Coronet Theatre in February 1965.) Mimeographed
sheets in brad-bound yellow printed wraps. About
35 to 40 copies (Lloyd Currey 8/92) $175.

021a: THE VINTAGE BRADBURY Vintage
Books NY (1965) [1] Library edition in buckram
without dustwrapper $300.

021b: THE VINTAGE BRADBURY Vintage
Books NY (1965) [1] Wraps. Price of $1.45 on
cover and "First Vintage Edition, September, 1965"
on copyright page $60.

022a: TWICE 22 Doubleday Garden City 1966 [0]
"47G" at bottom of p.405 (N. Certo 12/92). (Later
printings drop "1966" from title page) $40/200

023a: THE DAY IT RAINED FOREVER *A
Comedy in One Act* Samuel French NY/Hywd/L/T
(1966) [0] Blue wraps. Price of 75¢ at base of front
cover. While there was only one printing of this
edition, the price was raised with later sales by
over-stamping with higher prices. Not to be con-
fused with 1988 edition in pink wraps with no price
(ref.c) $75.

024a: THE PEDESTRIAN A FANTASY IN ONE
ACT   Samuel French NY/Hollywood/L/T (1966)
[0] Wraps. While there was only one printing of
this edition, the price was raised with later sales by
over-stamping with higher prices (ref.c) $75.

025a: S IS FOR SPACE Doubleday Garden City
1966 [1]   Code "H27" on bottom p.[238] (later
printings drop "1966" from title page. Includes
three previously uncollected stories $35/175

025b: S IS FOR SPACE Doubleday Garden City
1966 [0]   Library edition in pictorial cloth. Code
"H27" bottom p.[239]. Later printings drop "1966"
from title page $75/125

025c: S IS FOR SPACE Rupert Hart-Davis L 1968
[1] $25/100

026a: CREATIVE MAN AMONG HIS SERVANT
MACHINES   (Stromberg Data-graphix)   San
Diego, CA 1967 [0] Photocopied on both sides of
12 stapled leaves of stiff paper (ref.c) $350.

026b: CREATIVE MAN AMONG HIS SERVANT
MACHINES (Stromberg Data-graphix) San Diego,
CA 1967 [0] Reprint of above but xeroxed on only
one side of 23 pages on regular weight paper with
pages numbered "v-1", "v-2", etc. (ref.c) $150.

027a: BLOCH AND BRADBURY   Tower (NY
1969) [0] Wraps $40.

027b: FEVER DREAM AND OTHER FAN-
TASIES Sphere Books L (1970) [1] New title.
Wraps (ref.b) $40.

028a: I SING THE BODY ELECTRIC Knopf NY
1969 [1] $20/100

028b: I SING THE BODY ELECTRIC   Rupert Hart-Davis L (1970) [1] Black cloth. (1 copy has been seen in orange cloth) (ref.c) $20/75

029a: CHRISTUS APOLLO (UCLA LA 1969) [0] Mimeographed on both sides of 3 stapled leaves (ref.c) $175.

030a: OLD AHAB'S FRIEND, AND FRIEND TO NOAH, SPEAKS HIS PIECE   (Roy A. Squires Glendale, CA 1971) [2] Wraps. Copies numbered "1" to "40" signed for subscribers and issued in unprinted dustwrapper in plain envelope (ref.c) $250.

030b: OLD AHAB'S FRIEND, AND FRIEND TO NOAH, SPEAKS HIS PIECE   (Roy A. Squires Glendale, CA 1971) [2] Wraps. Copies numbered "41" to "485" in plain envelope (ref.c) $60.

030c: OLD AHAB'S FRIEND, AND FRIEND TO NOAH, SPEAKS HIS PIECE   (Roy A. Squires Glendale, CA 1971) [2] Wraps. Variant of 030b bound in a darker brown cover stock with title in dark green instead of brown (ref.c) $75.

031a: TEACHER'S GUIDE SCIENCE FICTION Bantam Books NY (1971) [] Wraps. 10 titles by RB listed on p.15 (later printing circa 1973 lists 11 titles, among other differences) (ref.c) $75.

032a: SCIENCE FICTION: WHY BOTHER? Bantam Books NY (1971) [0] Large sheet of stiff paper folded into 4 pages and again folded for mailing (ref.c) $75.

033a: THE WONDERFUL ICE CREAM SUIT *And Other Plays* Bantam Pathfinder Edition T/NY/L (1972) [1] Wraps $35.

033b: THE WONDERFUL ICE CREAM SUIT *And Other Plays* Bantam Books T/NY/L (1972) [1] Wraps. "Special Edition No. 1963" on cover, book club edition, probably simultaneous (ref.c) $25.

033c: THE WONDERFUL ICE CREAM SUIT *And Other Plays* Hart-Davis, MacGibbon L (1973) [1] (ref.b) $15/75

034a: MADRIGALS FOR THE SPACE AGE Associated Music Publ. NY/L 1972 [0] Wraps. Music by Lalo Schifrin. First printing has "$1.50" on front cover (ref.c) $60.

035a: PILLAR OF FIRE *A Drama* (Starlite L.A. 1972) [] 74 leaves mimeographed on white paper and brad-bound in orange printed wraps. About 35 to 40 copies (Lloyd Currey 8/92) $225.

036a: THE HALLOWEEN TREE   Knopf NY (1972) [1] $25/100

035b: THE HALLOWEEN TREE   Knopf NY (1972) [1]   Library edition with pictorial cover without dustwrapper. Issued simultaneously (ref.b) $75.

036c: THE HALLOWEEN TREE   Hart-Davis, MacGibbon L (1973) [1] $15/75

037a: ZEN AND THE ART OF WRITING Capra Press Santa Barbara 1973 [2] 250 sgd no cc. Hard cover bound by hand $125.

037b: ZEN AND THE ART OF WRITING Capra Press Santa Barbara 1973 [0] Wraps $30.

038a: WHEN ELEPHANTS LAST IN THE DOORYARD BLOOMED Knopf NY 1973 [1] $10/40

038b: WHEN ELEPHANTS LAST IN THE DOORYARD BLOOMED   Hart-Davis, MacGibbon L (1975) [1] (Ref.c) $10/40

039a: THAT SON OF RICHARD III   Roy A. Squires (Glendale, CA) 1974 [2] Wraps. Copies numbered "I" to "LXXXV" signed for subscribers in unprinted dustwrapper in printed envelope (ref.c) $125/150

039b: THAT SON OF RICHARD III   Roy A. Squires (Glendale, CA) 1974 [2] 400 no cc. Wraps in printed envelope (ref.c) $50/60

040a: BYZANTIUM I COME NOT FROM   (Fullerton College Fullerton, CA 1975) [0] Broadside (ref.c) $200.

041a: 1984 WILL NOT ARRIVE: A PREDICTION FOR THE GREENING OF SCRIPPS   (Grant Dahlstrom, The Castle Press Pasadena, CA 1975) [0] Wraps (ref.c) $75.

042a: BRADBURY READS BRADBURY Listening Library (Old Greenwich, CT   1975)   [0] Wraps. Text to accompany recordings (ref.c) $40.

043a: RAY BRADBURY   Harrap L (1975) [1] Flexible cloth wraps (ref.b) $40.

044a: PILLAR OF FIRE AND OTHER PLAYS Bantam Books T/NY/L (1975) [1] Wraps. No. "N2173" (ref.b). (Also see 035a.) $25.

045a: CHRISTMAS WISHES 1975 (Printed for author LA 1975) [0] Broadside. Issued on plain white and on stiff textured parchment-like papers (ref.c) $60.

046a: THAT GHOST, THAT BRIDE OF TIME *Excerpts from a Play-in-Progress* (Roy A. Squires Glendale, CA 1976) [2] Copies numbered "1" to "150." Signed for subscribers. Wraps in dustwrapper in printed envelope (ref.c) $100/125

046b: THAT GHOST, THAT BRIDE OF TIME *Excerpts from a Play-in-Progress* (Roy A. Squires Glendale, CA 1976) [2] Copies numbered "151" to "280." Wraps in dustwrapper in printed envelope (ref.c) $30/40

046c: THAT GHOST, THAT BRIDE OF TIME *Excerpts from a Play-in-Progress*   (Roy A. Squire

Glendale, CA 1976) [2] Copies numbered "281" to
"400." Variant printing of 046b with 30 lines on
p.9 instead of 31. These were actually the first
printed before correction, but saved till last and
bound later, per publisher (ref.c) $40/50

047a: THE DOGS THAT EAT SWEET GRASS
Morgan Press Greentown 1965 (really LA 1976)
[2] 16 numbered copies. Offset printed. Pirated
from a xerox in the UCLA Library. Buckram binding, no dustwrapper (ref.c) $3,000.

048a: LONG AFTER MIDNIGHT Knopf NY
1976 [1] Wraps. First state proof copy with "I
Rocket" (replaced with "The Better Part of
Wisdom" in published book {ref.b}) $300.

048b: LONG AFTER MIDNIGHT Knopf NY
1976 [1] Wraps. Second state proof copy with "I
Rocket" cut out (ref.b) $200.

048c: LONG AFTER MIDNIGHT Knopf NY
1976 [1] (Ref.b) $10/50

048d: LONG AFTER MIDNIGHT   Hart-Davis,
MacGibbon L (1977) [1] (Ref.c) $10/40

049a: WRITER'S DIGEST INTERVIEWS BRAD-
BURY Writer's Digest NY 1976 [0] Wraps (ref.c) $40.

050a: MAN DEAD? THEN GOD IS SLAIN! Santa
Susana Press Ca. State Univ. Northridge Lib. 1977
[2] 26 sgd no cc. Boxed with 5 signed prints by
Hans Burkhardt. Not published for sale. (ref.c) $800/1,000

050b: MAN DEAD? THEN GOD IS SLAIN!
Santa Susana Press Ca. State Univ. Northridge
Lib. 1977 [2] 1 sheet folded into 4 pages. Not
published for sale. 1 copy, among possible variations, has been seen with title in 5/8" high type
instead of 3/8" (ref.c) $100.

051a: WHERE ROBOT MICE AND ROBOT MEN RUN ROUND IN ROBOT TOWNS   Knopf NY 1977 [1] (Ref.c) $5/30

051b: WHERE ROBOT MICE AND ROBOT MEN RUN ROUND IN ROBOT TOWNS   Hart-Davis, MacGibbon L/T/Sidney/NY (1979) [1] (Ref.c) $7/35

052a: THE MUMMIES OF GUANAJUATO Abrams NY 1978 [0] (Ref.c) $30/100

052b: THE MUMMIES OF GUANAJUATO Abrams NY 1978 [0] Wraps (ref.c) $30.

053a: TWIN HIEROGLYPHS THAT SWIM THE RIVER DUST   Lord John Press   Northridge, CA (1978) [2] 26 sgd ltr cc. Issued in full leather (ref.c) $300.

053b: TWIN HIEROGLYPHS THAT SWIM THE RIVER DUST   Lord John Press   Northridge, CA (1978) [2] 300 sgd no cc (ref.c) $100.

054a: THE GOD IN SCIENCE FICTION Santa Susana Press   Calif. State Univ   Northridge Lib. 1978 [0] Wraps (ref.c) $50.

055a: THE BIKE REPAIRMEN   (Santa Susana Press   Calif. State Univ. Northridge Lib. 1978) [0] Broadside.   First state printed in red and black. Approximately 400 copies (ref.c) $75.

055b: THE BIKE REPAIRMEN   (Santa Susana Press   Calif. State Univ. Northridge Lib. 1978) [0] Broadside.   Second state printed in black only on thinner and larger paper. Approximately 200 copies (ref.c) $50.

056a: CHRISTMAS GREETINGS 1978   (Printed for author LA 1978) [0] Broadside (ref.c) $40.

057a: TO SING STRANGE SONGS   Wheaton & Co. (Exeter 1979) [1] Wraps (ref.c) $20.

058a: THE FOGHORN AND OTHER STORIES
(Taiyosha Tokyo 1979) [0] Wraps in dustwrapper
(ref.c) $50/75

059a: THE POET CONSIDERS HIS RESOURCES
The Lord John Press Northridge, CA 1979 [2]
Approximately 12 copies. Broadside marked "Pre-
sentation Copy" (ref.c) $225.

059b: THE POET CONSIDERS HIS RESOURCES
The Lord John Press Northridge, CA 1979 [2] 26
sgd ltr cc. Broadside on handmade paper (ref.c) $150.

059c: THE POET CONSIDERS HIS RESOURCES
The Lord John Press Northridge, CA 1979 [2] 200
sgd no cc. Broadside (ref. c) $65.

060a: BEYOND 1984 - A REMEMBRANCE OF
THINGS FUTURE Targ Editions (NY 1979) [2]
Marked "Out of Series" for presentation by author
(ref.c) $125.

060b: BEYOND 1984 - A REMEMBRANCE OF
THINGS FUTURE Targ Editions (NY 1979) [2]
350 sgd no cc (ref.c) $100.

061a: THE AQUEDUCT Roy A. Squires (Glendale, CA) 1979 [2] 230 no cc. Wraps. In unprinted
dustwrapper in printed envelope (ref.c) $100/125

062a: CHRISTMAS GREETINGS 1979 (Printed
for author LA 1979) [0] Broadside (ref.c) $60.

063a: THIS ATTIC WHERE THE MEADOW
GREENS Lord John Press Northridge, CA 1979
[2] Approximately 12 cc. Marked "Presentation
Copy" and signed (ref.c) $200.

063b: THIS ATTIC WHERE THE MEADOW
GREENS Lord John Press Northridge, CA 1979
[2] 75 deluxe sgd no cc. Issued in half leather
(ref.c) $150.

063c: THIS ATTIC WHERE THE MEADOW
GREENS Lord John Press Northridge, CA 1979
[2] 300 sgd no cc (ref.c) $75.

064a: ABOUT NORMAN CORWIN Santa Susana
Press Calif. State Univ. Northridge (Library) 1979
[2] 60 sgd no cc. Folio, boxed with 12 original
signed and numbered photos by Amanda Blanco
(ref.c) $500.

065a: DOING IS BEING WED Imagineers (LA)
1980 [1] Signed broadside (ref.c) $200.

066a: THE LAST CIRCUS & THE ELECTRO-
CUTION Lord John Press Northridge, CA 1980
[2] Approximately 12 cc. Marked "Presentation
Copy" and signed by Bradbury, William F. Nolan
(introduction) and Joseph Mugnaini (illustrations)
(ref.c) $200.

066b: THE LAST CIRCUS & THE ELECTRO-
CUTION   Lord John Press Northridge, CA 1980
[2] 100 deluxe no cc. Signed by Bradbury, Nolan,
and Mugnaini in slipcase (ref.c) $125/150

066c: THE LAST CIRCUS & THE ELECTR-
OCUTION Lord John Press Northridge, CA 1980
[2] 300 no cc sgd by Bradbury and Nolan in
slipcase (ref.c) $50/75

066d: THE LAST CIRCUS & THE ELECTRO-
CUTION   Lord John Press Northridge, CA 1980
[1] Approximately 100 cc. First state dustwrapper
in red on yellow per publisher $7/40

066e: THE LAST CIRCUS & THE ELECTRO-
CUTION   Lord John Press Northridge, CA 1980
[1] Approximately 500 cc. Second state dustwrap-
per in black on yellow per publisher $7/30

067a: FANTASMAS PARA SIEMPRE Ediciones
Libreria La Ciudad Buenos Aires 1980 [2] 4,000 no
cc. Precedes the English language edition, 067b
(ref.c) $100/200

067b: THE GHOSTS OF FOREVER Rizzoli NY
(1981) [1] 1,500 cc (Fine Book Co. 1/94) $30/75

068a: THE STORIES OF RAY BRADBURY
Knopf NY 1980 [1] Wraps. Proof copy with the
first appearance in print of "Heart Transplant" (not
in published version) "Ray Bradbury" and Borzoi
design on spine (ref.c) $350.

068b: THE STORIES OF RAY BRADBURY
Knopf NY 1980 [1] Second state of proof, as 068a
except has "RAY BRADBURY" in caps and
"Knopf" instead of Borzoi design $275.

068c: THE STORIES OF RAY BRADBURY
Knopf NY 1980 [2] 60 specially bound presenta-
tion copies for author (ref.c) $650.

068d: THE STORIES OF RAY BRADBURY
Knopf NY 1980 [1] (ref.c) $20/60

068e: THE STORIES OF RAY BRADBURY
Granada L/Toronto 1981 [1] (ref.c) $8/40

069a: CHRISTMAS GREETINGS 1980 (Printed
for author LA 1980) [0] Broadside (ref.c) $40.

070a: THE FOGHORN AND OTHER STORIES
Kinseido Tokyo (1981) [0] Wraps in dustwrapper.
Note: same title as 058a but different stories (ref.c) $25/50

071a: IMAGINE Lord John Press Northridge, CA
1981 [2] Broadside. 150 no cc. Signed by
Bradbury and artist Joseph Mugnaini (ref.c). See
also Item 080a $75.

072a: THE HAUNTED COMPUTER AND AN-
DROID POPE Knopf NY 1981 [1] (Ref.c) $6/30

072b: THE HAUNTED COMPUTER AND AN-
DROID POPE Granada L/T (1981) [1] (Ref.c)　　　$8/40

073a: LONG AFTER MIDNIGHT AND OTHER
STORIES Nan'Un-Do Tokyo (1981) [0] Wraps
(Ref.c)　　　$40.

074a: THEN IS ALL LOVE? IT IS, IT IS! Orange
County Book Soc. Orange, CA 1981 [2] Broad-
side. 230 cc. Signed by Bradbury and artist Scott
Fitzgerald (ref.c)　　　$100.

074b: THEN IS ALL LOVE? IT IS, IT IS!
CHRISTMAS WISHES 1981 (Printed for author
LA 1981) [0] Broadside (ref.c)　　　$40.

075a: THERE IS LIFE ON MARS (Readers Digest
Pleasantville, NY 1981) [0] Wraps (ref.c)　　　$35.

076a: THE OTHER FOOT Perfection Form Co.
(Logan, Iowa) 1982 [0] Wraps. First separate
printing (ref.c)　　　$5.

077a: THE VELDT Perfection Form Co. (Logan,
Iowa) 1982 [0] Wraps. First separate printing (ref.c)　　　$5.

078a: THE COMPLETE POEMS OF RAY BRAD-
BURY Del Rey/Ballantine NY (1982) [1] Wraps
(ref.c)　　　$15.

079a: THE LOVE AFFAIR   Lord John Press
Northridge, CA 1982 [2] Approximately 12 cc.
Marked "Presentation Copy" and signed by Brad-
bury and artist Joseph Mugnaini (ref.c)　　　$250.

079b: THE LOVE AFFAIR   Lord John Press
Northridge, CA 1982 [2] 100 deluxe no cc. Signed
by Bradbury and Mugnaini (ref.c)　　　$125.

079c: THE LOVE AFFAIR   Lord John Press
Northridge, CA 1982 [2] 300 sgd no cc. Issued in
dustwrapper. Simulated leather spine (ref.c)　　　$50/75

079d: THE LOVE AFFAIR   Lord John Press
Northridge, CA 1982 [2]   Variant binding with
cloth spine (ref.c) $40/60

080a: CHRISTMAS GREETINGS 1982   (Printed
for author L.A. 1982) [0] Broadside. Although not
so titled, it is actually "IMAGINE" (item 071a)
(ref.c) $50.

081a: AMERICA   Herb Yellin for Pat Reagh &
Richard Gurewitz (CA 1983) [2] Approximately
12 cc. Marked "Presentation Copy" (ref.c) $175.

081b: AMERICA   Herb Yellin for Pat Reagh &
Richard Gurewitz   (CA 1983) [2] 26 sgd ltr cc.
Broadside (ref.c) $150.

081c: AMERICA   Herb Yellin for Pat Reagh &
Richard Gurewitz (CA 1983) [2] 300 sgd no cc.
Broadside (ref.c) $50.

081d: AMERICA   Herb Yellin for Pat Reagh &
Richard Gurewitz (CA 1983) [0] Broadside. Trade
issue with facsimile signature (ref.c) $20.

082a: DINOSAUR TALES Bantam Books T/NY/L
and Sydney (1983) [1] Large wraps (ref.c) $30.

083a: TO IRELAND Santa Susana Press Northridge, CA 1983 [0] Approximately 500 cc. Broadside (ref.c) $50.

084a: OCTOBER Walt Daugherty LA 1983 [1]
Approximately 150 cc. Wraps. Not published for
sale (ref.c) $75.

085a: CHRISTMAS GREETINGS 1983 [] (Printed
for author LA 1983) [0] Broadside (ref.c) $40.

086a: A MEMORY OF MURDER Dell (NY 1984)
[1] Wraps (ref.c) $25.

087a: FOREVER AND THE EARTH Croissant & Co. (Athens, OH 1984) [2] 300 sgd no cc. Issued in tissue wrapper (the signature page is tipped-in 2 ways, either facing p.[44] or facing the colophon page {ref.c}) $75.

088a: THE NOVELS OF RAY BRADBURY Granada L/Toronto (1984) [1] Contains *Something Wicked This Way Comes, Fahrenheit 451,* and *Dandelion Wine* (ref.c) $15/50

089a: THE LAST GOOD KISS Santa Susana Press Calif. State Univ. Northridge Library 1984 [2] Approximately 5 cc. Marked "Presentation Copy." Boxed with 3 signed prints by Hans Burkhardt. (ref.c) $500/600

089b: THE LAST GOOD KISS Santa Susana Press Calif. State Univ. Northridge Library 1984 [2] 60 sgd no cc. Boxed with 3 signed prints by Hans Burkhardt (ref.c) $500/600

090a: CHRISTMAS GREETINGS 1984 (Printed for the author LA 1984) [0] Broadside (ref.c) $40.

091a: THE VISION   (World Inter-Dependence Fund Beverly Hills, CA 1985 {on back cover}) [0] Wraps (ref.c) $60.

092a: WORLD INTER-DEPENDENCE FUND (World Inter-Dependence Fund Beverly Hills, CA {on back cover}) (no-date) [0] Wraps (ref.c) $60.

093a: LONG AFTER ECCLESIASTES Gold Stein Press Santa Ana, CA 1985 [2] 10 artist proofs marked "A.P." Signed. A miniature book bound in leather in slipcase (ref.c) $150/200

093b: LONG AFTER ECCLESIASTES Gold Stein Press Santa Ana, 1985 [2] 75 sgd no cc. Miniature book in leather in slipcase (ref.c) $100/150

094a: THE ART OF PLAYBOY   Alfred Van Der
Marck NY (1985) [1] Text by Bradbury (ref.c) $15/40

095a: DEATH IS A LONELY BUSINESS Knopf
NY 1985 [1] Dustwrapper priced at $16.95 (very
scarce). (Published in October.) (Ref.c) $7/200

095b: DEATH IS A LONELY BUSINESS Knopf
NY 1985 [1] Dustwrapper priced at $15.95 with
minor design changes. (Published in October.)
(Ref.c) $7/35

095c: DEATH IS A LONELY BUSINESS Franklin
Library Franklin Ctr PA 1985 [2] Approximately
13,000 cc.   "Signed Limited Edition" with new
introduction by author.   Bound in full leather.
(Published in November.) (Ref.c) $85.

095d: DEATH IS A LONELY BUSINESS Knopf
NY 1985 [1] 70 specially bound presentation copies
for author (Fine Book Co. cataloged "one of 60
copies"). Full black cloth with gold stamping,
without dustwrapper.   (Published in December.)
(Ref.c) $500.

095e: DEATH IS A LONELY BUSINESS Grafton
Books L... (1986) [1] (Ref.c) $10/40

096a: THE WONDERFUL DEATH OF DUDLEY
STONE   Pyewacket Press   North Hampton, MA
1985 [2] 29 no. cc. Signed by printer, without dustwrapper (ref.c) $500.

097a: A CHRISTMAS WISH 1985 (Printed for
author LA 1985) [0] Broadside (ref.c) $40.

098a: THE FLYING MACHINE Dramatic Publ.
Co. Woodstock, IL (1986) [0] Wraps (ref.c) $15.

099a: THE MARTIAN CHRONICLES Dramatic
Publ. Co. Woodstock, IL (1986) [0] Wraps. (A
play) (ref.c) $10.

100a: FAHRENHEIT 451   Dramatic Publ. Co. Woodstock, IL (1986) [0] Wraps. (A play.) (Ref.c) $10.

101a: WONDERFUL ICE CREAM SUIT   Dramatic Publ. Co. Woodstock, IL (1986) [0] Wraps. (A play.) (Ref.c) $10.

102a: KALEIDOSCOPE   Dramatic Publ. Co. Woodstock, IL (1986) [0] Wraps. (A play.) (Ref.c) $10.

103a: A DEVICE OUT OF TIME Dramatic Publ. Co. Woodstock, IL (1986) [0] Wraps. (A play.) (ref.c) $10.

104a: THE PAINTED SPEECH OF RAY BRAD-BURY Art Center College of Design Pasadena, CA 1986 [2] 100 sgd no cc. Portfolio (ref.c) $250.

105a: CHRISTMAS WISHES 1986 (Printed for the author 1986) [0] Broadside (ref.c) $35.

106a: DEATH HAS LOST ITS CHARM FOR ME Lord John Press Northridge, CA 1987 [2] Approximately 25 cc. Marked "Presentation Copy" (ref.c) $200.

106b: DEATH HAS LOST ITS CHARM FOR ME Lord John Press Northridge, CA 1987 [2] 26 sgd ltr cc. Bound in half leather (ref.c) $250.

106c: DEATH HAS LOST ITS CHARM FOR ME Lord John Press Northridge, CA 1987 [2] 150 sgd no cc (ref.c) $100.

106d: DEATH HAS LOST ITS CHARM FOR ME Lord John Press Northridge, CA 1987 [1] $6/30

107a: FEVER DREAMS St. Martins NY (1987) [0] (Ref.c) $5/25

108a: LIPSYNC, DALI'S DILEMMA   (Bernard Kordell LA 1987) [2] 67 no cc. Broadside (ref.c) $150.

109a: RAY BRADBURY Octopus/Heinemann (NY 1987) [1] Contains *Fahrenheit 451, The Illustrated Man, Dandelion Wine, The Golden Apples of the Sun* and *The Martian Chronicles* (ref.c) $10/25

110a: THE APRIL WITCH Creative Education no place? 1987 [] (Ref.c) $5.

111a: THE FOG HORN Creative Education no place? 1987 [] (Ref.c) $5.

112a: THE OTHER FOOT Creative Education no place? 1987 [] (Ref.c) $5.

113a: THE VELDT Creative Education no place? 1987 [] (Ref.c) $5.

114a: CHRISTMAS WISHES 1987 (printed for the author LA 1987) [0] Broadside (ref.c) $35.

115a: THE DRAGON (Footsteps Press Round Top, NY 1988) [2] 10 cc. Artist proofs marked "A/P" $60.

115b: THE DRAGON (Footsteps Press Round Top, NY 1988) [2] Wraps. 26 ltr cc signed in red, with illustrated cover in blue mylar (ref.c) $125.

115c: THE DRAGON (Footsteps Press Round Top, NY 1988) [2] Wraps. 16 double-lettered, signed copies for presentation $100.

115d: THE DRAGON (Footsteps Press Round Top, NY 1988) [2] Wraps. 300 no cc sgd in blue, with illustrated cover in red mylar $40.

116a: THE TOYNBEE CONVECTOR Knopf NY 1988 [] Uncorrected proofs in blue printed wraps (Bert Babcock 11/89) $75.

116b: THE TOYNBEE CONVECTOR Knopf NY 1988 [2] 350 sgd no cc. Issued without dustwrapper in illustrated slipcase (ref.c) $100/150

116c: THE TOYNBEE CONVECTOR Knopf NY
1988 [1] (Published June 1988 at $17.95) (ref.c) $5/25

116d: THE TOYNBEE CONVECTOR Grafton L
(1989) [1] "Published by Grafton Books 1989" $10/40

117a: WHERE WAS GEORGE? A.B. Laffer
Assoc. Lomita, Ca 1988 [0] 5 stapled leaves
printed on both sides $60.

118a: FALLING UPWARD Dramatic Publ.
(Woodstock, IL 1988) [0] Wraps $10.

119a: A CHRISTMAS WISH 1988 (Printed For
Author L.A. 1988) [0] Broadside poem $35.

120a: THERE WILL COME SOFT RAINS Perfection Form Co. Logan, Iowa 1989 [0] Wraps $5.

121a: THE CLIMATE OF PALETTES Lord John
Press Northridge, CA 1989 [2] 26 sgd ltr cc. A
miniature book in slipcase (There were also a
number of presentation copies) $150/175

121b: THE CLIMATE OF PALETTES Lord John
Press Northridge, CA 1989 [2] 150 sgd no cc.
Miniature book. Issued without slipcase $75.

122a: KALEIDOSCOPE + Livre de Poche (Paris
1989) [0] Wraps. (Used for teaching English) $35.

123a: A CHRISTMAS WISH 1989 (Printed For
Author L.A. 1989) [0] Broadside poem $35.

124a: CLASSIC STORIES I Bantam NY (1990)
[0] Wraps. "Bantam Edition/ May 1990. KR 10
9...1." Priced at $3.95 $10.

125a: CLASSIC STORIES II Bantam NY (1990)
[0] Wraps. "Bantam Edition/ May 1990. KR 10
9...1." Priced at $3.95 $7.

126a: A GRAVEYARD FOR LUNATICS Grafton
L 1990 [] (Precedes U.S. -Barry Levin) $8/40

126b: A GRAVEYARD FOR LUNATICS Knopf
NY 1990 [1] Uncorrected proof in blue wraps
which was edited and changed by Bradbury for the
published edition $100.

126c: A GRAVEYARD FOR LUNATICS Knopf
NY 1990 [1] (Published July 1990 at $18.95) $6/30

127a: GREEN SHADOWS WHITE WHALE
Knopf NY 1992 [1] Uncorrected proof in lime-
green wraps (Bev Chaney 10/95) $60.

127b: GREEN SHADOWS WHITE WHALE
Knopf NY 1992 [1] (Published 5/92 at $21) $5/25

127c: GREEN SHADOWS WHITE WHALE
Ultramarine Press NY 1992 [2] 12 sgd ltr cc.
Issued in full leather $450.

128d: GREEN SHADOWS WHITE WHALE
Ultramarine Press NY 1992 [2] 38 sgd no cc.
Issued in quarter leather (The Fine Books Co. 1/95) $325

127d: GREEN SHADOWS WHITE WHALE
Ultramarine Press NY 1992 [2] 100 sgd ltd cc.
Issued without dustwrapper in slipcase $100/150

127e: GREEN SHADOWS   WHITE WHALE
Harper Collins L 1992 [] $5/30

128a: THE R.B., G.K.C., AND G.B.S. FOREVER
ORIENT EXPRESS   (Joshua O'Dell Editions
Santa Barbara 1994) [] Advance excerpt from
Journey to Far Metahor. Unbound sheets laid into
very tall, stiff red wraps (Between The Covers
12/94) $50.

128b: THE R.B., G.K.C., AND G.B.S. FOREVER
ORIENT EXPRESS   (Joshua O'Dell Editions
Santa Barbara 1994) [] 700 cc. Broadside. Double-

sided in folding jacket. A long poem (Vagabond Books 4/95) $20.

EDITED BY BRADBURY

129a: FUTURIA FANTASIA Vol. 1, No. 1, Summer 1939 (Printed by author LA 1939) [0] Printed on both sides of 6 stapled leaves $500.

130a: FUTURIA FANTASIA Vol. 1, No. 2, Fall 1939 (Printed by author LA 1939) [0] Printed on both sides of 10 stapled leaves $500.

131a: FUTURIA FANTASIA Vol. 1, No. 3, Winter 1940 (Printed by author LA 1940) [0] Printed on both sides of 10 stapled leaves $500.

132a: FUTURIA FANTASIA Vol. 1 No. 4 (Printed by the author LA 1940) [0] Printed on both sides of 10 stapled leaves $500.

133a: TIMELESS STORIES FOR TODAY AND TOMORROW Bantam Books NY (1952) [1] Wraps. First issue with price of 35¢ (ref.c) $60.

134a: TIMELESS STORIES FOR TODAY AND TOMORROW Bantam Books NY (1952) [1] Wraps. Second issue with price of 50¢ $35.

135a: THE CIRCUS OF DR. LAO AND OTHER IMPROBABLE STORIES Bantam Books NY (1956) [1] Wraps $40.

ADAPTATIONS OF BRADBURY'S WORKS

136a: THE AUTUMN PEOPLE Ballantine Books NY (1965) [1] Wraps. Comic illustrated versions of stories by "E. C." artists (Ref.c) $50.

137a: TOMORROW MIDNIGHT Ballantine
Books NY (1966) [1] Wraps. Comic illustrated
versions of stories by "E. C." artists (Ref.c) $50.

138a: ILS ETAIENTS NOIRS, AUX YEUX D'OR
(Dark They Were And Golden Eyed) Edwin Arnold
(L 1972) [1] Wraps. Adapted and enlarged by Anne
Jacobs (Ref.c) $30.

139a: IT CAME FROM OUTER-SPACE (Crest-
wood House Mankato, MN) 1982 [0] Pictorial
cloth without dustwrapper. Adapted by Ian Thorne
(Ref.c) $40.

139b: IT CAME FROM OUTER-SPACE (Crest-
wood House Mankato, MN) 1982 [0] Wraps.
Adapted by Ian Thorne (ref.c) $15.

140a: FROST AND FIRE (D.C. Comics NY 1985)
[0] Wraps. Comic illustrated adaptation by Klaus
Janson (ref.c) $25.

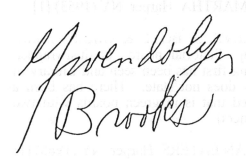

GWENDOLYN BROOKS

Brooks was born in Topeka, Kansas, in 1917 but was raised and spent most of her life in Chicago. She began submitting poems for publication during her high school years. In the 1940s she won a number of first prizes from the Midwestern Writers' Conference; as well as an American Academy of Arts and Letters award and a Guggenheim fellowship. She has taught at Columbia, Elmhurst, and the City College of New York, among others. Brooks was awarded a Pulitzer Prize in 1950; has been the Poet Laureate of Illinois; and the poetry consultant at the Library of Congress.

We are not aware of a bibliography on Brooks. The information herein was based on a private collection.

001a: SONG AFTER SUNSET 1936 [] One known
copy $5,000

002a: A STREET IN BRONZEVILLE Harper NY
1945 [1] $100/400

003a: WE'RE THE ONLY COLORED PEOPLE
HERE Black Sun Press Washington, D.C. 1946 []
12" x 16" broadside. Printed on both sides in portfolio. Black Sun Portfolio, Volume 3 (Waverly
4/94) $150.

004a: ANNIE ALLEN Harper NY (1949) [1] 1950
Pulitzer Prize for Poetry $75/300

005a: MAUD MARTHA Harper NY (1953) [1] $75/200

006a: BRONZEVILLE BOYS & GIRLS Harper NY (1956) [0] Pictorial boards in dustwrapper. (No copy stating first has been seen and Library of Congress copy does not state. There has been a later copy noted that is in green boards with two children in corners) $75/250

007a: THE BEAN EATERS Harper NY (1960) [1] 60/300

008a: SELECTED POEMS Harper NY (1963) [1] $25/125

008b: SELECTED POEMS Harper NY 1963 [1] Wraps $35.

009a: NEW NEGRO POETS: USA Indiana University Press Bloomington (1964) [0] (Assume wraps.) Edited by Langston Hughes, foreword by Gwendolyn Brooks $125

010a: IN THE TIME OF DETACHMENT, IN THE TIME OF COLD Civil War... Springfield 1965 [2] Single folded sheet with stamped number on back cover but no total limitation (Lib. of Congress had #275; but Beasley Books in 3/93 cataloged a copy with #545 so there are at least that many) $75.

011a: WE REAL COOL Broadside Press Detroit 1966 [0] 8 1/2" x 12" broadside $75.

012a: THE WALL Broadside Press Detroit 1967 [0] Broadside $75.

013a: A PORTION OF THAT FIELD+ University of Illinois Urbana 1967 [0] $35/175

014a: IN THE MECCA Harper NY (1968) [1] $25/125

015a: MARTIN LUTHER KING, JR. Broadside Press Detroit 1968 [2] 200 sgd no cc. Broadside $100.

016a: FOR ILLINOIS 1968: A SESQUICENTEN-
NIAL POEM Sesquicentenial Comm. (Chicago
1968) [2] Sgd/ltd. Wraps. Not numbered and no
total quantity indicated $150.

017a: RIOT Broadside Press Detroit (1969) [1]
Wraps. First issue with "these" for "there" on p.22
(Beasley Books #14) $75.

017b: RIOT Broadside Press Detroit (1969) [1]
P.22 corrected $40.

018a: FAMILY PICTURES   Broadside Press
Detroit 1970 [1] Wraps $75.

018b: FAMILY PICTURES   Broadside Press
Detroit   1971 [] Issued without dustwrapper
(Thomas Goldwasser 10/92) $75.

019a: ALONENESS Broadside Press Detroit 1971
[1] $25/75

019b: ALONENESS Broadside Press Detroit 1971
[1] Wraps $35.

020a: A BROADSIDE TREASURY   Broadside
Press Detroit (1971) [1] Edited by Brooks, issued
without dustwrapper $75.

020b: A BROADSIDE TREASURY   Broadside
Press Detroit (1971) [1] Wraps. Edited by Brooks $35.

021a: BLACK STEEL   Broadside Press   Detroit
1971 [1] Broadside $50.

022a: TO GWEN WITH LOVE   Johnson Publ.
Chicago 1971 [0] Foreword by Brooks $25/75

022b: TO GWEN WITH LOVE   Johnson Publ.
Chicago 1971 [0] Wraps $35.

023a: JUMP BAD: A NEW CHICAGO ANTHOL-
OGY Broadside Press Detroit (1971) [1] Wraps.
An anthology presented by Brooks $75.

024a: THE WORLD OF GWENDOLYN BROOKS
Harper NY (1971) [1] Also has "...1" on last page
and "0971" on dustwrapper flap. (Later printings
continue to state first edition) $25/125

025a: WE ASKED GWENDOLYN BROOKS
ABOUT THE CREATIVE ENVIRONMENT IN
ILLINOIS   Illinois Bell Telephone (Chicago) [no-
date] [0] Wraps $60.

026a: AURORA Broadside Press Detroit 1972 [2]
500 cc $60.

027a: REPORT FROM PART ONE   Broadside
Press Detroit (1972) [1] Advance copy. Perfect
bound without front cover and with heavy
cardboard on back $125.

027b: REPORT FROM PART ONE   Broadside
Press Detroit (1972) [1] Issued without dustwrapper $75.

028a: THE TIGER WHO WORE WHITE
GLOVES... Third World Press Chicago (1974) [1] $25/100

028b: THE TIGER WHO WORE WHITE
GLOVES... Third World Press Chicago (1974) [1]
Wraps $35.

029a: BECKONINGS: POEMS Broadside Press
Detroit (1975) [1] Wraps $60.

030a: A CAPSULE COURSE IN BLACK
POETRY WRITING Broadside Press Detroit 1975
[] Wraps. Brooks and others $50.

031a: TO YOUNG READERS Chicago Public
Library Chicago 1979 [0] Small broadside $40.

032a: PRIMER FOR BLACKS   Brooks Press
(Chicago 1980) [1] Wraps $60.

033a: YOUNG POET'S PRIMER   Brooks Press
(Chicago 1980) [0] Wraps $60.

034a: TO DISEMBARK   Third World Press   Chicago (1981) [0] $25/75

034b: TO DISEMBARK   Third World Press   Chicago (1981) [0] Wraps $30.

035a: THE PROGRESS   Turtle Press   (no-place)
1982   [2]   300 cc.   Wraps.   Reprinted from *The
World of Gwendolyn Brooks* with new "Afternote" $75.

036a: BLACK LOVE (Brooks Press   Chicago
1982) [0] Wraps $40.

037a: VERY YOUNG POETS Brooks Press (Chicago 1983) [] Wraps $40.

038a: MAYOR HAROLD WASHINGTON Brooks
Press (Chicago 1983) [1] Wraps $40.

039a: THE NEAR - JOHANNESBURG BOY+
David Co. Chicago (1986) [] Wraps $35.

040a: BLACKS   David Co.   Chicago (1987) [0]
(Published at $25) $15/60

041a: GOTTSCHALK AND THE GRANDE TAR-
ANTELLE   David Co.   Chicago   (1988)   [1]
Leatherette   without   dustwrapper   (Thomas
Goldwasser 11/94) $75.

041b: GOTTSCHALK AND THE GRANDE TAR-
ANTELLE David Co. Chicago (1988) [1] Wraps $30.

042a: WINNIE   David Co.   Chicago (1988) [1]
Wraps $30.

043a: THE SECOND SERMON ON THE WARP-
LAND Chax Press (Tucson) 1988 [] 10" x 15"
broadside (Am Here Books 5/92) $30.

044a: JANE ADDAMS *San Francisco Examiner*
San Francisco   1990 []   13" x 7 1/4" poetry
broadside in two colors $30.

045a: THE BEAN EATERS (Poem) (Kutztown
Univ. Pennsylvania 1991) [2] 25 sgd no cc. 8 1/2"
x 11" broadside $75.

045b: THE BEAN EATERS (Poem)   (Kutztown
Univ. Pennsylvania 1991) [2] 175 cc. Broadside $50.

046a: CHILDREN COMING HOME   David Co.
Chicago (1991) [] Wraps (Antic Hay 2/93) $25.

Chandler Brossard (signature)

CHANDLER BROSSARD

Born in 1922 in Idaho into a Mormon family, Brossard left school at the age of 11. His first two novels have been classed as early Beat novels by some, but he has moved in a more European avant-garde direction ever since. His numerous short story anthologies contain many of his own stories, most under female pseudonyms. He has worked at such magazines as the *New Yorker*, *Time*, *American Mercury*, and *Look* and has had brief stints of teaching at a variety of colleges. He has lived abroad many years, but now resides on New York's upper West side.

We would like to thank Steven Moore for the preparation of the initial bibliographical information herein.

001a: WHO WALK IN DARKNESS New Directions (NY 1952) [0] $25/100

001b: WHO WALK IN DARKNESS John Lehmann L (1952) [] $15/75

001c: WHO WALK IN DARKNESS New Directions (NY 1952) [0] Wraps. Remaining sheets of 001a bound as NDP 116 (3/21/62) per *New Directions Reader* $40.

001d: WHO WALK IN DARKNESS Harper & Row NY (1972) [1] Wraps. Unexpurgated edition $25.

002a: THE BOLD SABOTEURS Farrar, Straus NY (1953) [1] $15/60

003a: PARIS ESCORT by "Daniel Harper" Eton Books NY (1953) [0] Wraps. (Also see item 016a) $75.

004a: THE WRONG TURN   by "Daniel Harper"
Avon NY (1954) [0] Wraps $60.

005a: ALL PASSION SPENT Popular Library NY
(1954) [] Wraps. (Reissued as *Episode with Erika*
in 1963) $60.

006a: THE SCENE BEFORE YOU: A NEW AP-
PROACH TO AMERICAN CULTURE Rinehart
NY (1955) [5] Edited by Brossard $20/60

007a: THE FIRST TIME Pyramid NY (1957) []
Wraps. Edited by Brossard $40.

008a: THE DOUBLE VIEW Dial NY 1960 [0] $10/40

009a: DEAD OF NIGHT | THE DENTIST   NY
Film Society Winter 60-61 [0] Single folded sheet
making four pages with notes by Brossard $35.

010a: THE GIRLS IN ROME   New American
Library (Signet) (NY 1961) [1] Wraps. (Reissued
as *We Did the Strangest Things* in 1968) $40.

011a: DESIRE IN THE SUBURBS Lancer NY
(1962) [] Wraps. Edited by Brossard $40.

012a: THE PANGS OF LOVE   Regency Books
Evanston, IL (1962) [] Wraps. Edited by Brossard $40.

013a: THE NYMPHETS   Edited by "Daniel
Harper" Lancer NY (1963) [0] Wraps $40.

014a: 18 BEST STORIES BY EDGAR ALLAN
POE Dell (NY 1965) [1] Wraps. Edited by
Brossard and Vincent Price $35.

015a: WIVES AND LOVERS Dell (NY 1965) [1]
Wraps. Edited by Brossard $35.

016a: A MAN FOR ALL WOMEN Fawcett Greenwich, CT (1966) [0] Wraps. (An expanded version of *Paris Escort*) $25.

017a: ILLYA: THAT MAN FROM U.N.C.L.E. by "Iris-Marie Brossard" Pocket Books NY (1966) [0] Wraps $50.

018a: THE INSANE WORLD OF ADOLF HIT- LER Fawcett (Greenwich, CT 1966) [0] Wraps $35.

019a: LOVE ME, LOVE ME! Fawcett Greenwich, CT (1966) [0] Wraps. Edited by Brossard $30.

020a: MARRIAGE GAMES Pyramid Books NY (1967) [0] Wraps. Edited by Brossard $30.

021a: I WANT MORE OF THIS Dell (NY 1967) [1] Wraps. Edited by Brossard $30.

022a: THE SPANISH SCENE Viking NY (1968) [1] $10/40

023a: WAKE UP. WE'RE ALMOST THERE Richard Baron NY 1970 [] "Uncorrected Proof" in blue printed wraps $50.

023b: WAKE UP. WE'RE ALMOST THERE Richard Baron NY 1970 [1] $10/35

024a: DID CHRIST MAKE LOVE? Bobbs-Merrill Indianapolis (1973) [0] 4,000 cc $10/35

025a: DIRTY BOOKS FOR LITTLE FOLKS (Daniel Cointe La Chapelle la Reine, France 1978) [0] Wraps $50.

026a: RAGING JOYS, SUBLIME VIOLATIONS Cherry Valley (Silver Spring, MD 1981) [2] 26 copies signed by Brossard on half-title $60.

026b: RAGING JOYS, SUBLIME VIOLATIONS Cherry Valley (Silver Spring, MD 1981) [1] 200 cc $10/35

026c: RAGING JOYS, SUBLIME VIOLATIONS
Cherry Valley (Silver Spring, MD 1981) [] 600 cc.
Wraps $15.

027a: A CHIMNEY SWEEP COMES CLEAN Re-
alities Library (San Jose, CA 1985) [0] 2,000 cc.
Wraps $15.

028a: CLOSING THE GAP Redbeck Press (Hes-
lington, Yorkshire) 1986 [2] 26 sgd ltr cc. Wraps $50.

028b: CLOSING THE GAP Redbeck Press (Hes-
lington, Yorkshire) 1986 [1] 474 cc. Wraps $15.

029a: POSTCARDS   Redbeck Press (Heslington,
Yorkshire) 1987 [] (Not seen) $25.

030a: CHANDLER BROSSARD   Review of Contemporary Fiction 1987 [] Wraps. Brossard issue,
by and about (Water Row Books) $10.

031a: AS THE WOLF HOWLS AT MY DOOR
Dalkey Archive no place? 1992 [] (Published 4/92
at $21.95) $5/25

Truman Capote (signature)

TRUMAN CAPOTE
1924 - 1985

Truman Capote was born in New Orleans and educated in New York and Connecticut. He worked in the Art Department of *The New Yorker* and as a writer on a television show before going on his own as a full-time writer. His first novel at age 24 brought him literary fame and a following, which continued throughout his life probably reaching a peak with the success of his "non-fiction" true crime novel *In Cold Blood.*

We would like to thank D. Edmond Miller for his assistance on the preliminary bibliographic research for this guide.

REFERENCES:

(a) Lepper, Gary M. A BIBLIOGRAPHICAL REFERENCE TO SEVENTY-FIVE MODERN AMERICAN AUTHORS. Berkeley: Serendipity Books, 1976.

(b) Wilson, Robert A. *Truman Capote: A Bibliographical Checklist* in *American Book Collector*. Vol. 1, No. 4, July/August, 1980.

(c) Eppard, Philip B., editor. FIRST PRINTINGS OF AMERICAN AUTHORS. Volume 5. Detroit: Gale Research Company (1987).

(d) D. Edmond Miller or inventory.

001a: OTHER VOICES, OTHER ROOMS Random House NY (1948) [1] 10,000 cc per introduction to the first French edition (ref.d). (William Reese Catalog 46 noted 3 variants: top edge stained gray-green; stained gray; and unstained $100/400

001b: OTHER VOICES, OTHER ROOMS William Heinemann Ltd. L (1948) [1] Ref.b $40/200

001c: OTHER VOICES, OTHER ROOMS Random House NY (1968) [0] 20th anniversary edition. New preface by Capote $10/40

001d: OTHER VOICES, OTHER ROOMS Heine-mann L 1968 [] 20th anniversary edition. New preface by Capote (ref.c) $10/40

001e: OTHER VOICES, OTHER ROOMS Franklin Library Franklin Center 1979 [2] Signed "limited" edition. Numer of copies not specified. Same preface as in 001c. Adds new 4-page "special message" by Capote. Leather binding (ref.c) $150.

002a: A TREE OF NIGHT *and Other Stories* Random House NY (1949) [1] Also see 004e $40/200

002b: A TREE OF NIGHT *and Other Stories* William Heinemann Ltd L (1950) [1] Wraps. Proof copy in off-white printed wraps (Gotham Book Mart) $350.

002c: A TREE OF NIGHT *and Other Stories* William Heinemann Ltd L (1950) [1] Ref.b $25/125

003a: LOCAL COLOR Random House NY (1950) [1] $50/250

003b: LOCAL COLOR William Heinemann Ltd. L (1950) [2] 200 no. cc. Ref.c gives date as "1955." Full leather in cellophane dustwrapper (ref.b) $500.

004a: THE GRASS HARP Random House (NY 1951) [1] Rough beige cloth; brown, green and black stamping $75/250

004b: THE GRASS HARP Random House (NY 1951) [1] Second binding: smooth, fine grained beige cloth. Dustwrapper is the same as 004a $25/150

004c: THE GRASS HARP Heinemann L (1952) [] Wraps. "Proof copy for personal reading" (Gotham Book Mart) $300.

004d: THE GRASS HARP   William Heinemann
Ltd L (1952) [1] Ref.b. (Published 10/13/52) $25/125

004e: THE GRASS HARP and A TREE OF
NIGHT Signet (NY 1956) [] Wraps (ref.d) $30.

005a: THE GRASS HARP *A Play* Random House
NY (1952) [1] Reportedly only 500 cc $75/350

005b: THE GRASS HARP *A Play* Dramatists Play
Service (NY 1954) [0] Wraps. List of new titles
on back cover begins with *Inherit the Wind* (ref.b) $40.

006a: THE MUSES ARE HEARD   *An Account.*
Random House NY (1956) [1] $20/100

006b: THE MUSES ARE HEARD *An Account of
the Porgy and Bess Visit to Leningrad.* Heine-mann
L (1957) [1] Wraps.   Uncorrected proof copy in
light steel gray wraps printed in red (ref.d) $350.

006c: THE MUSES ARE HEARD *An Account of
the Porgy and Bess Visit to Leningrad.* Heinemann
L (1957) [1] Ref.b $15/75

007a: BREAKFAST AT TIFFANY'S   Random
House NY (1958) [1] $75/350

007b: BREAKFAST AT TIFFANY'S   Hamish
Hamilton L (1958) [1] Ref.b $20/100

008a: OBSERVATIONS Simon & Schuster NY
(1959) [0] Acetate dustwrapper in slipcase, photographs by Richard Avedon $100/350

008b: OBSERVATIONS Weidenfeld and Nicolson
L (1959) [0] Acetate dustwrapper in slipcase
(ref.b) $100/350

009a: SELECTED WRITINGS   Random House
NY (1963) [1] $30/150

009b: SELECTED WRITINGS   Modern Library
NY (1963) [1] Same plates as 009a with new title
page (Andes {Modern Library Bibliography} p.38) $8/40

009c: SELECTED WRITINGS   Hamish Hamilton
L (1963) [1] Ref.b $15/75

010a: VOCAL SELECTIONS FROM "HOUSE OF
FLOWERS"   Harwin Music Corp. NY 1963 [1]
Wraps. Lyrics by Capote and Harold Arlen (ref.c
lists but notes "not seen") $100.

010b: VOCAL SELECTIONS FROM "HOUSE OF
FLOWERS"   Harwin Music Corp. NY 1968 []
Wraps. Enlarged edition (ref.c lists but notes "not
seen") $40.

011a: IN COLD BLOOD   Random House   NY
(1965) [0] "Advance Proof Uncor..." in tall narrow
blue printed wraps with blue spiral binding. Printed
on rectos only (ref.d) $1,500.

011b: IN COLD BLOOD   Random House   NY
(1965) [1] 500 cc. Wraps. Advance Reading Copy
in which wrap is formed by dustwrapper and glued
to signatures at spine $300.

011c: IN COLD BLOOD   Random House   NY
(1965) [2] 500 sgd no cc. Black cloth, maroon
slipcase $500/600

011d: IN COLD BLOOD   Random House   NY
(1965) [1] Small number issued (exact quantity
unknown). Tipped-in leaf signed by Capote inserted
after front free endpaper.   Maroon cloth; gold
stamped $300/350

011e: IN COLD BLOOD   Random House   NY
(1965) [1] Maroon cloth; gold stamping.   First
dustwrapper has "1/66" on front flap. Also noted
that the first dustwrapper has 2 extra lines at bottom
of back flap: "Publishers of the American College

Dictionary and the Modern Library" (not on BOM
Club edition) $15/60

011f: IN COLD BLOOD Hamish Hamilton L
(1966) [1] Ref.b $15/60

012a: A CHRISTMAS MEMORY Random House
NY (1966) [2] 600 sgd no cc. Green cloth with
gold stamping. Issued with acetate dustwrapper in
bright red slipcase (Published November 4, 1966) $400/500

012b: A CHRISTMAS MEMORY Random House
NY [1966] [0] "1966" not in book, copyright 1956.
Beige boards with teal blue cloth spine and gold
stamping. Issued without dustwrapper in maroon
slipcase (Also noted in black cloth with gold
stamping in bright red slipcase) $25/75

012c: A CHRISTMAS MEMORY Hamish
Hamilton L 1966? [] (Ref.d) $25/75

012d: A CHRISTMAS MEMORY Creative
Education Mankato, MN (1984) [0] 5,000 cc.
(Ref.d) $6/30

012e: A CHRISTMAS MEMORY Knopf NY
(1989) [3] Illustrated by Beth Peck. First thus $6/30

013a: THE THANKSGIVING VISITOR Random
House NY (no-date [1968]) [2] 300 sgd no cc.
Grayish-green cloth with gold stamping. Issued in
acetate dustwrapper and green slipcase. (Published
11/21/68). Last date on copyright page is 1967
which is date of publication given in ref.a & b $400/600

013b: THE THANKSGIVING VISITOR Random
House NY (1968) [1] Beige boards with red cloth
spine and gold stamping. Issued in green or brown
slipcase, priority unknown (ref.b) $35/100

013c: THE THANKSGIVING VISITOR Hamish
Hamilton L (1969) [1] Ref.b $12/60

013d: THE THANKSGIVING VISITOR *A Christmas Memory* Random House NY (no-date) [0] First combined edition. Issued without dustwrapper in slipcase by Book-of-the-Month Club $5/35

014a: HOUSE OF FLOWERS Random House NY (1968) [0] Musical comedy. Written with Harold Arlen. (See also 010) $100/400

015a: TRILOGY *An Experiment of Multimedia* Macmillan Co. (NY 1969) [1] Written with Eleanor and Frank Perry $25/125

016a: THE DOGS BARK... Random House NY (1973) [] Uncorrected "First" proof in wraps. The preface is not typeset but in the form of a photocopied typescript and laid (or paper clipped) in (Wm. Reese Co. 4/95) $200.

016b: THE DOGS BARK... Random House NY (1973) [1] Wraps. "Uncorrected Proof" in red printed wraps (ref.d) $150.

016c: THE DOGS BARK... Random House NY (1973) [1] $10/50

016d: THE DOGS BARK...   Weidenfeld and Nicolson L (1974) [1] "First published ..." (ref.b) $10/50

017a: MUSIC FOR CHAMELEONS   Franklin Library Franklin Center, Pa. 1980 [1] Includes special message by Capote for members of First Edition Society not in Random House edition. Leather. (Ref.c) $125.

017b: MUSIC FOR CHAMELEONS   Random House NY (1980) [1] Wraps. "Uncorrected First Proof" in red printed wraps (ref.d) $200.

017c: MUSIC FOR CHAMELEONS   Random House NY (1980) [2] 350 sgd no cc. Brown cloth in dark brown slipcase (ref.d). (Published August 11, 1980) $200/300

017d: MUSIC FOR CHAMELEONS   Random House NY (1980) [] 25 cc. Bound for Capote in brown cloth and tan slipcase (Gotham Book Mart) $250/275

017e: MUSIC FOR CHAMELEONS   Random House   NY (1980) [1] Signed on tipped-in leaf (Alphabet Books 8/92) $150/200

017f: MUSIC FOR CHAMELEONS   Random House NY (1980) [1] (Ref.c) $7/35

017g: MUSIC FOR CHAMELEONS Hamilton L (1981) [] "Uncorrected Advance Proof" in light green printed wraps (Gotham Book Mart) $150.

017h: MUSIC FOR CHAMELEONS Hamilton L (1981) [] (Ref.c) $8/40

018a: MIRIAM   Creative Education   Mankato, Minn. (1982) [0]   Issued without dustwrapper. Also noted in library binding without dustwrapper (Steven Bernard 12/90) $50.

019a: A CHRISTMAS MEMORY   (Tales For Travellers S.F. 1982) [0] Single sheet map folded to make 24 pages (Boston Book Annex #31). (Probably the same text as 012) $25.

019b: A CHRISTMAS MEMORY   Creative Education (Mankato   1984) []   Issued without dustwrapper (Ampersand 9/88). (Probably the same text as 012) $25.

020a: ONE CHRISTMAS *Ladies Home Journal* NY 1982 [] Wraps. White printed in gray (Gotham Book Mart) $250.

020b: ONE CHRISTMAS Random House NY (1983) [1]   Wraps. "Uncorrected proof" in red printed wraps (Gotham Book Mart) $150.

020c: ONE CHRISTMAS   Random House NY (1983) [2] 500 sgd no cc.   Issued without dustwrapper in slipcase (ref.d) $250/350

020d: ONE CHRISTMAS   Random House NY (1983) [1] Trade edition also issued without dust-wrapper in slipcase (ref.d) $25/75

020e: ONE CHRISTMAS Hamish Hamilton L (1983) [] $12/60

021a: CONVERSATIONS WITH CAPOTE New American Lib. NY (1985) [1] Transcriptions of interviews with Capote by Lawrence Grobel. Foreword by James Michener (ref.d) $10/50

022a: THREE BY TRUMAN CAPOTE   Random House NY (1985) [1] Includes *Other Voices, Other Rooms*; *Breakfast at Tiffany's* and *Music For Chameleons* (ref.c) $10/50

023a: JUG OF SILVER   Creative Education Mankato (1986) [] First separate edition. Issued in pictorial boards without dustwrapper $75.

024a: ANSWERED PRAYERS Hamish Hamilton L (1986) [1] Precedes U.S. edition $10/50

024b: ANSWERED PRAYERS   Random House NY (1987) [] Uncorrected proof in yellow wraps (Joseph Dermont 5/88) $125.

024c: ANSWERED PRAYERS   Random House NY (1987) [4] 35,000 cc (PW). (Published 9/21/87 at $16.95) $7/35

025a: TRUMAN CAPOTE CONVERSATIONS University Press of Mississippi. Jackson (1987) [] Collected interviews from 1948 to 1980 edited by W. Thomas Inge $15/40

025b: TRUMAN CAPOTE CONVERSATIONS University Press of Mississippi Jackson (1987) [] Wraps $25.

026a: I REMEMBER GRANDPA Peachtree Atlanta 1987 [] Uncorrected proof in pictorial white wraps. Issued without plates by Barry Moser (Waiting for Godot 10/90) $100.

026b: I REMEMBER GRANDPA Peachtree Atlanta 1987 [1] 50,000 cc (PW). Illustrated by Barry Moser. (Published 9/1/87 at $14.95) (ref.d) $7/35

027a: THE WHITE ROSE Tamazunchale Press Newton, Iowa (1987) [2] 250 no. cc. Miniature book bound in vellum (Published at $49.50) $100.

028a: A CAPOTE READER Random House NY 1987 [4] Uncorrected proof in yellow wraps (Chloe's Books 7/89) $125.

028b: THE CAPOTE READER Random House NY 1987 [4] 35,000 cc (PW). (Published 9/21/87 at $25) $7/35

Chas W. Chesnutt

CHARLES W. CHESNUTT
(1858 - 1932)

Born in Cleveland, Ohio, in 1858, Chesnutt spent the 1860s and 1870s in Fayetteville, N.C., and began teaching at the age of sixteen. His first book was a collection of tales of plantation life in the Old South presented through the comments of an ex-slave denizen of the region. Chesnutt was a black man but very light skinned and barely distinguished from a white. He is sometimes called the first negro novelist. His later books dealt with racial prejudice. In 1928 he received the Springarn Gold Medal for his pioneer work in depicting the struggles of American blacks.

Prices are for very good to fine copies without dustwrapper prior to 1920.

REFERENCES:

(a) Bruccoli & Clark. FIRST PRINTINGS OF AMERICAN AUTHORS. Volume 3. Detroit: Gale Research (1978).

(b) Andrews, William L. THE LITERARY CAREER OF CHARLES W. CHESNUTT. Baton Rouge: Louisiana State University (1980).

001a: THE CONJURE WOMAN (Houghton Mifflin) Boston 1899 [2] 150 numbered large paper copies printed at the Riverside Press. Two signed copies have been noted but not known whether all were. It was issued with a dustwrapper. (A copy was catalogued for $3,700) $1,500.

001b: THE CONJURE WOMAN Houghton Mifflin Boston 1899 [0] Trade edition $500.

001c: THE CONJURE WOMAN Gay & Bird London 1899 [] $350.

001d: THE CONJURE WOMAN Houghton Mifflin Boston 1927 [] New edition $25/100

002a: FREDERICK DOUGLASS Small Maynard Boston 1899 [0] Limp leather (Bradley's *Handbook of Values*) $750.

002b: FREDERICK DOUGLASS Kegan Paul London 1899 [] $350.

003a: THE WIFE OF HIS YOUTH + Houghton Mifflin Boston 1899 [0] $500.

004a: THE HOUSE BEHIND THE CEDARS Houghton Mifflin Boston 1900 [0] $600.

005a: THE MARROW OF TRADITION Houghton Mifflin Boston 1901 [] Noted in either green, red, or yellow cloths, priority unknown $500.

006a: THE COLONEL'S DREAM Doubleday Page NY 1905 [1] "Published September 1905." Chesnutt's name mis-spelled "Chestnutt" on spine and front cover $450.

006b: THE COLONEL'S DREAM Doubleday Page NY 1905 [1] Name spelled correctly $350.

006c: THE COLONEL'S DREAM Constable London 1905 [] $250.

007a: BAXTER'S PROCRUSTES Cleveland 1966 [2] 180 copies $150.

008a: THE SHORT FICTION OF CHARLES W. CHESNUTT Howard Univ. Press Washington, D.C. 1974 [0] Edited by Sylvia Lyons Render $15/60

009a: THE JOURNAL OF CHARLES W. CHESNUTT Duke University Durham, NC 1993 [] Edited by Richard D. Brodhead. (Published at $34.95)

009b: THE JOURNAL OF CHARLES W. CHES-
NUTT   Duke University   Durham, NC   1993 []
Wraps. (Published at $12.95)

010a: CONJURE   WOMAN   AND   OTHER
STORIES Duke University Durham, NC 1993? []
Assume includes stories not in 1899 edition. (Pub-
lished at $34.95)

010b: CONJURE   WOMAN   AND   OTHER
STORIES Duke University Durham, NC 1993? []
Wraps. (Published at $12.95)

Agatha Christie (signature)

AGATHA CHRISTIE
(1890 - 1976)

Agatha Mary Clarissa Miller was the third child of Frederick Miller, an American, and Clarissa his English wife. She was educated at home and sent to finishing school in Paris. She met her first husband, Archibald Christie, on a trip to Egypt. They were married from 1914 to 1926. She met her second husband, Max Mallowan, on a trip to Baghdad. They were married from 1932 until her death.

She worked as a nurse during WWI and had been writing romantic fiction when her sister suggested she try a detective story. Her first priority was to create a detective and a tidy little man named Poirot emerged. (He had been retired quite some time in 1920 and Julian Symons estimated his age at over 130.) The first book was turned down by a number of publishers before John Lane agreed to publish it. He published the first six books and it is reported that the success of these books helped to reverse the firm's financial decline.

The titles, publishers and dates were taken from Robert Bonnard's *A Talent To Deceive: An Appreciation of Agatha Christie*, London: Collins, 1980, which includes an excellent checklist of the hardback and paperback editions. The identification codes for the first editions were obtained from Library of Congress copyright copies, books in inventory, or from Charles Vukotich, Jr., who we thank for his assistance. Although there were many titles not seen (these are denoted by empty brackets []), as far as we know neither Dodd, Mead, nor Collins was in the habit of stating "first edition." Therefore, if there is no statement of a later printing, one can assume the book is a first, at least before 1960.

001a: THE MYSTERIOUS AFFAIR AT STYLES
Lane NY 1920 [] $2,000/15,000

001b: THE MYSTERIOUS AFFAIR AT STYLES
Lane L 1921 [] $2,000/12,500

002a: THE SECRET ADVERSARY Lane L 1922
[] $750/3,500

002b: THE SECRET ADVERSARY Dodd, Mead
NY 1922 [] $600/2,500

003a: MURDER ON THE LINKS Lane L 1923 [] $850/4,000

003b: MURDER ON THE LINKS Dodd, Mead
NY 1923 [0] $750/3,500

004a: THE MAN IN THE BROWN SUIT Lane L
1924 [] $850/3,500

004b: THE MAN IN THE BROWN SUIT Dodd,
Mead NY 1924 [0] $600/2,500

005a: THE ROAD OF DREAMS Geoffrey Bles L
1924 [] $350/1,250

006a: POIROT INVESTIGATES Lane L (1924) [] $750/3,000

006b: POIROT INVESTIGATES Dodd, Mead NY
1925 [0] $600/2,500

007a: THE SECRET OF CHIMNEYS Lane L
(1925) [1] $650/2,500

007b: THE SECRET OF CHIMNEYS Dodd, Mead
NY 1925 [0] $450/2,000

008a: THE MURDER OF ROGER ACKROYD
Collins L 1926 [0] Haycraft-Queen Cornerstone.
Blue cloth with red letters. Variant: green cloth with
mustard-yellow letters $1,000/5,000

008b: THE MURDER OF ROGER ACKROYD
Dodd, Mead NY 1926 [] $750/3,000

009a: THE BIG FOUR Collins L (1927) [0] $600/2,500

009b: THE BIG FOUR Dodd, Mead NY 1927 [0] $400/1,750

010a: THE MYSTERY OF THE BLUE TRAIN
Collins L 1928 [] $500/2,000

010b: THE MYSTERY OF THE BLUE TRAIN
Dodd, Mead NY 1928 [0] $200/1,000

011a: THE SEVEN DIALS MYSTERY Collins L
1929 [] Blue cloth lettered in black on front and
spine. Also noted in black cloth with red lettering
(Janus Books) $600/2,500

011b: THE SEVEN DIALS MYSTERY Dodd,
Mead NY 1929 [0] Noted with wrap-around band
"Detective Story Club Selection" (Mordida 11/88) $200/750

012a: ALIBI French L 1929 [] Wraps. Dramatization of Item 008a $100.

013a: PARTNERS IN CRIME Collins L 1929 [] $500/2,000

013b: PARTNERS IN CRIME Dodd, Mead NY
(1929) [0] $200/1,000

014a: THE UNDERDOG Reader's Library L
(1929) [] With *Blackman's Wood* by E. Phillips
Oppenheim $100/500

015a: THE MURDER AT THE VICARAGE
Collins L 1930 [] $500/2,000

015b: THE MURDER AT THE VICARAGE
Dodd, Mead NY 1930 [0] $200/850

016a: THE MYSTERIOUS MR. QUIN Collins L
1930 [] $450/1,750

016b: THE MYSTERIOUS MR. QUIN   Dodd,
Mead NY 1930 [0] $150/750

017a: GIANT'S BREAD Collins L 1930 [] Writ-
ten as Mary Westmacott $100/500

017b: GIANT'S BREAD Doubleday GC 1930 [1]
Written as Mary Westmacott $75/350

018a: THE SITTAFORD MYSTERY Collins L
1931 [] Noted in orange or black covers, priority
unknown (Ergo Books 12/90) $200/1,000

018b: THE MURDER AT HAZELMOOR Dodd,
Mead NY 1931 [0] New title $200/850

019a: AN AGATHA CHRISTIE OMNIBUS Lane
L 1931 [] $75/350

020a: PERIL AT END HOUSE Collins L 1932 [] $200/1,250

020b: PERIL AT END HOUSE Dodd, Mead NY
1932 [0] $125/600

021a: THE THIRTEEN PROBLEMS Collins L
(1932) [0] $250/1,500

021b: THE TUESDAY CLUB MURDERS Dodd,
Mead NY 1933 [0] New title $200/750

022a: AN AGATHA CHRISTIE OMNIBUS OF
CRIME Collins L 1932 [] $75/350

023a: LORD EDGWARE DIES Collins L 1933 [] $300/1,500

023b: THIRTEEN AT DINNER Dodd, Mead NY
1933 [0] New title $125/600

024a: THE HOUND OF DEATH AND OTHER
STORIES Odhams L (1933) [0] "Copyright 1933" $200/1,000

025a: PARKER PYNE INVESTIGATES   Collins
L 1934 [] $200/1,000

025b: MR PARKER PYNE, DETECTIVE Dodd, Mead NY 1934 [0] New title $150/750

026a: THE LISTERDALE MYSTERY AND OTHER STORIES Collins L 1934 [] $250/1,250

027a: BLACK COFFEE Ashley L 1934 [] $150/650

028a: WHY DIDN'T THEY ASK EVANS? Collins L 1934 [] $250/1,250

028b: BOOMERANG CLUE Dodd, Mead NY 1935 [0] New title $150/600

029a: MURDER ON THE ORIENT EXPRESS Collins L (1934) [] Uncorrected proof in blue wraps with printed label. Printed on rectos only (Swann Galleries 2/91) $4,000.

029b: MURDER ON THE ORIENT EXPRESS Collins L (1934) [] $600/3,500

029c: MURDER ON THE ORIENT EXPRESS Dodd, Mead NY 1934 [0] Unspecified number of copies for publisher's presentation (Pepper & Stern 11/89) $300/1,500

029d: MURDER IN THE CALAIS COACH Dodd, Mead NY 1934 [0] New title $175/850

030a: MURDER IN THREE ACTS Dodd, Mead NY (1934) [0] $175/850

030b: THREE ACT TRAGEDY Collins L 1935 [] New title $200/1,000

031a: UNFINISHED PORTRAIT Collins L 1934 [] Written as Mary Westmacott $150/750

031b: UNFINISHED PORTRAIT Doubleday GC 1934 [1] Written as Mary Westmacott $100/500

031c: UNFINISHED PORTRAIT   Arbor House
NY 1973 [] $10/40

032a: DEATH IN THE CLOUDS Collins L 1935
[] $200/1,000

032b: DEATH IN THE AIR   Dodd, Mead   NY
1935 [0] New title $125/600

033a: THE A.B.C. MURDERS: A NEW POIROT
MYSTERY Collins L 1936 [] $200/1,000

033b: THE A.B.C. MURDERS: A NEW POIROT
MYSTERY Dodd, Mead NY 1936 [0] $125/600

034a: CARDS ON THE TABLE Collins L 1936 [] $200/850

034b: CARDS ON THE TABLE Dodd, Mead NY
1937 [0] $100/500

035a: HERCULE POIROT: MASTER DETEC-
TIVE Dodd, Mead NY 1936 [0] $100/500

036a: MURDER IN MESOPOTAMIA Collins L
1936 [0] $200/1,000

036b: MURDER IN MESOPOTAMIA   Dodd,
Mead NY 1936 [0] $125/600

037a: THREE CHRISTIE CRIMES   Grosset &
Dunlap NY 1937 [] $35/175

038a: MURDER IN THE MEWS AND OTHER
STORIES Collins L (1937) [0] $250/1,250

038b: MURDER IN THE MEWS AND OTHER
STORIES Odhams L (1937?) [] Assume reprint
(Limestone Hills Books 3/90) $20/100

038c: DEAD MAN'S MIRROR AND OTHER
STORIES Dodd, Mead NY 1937 [0] New title $100/400

039a: LOVE FROM A STRANGER: A PLAY
French L 1937 [] Wraps. A dramatization of
Philomel Cottage by Frank Vosper $100.

040a: DEATH ON THE NILE Collins L 1937 [0] $200/1,000

040b: DEATH ON THE NILE Dodd, Mead NY
1938 [0] Advance proof in aqua wraps with "The
big Detective Story for 1938!" on front cover (no
title on cover) $450.

040c: DEATH ON THE NILE Dodd, Mead NY
1938 [0] On back flap of dustwrapper the author of
Fast Company (Harry Kurnitz) is overprinted in
black "By Marco Page," all copies? $100/500

041a: DUMB WITNESS Collins L (1937) [0] $150/850

041b: POIROT LOSES A CLIENT Dodd, Mead
NY 1937 [0] New title $125/600

042a: APPOINTMENT WITH DEATH: *A Poirot
Mystery* Collins L 1938 [] $250/1,250

042b: APPOINTMENT WITH DEATH: *A Poirot
Mystery* Dodd, Mead NY 1938 [0] $150/750

043a: THE REGATTA MYSTERY AND OTHER
STORIES Dodd, Mead NY 1939 [0] $125/600

044a: HERCULE POIROT'S CHRISTMAS Col-
lins L 1939 [] Published in 1938 but dated ahead to
1939 $175/850

044b: MURDER FOR CHRISTMAS: *A Poirot
Story* Dodd, Mead NY 1939 [0] New title $125/600

045a: MURDER IS EASY Collins L 1939 [0] $200/850

045b: EASY TO KILL Dodd, Mead NY 1939 [0]
New title. Blue cloth. Dustwrapper price: $2.00 $100/500

046a: TEN LITTLE NIGGERS (novel) Collins L
(1939) [0] $400/2,000

046b: AND THEN THERE WERE NONE Dodd,
Mead NY 1940 [] New title $125/600

047a: ONE, TWO, BUCKLE MY SHOE Collins
L 1940 [] $200/1,000

047b: THE PATRIOTIC MURDERS Dodd, Mead
NY 1941 [0] New title $100/500

048a: TWO DETECTIVE STORIES... Dodd, Mead
NY 1940 []   Contains *The Mysterious Affair at
Styles* and *Murder on the Links* $40/200

049a: SAD CYPRESS Collins L (no-date [1940])
[0] $200/1,000

049b: SAD CYPRESS Dodd, Mead NY 1940 [0] $100/450

050a: EVIL UNDER THE SUN Collins L 1941 [] $200/1,000

050b: EVIL UNDER THE SUN Dodd, Mead NY
1941 [0]   Advance copy. Perfect bound in dustwrapper with flaps $400.

050c: EVIL UNDER THE SUN Dodd, Mead NY
1941 [0] $100/400

051a: POIROT AND THE REGATTA MYSTERY
Vallancey Press L (no-date [1941?]) [0] Cardboard
covers (Also listed as 1944?) $350.

052a: N OR M? Collins L 1941 [] $125/600

052b: N OR M? Dodd, Mead NY 1941 [0] $75/350

053a: THE BODY IN THE LIBRARY Collins L
1942 [] $200/1,000

053b: THE BODY IN THE LIBRARY   Dodd,
Mead NY 1942 [0] $125/600

054a: THE MOVING FINGER Dodd, Mead NY 1942 [0] $100/500

054b: THE MOVING FINGER Collins L (1943) [0] $175/850

055a: FIVE LITTLE PIGS Collins L 1942 [0] $150/750

055b: MURDER IN RETROSPECT Dodd, Mead NY 1942 [0] New title $100/400

056a: TRIPLE THREAT Dodd, Mead NY 1943 [0] $60/300

057a: DEATH COMES AS THE END   Dodd, Mead NY 1944 [0] $75/350

057b: DEATH COMES AS THE END Collins L 1945 [0] $60/300

058a: CRIME IN CABIN 66 Vallancey Press L 1944 [0] Wraps $350.

059a: TOWARDS ZERO Collins L 1944 [] $150/750

059b: TOWARDS ZERO Dodd, Mead NY 1944 [0] (Presumed second issue has "Distributed by Blakiston..." on title page {William Dunn 8/91}) $75/350

060a: AGATHA CHRISTIE'S CRIME READER World Cleveland 1944 [] $20/100

061a: ABSENT IN THE SPRING Collins L 1944 [] Written as Mary Westmacott $75/350

061b: ABSENT IN THE SPRING Farrar & Rinehart NY (1944) [0] Written as Mary Westmacott $50/250

062a: TEN LITTLE NIGGERS (play) French L (1945) [0] Sea-green wraps $100.

062b: TEN LITTLE INDIANS French (NY) 1946 [0] Wraps. New title $35.

063a: SPARKLING CYANIDE Collins L (1945) [0] $125/600

063b: REMEMBERED DEATH Dodd, Mead NY 1945 [0] New title $60/300

064a: APPOINTMENT WITH DEATH (play) French L 1945 [] $60.

065a: PERIL AT END HOUSE A Play French L 1945 [] Wraps. Dramatization by Arnold Ridley $50.

066a: THE HOLLOW Collins L 1946 [0] $60/300

066b: THE HOLLOW Dodd, Mead NY 1946 [0] $50/250

067a: POIROT KNOWS THE MURDERER Poly Books L/NY 1946 [] $60/300

068a: POIROT LENDS A HAND Poly Books L/NY 1946 [] $60/300

069a: COME TELL ME HOW YOU LIVE (travel) Collins L 1946 [0] Red cloth, lettered in gilt on spine. 16 illustrations and map $60/300

069b: COME TELL ME HOW YOU LIVE (travel) Dodd, Mead NY 1946 [] $50/250

070a: THE LABOURS OF HERCULES Collins L (1947) [0] $100/500

070b: LABORS OF HERCULES Dodd, Mead NY 1947 [0] $50/250

071a: MURDER ON THE NILE (play) French L 1948 [0] $50.

071b: MURDER ON THE NILE (play) French (NY) 1948 [] $40.

072a: TAKEN AT THE FLOOD Collins L (1948) [0] $50/250

072b: THERE IS A TIDE... Dodd, Mead NY 1948 [0] New title $35/175

073a: THE ROSE AND THE YEW TREE Heinemann L 1948 [] Written as Mary Westmacott $35/175

073b: THE ROSE AND THE YEW TREE Rinehart NY (1948) [5] Written as Mary Westmacott. (Note: the Arbor reprint in 1971 states first) $25/125

073c: THE ROSE AND THE YEW TREE Arbor NY (1971) [1] $10/40

074a: WITNESS FOR THE PROSECUTION Dodd, Mead NY (1948) [0] $75/350

THREE BLIND MICE *And Other Stories* See 078a

075a: CROOKED HOUSE Collins L (1949) [0] Scarlet cloth, lettered in black on spine $60/300

075b: CROOKED HOUSE Dodd, Mead NY (1949) [0] $40/200

076a: A MURDER IS ANNOUNCED Collins L 1950 [0] $50/250

076b: A MURDER IS ANNOUNCED Dodd, Mead (NY 1950) [] Advance copy perfect bound in wraps and dustwrapper $250.

076c: A MURDER IS ANNOUNCED Dodd, Mead (NY 1950) [0] $25/125

077a: THE MURDER AT THE VICARAGE French L (1950) [0] Dramatization by Moie Charles and Barbara Toy $50.

078a: THREE BLIND MICE AND OTHER STORIES Dodd, Mead NY [1950] [0] Last copyright date is 1948, but published in 1950 $50/250

078b: THE MOUSETRAP   Dell   NY   1952   []
Wraps. New title $50.

079a: UNDERDOG AND OTHER STORIES
Dodd, Mead NY (no date [1951]) [0] $30/150

080a: THEY CAME TO BAGHDAD Collins L
1951 [0] $50/250

080b: THEY CAME TO BAGHDAD Dodd, Mead
NY 1951 [0] $25/125

081a: THE HOLLOW (play) French L (1952) [0]
Wraps $40.

081b: THE HOLLOW (play) French (NY) 1952 []
Wraps $40.

082a: THEY DO IT WITH MIRRORS Collins L
(1952) [0] Red cloth, blocked and lettered in black
on spine $40/200

082b: MURDER WITH MIRRORS Dodd, Mead
NY (1952) [0] New title $30/150

083a: MRS McGINTY'S DEAD Collins L (1952)
[0] $35/175

083b: MRS McGINTY'S DEAD Dodd, Mead NY
(1952) [0] $30/150

084a: A DAUGHTER'S A DAUGHTER   Heine-
mann L (1952) [1] Written as Mary Westmacott $25/125

084b: A DAUGHTER'S A DAUGHTER Dell NY
1963 [] Wraps $40.

084c: A DAUGHTER'S A DAUGHTER   Arbor
House NY (no-date [1971]) [0] First U.S. hardback $10/40

085a: AFTER THE FUNERAL Collins L (1953)
[0] $30/150

085b: FUNERALS ARE FATAL Dodd, Mead NY (1953) [0] New title $20/100

086a: A POCKET FULL OF RYE Collins L (1953) [0] $25/125

086b: A POCKET FULL OF RYE Dodd, Mead NY (1954) [0] $20/100

087a: WITNESS FOR THE PROSECUTION (play) French L (1954) [] Wraps $50.

087b: WITNESS FOR THE PROSECUTION (play) French (NY) 1954 [] Wraps $40.

088a: THE MOUSETRAP (play) French L 1954 [] Wraps $100.

088b: THE MOUSETRAP *and Other Plays* Dodd, Mead NY 1978 [] $15/75

089a: PERILOUS JOURNEYS OF HERCULE POIROT Dodd, Mead NY 1954 [] $25/125

090a: DESTINATION UNKNOWN Collins L (1954) [0] $30/150

090b: SO MANY STEPS TO DEATH Dodd, Mead NY (1955) [0] New title $20/100

091a: HICKORY, DICKORY, DOCK Collins L (1955) [0] $20/100

091b: HICKORY, DICKORY, DEATH Dodd, Mead NY (1955) [0] New title $15/75

092a: SURPRISE ENDINGS BY HERCULE POIROT Dodd, Mead NY 1956 [0] $25/125

093a: DEAD MAN'S FOLLY Collins L (1956) [0] $20/100

093b: DEAD MAN'S FOLLY Dodd, Mead NY (1956) [0] $15/75

094a: APPOINTMENT WITH DEATH *A Play* French L 1956 [] Wraps — $50.

095a: THE BURDEN Heinemann L (1956) [1] Written as Mary Westmacott — $25/125

095b: THE BURDEN Dell NY 1963 [] Wraps. "First publ...in 1956" — $40.

095c: THE BURDEN Arbor House NY (no-date [1973]) [0] — $7/35

096a: THE SPIDER'S WEB French L (1957) [] Wraps — $40.

097a: TOWARDS ZERO Dramatists Play Service NY 1957 [] Wraps — $40.

097b: TOWARDS ZERO French L 1958 [] Wraps — $40.

098a: CHRISTIE CLASSICS Dodd, Mead NY 1957 [0] — $15/75

099a: 4-50 FROM PADDINGTON Collins L (1957) [0] — $20/100

099b: WHAT MRS. McGILLICUDDY SAW! Dodd, Mead NY (1957) [0] New title — $15/75

100a: VERDICT (play) French L 1958 [] Wraps — $40.

101a: THE UNEXPECTED GUEST (play) French L (1958) [0] Wraps — $40.

102a: ORDEAL BY INNOCENCE Collins L (1958) [0] — $20/100

102b: ORDEAL BY INNOCENCE Dodd, Mead NY 1959 [0] — $15/75

103a: CAT AMONG THE PIGEONS Collins L (1959) [0] — $20/100

103b: CAT AMONG THE PIGEONS Dodd, Mead NY 1960 [0] $15/75

104a: THE ADVENTURE OF THE CHRISTMAS PUDDING Collins L (1960) [0] $25/125

105a: MURDER PREFERRED Dodd, Mead NY 1960 [0] $15/75

106a: GO BACK FOR MURDER (play) French L 1960 [] Wraps. An adaptation of *Five Little Pigs* $40.

107a: DOUBLE SIN AND OTHER STORIES Dodd, Mead NY 1961 [0] $15/75

108a: 13 FOR LUCK Dodd, Mead NY 1961 [] $12/60

108b: 13 FOR LUCK Collins L 1966 [1] $20/100

109a: THE PALE HORSE Collins L (1961) [0] Uncorrected proof in pictorial wraps (Swann Galleries 2/91) $200.

109b: THE PALE HORSE Collins L (1961) [0] $20/100

109c: THE PALE HORSE Dodd, Mead NY 1962 [0] $12/60

110a: THE MIRROR CRACK'D FROM SIDE TO SIDE Collins L (1962) [0] $20/100

110b: THE MIRROR CRACK'D Dodd, Mead NY 1963 [1] $12/60

111a: MAKE MINE MURDER Dodd, Mead NY 1962 [0] $15/75

112a: RULE OF THREE French L 1963 [] Wraps. Includes *Afternoon at the Seaside*, *The Patient* and *The Rats* $40.

113a: THE RATS French L (1963) [0] Wraps $40.

114a: THE PATIENT French L (1963) [0] Wraps $40.

115a: AFTERNOON AT THE SEASIDE French
L (1963) [] Wraps $40.

116a: THE CLOCKS Collins L (1963) [0]
Uncorrected proof in pictorial wraps (Swann
Galleries 2/91) $200.

116b: THE CLOCKS Collins L (1963) [0] $15/75

116c: THE CLOCKS Dodd, Mead NY 1964 [1] $10/50

117a: A CARIBBEAN MYSTERY Collins L
(1964) [0]   Uncorrected proof in red wraps
(Alphabet 5/92) $200.

117b: A CARIBBEAN MYSTERY Collins L
(1964) [0] $20/100

117c: A CARIBBEAN MYSTERY Dodd, Mead
NY [0] Advance copy perfect bound in
pictorial wraps (Cardinal Books 2/91). Bound in
dustwrapper (Else Fine 8/91) $125.

117d: A CARIBBEAN MYSTERY Dodd, Mead
NY (1965) [1] $12/60

118a: MURDER INTERNATIONAL Dodd, Mead
NY 1965 [0] $12/60

119a: STAR OVER BETHLEHEM AND OTHER
STORIES Collins L 1965 [0] Written as A.C.
Mallowan $12/60

119b: STAR OVER BETHLEHEM AND OTHER
STORIES Dodd, Mead NY 1965 [0] Written as
A.C. Mallowan $10/50

120a: SURPRISE! SURPRISE! Dodd, Mead NY
(1965) [0] (Stories) $15/75

121a: AT BERTRAM'S HOTEL Collins L (1965) [0] $20/100

121b: AT BERTRAM'S HOTEL Dodd, Mead NY (1966) [1] $12/60

122a: THIRTEEN CLUES FOR MISS MARPLE Dodd, Mead NY (1966) [0] $15/75

123a: THIRD GIRL Collins L 1966 [0] $15/75

123b: THIRD GIRL Dodd, Mead NY (1967) [1] "First published in book form ..." $10/50

124a: MURDER IN OUR MIDST Dodd, Mead NY (1967) [0] $10/50

125a: ENDLESS NIGHT Collins L 1967 [0] $15/75

125b: ENDLESS NIGHT Dodd, Mead NY (1968) [1] $10/50

126a: SPIES AMONG US Dodd, Mead NY (1968) [0] $15/75

127a: BY THE PRICKING OF MY THUMBS Collins L 1968 [0] Green or red cloth; no priority, although red scarcer (Ian McKelvie 8/90) $15/75

127b: BY THE PRICKING OF MY THUMBS Dodd, Mead NY (1968) [0] $10/50

128a: SELECTED STORIES   Progress Publ. Moscow 1969 [0] Wraps. (Text in English) $75.

129a: HALLOWE'EN PARTY Collins L (1969) [0] $15/75

129b: HALLOWE'EN PARTY Dodd, Mead NY 1969 [0] $10/50

130a: PASSENGER TO FRANKFURT Collins L (1970) [0] Scarlet boards blocked and lettered in gilt

on spine. Variant without price on dustwrapper flap
(Janus Books 6/89) $15/75

130b: PASSENGER TO FRANKFURT   Dodd,
Mead NY (1970) [0] $10/50

131a: THE NURSERY RHYME MURDERS
Dodd, Mead NY 1970 [] $15/75

132a: NEMESIS Collins L (1971) [1] $15/75

132b: NEMESIS Dodd, Mead NY (1971) [0] $8/40

133a: THE GOLDEN BALL AND OTHER
STORIES Dodd, Mead NY (1971) [0] $12/60

THE ROSE AND THE YEW TREE See 073c

134a: ELEPHANTS CAN REMEMBER (Collins)
Crime Club L 1972 [] Uncorrected advance proof
in red wraps (David Mayou 7/91), blue wraps
(Swann Galleries 2/91). Priority unknown $125.

134b: ELEPHANTS CAN REMEMBER (Collins)
Crime Club L 1972 [1] $15/75

134c: ELEPHANTS CAN REMEMBER Dodd,
Mead NY (1972) [0] Uncorrected proof in orange
wraps $100.

134d: ELEPHANTS CAN REMEMBER Dodd,
Mead NY (1972) [0] $8/40

135a: MURDER-GO-ROUND Dodd, Mead NY
1972 [0] $12/60

136a: POSTERN OF FATE (Collins) Crime Club
L (1973?) [1] $12/60

136b: POSTERN OF FATE Dodd, Mead NY
(1973) [0] $8/40

UNFINISHED PORTRAIT. See 031c.

137a: AKHNATON (play) Collins L 1973 [1] $10/50

137b: AKHNATON (play) Dodd, Mead NY 1973 [1] $8/40

138a: POEMS Collins L 1973 [] Advance uncorrected proof in plain wraps with label on cover (Black Sun Books 3/91); in cloth backed red wraps (Swann Galleries 2/91); original red wraps with with label, also no-place or date on title page (Geo. Robert Minkoff 9/91, 1/95) $125.

138b: POEMS Collins L 1973 [1] $12/60

138c: POEMS Dodd, Mead NY 1973 [1] Issued without dustwrapper (Mordida Books 7/90) $60.

139a: POIROT'S EARLY CASES Collins L 1974 [0] Uncorrected proof in red printed wraps (Swann Galleries 2/91) $100.

139b: POIROT'S EARLY CASES Collins L 1974 [0] $10/50

139c: HERCULE POIROT'S EARLY CASES Dodd, Mead NY (1974) [0] New title $8/40

140a: MURDER ON BOARD: THREE COMPLETE MYSTERY NOVELS Dodd, Mead NY (1974) [0] Includes *The Mystery of The Blue Train, Death in The Air* and *What Mrs. McGillicuddy Saw!* $12/60

141a: POIROT'S LAST CASE Collins L 1975 [] Uncorrected proof in red printed wraps (Swann Galleries 2/91)   100.

141b: CURTAIN: HERCULE POIROT'S LAST CASE Collins L 1975 [1] New title $10/50

141c: CURTAIN: POIROT'S LAST CASE Dodd, Mead NY (1975) [0] Uncorrected proof in red wraps. New title   100.

141d: CURTAIN: HERCULE POIROT'S LAST CASE Dodd, Mead NY (1975) [0] Later proof with published title. Also in red wraps and slightly heavier (Swann Galleries 2/91) $75.

141e: CURTAIN: HERCULE POIROT'S LAST CASE Dodd, Mead NY (1975) [0] $8/40

142a: SLEEPING MURDER Collins L (1976) [1] Uncorrected proof in red wraps (Swann 2/91)   100.

142b: SLEEPING MURDER Collins L (1976) [1] $8/40

142c: SLEEPING MURDER Dodd, Mead NY (1976) [0] $7/35

143a: A POIROT QUINTET Collins L 1977 [] $10/50

144a: MASTERPIECES OF MURDER Dodd, Mead NY 1977 [] $8/40

145a: STARRING MISS MARPLE Dodd, Mead NY (1977) [0] $5/35

146a: AN AUTOBIOGRAPHY Collins L 1977 [] Uncorrected proof in pink wraps. (Not published until 1979 - Nigel Williams 9/94) $125.

146b: AN AUTOBIOGRAPHY Collins L 1977 [] $8/40

146c: AN AUTOBIOGRAPHY Dodd, Mead NY (1977) [3] $7/35

147a: A MISS MARPLE QUINTET Collins L 1978 [] $10/50

148a: A MURDER IS ANNOUNCED French L 1978 [] Wraps. Dramatization by L. Darbon $30.

THE MOUSETRAP... See 088b

149a: MISS MARPLE'S 6 FINAL CASES AND TWO OTHERS Collins L (1979) [1] Uncorrected proof in orange wraps (Nigel Williams 2/93) $100.

149b: MISS MARPLE'S 6 FINAL CASES AND TWO OTHERS Collins L (1979) [1] $10/50

150a: THE BEST OF POIROT Collins L 1981 [] $8/40

151a: THE AGATHA CHRISTIE HOUR Collins L 1982 [1] Collection of short stories selected for TV series (Mordida Books 7/89) $10/50

152a: THE WESTMACOTT-CHRISTIE READER Dodd Mead NY (1983) [] $7/35

153a: THE AGATHA CHRISTIE MYSTERY COLLECTION Bantam NY 1983 [] 74 volumes in full leather (Fine Book Co. 5/92) $500.

154a: HERCULE POIROT'S CASEBOOK Dodd, Mead NY 1984 [] $6/30

155a: MISS MARPLE-THE COMPLETE SHORT STORIES Dodd Mead NY 1985 [1] $6/30

156a: PROBLEMS AT POLLENSA BAY + Harper/Collins NY/L 1991 [] 8 short stories, 4 of which have never been published before $6/30

PAT CONROY

Pat Conroy was born in Atlanta, Georgia, in 1945. He graduated from the Citadel and then worked as a teacher for a year, which gave him material for his second book. His father was the model for *The Great Santini.*

We would like to thank Cliff Graubart of Old New York Book Shop in Atlanta for his assistance, and Colonel Thomas Nugent Courvoisie (the "Boo"), and Roy Bemis for quantities on the first two entries.

Conroy has also written at least three screen plays. *The Prince of Tides* (with Becky Johnston), *EX* (with Doug Marlette), and *Hard News* (with Wendell Rawls, Jr.). All were "published" by Warner Bros. Burbank in 1989 in printed studio wrappers and are valued at about $100. each.

001a: THE BOO McClure Press Verona, VA (1970) [] Uncorrected proof in plain wraps with a business size card with details about the book, glued to front cover. "New Book | The Boo | (A Saga of the Citadel 1961 - 1968) | ..." (Old New York Book Shop 9/95) $5,000.

001b: THE BOO McClure Press Verona, VA (1970) [1] 2,000 cc (Courvoisie). 5"x8" card entitled "Boo's Immortals" laid in some copies $400/2,500

001c: THE BOO Pinnacle Books NY 1981 [1] Wraps. "Published November 1981." New 9-page introduction $75.

001d: THE BOO Old New York Book Shop Atlanta 1988 [2] 20 sgd ltr cc. Issued without dustwrapper in slipcase. Signed by Conroy who wrote a new (last) introduction, Col. Courvoisie (The Boo), and Donald Conroy (The Great Santini). Each copy in this issue includes a page of the original typed manuscript of the new introduction — $700/750

001e: THE BOO Old New York Book Shop Atlanta 1988 [2] 250 sgd no. cc. Issued without dustwrapper in slipcase. Also signed by all three. Although dated 1988, this edition was not actually distributed until late 1990 — $300/350

001f: THE BOO Old New York Book Shop Atlanta 1988 [0] 1,000 cc. Trade edition issued at $15.95 — $15/60

002a: THE WATER IS WIDE Houghton Mifflin Boston 1972 [1] 10,000 cc. Red cloth printed in blue (title/publisher) and white (author) on spine only — $125/600

003a: THE GREAT SANTINI Houghton Mifflin Boston 1976 [3] Uncorrected proof in salmon colored wraps (also seen listed as in "orange" and "burnt orange" - same color just described differently) — $400.

003b: THE GREAT SANTINI Houghton Mifflin Boston 1976 [3] 35 to 50 copies of the uncorrected proof bound with dustwrapper which states on front flap "daughters to provide their husbands (Marines, naturally) with a good lay and more fodder for the Corps." Imitation leather of various colors, bound by National Library Bindery for Norman Berg — $1,000.

003c: THE GREAT SANTINI Houghton Mifflin Boston 1976 [3] 10,000 cc. Orange-red cloth printed in black on spine only. Dustwrapper flap changed to read "... with a good <u>home</u> ..." (first dustwrapper was never issued except with proof copies) — $40/200

003d: THE GREAT SANTINI Collins London 1977 [] — $20/100

004a: THE LORDS OF DISCIPLINE Houghton
Mifflin Boston 1980 [3] Advance reading copy in
printed white wraps .... $175.

004b: THE LORDS OF DISCIPLINE Houghton
Mifflin Boston 1980 [3] 25,000 cc (b&c).
(Published 10/6/80 at $12.95.) Black cloth spine
stamped in gold and blue paper covered boards
blind stamped with title. First dustwrapper has
review by James Dickey on back panel $25/125

004c: THE LORDS OF DISCIPLINE Houghton
Mifflin Boston 1980 [3] Second issue dustwrapper
has four reviews on back panel (usually not found
on a first printing) $25/75

004d: THE LORDS OF DISCIPLINE Secker &
Warburg L (1981) [1] $20/100

005a: THE PRINCE OF TIDES Houghton Mifflin
Boston 1986 [0] Advance Uncorrected Proof in
pictorial wraps given out at ABA Convention ...... $75.

005b: THE PRINCE OF TIDES Houghton Mifflin
Boston 1986 [2] 20 sgd no cc (numbered 1 to 20.
Reserved for Special Friends of the Author).
Advance uncorrected proof bound in dark brown or
burgundy simulated leather (Old New York Book
Store) .... $1,000.

005c: THE PRINCE OF TIDES Houghton Mifflin
Boston 1986 [2] 35 sgd cc (unnumbered, given to
sales reps and other individuals). Advance proof
bound in blue vinyl simulated leather (Old New
York Book Store) .... $850.

005d: THE PRINCE OF TIDES Houghton Mifflin
Boston 1986 [3] 250,000 cc. (Published 10/21/86 at
$19.95) $10/50

005e: THE PRINCE OF TIDES Bantam/Trans-
world London 1987 [] $10/50

005f: THE PRINCE OF TIDES *A Screenplay* Triad Artist no-place (1988) [] Pinned wraps. Written with Becky Johnston $300.

005g: THE PRINCE OF TIDES (San Francisco Public Library San Francisco 1992) [] Broadside. 6 1/2" x 12 1/2" $50.

006a: CONROY'S WORLD Bantam NY 1987 [] Wraps. Excerpts from four novels $25.

007a: MILITARY BRATS Crown/Harmony New York 1991 [] (Published 4/91 at $20.) Introduction by Conroy $6/30

008a: "TO DESCRIBE OUR GROWING UP IN THE LOW COUNTRY..." *San Francisco Examiner* San Francisco 1992 [] Broadside in two colors. 12 1/2" x 6 1/2" $50.

009a: BEACH MUSIC Doubleday (New York) 1995, but 1994 [0] Broadside. 8 1/2" x 17". Excerpt from upcoming book. Given out at the 1994 ABA so probably 3,000 copies but most will have been thrown away or ruined. Interesting to note that in the third person ("Jack had no idea...") while the published book is in first person ("I had no idea..."). (Note: there is a reprint of this broadside by Bay Street Books, the same except it is 11"x17 1/2" and does not have the small sunrise picture in upper left hand corner) $50.

009b: BEACH MUSIC Doubleday (New York) 1995 [] "Final Proof," so stated. Photocopied loose sheets which were shot from final printer's setting. They were sent out about two months before publication. No bound proofs were produced (Waverly Books 8/95) $150.

009c: BEACH MUSIC Doubleday (New York) 1995 [2] 350 sgd no cc. (Published at $150 but sold out) $200.

009d: BEACH MUSIC   Doubleday   (New York)
1995 [] (Published at $25)

JAMES CRUMLEY

Crumley was born October 12, 1939, in Three Rivers, Texas. After a brief stint as a student at the Georgia Institute of Technology, he served as an enlisted man in the U.S. Army from 1958 to 1961 then returned to school again, this time getting a B.A. from Texas A & I (1964) and an M.F.A. from the University of Iowa (1966). He has also worked as a roughneck, a bartender, and a college professor. His academic peregrinations have taken him all across the west. For a while he divided his time between Karnes County, Texas, and Missoula, Montana, but now he lives and writes in Missoula. In addition to the published works listed below, Crumley has written for little magazines, popular periodicals, and the silver screen.

We would like to acknowledge the assistance of John Koontz in preparing this guide. The quantities were given by Crumley in an interview printed in the book *Whores* (McMillan, Missoula, 1988).

001a: ONE TO COUNT CADENCE   Random House NY 1969 [1] 17,500 cc. Brown cloth $60/350

001b: ONE TO COUNT CADENCE Picador L 1994 [] Wraps (Nicholas Burrows 11/94) $25.

002a: THE WRONG CASE Random House NY (1975) [4] 5,000 cc. Blue cloth spine and pale green boards. (There may be as many as 5,500 cc) $125/600

002b: THE WRONG CASE   Hart-Davis, Mac-Gibbon London (1976) [1] Brown cloth (or simu-

lated), gold lettering on spine. Dustwrapper price:
£3.95 net $40/200

003a: "Whores" in THE PUSHCART PRIZE III:
BEST OF THE SMALL PRESSES Pushcart Press
Yonkers, NY 1978 [1] Edited by Bill Henderson.
Green cloth $10/50

004a: THE LAST GOOD KISS Random House
NY 1978 [4] "Uncorrected Proof" in red wraps $300.

004b: THE LAST GOOD KISS Random House
NY 1978 [4] 9-10,000 cc. Burgundy cloth over rose
boards. P.234:15 "found" vs "fond" (all copies?) $20/100

004c: THE LAST GOOD KISS Granada Hert-
fordshire (1979) [1] $12/60

005a: "Cairn" in TEXAS STORIES AND POEMS
Texas Center for Writers Press Dallas 1978 [0]
Wraps $40.

006a: DANCING BEAR Random House NY
(1982) [4] Uncorrected Proof in red wraps. First
state: name misspelled "Crumly" on spine and title
page. (Pettler & Lieberman 12/90) $175.

006b: DANCING BEAR Random House NY
(1982) [4] Uncorrected Proof. Second state: name
correctly spelled $125.

006c: DANCING BEAR Random House NY 1983
[4] "First edition 2 3 4..." Black cloth over boards
(Crumley stated 6,000 in first printing and 3,000 in
second printing) $15/75

006d: DANCING BEAR Random House NY 1983
[0] Black cloth over boards. (A review copy was
seen that did not state "First edition 2 3 4...") $6/30

006e: DANCING BEAR Penguin Harmondsworth
1987 [] Wraps. No UK hardback (Ian McKelvie
8/92) $35.

007a: THE MUDDY FORK *A Work in Progress*
Lord John Press Northridge 1984 [2] 50 sgd no cc.
Deluxe edition, quarterbound burgundy leather over
orange and violet marbled boards $400.

007b: THE MUDDY FORK *A Work in Progress*
Lord John Press Northridge 1984 [2] 200 sgd no cc.
Brown cloth over tan decorated boards $150.

008a: THE PIGEON SHOOT   Neville   Santa
Barbara 1987 [2] 26 sgd ltr cc. Full leather without
dustwrapper in slipcase $400.

008b: THE PIGEON SHOOT   Neville   Santa
Barbara 1987 [2] 15 sgd presentation copies. Issued
in unprinted white wrappers. (Proof copies per Ken
Lopez) $200.

008c: THE PIGEON SHOOT   Neville   Santa
Barbara 1987 [2] 350 sgd no cc. Issued in clear
acetate dustwrapper $125.

009a: WHORES Dennis McMillan (Missoula,
Montana) 1988 [2] 26 sgd ltr cc. Issued in full
leather $400.

009b: WHORES   Dennis McMillan (Missoula,
Montana) 1988 [2] 13 sgd unlettered cc in leather $200.

009c: WHORES   Dennis McMillan   (Missoula,
Montana) 1988 [2] 475 sgd no cc.   Issued in
dustwrapper $175.

009d: WHORES Dennis McMillan (Missoula,
Montana) 1988 [] Wraps (Between The Covers
10/90) $25.

010a: THE MUDDY FORK *And Other Things*
Clark City Press Livingston (1991) [1] Uncorrected
proof in cream wraps. Reportedly only 10 copies
(Dennis McMillan) $300.

010b: THE MUDDY FORK *And Other Things*
Clark City Press Livingston (1991) [1] Advance
reading copy in pictorial wraps (Waiting For Godot
2/92) $75.

010c: THE MUDDY FORK *And Other Things*
Clark City Press Livingston (1992) [2] 125 sgd
no cc in slipcase (The Captain's Bookshelf 2/95) $200.

011a: THE JAMES CRUMLEY TRILOGY
Picador L 1991 [] Uncorrected proof in printed
wraps (Nicholas Pounder) $50.

011b: JAMES CRUMLEY: THE COLLECTION
Picador (L 1991) [1] 1,200 cc. New title. Contains
The Wrong Case, *The Last Good Kiss* and *Dancing
Bear*, and new introduction. No US edition. (Pettler
& Lieberman 3/93) $25/100

011c: JAMES CRUMLEY: THE COLLECTION
Picador (L 1991) [] Wraps $25.

012a: THE MEXICAN TREE DUCK Mysterious
Press   NY 1993 [] Advance reading copy in
pictorial wraps $50.

012b: THE MEXICAN TREE DUCK James Cahill
Publishing Huntington Beach, Calif. 1993 [2] 150
sgd no cc. Issued in slipcase. Mysterious Press
sheets with additional title page (Published August
1993) $150.

012c: THE MEXICAN TREE DUCK Mysterious
Press NY 1993 [] 28,000 cc (Crumley), 50,000 cc
(PW). (Published September 1993 at $19.95) $5/25

012d: THE MEXICAN TREE DUCK Scorpion
Press Bristol 1993 [2] 75 sgd no cc. With an
appreciation by Maxim Jakubowski. Quarter
imitation morocco in glassine dustwrapper $150.

012e: THE MEXICAN TREE DUCK Picador (L 1993) []   Uncorrected proof in dustwrapper (Nicholas and Helen Burrows 1/95) $40/75

012f: THE MEXICAN TREE DUCK Picador (L 1994) [3]   Also states "First published in Great Britain 1994..." $10/40

Countée Cullen (signature)

COUNTEE CULLEN
(1903-1946)

Cullen was born in New York City in 1903. In 1918, *Modern School Magazine* printed "To a Swimmer," a poem he had written the previous year at age fourteen. He graduated Phi Beta Kappa from New York University in 1925 and received his masters in English literature from Harvard the following year. He was assistant editor of *Opportunity: A Journal of Negro Life* from 1926 to 1928 and then studied abroad on a Guggenheim Fellowship. Thereafter he turned to teaching and for the last 11 years he taught French at Frederick Douglass High School. Cullen's last work was a play that he was writing with Arna Bontemps, *St. Louis Woman*.

001a: COLOR Harper NY 1925 [1] $125/500

002a: COPPER SUN Harper NY 1927 [2] 100 sgd no cc. Issued in glassine dustwrapper and slipcase (Waiting For Godot 6/88) $500/600

002b: COPPER SUN Harper NY 1927 [2] 500 cc. Issued in slipcase $250/350

002c: COPPER SUN Harper NY 1927 [1] (Also noted a variant in publisher's soft red leather {Country Lane Books 10/95}) $75/300

003a: THE BALLAD OF THE BROWN GIRL Harper NY 1927 [2] 500 no cc. Issued by *Opportunity*. Issued without dustwrapper in slipcase $250/350

003b: THE BALLAD OF THE BROWN GIRL
Harper NY 1927 [1] Issued without dustwrapper in
slipcase $60/30

004a: CAROLING DUSK Harper NY 1927 [1]
Edited by Cullen $40/200

005a: THE BLACK CHRIST *And Other Poems*
Harper NY 1929 [2] 128 sgd no cc. Issued in
slipcase (Heritage Book Shop 10/90) $500/600

005b: THE BLACK CHRIST *And Other Poems*
Harper NY 1929 [1] $60/300

005c: THE BLACK CHRIST *And Other Poems*
Putnam L 1929 [] (Bolerium Books 9/92) $40/200

006a: ONE WAY TO HEAVEN Harper NY 1932
[1] Noted in red buckram library binding with blue
printed silver foil labels; and in decorated boards
with same labels, priority unknown (Waiting For
Godot 10/88) $100/500

007a: THE MEDIA *And Some Other Poems* Harper
NY 1935 [1] $50/250

008a: THE LOST ZOO Harper NY (1940) [1]
Written with "Christopher Cat" $40/200

009a: MY LIVES AND HOW I LOST THEM
Harper NY (1942) [1] "First Edition C-R" $50/250

010a: ON THESE I STAND Harper NY (1947) [1]
Anthology selected by Cullen. Includes six new
poems $30/150

011a: MY SOUL'S HIGH SONG *The Collected
Writings...* Doubleday NY 1991 [] Edited by
Gerald Early. (Published at $24.95) $

011b: MY SOUL'S HIGH SONG *The Collected Writings...*   Doubleday   NY   1991 [] Wraps. (Published at $14.95) $

DON DeLILLO

DeLillo was born in the Bronx in 1936. He graduated from Fordham University. *White Noise* won the American Book Award for Fiction in 1985. There is not much biographical information furnished in Contemporary Authors or any of the dustwrapper blurbs.

We thank Houghton Mifflin for supplying the quantities shown.

REFERENCES:

(a) Bruccoli & Clark. FIRST PRINTINGS OF AMERICAN AUTHORS. Volume 1. Detroit: Gale Research (1977).

(b) After 1977 the information is from inventory or as noted.

001a: AMERICANA   Houghton Mifflin   Boston
1971 [1] 4,500 cc $75/350

002a: END ZONE Houghton Mifflin Boston 1972
[1] 6,500 cc. (Published 3/27/72 at $5.95) $35/175

002b: END ZONE Deutsch London 1973 [] $15/75

002c: END ZONE   (Deutsch/Wildwood House
London   1973) []   Pictorial wraps. Simultaneous
issue (N. Williams 11/94) $25.

003a: GREAT JONES STREET Houghton Mifflin
Boston 1973 [1] 12,500 cc $30/150

003b: GREAT JONES STREET Deutsch (London 1974) [1] (Ref.b) $15/75

003c: GREAT JONES STREET   Wildwood House London 1974 [] Wraps. Simultaneous issue (Peter Selley 5/92) $25.

004a: RATNER'S STAR Knopf NY 1976 [1] "Uncorrected Proof" in blue-green wraps (H.E. Turlington #28) $150.

004b: RATNER'S STAR Knopf NY 1976 [1] (Ref.c) $25/125

005a: PLAYERS Knopf NY 1977 [1] Uncorrected proof in tall thin blue printed wraps $125.

005b: PLAYERS Knopf NY 1977 [1] $15/75

005c: PLAYERS Vintage L 1991 [] Wraps. No UK hard cover edition (Andrew Selanders 11/94) $25.

006a: RUNNING DOG Knopf NY 1978 [1] Uncorrected proof in gray wraps $100.

006b: RUNNING DOG Knopf NY 1978 [1] $12/60

006c: RUNNING DOG Gollancz London 1978 [0] Red boards, gold letters on spine $10/50

007a: AMAZONS Holt Rinehart NY (1980) [3] Written as Cleo Birdwell. Advance Review copy in pictorial wraps as trade dustwrapper $50.

007b: AMAZONS Holt Rinehart NY (1980) [3] $8/40

007c: AMAZONS Granada L 1980 [] (David Rees 3/90) $10/50

008a: THE NAMES Knopf NY 1982 [1] Uncorrected proofs in printed blue wraps $125.

008b: THE NAMES Knopf NY 1982 [1] $10/60

008c: THE NAMES Harvester (Brighton 1983) []
(Bert Babcock #53) $8/40

009a: WHITE NOISE   Viking   (NY 1985) [1]
Uncorrected proof in white and black printed wraps $100.

009b: WHITE NOISE   Viking   (NY 1985) [1]
25,000 cc (PW). Winner of the American Book
Award for Fiction in 1985 $12/60

009c: WHITE NOISE Picador London (1985) []
Noted with wrap-around band with "Winner of..." $10/50

010a: THE DAY ROOM (*American Theatre* NY
1986) [] Wraps. Play inserted in September issue of
magazine. Separate pagination (Euclid Books #4) $40.

010b: THE DAY ROOM, A PLAY Knopf NY
1987 [] Uncorrected proof in gray wraps (Bev
Chaney 11/88) $60.

010c: THE DAY ROOM, A PLAY   Knopf NY
1987 [1] $8/40

011a: LIBRA Viking (no-place [NY] no-date
[1988]) [0] "Advance Reading Copy" in pictorial
wraps $60.

011b: LIBRA   Viking (NY 1988) [0] 50,000 cc
(PW). (Published 8/88 at $19.95) $7/35

011c: LIBRA Viking L 1988 [] (Andrew Sclanders
11/94) $10/40

012a: MAO II Viking (no-place [NY] 1991) []
Uncorrected proof in glossy pictorial wraps $50.

012b: MAO II   Viking (no-place [NY] 1991) []
75,000 cc (PW) $6/30

012c: MAO II   Jonathan Cape   L 1991 []
Uncorrected proof in pictorial wraps (Polyanthos
Park Avenue Books 9/95) $60.

012d: MAO II   Jonathan Cape   L 1991 [] (Nigel
Williams 2/95) $6/30

013a: "MASTER LEADS THE CHANT..."   Black
Oak Books   Berkeley   (1991) [] 7 1/2" x 13"
broadside (Am Here Books 5/92).   Also noted as
MANSEI *From Mao II*   Black Oak Books/Okeanos
Press Berkeley 1991 [] 7 1/2" x 13" broadside (Am
Here Books 5/92).   An excerpt from *Mao II* issued
on the occasion of a reading by the author at Black
Oak Books (Ken Lopez 12/94). Assume the same $35.

014a: *"On February 14, 1989..."* (Rushdie Defense
Committee USA   no-place 1994) [0] 450,000 cc.
One page folded to make four pages. Flyer issued
in support of Salman Rushdie on the fifth
anniversary of the Iranian death edict issued against
him in response to *The Satanic Verses*.   Text is
attributed to DeLillo (Ken Lopez 3/95) $30.

E.L. DOCTOROW

Doctorow was born in New York City in 1931. He attended Kenyon College and Columbia University, and has taught at Sarah Lawrence College and Princeton University. *Ragtime* won the 1976 National Book Critics Award. *Billy Bathgate* won both the National Book Critics Circle Award and the PEN/Faulkner Award.

REFERENCES:

(a) Bruccoli & Clark. FIRST PRINTINGS OF AMERICAN AUTHORS. Volume 1. Detroit: Gale Research (1977).

(b) Inventory.

(c) Cumulative Book Index.

001a: WELCOME TO HARD TIMES   Simon & Schuster NY 1960 [1] Printed on very cheap paper which has usually turned brown $150/750

001b: BAD MAN FROM BODIE Deutsch (London 1961) [] New title $60/300

002a: BIG AS LIFE Simon & Schuster NY (1966) [1] $100/500

003a: THE BOOK OF DANIEL   Random House NY (1971) [1] Uncorrected proof in green wraps (Joseph Dermont 11/89) $150.

003b: THE BOOK OF DANIEL   Random House NY (1971) [1] Complimentary copy without front endpaper and previous titles printed on front pastedown (ref.b) $50/100

003c: THE BOOK OF DANIEL Random House NY (1971) [1] $15/75

003d: THE BOOK OF DANIEL Macmillan (London 1972) [0] $12/60

004a: RAGTIME Random House NY (1975) [] Uncorrected proof in tall red wraps $250.

004b: RAGTIME Random House NY (1975) [2] 150 sgd no cc. Issued in white cloth without dust-wrapper in slipcase. Winner of the National Book Critics Award for 1976 $200/250

004c: RAGTIME Random House NY (1975) [2] 2,000 cc. "For friends of the author." Issued in plain acetate dustwrapper. (Also noted in printed dust-wrapper. {Bert Babcock #55}) $75.

004d: RAGTIME Random House NY (1975) [4] Unspecified number in brown cloth with signed tipped-in sheet, perhaps with different dustwrapper? $75/125

004e: RAGTIME Random House NY (1975) [4] Brown cloth and dustwrapper without review on back flap. Both 004e and f have "7/75" at bottom of back flap. (Book Club edition has "MP5E." Joseph Zabel) $15/75

004f: RAGTIME Random House NY (1975) [4] Review on back flap of dustwrapper $15/50

004g: RAGTIME M(acmillan) L 1976 [] Proof in plain brown wraps and proof dustwrapper (Dalian) $125.

004h: RAGTIME M(acmillan) London 1976 [] Ref.c (in variant? green cloth {Bert Babcock #55}) $10/50

004i: RAGTIME Bantam NY 1976 [] Yellow and green mixed weave-textured boards (Robert Temple 11/91). Assume issued without dustwrapper $30.

004j: RAGTIME Bantam NY (1976) [] Wraps.
First illustrated edition in slipcase $10/35

005a: DRINKS BEFORE DINNER Random House
NY (1979) [] "Uncorrected Proof" in red printed
wraps (Phoenix #205) $125.

005b: DRINKS BEFORE DINNER *A Play* Random House NY (1979) [4] $12/60

005c: DRINKS BEFORE DINNER *A Play* Macmillan London 1980 [] (Ref. c) $10/50

006a: LOON LAKE Random House NY (1980)
[4] "Uncorrected Proof" in red wraps (H.E.
Turlington #28) $75.

006b: LOON LAKE Random House NY (1980)
[2] 350 sgd no cc. Issued without dustwrapper in
slipcase (ref.b) $75/125

006c: LOON LAKE Franklin Press Franklin, PA
1980 [2] Limited edition in full leather. With
special message to subscribers from the author
(Between The Covers 12/94) $75.

006d: LOON LAKE Random House NY (1980)
[4] Signed tipped-in page (Aspidistra Bookshop
#6) $35/50

006e: LOON LAKE Random House NY (1980)
[2] Presentation edition (1000 copies) not signed.
Black cloth issued without dustwrapper (Magnum
Opus #6) $30.

006f: LOON LAKE Random House NY (1980) [4]
(Published 9/25/80 at $11.95.) (Ref.b) $7/35

006g: LOON LAKE M(acmillan London 1980) []
Proof in cream printed wraps (Dalian Books) $75.

006h: LOON LAKE M(acmillan London 1980) [1]
(Ref.c) $7/35

007a: AMERICAN ANTHEM Stewart, Tabori & Chang NY (1982) [2] 1,000 sgd no cc. Issued in clear plastic dustwrapper and slipcase. Signed by Doctorow and J.C. Suares (one of the photographers) (Steven Bernard 11/89) $75/125

007b: AMERICAN ANTHEM Stewart, Tabori & Chang NY (1982) [] Trade edition without dustwrapper or slipcase (Steven Bernard 11/89) $35.

008a: ESSAYS & CONVERSATIONS *Ontario Review* Princeton 1983 [] (Euclid Books 4/89) $10/40

009a: LIVES OF THE POETS Random House NY (1984) [] Uncorrected proof in yellow wraps $75.

009b: LIVES OF THE POETS Random House NY (1984) [2] 350 sgd no cc. Issued without dustwrapper in slipcase (ref.b) $50/100

009c: LIVES OF THE POETS Random House NY (1984) [4] $7/35

009d: LIVES OF THE POETS Michael Joseph London (1985) [] $7/35

010a: WORLD'S FAIR Random House NY (1985) [] Advance reading copy in pictorial wraps $60.

010b: WORLD'S FAIR Random House NY (1985) [2] 300 sgd no cc. Issued without dustwrapper in slipcase $60/10

010c: WORLD'S FAIR Random House NY (1985) [4] Signed on tipped-in leaf $35/50

010d: WORLD'S FAIR Random House NY (1985) [4] 100,000 cc (PW) $7/35

010e: WORLD'S FAIR Michael Joseph L (1986) [] (Keane-Egan Books 12/94) $8/40

011a: BILLY BATHGATE Random House NY (1989) [] Uncorrected proofs in yellow wraps (Bev Chaney 3/89). Winner of both the National Book Critics Circle Award and the PEN/Faulkner Award $150.

011b: BILLY BATHGATE Franklin Library Franklin Center 1989 [2] Signed "Limited First Edition" with special note by author $100.

011c: BILLY BATHGATE Random House NY (1989) [2] 300 sgd no cc. Issued without dustwrapper in slipcase. Published at $100. $100/150

011d: BILLY BATHGATE Random House NY (1989) [] 100,000 cc (PW). (Published Febrary 1989 at $19.95) $6/30

011e: BILLY BATHGATE Macmillan London 1989 [2] 50 sgd no cc. Issued in wraps (Any Amount of Books 3/93) $100.

011f: BILLY BATHGATE Macmillan London 1989 [] (Nicholas Burrows 11/94) $6/30

012a: SCENES AND SEQUENCES Peter Blum Editions NY 1989 [2] 55 sgd no cc. Oblong folio in cloth-backed boards and slipcase. Text by Doctorow and 58 illustrations by Eric Fischl with an original signed monotype by Fischl (Geo. Robert Minkoff) $5,500

012b: SCENES AND SEQUENCES Peter Blum Editions NY 1989 [] 1,600 cc. Oblong folio in cloth-backed boards and slipcase with text by Doctorow and 58 illus by Eric Fischl $350.

013a: AN OPEN LETTER TO THE PRESIDENT Midwest Booksellers for Social Responsibility St. Paul [1991] [] One sheet folded to make 4 pages (Waverly Books 9/91) $75.

014a: THE PEOPLE'S TEXT *A Citizen Reads the Consititution* Nouveau Press Jackson, Miss. 1992

[2] 40 sgd no (Roman-numerals) cc. Issued in quarter morocco. Signed by author and Barry Mosher (illustrator) with an extra signed frontispiece wood engraving laid in $250.

014b: THE PEOPLE'S TEXT *A Citizen Reads the Constitution* Nouveau Press Jackson, Miss. 1992 [2] 200 sgd no cc. Hand bound in Dutch cloth with printed Fabriano cover papers. Signed by author and Barry Mosher (illustrator) $125.

015a: JACK LONDON, HEMINGWAY, AND THE CONSTITUTION Random House NY (1993) [] Uncorrected proof in patterned wraps (Ken Lopez 2/95) $60.

015b: SELECTED ESSAYS 1977-1992 Random House NY 1993 [] New title $6/30

016a: THE WATERWORKS Random House NY (1994) [2] 150 sgd no cc. Issued without dustwrapper in slipcase $100/150

016b: THE WATERWORKS Random House NY (1994) [4] (Published June 1994 at $23) $5/25

016c: THE WATERWORKS Macmillan London 1994 [] Uncorrected proof in pictorial wraps $60.

016d: THE WATERWORKS Macmillan London 1994 [] $6/30

017a: *"Ever since this day I have dreamt sometimes..."* Black Oak Books Berkeley 1994 [] 9 1/2" x 6 1/2" broadside. Excerpt taken from *The Water Works* (Chloe's Books 2/95) $15.

T. S. Eliot signature

T. S. ELIOT
(1888 - 1965)

Eliot was born in St. Louis, Missouri, where he lived and attended school until 1906 before beginning his studies at Harvard University. At Harvard he completed his undergraduate work in three years and took a M.A. in his fourth year, the year he also edited *The Harvard Advocate*. He then spent a year at the Sorbonne before returning to Harvard for three years to work on a Ph.D. in philosophy. His dissertation on F.H. Bradley and Meinong's *Gegenstandstheorie* was accepted, he said "because it was unreadable." He never took the degree but instead visited Germany and England on a traveling scholarship. He married Vivian Haigh-Wood of London in 1915 and earned his living teaching at Highgate School, working at Lloyd's Bank and then as a literary editor at Faber & Faber. He became a British subject in 1927 and published his own magazine, *The Criterion*, from 1922 to 1939.

He was awarded a Nobel Prize in literature in 1948 and won general attention and popularity in the 1950s with his two verse dramas *The Cocktail Party* and *The Confidential Clerk*. *The Wasteland* and the *Four Quartets* are regarded as among the most influential works of this century. More recently, his name has again been before the public due to the immense popularity of the play CATS adapted from his *Old Possum's Book of Practical Cats*.

We would like to acknowledge the assistance of Carl Hahn who prepared the basic bibliographical information from Dr. Gallup's bibliography, which is one of the best in that it provides exact information on first edition identification and also provides the printing quantities which are lacking from the vast majority of bibliographies.

REFERENCES:

(a) Gallup, Donald. T.S. ELIOT A BIBLIOGRAPHY. New York: Harcourt (1969).

(b) Methuen records at the Lilly Library furnished by William Cagle.

(c) Woolmer, J. Howard. A CHECKLIST OF THE HOGARTH PRESS. Andes, New York: Woolmer/Brotherson, 1976.

(d) Bradley, Van Allen. THE BOOK COLLECTOR'S HANDBOOK OF VALUES 1982-1983. New York: Putnam, 1982.

(e) Various dealer catalogs.

001a: PRUFROCK AND OTHER OBSERVA-TIONS The Egoist Ltd. L 1917 [0] 500 cc. Wraps. Connolly's *Modern Movement* $7,500.

002a: EZRA POUND HIS METRIC AND POETRY Knopf NY 1917 [0] 1,000 cc. Rose paper boards and plain buff dustwrapper. (Eliot's authorship not revealed until 1920) $600/650

003a: POEMS Hogarth Pr. Richmond 1919 [0] 250 cc. Wraps. First issue: p.13:6 "aestival" for "estivale" and p.13:12 "capitaux" for "chapitaux" $6,000.

    (Note: there were fewer than 250 copies in both issues 3a and 3b combined.) Various types of wraps with red printed label.

003b: POEMS Hogarth Pr. Richmond 1919 [0] Wraps. Misprints corrected. Later copies in marbled wraps, most with black-printed label (although at least one copy has been noted in this binding and with errors) $5,500.

004a: ARA VUS PREC The Ovid Pr. (L 1920) [2] 4 copies numbered 1-4 on Japan vellum in various bindings. Not For Sale. Error "Vus" for "Vos" on title page. (The title, *Ara Vos Prec*, is correct on the cover) $7,500.

004b: ARA VUS PREC The Ovid Pr. (L 1920) [2]
30 sgd no cc. Numbered 5-34 with error on title
page, early numbers in black boards, later adds
yellow cloth spine $6,500.

004c: ARA VUS PREC The Ovid Pr. (L 1920) [2]
220 no. cc. Numbered 35-255 with error on title
page, issued in both bindings as in 4b $3,500.

004d: ARA VUS PREC The Ovid Pr. (L 1920) [2]
10 cc not numbered. Ref.a suggests (and our own
observation would indicate) more than 10
unnumbered copies may have been printed. Title
error still present $1,750.

004e: POEMS Knopf NY 1920 [0] New title. Tan
paper boards and yellow dustwrapper printed in
green or brown $300/1,500

005a: THE SACRED WOOD Methuen L (1920)
[1] 1,135 cc (a+b). First state: "Methuen" at foot of
spine in letters approximately 3mm in height and
dustwrapper without subtitle on front $400/1,000

005b: THE SACRED WOOD Methuen L (1920)
[1] (Issued 1921.) Second state: letters 3.5mm,
dustwrapper includes subtitle and adds "Books by
A. Clutton-Brock" on back (ref.a). Records indicate
5a, b, c and d sheets were all printed in October
1920 (ref.b) $150/600

005c: THE SACRED WOOD Methuen L (1920)
[1] 500 cc. Third state: adds 8 pages of publisher's
ads inserted after p.156 (ref.a). Bound in June 1925 $100/400

005d: THE SACRED WOOD Methuen L (1920)
[1] "Hybrid State" has features of the first and third
bindings: the imprint at the base of the spine is in 3
mm letters and 8 pages of publisher's ads are
inserted at rear (MacDonnell Rare Books 11/94) $150/500

005e: THE SACRED WOOD Knopf NY 1921 [0] 365 cc. English sheets. No dustwrapper mentioned in Ref.a but copy in dustwrapper at auction in 1982 $300/1,000

005f: THE SACRED WOOD Methuen L (1928) [] 1,497 cc (5f+g). Blue cloth boards and buff dustwrapper printed in blue. "Second Edition" $75/250

005g: THE SACRED WOOD Knopf NY 1930 [0] 500 cc. English second edition sheets. No dustwrapper mentioned in ref.a. Ref.b indicates 520 sets actually sent in May 1930. Assume dustwrapper $75/350

006a: THE WASTE LAND Boni & Liveright NY 1922 [2] 1,000 no. cc in total. Approximately 500 copies in first state: flexible cloth boards and "mountain" correctly spelled on p.41, number on colophon 5mm high $2,000/6,500

006b: THE WASTE LAND Boni & Liveright NY 1922 [2] 1,000 no. cc in total. Approximately 500 copies in second state: stiff cloth boards and "mount in" for "mountain" on p.41. Number on colophon 2mm high $1,000/5,000

006c: THE WASTE LAND Boni & Liveright NY (1923) [2] 1,000 no. cc. Misprint "mount in" remains. "Second Edition." No dustwrapper mentioned in ref.a but copy with dustwrapper catalogued (Anacapa #51) $350/1,500

006d: THE WASTE LAND Hogarth Richmond 1923 [0] Approximately 460 cc. 3 states of label exist: with border of asterisks; with single rule above and below title; without rules. Ref.a states "used, apparently simultaneously, in three states." Ref.c assigns no label priority. Ref.d states label with asterisks is the "first issue" $3,500.

006e: THE WASTE LAND Faber & Faber L (1961) [2] 300 sgd no cc. Marbled paper boards and white parchment spine in marbled paper covered box (signed 1961/published 1962) $2,750/3,000

006f: THE WASTE LAND Faber & Faber L (1971) [2] 500 cc. Facsimile and transcript of original draft edited by Valerie Eliot. Cloth in slipcase without dustwrapper (ref.e) $200/300

Also see 043.

006g: THE WASTE LAND Faber & Faber L (1971) [1] $15/75

006h: THE WASTE LAND Harcourt Brace NY (1971) [2] 250 no cc $250/350

006i: THE WASTE LAND Harcourt Brace NY (1971) [1] $12/60

007a: HOMAGE TO JOHN DRYDEN THREE ESSAYS... Hogarth L 1924 [0] Approximately 2,000 cc. Wraps $350.

007b: HOMAGE TO JOHN DRYDEN [Haskell House NY 1964] [0] Wraps. Off-print of pages 197-239 from an anthology. No indication of publisher, place or date. First US edition $100.

008a: POEMS 1909-1925 Faber & Gwyer L 1925 [0] 1,460 cc. Blue cloth boards with cream dustwrapper printed in blue $150/750

008b: POEMS 1909-1925 Faber & Gwyer L 1925 [2] 85 sgd no cc of which 75 were for sale (actually issued in 1926). Glassine dustwrapper $3,000.

008c: POEMS 1909-1925 Harcourt, Brace & Co. NY/Chicago (1932) [0] 4,080 cc. Cream dustwrapper printed in blue without price at bottom of back flap. Printed on laid paper watermarked with a crown and "ANTIQUE DE LUXE BCMSH." Bound in blue cloth

$100/400

008d: POEMS 1909-1925 Harcourt.. NY/Chicago (no-date) [0] Second printing (probably 1933). On wove unwatermarked paper, lavender dustwrapper with price on bottom back flap. (Later printing dustwrapper has advertisement for *After Strange Gods* and is priced $2.00 on front flap)

$25/75

009a: JOURNEY OF THE MAGI (Faber & Gwyer L 1927) [0] 5,000 cc. Wraps. Note: unsold copies were reissued in 1938 in mauve paper envelopes printed in black "The Original First..."

$100.

009b: JOURNEY OF THE MAGI (Faber & Gwyer L 1927) [2] 350 no. cc (not signed). Yellow boards in glassine dustwrapper

$250.

009c: JOURNEY OF THE MAGI Wm. Edwin Rudge NY 1927 [2] 27 no. cc. Wraps. 12 copies were for sale (to secure copyright in U.S.)

$1,500.

009d: JOURNEY OF THE MAGI (No-publisher) Iowa City, Iowa 1953 [2] 260 cc. Issued gratis and mailed in blue paper envelope (for friends of G. & C. Coleman)

$150.

010a: SHAKESPEARE AND THE STOICISM OF SENECA Oxford Univ. Press L 1927 [0] Wraps

$300.

011a: A SONG FOR SIMEON (Faber & Gwyer L 1928) [0] 3,500 cc. Wraps. Note: unsold copies reissued in 1938 in gray paper envelopes printed in red "The Original First ..."

$100.

011b: A SONG FOR SIMEON Faber & Gwyer L 1928 [2] 500 sgd no cc. Off-white paper boards, issued without dustwrapper

$450.

012a: FOR LANCELOT ANDREWES   Faber &
Gwyer L (1928) [1] 1,500 cc $100/400

012b: FOR LANCELOT ANDREWES   Double-
day Garden City 1929 [1] 2,000 cc $60/300

013a: DANTE   Faber & Faber L (1929) [1] 2,000
cc. Gray dustwrapper printed in blue and black. Earliest state of dustwrapper has no review excerpts on
front flap and back cover $60/300

013b: DANTE   Faber & Faber L (1929) [2] 125 sgd
no cc.   Blue-green cloth boards lettered in gold,
glassine dustwrapper $1,250.

014a: ANIMULA   (Faber & Faber L 1929) [0]
3,000 cc. Wraps. Note: unsold copies reissued in
1938 in green paper envelopes printed in brown
"The Original First..." $100.

014b: ANIMULA (Faber & Faber) L 1929 [2] 400
sgd no cc. Yellow paper boards, issued without
dustwrapper $500.

015a: ASH-WEDNESDAY   Fountain Pr/Faber &
Faber   NY/L   1930   [2] 600 sgd no cc.   In
cellophane dustwrapper with white paper flaps and
in plain brown cardboard box (200 copies for
UK/400 copies for US) $600/750

015b: ASH-WEDNESDAY   Faber & Faber   L
1930 [1] 2,000 cc.   Connolly's *The Modern
Movement #65* $75/350

015c: ASH-WEDNESDAY   Putnam's Sons NY/L
1930 [1] 2,000 cc. Issued in glassine dustwrapper $50/250

016a: ANABASIS A POEM BY ST.-J. PERSE
Faber & Faber L 1930 [2] 350 sgd no cc. Issued in
cellophane dustwrapper and plain green cardboard
box $500/600

016b: ANABASIS A POEM BY ST.-J. PERSE
Faber & Faber L 1930 [0] 549 cc. Blue green cloth,
top edge green, in white dustwrapper printed in
green, black and red $75/350

016c: ANABASIS A POEM BY ST.-J. PERSE
Faber & Faber L 1930 [0] 1,101 cc. (From first
edition sheets cut down, bound and reissued in
1937.) Green cloth boards, green dustwrapper
printed in purple $35/150

016d: ANABASIS A POEM BY ST.-J. PERSE
Harcourt, Brace NY 1938 [1] 1,000 cc. Revised and
corrected by Eliot per information on dustwrapper
(ref.a) $50/200

016e: ANABASIS A POEM BY ST.-J. PERSE
Harcourt, Brace NY (1949) [1] 3,000 cc. "Revised
and corrected edition, 1949" (includes note by Eliot) $20/100

016f: ANABASIS A POEM BY ST.-J. PERSE
Faber & Faber L (1959) [] Proof copy in brown
wrappers (R.A. Gekoski 12/91) $200.

016g: ANABASIS A POEM BY ST.-J. PERSE
Faber & Faber L (1959) [1] 3,000 cc. Revised
edition $25/75

017a: MARINA (Faber & Faber L 1930) [0] 2,000
cc. Wraps $100.

017b: MARINA Faber & Faber L 1930 [2] 400 sgd
no cc. Issued in glassine dustwrapper $500.

018a: THOUGHTS AFTER LAMBETH Faber &
Faber L (1931) [1] 300 cc. Gray cloth boards,
double endpapers, glassine dustwrapper $350.

018b: THOUGHTS AFTER LAMBETH Faber &
Faber L (1931) [1] 3,000 cc. Wraps $100.

019a: TRIUMPHAL MARCH (Faber & Faber L
1931) [0] 2,000 cc. Wraps $100.

019b: TRIUMPHAL MARCH   Faber & Faber L 1931 [2] 300 sgd no cc. Issued without dustwrapper $600.

020a: CHARLES WHIBLEY A MEMOIR (Oxford Univ. Pr. L) 1931 [0] Approximately 1945 cc. Pamphlet No. 80. Gray wraps. (Approximately 2,055 additional copies were bound without wraps, see following entries) $100.

020b: THE ENGLISH ASSOCIATION PAMPHLETS WRITERS POETS & PLAYWRIGHTS Heffer Cambridge (1964) [0] 1,205 cc.   Issued without wraps and bound with other pamphlets in blue cloth and buff dustwrapper $50/200

020c: THE ENGLISH ASSOCIATION PAMPHLETS A SELECTED MISCELLANEA Heffer Cambridge (1964) [0] Approximately 850 cc. Bound without wrapper with other pamphlets; gray-green cloth boards and buff dustwrapper $25/125

021a: DEATH BY WATER   (No-publisher [Frederic Prokosch]) New Haven 1932 [2] 5cc. Wraps. Hand-illuminated, hand-bound (Black Sun #L-85-8) $1,500.

022a: SELECTED ESSAYS 1917-1932 Faber & Faber L (1932) [2] 115 sgd no cc.   Issued in cellophane dustwrapper $2,000.

022b: SELECTED ESSAYS 1917-1932 Faber & Faber L (1932) [1] 3,000 cc.   Issued in white dustwrapper (ref.a).   Also noted in a green dustwrapper $100/500

022c: SELECTED ESSAYS 1917-1932 Harcourt, Brace NY (1932) [1] 3,700 cc $50/250

022d: SELECTED ESSAYS New Edition Harcourt, Brace NY (1950) [0] 5,000 cc. Four additional essays, new note $25/100

023a: JOHN DRYDEN THE POET... Terence &
Elsa Holliday NY 1932 [2] 110 cc of which 100 are
signed. Issued in cellophane dustwrapper $1,250.

023b: JOHN DRYDEN THE POET... Terence &
Elsa Holliday NY 1932 [0] 1,000 cc. Assume issued
without dustwrapper $250.

024a: SWEENEY AGONISTES... Faber & Faber L
(1932) [1] 4,100 cc (total a+b). First state: blue
paper boards $50/250

024b: SWEENEY AGONISTES... Faber & Faber
L (1932) [1] Second state: blue-green paper boards $30/150

025a: O CITY CITY (No-publisher [Frederic
Prokosch]) New Haven 1932 [2] Wraps. 5 cc (2 of
which were reportedly done in 1948 {Black Sun
#73}) $2,000.

026a: AFTER THE TORCHLIGHT (No-publisher
[Frederic Prokosch]) New Haven 1933 [2] Wraps.
5cc (of which 2 copies were reportedly done in
1948 {Black Sun #73}) $2,000.

027a: THE USE OF POETRY AND THE USE OF
CRITICISM... Faber & Faber L (1933) [1] 2,500
cc. Top edge stained blue (variant with top edge not
stained blue also noted - Steven Temple 6/89) $75/350

027b: THE USE OF POETRY AND THE USE OF
CRITICISM... Harvard University Press
Cambridge, MA 1933 [0] 1,500 cc $60/300

028a: AFTER STRANGE GODS Faber & Faber L
1933 [1] 3,000 cc $60/300

028b: AFTER STRANGE GODS Harcourt, Brace
NY 1933 [1] 1,500 cc $50/250

029a: MORNING AT THE WINDOW (No-
publisher [Frederic Prokosch]) New Haven 1933
[2] 5cc. Wraps. Hand-illuminated, hand-bound $1,750.

030a: EXCERPT FREDERIC PROKOSCH (No-publisher [Frederic Prokosch]) New Haven 1933 [2] 5cc. Wraps. Hand-illuminated, hand-bound $1,750.

031a: LADY OF SILENCES (No-publisher [Frederic Prokosch]) New Haven 1933 [2] 5cc. Wraps. Hand-illuminated, hand-bound $1,750.

032a: THE ROCK *A Pageant Play* Faber & Faber L 1934 [1] 2,000 cc. Wraps. Black printing on spine, note on Iconoclasm scene laid-in some copies. Priced at 1 shilling. Heavy gray wraps have flaps folded over first and last blank leaves $150.

032b: THE ROCK *A Pageant Play* Faber & Faber L (1934) [1] 1,000 cc. Gray paper boards, blue lettering on spine. White dustwrapper printed in gray and red $50/250

032c: THE ROCK *A Pageant Play* Harcourt, Brace NY 1934 [1] 1,500 cc. One line of text that appeared in UK edition has been deleted $50/200

033a: ELIZABETHAN ESSAYS Faber & Faber L (1934) [1] 4,000 cc in total. First issue: misprint on half title "No. 21" for "No. 24", spine stamped in gold $150/350

033b: ELIZABETHAN ESSAYS Faber & Faber L (1934) [1] Second issue: cancel half-title leaf corrects error above. Spine stamped in silver $50/250

033c: ELIZABETHAN ESSAYS Faber & Faber L (1934) [1] Third state: copies measure 18cm in height, half-title correctly reprinted, spine stamped in silver $25/125

033d: ESSAYS ON ELIZABETHAN DRAMA Harcourt, Brace NY (1956) [0] 15,000 cc. Wraps. New title. "Harvest Book 18." Deletes three essays and adds one from UK edition, new preface $60.

033e: ELIZABETHAN DRAMATISTS   Faber &
Faber L (1963) [1] 13,450 cc. Wraps. New title.
Preface slightly revised from American edition $50.

034a: WORDS FOR MUSIC ("Bryn Mawr Press")
Bryn Mawr, Pa. (1935) [2] 2 ltr cc.   Wraps.
Lettered "A" and "B." Privately printed for Frederic
Prokosch. Bound in red and gold wraps and a
cellophane dustwrapper $3,500.

034b: WORDS FOR MUSIC ("Bryn Mawr Press")
Bryn Mawr, Pa. (1935) [2] 6 ltr cc.   Wraps.
Lettered a-f. Privately printed for Frederic
Prokosch. Bound in gold paper wraps with white
paper label (no dustwrapper) $3,000.

034c: WORDS FOR MUSIC ("Bryn Mawr Press")
Bryn Mawr, Pa. (1935) [2] 6 no. cc.   Wraps.
Numbered 1-6. Privately printed for Frederic
Prokosch. Bound in marbled paper wraps with
white paper label (no dustwrapper) $3,000.

034d: WORDS FOR MUSIC ("Bryn Mawr Press")
Bryn Mawr, Pa. (1935) [2] 6 no cc.   Wraps.
Numbered I-VI. Privately printed for Frederic
Prokosch. Issued in decorated paper wraps with
silver paper label (no dustwrapper) $3,000.

> NOTE: there are indications that the total
> edition of *Words for Music* exceeds the above
> 20 copies.

035a: MURDER IN THE CATHEDRAL   H.J.
Goulden, Ltd. (no-place) 1935 [0] 750 cc. Gray
paper wraps printed in blue (Acting Edition) $450.

035b: MURDER IN THE CATHEDRAL   H.J.
Goulden, Ltd. (no-place) 1935 [0] A few copies for
the members of the cast in plain white wraps
(Acting Edition) $600.

035c: MURDER IN THE CATHEDRAL Faber &
Faber L (1935) [1] 3,000 cc $60/300

035d: MURDER IN THE CATHEDRAL Harcourt, Brace NY (1935) [1] 1,500 cc $50/250

035e: THE FILM OF MURDER IN THE CATHEDRAL Faber & Faber L (1952) [1] 10,000 cc (e&f). First state: mauve cloth, spine stamped in blue and silver $50/100

035f: THE FILM OF MURDER IN THE CATHEDRAL Faber & Faber L (1952) [1] Second state: blue boards with spine stamped in red and silver. (Copy in blue cloth noted by Leaves of Grass 2/91) $25/75

035g: THE FILM OF MURDER IN THE CATHEDRAL Harcourt, Brace NY (1952) [1] 3,000 cc. Black cloth stamped in silver $25/75

035h: THE FILM OF MURDER IN THE CATHEDRAL Harcourt, Brace NY (1952) [1] 2,000 cc. Green cloth spine printed in black $15/60

036a: TWO POEMS Cambridge Univ. Pr. Cambridge 1935 [2] 22 cc. Wraps. 5 copies on Arches (numbered 1-5); 5 copies on Normandie (numbered I-V); 5 copies on Bremen (lettered a-e); 5 copies on Brussels (lettered A-E); 2 copies on Brussels (lettered x and xx). (Also a proof copy noted -Glenn Horowitz 6/90) $2,500.

037a: ESSAYS ANCIENT AND MODERN Faber & Faber L (1936) [1] 2,500 cc. A reissue of FOR LANCELOT ANDREWES with a new preface and five previously uncollected essays. Also deletes three essays from earlier book $50/250

037b: ESSAYS ANCIENT AND MODERN Harcourt, Brace NY (1936) [1] 2,500 cc. Blue cloth. Later dark blue $40/200

038a: COLLECTED POEMS 1909-1935 Faber & Faber L (1936) [1] Uncorrected proof in yellow wraps (Glenn Horowitz 6/90) $1,500.

038b: COLLECTED POEMS 1909-1935 Faber &
Faber L (1936) [1] 6,000 cc $60/300

038c: COLLECTED POEMS 1909-1935 Harcourt,
Brace NY (1936) [1] 4,700 cc $40/200

039a: THE REVENGER'S TRAGEDY A.D.C. &
Marlowe Soc. Cambridge (1937) [] Wraps. 8vo.
Wire-stitched program for the production of
Tourneur's Tragedy. Includes 500 word essay by
Eliot. Unrecorded (Ian McKelvie 11/90) $1,250.

040a: THE FAMILY REUNION Faber & Faber L
(1939) [] Uncorrected proof in yellow wraps with
minor changes (Glenn Horowitz 6/90) $1,250.

040b: THE FAMILY REUNION Faber & Faber L
(1939) [1] 6,375 cc. Dustwrapper in red, green and
black $40/200

040c: THE FAMILY REUNION Faber & Faber L
(1939) [1] Mauve dustwrapper, printed in black $40/150

040d: THE FAMILY REUNION Harcourt, Brace
NY (1939) [1] 2,500 cc $35/175

041a: OLD POSSUM'S BOOK OF PRACTICAL
CATS Faber & Faber L (1939) [] Uncorrected
proof in yellow wraps (Glenn Horowitz 6/90) $2,000.

041b: OLD POSSUM'S BOOK OF PRACTICAL
CATS Faber & Faber L (1939) [1] 3,005 cc $125/600

041c: OLD POSSUM'S BOOK OF PRACTICAL
CATS Harcourt, Brace NY (1939) [1] 2,000 cc $100/500

041d: OLD POSSUM'S BOOK OF PRACTICAL
CATS Faber & Faber L (1940) [1] 3,025 cc. First
illustrated edition $50/250

041e: OLD POSSUM'S BOOK OF PRACTICAL
CATS Harcourt, Brace NY (1982) [3] Also states

"First Edition." Illustrated by Edward Gorey (first thus) $10/50

042a: THE IDEA OF A CHRISTIAN SOCIETY
Faber & Faber L (1939) [1] 2,000 cc $60/300

042b: THE IDEA OF A CHRISTIAN SOCIETY
Harcourt, Brace NY (1940) [1] 3,000 cc $30/150

043a: THE WASTE LAND AND OTHER POEMS
Faber & Faber L (1940) [1] 5,000 cc. Note: none of
the poems are a first appearance. First edition
dustwrapper has ads for four "Sesame Books" on
back panel $40/200

043b: THE WASTE LAND AND OTHER POEMS
Harcourt, Brace NY (1955) [0] 20,000 cc. Wraps.
("Harvest Books 1") $50.

044a: EAST COKER   The New English Weekly
(Supplement) L 1940 [0] unbound supplemental
printing of "The New English Weekly Easter No.,
1940" $1,250.

044b: EAST COKER A POEM BY T.S. ELIOT
"New English Weekly" L 1940 [0] 500 cc.
("Reprinted from the Easter Number.") Wire-
stitched $600.

044c: EAST COKER Faber & Faber L (1940) [1]
9,030 cc. Yellow wraps $250.

045a: BURNT NORTON Faber & Faber L (1941)
[1] 4,000 cc. Wraps. (First separate edition) $200.

046a: POINTS OF VIEW Faber & Faber L (1941)
[] Uncorrected proof on cheap pulp paper in light
green wraps (Glenn Horowitz 6/90) $500.

046b: POINTS OF VIEW Faber & Faber L (1941)
[1] 4,000 cc $40/200

047a: THE DRY SALVAGES Faber & Faber L
(1941) [1] 11,223 cc. Wraps. Some copies printed
on slightly thicker paper without "ADELPHI"
watermark. $150.

048a: THE CLASSICS AND THE MAN OF
LETTERS Oxford Univ. Press L/NY/T 1942 [0]
5,017 total cc (a+b). Wraps. (First copies the "t" of
"the" in line 6 of title page correctly printed) $125.

048b: THE CLASSICS AND THE MAN OF
LETTERS Oxford Univ. Press L/NY/T 1942 [0]
Wraps. (Later copies the "t" of "the" in line 6 of
title page 'registers so weakly as almost to
disappear' {Gallup}) $75.

048c: THE CLASSICS AND THE MAN OF
LETTERS Oxford Univ. Press L/NY/T 1942 [0]
Two sewn signatures specially issued for Classical
Association, which usually distributed copies in
unbound form (Bell, Book & Radmall 7/93) $150.

049a: THE MUSIC OF POETRY Jackson, Son &
Co. Glasgow 1942 [0] 1,000 cc. Wraps. (Note:
Jackson, Son & Co. were publishers for Oxford
University) $150.

050a: LITTLE GIDDING Faber & Faber L (1942)
[1] 16,775 total (a+b). Wraps. Earliest copies were
sewn $200.

050b: LITTLE GIDDING Faber & Faber L (1942)
[1] Wraps. Later copies were wire-stitched $150.

051a: FOUR QUARTETS Harcourt, Brace NY
(1943) [1] 788 cc. (4,165 copies printed but 3,377
copies destroyed.) Copies state "First Amer.."
(Connolly's *Modern Movement* #92) Back panel of
dustwrapper has heavy block letters with nine titles
listed on back thru *Possum*... Priced $2.00 with 20
lines of text and publisher on front flap. Back flap
blank $500/2,000

051b: FOUR QUARTETS   Harcourt, Brace NY (1943) [0] 3,500 cc. First edition, second impression: does not state "first" and no code designation within brackets on title page verso. Dustwrapper as described above $100/500

It should be noted that the book was reprinted from 1943 to 1948 without any code designation on copyright page in two other dustwrappers:

(1) lighter type with *Essays Ancient & Modern* as one of the six titles and publisher's address as "New York"

(2) heavy block letters with *Family Reunion* as one of the six titles and address as "New York 17"

We are assuming the dustwrapper **without** "NY 17" is first but do not know. After 1948 it was still reprinted without codes but the dustwrapper mentions the Nobel Prize and is priced at $2.50.

051c: FOUR QUARTETS Faber & Faber L (1944) [1] 6,000 cc $100/400

051d: FOUR QUARTETS Faber & Faber L (1960) [2] 290 sgd no cc. Marbled paper boards, issued in marbled paper cardboard box $3,000.

052a: REUNION BY DESTRUCTION   (The Council for the Def.. L   1943) [0] Wraps.   Gray-brown or tan. Pamphlet No. 7. (Price correction on pamphlet "no. 1" and back wrapper in copies seen by Gallup) $175.

053a: WHAT IS A CLASSIC? Faber & Faber L (1945) [1] 500 cc. Heavy green paperwraps (Virgil Society issue) contains statements on the aims of the Virgil Society by Eliot and others which were not included in the next entry $300.

053b: WHAT IS A CLASSIC? Faber & Faber L (1945) [1] 4,500 cc $25/125

054a: DIE EINHEIT DER EUROPAISCHEN KULTUR Carl Habel Berlin 1946 [0] Wraps. Pages 58 and 59 numbered $250.

054b: DIE EINHEIT DER EUROPAISCHEN KULTUR Carl Habel Berlin 1946 [0] Wraps. Later impression, pg. 58 and 59 unnumbered $75.

054c: THE UNITY OF EUROPEAN CULTURE Verlag Lipsius & Tischer Kiel 1951 [] Buff wraps. First separate appearance in English? First English text published in Germany, with notes in German. The English text first appeared as a an appendix to the English and American editions of *Notes Toward The Definition Of Culture*, 1948 and 1949, respectively (Buddenbrooks 3/95) $125.

055a: A PRACTICAL POSSUM Harvard Printing Office Cambridge, Ma. (1947) [2] 60 no. cc. Wraps. (States 80 cc but actually only 60 were printed) $1,750.

056a: GERONTION Univ of Va. (Charlottesville) 1947 [0] Wraps. Published March 21, 1947, for McGregor Room Seminars (H.E. Turlington 9/85) $250.

057a: ON POETRY (Concord Academy) Concord, Ma 1947 [2] 750 no. cc (number written on inside front cover). Olive-green wraps $650.

058a: MILTON Geoffrey Cumberlege L 1947 [0] 500 cc. Gray paper wraps printed in black. Sewn. Page 20: "Printed in Great Britain at the University Press Oxford ..." Ref.a notes that the second printing is so noted on p.[ii] of cover. There were several reprints most are easily identified. (An unauthorized reprint (Haskell House? {1965?}) was wire stitched vs sewn and 23.3cm tall vs 25.8cm) $175.

059a: A SERMON   Cambridge University Press Cambridge 1948 [0] 300 cc. Unbound, sewn $300.

060a: SELECTED POEMS   British Publ. Guild Vienna (1946) [] Guild Books No. A9. (Bell, Book & Radmall 11/90) $75.

060b: SELECTED POEMS   Penguin Books Middlesex (1948) [1] 50,000 cc. Wraps. "First Published in Penguin Books.." (Contains no first appearances) $50.

060c: SELECTED POEMS   Faber   L (1954) [1] First hardback edition in blue cloth $15/75

060d: SELECTED POEMS   Harcourt, Brace NY [1967] [1] 50,000 cc. Wraps. Last date on copyright page is 1964 $35.

061a: NOTES TOWARDS THE DEFINITION OF CULTURE   Faber & Faber   L (1948) [] Uncorrected proof in yellow wraps (Wm. Reese Co. 10/92) $500.

061b: NOTES TOWARDS THE DEFINITION OF CULTURE   Faber & Faber   L (1948) [1] 18 cc. Error "a" for "the" in title on spine. Ref.a states none sold but copies auctioned in 1977 ($475) $800/900

061c: NOTES TOWARDS THE DEFINITION OF CULTURE Faber & Faber L (1948) [1] 5,988 cc $30/150

061d: NOTES TOWARDS THE DEFINITION OF CULTURE Harcourt, Brace NY (1949) [1] 7,500 cc (57d+e). Earliest dustwrapper state has 10 items listed under "Books by T.S. Eliot" on back panel $25/100

061e: NOTES TOWARDS THE DEFINITION OF CULTURE Harcourt, Brace NY (1949) [1] Later state of dustwrapper has 8 items listed under "Books by T.S. Eliot" $15/75

062a: FROM POE TO VALERY Harcourt, Brace NY (1948) [2] 1,500 cc. Issued in green paper mailing envelope and glassine dustwrapper (ref.e) $150.

062b: FROM POE TO VALERY (Library of Congress) Washington, DC 1949 [0] 1,000 cc. Wraps $100.

063a: THE UNDERGRADUATE POEMS... The Harvard Advocate Cambridge, Ma. (1949) [0] Approximately 1,000 cc. Wraps. Unauthorized publication reprinted from the *Harvard Advocate* (Nov. 1948) of which 750 copies were supposedly withdrawn from sale $200.

064a: THE AIMS OF POETIC DRAMA Poets Theatre Guild L 1949 [0] 5,000 cc. Unbound, wire-stitched $150.

065a: THE COCKTAIL PARTY Faber & Faber L (1950) [1] Wraps. Gray paper proof copy $500.

065b: THE COCKTAIL PARTY Faber & Faber L (1950) [1] 19,950 cc (61b+c). Ref.a states "about half" of the copies have misprint "here" for "her" p.29:1 $50/150

065c: THE COCKTAIL PARTY Faber & Faber L (1950) [1] Error corrected $15/100

065d: THE COCKTAIL PARTY Harcourt, Brace NY (1950) [0] Advance reading copy in wraps with pp.35-36 printed on uncancelled leaf (Joseph the Provider #31). Also unbound signatures (Glenn Horowitz 6/90) $750.

065e: THE COCKTAIL PARTY Harcourt, Brace NY (1950) [0] Approximately 10 cc with pp. 35-36 printed on uncancelled leaf $700/750

065f: THE COCKTAIL PARTY Harcourt, Brace NY (1950) [0] 10,000 cc with pp. 35-36 printed on cancel leaf. (Note: later printings have code letters/ numbers below copyright notice $15/75

065g: THE COCKTAIL PARTY Faber & Faber L (1950) [] 20,000 cc. Revised English edition. Title page says "Fourth Impression (revised).." $10/40

065h: THE COCKTAIL PARTY French NY (1950) [0] Wraps. 1,033 cc $75.

066a: POEMS WRITTEN IN EARLY YOUTH Privately Printed Stockholm 1950 [2] 12 no. cc $850.

066b: POEMS WRITTEN IN EARLY YOUTH Faber & Faber L (1967) [1] 15,000 cc $12/60

066c: POEMS WRITTEN IN EARLY YOUTH Farrar, Straus & Giroux NY (1967) [1] 3,500 cc $12/60

067a: POETRY OF T.S. ELIOT (University of Chicago 1950) [0] Wraps. 16 page pamphlet plus cover. No title page. Transcript of a broadcast on NBC by Eliot who made preliminary and closing remarks and read a selection of his poetry $100.

068a: POETRY AND DRAMA Harvard Univ. Press Cambridge, MA 1951 [0] 5,000 cc $15/75

068b: POETRY AND DRAMA Faber & Faber L (1951) [] Uncorrected proof in plain brown wraps (Glenn Horowitz 6/90) $350.

068c: POETRY AND DRAMA Faber & Faber L (1951) [1] 10,000 cc $15/75

069a: THE VALUE AND USE OF CATHEDRALS... Friends.. Chichester Cath. (Chichester 1952) [0] Approximately 2,000 cc. Wraps. First edition has printed on back cover "On sale at S.P.C.K. Bookshops One Shilling" (later printing at 2s) $100.

070a: AN ADDRESS TO MEMBERS OF THE
LONDON LIBRARY (London Library L 1952) [2]
500 cc. Wraps $150.

070b: AN ADDRESS TO MEMBERS OF THE
LONDON LIBRARY The Providence Athenaeum
Providence, RI 1953 [0] 1,100 cc. Unbound, wire-
stitched $100.

071a: THE COMPLETE POEMS AND PLAYS
Harcourt, Brace NY (1952) [1] 12,600 cc $15/75

072a: SELECTED PROSE   Penguin Books
Melbourne/Harmondsworth/Baltimore (1953) [1]
Approximately 40,000 cc. Wraps $35.

073a: THE HOLLOW MEN   (W.A.M. Press|
Reopel & Sorensen no-place 1953) [2] Paper
covered boards. 5 no. cc on Fabriano and 15 no. cc
on quality bond (Also see entry 092) $400.

073b: THE HOLLOW MEN School of Art Press
Oxford 1964 [] Issued without dutwrapper $300.

074a: AMERICAN LITERATURE AND THE
AMERICAN LANGUAGE Washington University
St. Louis (1953) [0] 500 cc. Wraps $200.

075a: THE THREE VOICES OF POETRY
Cambridge University Press 1953 [0] 7,000 cc.
Wraps. (Also noted with a Macmillan of Canada
review slip laid in. Assume no Canadian issue but
U.K. were distributed by McMillan) $60.

075b: THE THREE VOICES OF POETRY
Cambridge University Press NY 1954 [0] 3,000 cc $15/60

076a: THE CONFIDENTIAL CLERK   Faber &
Faber L (1954) [] Uncorrected proof in printed
brown wraps (Glenn Horowitz 6/90) $600.

076b: THE CONFIDENTIAL CLERK   Faber &
Faber L (1954) [1]   20,000 cc (b+c). Misprint

"Ihad" for "I had" on page 7, the penultimate line. First state of dustwrapper with price of 10s6d $25/100

076c: THE CONFIDENTIAL CLERK Faber & Faber L (1954) [1] Later state dustwrapper with price of 12s6d and misprint corrected $15/60

076d: THE CONFIDENTIAL CLERK Harcourt, Brace NY (1954) [1] 26,000 cc. Also seen in promotional dustwrapper with "Place your order now..." "To be published in a companion format to *The Cocktail Party*...$3.00...March 8, 1954" (In Our Time 10/90) $12/60

077a: RELIGIOUS DRAMA: MEDIAEVAL AND MODERN House of Books NY 1954 [2] 26 sgd ltr cc. Issued in glassine dustwrapper. Limitation page inserted $1,500.

077b: RELIGIOUS DRAMA: MEDIAEVAL AND MODERN House of Books NY 1954 [2] 300 sgd no cc. Issued in glassine dustwrapper. Limitation page inserted $600.

078a: THE CULTIVATION OF CHRISTMAS TREES Faber & Faber L (1954) [1] 10,140 cc. Wraps. Issued in pale pink paper mailing envelope printed in black $50/75

078b: THE CULTIVATION OF CHRISTMAS TREES Farrar, Straus & Cudahy NY (1956) [1] 30,000 cc. Boards issued in yellow paper mailing envelope printed in black. "First Edition" front pastedown $40/60

078c: THE CULTIVATION OF CHRISTMAS TREES Farrar, Straus & Cudahy NY (1956) [0] Second printing published in September 1957. Cloth boards in dustwrapper (also noted 78b in 78c dustwrapper, perhaps remainder?) $10/50

079a: THE LITERATURE OF POLITICS
Conservative Political Center (L 1955) [1] 6,160 cc.
Wraps $75.

080a: THE FRONTIERS OF CRITICISM
(University of Minnesota Press Minnesota 1956)
[0] 10,050 cc. Wraps. Issued in white mailing
envelope printed with return address of *Minnesota
Star & Tribune* or University of Minnesota $60/100

081a: ON POETRY AND POETS Faber & Faber L
(1957) [] Uncorrected proof in blue wraps (Glenn
Horowitz 6/90) $350.

081b: ON POETRY AND POETS Faber & Faber
L (1957) [1] 6,180 cc $15/75

081c: ON POETRY AND POETS Farrar, Straus
NY 1957 [1] 15,000 cc $12/60

082a: THE ELDER STATESMAN Faber & Faber
L (1959) [] Uncorrected proof in blue wraps with
"T.S. Elliot" on cover (Robert Temple 11/39) $350.

082b: THE ELDER STATESMAN Faber & Faber
L (1959) [1] 15,000 cc $12/60

082c: THE ELDER STATESMAN Farrar, Straus
& Giroux NY (1959) [] Galley proof on 40 narrow
folio leaves printed on rectos only (Glenn Horowitz
6/90) $400.

082d: THE ELDER STATESMAN Farrar, Straus
& Giroux NY (1959) [1] 10,000 cc $10/50

083a: ON TEACHING THE APPRECIATION OF
POETRY   Teachers College Record   No-place
1960 [] 6 pages, stapled. Off-print (R.A. Gekoski
12/90) $300.

084a: GEOFFREY FABER 1889-1961 Faber &
Faber L (1961) [2] 100 no. cc. Issued in cellophane

dustwrapper. Later copies issued in plain brown paper covered box $750.

084b: GEOFFREY FABER 1889-1961 Reprint Society L 1969 [] Issued without dustwrapper? (Waiting For Godot 6/94) $75.

085a: HE WHO CEASELESS LABOURS TOOK DELIGHT No publisher or place 1961 [] 30 cc. Card folded three times for dinner for W.J. Crawley. With special poem by TSE $500.

086a: COLLECTED PLAYS Faber & Faber L (1962) [] Uncorrected proof in blue wraps (Bernard Quarich 2/93) $300.

087a: COLLECTED PLAYS Faber & Faber L (1962) [1] 15,000 cc $15/75

087b: THE COMPLETE PLAYS OF T.S. ELIOT Harcourt, Brace NY (1967) [1] $15/75

088a: GEORGE HERBERT Longmans, Green (L 1962) [1] 8,000 cc. Wraps. Also noted: Second issue with small white cancellation slip altering the price to "Three shillings and sixpence net" (Robert Temple 3/95) $50.

088b: GEORGE HERBERT University of Nebraska Lincoln [Nebraska] (1964) [0] 5,000 cc. Wraps. Included with essay by Frank Kermode and Margaret Willy $50.

089a: COLLECTED POEMS 1909-1962 Faber & Faber L (1963) [] Uncorrected proof in cream-colored wraps (Glenn Horowitz 6/90) $400.

089b: COLLECTED POEMS 1909-1962 Faber & Faber L (1963) [1] 15,090 cc $15/75

089c: COLLECTED POEMS 1909-1962 Harcourt, Brace & World NY (1963) [1] 8,000 cc $17/75

089d: COLLECTED POEMS 1909-1962 Franklin
Library   Franklin   Center   1978 [2] "Limited
Edition" in full leather $100.

090a: KNOWLEDGE   AND   EXPERIENCE...
Faber & Faber L (1963) [] Uncorrected proof in
cream wraps.   45 copies but most recalled and
destroyed $1,000.

090b: KNOWLEDGE   AND   EXPERIENCE...
Faber & Faber L (1963) [1] 4,961 sets printed
(2,961 bound, 2,000 pulped, most of bound copies
subsequently destroyed by publisher) $1,750.

090c: KNOWLEDGE   AND   EXPERIENCE...
Faber & Faber L (1964) [1] 5,040 cc $15/75

090d: KNOWLEDGE   AND   EXPERIENCE...
Farrar, Straus NY (1964) [1] 5,000 cc $15/60

091a: TO CRITICIZE THE CRITIC AND OTHER
WRITINGS   Faber & Faber   L (1965) []
Uncorrected proof in brown wraps with publication
date of 10/28 vs. Gallup's 11/11 (Waiting for Godot
4/90) $300.

091b: TO CRITICIZE THE CRITIC AND OTHER
WRITINGS Faber & Faber L (1965) [1] 6,000 cc $15/60

091c: TO CRITICIZE THE CRITIC AND OTHER
WRITINGS Farrar, Straus & Giroux NY (1965) [1]
7,500 cc. 10,000 sets of sheets printed, of which
2,500 used for second issue $15/50

091d: TO CRITICIZE THE CRITIC AND OTHER
WRITINGS Farrar, Straus & Giroux NY (1967) [1]
2,500 cc. Wraps. "Noonday 322." 2,500 copies of
first edition sheets $35.

092a: THE HOLLOW MEN: 1925 School of Art
Press Oxford 1964 [] About 50 copies. Not for
sale. (Ulysses Bookshop 6/92) $150.

092b: THE HOLLOW MEN: 1925 (Dartmouth College) Hanover (1966) [2] 20 no cc. Wraps. (Joseph The Provider #33) (Also see entry 073a) $250.

093a: WE HAVE LINGERED IN THE CHAMBERS OF THE SEA Publisher or place? 1966 [] Multicolored broadside. About 6"x9" (Alphabet Books 4/95) $75.

094a: THE COMPLETE POEMS AND PLAYS... Faber & Faber L (1969) [] $15/75

095a: SELECTED PROSE OF T.S. ELIOT Faber & Faber L (1975) [1] Edited and introduction by Frank Kermode. Cloth $12/60

095b: SELECTED PROSE OF T.S. ELIOT Faber & Faber L (1975) [1] Wraps $25.

COLLECTED POEMS 1909-1962 See 089d.

096a: (MISS HARRIETT WEAVER) (University of Tulsa 1978) [2] Wraps. 2,500 cc. Draft of letter by Eliot published by McFarlin Library as Keepsake No. 1 $75.

097a: CONFERMENT BY NEEDLE Ronart Press St. Louis 1980 [2] 230 no. cc. Wraps. An exchange of letters with Vincent Starrett (Pepper & Stern List S) $60

098a: The following were illustrated and signed by Frederic Prokosch using Prometheus Press, Grasse (France) 1983. Each states: "Limited to five hand-illustrated copies, one on Velin Provence numbered Alpha, one on Guerimand (Beta), one on Les Aubiers (Gamma), one on Extra Strong (Delta) and one on Japon (Epsilon)"

    a. DESCEND LOWER
    b. DESIRE ITSELF

c. GARLIC AND SAPPHIRE
d. TIME AND THE BELL
e. WORDS MORE, MUSIC MOVES — $500.

099a: OF THE AWEFUL BATTLE OF THE PEKES AND THE POLLICLES Eden Press Toronto 1984 [] 20 cc. Wraps. (140 copies were printed in total but 120 were included in *Waygoose Anthology*. (Thomas A. Goldwasser 5/95) — $350.

100a: GROWTIGER'S LAST STAND + (Faber & Faber L 1986) [1] Copyright information on last page. Text from *Old Possum's...* Pictorial boards in dustwrapper. Illustrated by Errol LeCain — $10/40

100b: GROWLTIGER'S LAST STAND + Farrar/Harcourt NY (1987) [] — $10/40

101a: PRELUDES (Lumiere Press Toronto 1987) [2] 100 cc. Tall, tied printed wraps with tipped-in photograph by Michael Torosian (Wilder Books 12/89) — $150.

102a: PRELUDE I Poems on the Underground L (no date) [] Oblong broadside. 24"x11". "Prelude I" from *Prufrock*. (J. Howard Woolmer 3/95. Mr. Woolmer thinks this was probably done in the late 1980s so, we have placed with "Preludes") — $35.

103a: THE LETTERS OF T.S. ELIOT Volume I 1898-1922 Faber & Faber L (1988) [1] — $10/40

103b: THE LETTERS OF T.S. ELIOT Volume I 1898-1922 [Harcourt Brace NY 1988] [] Uncorrected Proof in printed blue wraps (Alphabet Books 7/95) — $150.

103c: THE LETTERS OF T.S. ELIOT Volume I 1898-1922 Harcourt Brace (NY 1988) [] (Published September 1988 at $29.95) — $10/40

103d: THE LETTERS OF T.S. ELIOT Faber/ Harcourt (L/NY 1988) [2] 500 no cc. Signed by Valerie Eliot. Issued without dustwrapper in slipcase (1-250 for UK and 251-599 for US) (Published at $150. in US) $100/150

104a: "NOT IN GALLUP" (cover title) (Perpetua Press Oxford 1988) [2] 150 cc. Wraps. Facsimile of T.S.E.'s preface to "The Merry Masque of Our Lady In London Tower" $75.

105a: MR.   MOSTOFFELEER   WITH MUNGOJERRIE   AND   RUMPELTEAZER Harcourt Brace Jovanovich/Farrar... (no place 1991) [3] "First U.S. Edition 1991 ABCDE" $10/40

106a: EELDROP AND APPLEPLEX The Foundation Press   (Kent) 1992 [2] 500 no cc. Wraps and dustwrapper (Keane-Egan Books 12/94) $50/100

107a: THE VARIETIES OF METAPHYSICAL POETRY Harcourt Brace San Diego (1993) [] Uncorrected Proof in printed blue wraps. The Clark lectures delivered at Trinity College in 1926 (Bev Chaney, Jr. 1/95) $50.

107b: THE VARIETIES OF METAPHYSICAL POETRY Harcourt Brace NY (1993) [] (Also noted as "1994" {Stephen Lupac 7/95}) $

William Faulkner (signature)

WILLIAM FAULKNER
(1897-1962)

William Faulkner was born near Oxford, Mississippi, where he spent most of his life. In his fourth book, *Sartoris*, he found the subject that was to be used in his major works. He created a town named "Jefferson" and a county named "Yoknapatawpha" and populated them. He won the Nobel Prize for Literature in 1949 and the Pulitzer Prize in 1955 (*A Fable*) and 1963 (*The Reivers*).

Our practice has been to use one reference work for basic bibliographic information and then note other references as they apply. For this guide we used reference (a) [see references below] for the basic bibliographical information because it was the reference that actually indicated whether or not the place and date appeared on the title page and if the copyright page actually stated "first edition," "first printing," etc. Reference (b) included quantities for the British editions and reference (c) included quantities for the early American editions which were taken from a catalog of an exhibit at Yale prepared by Robert Daniel (not seen).

REFERENCES:

(a) Massey, Linton R. "MAN WORKING" 1919-1962 WILLIAM FAULKNER. Charlottesville: University Press Of Virginia (1968).

(b) Meriwether, James B. THE LITERARY CAREER OF WILLIAM FAULKNER - *A Bibliographic Study.* Princeton: Princeton University Press, 1961.

(c) Petersen, Carl. EACH IN ITS ORDERED PLACE *A Faulkner Collector's Notebook.* Ann Arbor: Ardis (1975); and Petersen, Carl. ON THE TRACK OF THE DIXIE LIMITED. La Grange: Colophon Book Shop, 1979.

(d) FIRST PRINTINGS OF AMERICAN AUTHORS. Volume One. Detroit: Gale (1977).

(e) Brodsky, Louis Daniel, and Hamblin, Robert W. FAULKNER - *A Comprehensive Guide to the Brodsky Collection.* Volume One:

The Bibliography.   Jackson: University Press of Mississippi (1982).

(f) Inventory or dealer catalogs.

> Note: throughout the guide we cite Serendipity's catalog of the Peterson collection issued in 1991. In many cases the prices therein are higher than our estimates now. This is particularly true for English editions, but also true for uncorrected proofs and some of the signed limited editions. This is because the condition of the books in the Peterson collection was unusually fine.

001a: THE MARBLE FAUN Four Seas Boston (1924) [0] Approximately 500 cc. (Published December 15, 1924) $10,000/20,000

001b: THE MARBLE FAUN AND A GREEN BOUGH Random House NY 1965 [1] $15/75

002a: SOLDIERS' PAY Boni & Liveright NY 1926 [0] 2,500 cc. (Published February 25, 1926) $750/15,000

002b: SOLDIERS' PAY Chatto & Windus L 1930 [0] 2,000 cc. Preface by Richard Hughes $200/1,500

003a: SHERWOOD ANDERSON & OTHER FAMOUS CREOLES Pelican New Orleans 1926 [2] 50 sgd no cc (numbered 1-40 or 50). Faulkner introduction, Wm. Spratling caricatures. 40 or 50 copies bound in decorative boards with frontis and illustrations hand-tinted by Spratling, who signed the book $8,500.

003b: SHERWOOD ANDERSON & OTHER FAMOUS CREOLES Pelican New Orleans 1926 [2] 200 no cc. Green boards; limitation notice indicates 250 copies (numbered 51 to 250) (Published December 16, 1926) $2,500.

003c: SHERWOOD ANDERSON & OTHER
FAMOUS CREOLES Pelican New Orleans 1926
[2] 150 cc. Label is pasted over original limitation
statement stating "Second Issue 150 copies January
1927." All 400 copies (a,b&c) were printed at same
time. Also has Hemingway poem on back cover $1,500.

003d: SHERWOOD ANDERSON & OTHER
FAMOUS CREOLES University of Texas Press
Austin (1967) [0] Reprint. Includes an article by
Spratling on Faulkner, and on Spratling by Robt.
David Duncan (ref.c) $25/75

004a: MOSQUITOES Boni & Liveright NY 1927
[0] 3,047 cc (4a & 4b). Red on green dustwrapper
with mosquito (Published April 30, 1927) $600/3,000

004b: MOSQUITOES Boni & Liveright NY 1927
[0] Dustwrapper with card players on yacht and
Boni & Liveright as publisher $600/8,500

004c: MOSQUITOES Boni & Liveright NY 1927
[0] Dustwrapper has "Horace Liveright, Inc." on
spine. (Serendipity Books 12/91 notes that name
change of firm took place in 1930 and that it is
obviously the remainder of the first printing with a
new dustwrapper) $600/2,500

004d: MOSQUITOES Horace Liveright NY
(1931) [1] "Second printing, September 1931."
Card players on dustwrapper with "New Edition" on
front flap $50/400

004e: MOSQUITOES Chatto & Windus L 1964
[0] Wraps. "Proof Copy" in gray wraps $750.

004f: MOSQUITOES Chatto & Windus L 1964 [0]
Introduction by Richard Hughes. (Published
October 1964.) First binding: gray-brown imitation
cloth paperboards with a vertical and horizontal
pattern (Serendipity Books 12/91) $15/75

004g: MOSQUITOES Chatto & Windus L 1964
[0]   Second binding: gray imitation cloth paper
boards with a tiny diamond design (Serendipity
Books 12/91) $12/60

005a: SARTORIS Harcourt, Brace NY (1929) [0]
1,998 cc. (Published January 31, 1929.) Also see
Flags In The Dust (1973) $600/3,500

005b: SARTORIS Chatto & Windus L 1932 [0]
2,000 cc (5b&c). Blue cloth. Top edge stained blue.
(Published February 18, 1932) $150/1,750

005c: SARTORIS Chatto & Windus L 1932 [0]
Tan cloth. Top edge unstained. "Cheap Edition" on
dustwrapper (ref.c). Cloth color described as orange
by both Robert Dagg and Serendipity Books 12/91 $50/450

006a: THE SOUND AND THE FURY Cape &
Smith NY (1929) [1] Wraps. Advance copies issued
in dustwrapper but without printing on back $12,500.

006b: THE SOUND AND THE FURY Cape &
Smith NY (1929) [1] 1,789 cc. (Published October
7, 1929.) Dustwrapper not priced, ad for *Humanity
Uprooted,* on rear dustwrapper panel, offering **that
book** at $3.00 (Jeffrey Marks). (Note: price for
dustwrapper based on very good to fine, with only
slightly faded spine. A copy in new condition
would sell for much more) $500/5,000

006c: THE SOUND AND THE FURY Cape &
Smith NY (1929) [1] Dustwrapper not priced, ad
for *Humanity Uprooted,* on rear panel, offering **that
book** at $3.50 $500/4,000

006d: THE SOUND AND THE FURY Chatto &
Windus L 1931 [0] 2,000 cc. Introduction by
Richard Hughes. Bound in black cloth, top edge
stained red. (Published April 16, 1931) $150/1,750

006e: THE SOUND AND THE FURY Chatto &
Windus L 1931 [0] Later issue with same sheets

bound in a mustard cloth stamped in red. Top page edge unstained, no publisher's imprint on spine. 4 pages of ads at rear would indicate 1935 or later. Dustwrapper appears to be the same (Steven Temple 6/89) $50/750

006f: THE SOUND AND THE FURY Random House NY 1984 [] Corrected edition $10/50

006g: WILLIAM FAULKNER MANUSCRIPTS : THE SOUND AND THE FURY Random House NY 1987 [] Two oversized volumes. Volume I: reproduces holograph manuscript. Volume II: reproduces carbon typescript. Issued without dustwrappers at $195 $200

007a: AS I LAY DYING Cape & Smith NY (1930) [1] 2,522 cc (7a & 7b). Beige cloth with top page edge stained brown. Initial capital "I" at p.ll:l not aligned (dropped so that the top of the letter is almost at the bottom of the first line of text). (Published October 6, 1930.) Preferred state of binding has lettering complete and undamaged $750/3,500

007b: AS I LAY DYING Cape & Smith NY (1930) [1] Initial capital "I" at p.11:l correctly aligned $100/2,000

007c: AS I LAY DYING Chatto & Windus L 1935 [0] 1,500 cc. Blue cloth stamped in white, top page edge stained blue. (Published September 26, 1935) $250/2,500

008a: SANCTUARY Cape & Smith NY (1931) [1] Magenta paper boards, gray cloth spine, gray endpapers. (Published September 26, 1931) $500/3,000

008b: SANCTUARY Cape & Smith NY (1931) [1] As above but with solid magenta endpapers (Serendipity Books 12/91). (Note: the later printings also had magenta endpapers. Peter Howard surmises that the publisher ran out of the gray paper and switched to magenta on the final copies of the first printing) $200/2,500

008c: SANCTUARY Chatto & Windus L 1931 [0] 2,000 cc (8c & 8d). First binding: wine-red cloth stamped in gold. Top page edges stained gray. Four pages of ads. (Published September 10, 1931) $150/1,750

008d: SANCTUARY Chatto & Windus L 1931 [0] Second binding: bright red cloth stamped in black. No ads $50/1,500

008e: SANCTUARY Modern Library NY (1932) [1] "First Modern Library Edition." Introduction by author. Noted in various colors. (Published March 25, 1932) $25/125

008f: FAULKNER'S REVISION OF *SANCTUARY* University of Texas Austin (1972) [] Issued without dustwrapper? $60.

008g: SANCTUARY *The Original Text* Random House NY 1981 [] Edited and notes by Noel Polk (ref.e) $8/40

008h: SANCTUARY *The Original Text* Chatto & Windus L 1981 [] $8/40

009a: THESE 13 Cape & Smith NY (1931) [2] 299 sgd no cc. Large paper edition issued in tissue wrapper $2,000.

009b: THESE 13 Cape & Smith NY (1931) [1] Endpapers noted in various shades of blue (no priority). (Published September 21, 1931) $200/1,000

009c: THESE 13 Chatto & Windus L 1933 [0] 1,500 cc. Blue cloth stamped in gold, top page edge stained green. (Published September 21, 1933) $200/2,250

010a: IDYLL IN THE DESERT Random House
NY 1931 [2] 400 sgd no cc. Issued in glassine
wrapper. (Published December 10, 1931) $1,500.

011a: SALMAGUNDI Casanova Press ML 1932
[2] 525 no. cc. Wraps. First 26 copies have bottom
edge untrimmed and top edge even with top of
cover. Issued in box. (Published April 30, 1932) $2,250/2,500

011b: SALMAGUNDI Casanova Press ML 1932
[2] Wraps. Numbered 27 through 525. Trimmed on
three sides and centered within cover. Issued in box $600/750

012a: MISS ZILPHIA GANT Book Club of Texas
(Dallas) 1932 [2] 300 no cc. Issued in glassine
wrapper. (Published June 27, 1932) $1,750.

013a: LIGHT IN AUGUST Smith & Haas NY
(1932) [1] 8,500 cc. First binding: coarse tan cloth,
stamped in orange on front cover, and in blue and
orange on spine. Top page edges stained orange
(Serendipity Books 12/91). Sheets bulk 1 1/16" with
overall thickness 1 5/16" (Pepper & Stern 12/94).
Issued with a glassine over-wrapper. Merle Johnson
included a "point" of "Jefferson" vs "Mottstown" on
p.340:1; but it is in all copies and therefore, a moot
point. (Published October 6, 1932.) (Note: Pepper &
Stern 12/94 catalogued an "unrecorded variant"
with top page edge stained reddish-brown and
sheets bulking 1 3/16", overall thickness 1 3/8" at
$1,450) $200/1,000

013b: LIGHT IN AUGUST Smith & Haas NY
(1932) [1] Second binding: coarse tan cloth stamped
in blue on cover and in blue [only] on spine
(Serendipity Books 12/91 surmises that the last of
the first printing sheets were bound with the blue
stamping only, as were the second through the
fourth binding) $75/750

013c: LIGHT IN AUGUST Chatto & Windus L
1933 [0] 2,500 cc. Brick red cloth stamped in gold,

top page edges stained reddish-brown. (Published
January 26, 1933) $150/1,250

013d: LIGHT IN AUGUST Random House NY
1987 [] Two oversized volumes. Volume I:
reproduces holograph manuscript. Volume II:
reproduces carbon typescript. Issued without
dustwrappers at $215. $200.

014a: THIS EARTH Equinox NY 1932 [0] 1,000
cc. 8 pages, stiff tan wrappers in plain white
envelope $350.

015a: A GREEN BOUGH Smith & Haas NY 1933
[2] 360 sgd no cc. Issued without dustwrapper $1,250.

015b: A GREEN BOUGH Smith & Haas NY 1933
[0] (Published April 20, 1933) $125/600

016a: DOCTOR MARTINO AND OTHER
STORIES Smith & Haas NY 1934 [2] 360 sgd no
cc. Issued in tissue wrapper (Petersen reported a
copy in dustwrapper but it may have been an
untrimmed trade edition). Also in slipcase
(Christie's Gilvarry Sale in February 1986) $1,250/1,500

016b: DOCTOR MARTINO AND OTHER
STORIES Smith & Haas NY 1934 [0] (Published
April 16, 1934) $200/1,000

016c: DOCTOR MARTINO AND OTHER
STORIES Chatto & Windus L 1934 [0] 1,500 cc.
Red-orange cloth stamped in gold, top page edges
stained red. (Published September 1934) $150/1,250

017a: PYLON Smith & Haas NY 1935 [1]
Wraps. Advance copies with front of trade dust-
wrapper pasted on as cover or bound in dustwrapper
(Wm Reese Co. Cat. 40) $3,000.

017b: PYLON Smith & Haas NY 1935 [2] 310
sgd no cc. Issued without dustwrapper in slipcase $1,250/1,500

017c: PYLON   Smith & Haas   NY 1935   [1] (Published March 25, 1935 although states "February 1935".) (Note: Meriwether reported to David Mason that in the 1950's the second printing was remaindered in an unpriced dustwrapper which was blank on back) $175/850

017d: PYLON Chatto & Windus L 1935 [0] 2,900 cc (both d&e). First binding: rose-brown. Top page edge stained rose; bottom edge untrimmed. Two leaves of ads at end. (Published March 25, 1935) $150/1,750

017e: PYLON   Chatto & Windus L 1935 [0] Second binding: bright red. Top page edge unstained, bottom edge trimmed. No ads $50/1,500

018a: ABSALOM, ABSALOM!   Random House NY 1936 [0] Salesman's dummy in flexible cover. Ten pages of text $10,000.

018b: ABSALOM, ABSALOM!   Random House NY 1936 [2] 300 sgd no cc.   Issued without dustwrapper or slipcase $4,000.

018c: ABSALOM, ABSALOM!   Random House NY 1936 [0] (Published October 26, 1936) $250/1,250

018d: ABSALOM, ABSALOM! Chatto & Windus L (1937) [0] 1,750 cc. Glassine dustwrapper with glued on printed flaps. Cream cloth stamped in red and black. Top page edge stained red (ref.c). (Ref.e notes a copy stamped in red only, top page edge unstained. Presumed trial binding.) (Published February 11, 1937) $200/2,000

018e: ABSALOM, ABSALOM!   Franklin Press Franklin Center   1978 [2] "Limited Edition" in full leather $100.

018f: ABSALOM, ABSALOM! *The Corrected Text* Random House NY (1986) [4] Uncorrected proof in yellow wraps and dustwrapper $75.

018g: ABSALOM, ABSALOM! *The Corrected Text* Random House NY (1986) [4] $10/40

019a: THE UNVANQUISHED Random House NY (1938) [2] 250 sgd no cc. Issued without dustwrapper or slipcase $3,500.

019b: THE UNVANQUISHED Random House NY (1938) [1] (Published February 15, 1938) $200/1,000

019c: THE UNVANQUISHED Chatto & Windus L 1938 [0] 1,750 cc. Pale blue cloth decorated in black. Top page edges stained maroon. Clear wrapper glued to paper flaps and priced 7/6. The dustwrapper is rare. (Serendipity Books 12/91). (Published May 12, 1938) $200/2,000

020a: THE WILD PALMS Random House NY (1939) [1] Wraps. Advance copy, perfect bound in trade dustwrapper $1,500.

020b: THE WILD PALMS Random House NY (1939) [2] 250 sgd no cc. Issued in glassine wrapper without slipcase $2,500.

020c: THE WILD PALMS Random House NY (1939) [1] Tan cloth, stamped in gold and green on spine. Top page edges stained matte dark green. (Published January 1, 1939) $200/1,000

020d: THE WILD PALMS Random House NY (1939) [1] Tan (beige {Thomas Goldwasser}) cloth, stamped in brown and green on spine $75/750

020e: THE WILD PALMS Chatto & Windus L 1939 [0] 2,000 cc. (Published March 16, 1939) $150/1,250

020f: THE WILD PALMS Penguin NY (1948) [1] Wraps. First separate edition. "First Printing January 1948" $50.

020g: THE OLD MAN   New American
Library/Signet (NY 1948) [1] Wraps. First separate
edition. "First Printing, November 1948" $60.

021a: TURN ABOUT   Massiah Ottawa 1939 [0]
Estimated at 50 copies or so; about half dozen
known. Purple velour wrappers. 30 pp. Published
late in that year as a season's greeting. (There was
also a script done for MGM Script Dept. Culver
City   July 26, 1932. Blue stenciled wraps with 2
pins and label. 8 1/2" x 11". 42 pages. {Seren-
dipity Books 12/91 cataloged at $30,000}) $15,000.

022a: THE HAMLET Random House NY 1940
[] Uncorrected proof bound in manila boards with
black tape on spine $7,500.

022b: THE HAMLET Random House NY 1940
[2] 250 sgd no cc. Boxed $3,250/3,500

022c: THE HAMLET Random House NY 1940
[1] Back of dustwrapper has ads for other Random
House titles. (Published April 1, 1940) $200/1,000

022d: THE HAMLET Random House NY 1940
[1] Back of dustwrapper has reviews of this book $200/500

022e: THE HAMLET Chatto & Windus L 1940 [0]
2,000 cc. Yellow cloth stamped in green. Top page
edges stained yellow. (Published September 12,
1940) $150/1,000

022f: THE LONG HOT SUMMER   New Amer.
Library NY (1958) [1] Wraps. Book three of *The
Hamlet*. First separate edition $50.

023a: GO DOWN, MOSES AND OTHER
STORIES Random House NY (1942) [0] Advance
copy in patterned gray wraps. Top edges stained
red. (Serendipity Books catalogued "only known
copy" signed by Faulkner at $15,000 12/91) $10,000.

023b: GO DOWN, MOSES AND OTHER
STORIES Random House NY (1942) [2] 100 sgd
no cc $20,000.

023c: GO DOWN, MOSES AND OTHER
STORIES Random House NY (1942) [1] Black
cloth. Top page edge stained red. (Published May
11, 1942) $200/1,000

023d: GO DOWN, MOSES AND OTHER
STORIES Random House NY (1942) [1] Various
colors of cloth with top page edges unstained (ref.c
reports 9 variants in total) $150/750

023e: GO DOWN, MOSES AND OTHER
STORIES Chatto & Windus L 1942 [0] 2,500 cc.
Dark green cloth stamped in white. (Published
October 8, 1942) $150/750

024a: A ROSE FOR EMILY AND OTHER
STORIES Armed Services Edition (NY 1945) [0]
Wraps. 8 stories. Ref.e notes two states on verso of
title page: with "Manufactured in U.S." and one
with floor plan of "main floor." Priority unknown.
(Published April 1945) $350.

024b: A ROSE FOR EMILY AND OTHER
STORIES Nan'un-do Tokyo 1956 [0] Wraps. 4
stories (in English) $200.

024c: A ROSE FOR EMILY AND OTHER
STORIES Perfection Form Co. Logan, Iowa 1990
[] Wraps. First separate edition $25.

025a: THE PORTABLE FAULKNER Viking NY
1946 [1] (Published April 29, 1946.) (Same
contents were reissued in 1950 as *The Indispensable
Faulkner*) $35/175

025b: THE PORTABLE FAULKNER Viking NY
1967 [1] "Revised and Expanded Edition". About
20,000 words longer per Cowley. Library binding
without dustwrapper $75.

025c: THE PORTABLE FAULKNER Viking NY
1967 [1] Wraps $40.

025d: THE PORTABLE FAULKNER   Chatto &
Windus L 1967 [] Wraps $40.

THE WILD PALMS and THE OLD MAN see 020f
and 020g

026a: INTRUDER IN THE DUST Random House
NY (1948) [1] Wraps. Uncorrected proof in blue
wraps -"For Advance Readers" $4,500.

026b: INTRUDER IN THE DUST Random House
NY (1948) [1] (Published September 27, 1948) $50/250

026c: INTRUDER IN THE DUST   Chatto &
Windus L 1949 [0] 2,000 cc. Blue cloth stamped in
gold. Top page edge stained blue-green. (Published
September 29, 1949) $40/200

027a: KNIGHT'S GAMBIT Random House NY
(1949) [0] Wraps. Proof tied in blue wraps - "For
Advance Readers" $4,000.

027b: KNIGHT'S GAMBIT Random House NY
(1949) [0] (Published November 7, 1949) $50/250

027c: KNIGHT'S GAMBIT Chatto & Windus L
1951 [] Advance Review copy in blue wraps $600.

027d: KNIGHT'S GAMBIT Chatto & Windus L
1951 [0] 4,000 cc. Blue cloth lettered in gold. Top
page edge stained gray. (Published April 16, 1951) $40/200

THE INDISPENSABLE FAULKNER see 025a

028a: COLLECTED STORIES OF WILLIAM
FAULKNER Random House NY (1950) [1] Gray
cloth. Title page printed in blue and black. Top page
edge stained blue. Spine reads "The Collected
Stories of William Faulkner" (ref.e) $100/350

028b: COLLECTED STORIES OF WILLIAM FAULKNER Random House NY (1950) [1] Top page edge unstained and corrects spine title (deletes "The")

$50/250

028c: COLLECTED STORIES OF WILLIAM FAULKNER Chatto & Windus L 1951 [0] 1,526 cc. (Published October 18, 1951)

$150/750

028d: THE COLLECTED SHORT STORIES OF WILLIAM FAULKNER Chatto & Windus L 1958 [0] 6,000 cc. (Published March 24, 1958.) Volume I: *Uncle Willy and Other Stories*

$35/175

028e: THE COLLECTED SHORT STORIES OF WILLIAM FAULKNER Chatto & Windus L 1958 [0] 6,000 cc. (Published September 18, 1958.) Volume II: *These Thirteen*

$30/150

028f: THE COLLECTED SHORT STORIES OF WILLIAM FAULKNER Chatto & Windus L 1959 [0] 6,000 cc. (Published February 5, 1959.) Volume III: *Dr. Martino and Other Stories*

$25/125

029a: TO THE VOTERS OF OXFORD... (Privately printed Oxford, Miss. 1950) [0] "Beer Broadside" printed at the Eagle Press and distributed in September 1950

$2,000.

029b: TO THE VOTERS OF OXFORD... Palaemon Press (Winston-Salem) 1978 [2] 26 ltr cc. (Ref.e)

$250.

029c: TO THE VOTERS OF OXFORD... Palaemon Press (Winston-Salem) 1978 [2] 100 no. cc. (Ref.e)

$75.

029d: TO THE VOTERS OF OXFORD... Stuart Wright (Winston-Salem) 1980 [2] 25 cc for presentation. Single sheet (Joseph Dermont 8/89)

$150.

030a: NOTES ON A HORSETHIEF Levee Press Greenville, Miss. 1950 [2] 975 sgd no cc. Copyrighted in February 1951 but according to colophon printed November 4, 1950. Issued in tissue dustwrapper without slipcase (ref.b) $1,000.

031a: THE NOBEL PRIZE SPEECH (Spiral Press NY 1951) [2] 1,500 cc. Wraps. Published approximately March 15, 1951 (ref.b) $150.

031b: THE NOBEL PRIZE SPEECH (Spiral Press NY 1951) [2] 2,550 cc. Published March 25, 1951 (ref.b). Ref.e states second printing was 1,000 copies $75.

031c: THE NOBEL PRIZE SPEECH (Spiral Press NY 1951) [2] 1,150 cc. Published "March (actually April 10) 1951" (ref.c). Ref.e states third printing was 1,000 copies $75.

031d: THE NOBEL PRIZE SPEECH Hunterdon Press NY 1951 [2] 200 cc. Wraps. Issued in envelope $150.

031e: THE NOBEL PRIZE SPEECH (Chatto & Windus L 1951) [] Wraps (Joseph the Provider Cat. 30) $150.

031f: THE NOBEL PRIZE SPEECH (Cowell Press Santa Cruz 1972) [2] 60 cc. Student project (Wm. Reese Co. 4/89) $50.

031g: THE NOBEL PRIZE SPEECH King Library Press (no-place) 1986 [2] 100 no cc. Broadside $60.

032a: REQUIEM FOR A NUN Random House NY (1951) [2] 750 sgd no cc. Issued in acetate dustwrapper. Not issued in slipcase $850.

032b: REQUIEM FOR A NUN Random House NY (1951) [0] Pale green cloth. Textured black cloth backstrip. Top edge stained dark gray. Presumed first issue. Dustwrapper artist E. McKnight

Kauffer is incorrectly identified as "M. McKnight Kauffer" (Serendipity Books 12/91) $50/200

032c: REQUIEM FOR A NUN   Random House NY (1951) [0] Dark green cloth. Top page edge unstained. Note: Petersen felt this was so shabby a production that it might have been a trial or advance copy $50/200

032d: REQUIEM FOR A NUN   Chatto & Windus L 1953 [0] 5,500 cc (ref.c). (4,000 copies - Serendipity Books 12/91.) (Published February 9, 1953) $30/150

033a: AN ADDRESS DELIVERED BY WILLIAM FAULKNER ... AT ... DELTA COUNCIL... Delta State Cleveland, Miss. (1952) [0] 5,000 cc. 8 page pamphlet (Glenn Horowitz #11) $2,500.

034a: COMMENCEMENT ADDRESS   Pine Manor Junior College Wellesley, Mass. 1953 [] 11 pp. 8"x11", one staple. Printed on one side only. A second printing has 10 pages and was distributed shortly after Faulkner's address (Serendipity Books 12/91 cataloged for $5,500) $NVA

035a: MIRRORS OF CHARTRES STREET (Faulkner Studies Minneapolis 1953) [2] 1,000 no cc. Tan cloth, spine stamped in red $75/350

035b: MIRRORS OF CHARTRES STREET (Faulkner Studies Minneapolis 1953) [2] Gray cloth stamped in red and black. Press overrun of 13 copies $100/400

035c: MIRRORS OF CHARTRES STREET (Pirated reissue) [0] Red buckram, no limitation page (ref.d) $60.

036a: THE FAULKNER READER   Random House NY (1954) [0] Foreword by Faulkner. Blue cloth, top page edge stained red with no BOM Club stamp on rear cover. (Published January 1, 1954) $50/250

036b: THE FAULKNER READER   Modern Library NY (1959) [1] $15/75

037a: A FABLE Random House (NY 1954) [] Wraps. 8 1/4"x12". Uncorrected proof in blue covers with white cloth ribbon tied at the top (Serendipity 12/91) $4,000.

037b: A FABLE Random House NY (1954) [2] 1,000 sgd no cc. Issued in glassine dustwraper and slipcase $750.

037c: A FABLE   Random House NY (1954) [1] Maroon cloth with top page edge blue-gray (ref.a&c. Ref.d describes staining on top page edge as "gray"). Won the 1955 Pulitzer Prize for Literature and the National Book Award. (Published August 2, 1954) $30/150

037d: A FABLE Chatto & Windus L 1955 [0] Wraps. Advance copy in printed gray wrappers. (Also noted in plain wraps) $1,000.

037e: A FABLE   Chatto & Windus L 1955 [0] 13,160 cc. Red cloth stamped in gold. (Published June 9, 1955.)   Also noted with "Book Society Recommendation" wrap-around band (John Butterworth 10/92) $35/175

038a: ADDRESS OF WILLIAM FAULKNER, NATIONAL BOOK AWARD (Random House) NY 1955 [0] 2 leaves, stapled. Mimeographed typescript (Wm. Resse Co. 11/91) $1,500.

039a: NEW ORLEANS SKETCHES Hoku-seido Press (Tokyo 1955) [0] 13 sketches. Dark blue and medium blue cloth bindings (ref.e). (Published January 1, 1955) $100/400

039b: NEW ORLEANS SKETCHES Hoku-seido Press (Tokyo 1955) [0] Wraps. Ref.c notes both pink mottled wraps and tan mottled wraps (priority unknown) — $175.

039c: NEW ORLEANS SKETCHES Rutgers University Press New Brunswick 1958 [1] Includes all 16 sketches — $30/150

039d: NEW ORLEANS SKETCHES Sidgwick & Jackson L (1959) [1] Black, blue, or tan boards; priority unknown. Edited by Carvel Collins — $25/100

039e: NEW ORLEANS SKETCHES Random House NY (1968) [1] Adds an essay on Sherwood Anderson as appendix — $25/100

039f: NEW ORLEANS SKETCHES Chatto & Windus L (1968) [0] — $15/75

040a: FAULKNER'S COUNTY *Tales of Yoknapatawpha County* Chatto & Windus L 1955 [0] Wraps. Advance copies in plain wrappers — $500.

040b: FAULKNER'S COUNTY *Tales of Yoknapatawpha County* Chatto & Windus L 1955 [0] 5,000 cc (Serendipity Books 12/91) — $35/175

040c: THE BEST OF FAULKNER Reprint Society L (1955) [1] New title — $12/60

040d: THE BEST OF FAULKNER World Books Society Toronto (1955) [] UK sheets (Alphabet Bookshop) — $12/60

041a: TO THE YOUTH OF JAPAN (NIHON NO SEINEN E) United States Information Service Tokyo August 1955 [] Wraps. 5" x 7 1/18". 9 pp. (Serendipity Books 12/91) — $1,750.

042a: FAULKNER ON TRUTH AND FREEDOM
Philippine Writers' Association Manila 1955 []
Wraps. 5"x7". 18 pp. (Serendipity Books 12/91) $1,500.

043a: JEALOUSY AND EPISODE Faulkner
Studies Minneapolis 1955 [2] 500 no cc. First
separate appearance of two sketches of the 13 in
New Orleans Sketches. Issued without dustwrapper.
(Published September 1, 1955) $450.

044a: BIG WOODS Random House NY (1955) [1]
All stories had appeared in book form before, but
some revisions were made. (Published October 14,
1955) $40/200

045a: FAULKNER AT NAGANO Kenkyusha Ltd.
Tokyo (1956) [1] Also had cellophane dustwrapper
over regular dustwrapper (Old New York Bookshop
Cat. 4) $75/300

046a: THREE VIEWS OF SEGREGATION
DECISION Southern Regional Council Atlanta
1956 [0] Gray wraps. Faulkner, Benjamin Mays and
Cecil Sims. *"Three Views ..."* is cover title, *"The
Segregation Decision..."* is title on copyright page.
Faulkner's piece entitled: *"American Secregation
and theWorld Crisis"* (ref.f) $300.

046b: THREE VIEWS OF SEGREGATION
DECISION Southern Regional Council Atlanta
1956 [] Second printing, same, but off-white wraps
(Serendipity Books 12/91) $125.

047a: THE TOWN Random House NY (1957) [2]
450 sgd no cc. Issued in acetate dustwrapper
without slipcase $1,250.

047b: THE TOWN Random House NY (1957) [1]
Red cloth. Top edge stained gray. Dustwrapper
priced $3.95 and has "5/57" on bottom of front flap.
Threaded gray endpapers (ref.e). (Published May 1,
1957) $35/125

047c: THE TOWN Random House NY (1957) [1]
Various cloths, plain endpapers, various top edge
colors without "5/57" on dustwrapper. Ref.e notes
two variants with dustwrapper point and one
presumed first issue without dustwrapper point $15/60

047d: THE TOWN Chatto & Windus L 1958 [0]
10,000 cc. (Published January 30, 1958) $20/100

THE LONG HOT SUMMER see 022f

048a: THE BEAR Paderburn (Germany) 1958 []
Wraps. First separate edition. In English with
German notes. An abridged version used as
teaching aid (Between The Covers 2/91) $100.

THE FAULKNER READER see 036b

049a: REQUIEM FOR A NUN *A Play...* Random
House NY (1959) [1] Adaptation by Ruth Ford.
(Published January 30, 1959) $20/100

050a: THE MANSION Random House NY (1959)
[1] Wraps. Uncorrected proof in spiral bound blue
wraps $3,500.

050b: THE MANSION Random House NY (1959)
[2] 500 sgd no cc. Issued in acetate dustwrapper
without slipcase $950.

050c: THE MANSION Random House NY (1959)
[1] "10 59" on front flap of dustwrapper. (Published
November 13, 1959) $25/125

050d: MAN WORKING Alderman Library
(Charlottesville) 1959 [0] New title. One sheet
folded to make four pages. Reproduces first page of
corrected typescript of *The Mansion* (Pharos Books
5/89) $100.

050e: THE MANSION Chatto & Windus L 1961
[0] Proof in gray wraps $500.

050f: THE MANSION Chatto & Windus L 1961
[0] Dull orange imitation cloth boards. Top page
edge stained orange (Serendipity Books 12/91) $20/100

051a: ACCEPTANCE [ADDRESS], GOLD
MEDAL FOR FICTION OF THE NATIONAL
INSTITUTE OF ARTS AND LETTERS (New
York City) May 24, 1962 [] 2 sheets, 8"x11",
stapled.   Printed on one side only (Serendipity
Books 12/91 cataloged for $1,250) $NVA

052a: FAULKNER IN THE UNIVERSITY
University of Virginia Press Charlottesville 1959
[0] Edited by Frederick L. Gwynn and Joseph L.
Blotner $25/100

053a: THE REIVERS Random House NY (1962)
[0] Wraps. "Advance Proofs." Unbound full galley
sheets $3,500.

053b: THE REIVERS Random House NY (1962)
[2] 500 sgd no cc. Issued in acetate dustwrapper
without slipcase $950.

053c: THE REIVERS Random House NY (1962)
[1] Red cloth. Top page edge stained red and
without BOM Club blind stamp on back cover.
Winner of 1963 Pulitzer Prize for Literature $25/100

053d: THE REIVERS Chatto & Windus L 1962
[0] Proof copy in blue wraps $450.

053e: THE REIVERS Chatto & Windus L 1962
[0] $12/60

053f: THE REIVERS Franklin Library Franklin
Center 1979 [] Full leather $75.

054a: FAULKNER'S UNIVERSITY PIECES
Kenkyusha Ltd. Tokyo 1962 [0] English text $200.

055a: EARLY PROSE AND POETRY   Little Brown   Boston (1962) [1] Wraps. Uncorrected advance proof in spiral bound pale blue wraps $450.

055b: EARLY PROSE AND POETRY   Little, Brown Boston (1962) [1] Simulated cloth boards. Edited by Carvel Collins $15/75

055c: EARLY PROSE AND POETRY   Little, Brown   Boston   (1962) [1] Wraps. Simultaneous issue $25.

055d: EARLY PROSE AND POETRY Cape L (1963) [1] Wraps. Advance copies in printed wraps $250.

055e: EARLY PROSE AND POETRY Cape L (1963) [1] Green boards. Top page edge stained dark gray. Edited by Carvel Collins $12/60

056a: SELECTED SHORT STORIES OF WILLIAM FAULKNER   Modern Library   NY (1962) [1] "ML 324." Contains 13 stories $15/75

057a: THREE PLAYS Harcourt, Brace NY 1962 [] Wraps. By Horton Foote. Harvest Paperbook 45. Includes adaptation of "Old Man" and "Tomorrow" $40.

058a: FAULKNER AT WEST POINT   Random House   NY (1964) [] Spiral bound uncorrected galley proofs in plain wraps (Wm. Reese Co. 5/89) $450.

058b: FAULKNER AT WEST POINT   Random House NY (1964) [1] Edited by Joseph L. Fant and Robert Ashley $15/75

059a: BEAR, MAN, AND GOD: SEVEN APPROACHES TO WILLIAM FAULKNER'S THE BEAR Random House NY 1964 [] Wraps. Edited by F.L. Utley, L.Z. Bloom and A.F. Kinney. Includes texts of two versions of "The Bear," the "Nobel Prize Speech," "Delta Autumn" and critical work relating to "The Bear" $50.

060a: ESSAYS SPEECHES & PUBLIC LETTERS
Random House NY (1965 [1966]) [1] Edited by
James B. Meriwether. Copyrighted in 1965.
(Published January 7, 1966) $15/75

060b: ESSAYS SPEECHES & PUBLIC LETTERS
Chatto & Windus L 1967 [1967] [1] "First
published in Great Britain in 1966." (Published
November 1967) $12/60

061a: THE FAULKNER-COWLEY FILE Viking
Press NY (1966) [1] Edited by Malcolm Cowley $12/60

061b: THE FAULKNER-COWLEY FILE Chatto
& Windus L (1966) [] $10/50

062a: THE WISHING TREE Random House NY
(1967) [1] Wraps. Uncorrected proof in pale blue
wraps $750.

062b: THE WISHING TREE Random House NY
(1967) [2] 500 no cc. Issued in dustwrapper and
slipcase $50/250

062c: THE WISHING TREE Random House NY
(1967) [1] (Published April 11, 1967) $25/100

062d: THE WISHING TREE Chatto & Windus L
1967 [0] $20/100

063a: A LION IN THE GARDEN *Interviews ...*
1926-1962   Random House NY (1968) []
Uncorrected proof in oversize printed blue wraps
with blue plastic spine. Pages printed on rectos only
(Serendipity Books 12/91) $250.

063b: LION IN THE GARDEN *Interviews ...*
1926-1962 Random House NY (1968) [1] Edited
by James B. Meriwether and Michael Millgate $15/75

063c: LION IN THE GARDEN *Interview*
University of Nebraska 1980 [] Edited by
Meriwether and Milgate $10/40

Faulkner

063d: LION IN THE GARDEN *Interview* University of Nebraska 1980 [] Wraps $15

064a: PREFATORY NOTE BY FAULKNER FOR HIS "APPENDIX: COMPSON, 1699-1945 Friends of Coindreau..." (no-place 1970) [2] 25 cc. Christmas Greeting. Broadside. French translation was published six months previously $850.

065a: BARN BURNING+ Chatto & Windus L (1971) [1] "First Published in Queen's Classics 1971" $25/125

065b: BARN BURNING+ Perfection Form Co. (Logan, Iowa 1979) [] Wraps $25.

066a: FLAGS IN THE DUST Random House NY (1973) [] Uncorrected proof in tall red wraps (Key West Island Books 9/95) $250.

066b: FLAGS IN THE DUST Random House NY (1973) [1] Edited by Douglas Day. The original version of *Sartoris* $20/100

067a: WM. FAULKNER'S FIRST BOOK: THE MARBLE FAUN FIFTY YEARS LATER Pigeon Roost Press Memphis 1974 [1975] [2] 1,000 cc. Wraps. Issued in dustwrapper. "Copyright 1975" $25/75

068a: FAULKNER ON LOVE: A LETTER TO MARJORIE LYONS Merrykit Press Fargo (1974) [2] 10 no cc. Numbered I-X. Wraps in dustwrapper (ref.e) $350.

068b: FAULKNER ON LOVE: A LETTER TO MARJORIE LYONS Merrykit Press Fargo (1974) [2] 100 no cc. Plain white wrappers in red printed dustwrapper $250.

069a: A FAULKNER MISCELLANY University Press of Mississippi Jackson 1974 $10/50

-165-

070a: THE MARIONETTES *A Play in One Act*
University Press of Virginia (Charlottesville 1975)
[2] 26 ltr cc. Unbound gatherings on Arches paper
in box. One-act play Faulkner wrote in 1920 (ref.e) $600.

070b: THE MARIONETTES *A Play in One Act*
University Press of Virginia (Charlottesville 1975)
[2] 100 no cc. Unbound in slipcase (ref.e&f) $400.

070c: THE MARIONETTES *A Play in One Act*
Yoknapatawpha Press Oxford (Miss.) 1975 [2] 10
ltr cc. Facsimile edition in boards with monograph
by Ben Wasson, *A Memory of Marionettes*, a
pamphlet. Both laid in brown clam shell box. Not
for Sale. (Ref.e) $750.

070d: THE MARIONETTES *A Play in One Act*
Yoknapatawpha Press Oxford (Miss.) 1975 [2] 500
no cc (d&e). (Assume only 180 copies sold - see
next entry) $300/350

070e: THE MARIONETTES *A Play in One Act*
Yoknapatawpha Press Oxford (Miss.) 1975 [2]
Same as above with new label pasted over original
limitation: "This second issue...consists of 320
unnumbered copies, November 1979." (Ref.e.) In
box $150/200

070f: THE MARIONETTES *A Play in One Act*
University Press of Virginia Charlottesville 1977 []
First trade edition with introduction by Noel Polk
(ref.e) $10/50

071a: A FLIGHT COMMANDER Sandhill Press
(no place) 1975 [2] 15 cc. issued in printed brown
boards without dustwrapper (John DePaovo 12/90) $NVA

072a: THE PRIEST Mississippi Quarterly no place
1976 [] Wraps. 20cc. (6)pp. Offprint (Chapel Hill
Rare Books 11/94) $350.

073a: FAIRCHILD'S STORY Warren Editions L 1976 [2] 175 cc. Wraps. An excerpt from *Mosquitoes* (Pepper & Stern 5/92) $250

074a: MAYDAY University of Notre Dame Press Notre Dame/L (1977) [2] 26 presentation copies. Laid in box (Evlen Books). "Printed in Atlanta 1977" on copyright page $350/400

074b: MAYDAY University of Notre Dame Press Notre Dame/L (1977) [2] 125 no cc. Boards with paper spine label. Facsimile of Faulkner's 1926 work. Also includes Carvel Collins' *Faulkner's Mayday* which is in wraps. Issued together in slipcase (ref.e). "Printed in Atlanta 1977" on copyright page $300/350

074c: MAYDAY University of Notre Dame Press Notre Dame/L (1978) [0] Advance proof laid in trade dustwrapper $300.

074d: MAYDAY University of Notre Dame Press Notre Dame/L (1978) [0] (Ref.e) $10/40

074e: MAYDAY University of Notre Dame Press Notre Dame/L (1978) [0] Wraps $15.

075a: SELECTED LETTERS OF WILLIAM FAULKNER Random House NY 1977 [] Wraps. Long unbound galley sheets which include letters deleted before publication. Edited by Joseph Blotner (ref.e) $600.

075b: SELECTED LETTERS OF WILLIAM FAULKNER Franklin Library Franklin Center 1976 [2] "Limited Edition." Issued without dustwrapper. Accompanied by a 143 page book in wraps entitled *A Faulkner Perspective*. For both: $150.

075c: SELECTED LETTERS OF WILLIAM FAULKNER Random House NY 1977 [4] (Ref.f) $10/40

075d: SELECTED LETTERS OF WILLIAM
FAULKNER Scholar Press L 1977 [] (Ref.e) $10/40

076a: WILLIAM FAULKNER'S LETTERS TO
MALCOLM FRANKLIN Society for the Study of
Traditional Culture Irvin, Texas 1976 [] 40 cc.
8"x11". Printed white wraps (Serendipity Books
12/91), cream colored wraps (ref.e). Proof of
"Appendix" used that year in *Bitterweeds* by
Malcolm Franklin. Actually 47 copies (Chapel Hill
Rare Books 12/94) $350.

077a: FRANKIE AND JOHNNIE   Mississippi
Quarterly (no place) 1978 [] Wraps. 20 cc. 12
page offprint (Chapel Hill Rare Books 11/94) $300.

078a: UNCOLLECTED STORIES OF WILLIAM
FAULKNER Random House NY 1979 [] Edited
and introduction by Joseph Blotner. Uncorrected
advance page proof in red wraps (ref.e) $600.

078b: UNCOLLECTED STORIES OF WILLIAM
FAULKNER Franklin Library Franklin Center
1979 [2] "Limited Edition" in full leather $125.

078c: UNCOLLECTED STORIES OF WILLIAM
FAULKNER Random House NY (1979) [3]
Edited and introduction by Joseph Blotner $12/60

078d: UNCOLLECTED STORIES OF WILLIAM
FAULKNER Chatto & Windus L 1980 [0] $10/50

079a: MISSISSIPPI POEMS   (Yoknapatawpha
Press Oxford 1979) [] 3 cc. Sample copy in white
printed wraps with poems in incorrect order and
lacking Brodsky's "Afterword" $300.

079b: MISSISSIPPI POEMS   Yoknapatawpha
Press Oxford 1979 [2] 101 cc. Introduction by
Joseph Blotner and afterword by Louis Daniel
Brodsky. Advance copy in white printed wraps.
Includes limitation page "..one of 125...review
copies" (see next entry) $200.

079c: MISSISSIPPI POEMS Yoknapatawpha Press Oxford 1979 [2] 24 cc. Black cloth stamped in gold. 24 copies of the proof (item b) bound 12/10/80. 2 lacked limitation page (Evlen Books #1 catalogued one of 25 advance review copies - same?) $200.

079d: MISSISSIPPI POEMS Yoknapatawpha Press Oxford 1979 [2] 20 sgd ltr cc. Signed by Blotner and Brodsky; issued in brown cloth slipcase $350.

079e: MISSISSIPPI POEMS Yoknapatawpha Press Oxford 1979 [2] 500 no cc. Issued in brown cloth slipcase without dustwrapper (Beasley Books #25 catalogued one of 500 numbered copies in dustwrapper for $150. -another issue?) $150.

080a: "I BELIEVE THAT MAN WILL NOT MERELY ENDURE..." Container Corporation of America (no place or date but circa 1970s?) [] Broadside. Single sheet printed on glossy stock paper measuring 11" x 14". Prints an excerpt from the Noble Prize acceptance speech. Illustrated by Jerry Uelsman (Waiting For Godot 2/95) $50.

081a: THE GHOSTS OF ROWAN OAK (Yoknapatawpha Press Oxford 1980) [] Stapled proof in plain white wraps. Faulkner's children's stories recounted by Dean Faulkner Wells $250.

081b: THE GHOSTS OF ROWAN OAK Yoknapatawpha Press Oxford 1980 [2] 12 ltr cc. (Not For Sale.) Introduction by Willie Morris. Issued in dustwrapper $300/350

081c: THE GHOSTS OF ROWAN OAK Yoknapatawpha Press Oxford 1980 [2] 150 no cc. Issued in dustwrapper $60/125

081d: THE GHOSTS OF ROWAN OAK Yoknapatawpha Press Oxford 1980 [0] Trade edition $10/40

082a: TO HAVE AND HAVE NOT   University of Wisconsin Press   (Madison 1980) [1] 1,036 cc. Screenplay by Faulkner and Jules Furthman of Hemingway's novel (Pepper & Stern 6/89) $25/100

082b: TO HAVE AND HAVE NOT   University of Wisconsin Press   (Madison 1980) [1] 4,310 cc. Wraps $35.

083a: THE UNCUT TEXT OF FAULKNER'S REVIEW OF *TEST PILOT*   Mississippi Quarterly (no place) 1980 [] Wraps. 20 cc. Offprint, (6)pp. Errata slip laid in (Chapel Hill Rare Books 11/94) $300.

084a: HELEN: A COURTSHIP   Tulane University/ Yoknapatawpha Press   (Oxford 1981) [2] 20 ltr cc. Facsimile of Faulkner's 1926 work.   Issued in boards. Also includes Carvel Collins' background of Helen. Wraps. Both laid in blue clamshell box $250/300

084b: HELEN: A COURTSHIP   Tulane University/ Yoknapatawpha Press (Oxford 1981) [2] 150 no cc. Issued in box $200/250

084c: HELEN: A COURTSHIP   Tulane University/ Yoknapatawpha   Press   (Oxford   1981)   [0] Introductory essays by Collins and Joseph Blotner, errata slip laid in $10/40

085a: AN ADDRESS BY WILLIAM FAULKNER Delta State Teachers' College   Cleveland, Miss. 1981 [] Thin, narrow pamphlet reprinting speech by Faulkner (Ken Lopez 12/93) $NVA

086a: THE ROAD TO GLORY *A Screenplay* Southern Illinois University   Carbondale (1981) [] Written with Joel Sayre, afterword by George Garrett $25/75

086b: THE ROAD TO GLORY *A Screenplay* Southern Illinois University   Carbondale (1981) [] Wraps $25.

087a: FAULKNER'S MGM SCREENPLAYS University of Tennessee Press Knoxville (1982) [] Edited with an introduction and commentaries by Bruce F. Kawin (Serendipity Books 12/91)　　$25/75

087b: FAULKNER'S MGM SCREENPLAYS University of Tennessee Press Knoxville (1982) [] Wraps　　$25.

088a: FAULKNER: A COMPREHENSIVE GUIDE TO THE BRODSKY COLLECTION Volume I: *The Biobibliography* University Press of Mississippi Jackson (1982) [0] 1,540 cc. By Louis Daniel Brodsky and Robt W. Hamblin. Cloth　　$50/100

　　Note: Quantities on this and later volumes supplied by the publisher

089a: FAULKNER: A COMPREHENSIVE GUIDE TO THE BRODSKY COLLECTION Volume II: *The Letters* University Press of Mississippi Jackson (1983) [0] 1,047 cc. Edited by Brodsky and Hamblin. Cloth　　$25/75

089b: FAULKNER: A COMPREHENSIVE GUIDE TO THE BRODSKY COLLECTION Volume II: *The Letters* University Press of Mississippi Jackson (1983) [0] 1,560 cc. Wraps　　$25.

090a: PIERROT, SITTING BESIDE THE BODY OF COLUMBINE, SUDDENLY SEES HIMSELF IN A MIRROR Mississippi Quarterly (no place) 1982 [] Wraps. Offprint, (4) pp. First separate edition of this poem written by Faulkner in 1921 (Chapel Hill Rare Books 11/94)　　$200.

091a: FAULKNER'S SPEECH AT NAGANO .... Mississippi Quarterly (no place) 1982 [] Wraps. 40cc. Offprint, (4) pp. First separate edition (Chapel Hill Rare Books 11/94)　　$200.

092a: FATHER ABRAHAM Red Ozier Press NY
1983 [] Prospectus. Single leaf folded to make four
pages $35.

092b: FATHER ABRAHAM Red Ozier Press NY
1983 [2] 210 no cc. Issued without dustwrapper,
although a special solander case was made available $600/700

092c: FATHER ABRAHAM Random House NY
(1983) [4] Edited by James B. Meriwether, wood
engravings by John DePol $10/50

093a: A SORORITY PLEDGE   Seajay Press
Northport 1983 [2] 26 ltr cc. Wraps $300.

093b: A SORORITY PLEDGE   Seajay Press
Northport 1983 [2] 100 no cc. Wraps $200.

094a: ELMER Seajay Press Northport 1984 [2] 26
ltr cc. Edited by Dianne L. Cox. Foreword by James
B. Meriwether. Issued without dustwrapper or
slipcase $450.

094b: ELMER Seajay Press Northport 1984 [2]
200 no cc $350.

095a: FAULKNER: A COMPREHENSIVE
GUIDE TO THE BRODSKY COLLECTION
Volume III: *The DeGaulle Story* University Press
of Mississippi Jackson (1984) [0] 985 cc. Edited
by Brodsky and Hamblin (Ref.e) $25/75

095b: FAULKNER: A COMPREHENSIVE
GUIDE TO THE BRODSKY COLLECTION
Volume III: *The DeGaulle Story* University Press
of Mississippi Jackson (1984) [0] 1,000 cc. Wraps
(ref.e) $25.

096a: VISION OF SPRING University of Texas
Austin (1984) [] Unbound advance sheets.
Reportedly only 5 copies (Watermark West 12/91) $150.

096b: VISION OF SPRING   University of Texas Austin (1984) [1] $10/50

097a: FAULKNER: A COMPREHENSIVE GUIDE TO THE BRODSKY COLLECTION Volume IV: *Battle Cry*   University Press of Mississippi Jackson (1985) [0] 1,500 cc. Edited by Brodsky and Hamblin (ref.e). No wraps edition $15/60

098a: TOMORROW AND TOMORROW AND TOMORROW   University Press of Mississippi Jackson (1985) [] Faulkner's story and two treatments by Horton Foote. Foreword by Judith Crist. Edited by David Yellin and Marie Connors (ref.e) $10/40

099a: AS I LAY DYING   Mississippi Quarterly (no place) 1986 [] Wraps. 20 cc. Offprint, (18) pp. First separate edition. This previously unpublished short story was probably written by Faulkner in the fall of 1928, and apparently unrelated to his famous novel of the same title (Chapel Hill Rare Books 11/94) $300.

100a: COUNTRY LAWYER+   University Press of Mississippi   Jackson (1987) [0] 3,000 cc (Bev Chaney #6). Edited by Brodsky and Hamblin $15/50

100b: COUNTRY LAWYER+   University Press of Mississippi Jackson (1987) [0] Wraps $25.

101a: HUNTING STORIES Limited Editions Club (NY 1988) [2] 850 sgd no cc. Etchings by Neil Welliver. Introduction by Cleanth Brooks (signed by both). In goatskin and linen in slipcase $500.

102a: STALLION ROAD   University Press of Mississippi Jackson 1989 [] Screenplay. Edited by Louis Daniel Brodsky and Robert Hamblin. Foreword by Stephen Longstreet $10/40

103a: SPOTTED HORSES   University of South
Carolina Press   Columbia 1990 [2] 600 sgd no cc.
Issued in slipcase with extra lithograph laid in. First
separate edition, illustrated and signed by Boyd
Saunders. Published at $350 $350.

104a: AFTERNOON OF A COW   Windhover
Press/University of Iowa (Ames?) 1991 [] 200 cc.
Issued in printed wraps. Written as Ernest V.
Trueblood. First separate edition of this story (Bert
Babcock 2/95) $100.

105a: THINKING OF HOME *William Faulkner's
Letters to His Mother and Father 1918-1925* W.W.
Norton NY (1992) [2] 71 no. cc. No limitation
given but issued with special printed front endpaper
and in dustwrapper (all price clipped). There were
to be 75 copies but only received 71 from printer.
(Howard Woolmer 7/92) $125/175

105b: THINKING OF HOME *William Faulkner's
Letters to His Mother and Father 1918-1925* W.W.
Norton NY (1992) [3] Also states "First Edition".
(Published January 1992 at $22.95) $5/25

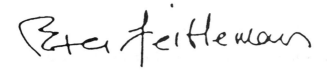

PETER S. FEIBLEMAN

Peter S(teinam) Feibleman was born in New York City in 1930. He studied acting at Carnegie Institute of Technology and attended Columbia University. He was an actor in radio productions in the 1940s and appeared in a number of Spanish, Italian and French films in the 1950s, before becoming a full-time writer.

001a: A PLACE WITHOUT TWILIGHT   World
Cleveland/NY (1958) [1] $15/75

001b: A PLACE WITHOUT TWILIGHT   M.
Joseph L (1958) [1] $12/60

002a: THE DAUGHTERS OF NECESSITY World
NY (1959) [] $10/50

002b: THE DAUGHTERS OF NECESSITY   M.
Joseph L (1960) [1] $8/40

003a: TIGER TIGER BURNING BRIGHT World
Cleveland (1963) [] (We have not seen one that
states first??) $12/60

004a: STRANGERS AND GRAVES *Four Short
Novels* Atheneum NY 1966 [] Uncorrected Galleys
in spiral bound wraps (William Resse Co. 11/91) $75.

004b: STRANGERS AND GRAVES *Four Short
Novels* Atheneum NY 1966 [1] 4,000 cc $12/60

004c: STRANGERS AND GRAVES Gollancz L
1967 [] $8/40

005a: THE COOKING OF SPAIN & PORTUGAL
Time-Life NY 1969 [] Issued without dustwrapper $30.

006a: AMERICAN COOKING: CREOLE &
ACADIAN Time-Life Books NY 1971 [] (PSF
and the editors of Time-Life). Laminated boards.
Issued without dustwrapper $30.

007a: THE COLUMBUS TREE Atheneum NY
1973 [1] 20,000 cc $8/40

007b: THE COLUMBUS TREE Gollancz L 1973
[] $7/35

008a: THE BAYOUS Time-Life NY 1973 []
American Wilderness Series. (PSF and the editors
of Time-Life) $40.

009a: CHARLIE BOY Little Brown B (1980) [1]
"Uncorrected proof" in blue printed wraps $40.

009b: CHARLIE BOY Little Brown B (1980) [1]
20,000 cc $6/30

010a: EATING TOGETHER Little Brown   B
(1984) [1] 15,397 cc (a&b). No copyright date.
Written with Lillian Hellman $15/40

010b: EATING TOGETHER Little Brown   B
(1984) [1] "1984" stamped on copyright line $6/30

011a: LILLY: REMINISCENCES OF LILLIAN
HELLMAN Morrow NY 1988 [] 65,000 cc (PW).
(Publ 9/88 at $18.95) $5/25

C.S. Forester [signature]

C.S. FORESTER
(1899-1966)

Born Cecil Lewis Troughton Smith, he broke with his family in 1921 and took the name C.S. Forester [Sanford Sternlicht. *C.S. Forester*. Boston: Twayne (1981)]. He was born in Cairo, Egypt, and lived in Corsica, Spain, and France before the family moved to a London suburb. He attended Dulwich College and then studied medicine at Guy's Hospital for a time before deciding for a number of reasons - including "laziness and indiscipline" - that a writing career was what he really wanted in life. His first major success was with his fifth book, *Payment Deferred*. *The General* (1936), a study of the mentality and behavior of some of the higher command during World War I, had a large sale in Germany where it was regarded by the Nazis (to the surprise of the author) as a sublime deification of the militaristic spirit. Forester worked as a journalist for the *Times* in Spain in 1936-37 and covered Prague during the Nazi occupation of Czechoslovakia. He spent much time in California - particularly after the successes of *The African Queen* and his perennial favorite, Hornblower - and eventually made his permanent home in Berkeley, California.

We would like to acknowledge the assistance of Edwin Feldman and particularly George M. Barringer (reference.a), for their invaluable aid in preparing this list. Mr. Barringer continues to work on a definitive bibliography of C.S. Forester.

Little Brown, Michael Joseph and William Cagle (Methuen records at the Lilly Library) were kind enough to provide the printing quantities.

001a: A PAWN AMONG KINGS Methuen L
(1924) [1] 1,740 cc. Sheets received January 30 and
bound over a two year period $500/2,000

001b: A PAWN AMONG KINGS Macmillan T
(1924) [1] 260 cc. English sheets $400/1,750

002a: NAPOLEON AND HIS COURT Methuen L
(1924) [1] 2,000 cc. "Published 1924" on copyright
page. Sheets received in June, bound over a 5 year
period. First issue in blue-green cloth (Ian
McKelvie 11/89) with ads dated "324" at rear. Front
cover stamped in gilt (later blind stamped) $400/1,750

002b: NAPOLEON AND HIS COURT Dodd,
Mead NY 1924 [0] $250/1,250

003a: THE PAID PIPER Methuen L (1924) [1]
1,740 cc (a&c). Sheets received in July, bound over
a 2 year period. Ads dated September 1923 $600/3,000

003b: THE PAID PIPER Macmillan T (1924) [1]
260 cc. English sheets $400/2,000

003c: THE PAID PIPER Methuen L (1924) [1]
Ads dated May 1925 $350/2,000

004a: JOSEPHINE, NAPOLEON'S EMPRESS
(Methuen) L (1925) [0] 2,000 cc (a&b). "Published
1925" on copyright page. Spine stamped in gilt;
later, in black (ref.a). Sheets bound over a 4 year
period $250/1,250

004b: JOSEPHINE, NAPOLEON'S EMPRESS
(Methuen) L (1925) [0] Ads dated June 1928 $100/750

004c: JOSEPHINE, NAPOLEON'S EMPRESS
Dodd, Mead NY 1925 [0] $150/600

005a: PAYMENT DEFERRED John Lane L
(1926) [1] $400/2,000

005b: PAYMENT DEFERRED by Jeffrey Dell
Samuel French L 1934 [1] Wraps. Play based on
Forester's novel of the same name $75.

005c: PAYMENT DEFERRED Little Brown B
1942 [1] 5,000 cc. "Published January 1942" on
copyright page $50/250

006a: LOVES LIES DREAMING John Lane L
(1927) [1] $250/1,000

006b: LOVES LIES DREAMING Bobbs Merrill
Indianapolis (1927) [0] First issue: "C.E. Forester"
vs "C.S. Forester" on cover. Royalties paid on 1,629
copies. (Bobbs Merrill records at Lilly Library) $125/500

007a: VICTOR EMMANUEL II... Methuen L
(1927) [1] 1,500 cc (a&b). First issue with blue
cover. Sheets were bound over a 6 year period in a
number of different bindings. Ads dated October
1926 $150/750

007b: VICTOR EMMANUEL II... Methuen L
(1927) [1] Light yellow-green cloth. Ads dated
September 1932 $75/500

007c: VICTOR EMMANUEL II... Dodd, Mead
NY 1927 [0] $125/500

008a: THE WONDERFUL WEEK John Lane L
(1927) [1] Tan cloth stamped in reddish-brown
(ref.a) $250/1,000

008b: ONE WONDERFUL WEEK Bobbs Merrill
Indianapolis (1927) [0] New title. Royalties paid on
1,106 copies (Bobbs Merrill records at Lilly
Library). Light green cloth stamped in orange
(ref.a) $150/600

009a: LOUIS XIV... Methuen L (1928) [1] 1,700
cc. Sheets were bound over a 2 year period. Ads
dated February 1928 $150/750

009b: LOUIS XIV... Dodd, Mead NY 1928 [0] $100/400

010a: THE SHADOW OF THE HAWK John Lane
L (1928) [1] $400/1,750

010b: THE DAUGHTER OF THE HAWK Bobbs
Merrill Indianapolis (1928) [1] New title. Royalties
paid on 844 copies (Bobbs Merrill records at Lilly
Library) $150/600

011a: BROWN ON RESOLUTION John Lane L
(1929) [1] Uncorrected proof in peach colored cloth
with "Advance Proof" printed on front cover
(Robert Dagg 3/91) $500.

011b: BROWN ON RESOLUTION John Lane L
(1929) [1] $250/1,000

011c: SINGLE-HANDED Putnam NY 1929 [1]
New title $125/500

012a: THE VOYAGE OF THE ANNIE MARBLE
John Lane L (1929) [1] No "Bodley's Head" logo
on spine (ref.a) $150/750

013a: NELSON John Lane L (1929) [1] First 500
copies are 9x6 inches (per *Hornblower - One More
Time*). Blue cloth stamped in gilt (ref.a) $150/600

013b: NELSON John Lane L (1929) [1] Second
issue is smaller (per *Hornblower - One More Time*) $75/300

013c: LORD NELSON Bobbs Merrill Indianapolis
(1929) [1] New title. Royalties paid on 800 copies
(Bobbs Merrill records at Lilly Library).
Black/yellow letters $100/400

013d: LORD NELSON Bobbs Merrill Indianapolis (1929) [1] Tan/blue letters $50/250

014a: THE ANNIE MARBLE IN GERMANY
John Lane L (1930) [1] $150/750

015a: PLAIN MURDER John Lane L (1930) [1] $300/1,500

015b: PLAIN MURDER Dell (NY 1954) [0] "NOT A REPRINT" on front cover $40.

016a: U-97 John Lane L (1931) [1] A play $150/750

017a: TWO-AND-TWENTY John Lane L (1931) [1] $150/750

017b: TWO-AND-TWENTY Appleton NY 1931 [5] $100/500

018a: DEATH TO THE FRENCH Lane L (1932) [1] No "Bodley's Head" logo on spine (ref.a) $250/1,000

018b: RIFLEMAN DODD and THE GUN Readers Club NY (1942) [0] New title $20/100

018c: RIFLEMAN DODD and THE GUN Little Brown B (1943) [1] 4,000 cc. "Published March 1943" on copyright page $400/200

019a: NURSE CAVELL J. Lane L (1933) [1] A play with C. E. Bechhofer Roberts $250/1,000

019b: NURSE CAVELL J. Lane L (1933) [1] Wraps. Issued simultaneously $350.

020a: THE GUN Lane L (1933) [1] $250/1,000

020b: THE GUN Little Brown B 1933 [1] 2,000 cc. "Published August 1933" on copyright page $100/400

020c: THE PRIDE AND THE PASSION Dell NY no date [] New title. (#824.) "A Movie Classic" on cover. Comic book (movie tie-in) based on Forester's *The Gun* $60.

PAYMENT DEFERRED (play) See 005b

021a: THE PEACEMAKER Heinemann L (1934) [1] $150/750

021b: THE PEACEMAKER Little Brown B 1934
[1] 2,500 cc $100/400

022a: THE AFRICAN QUEEN Heinemann L
(1935) [1] $500/2,500

022b: THE AFRICAN QUEEN Little Brown B
1935 [1] 2,500 cc. Text differs from English edition
(severely truncated at end) $350/1,750

022c: THE AFRICAN QUEEN Modern Library
NY 1940 [1] Gray binding. No. 102. First complete
edition in U.S. Adds new foreword $25/125

023a: THE GENERAL Little Brown B 1936 [1]
2,000 cc. Precedes UK edition (ref.a) $75/400

023b: THE GENERAL M. Joseph L (1936) [1]
5,000 cc $100/500

023c: THE GENERAL Little Brown B 1947 [1]
3,000 cc. "Republished June 1947" on copyright
page. Adds new introduction $20/100

024a: MARIONETTES AT HOME M. Joseph L
(1936) [1] 1,500 cc (a&b). Matte-finished siena
cloth stamped in silver (ref.a). Dustwrapper without
"3/6 net" on spine $150/750

024b: MARIONETTES AT HOME M. Joseph L
(1936) [1] Orange cloth with "3/6 net" on spine of
dustwrapper (ref.a) $100/500

025a: THE HAPPY RETURN M. Joseph L
(1937) [1] 12,000 cc. Dustwrapper has ad for *The
General* on back $150/750

025b: BEAT TO QUARTERS Little Brown B
1937 [1] New title. (Mr. Barringer {ref.a} believes
that the first dustwrapper has blurbs by Hemingway,
Hall and Riesenberg for BTQ. Later dustwrappers
have ad for *A Ship of The Line* and *Flying Colours*
on back) $150/500

025c: BEAT TO QUARTERS Armed Services NY (no date) [] Wraps. "Copyright 1937, 1939" on title page. Assume published around 1945 — $75.

026a: A SHIP OF THE LINE Little Brown B 1938 [1] 6,000 cc. Also states "Published March 1938" on copyright page. Precedes UK edition (ref.a) — $100/500

026b: A SHIP OF THE LINE M. Joseph L (1938) [1] 15,000 cc — $200/1,000

026c: A SHIP OF THE LINE R. Saunders Toronto (1938) [] Printed in England with title page and verso reset (ref.a) — $50/250

027a: FLYING COLOURS *including* A SHIP OF THE LINE M. Joseph L (1938) [1] 7,400 cc — $100/400

027b: FLYING COLOURS M. Joseph L (1938) [1] 12,000 cc. First separate edition. Issued one day after 027a — $150/600

027c: FLYING COLOURS R. Saunders Toronto (1938) [] Printed in England with title page and verso reset — $75/300

027d: FLYING COLOURS Little Brown B 1939 [1] 5,000 cc — $75/400

028a: TO THE INDIES Little Brown B 1940 [1] 12,000 cc. Precedes UK edition (ref.a) — $50/200

028b: TO THE INDIES R. Saunders Toronto 1940 [] Printed in US with title page and verso reset (ref.a) — $30/150

028c: THE EARTHLY PARADISE M. Joseph L (1940) [1] 15,000 cc. New title. Also noted in "Book Society Choice" wrap-around band — $50/250

029a: THE CAPTAIN FROM CONNECTICUT Little Brown B 1941 [1] 25,000 cc. Precedes UK edition (ref.a) $75/300

029b: THE CAPTAIN FROM CONNECTICUT M. Joseph L (1941) [1] 15,000 cc. Yellow cloth stamped in blue (ref.a) $100/400

RIFLEMAN DODD see 018b & c
PAYMENT DEFERRED see 005c

030a: POO-POO AND THE DRAGONS Little Brown B 1942 [1] 10,000 cc. "Published August 1942" on copyright page. Precedes UK edition (ref.a) $125/500

030b: POO-POO AND THE DRAGONS M. Joseph L (1942) [1] 5,000 cc $150/600

031a: THE SHIP Little Brown B 1943 [1] 12,000 cc. Dustwrapper illustrated by Tom Lea. Precedes UK edition (ref.a) $30/150

031b: THE SHIP M. Joseph L (1943) [1] 20,000 cc. Some copies in wrap-around band (Peter Joliffe Catalog 29) $50/250

031c: THE SHIP Reginald Saunders T 1943 [1] "Published June 1943" on copyright page $20/100

032a: THE BEDCHAMBER MYSTERY Saunders T (1944) [1] $50/250

033a: THE COMMODORE M. Joseph L (1945) [1] 50,000 cc. Issued in light brown, thin, hard boards. Dustwrapper in black, orange and yellow (Robert Temple 1/91) $30/150

033b: THE COMMODORE M. Joseph L/Augus and Robertson Sydney 1945 [] Printed in Australia $20/100

033c: COMMODORE HORNBLOWER   Little Brown B 1945 [1] 34,500 cc. New title. Also states "Published May 1945" on copyright page. Dustwrapper illustrated by N.C. Wyeth. (We had a proof in sewn signatures with slip on front "To the literary Editor: This book will be published on May 21, 1945..." Probably had wraps which were missing on our copy) $25/125

033d: COMMODORE HORNBLOWER   Reginald Saunders (no place [Toronto]) 1945 [1] "Printed in Canada" on copyright page. Larger size than U.S. edition $20/100

033e: COMMODORE HORNBLOWER   Armed Services Edition NY (1945) [0] Oblong wraps $75.

033f: THE COMMODORE M. Joseph L/Thacker & Co. Bombay 1946 [1] "First Indian Edition 1946" on verso of title page $15/75

034a: LORD HORNBLOWER   Little Brown B 1946 [1] 40,000 cc. Blue-green binding. 322 pages. Dustwrapper illustrated by Andrew Wyeth. (Also noted in plain printed dustwrapper due to strike. Letter from publisher stated that pictorial dustwrapper would be sent later but that the book was a normal first edition {Turtle Island Booksellers 8/92}. Mr. Barringer notes that the plain dustwrapper and letter pertain to the Literary Guild edition that inaccurately still states first edition.) Precedes U.K. edition (ref.a) $25/125

034b: LORD HORNBLOWER M. Joseph L (1946) [1] 50,000 cc. Also noted with "Colonial Edition" stamped on flyleaf $25/125

034c: LORD HORNBLOWER Ryerson Press T (1946) [0] Same dustwrapper illustration as 034a $15/75

035a: THE SKY AND THE FOREST Little Brown B 1948 [1] 25,000 cc. Precedes UK edition (ref.a) $10/50

035b: THE SKY AND THE FOREST M. Joseph L (1948) [1] 40,000 cc. First state with full stop at end of last line on p.210. Dustwrapper printed in orange-red and yellow with "s" in Forest damaged (Robert Temple 12/90 thinks that on the second issue dustwrapper the "s" is undamaged) $40/200

035c: THE SKY AND THE FOREST M. Joseph L (1948) [1] Second issue without full stop at end of last line on p.210 $15/75

035d: THE SKY AND THE FOREST M. Joseph Toronto (1948) [] Printed in Canada (ref.a) $12/60

036a: MR. MIDSHIPMAN HORNBLOWER Little Brown B 1950 [1] 20,100 cc. Dustwrapper illustrated by Andrew Wyeth. Precedes UK edition (ref.a) $25/125

036b: MR. MIDSHIPMAN HORNBLOWER M. Joseph L (1950) [1] 25,000 cc. Also states "Published March 1950" on copyright page $30/150

037a: RANDALL AND THE RIVER OF TIME Little Brown B 1950 [1] 20,000 cc $15/75

037b: RANDALL AND THE RIVER OF TIME M. Joseph L (1951) [1] 30,000 cc. Title leaf a cancel $30/100

037c: RANDALL AND THE RIVER OF TIME M. Joseph L (1951) [1] Title leaf integral $12/60

038a: LIEUTENANT HORNBLOWER M. Joseph L (1952) [1] 50,000 cc. (Also noted with wrap-around band - David Mason #22) $20/100

038b: LIEUTENANT HORNBLOWER Little Brown B 1952 [1] 15,158 cc. Dustwrapper illustrated by Andrew Wyeth $25/125

039a: HORNBLOWER AND THE ATROPOS Little Brown B (1953) [1] 15,302 cc. Precedes UK edition (ref.a) $25/125

039b: THE CAPTAIN OF THE ATROPOS M. Joseph L (1953) [1] New title. Proof in printed wraps (Ferret Fantasy 6/93) $250

039c: HORNBLOWER AND THE ATROPOS M. Joseph L (1953) [1] 50,000 cc. Title changed before publication $25/125

040a: THE BARBARY PIRATES Random House NY (1953) [0] Red cloth. Buff and blue endpapers. Ads on verso of p.187 and on back panel of dustwrapper for Landmark Books 1-40 and World Landmarks 1-10 (Note: Book club is in light tan cloth and the dustwrapper has "Young Readers of America" and no price top of front flap. There are no ads in back). Mr. Barringer notes that this book in dustwrapper is quite scarce $50/250

040b: THE BARBARY PIRATES MacDonald L (1956) [1] $40/200

041a: THE ADVENTURES OF JOHN WETHERELL Doubleday GC 1953 [1] Edited and introduction by Forester.   Dustwrapper illustrated by Edward Gorey $15/75

041b: THE ADVENTURES OF JOHN WETHERELL M. Joseph L (1954) [1] 4,000 cc $25/125

PLAIN MURDER see 015b

042a: THE NIGHTMARE Little Brown B (1954) [1] 7,000 cc. Precedes UK edition (ref.a) $20/100

042b: THE NIGHTMARE M. Joseph L (1954) [1] 20,000 cc $20/100

043a: THE GOOD SHEPHERD Little Brown B (1955) [1] 20,000 cc. Black cloth. Precedes UK edition (ref.a) $10/50

043b: THE GOOD SHEPHERD M. Joseph L (1955) [1] 40,000 cc $10/50

044a: THE AGE OF FIGHTING SAIL Doubleday GC 1956 [1] $25/100

044b: THE NAVAL WAR OF 1812 M. Joseph L (1957) [1] 7,500 cc. New title $25/100

045a: ADMIRAL HORNBLOWER IN THE WEST INDIES Little Brown B (1958) [1] 15,000 cc. Precedes UK edition (ref.a) $25/100

045b: HORNBLOWER IN THE WEST INDIES M. Joseph L (1958) [1] 40,000 cc. New title $25/100

046a: THE LAST NINE DAYS OF THE BISMARCK Little Brown B (1959) [1] 15,200 cc. Precedes UK edition (ref.a) $15/75

046b: HUNTING THE BISMARCK M. Joseph L (1959) [1] 25,000 cc. New title $15/75

047a: HORNBLOWER AND THE HOTSPUR M. Joseph L (1962) [1] 40,000 cc $25/125

047b: HORNBLOWER AND THE HOTSPUR Little Brown B (1962) [] Uncorrected proof in pink wraps giving publication date as August 1, 1962 $175.

047c: HORNBLOWER AND THE HOTSPUR Little Brown B (1962) [1] 20,316 cc $20/100

048a: THE HORNBLOWER COMPANION Little Brown B (1964) [1] 8,175 cc. Precedes UK edition (ref.a) $75/200

048b: THE HORNBLOWER COMPANION M. Joseph L (1964) [1] 10,000 cc $75/200

049a: HORNBLOWER AND THE CRISIS M. Joseph L (1967) [1] 25,000 cc $15/75

049b: HORNBLOWER DURING THE CRISIS Little Brown B (1967) [] Uncorrected proof in tall green wraps (Detering Book Gallery 7/95) $175.

049c: HORNBLOWER DURING THE CRISIS Little Brown B (1967) [1] 15,352 cc $15/75

050a: LONG BEFORE FORTY M. Joseph L (1967) [1] 5,000 cc $20/100

050b: LONG BEFORE FORTY Little Brown B 1968 [1] 7,743 cc $15/75

051a: THE MAN IN THE YELLOW RAFT M. Joseph L (1969) [1] 10,000 cc $15/75

051b: THE MAN IN THE YELLOW RAFT Little Brown B (1969) [1] 9,950 cc $12/60

052a: GOLD FROM CRETE Little Brown B (1970) [1] 12,150 cc $12/60

052b: GOLD FROM CRETE M. Joseph L (1971) [1] 10,000 cc $12/60

053a: HORNBLOWER--ONE MORE TIME Non-Profit Press Tacoma, WA (1976) [2] 25 cc. Printed on special paper (for presentation only) and signed by Alexander Kent $300/350

053b: HORNBLOWER--ONE MORE TIME Non-Profit Press Tacoma, WA (1976) [2] Ltd to 350 cc (300 for sale) $100/200

ANTHOLOGIES AND OTHER EDITIONS

054a: CAPTAIN HORATIO HORNBLOWER Little Brown B 1939 [1] 10,000 cc. "Published April 1939" on copyright page. One volume in red cloth. (Book-of-Month Club issued in 3 volumes in slipcase without dustwrappers) $75/150

054b: CAPTAIN HORNBLOWER RN M. Joseph L (1939) [] 5,000 cc. New title $50/250

055a: HORATIO HORNBLOWER M. Joseph L (1952) [1] 7,500 cc. (*The Commodore* and *Lord Hornblower*) $20/100

056a: HORNBLOWER GOES TO SEA M. Joseph L (1954) [1] 15,000 cc. Cadet Edition. Volume One $20/100

056b: HORNBLOWER GOES TO SEA   Little Brown B 1965 [] 5,350 cc. Cadet Edition $20/100

057a: HORNBLOWER TAKES COMMAND M. Joseph L (1954) [1] 15,000 cc. Cadet Edition. Volume Two $20/100

057b: HORNBLOWER TAKES COMMAND Little Brown B 1965 [] 5,350 cc. Cadet Edition $20/100

058a: HORNBLOWER IN CAPTIVITY M. Joseph L (1955) [1] 15,000 cc (assumed). Cadet Edition. Volume Three $20/100

058b: HORNBLOWER IN CAPTIVITY   Little Brown B 1965 [1] 5,350 cc. Cadet Edition $20/100

059a: HORNBLOWER'S TRIUMPH M. Joseph L (1955) [1] 15,000 cc. Cadet Edition. Volume Four $20/100

059b: HORNBLOWER'S TRIUMPH Little Brown B (1965) [1] 4,671 cc. Cadet Edition $20/100

060a: THE YOUNG HORNBLOWER   Little Brown B 1960 [] 3,500 cc $30/150

060b: THE YOUNG HORNBLOWER M. Joseph L (1964) [1] 15,000 cc $15/75

061a: THE INDOMITABLE HORNBLOWER
Little Brown B (no date [1963]) [0] 5,000 cc. "A"
on copyright page. Top page edge not stained (ref.a) $25/125

062a: CAPTAIN HORNBLOWER, RN   M. Joseph
L 1965 [] 15,000 cc. Omnibus edition $20/100

062b: CAPTAIN HORNBLOWER, RN   M. Joseph
L 1969 [1] 7,500 cc. Another Omnibus edition with
different contents $20/100

063a: ADMIRAL HORNBLOWER   M. Joseph L
(1966) [1] 15,000 cc $15/75

064a: C.S. FORESTER THE SHIP AND FIVE
OTHERS Heinemann / Octopus (L 1977) [1] Also
noted with wrap-around band and optional plastic
jacket cover $25/50

Wmṃ̇ Gaddis (signature)

WILLIAM GADDIS

Gaddis was born in New York City in 1922. He was educated at Harvard. His first book was not well received here or in England, where it was published seven years later. However, his second book received the National Book Award for 1976.

We wish to thank Steven Moore for providing much of the detailed bibliographical information herein.

001a: THE RECOGNITIONS Harcourt Brace and Co. NY (1955) [1] Approximately 220 copies. "Advance Review Copy" (on first page). Issued in black wraps with a cream colored spine. $750.

001b: THE RECOGNITIONS Harcourt Brace and Co. NY (1955) [1] 4,885 cc. Black cloth. Note: the second printing has "B.4.64" on copyright page and may have "Harcourt, Brace & World" on dustwrapper which would be a later state (Wm. Reese Co. 2/90) $100/500

001c: THE RECOGNITIONS MacGibbon & Kee Ltd L (1962) [1] 1,500 cc. "First published in Great Britain by MacGibbon & Kee Ltd" (no date) on copyright page. Dark blue cloth. Also noted in blue-gray cloth in advance dustwrapper with provisional publication date on inner flap (Ian McKelvey #62-1). Exported from Meridian's corrected trade paper edition of 1962. The 1985 Penguin re-issue has further corrections and constitutes the definitive edition $40/200

002a: JR Knopf NY 1975 [1] Uncorrected proof in red wraps with a number of differences from published edition $500.

002b: JR   Knopf NY 1975 [1] Small first printing (may be as little as 2,000 copies) due to simultaneous paperback edition. Black cloth $40/200

002c: JR Knopf NY 1975 [1] Wraps. 40,000 cc. (Issued simultaneously with hardback) $40.

002d: JR   Jonathan Cape L (1976) [] Red paper covered boards. Presumed small first printing due to simultaneous paper edition.   First issue dustwrapper does not have the word "condom" crossed out on front flap (Peter Jolleff 7/90) $25/125

002e: JR Jonathan Cape L (1976) [] Wraps $30.

003a: READER'S   GUIDE   TO   WILLIAM GADDIS'S *THE RECOGNITIONS*   Univ. of Nebraska Press 1982 [] Written by Steven Moore. Includes the first book appearance of three Gaddis essays $25/50

004a: CARPENTER'S GOTHIC   Viking   (NY 1985) [1] "Unrevised and Unpublished Proofs" in orange printed wraps $125.

004b: CARPENTER'S GOTHIC   Viking   (NY 1985) [1] 24,600 cc. Light cream cloth spine and pink-brown boards. (Published July 1, 1985 [] $16.95) $8/40

004c: CARPENTER'S GOTHIC   A. Deutsch (L 1986) [] Red cloth (Ian McKelvie #62-1) $10/40

005a: From "A Frolic of His Own"   Lannan Foundation L.A. 1994 [] 6-page excerpt in stapled wraps $35.

005b: A FROLIC OF HIS OWN   Poseidon NY (1994) [] Advance pad-bound photocopied galley proof (James Jaffe 5/95) $250.

005c: A FROLIC OF HIS OWN   Poseidon NY
(1994)   [] Uncorrected Proof in pale blue printed
wraps (Lame Duck Books 12/94) $125.

005c: A FROLIC OF HIS OWN Viking L (1994)
[] $5/25

ERNEST J. GAINES

Gaines was born in Louisiana in 1933. He served in the U.S. Army and then attended San Francisco State College (B.A. 1957) and Stanford University (1958/59). He has been the recipient of a number of awards and grants and presently divides his time between San Francisco and Lafayette, Louisiana, where he is a visiting professor in creative writing at the University of Southwestern Louisiana.

REFERENCES:

(a) Bruccoli & Clark. FIRST PRINTINGS OF AMERICAN AUTHORS, Volume 1. Detroit: Gale Research (1977).

(b) Inventory.

001a: CATHERINE CARMIER Atheneum NY 1964 [1] Reportedly no more than 1,000 copies (Steven C. Bernard 2/91)	$100/400
001b: CATHERINE CARMIER Secker & War-burg L (1966) [1]	$30/150
002a: OF LOVE AND DUST Dial NY 1967 [1]	$50/250
002b: OF LOVE AND DUST Secker & Warburg L 1968 []	$20/100

003a: BLOODLINE Dial NY 1968 [] "Uncorrected proof" spiral bound in printed wraps (Wm.
Reese 5/89) $250.

003b: BLOODLINE Dial NY 1968 [1] $30/150

004a: THE AUTOBIOGRAPHY OF MISS JANE
PITTMAN Dial NY 1971 [] "Uncorrected proof"
in tall cream/buff wraps. Typeset but page numbers
written in (ref.b) $400.

004b: THE AUTOBIOGRAPHY OF MISS JANE
PITTMAN Dial NY 1971 [1] $30/150

004c: THE AUTOBIOGRAPHY OF MISS JANE
PITTMAN M. Joseph L (1973) [1] $20/100

005a: A LONG DAY IN NOVEMBER Dial Press
NY (1971) [1] (Also issued with library binding per
Cumulative Book Index) $30/150

006a: IN MY FATHER'S HOUSE Knopf NY
1978 [1] "Uncorrected proof" in light gray printed
wraps (ref.b) $125.

006b: IN MY FATHER'S HOUSE Knopf NY
1978 [1] (Published June 25, 1978 at $8.95) (ref.b) $15/75

007a: A GATHERING OF OLD MEN Knopf NY
1983 [1] (ref.b) $12/60

007b: A GATHERING OF OLD MEN Heine-
mann L (1984) [1] $8/40

008a: PORCH TALK WITH ERNEST GAINES
Lousiana State Press Baton Rouge 1990 []
(Published October 1990) Conversations with
Marcia Gaudet and Carl Wooton $20/40

009a: A LESSON BEFORE DYING Knopf NY
1993 [1] Uncorrected proof in mauve wraps
(Monroe Stahr 3/93), brown wraps (Waverly
Books), tan wraps (Bev Chaney Books) $100.

009b: A LESSON BEFORE DYING Knopf NY 1993 [1] Advance copy in pictorial wraps. Signed on flyleaf. Issued in pictorial slipcase $60/100

009c: A LESSON BEFORE DYING Knopf NY 1993 [1] (Published April 1993 at $21) $6/30

009d: BROADSIDE: FROM A LESSON BEFORE DYING Black Oak Books Berkeley 1994 [] 7 1/4" x 11 1/2". "Jefferson was sitting on the bunk..." $25.

010a: OBSESSION Quill & Brush Rockville 1994 [1] 600 cc. Wraps. Issued for PEN/Faulkner. Chapbook Series No. 1. Anthology of original essays by 15 authors. (In print at $15)

010b: OBSESSION Quill & Brush Rockville 1994 [2] 200 sgd no cc. Signed by the 15 contributing authors. Gray cloth with an original numbered and signed silkscreen by Lou Stovall held in place by silk ties on inside book cover. Issued in slipcase. (In print at $100)

010c: OBSESSION Quill & Brush Rockville 1994 [2] 26 sgd ltr cc. Signed by the 15 contributing authors. Full gray leather. Original signed and numbered silkscreen by Lou Stovall held in place by silk ties inside top of black cloth clamshell case. (Published price: $200)

011a: CONVERSATION WITH ERNEST GAINES University Press of Mississippi Jackson (1995) [] (Bev Chaney, Jr. 10/95) $15/40

011b: CONVERSATION WITH ERNEST GAINES University Press of Mississippi Jackson (1995) [] Wraps $15.

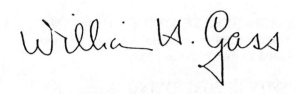

WILLIAM H. GASS

Gass was born in Fargo, North Dakota in 1924. He attended Kenyon College and Ohio Wesleyan; and received a Ph.D. from Cornell. He served in the Navy during WWII and has taught English and Philosophy at various universities.

REFERENCES:

(a) Lepper, Gary M. A BIBLIOGRAPHICAL INTRODUCTION TO SEVENTY-FIVE MODERN AMERICAN AUTHORS. Berkeley: Serendipity Books, 1976.

(b) Inventory or dealer catalogs.

(c) Bruccoli & Clark. FIRST PRINTINGS OF AMERICAN AUTHORS, Volume 4. Detroit: Gale Research (1979).

001a: OMENSETTER'S LUCK   New American Library (NY 1966) [1] 2,700 cc $40/200

001b: OMENSETTER'S LUCK   Collins   L 1967 [0] (Ref.b) $25/125

002a: IN THE HEART OF THE HEART OF THE COUNTRY Harper NY (1967) [] Spiral bound uncorrected proof (Anacapa Books) $300.

002b: IN THE HEART OF THE HEART OF THE COUNTRY Harper NY (1968) [1] $20/100

002c: IN THE HEART OF THE HEART OF THE COUNTRY Jonathan Cape L (1969) [] Uncorrected proof in red decorated wraps (Waiting For Godot 2/91) $100.

002d: IN THE HEART OF THE HEART OF THE
COUNTRY Jonathan Cape L (1969) [1] (Ref.b) $15/75

003a: WILLIE MASTERS' LONESOME WIFE
(Northwestern University Press Evanston 1968) [2]
100 sgd no cc (total of 400 copies in limited
edition). Issued without dustwrapper $300.

003b: WILLIE MASTERS' LONESOME WIFE
(Northwestern University Press Evanston 1968) [2]
300 cc (not signed or numbered). Issued without
dustwrapper $125.

003c: WILLIE MASTERS' LONESOME WIFE
(Northwestern University Press Evanston 1968) [0]
Wraps. *Tri-Quarterly* Supplement #2 $40.

003d: WILLIE MASTERS' LONESOME WIFE
Knopf NY 1971 [0] (Ref.b) $8/40

004a: FICTION AND THE FIGURES OF LIFE
Harper & Row NY 1970 [1] Wraps. Uncorrected
proof. (Note: after proof was issued the book was
then published by Knopf) $175.

004b: FICTION AND THE FIGURES OF LIFE
Knopf NY 1970 [1] New publisher $15/75

005a: THE GEOGRAPHICAL HISTORY OF
AMERICA... Vintage NY (1973) [1] Wraps.
Gass's introduction to Gertrude Stein's book $35.

006a: ON BEING BLUE Godine B (1975) []
Advance copies with sewn signatures. Publisher's
label taped on (H.E. Turlington Cat.28) $175.

006b: ON BEING BLUE Godine B (1976) [2]
225 sgd no cc. Issued without dustwrapper in
slipcase (ref.c) $100/150

006c: ON BEING BLUE Godine B (1976) [2]
3,000 cc. (Ref.c) $10/50

006d: ON BEING BLUE   Carcanet Press
Manchester (England) (1979) [] Wraps. (Am Here
Books 5/91) $35.

007a: MAD MEG IN THE MAELSTROM (No.
Mountains Poetry Project Chicago 1976) [2] 150
sgd cc. Broadside (ref.c) $75.

008a: THE WORLD WITHIN THE WORD Knopf
NY 1978 [1] Uncorrected proof in sea-green wraps
with page numbers not typeset $100.

008b: THE WORLD WITHIN THE WORD Knopf
NY 1978 [1] (Published 5/23/78 at $10) $10/50

009a: THE FIRST WINTER OF MY MARRIED
LIFE Lord John Press Northridge 1979 [2] 26 sgd
ltr cc. Issued without dustwrapper in slipcase
(Ref.b) $175/200

009b: THE FIRST WINTER OF MY MARRIED
LIFE Lord John Press Northridge 1979 [2] Signed
copies marked "Presentation Copy" (quantity
unknown). Issued without dustwrapper or slipcase $100.

009c: THE FIRST WINTER OF MY MARRIED
LIFE Lord John Press Northridge 1979 [2] 275 sgd
no cc (ref.b).   Issued without dustwrapper or
slipcase $100.

010a: HABITATIONS OF THE WORD Simon &
Schuster NY (1984) [3]   "Advance Uncorrected
Proofs" in yellow printed wraps (ref.b) $75.

010b: HABITATIONS OF THE WORD Simon &
Schuster NY (1984) [3] 7,500 cc (publishers'
records). (Published November 1984 at $17.95) $10/50

011a: CULP Grenfell Press NY 1985 [2] 15 sgd no
cc. Bound in full limp vellum in clamshell (full
linen) box, vellum label. Signed by Gass and
Malcolm Morley. The first publication of a portion
of *The Tunnel* (see 015) $1,250.

011b: CULP Grenfell Press NY 1985 [2] 85 sgd
no cc. Quarter vellum and boards $450.

012a: ON PLACE Walker Art Ctr Minn 1985 [2]
300 sgd no cc. 13" x 10" Broadside $45.

013a: A TEMPLE OF TEXTS: FIFTY LITERARY
PILLARS Olin Library Washington University
(St. Louis) 1991 [0] Selfwraps. An exhibit to
inaugurate the International Writer's Center.
Selected by Gass (the director). Assume it was
written by him $40.

014a: A FUGUE: READING & CONVERSA-
TIONS Center Green Theatre/Pacific Design
Center L 1992 [] Wraps. 4-page pamphlet, first
separate edition (Waverly Books 6/92) $40.

015a: THE TUNNEL Knopf NY 1995 []
Uncorrected proof in white wraps (Jaffe 1/95). Also
see 011a $100.

015b: THE TUNNEL Knopf NY 1995 [1]
(Published February 1995 at $30)

NADINE GORDIMER

Gordimer was born in South Africa in 1923 and currently lives in Johannesburg. She has devoted her life to writing, beginning with her first published short story at the age of 15. She has also been a visiting lecturer at many universities in the United States. She feels that "if you write honestly about life in South Africa, apartheid damns itself." She herself has been damned frequently by the South African censors, who have banned several of her books in her own country. It would appear that with the election of Nelson Mandela, she is vindicated.

REFERENCES:

(a) Inventory

(b) CONTEMPORARY NOVELISTS, Second Edition. New York: St. Martin's Press (1976).

001a: FACE TO FACE: *Short Stories* Silver Leaf
Books Johannesburg (1949) [1] 16 stories $250/1,250

002a: THE SOFT VOICE OF THE SERPENT *and
Other Stories* Simon & Schuster NY 1952 [1] 21
stories including 13 from first book $50/250

002b: THE SOFT VOICE OF THE SERPENT *and
Other Stories* Gollancz L 1953 [] Ref.b $40/250

003a: THE LYING DAYS Gollancz L 1953 [0] $40/200

003b: THE LYING DAYS Simon & Schuster NY
1953 [] Ref.b $30/150

004a: SIX FEET OF COUNTRY: *Short Stories*
Gollancz L 1956 [0] $50/250

004b: SIX FEET OF COUNTRY: *Short Stories* Simon & Schuster NY 1956 [] Ref.b $25/125

005a: A WORLD OF STRANGERS Gollancz L 1958 [0] $30/150

005b: A WORLD OF STRANGERS Simon & Schuster NY 1958 [1] Ref.b $20/100

006a: FRIDAY'S FOOTPRINT *and Other Stories* Gollancz L 1960 [0] $30/150

006b: FRIDAY'S FOOTPRINT *and Other Stories* Viking NY 1960 [1] "Published in 1960..." on copyright page $20/100

007a: OCCASION FOR LOVING Gollancz L 1963 [] Ref.b $20/100

007b: OCCASION FOR LOVING Viking NY (1963) [1] "Published in 1963 by Viking" on copyright page (ref.b) $15/75

008a: NOT FOR PUBLICATION *and Other Stories* Gollancz L 1965 [] Ref.b $30/150

008b: NOT FOR PUBLICATION *and Other Stories* Viking NY 1965 [] Ref.b $15/75

009a: THE LATE BOURGEOIS WORLD Gollancz L 1966 [] Ref.b $25/125

009b: THE LATE BOURGEOIS WORLD Viking NY (1966) [1] $15/75

010a: SOUTH AFRICAN WRITING TODAY Penguin L 1967 [] Wraps. Edited with Lionel Abrahams (Ref.b) $75.

011a: MODERN AFRICAN WRITING Mich. Quarterly Rev. Ann Arbor (1970) [0] An offprint in stapled wraps (Glenn Horowitz #7) $200.

012a: A GUEST OF HONOR Viking NY (1970)
[1] "Published in 1970..." on copyright page $15/75

012b: A GUEST OF HONOR Jonathan Cape L
(1971) [1] $15/75

013a: LIVINGSTON'S COMPANIONS Viking
NY 1971 [] Ref.b $10/50

013b: LIVINGSTON'S COMPANIONS Jonathan
Cape L (1972) [1] $10/50

014a: AFRICAN LITERATURE: *The Lectures
Given on This Theme at The University of Cape
Town's Public Summer School February 1972*
University of Cape Town 1972 [0] Tall blue wraps
with black cloth tape spine. Three lectures. 28
leaves plus cover $250.

015a: ON THE MINES C. Struik Cape Town 1973
[] Written with David Goldblatt (Ref.b) $50/250

016a: THE BLACK INTERPRETERS Spro-
cas/Raven (Johannesburg 1973) [1] Wraps $125.

017a: THE CONSERVATIONIST Jonathan Cape
L (1974) [] Uncorrected proof in Cape logo
decorated wraps (William Reese Co. 5/92) $100.

017b: THE CONSERVATIONIST Jonathan Cape
L (1974) [1] Shared the British Booker Prize $15/75

017c: THE CONSERVATIONIST Viking NY
(1975) [1] "Published in 1975..." on copyright page $10/50

018a: SELECTED STORIES Jonathan Cape L
(1975) [1] "This Selection First Publ 1975".
Uncorrected proof in printed pale green wraps $125.

018b: SELECTED STORIES Jonathan Cape L
(1975) [1] $12/60

018c: SELECTED STORIES Viking NY (1976)
[1] "Published in 1976 by..." on copyright page $10/50

019a: BURGER'S DAUGHTER Jonathan Cape L
(1979) []   Uncorrected proof in dark blue wraps
(Monroe Stahr 6/92) $75.

019b: BURGER'S DAUGHTER Jonathan Cape L
(1979) [1] $12/60

019c: BURGER'S DAUGHTER   Viking   NY
(1979) [1] "Published in 1979 by ..." on copyright
page $8/40

020a: A SOLDIER'S EMBRACE Jonathan Cape L
(1980) [1] $12/60

020b: A SOLDIER'S EMBRACE   Viking   NY
(1980) [1] $8/40

021a: WHAT HAPPENED TO BURGER'S
DAUGHTER; or, How South African Cencorship
Works   Taurus   (Emmarentia 1980) [0] Wraps.
Includes preface and defense of book by Gordimer $75.

022a: TOWN AND COUNTRY LOVERS   Sylvester & Orphanos LA 1980 [2] 4 sgd cc for private
distribution $400.

022b: TOWN AND COUNTRY LOVERS   Syl-
vester & Orphanos LA 1980 [2] 26 sgd ltr cc $250.

022c: TOWN AND COUNTRY LOVERS   Syl-
vester & Orphanos LA 1980 [2] 300 sgd no cc $125.

023a: JULY'S PEOPLE   Raven Press (Pretoria,
S.A. 1981) [1] (Watermark West 12/91) (We
assume this precedes Cape edition) $25/100

023b: JULY'S PEOPLE Jonathan Cape L (1981)
[1] $12/60

023c: JULY'S PEOPLE Viking NY (1981) [1] $7/35

024a: BUT USUALLY PEOPLE... Toothpaste Press for Bookslinger/Walker Art Ctr Minn (1982) [2] 90 sgd no cc. Broadside (Bert Babcock 1/89) $100.

025a: SOMETHING OUT THERE Viking NY (no date) [] "Unrefined and unpublished proofs" in gray printed wraps. "June 1984 publication" $100.

025b: SOMETHING OUT THERE Viking NY (1984) [1] "Published in 1984 by Viking..." on copyright page $7/35

025c: SOMETHING OUT THERE Jonathan Cape L (1984) [1] $10/50

026a: A CORRESPONDENCE COURSE *and Other Stories* Eurographica Helsinki 1986 [2] 350 sgd no cc $125.

027a: LIFETIMES: UNDER APARTHEID Jonathan Cape L 1986 [] Illustrated with photos by David Goldblatt $25/75

027b: LIFETIMES: UNDER APARTHEID Knopf NY 1986 [] $12/60

028a: A SPORT OF NATURE Jonathan Cape L (1987) [] (We assume the U.K. edition was published first) $10/50

028b: A SPORT OF NATURE Knopf NY 1987 [1] Uncorrected proof in salmon wraps. First issue (Ken Lopez 12/90) $75.

028c: A SPORT OF NATURE Knopf NY 1987 [1] Uncorrected proof in white wraps (Ken Lopez #33) $60.

028d: A SPORT OF NATURE Knopf NY 1987 [1] 35,000 cc. (Published April 27, 1987 at $18.95) $7/35

029a: WHY HAVEN'T YOU WRITTEN Tales for Travellers (Napa, CA 1987) [0] Map-folded excerpt from *Livingstone's Companion* — $25.

030a: THE ESSENTIAL GESTURE Jonathan Cape L (1988) [1] (We assume the U.K. edition preceded the U.S.) — $8/40

030b: THE ESSENTIAL GESTURE: *Writing, Politics and Places* Knopf NY 1988 [] Uncorrected proof in green wraps (Waverly 11/88) — $60.

030c: THE ESSENTIAL GESTURE: WRITING, POLITICS AND PLACES Knopf NY 1988 [1] (Published October 1988 at $19.95) — $5/25

031a: MY SON'S STORY Bloomsbury L 1990 [] (We assume this was published first) — $7/35

031b: MY SON'S STORY Farrar NY (1990) [] Uncorrected proof in gray wraps (Bev Chaney 1/90) — $50.

031c: MY SON'S STORY Farrar NY (1990) [] 27,000 cc. (Published October 1990 at $19.95) — $5/25

032a: CONVERSATIONS WITH NADINE GORDIMER University Press of Mississippi Jackson 1990 [] — $20/40

032b: CONVERSATIONS WITH NADINE GORDIMER University Press of Mississippi Jackson 1990 [] Wraps — $25.

033a: JUMP *and Other Stories* Bloomsbury L 1990 [] (Nicholas Burrows 2/93) — $7/35

033b: JUMP *and Other Stories* Bloomsbury L 1990 [] David Phillip Cape Town (1991) [] (Ken Lopez 5/95) — $10/50

033c: JUMP *and Other Stories* Franklin Library Franklin Center 1991 [2] Sgd ltd ed. Full leather — 75.

033d: JUMP *and Other Stories* Farrar Straus NY (1991) [] Uncorrected proof in gray wraps (Waiting for Godot 2/92) $40.

033e: JUMP *and Other Stories* Farrar, Straus & Giroux NY (1991) [] $5/25

034a: CRIMES OF CONSCIENCE Heinemann (Oxford/Portsmouth, NH 1991) [3] Wraps. (Published June 3, 1991 at $8/95) $15.

035a: NONE TO ACCOMPANY ME Farrar, Straus & Giroux NY (1994) [] Advance reading copy in glossy pictorial wraps (Bev Chaney 1/95) $35.

035b: NONE TO ACCOMPANY ME Farrar, Straus & Giroux NY (1994) [] (Published September 1994 at $22)

SHIRLEY ANN GRAU

Grau was born in New Orleans in 1929. She graduated from Tulane University and attended graduate school for a time before deciding to write full-time. Her fourth book *The Keepers of The House* won a Pulitzer in 1965.

REFERENCES:

(a) Lepper, Gary M. A BIBLIOGRAPHICAL INTRODUCTION TO SEVENTY-FIVE MODERN AMERICAN AUTHORS. Berkeley: Serendipity Books, 1976.

(b) CONTEMPORARY NOVELISTS, Second Edition. New York: St. Martin's Press (1976). Edited by James Vinson.

(c) FIRST PRINTINGS OF AMERICAN AUTHORS, Volume 4. Matthew J. Bruccoli and C.E. Frazer Clark, Jr., Editors. Detroit: Gale Research Co. (1979).

(d) Inventory.

001a: THE BLACK PRINCE *And Other Stories* Knopf NY 1955 [1] First issue dustwrapper without reviews (Firsts & Company -List 101) $25/125

001b: THE BLACK PRINCE AND OTHER STORIES *And Other Stories* Knopf NY 1955 [1] Second issue dustwrapper with reviews $25/75

001c: THE BLACK PRINCE AND OTHER STORIES Heinemann L (1956) [1] (Ref.d) $15/75

002a: THE HARD BLUE SKY Knopf NY 1958 [1] $12/60

002b: THE HARD BLUE SKY   Heinemann   L
1959 [] (Ref.b) $8/40

003a: THE HOUSE ON COLISEUM STREET
Knopf NY 1961 [1] $8/40

003b: THE HOUSE ON COLISEUM STREET
Heinemann L 1961 [] (Ref.b) $7/35

004a: OLD CREOLE DAYS   Signet/New
American Library (NY 1961) [1] 67,300 cc. Wraps.
Foreword by Grau to Cable's book (Ref.c) $25.

005a: THE KEEPERS OF THE HOUSE   Knopf
NY 1964 [1] Pulitzer Prize for Fiction for 1965 $15/75

005b: THE KEEPERS OF THE HOUSE   Long-
mans L 1964 [] (Ref.b) $8/40

005c: THE KEEPERS OF THE HOUSE Franklin
Library   Franklin Center 1977 [2] "Limited
Edition". Issued in full leather $75.

006a: CROSS CREEK   Time   NY (1966) [0]
Introduction by Grau to Rawlings' book. One "x" on
last page $30.

007a: THE CONDOR PASSES Knopf NY 1971
[] Advance Reading Copy in white printed wraps
(Waiting For Godot Books 2/91) $60.

007b: THE CONDOR PASSES Knopf NY 1971
[1] $8/40

007c: THE CONDOR PASSES Longmans L 1972
[] (Ref.b) $7/35

008a: THE WIND SHIFTING WEST Knopf NY
1973 [1] $7/35

008b: THE WIND SHIFTING WEST Chatto &
Windus L 1974 [] (Ref.b) $7/35

009a: EVIDENCE OF LOVE Knopf NY 1977 [1] $6/30

009b: EVIDENCE OF LOVE   Franklin Library
Franklin Center 1977 [2] "Limited Edition". Issued
in full leather (Ref.c) $40.

009c: EVIDENCE OF LOVE Hamish Hamilton L
(1977) [1] $6/30

010a: NINE WOMEN   Knopf   NY 1986 [1]
Uncorrected proof in pink wraps (Waverly 4/89) $40.

010b: NINE WOMEN Franklin Library Franklin
Center 1986 [2] "Signed Limited Edition". Issued
in full leather with "Special Message" from the
author not in trade edition $40.

010c: NINE WOMEN Knopf NY 1986 [1] $5/25

011a: ROADWALKERS Knopf NY 1994 []
Uncorrected proof in green wraps (Waiting For
Godot 2/95) $40.

011b: ROADWALKERS Knopf NY 1994 [1]
(Published July 1994 at $23.00)

Robert Graves

ROBERT GRAVES
(1895 - 1985)

Robert Graves was born in London, England, the son of Alfred Perceval Graves, an Irish poet and ballad writer. After World War I, during which he was severely wounded and actually reported dead, he graduated from Oxford (1926). He moved to Majorca in 1929, reportedly at Gertrude Stein's urging, and resided there until his death. He supported himself for most of his career with his successful and highly readable historical fiction. He was a prolific poet, novelist, essayist and translator, and his first editions have been collected for decades.

We have made some changes in the first edition identification codes that we found were in error. Higginson/Williams, although excellent, was not precise on exactly what information appeared on the copyright page and may have had later printings of the Doubleday books as there seem to be a few cases where "First Edition" is stated but not mentioned in the bibliography. In addition, there have been many variants discovered and documented by Carl Hahn, which are incorporated herein.

REFERENCES:

(a) Higginson, Fred H. A BIBLIOGRAPHY OF THE WRITINGS OF ROBERT GRAVES. Second Edition. Revised by William Proctor Williams. (Hampshire, England): St. Paul's Bibliographies, 1987.

(b) Edwards, A.S.G. and Diane Tolomeo. "ROBERT GRAVES: A Checklist of his Publications 1965-1974." *Malahat Review 35,* pp. 168-179, 1975.

(c) Edwards, A.S.G. "Robert Graves Bibliography: Addenda and Corrigenda." Dekalb, Ill.: *Analytical and Enumerative Bibliography*, 4: pp. 37-39, 1980.

(d) Edwards, A.S.G. "Further Addenda to Higginson: The Bibliography of Robert Graves" *Papers of the Bibliography Society of America*, 75(2): pp. 210-211, 1981.

(e) Mason, Ellsworth. "The Robert Graves and Laura Riding Jackson Collections of Ellsworth Mason." Unpublished (c.1976). (An annotated list of Mason's collection acquired by the University of Tulsa in 1976.)

(f) Mason, Ellsworth. "Emendations and Extensions of the Bibliography of Robert Graves" Dekalb, Ill.: *Analytical and Enumerative Bibliography*, 2: pp 265-315, 1978.

(g) Woolmer, J. Howard. "A Checklist of the Hogarth Press 1917-1938" Andes, NY: Woolmer-Brotheson, 1976.

(h) Carl Hahn collection.

This guide was prepared with a great deal of assistance from Mr. Hahn.

001a: OVER THE BRAZIER Poetry Bookshop L 1916 [0] Wraps. Also noted with "Presentation Copy" stamped on title page in purple ink (ref.h). Also, note comment in next entry $1,250.

001b: OVER THE BRAZIER Poetry Bookshop L 1917 [0] Wraps. "Second Impression" on front cover (which has been erased on a number of copies we've seen so check for this alteration) $350.

001c: OVER THE BRAZIER Poetry Bookshop L (1920) [1] 1,000 cc. New foreword. Omits two poems and includes "alterations in the text" (Graves' foreword). Noted with front cover printed in blue as called for by ref.a and also in blue with fire in brazier on front cover printed in red $150/500

001d: OVER THE BRAZIER   Norwood (Norwood, Pa.) [2] 100 cc $50.

002a: GOLIATH AND DAVID (Chiswick Press [blind stamped on title page] L [1917] [0] Page Proof, unbound, stitched; only known copy has Siegfried Sassoon's handwritten notes and corrections. On title page Sassoon has written "Send another proof. The wrapper is too *shiny*, and must be *red, not* magenta-pink." The fate of the proof in the magenta-pink wrapper is unknown. Ref. a notes that "Graves himself now 'guesses' that (*Goliath and David*) was published in late 1916..." But, this proof is dated "27.1.17" and Sassoon himself recorded on 18 January 1917: "This afternoon I sent Robert's new poems to the Chiswick Press. Only nine of them -but the best work he has done, or will do for sometime, I am afraid...," presumably referring to an earlier set of proofs. Clearly *Goliath and David* could not have appeared with these corrections in 1916 and so 1917 has been given as the date of the work. (Sotheby's sale of July 18, 1991.) The proof brought £4,950 $7,500.

002b: GOLIATH AND DAVID (Chiswick L 1917) [0] 200 cc. Wraps $2,500.

003a: FAIRIES AND FUSILIERS Heinemann L (1917) [0] 1,000 cc. First binding: orange-red 'B'-type cloth (see BAL) stamped in gilt. Publisher's imprint on spine 5/8" across (ref.a) $200/850

003b: FAIRIES AND FUSILIERS Heinemann L (1917) [0] Second binding: red 'CM'-type cloth (see BAL), stamped in green, publisher's imprint 3/4" across (ref.h) $100/750

003c: FAIRIES AND FUSILIERS Knopf NY 1918 [0] Blue boards (ref.h) $175/750

003d: FAIRIES AND FUSILIERS Knopf NY 1919 [1] (Second Printing stated.) Ref.a calls for maroon cloth, but better termed burgundy. Also noted in blue boards, the same as in the first printing (ref.h) $50/250

003e: FAIRIES AND FUSILIERS   Folcroft
(Folcroft, Pa.) 1971 [2] 150 cc (ref.h) $50.

004a: FINLAND Poetry Bookshop L (1917) [0]
"New Poetry Broadside No. 14." First separate
appearance (ref.h) $350.

005a: TREASURE BOX (Chiswick Press L 1919)
[0] Proof copy, unbound, stitched with yellow
ribbon. A copy with corrections in Graves'
handwriting was offered at Sotheby's sale of July
18, 1991, realizing £1,760 $2,750.

005b: TREASURE BOX (Chiswick L 1919) [0]
200 cc. Wraps. Ref.a states pages stapled at center
but all copies we've seen have been sewn $2,250.

006a: COUNTRY SENTIMENT Martin Secker L
(1920) [1] 1,000 cc $100/400

006b: COUNTRY SENTIMENT Knopf NY 1920
[0] Ref.a calls for blue boards, but have also noted
two variants in dark blue pebbled cloth and in a
burgundy cloth (ref.h) $100/400

007a: CHRISTMAS 1920 (Lund Murphies & Co.
L) 1920 [0] Wraps. Stiff white card folded. Nancy
Nicholson designed cover $NVA

008a: THE PIER-GLASS Martin Secker L (1921)
[0] 500 cc $175/750

008b: THE PIER-GLASS Knopf NY 1921 [0]
Bound in green cloth. Mason assumes this precedes
boards (ref.e) $150/500

008c: THE PIER-GLASS Knopf NY 1921 [0]
Bound in orange paper covered boards $75/400

009a: ON ENGLISH POETRY Knopf NY 1922
[1] "Published, May, 1922" on copyright page.
Bound in orange paper covered boards printed in

red. Red paper spine label printed in gray-blue: "ON | ENGLISH | POETRY | [device] | ROBERT | GRAVES | 1922" [All enclosed in heavy ruled rectangle, enclosing light ruled rectangle]. Leaves 93/94, 97/98, 125/126, and 133/134 are cancels. On page 145:5 "have" instead of "how" (009 a to d have this error.) The William Reese Co. (Catalogue 137, 10/94) in reference to this issue in orange boards states, "First edition in the binding the bibliographers describe as 'variant' and 'not seen', but which is actually the common primary binding for this book." The William Reese Co. Catalogue 103, 11/91 also in reference to this book states, "To date, every contemporary presentation to a notable we have seen, including to Siegfried Sassoon, has been in this 'variant' binding." $150/600

009b: ON ENGLISH POETRY Knopf NY 1922 [1] "Published, May, 1922" on copyright page. Bound in cream boards printed in red on front and spine. No spine label. $125/500

009c: ON ENGLISH POETRY Heinemann L 1922 [0] Yellow cloth with cobbled design on front (but not on spine). 1,560 copies (c and d). Presumed first issue dustwrapper with last line on rear panel reading, "LONDON: WILLIAM HEINEMANN". $100/400

009d: ON ENGLISH POETRY Heinemann L 1922 [0] Buff boards with cobbled design (including spine). Presumed second issue dustwrapper with last line on rear panel reading, "LONDON: WILLIAM HEINEMANN LTD". $75/350

009e: ON ENGLISH POETRY Haskell House NY 1972 [] (In print) $75.

009f: ON ENGLISH POETRY Folcroft Library Edition no place 1975 [0] Issued without dustwrapper $40.

009g: ON ENGLISH POETRY Richard West Ph 1977 [2] 100 cc $35.

010a: WHIPPERGINNY Heinemann L (1923) [1] 1,000 cc $100/400

010b: WHIPPERGINNY Knopf NY 1923 [1] $150/600

010c: WHIPPERGINNY Norwood (Norwood, Pa.) 1977 [2] 100 cc $40.

011a: THE FEATHER BED Hogarth Richmond 1923 [2] 250 sgd no cc (254 copies per ref.a) $750.

012a: MOCK BEGGAR HALL Hogarth L 1924 [0] $650.

013a: THE MEANING OF DREAMS   Cecil Palmer (L 1924) [1] Ref.a calls for dark blue cloth, top edges only trimmed. (Book & Radmall catalogued a variant in black cloth with top and fore-edges trimmed) $200/750

013b: THE MEANING OF DREAMS Greenberg NY 1925 [0] Bound in coarse purple cloth per ref.f. Neither ref.a nor ref.b note that the title leaf is a cancel, but it is in ref.h $150/600

014a: POETIC UNREASON Cecil Palmer (L 1925) [1] $100/400

015a: JOHN KEMP'S WAGER Blackwell Oxford 1925 [0] 750 cc. Paper covered flexible boards $300.

015b: JOHN KEMP'S WAGER Blackwell Oxford 1925 [2] 100 sgd no cc. Spine lettering reads from bottom to top - not top to bottom as ref.a states (ref.h). Issued without dustwrapper $1,250.

015c: JOHN KEMP'S WAGER   Samuel French NY 1925 [0] 250 cc. Wraps $250.

015d: JOHN KEMP'S WAGER   Richard West Ph
1978 [2] 100 cc (ref.h) $40.

016a: MY HEAD! MY HEAD! Martin Secker L
1925 [0] 1,000 cc $125/500

016b: MY HEAD! MY HEAD! Knopf NY 1925
[0] 500 cc $125/500

017a: CONTEMPORARY TECHNIQUES OF
POETRY Hogarth L 1925 [0] Wraps. Ref.a calls
the binding blue boards but actually they are closer
to stiff wraps $250.

017b: CONTEMPORARY TECHNIQUES OF
POETRY Folcroft (Folcroft, Pa.) 1971 [0] (Ref.h) $40.

017c: CONTEMPORARY TECHNIQUES OF
POETRY Norwood (Norwood, Pa.) 1978 [2] 100
cc (ref.h) $50.

018a: WELCHMAN'S HOSE Fleuron L 1925 [2]
525 cc.   Issued in transparent parchment
dustwrapper $350/400

018b: WELCHMAN'S HOSE Folcroft (Folcroft,
Pa.) 1971 [] $40.

019a: ROBERT GRAVES Ernest Benn L (1925)
[0] Wraps. Publisher's address: 8, Bouverie Street $125.

019b: ROBERT GRAVES Ernest Benn L (1932)
[0] Wraps. Date of 1933 (ref.a) is probably
incorrect per ref.f. Publisher's address: Bouverie
House/Fleet Street. Copies stapled or stitched noted
(ref.e) $60.

020a: THE MARMOSITE'S MISCELLANY
Hogarth (L) 1925 [0] Written under pseudonym
John Doyle. Issued without dustwrapper $1,000.

020b: THE MARMOSITE'S MISCELLANY
Pharos Victoria, B.C. 1975 [2] 80 sgd no cc (num-

bered 1-80). Issued without dustwrapper in slipcase
(ref.h) $300/350

020c: THE MARMOSITE'S MISCELLANY
Pharos Victoria, B.C. 1975 [2] 670 no cc
(numbered 81-750). Issued without dustwrapper or
slipcase (ref.h.) $175.

021a: ANOTHER FUTURE OF POETRY Hogarth
L 1926 [0] 600 cc. Issued in heavy pictorial
wraps without dustwrapper. (1,000 copies printed
but 400 were pulped per ref.g) $200.

022a: THE ENGLISH BALLAD Ernest Benn L
1927 [0] Presumed first issue binding bright red
cloth, top edge only trimmed. Book height is 19.5
cm; dustwrapper height is 19.8 cm $100/400

022b: THE ENGLISH BALLAD Ernest Benn L
1927 [0] Presumed later issue binding: dull red
cloth having a faded appearance, all edges trimmed.
Book and dustwrapper height is 19.0 cm $50/300

   Note: Higginson describes a book "bound in
   red cloth" ... "top edges only trimmed"; height
   = "18.8" cm.

022c: ENGLISH AND SCOTTISH BALLADS
Heinemann L (1957) [1] Revised introduction.
New title $50/150

022d: ENGLISH AND SCOTTISH BALLADS
Macmillan NY (1957) [0] $50/150

023a: LARS PORSENA... Kegan Paul.. L (1927)
[0] Two states of the publisher's advertisements
which are bound in at the end and two states of the
dustwrapper have been noted. Presumed earliest
state: 15 pages of publisher's ads bound in at rear
with this title on p.12 under the heading, "Nearly
Ready;" in dustwraper with this book listed fourth
from bottom on rear panel. Presumed later state: 16
pages of publisher's ad with this title on p.13 under

the heading, "Just Published;" in dustwrapper with
this book listed sixth from bottom and publisher's
slug at end of list. This state of the dustwrapper
adds at the end of the list of titles, "Kegan Paul,
Trench, Trubner & Co, Ltd., London, E. C. 4."
(ref.h) $100/350

023b: LARS PORSENA...   Dutton   NY no date
[1927] [0] 1,200 cc. Ref.a calls for blue cloth and a
variant in light olive-green with buff labels. Ref.h
includes   two   variants   (priority   unknown),   as
follows:

> 1. Orange-red cloth with white label on cover
> printed in black; rectangular box enclosing
> printing on front label.
>
> 2. Bright green cloth, 14.8 x 10.8 cm, white
> label on cover printed in black without box
> enclosing text $75/300

023c: THE FUTURE OF SWEARING...   Kegan
Paul.. L 1936 [0] New title. "First published under
title Lars Porsena ... rewritten 1936" $25/125

023d: LARS PORSENA..   Brian & O'Keefe L
1972 [2] 100 sgd no cc. Buckram in glassine and
slipcase. New foreword by author $150/200

023e: LARS PORSENA..   Brian & O'Keefe   L
(1972) [1] 1,000 cc.   "This edition published in
1972." Brown cloth and green dustwrapper $15/60

024a: IMPENETRABILITY... Hogarth L 1926 [0]
600 cc. (Actually published March 1927.) Not
issued in dustwrapper. (1,000 copies printed but 400
pulped per ref.g) $300.

025a: POEMS (1914-1926) Heinemann L 1927
[0] 1,000 cc $125/500

025b: POEMS (1914-26) Doubleday NY 1929 [0]
Ref.a erroneously gives the title as printed on the

title page as *Poems* (1914-1926). Front cover and dustwrapper title is *Collected Poems 1914-1926.* $125/500

026a: POEMS (1914-1927) Heinemann L 1927 [2] 115 sgd no cc. Issued with dustwrapper in plain white slipcase $1,000/1,250

027a: JOHN SKELTON Ernest Benn L (1927) [0] Wraps. Poems modernized by Graves. No errata. P.22 (footnote 10): broken "c" in "can" (ref.f); "note" initialed "R.G." (printed) $250.

027b: JOHN SKELTON Ernest Benn L (1927) [0] Wraps. Contains errata.Pp.22 (footnote 10): "c" in "can" unbroken $125.

027c: JOHN SKELTON (No publisher, place or date) [0] Wine red simulated cloth cover pasted to 027b with cut-out to see old cover. Assume remainder binding, perhaps published by Eyre & Spottiswoode (covers look the same as *Augustan Poets* published by them in 1943) $75.

028a: LAWRENCE AND THE ARABS Jonathan Cape L (1927) [] Proof in brown wraps printed in black. Also noted another proof in gray paper wraps (Harvey Sarner) $1,000.

028b: LAWRENCE AND THE ARABS Jonathan Cape L (1927) [1] William Reese Co. (Catalogue 103, 11/93) states that the light yellow-orange cloth is probably primary in that it appears on several presentation copies from Graves that are contemporary with publication and on at least one presentation copy from T. E. Lawrence. Ref.a calls for mustard-orange cloth which we assume means a dark, almost brown color (reddish brown), which seems to be the most common. Robert Temple catalogued a copy in sand colored cloth which seems to be the same as Reese's "light yellow-orange". 60,000 copies in four printings with quantity in first unknown $125/500

028c: LAWRENCE AND THE ARABIAN ADVENTURE Doubleday GC 1928 [1] 20,000 cc $75/300

029a: THE LESS FAMILIAR NURSERY... Ernest Benn L (1927) [0] Wraps $300.

030a: A SURVEY OF MODERNIST POETRY Heinemann L 1927 [0] 1,000 cc. Written with Laura Riding $125/400

030b: A SURVEY OF MODERNIST POETRY Doubleday GC 1928 [0] 500 cc. Written with Laura Riding $125/450

030c: A SURVEY OF MODERNIST POETRY Haskell House (NY) 1969 [] Reprint of English edition. (In print) $75.

030d: A SURVEY OF MODERNIST POETRY Folcroft Library (Folcroft, PA) 1971 [2] 150 cc $50.

030e: A SURVEY OF MODERNIST POETRY Scholarly Press (St. Clair Shores) 1972 [] A reprint of first American edition $50.

031a: A PAMPHLET AGAINST ANTHOLOGIES Jonathan Cape L (1928) [1] Written with Laura Riding $75/350

031b: A PAMPHLET AGAINST ANTHOLOGIES Doubleday GC 1928 [0] buff paper over boards $75/300

031c: A PAMPHLET AGAINST ANTHOLOGIES AMS Press (NY) 1970 [] Issued without dustwrapper $35.

032a: MRS. FISHER... Kegan Paul.. L 1928 [0] All copies we've seen have 24 pages of ads at rear vs. 20 pages as called for in ref.a, we believe ref.a is in error $75/250

032b: MRS. FISHER... Folcroft (Folcroft, Pa.) 1974 [] Issued without dustwrapper $40.

032c: MRS. FISHER... Richard West (Ph) 1977 [2] 100 cc (ref.h). Issued without dustwrapper $50.

033a: THE SEIZIN PRESS-NECESSARY BOOKS (Seizin Hammersmith) 1929 [0] Wraps. Folio sheet folded twice to make 4 pp. Lists Seizin books (ref.f) $250.

034a: THE SHOUT Mathews L 1929 [2] 530 sgd no cc $150/250

035a: GOOD-BYE TO ALL THAT Jonathan Cape L (1929) [1] Contains Sassoon poem on pp.341-3. Estimated at less than 100 copies by Faber & Foyle (*Modern First Editions: Second Series*, 1931); but a note in a 1932 catalog by Casanova, credited to the booksellers Wm. Jackson Ltd., stated "English exporters had their copies delivered a little in advance (Nov. 12) of actual publication date (Nov. 18). On Nov. 15th Cape attempted to recall all these copies. They were not entirely successful, however, and about 250 escaped, having already been dispersed to foreign booksellers. These, then, constitute the first issue" $400/1,250

035b: GOOD-BYE TO ALL THAT Jonathan Cape L (1929) [1] Asterisks in shape of "v" mark deletion of short passage on p.290 and Sassoon poem on pp.341-3. Seems to be much scarcer than 035a. 5,000 copies of this state printed in November 1929 $150/750

035c: GOOD-BYE TO ALL THAT Jonathan Cape L (1930) [1] 30,000 cc. Type reset to eliminate deletions $50/600

035d: GOOD-BYE TO ALL THAT Cape & Smith NY (1930) [1] Presumed advance copy in presumed advance dustwrapper without price and no mention of this book in ads on rear panel which is printed in black only. On the rear flap the advertisement for *The Paris Gun*, by Col. Henry W.

Miller reads, "To be published in February | Probable price, $3.50." Publisher's logo blind-stamped in middle of front cover (no lines, see below). Another state of this dustwrapper is identical except what may be production symbols are printed at the top of the rear flap of the dustwrapper. These read "OH477 | 100" (ref.h). William Reese Co. believe this may be a book club issue. If so, it may have preceded the trade issue based on the state of the ads for *The Paris Gun* (see below). $125/500

035e: GOOD-BYE TO ALL THAT Cape & Smith NY (1930) [1] Dustwrapper has printed price of $3.00 on front flap; this book listed in ads on rear panel of the dustwrapper which is printed in red and black; the advertisement for *The Paris Gun* on the rear flap suggests the book is now published and no longer lists a probable price, but reads "Illustrated, $3.50." Publisher's logo stamped in middle of front cover and double ruled lines run diagonally on both front and back cover $75/350

035f: GOOD-BYE TO ALL THAT (Revised) Anchor NY 1957 [1] 25,000 cc. Wraps $40.

035g: GOODBYE TO ALL THAT (Revised) Cassell L (1957) [0] Proof in tan wraps printed in black. In oversize proof dustwrapper slightly larger than the published dustwrapper (Ref. h) $250.

035h: GOODBYE TO ALL THAT (Revised) Cassell L (1957) [0] 6,027 cc $25/100

036a: POEMS 1929 Seizin L 1929 [2] 225 sgd no cc. Ref.a states yellow-green cloth, while ref.d notes green buckram per a Bertram Rota catalog. Spine usually faded $450.

037a: TEN POEMS MORE Hours Press P 1930 [2] 200 sgd no cc. Issued in transparent wrapper $650.

038a: BUT IT STILL GOES ON Jonathan Cape L (1930) [1] Refers to "the child she bare" first paragraph on p.157. Ref.a states there were 5,000 copies. Assume this is for all three states, but it seems more common than only 5,000 copies would imply. Dustwrapper is green printed in blue and black. Ref.a is incorrect in stating it is white printed in blue and black (at least we know of none) $100/400

038b: BUT IT STILL GOES ON Jonathan Cape L (1930) [1] "child she bare" deleted on p.157 which is on a stub $50/250

038c: BUT IT STILL GOES ON Jonathan Cape L (1930) [1] "child she bare" deleted but p.157 is not on a stub $25/125

038d: BUT IT STILL GOES ON Cape & Smith NY (1931) [1] "First Published in America, 1931." Ref.a calls for dark green cloth with top edges stained black. Also noted in light blue cloth with top edges red (ref.h) $50/250

039a: THE SEIZIN PRESS Seizin Press Mallorca (1931) [0] Broadside prospectus written with Laura Riding, containing Grave's poem (Anacapa Books) $250.

040a: THE SEIZIN PRESS   Seizin Press Deya, Mallorca (1931)   [0] Broadside advertising *No Trouble, Though Gently* and *To Whom Else?* as already printed and *Laura And Francisca* to be ready in the summer of 1931. Written with Laura Riding (Ref. h) $300.

041a: POEMS 1926-1930 Heinemann L 1931 [1] 1,000 cc. Extra spine label tipped in at rear $75/300

042a: TO WHOM ELSE? Seizin Mallorca 1931 [2] 200 sgd no cc. Issued in glassine dustwrapper which has buff paper attached to flaps (ref.f) $500/600

043a: NO DECENCY LEFT   Jonathan Cape   L
(1932)   [1]   Written with Laura Riding under the
pseudonym Barbara Rich $400/2,000

044a: THE REAL DAVID COPPERFIELD   A.
Barker   L   (1933)   [1] Ref.a states spine stamped in
gold, ref.f states gold was trial state. Ref.a states the
dustwrapper is light blue, printed in black and pink
on spine, while ref.f states lettering on spine is tan.
We suspect the "pink" and "tan" are the colors the
blue lettering on the spine becomes after fading. $300/500

044b: THE REAL DAVID COPPERFIELD   A.
Barker   L (1933)   [1] Spine stamped in black. Also
noted in green cloth over thin boards, spine stamped
in gold (possibly yellow), without publisher's name
on spine. Remainder binding? (Ref. h) $75/300

044c: DAVID COPPERFIELD   Harcourt...   NY
1934   [1] New title. Assume this was not issued in
dustwrapper because it was a textbook $200.

045a: POEMS 1930-1933   A. Barker   L 1933   [1]
Assume not issued in dustwrapper $300.

046a: OLD SOLDIERS NEVER DIE   Faber   L
(1933)   [0]   2,000 cc.   Published as written by Frank
Richards, but Graves rewrote $300/1,500

046b: OLD SOLDIERS NEVER DIE   Angus...
Sydney 1933   [1] 1,998 cc $200/1,000

046c: OLD SOLDIERS NEVER DIE   Faber   L
(1942)   [1] 25,000 cc.   Wraps and dustwrapper $50/150

046d: OLD SOLDIERS NEVER DIE   Faber   L
(1964)   [1] 10,068 cc.   Wraps.   First with a Graves'
introduction $60.

047a: I, CLAUDIUS   A. Barker   L 1934   [1]   Copy
seen with a wrap-around band (ref.h) $300/1,250

047b: I, CLAUDIUS   Smith & Haas   NY MCMXXXIV [1934] [0] Bound in dark slate-blue cloth with medallion blind stamped on front cover, but no gold stamping; publisher's name on spine, no publisher's emblem. Dustwrapper priced $3.00. Ref.a incorrectly calls for gold stamping on front cover, the publisher's emblem on spine and a dustwrapper priced $2.00 (ref.h) $150/600

047c: I, CLAUDIUS Time Reading Program/Time Inc. NY (1965) [0] Stiff wraps. The number of "X's" or "hourglass" figures on the last printed page indicates the printing for this series. Contains new introduction by Graves. Some copies noted with blue-gray bookmark printed in dark gray, loosely inserted. The bookmark quotes portions of Graves' introduction $50.

047d: I, CLAUDIUS   Paradine (no place or date [1977]) [2] 100 sgd no cc. Bound in full purple morocco without dustwrapper in slipcase (ref.h) $400/500

048a: CLAUDIUS THE GOD A. Barker L 1934 [1] Some copies with "Book Society" wrap-around band (Pepper & Stern 11/88) $75/350

048b: CLAUDIUS THE GOD Smith & Haas NY 1935 [0] Presumed first state of dustwrapper priced at $3.00 below text (not corner) with the first word on the rear jacket flap "suddenly". The book is in dark blue cloth, blind stamped on front, not stamped in gold as stated in ref.a $100/400

048c: CLAUDIUS THE GOD Smith & Haas NY 1935 [0] Presumed second state of dustwrapper, the same except the first word on the back flap is "At"; the book is dark blue with the front cover stamped in gold. This issue has elements of the presumed Book-of-the Month Club (BOMC) (see next entry) issue except the dustwrapper bears a printed price. In one copy examined, a BOMC flyer advertising

Claudius the God was pasted in at the rear of the book by a former owner. The status of this issue is uncertain (ref.h) $50/250

048d: CLAUDIUS THE GOD Smith & Haas NY 1935 [0] The presumed Book Club Edition has no price on front flap and "At" is first word on back flap. It is in dark blue or black cloth with front cover stamped in gold $10/40

049a: OLD-SOLDIER SAHIB Faber L (1936) [0] 5,000 cc. Published as written by Frank Richards, but rewritten by Graves. Bound in light blue cloth. Spine stamped in gold (ref.a). Also noted in rust colored cloth, spine stamped in blue (ref.h) $200/750

049b: OLD SOLDIER SAHIB Smith & Haas (NY 1936) [0] Introduction by Graves (not in English edition) $75/300

049c: OLD-SOLDIER SAHIB Faber L 1965 [1] 10,000 cc. Wraps. New foreword by Graves $40.

050a: ALMOST FORGOTTEN GERMANY Seizin M/L (1936) [1] Translation of George Schwarz's book by Graves and Riding $250/1,000

051a: ANTIGUA, PENNY, PUCE Seizin... M/L (1936) [1] "ytyle" for "style" on p.100:11 in all copies. Dustwrapper is priced "7/6 net" (ref.f) vs. the "10/6" in ref.a. The "7/6" is on cancel front flap. We have not seen a copy with "10/6". Also noted, a copy with priced clipped cancel front flap and "4/-" price sticker on spine (Ulysses 10/95). Also noted a copy of the first edition in dustwrapper with price clipped integral front flap and on spine: [printed in yellow] "Second | Printing | [printed in black] 3/6 | net". There is no known second printing, however (ref.h) $75/350

051b: ANTIGUA, PENNY, PUCE Macmillan T 1936 [1] (Ref.e&f.) U.K. sheets with typos of first

corrected. Precedes U.S. edition. Maroon cloth
lettered in white on spine (Steven Temple #23 -
7/88) $60/250

051c: THE ANTIGUA STAMP   Random House
NY (1937) [1] New title. Publisher's dummy with
title, prelims, and first 8 pages of text; in cloth with
stamp facsimile pasted on cover. Issued in
dustwrapper (Bell, Book & Radmall 11/90) $400/750

051d: THE ANTIGUA STAMP   Random House
NY (1937) [1] $50/200

052a: COUNT BELISARIUS   Cassell L (1938)
[1] 20,000 cc. Seen with "Book Society" wrap-
around band. 16,000 copies in dark blue-green
cloth: 4,000 copies, "Colonial" edition, in light
brown cloth $50/250

052b: COUNT BELISARIUS Random House NY
(1938) [1] Wraps.   Proof/advance copy perfect
bound in trade dustwrapper $200.

052c: COUNT BELISARIUS Random House NY
(1938) [1] Top edges stained green (ref.a), variant
with top edges not stained (ref.h) $30/150

053a: COLLECTED POEMS Cassell L (1938) [1] $200/1,000

053b: COLLECTED POEMS Random House NY
(1939) [1] English sheets $75/350

054a: T. E. LAWRENCE TO HIS BIOGRAPHER
Doubleday NY 1938 [2] 500 sgd no cc. Issued in
dustwrapper and slipcase with Liddell Hart's book
of same title. Price for both $600/750

054b: T. E. LAWRENCE TO HIS BIOGRAPHER
Faber L (1939) [2] 500 sgd no cc. Issued in
acetate dustwrapper with printed paper flaps in
slipcase with Hart's book of same title. Price for
both $600/750

054c: T. E. LAWRENCE TO HIS BIOGRAPHER
Cassell L (1963) [0] 2,062 cc $30/150

054d: T. E. LAWRENCE TO HIS BIOGRAPHER
Doubleday GC 1963 [0] 3,500 cc. "Johnathan" for
"Jonathan" on copyright page. Spine of dustwrapper
noted in three states (ref.h):

    1. Printed in orange, olive green and black
    (assume the norm as it matches front of
    dustwrapper)

    2. Printed in orange, bright green and black

    3. Printed in orange, yellow, bright green and
    black $25/100

055a: NO MORE GHOSTS Faber L (1940) [1]
2,000 cc $25/100

056a: SERGEANT LAMB OF THE NINTH
Methuen L (1940) [1] 10,000 cc $50/200

056b: SERGEANT LAMB'S AMERICA Random
House NY (1940) [1] Wraps. New title. Advance
reading copy with trade dustwrapper as cover. Top
page edge unstained $200.

056c: SERGEANT LAMB'S AMERICA Random
House NY (1940) [1] Noted with top edges stained
blue/gray (ref.h); also noted unstained (ref.a) and
stained light brown $30/150

057a: THE LONG WEEK-END Faber L (1940)
[1] 4,000 cc. Written with Alan Hodge. [Note: one
copy seen with "Special Presentation Edition"
stamped on verso of title page, but no other
differences (ref.h)] $75/200

057b: THE LONG WEEK-END Macmillan NY
1941 [1] Written with Alan Hodge $50/150

057c: THE LONG WEEK-END Faber L (1950) []
"Second impression, MCML". New note and some
rearrangement $25/75

057d: THE LONG WEEK-END   Four Square
Books L (1961) [1] Wraps. Revised with a new
note by Graves $35.

058a: PROCEED, SERGEANT LAMB   Methuen
L (1941) [1] 10,000 cc. Also noted, a variant
without two blank leaves before half title, *i.e,* the
book opens to the half title. Page height is 18.4 cm.
vs. 18.6 cm for the regular first edition and 18.2 cm.
for the second edition. A wartime economy
measure? (Ref. h) $50/200

058b: PROCEED, SERGEANT LAMB   Random
House NY (1941) [1] $30/150

058c: PROCEED, SERGEANT LAMB   Methuen
L (1947) [1] 5,000 cc. Second edition with new
foreword and note $25/75

059a: WORK IN HAND Hogarth L (1942) [1]
Written with N. Cameron and Alan Hodge $35/125

060a: WIFE TO MR. MILTON Cassell L (1943)
[1] 9,420 cc. Scarce in fine condition. Also noted
with "Overseas Edition" on dustwrapper flap (Peter
Jolliffe #29) $50/250

060b: WIFE TO MR. MILTON Creative Age NY
(1944) [0] $25/100

061a: THE READER OVER YOUR SHOULDER
Jonathan Cape L (1943) [1] Written with Alan
Hodge. Graves indicates 2,800 copies (*In Broken
Images*, p.316) $50/200

061b: THE READER OVER YOUR SHOULDER
Macmillan NY 1943 [1] Ref.a states 1944, which
is incorrect $35/100

061c: THE READER OVER YOUR SHOULDER
Jonathan Cape   L (1947) [] "Second Edition
(Abridged) 1947" $25/75

062a: ROBERT GRAVES (The Augustan Poets)
Eyre/Spottiswood (L 1943) [0] 5,000 cc. Wraps $60.

063a: THE GOLDEN FLEECE Cassell L (1944)
[1] 11,073 cc. Graves states 9,000 cc (*In Broken
Images*, p.327). Ref.a states spine stamped in
orange. All copies we've seen stamped in gold $35/175

063b: HERCULES, MY SHIPMATE Creative Age
NY (1945) [0] New title. All edges sprinkled blue
(ref.a). Variant: top edges stained blue (ref.h) $25/100

063c: HERCULES, MY SHIPMATE Farrar Straus
NY (1957) [1] $15/35

064a: POEMS 1938-1945   Cassell   L (1946) [1]
3,000 cc. (Correct date is 1946 per ref.e.) States
"First Published 1946" (ref.a states "Published
November 1945") $15/75

064b: POEMS 1938-1945   Creative Age   NY
(1946) [0] 5,500 cc $15/75

064c: POEMS 1938-1945   Farrar   NY (1967) [1]
(Ref.e&f) $15/35

065a: KING JESUS Creative Age NY (1946) [0]
Although not mentioned in ref.a, top edges stained
light green. Pages bulk 2.9 cm (ref.a). A variant has
also been noted with pages bulking 3.3 cm (ref.h)
and top edges stained dark green $25/100

065b: KING JESUS Cassell L (1946) [1] 10,152
cc. First printing dustwrapper has price of
"12s.6d.net"; front flap text begins "A recent book
by Robert Graves | [double rule] | The Golden
Fleece"; "Apt/G 416" at bottom of rear flap $25/125

065c: KING JESUS Farrar NY (1955) [1] $5/35

066a: THE HISTORIC LOGIC OF KING JESUS
Cornhill Magazine L? 1947 [] Offprint in wraps
with details of printing in red on front cover. First
separate edition (Harvey Sarner) $200.

067a: COLLECTED POEMS (1914-1947) Cassell
L (1948) [1] 2,962 cc $25/125

068a: THE WHITE GODDESS   Faber L (1948)
[1] 2,340 cc. First issue dustwrapper has no reviews
on front flap; rear flap unprinted; printed price of
"30s. | net". Yellow paper dustwrapper printed in
black and red $100/400

068b: THE WHITE GODDESS   Faber L (1948)
[1] Second issue dustwrapper: tan printed in black
and red with two reviews for this book added to text
on front flap; printed price of "30s. | net"; the rear
flap has advertisement for *The Gate of Horn* by G.
R. Levy. (The second impression (1948) dustwrapper is of yellow paper printed in black and red;
two reviews of this book are added to the text on the
front flap; three books are advertised on the rear
flap; the front flap bears a printed price of "35s |
net") $100/250

068c: THE WHITE GODDESS   Creative Age NY
1948 [1] $50/200

068d: THE WHITE GODDESS   Faber L (1952)
[1] 2,000 cc. Amended and enlarged edition $25/100

068e: THE WHITE GODDESS Farrar (NY 1958)
[0] Same as 068c- not revised $10/40

068f: THE WHITE GODDESS Vintage NY 1958
[0] Wraps. Amended and enlarged $35.

068g: THE WHITE GODDESS Faber L (1961)
[1] 10,000 cc. Wraps. New chapter XXVII added
(postscript 1960) $35.

069a: WATCH THE NORTH WIND RISE Creative Age NY 1949 [1] Tipped-in page signed by Graves $100/150

069b: WATCII TIIE NORTH WIND RISE Creative Age NY 1949 [1] $25/100

069c: SEVEN DAYS IN NEW CRETE Cassell L (1949) [1] 12,257 cc. Copies noted with page "v" actually printed on contents page are assumed to be the first issue (Robert Temple #42) $75/150

069d: SEVEN DAYS IN NEW CRETE Cassell L (1949) [1] Without "v" printed on page $25/100

069e: SEVEN DAYS IN NEW CRETE Cassell L (1949) [1] Issue with "OVERSEAS | EDITION" printed on front flap of dustwrapper. This issue does not have the "v" printed at the foot of the contents page (Ref. h) $25/100

070a: THE COMMON ASPHODEL Hamilton L (1949) [1] $25/125

070b: THE COMMON ASPHODEL Folcroft Folcroft, Pa. 1971 [] (Ref.h) $35.

071a: THE ISLANDS OF UNWISDOM Doubleday GC 1949 [1] 12,000 cc in two printings, it is not known how many copies are in each printing $25/75

071b: THE ISLES OF UNWISDOM Cassell L (1950) [1] 14,988 cc. New title. Also noted with "Overseas Issue" on dustwrapper flap (ref.h) $25/100

071c: THE ISLES OF UNWISDOM Cassell L (1950) [1] In dustwrapper priced "$2.50". First Canadian issue (ref.h) $25/300

072a: OCCUPATION: WRITER Creative Age NY 1950 [0] $25/100

072b: OCCUPATION: WRITER Cassell L 1951 [1] 7,500 cc $25/75

073a: THE TRANSFORMATIONS OF LUCIUS OTHERWISE KNOWN AS THE GOLDEN ASS Penguin   Middlesex   (1950)   [1] Higginson indicates this hardbound issued simultaneously with wraps edition $25/100

073b: THE TRANSFORMATIONS OF LUCIUS OTHERWISE KNOWN AS THE GOLDEN ASS Penguin Middlesex (1950) [1] Wraps $35.

073c: THE TRANSFORMATIONS OF LUCIUS OTHERWISE KNOWN AS THE GOLDEN ASS Penguin   Middlesex (1951)   [2] 2,000 sgd cc. Issued in dustwrapper and slipcase. Ref.e noted a trial copy with white endpapers (vs. gray) and the colophon leaf integral (cancel leaf in published book). An unknown portion of the 2,000 copies were made up for sale in the U.S. in a slipcase with red spine label printed in black "SIGNED | LIMITED | EDITION | $6.50" and label on front of slipcase "LIMITED EDITION | SIGNED BY ROBERT GRAVES | $6.50" (ref.h) $125/200

073d: THE TRANSFORMATION OF LUCIUS OTHERWISE KNOWN AS THE GOLDEN ASS Farrar Straus NY (1951) [5] $15/50

073e: THE TRANSFORMATION OF LUCIUS OTHERWISE KNOWN AS THE GOLDEN ASS Folio Society L 1960 [2] Illustrated by Michael Ayrton. Issued without dustwrapper in slipcase $25/50

074a: POEMS AND SATIRES Cassell L 1951 [1] Uncorrected proof in unprinted green wraps (Waiting For Godot 4/90) $200.

074b: POEMS AND SATIRES Cassell L 1951 [1] 2,000 cc $25/75

075a: POEMS 1953 Cassell L 1953 [2] 250 sgd no
cc. Transparent parchment wrapper $300/350

075b: POEMS 1953 Cassell L 1953 [1] 1,777 cc $25/75

076a: THE NAZARENE GOSPEL RESTORED
Cassell L 1953 [1] 2,981 cc. Written with Joshua
Podro $100/400

076b: THE NAZARENE GOSPEL RESTORED
Doubleday GC 1954 [1] 5,000 cc. Written with
Joshua Podro $75/300

076c: THE NAZARENE GOSPEL   Cassell L
1955 [0] 756 cc. Part III of "Gospel Restored" $125/400

077a: TO MAGDALENA MULET, MARGARITA
MORA AND LUCIA GRAVES (No publisher or
place) 1954 [0] Greeting card $NVA

078a: THE CROSS AND THE SWORD Indiana
University Bloomington (1954) [0] 2,000 cc.
Graves' translation of Manuel Galvan's work. $30/150

078b: THE CROSS AND THE SWORD Gollancz
L 1956 [0] 2,000 cc. Graves' translation of Manuel
Galvan's work $25/100

079a: HOMER'S DAUGHTER Cassell L (1955)
[1] 15,000 cc $25/75

079b: HOMER'S DAUGHTER Doubleday GC
1955 [1] 12,500 cc in three printings; unknown how
many copies in each printing $25/75

080a: THE GREEK MYTHS Penguin (Middlesex
1955) [1] Wraps. Two volumes. Issued in dustwrappers (ref.a),   although   we've   never   seen   in
dustwrappers $40/75

080b: THE GREEK MYTHS Penguin Baltimore
(1955) [1] 35,000 cc. Wraps. Two volumes $40.

080c: THE GREEK MYTHS Penguin Baltimore (1955) [1] 3,000 cc. New title. Hardbound in red cloth and in slipcase (ref.h). Issued without dustwrappers $50/100

080d: THE GREEK MYTHS Penguin Baltimore (1957) [] Two volumes. "First published 1955, reprinted Jan. 1957." In black cloth stamped in gold on spine, issued without dustwrappers, in slipcase (ref.h) $40/75

080e: THE GREEK MYTHS Penguin Baltimore (1957) [] "First published 1955, reprinted January 1957". 2 volumes in 1. In imitation black leather boards with gray cloth spine printed in black. No price on dustwrapper (ref.h) $20/60

080f: THE GREEK MYTHS Penguin Baltimore 1957 [] Same as 080e but date on title page and dustwrapper priced at $5. (ref.h) $20/50

080g: THE GREEK MYTHS (two volumes) Braziller NY 1957 [] "First published 1955 | Reprinted 1957". Issued without dustwrappers in slipcase $35/60

080h: THE GREEK MYTHS Braziller NY 1957 [] One volume edition. "First published 1955 | Reprinted 1957" $10/40

080i: GREEK MYTHS Cassell L (1958) [1] 2,999 cc. "This edition first published 1958..." Revised introduction and new note in chapter 104 (also noted with 1959 on title page) $15/75

081a: COLLECTED POEMS 1955 Doubleday GC 1955 [1] 3,500 cc in two printings. The number of copies in each printing is not known. The apparent first printing has "1955" printed above the publisher's name on title page. Ref. a says top edges stained light blue. [Note: of two copies examined one was stained light blue; the other dark blue (ref.h)] $25/75

081b: COLLECTED POEMS 1955 Doubleday GC 1955 [0] Possible second printing without first edition statement on verso of title page but, with "1955" printed on title page above publisher's name. Of four copies examined two have top edges stained dark blue, one stained light blue, the other is unstained. (Ref. h)　　　　　　　　　　　$15/50

081c: COLLECTED POEMS 1955 Doubleday GC (1955) [0] Possible second printing without first edition statement on verso of title page and without date above publisher's name on title page. Top edges stained dark blue in copy seen (Ref. h)　　$10/40

082a: ADAM'S RIB　Trianon (L 1955) [2] 26 sgd no cc. Issued in slipcase per ref.e　　　$400/500

082b: ADAM'S RIB　Trianon (L 1955) [2] 250 sgd no cc. Issued in slipcase　　　　　　$225/300

082c: ADAM'S RIB　Trianon (L 1955) [1] 1,750 cc　　$30/150

082d: ADAM'S RIB　Yoseloff NY (1958) [2] 100 sgd no cc. These may have been part of the original 250 copies by Trianon, with a new title page. The limitation notice (100 copies) is on a separate page from signature　　　　　　　　　　$175/250

082e: ADAM'S RIB　Yoseloff NY (1958) [0] 2,000 cc　　　　　　　　　　　　　　$25/75

083a: THE CROWNING PRIVILEGE　Cassell L (1955) [1] 3,012 cc　　　　　　　　　$25/75

083b: THE CROWNING PRIVILEGE Doubleday GC 1956 [1] 4,000 cc in two printings; it is not known how many copies in each printing. States "First published 1956 in the United States." Contents differ from English edition　　　$25/75

084a: THE INFANT WITH THE GLOBE　Trianon (L 1955) [0] Graves' translates and introduces Alarcon's book　　　　　　　　　　　$15/75

084b: THE INFANT WITH THE GLOBE Yoseloff NY (1959) [1] 1,500 cc. English sheets bound four years later $15/75

085a: WINTER IN MAJORCA Cassell L (1956) [1] 1,370 cc. Graves' annotations of Sand's and Quadrado's work $50/200

085b: WINTER IN MAJORCA Valldemosa M (1956) [1] 2009 cc (but see below). Wraps $35.

We have noted the following copies Rubber stamped: "CELDA | FEDERICO CHOPIN | Y | GEORGE SAND" (also noted in French); 11 Graves' books listed across from title page at top, off-set to left; top, center; or more centered on page. All copies we've seen have had the covers printed on white paper except one on light yellow paper (*below).

SIZE (cm)	COVER	STAMP	TITLES
21.5X14	dark yellow	half-title	offset top
21.7x14	sand	fep	offset top
19.7x13.3	lt yellow*	fep	center
21.x13.3	lt yellow	fep	center
21.5x13.4	lt yellow	fep	center top
21.5x14.5	sand	none	offset top
21.4x14.1	sand	none	offset top
21.6x14	sand	fep	offset top

We assume the Majorca Tourist bureau, if there is such, may have reprinted the title and that the copies with the titles offset to left at top would be the first, as the cloth edition was set that way. But we also assume that the number of copies far exceeds 2009 and the issue described by ref.a may not even be an early printing.

086a: CATACROK! Cassell L (1956) [1] 4,015 cc $25/75

087a: LUCAN PHARSALIA... Penguin (Middlesex 1956) [1] 30,000 cc. Wraps. Graves' translation $35.

087b: LUCAN PHARSALIA... Penguin (Baltimore 1957) [1] 3,000 cc $25/50

087c: LUCAN PHARSALIA... Penguin (Baltimore 1957) [1] 20,000 cc. Wraps. Price: 85¢ (changed to 95¢ with a sticker {ref.h}. Ref.a states 95¢ was printed but we have never seen one with 95¢ actually printed on cover) $35.

088a: THE TWELVE CAESARS Penguin (Middlesex 1957) [1] 40,000 cc. Wraps $50.

088b: THE TWELVE CAESARS Penguin no place [Baltimore] (1957) [1] 3,000 cc $50/200

088c: THE TWELVE CAESARS Penguin no place (Baltimore 1957) [1] 20,000 cc. Wraps $50.

088d: THE TWELVE CAESARS Cassell L (1962) [1] 3,104 cc $50/200

089a: JESUS IN ROME Cassell L (1957) [1] 3,006 cc. Written with Joshua Podro $25/125

090a: THEY HANGED MY SAINTLY BILLY Cassell L (1957) [1] 5,370 cc $15/75

090b: THEY HANGED MY SAINTLY BILLY Doubleday GC 1957 [1] 11,500 cc in two printings $15/50

091a: POEMS SELECTED BY HIMSELF Penguin (Middlesex 1957) [1] 24,660 cc. Wraps. "Published in Penguin Books 1957" $35.

091b: POEMS SELECTED BY HIMSELF Penguin (Middlesex 1961) [1] Wraps. "Revised and Enlarged Edition 1961" $30.

091c: POEMS SELECTED BY HIMSELF Penguin (Middlesex 1966) [0] Wraps. "Third Edition" with further revisions and new foreword $25.

092a: 5 PENS IN HAND Doubleday GC 1958 [1]
4,500 cc $25/75

093a: THE POEMS OF ROBERT GRAVES
Anchor GC 1958 [0] 25,000 cc. Wraps $35.

094a: STEPS Cassell L (1958) [] Uncorrected
proof in tan wraps printed in black (Bell, Book &
Radmall 7/95) $175.

094b: STEPS Cassell L (1958) [1] 2,996 cc $25/100

095a: COLLECTED POEMS Cassell L 1959 [1]
Uncorrected Proof in pale green wraps. Publication
date 23rd April 1959 (Dalian Books catalogued
copy in publisher's blue printed wraps 12/94,
probably the same as the color is very pale and
subtle) $150.

095b: COLLECTED POEMS 1959   Cassell   L
(1959) [1] 3,037 cc. First printing dustwrapper.
Printed in bright green and black $25/75

096a: FABLE OF THE HAWK AND THE
NIGHTINGALE Santuccio Lexington, Kentucky
1959 [2] 100 cc. Not issued in dustwrapper or
slipcase. In gray or brown paper covered boards.
Also noted in brick red Japanese paper covered
boards, with separate spine and cover labels; dark
gray non-conjugate endsheets; and variant binding
with sewn floating backstrip. There were 10 out-of-
series copies, one of which we would call oyster
shell (gray?) paper covered boards (Ref. h) $1,000.

097a: THE ANGER OF ACHILLES   Doubleday
GC 1959 [1] 11,000 cc in two printings; it is not
known how many copies in each printing $25/75

097b: THE ANGER OF ACHILLES   Cassell   L
(1960) [1] 3,967 cc $25/100

098a: FOOD FOR CENTAURS   Doubleday   GC
1960 [1] 5,500 cc in two printings. It is not known

how many copies in each printing. In dustwrapper with "F. F. C." above printed price at top of front flap. Also noted, a copy without first edition statement and in dustwrapper without "F. F. C." above printed price, the second printing (Ref. h) $25/75

099a: APHODITE AND OTHER MYTHS... Sunderland College of Art   no place or date (1960s?)   [0]   Pale green cloth. Illustrated and produced by John Mundy. Student exercise? (Sanders of Oxford 3/90) $250.

100a: GREEK GODS AND HEROES   Doubleday GC   1960   [1] 37,500 cc in five printings; it is not known how many copies are in each printing. In cloth, but also issued in a simultaneous(?) re-inforced library binding in pictorial cloth, reproducing the front panel of the dustwrapper. We have seen a later printing with the number series "98" at the bottom of copyright page in the library binding. It seemed to be Doubleday's practice with Graves' children's titles to issue the books simultaneously in trade and library bindings. $25/100

100b: MYTHS OF ANCIENT GREECE   Cassell L (1961) [1] 5,946 cc. New title $25/100

101a: THE PENNY FIDDLE   Cassell L (1960) [1] 6,238 cc $25/100

101b: THE PENNY FIDDLE   Doubleday   GC (1961) [1] 6,000 cc. Green cloth, white lettering on spine $25/75

101c: THE PENNY FIDDLE   Doubleday   GC (1961)   [1] 3,000 cc. Simultaneous issue in reinforced library binding. Pictorial blue cloth, reproducing the image on the front of the dustwrapper. "Doubleday Prebound Edition" printed in black on rear cover. Issued in dustwrapper $25/75

102a: MORE POEMS 1961   Cassell L (1961) [1] 3,913 cc $15/50

103a: SELECTED POETRY AND PROSE
Hutchinson (L 1961) [1] 6,000 cc. Chosen, introduced and annotated by J. Reeves, issued without
dustwrapper $60.

104a: COLLECTED POEMS Doubleday GC
1961 [1] 6,000 cc in two printings. It is not known
how many copies in each printing. Two states of the
dustwrapper have been seen, both printed on coated
paper. Seen with the letters "C.P." above price on
dustwrapper and without (signed copy at Lilly
Library has the letters as does ref.h's review and
inscribed copies). Priority unknown, but earliest
copies seem to have the letters "C.P." present.
Bound in gray cloth stamped in silver and brown.
[we have also examined the second printing
(without first edition statement), which was bound
as above and had the letters "C.P." present above
the price on the dustwrapper (ref. h)] $15/50

104b: COLLECTED POEMS Doubleday GC 1961
[1] Bound in red paper simulated cloth with black
cloth spine stamped in silver. Status of this binding
unknown, but apparently later. Noted in two
different dustwrappers, one of which is on coated
paper without the letters "C.P." The other is also
without "C.P." but is on uncoated paper. [Note: the
photo of Graves on the rear panel lacks the sharp
detail of the image on dustwrappers printed on
coated paper; it appears to be a copy of a copy
(ref.h)] $15/50

105a: THE MORE DESERVING CASES
Marlborough College Press no place 1962 [2] 400
sgd no cc in red morocco. Issued without
dustwrapper. Noted with and without "Printed in
England" stamped on rear endpaper (Harvey Sarner) $250.

105b: THE MORE DESERVING CASES
Marlborough College Press no place 1962 [2] 350
sgd no cc. Blue buckram without dustwrapper.
Ref.a appears to indicate this issue was printed later.

It may have been but have had a copy in red
numbered 510 which would indicate the sheets were
all signed at once and bound at random $200.

105c: THE MORE DESERVING CASES Folcroft
Folcroft, Pa. 1978 [] $35.

106a: OXFORD ADDRESSES ON POETRY
Cassell L (1962) [1] Uncorrected Proof in pale
apricot wraps printed in black (Ref. h) $150.

106b: OXFORD ADDRESSES ON POETRY
Cassell L (1962) [1] 2,951 cc $15/40

106c: OXFORD ADDRESSES ON POETRY
Doubleday GC 1962 [1] 4,000 cc in two printings;
number of copies in each printing unknown. States
"First Edition in the United States of America" $15/40

107a: THE COMEDIES OF TERENCE Anchor
Books GC 1962 [1] 10,000 cc. Wraps $35.

107b: THE COMEDIES OF TERENCE Aldine
Chicago (1962) [1] 2,000 cc. "...Aldine Library
Edition First Publ 1962" $25/75

107c: THE COMEDIES OF TERENCE Cassell L
(1963) [1] 2,866 cc. Ref.a calls for "brownish-gray"
cloth, but the many copies we've seen are in apricot
colored cloth $15/60

108a: ORATIO CREWEIANA (Oxford University
Oxford) 1962 [0] 1,400 cc. Wraps. Different text
than 1964 book of same title $200.

109a: THE BIG GREEN BOOK Crowell... (NY
1962) [1] Spine blank per ref.a, issued without
dustwrapper $75.

109b: THE BIG GREEN BOOK Crowell... (NY
1962) [1] Title, author, and publisher on spine per
ref.f. Issued without dustwrapper $60.

109c: THE BIG GREEN BOOK   Crowell   NY
(1968) [1] New format. This edition published in
dustwrapper $10/30

109d: THE BIG GREEN BOOK   Puffin Books
(Harmondsworth 1978) [1] 3,000 cc.   Wraps.
"Published in Puffin Books 1978" $35.

109e: THE BIG GREEN BOOK   Kestral (Mid-
dlesex 1979) [1] $10/30

110a: NEW POEMS 1962   Cassell L (1962) [1]
Uncorrected proof in pale gray unprinted wraps
(ref.h) $100.

110b: NEW POEMS 1962   Cassell L (1962) [1]
3,082 cc $10/50

110c: NEW POEMS   Doubleday   GC 1963 [1]
3,500 cc $10/50

111a: THE SIEGE AND FALL OF TROY Cassell
L (1962) [1] 7,553 cc $25/75

111b: THE SIEGE AND FALL OF TROY
Doubleday GC [1963] [1] 15,000 cc in trade issue
rust-brown cloth binding. Presumed first issue of
dustwrapper: without reviews of this book on rear
flap; publisher's emblem and publisher's name on
spine of dustwrapper; at top of front flap is
"T.S.A.F.O.T. | UP TO 16 | PRICE, $3.50."
(Published October 4, 1963. [Note: copyright date is
1962]). $25/75

111c: THE SIEGE AND FALL OF TROY
Doubleday GC (1963) [1] 5,000 cc issued
simultaneously in institutional (library) binding of
pictorial tan cloth with front cover printed in
yellow, orange and black and "Doubleday |
Prebound | Edition" printed in black on rear cover.
Seen in presumed first issue dustwrapper (Ref. h) $25/75

111d: THE SIEGE AND FALL OF TROY Doubleday GC (1963) [1] In presumed second issue dustwrapper: there are reviews for this book on the rear flap; publisher's name on spine of dustwrapper - publisher's emblem absent; at top of front flap, " T.S.A.F.O.T.| $3.50". (Ref. h) $25/50

112a: NINE HUNDRED IRON CHARIOTS M.I.T. Cambridge 1963 [0] 4,500 cc. Wraps $300.

113a: A NEW POEM Doubleday (GC 1963) [0] Wraps. Christmas greeting - The Bird of Paradise - illustrated by Leonard Baskin (ref.a&f) $150.

114a: MAMMON... School/Econ L 1964 [0] 500 cc. Wraps $500.

115a: THE HEBREW MYTHS Doubleday GC MCMLXIV [1] 6,500 cc. Written with Raphael Patai $25/100

115b: THE HEBREW MYTHS Cassell L (1964) [1] 4,022 cc $25/125

116a: COLLECTED SHORT STORIES Doubleday GC 1964 [1] Ref.a indicates 7,000 cc in two printings, it is not known how many copies in each printing $15/60

116b: COLLECTED SHORT STORIES Cassell L (1965) [1] 3,000 cc $20/75

117a: MAN DOES, WOMAN IS Cassell L 1964 [] Uncorrected proof in green wraps printed in black (Bell, Book & Radmall 7/95) $150.

117b: MAN DOES, WOMAN IS Cassell L 1964 [1] 4,010 cc $15/50

Note: dustwrapper on first printing of above has reviews of *New Poems 1962* on back, second printing dustwrapper has reviews for this book

117c: MAN DOES, WOMAN IS Cassell L 1964 [2] 26 sgd ltr cc. Issued in glassine dustwrapper without slipcase $450.

117d: MAN DOES, WOMAN IS Cassell L 1964 [2] 175 sgd no cc. Issued in glassine dustwrapper $200.

117e: MAN DOES, WOMAN IS Doubleday GC 1964 [1] 4,500 cc $10/40

118a: EL FENOMENO DEL TURISMO Ateneo Madrid 1964 [0] Wraps $200.

119a: THE POET IN A VALLEY OF DRY BONES (Houghton Mifflin NY no date, but possibly 1964) [0] Large 8vo stapled white wraps printed in purple throughout. Issued as *Literature Today, Number 8. A Service Bulletin on Literature.* Twelve pages, perforated at left edge for insertion in ring binder, as issued. The rear wrapper contains the notation "Ap.64.6M169" suggesting a publication date of April, 1964 in a quantity of 6,000 copies. First separate edition, not in ref.a which only notes a 1963 appearance in *Horizon* and a 1965 appearance in *Mammon and the Black Goddess* (Waiting for Godot Books 11/94) $75.

120a: ORATIO CREWEIANA (Oxford University Oxford) 1964 [0] 1,400 cc. Wraps. Different text than 1962 book of same title $200.

121a: ANN AT HIGHWOOD HALL Cassell L (1964) [1] 5,000 cc $25/75

121b: ANN AT HIGHWOOD HALL Doubleday GC [1966] [1] A review copy indicates that this book was published March 4, 1966 and the Library of Congress Catalog Card Number 66-10445, printed on the verso of the title page, also suggests a 1966 publication date. The book bears a copyright date of 1964, as does the English edition. The trade edition is in yellow-green cloth printed in black on the spine (not gold as called for by ref.a) $20/60

121c: ANN AT HIGHWOOD HALL   Doubleday GC [1966] [1] Simultaneous issue in a reinforced library binding with the front cover reproducing the pictorial image of the dustwrapper. Issued in dustwrapper $20/60

122a: MAMMON AND THE BLACK GODDESS Cassell L (1965) [1] 3,000 cc $15/60

122b: MAMMON AND THE BLACK GODDESS Doubleday GC 1965 [1] 4,000 cc $15/60

123a: MAJORCA OBSERVED   Cassell L (1965) [0] 4,935 cc $20/60

123b: MAJORCA OBSERVED   Doubleday   GC (1965) [0] 1,624 cc $30/150

124a: LOVE RESPELT   Cassell L (1965)   [2] 18 sgd ltr cc (lettered A-R). Not for sale $350/400

124b: LOVE RESPELT   Cassell   L   (1965)   [2] 250 sgd no cc. (Additional 30 copies out-of-series {ref.a}) $100/150

124c: LOVE RESPELT   Doubleday   GC   1966 [1] 4,000 cc Ref.a indicates the title on spine is in a dark brown rectangular box. All copies we've seen have title in black box $10/40

125a: COLLECTED POEMS 1965   Cassell   L (1965) [1] Uncorrected proof in white wraps (Wm. Reese Co. 4/90) $175.

125b: COLLECTED POEMS 1965   Cassell   L (1965) [1] 5,135 cc $25/75

125c: COLLECTED POEMS 1966 Doubleday   GC 1966 [1] Wraps. New title. No. A517. Cover price: $1.75. Painting by Robert Kipniss on front cover (ref.h) $35.

125d: COLLECTED POEMS Doubleday GC 1966 [1] Wraps. No. A517. Cover price: $1.75. Photo of Graves on front cover. Later issue of above (ref.h) Also noted, a presumed even later issue with a cover price of $2.50 $25.

126a: SEVENTEEN POEMS MISSING FROM... (Stellar Barnet) 1966 [2] 330 sgd no cc $125/175

127a: TWO WISE CHILDREN (Quist NY 1966) [1] Green cloth, covers blank, spine lettered in black. Dustwrapper price "$2.73 net" (ref.h) $25/75

127b: TWO WISE CHILDREN (Quist NY 1966) [1] Pictorial boards with picture of girl on front and back, green cloth spine lettered in gold. Dustwrapper price: "$2.75" $15/60

127c: TWO WISE CHILDREN Quist L 1967 [1] Noted with green or yellow endpapers, priority unknown (ref.h) $10/50

128a: POETIC CRAFT AND PRINCIPLE Cassell L 1967 [] Uncorrected proof in green wraps printed in black (Clearwater Books 8/95) $100.

128b: POETIC CRAFT AND PRINCIPLE Cassell L 1967 [1] $25/75

129a: COLOPHON TO LOVE RESPELT (Stellar Barnet) 1967 [2] 386 sgd no cc $100/150

130a: D.H. LAWRENCE AND ROBERT GRAVES (Poems) Longman L 1967 [0] Wraps. With D.H. Lawrence (ref.f & g) $50.

131a: SIXTEEN POEMS College of Technology Oxford 1967 [0?] 75 cc. (some numbered) Issued without dustwrapper. Ref.a calls for purple cloth and white end papers and does not mention numbered copies. Also seen in purple cloth with gray laid end papers; not numbered (ref. h). Harvey Sarner has two copies, both with yellow-green end papers and a Romayne Dawnay illustration on front cover with title stamped in gold. One (no. 54) is bound in white cloth; the other (no. 9) is bound in green cloth. Also noted, a numbered copy with full-page black-and-white illustrations by Romaine (sic) Dawnay in pictorial cloth covers (Ulysses Book Shop 6/93). It would appear that the book was not produced commercially, perhaps produced more for instructional purposes, thus could it be that no two copies are alike $350.

132a: THE RUBAIYYAT OF OMAR KHAYAAM Cassell L (1967) [1] $15/50

132b: THE ORIGINAL RUBAIYYAT OF OMAR KHAYAAM Doubleday GC 1968 [2] 500 sgd no cc. New title. Issued without dustwrapper in slipcase $150/200

132c: THE ORIGINAL RUBAIYYAT OF OMAR KHAYAAM Doubleday GC 1968 [1] 12,000 cc $10/40

133a: THE POOR BOY WHO FOLLOWED... Cassell L 1968 [1] Noted in medium blue and navy blue cloth, priority unknown (ref.h) $25/75

133b: THE POOR BOY WHO FOLLOWED... Doubleday GC (1969) [1] Trade issue in yellow cloth printed in black on spine, no endpapers $25/75

133c: THE POOR BOY WHO FOLLOWED... Doubleday GC (1969) [1] Simultaneous issue in library binding. Slick white cloth printed to match the dustwrapper which has a gold sticker "A Doubleday Reinforced Library Edition" on it. This issue has endpapers $25/75

134a: TETRASTICHON-KHAYAAM Narbulla L 1968 [] Translations by Graves, Edw. Fitzgerald, and Omar Ali-Shah (ref.b) $20/60

135a: GREEK MYTHS AND LEGENDS Cassell L (1968) [1] A combination of *Greek Gods and*

Heroes and *The Siege and Fall of Troy.* Issued
without dustwrapper $45.

136a: POEMS 1965-1968   Cassell L (1968) [1]
Proof in green wraps $75.

136b: POEMS 1965-1968 Cassell L (1968) [1] $10/40

136c: POEMS 1965-1968   Doubleday GC 1969
[1] $10/40

137a: LOVE RESPELT AGAIN Doubleday NY
(1969) [2] 1,000 sgd cc $50/75

138a: THE CRANE BAG... Cassell L (1969) [1] $25/75

139a: ON POETRY Doubleday GC 1969 [1] $20/60

140a: BEYOND GIVING: POEMS   (Stellar
Hatfield) 1969 [2] 536 sgd no cc $75/125

141a: POEMS ABOUT LOVE   Cassell L (1969)
[1] $20/60

141b: POEMS ABOUT LOVE Doubleday GC
1969 [1] $15/50

142a: QUEEN-MOTHER TO NEW QUEEN
(Gleeson Library   University of San Francisco
1970) [2] Wraps. 200 cc. Facsimile of manuscript
poem. Single leaf folded (ref.h) $75.

143a: POEMS 1968-1970 Cassell L (1970) [1]
Uncorrected Proof in green wraps printed in black
(Ref. h) $150.

143b: POEMS 1968-1970 Cassell L (1970) [1] $15/45

143c: POEMS 1968-1970   Doubleday GC 1971
[1] 4,500 cc $10/40

144a: ADVICE FROM A MOTHER Poem of the
Month L 1970 [0] Broadside (ref.e) $100.

145a: THE GREEN-SAILED VESSEL (Stellar Hatfield) 1971 [2] 536 sgd no cc $75/125

146a: POEMS: ABRIDGED FOR DOLLS AND PRINCES (Cassell L 1971) [1] $15/50

146b: POEMS: ABRIDGED FOR DOLLS AND PRINCES (Doubleday no place 1972) [2] 500 cc $20/60

147a: DEYA: A PORTFOLIO OF FIVE... Motif L 1972 [2] 75 sets. Five poems by Graves and lithographs by Paul Hogarth. Issued in portfolio $2,000.

148a: DIFFICULT QUESTIONS, EASY ANSWERS Cassell L (1972) [1] $15/50

148b: DIFFICULT QUESTIONS, EASY ANSWERS Doubleday GC 1973 [1] $10/40

149a: POEMS 1970-1972 Cassell L (1972) [1] All copies seen have gold stamped spine, not silver (ref.a) and blue, red and black printed dustwrapper not just blue & red (ref.a) $10/40

149b: POEMS 1970-1972 Doubleday GC 1973 [1] 4,500 cc. All copies seen have spine stamped in black (not gold as in ref.a) $10/35

150a: TIMELESS MEETING: POEMS (Steller Hatfield) 1973 [2] 536 sgd no cc $75/125

151a: THE SONG OF SONGS Potter NY (1973) [1] 10,000 cc $10/40

151b: THE SONG OF SONGS Collins (L 1973) [1] Illustrated by Hans Erni $10/40

152a: AT THE GATE: POEMS Stellar Hatfield 1974 [2] 536 sgd no cc $75/125

153a: COLLECTED POEMS 1975 Cassell L (1975) [1] Noted with title page cancel and with integral; priority unknown $20/50

153b: NEW COLLECTED POEMS Doubleday GC 1976 [1] New title. Uncorrected Proof in tall cream colored wraps printed in black (Ref. h) $125.

153c: NEW COLLECTED POEMS Doubleday GC 1977 [1] $10/30

153d: COLLECTED POEMS 1975 Oxford NY 1988 [1] Second American edition, the first under this title (Ref. h) $10/35

154a: CAMILO KERRIGAN (Majorca) 1976 [] Art exhibit card with text by Graves and facsimile signature $60.

155a: TWIN TO TWIN: TWO POEMS The Gruffygound Press Sidcot 1977 [2] 25 cc. One leaf, French folded, sewn at center $250.

156a: ADVICE TO COLONEL VALENTINE: TWO POEMS The Gruffyground Press Sidcot 1979 [2] 25 cc. One leaf folded and sewn in a yellow paper cover $250.

157a: IN THE WILDERNESS Seluzicki (L 1979) [2] 15 cc. Broadside signed by the artist $300.

158a: POEMS Limited Editions Club NY 1980 [2] 2,000 sgd cc. Illustrated by Paul Hogarth and signed by him, not Graves. In glassine dustwrapper and slipcase $75/125

159a: AN ANCIENT CASTLE Peter Owen L (1980) [1] 1,000 cc. The usual state of this book is brown simulated cloth stamped in silver on the spine; end paper before half title. (A review copy giving the date of publication as October 16 {1980} has the brown simulated cloth. Also noted in black simulated cloth, spine stamped in gold; endpaper and two blank leaves before half title. Priority unknown {ref. h}) $15/60

159b: AN ANCIENT CASTLE   Michael Kesend (NY 1981) [1] (Ref.h) — $15/40

160a: THE SECRET LAND   Charles Seluzicki Portland 1981 [2] 75 no cc. Broadside. Illustrated by Carol Blinn. (Not the first appearance of the poem {ref.h}) — $125.

161a: IN BROKEN IMAGES... Hutchinson L (1982) [1] 2,463 cc. Letters edited by Paul O'Prey — $15/45

161b: IN BROKEN IMAGES... Moyer Bell Mt. Kisco, NY (1988) [1] — $15/40

161c: IN BROKEN IMAGES... Moyer Bell Mt. Kisco, NY (1988) [1] Wraps — $20.

162a: TWO POEMS   Mercator Press   no place 1982 [2] 45 cc. Dutch translation by Willem Kramer with English text on verso. 20 pages bound in heavy gray wraps — $200.

163a: ELEVEN SONGS   (New Seizin Press Deya, Mallorca 1983) [2] 100 sgd no cc. Wraps in folding case. (Signed by illustrator and printer, not Graves.) (Also, one proof cataloged with word repeated in sixth stanza of "Song" {Words Etc. - 4/90}) — $175.

164a: BETWEEN MOON AND MOON... Hutchinson L (1984) [1] 1,726 cc. Letters edited by Paul O'Prey — $20/50

164b: BETWEEN MOON AND MOON... Moyer Bell Mount Kisco (1990) [1] Uncorrected proof in white wraps printed in black — $60.

164c: BETWEEN MOON AND MOON... Moyer Bell Mount Kisko and L (1990) [1] — $10/40

165a: SELECTED POEMS   Penguin Books (Harmondsworth, Middlesex 1986 [1] Wraps. "This

selection first published 1986." Reprinted in 1987
(Listed in Carter's *Robert Graves*, 1989) $15.

166a: GEORGE SAND IN MAJORCA   (New
Seizin Press Mallorca 1986) [2] 75 sgd no cc. Set
consists of three texts. (Original English, French
and Catalan.) Each folded and unbound. Nine
colored etchings each signed and numbered by Nils
Burwitz. Each book signed by Tomas Graves
(printer) and Lucia Graves (Catalan co-translator).
All laid in a cloth covered box with "Suite | Sand |
Graves | Nils Burwitz..." on cover (Bertram Rota
6/89) $900.

167a: POEMS ABOUT WAR Cassell (L 1988) [1]
"First published in Great Britain 1988." In
dustwrapper with a printed price of "£8.95 net."
Also noted in dustwrapper without a printed price
but with a publisher's white price sticker printed in
black "CASSELL | £ 8.95," which was also used on
the 1988 second printing (ref.h) $10/40

167b: POEMS ABOUT WAR Moyer Bell Limited
Mount Kisko and L (1990) [1] Uncorrected Proof
in white wraps printed in black (Ref. h) $50.

167c: POEMS ABOUT WAR Moyer Bell Limited
Mount Kisko and L (1990) [1] Wraps $20.

168a: CONVERSATIONS WITH ROBERT
GRAVES University Press of Mississippi Jackson
1989 [3] Edited by Frank Kersnowski. (Published
October 1989 at $28.95) $20/40

168b: CONVERSATIONS WITH ROBERT
GRAVES University Press of Mississippi Jackson
1989 [3] Wraps. (Published October 1989 at
$14.95) $20.

169a: CYNICS AND ROMANTICS Gruffyground
Press Sidcot 1989 [2] 150 cc. Wraps $75.

170a: LOVE POEMS Folio Society L 1990 [0] Selected and introduced by Sue Bradbury. Bound in quarter cloth and patterned paper-covered boards; in glassine dustwrapper. Lettering on spine reads "POEMS BY ROBERT GRAVES" (Biodata 5/92) $50.

171a: LIFE OF THE POET GNAEUS ROBERTULUS GRAVESEA New Seizin Press (Deya, Mallorca) 1990 [actually 1992] [2] 150 sgd no cc. (Signed by Alice Meyer-Wallace, the illustrator and by Tomas Graves and Carmen Garcia-Gutierrez). Bound in hand-lettered full limp vellum (ref.h) $150.

172a: ACROSS THE GULF New Seizin Press (Deya, Mallorca) 1992 [actually 1994] [2] 175 sgd no cc. 14 previously unpublished poems edited by Beryl and Lucia Graves with Dunstan Ward and signed by them. Issued in tissue dustwrapper $200.

173a: LOVE WITHOUT HOPE The Poetry Society/The British Council/ The British Library (L no date, but possibly 1994/1995) [0] First separate appearance. Issued in the "Poems on the Underground" series. Oblong broadside approx. 24 x 11 inches; glossy white paper printed in black, gray, red and blue (J. Howard Woolmer 3/95) $45.

174a: THE CENTENARY SELECTED POEMS Carcanet Manchester 1995 [1] Noted in gray paper covered boards, as well as black paper cover boards, priority unknown. (Published at £15.95 (Words Etcetera 7/95)

175a: COLLECTED WRITINGS ON POETRY
Carcanet Press/Alyschamps Press Manchester/Paris
(1995) [1] (Published at £35)

GRAHAM GREENE

Greene was born in Berkhamsted, England, in 1904. He has stated that he found himself prey to boredom, melancholy and disgust from an early age. He claims to have played Russian roulette eight times before becoming bored with it. He went into analysis at sixteen but didn't think it helped.

He graduated from Oxford in 1925 and converted to Roman Catholicism before his marriage in 1927. His early career was in journalism (editor and film critic). During the war he was employed in the Foreign Office.

We would like to thank Dr. R. A. Wobbe for permission to use his bibliography, and Joseph Jeffs and Bruce Howard for their assistance.

The Wobbe bibliography does not actually mention whether or not the individual books state "first published...," "first printing," etc.; but uses terms such as "publication," "publishing," "printing notices," therefore we checked a number of titles and believe the codes are correct. A "1" was used on Viking if it stated "Published in..." or "First published by Viking in..."

REFERENCES:

(a) Wobbe, R.A. GRAHAM GREENE: A BIBLIOGRAPHY AND GUIDE TO RESEARCH. New York/London: Garland Publishing, Inc., 1979. Used for all entries unless otherwise noted.

(b) Inventory or catalog entries.

(c) Information furnished by Joseph Jeffs.

001a: BABBLING APRIL   Basil Blackwell   Oxford   1925 [0] 500 copies were planned but only 300 or so ever issued (Blackwells of Oxford) $3,000/5,000

002a: THE MAN WITHIN   Wm. Heinemann   L (1929) [1] 2,500 cc.   Also noted with a wrap-around band: "Another Heinemann first novel discovery" (R.A. Gekoski) $500/2,500

002b: THE MAN WITHIN Doubleday, Doran   GC 1929   [1]   Ref.a calls for a white dustwrapper printed in blue with "Advertisements for other books published by Heinemann." We believe this may have been the description of the U.K. edition (Wobbe A2) as there is no dustwrapper description under A2. The only dustwrapper we've seen on the U.S. edition is primarily green with spine blocks in light green. $300/1,500

003a: THE NAME OF ACTION   Wm. Heinemann L (1930) [1] 2,000 cc sold. No other British edition exists. Ref.a calls for price of "7s6d" and dustwrapper with reviews of *The Man Within* on back cover $400/4,000

003b: THE NAME OF ACTION   Wm. Heinemann L (1930) [1] In dustwrapper with "3s6d" on spine and reviews on dustwrapper flap (R.A. Gekoski) $400/1,500

003c: THE NAME OF ACTION   Doubleday, Doran   GC   1931 [1] Publisher has said that no records survive of number of copies printed or sold (probably less than 1,000 copies sold) $250/1,750

> Note: "My second and third novels, *The Name of Action* and *Rumour at Nightfall,* published in 1930 and 1931, can now be found, I am glad to think, only in secondhand bookshops at an exaggerated price, since some years after their publication I suppressed them.   Both books are of a badness beyond the power of criticism properly to evoke the prose flat and stilted...the

characterization nonexistent." (*Ways Of Escape* pp.6-17)

004a: RUMOUR AT NIGHTFALL Wm. Heinemann L (1931) [1] 2,500 cc. 1,200 sold $400/4,000

004b: RUMOUR AT NIGHTFALL Doubleday, Doran NY 1932 [1] Doubleday reports 1,018 copies sold $200/2,000

005a: STAMBOUL TRAIN Wm. Heinemann L (1932) [] Uncorrected proof in red wraps. The proof does not have the changes mentioned in 005b (Lame Duck Books cataloged a copy for $9,000 in July 1993) $NVA

005b: STAMBOUL TRAIN Wm. Heinemann L (1932) [1] Approximately 13,000 cc. J.B. Priestley objected to the use of Q. C. Savory and the name was changed to Quin Savory on pages 77, 78, 82, 98 and 131. Although there were other places in the book where Q.C. was not changed to Quin. It is possible a few copies exist without these lines changed (this was mentioned by Greene in *A Sort of Life* but we thank Joseph Jeffs for providing detailed changes and page numbers). (Robert Temple cataloged a variant 186mm tall vs 189mm in February 1993) $300/3,000

005c: ORIENT EXPRESS Doubleday, Doran GC 1933 [1] 4,334 cc sold $200/2,000

006a: IT'S A BATTLEFIELD Wm. Heinemann L (1934) [1] First issue dustwrapper priced "7/6" $200/2,000

006b: IT'S A BATTLEFIELD Wm. Heinemann L (1934) [1] Second issue dustwrapper priced "3/6" (R. Gekoski 7/93) $200/1,250

006c: IT'S A BATTLEFIELD Doubleday, Doran GC 1934 [1] 1,960 cc sold $150/750

006d: IT'S A BATTLEFIELD Heinemann L (1948) [] Uniform Edition completely revised $25/75

006e: NEW INTRODUCTION TO IT'S A BATTLEFIELD Viking NY (1962) [] 4 pages stapled, distributed for review purposes (Joseph The Provider) $200.

006f: IT'S A BATTLEFIELD Viking NY (1962) [1] "Reissued in 1962 by Viking Press" (new introduction - revised text) $15/75

007a: THE OLD SCHOOL Jonathan Cape L (1934) [1] 1,517 cc. Essays edited by Greene $300/1,500

008a: ENGLAND MADE ME Wm. Heinemann L (1935) [1] $300/3,000

008b: ENGLAND MADE ME Doubleday, Doran GC 1935 [1] 2,102 cc sold $150/750

008c: SHIPWRECKED Viking NY 1953 [1] "Reissued by Viking Press in January 1953" (new title) $15/60

009a: THE BEAR FELL FREE Grayson & Grayson L 1935 [2] 285 cc of which 250 are signed and numbered (dark green cloth, although the British Library copy of the unnumbered edition is black) $1,500/2,500

009b: THE BEAR FELL FREE Folcroft Press (Folcroft, PA) no date [0] Library binding (ref.b) $40.

010a: THE BASEMENT ROOM *and Other Stories* Cresset Press Ltd. L (1935) [1] First issue green cloth (Ergo Book Catalog 501). (A later issue is not mentioned in ref.a) $250/2,500

010b: THE BASEMENT ROOM *and Other Stories* Cresset Press Ltd. L (1935) [1] Second binding in red cloth with black lettering (Hawthorn Books 10/89) $150/1,500

011a: JOURNEY WITHOUT MAPS Wm. Heinemann L/T (1936) [1] Book withdrawn by publisher per Helen MacLeod in *Book Collector* (U.K.) March, 1985 $400/4,000

011b: JOURNEY WITHOUT MAPS Doubleday, Doran GC 1936 [1] 2,200 cc sold $100/500

012a: THIS GUN FOR HIRE Doubleday, Doran GC 1936 [1] 2,100 cc sold. Published June 1936 $250/1,500

012b: A GUN FOR SALE Wm. Heinemann L (1936) [1] New title. Published one month after American edition $300/3,000

013a: BRIGHTON ROCK The Viking Press NY 1938 [1] 4,500 cc. "Published in June 1938." Also noted with wrap-around band (Pepper & Stern) $150/1,000

013b: BRIGHTON ROCK Wm. Heinemann L (1938) [1] About 8,000 cc sold per Greene. "Published July 1938" on copyright page. Red cloth. Variant binding in maroon cloth (Peter Ellis 5/91). (Perfect copy has sold for considerably more) $350/3,500

014a: TO BEG I AM ASHAMED Vanguard NY 1938 [0] By Sheila Cousins. Ghostwritten by Greene and Ronald Matthews. Effectively suppressed in England the same year (Joseph The Provider 5/92) $150/750

015a: THE LAWLESS ROADS Longmans, Green & Co. L/NY/T (1939) [1] Red cloth with letters in gold. (Also noted with black lettering {Nicholas Pounder 6/90}). All but one photo by Greene per acknowledgment on p.8. Maps on endpaper, 10 black-and-white photos. Photos vary in later printings (ref.a). $300/3,500

015b: THE LAWLESS ROADS Longmans, Green & Co. L/NY/T (1939) [1] Second binding: red cloth with blue letters (David Mayou 10/89) $150/1,500

015c: ANOTHER MEXICO The Viking Press NY 1939 [1] 2,000 cc. New title. "Published in June 1939" on copyright page. Adds 8 illustrations not in English edition and deletes 2 $100/500

016a: THE CONFIDENTIAL AGENT Wm. Heinemann L/T (1939) [1] $500/5,000

016b: THE CONFIDENTIAL AGENT The Viking Press NY 1939 [1] 3,600 cc $150/750

017a: THE POWER AND THE GLORY Wm. Heinemann L 1940 [] Uncorrected proof in buff wraps printed in red (Lakin & Marley Rare Books 7/95) $7,500.

017b: THE POWER AND THE GLORY Wm. Heinemann L (1940) [1] 3,500 cc (Greene estimate in *A Sort of Life*). Awarded Hawthornden Prize 1941; Connolly's Modern Movement #88 $450/4,500

017c: THE LABYRINTHINE WAYS The Viking Press NY 1940 [1] 3,500 cc for b&c. New title. A printing error resulted in the trasposition of p.165 and 256. The publisher tried to get back all copies but obviously some were missed. In the first state, p.165 starts "A voice said... " (ref.b) $300/1,000

017d: THE LABYRINTHINE WAYS The Viking Press NY 1940 [1] Second state, P.165 starts "A voice near his foot said..." (ref.b) $150/750

017e: THE POWER AND THE GLORY Viking NY 1946 [] "Reissued in 1946..." on copyright page. Yellow cloth with dark green lettering (American Book Co. 6/93) $15/60

017f: THE POWER AND THE GLORY Time Inc. NY (1962) [0] Wraps. New introduction. First printing has one "x" on last page $35.

017g: THE POWER AND THE GLORY
Heinemann L 1963 [] With new introduction.
Same as 017f? $15/60

017h: THE LABYRINTHINE WAYS Viking NY
1963 [1] Wraps. Compass Edition with new
introduction (same as 017f?) $25.

018a: BRITISH DRAMATISTS Wm. Collins L
1942 [1] $35/100

019a: THE MINISTRY OF FEAR Wm.
Heinemann L/T (1943) [1] Yellow cloth with black
letters (also noted in smooth beige cloth - Calif.
Book Auction #230) $200/2,000

019b: THE MINISTRY OF FEAR The Viking
Press NY 1943 [1] 4,000 cc $150/750

020a: THE LITTLE TRAIN (Eyre & Spottiswoode
L 1946) [0] Greene's name not on title page (is in
later editions). Illustrated by Dorothy Craigie.
Issued in dustwrapper although not noted in ref.a
(Bruce Howard) $250/1,000

020b: THE LITTLE TRAIN Lothrop, Lee &
Shepard NY (1958) [0] Illustrated by Dorothy
Craigie. Also noted in a reinforced library binding
and dustwrapper (Waiting For Godot 3/89) $125/350

020c: THE LITTLE TRAIN Bodley Head L 1973
[] Illustrated by Edward Ardizzone $25/75

020d: THE LITTLE TRAIN Doubleday GC
(1973) [1] Illustrated by Edward Ardizzone $25/75

021a: NINETEEN STORIES Wm. Heinemann
L/T (1947) [1] Eight of the stories first appeared in
The Basement Room. $75/350

021b: NINETEEN STORIES The Viking Press
NY 1949 [1] Signed on tipped-in leaf (Robert Dagg
3/94) $250/500

021c: NINETEEN STORIES   The Viking Press NY 1949 [1] 3,500 cc (b&c). Gray-green cloth, one of several variants (Alphabet Books 4/91) $40/200

022a: THE HEART OF THE MATTER Wm. Heinemann L/T(1948) [1] $35/175

022b: THE HEART OF THE MATTER   The Viking Press NY 1948 [2] 750 cc. Gray buckram cloth over boards without dustwrapper. "For the friends of Viking Press" $200.

022c: THE HEART OF THE MATTER   The Viking Press NY 1948 [1] 21,189 cc. Boards covered in maroon embossed paper with spine in ivory cloth per ref.a, but usually seen with gray-green cloth spine (Jeff Klaess) $25/125

023a: WHY DO I WRITE? Percival Marshall L (1948) [1] 1,300 cc. An exchange of letters among Greene, Eliz. Bowen and V.S. Pritchett. Issued in dustwrapper, although not noted in ref.a (Bruce Howard) $125/500

024a: AFTER TWO YEARS   Rosaio Press (Anacapri) 1949 [2] 25 no. cc. May not have been distributed.   3 known copies. (Hawthorn Books cataloged a copy for £15,000 in 1995) $NVA

025a: THE THIRD MAN: THE STORY FOR THE MOTION PICTURE The Viking Press NY 1950 [1]   10,000 cc.   "Published March 1950" on copyright page (Note: the Bantam Books edition which was printed in March 1950 and "Published April 1950," also preceded the U.K. edition) $50/250

025b: THE THIRD MAN AND THE FALLEN IDOL   Wm. Heinemann L (1950) [1] New title. Published July 1950, four months after American $100/500

025c: THE THIRD MAN: A FILM   Lorrimer L (1969) [1]   Wraps. New title. With Carol Reed.

(Ref.a notes published December 1968. It is
number 13 in the series "Modern Film Scripts") $50.

025d: THE THIRD MAN: A FILM   Simon &
Schuster NY (1969) [1] Wraps $40.

025e: THE THIRD MAN: A FILM   Eurographica
Helsinki 1988 [2] 500 sgd no cc. Issued in printed
acetate dustwrapper. Also "One of 20 additional
copies ... for ... author" Not numbered or signed
(Clearwater Books 9/95 cataloged for $200) $350/450

026a: THE LITTLE FIRE ENGINE (Max. Parrish
& Co. L 1950) [0] Illustrated by Dorothy Craigie.
Issued in dustwrapper, although not noted in ref.a
(Bruce Howard) $250/850

026b: THE LITTLE RED FIRE ENGINE Lothrop,
Lee & Shepard   NY (1953) [0] Illustrated by
Dorothy Craigie. (No dustwrapper mentioned in
ref.a) $200.

026c: THE LITTLE RED FIRE ENGINE Lothrop,
Lee & Shepard NY (1953) [] Wraps $75.

026d: THE LITTLE FIRE ENGINE Bodley Head
L (1973) [1] "This Edition First Published 1973" on
copyright page. Illustrated by Edw. Ardizzone $25/100

026e: THE LITTLE FIRE ENGINE   Doubleday
GC 1973 [] Illustrated by Edw. Ardizzone $25/75

027a: THE BEST OF SAKI   John Lane/Bodley
Head (no place 1950) [1] Wraps. Introduction by
Greene. First Guild Books edition $50.

027b: THE BEST OF SAKI The Viking Press NY
(1961) [1] Wraps $40.

028a: THE LOST CHILDHOOD *and Other Stories*
Eyre & Spottiswoode L 1951 [0] $40/200

028b: THE LOST CHILDHOOD *and Other Stories*
Viking Press NY (1952) [1] 3,500 cc $30/150

029a: THE END OF THE AFFAIR   Wm.
Heinemann L (1951) [] Proof copy in white wraps
printed in black (Glenn Horowitz 3/91) $750

029b: THE END OF THE AFFAIR   Wm.
Heinemann   L (1951) [1] (Also noted in "*Daily
Mail* Book Of The Month" wrap-around band - per
R.A. Gekoski 3/89) $25/125

029c: THE END OF THE AFFAIR   The Viking
Press NY 1951 [] Long folio gally sheets, string
tied in plain blue wraps (Black Sun 7/94) $600.

029d: THE END OF THE AFFAIR   The Viking
Press NY 1951 [1] 22,000 cc $15/75

030a: THE LITTLE HORSE BUS Max Parrish L
(1952) [0] Illustrated by Dorothy Craigie $200/750

030b: THE LITTLE HORSE BUS Lothrup, Lee &
Shepard NY (1954) [0] Illustrated by Dorothy
Craigie $100/500

030c: THE LITTLE HORSE BUS Bodley Head L
(1974) [1] "This edition first published 1974" on
copyright page. Illustrated by Edward Ardizzone $25/75

030d: THE LITTLE HORSE BUS Doubleday GC
1975 [] Illustrated by Edward Ardizzone $25/75

031a: THE LIVING ROOM Wm. Heinemann L
(1953) [1] (First appearance was a Swedish
translation published by P.A. Norstedt & Soners,
Stockholm, 1952) $30/150

031b: THE LIVING ROOM The Viking Press NY
1954 [1] 4,000 cc $15/75

031c: THE LIVING ROOM Samuel French NY (1955) [0] Wraps. "90¢" on cover (ref.b). Later blacked out and $1.00 stamped on $35.

032a: THE LITTLE STEAMROLLER *and Other Stories* Max Parrish L (1953) [0] Illustrated by Dorothy Craigie $150/600

032b: THE LITTLE STEAMROLLER *and Other Stories* Lothrup, Lee & Shepard NY 1955 [0] Illustrated by Dorothy Craigie $100/400

032c: THE LITTLE STEAMROLLER *and Other Stories* Bodley Head L (1974) [1] Illustrated by Edw. Ardizzone. "This edition first published 1974" on copyright page $25/75

032d: THE LITTLE STEAMROLLER *and Other Stories* Doubleday GC 1974 [1] Illustrated by Edw. Ardizzone. (Issued also in a reinforced library binding with dustwrapper) $25/75

033a: NINO CAFFE Knoedler NY (1953) [0] Wraps. 4-page pamphlet with 2 pages of text by Greene. Full color cover $250.

034a: ESSAIS CATHOLIQUES E'ditions du Seuil Paris (1953) [2] 630 cc. Wraps. No English edition. Translated into French by Marcelle Sibon. Usually has wrap-around band $75.

035a: TWENTY-ONE STORIES Wm. Heinemann L (1954) [1] No.12 of the "Uniform Edition." 4 new stories, 2 omitted from original *Nineteen Stories*, 1947 $15/75

035b: 21 STORIES The Viking Press NY (1962) [1] First U.S. appearance in book form for three of the stories $15/75

036a: LOSER TAKES ALL Wm. Heinemann L (1955) [1] Blue cloth. Ref.a describes a blue and yellow dustwrapper with a cafe table on left turning into a roulette wheel on right as later impression but does not describe first dustwrapper. We think this is first and movie photo is second $35/175

036b: LOSER TAKES ALL Wm. Heinemann L (1955) [1] Photo from film on front cover, assume second issue dustwrapper. A variant in bright green cloth also noted (David Mason) $35/125

036c: LOSER TAKES ALL Viking Press NY 1957 [1] Wraps. Stiff cover states "First U.S. Book Publication, Compass Books - 95¢" $40.

037a: THE QUIET AMERICAN Wm. Heinemann L (1955) [1] Some copies with wrap-around band (Maurice Neville) $30/150

037b: THE QUIET AMERICAN The Viking Press NY 1956 [1] 32,000 cc $15/75

038a: THE SPY'S BEDSIDE BOOK *and Other Stories* Rupert Hart-Davis L 1957 [0] Edited anthology with Hugh Green $20/100

039a: THE POTTING SHED *A Play in Three Acts* Viking Press NY 1957 [1] 4,000 cc. Third act differs from English Edition $25/100

039b: THE POTTING SHED *A Play in Three Acts* Samuel French NY (1957) [] Wraps. Actually printed in 1958 or later as it mentions the February 1958 play production (ref.c) $30.

039c: THE POTTING SHED *A Play in Three Acts* Heinemann L (1958) [1] Third act "As Greene originally wrote it" (ref.a). Not clear who rewrote third act for 039a $25/100

039d: THE POTTING SHED *A Play in Three Acts* Samuel French L (1959) [] Wraps $25.

040a: OUR MAN IN HAVANA Heinemann L (1958) [1] $25/125

040b: OUR MAN IN HAVANA The Viking Press
NY (1958) [1] 20,000 cc $15/75

041a: THE COMPLAISANT LOVER *A Comedy*
Heinemann L (1959) [1] $25/100

041b: THE COMPLAISANT LOVER *A Comedy*
French L 1959 [] Wraps $25.

041c: THE COMPLAISANT LOVER *A Comedy*
The Viking Press NY (1961) [1] (Publisher's
records do not show printing quantity) $25/75

041d: THE COMPLAISANT LOVER *A Comedy*
Samuel French NY (1961) [1] Wraps $25.

042a: A VISIT TO MORIN Heinemann L [1960]
[2] 250 cc. This was copyrighted in 1959 but ref.a
indicates it was distributed for Christmas 1960 $300/600

043a: A BURNT-OUT CASE Heinemann L
(1961) [1] Uncorrected proof in blue wraps with
textual variations (David Rees 3/90). (Published by
Gyldendel, Oslo 1960 as *Uterent*, preceding English
{Aubrey Bell 6/91}) $300.

043b: A BURNT-OUT CASE Heinemann L
(1961) [1] $25/100

043c: A BURNT-OUT CASE The Viking Press
NY 1961 [1] 22,000 cc $15/60

044a: IN SEARCH OF A CHARACTER The
Bodley Head L (1961) [] "Advance Unbound
Copy" in yellow wraps (Waiting For Godot 2/92) $300.

044b: IN SEARCH OF A CHARACTER *Two
African Journals* The Bodley Head L (1961) [1] $25/75

044c: IN SEARCH OF A CHARACTER *Two
African Journals* Viking NY (1961) [2] 600 cc.
Published in December 1961. Issued in acetate
dustwrapper without slipcase $175.

044d: IN SEARCH OF A CHARACTER *Two African Journals* Viking Press NY (1962) [1] 10,400 cc. Published June 1962 $15/60

045a: INTRODUCTION TO THREE NOVELS Norstedt & Soners Stockholm (1962) [0] Wraps. Preceded the appearance of these in the collected edition of Greene's work $250.

046a: A SENSE OF REALITY The Bodley Head L (1963) [] Uncorrected proof in lemon colored printed wraps (Sanders of Oxford 3/89) $250.

046b: A SENSE OF REALITY The Bodley Head L (1963) [1] $25/75

046c: A SENSE OF REALITY Viking Press NY (1963) [1] 10,000 cc $15/60

047a: THE REVENGE *An autobiographical fragment* Privately Printed (1963) [2] 300 cc. Wraps $500.

048a: CARVING A STATUE *A Play* The Bodley Head L (1964) [1] $25/125

049a: THE COMEDIANS (Viking) NY (1965) [2] 500 cc. "..For Friends of the Author for Christmas 1965." Issued in unprinted acetate dustwrapper $175.

049b: THE COMEDIANS The Bodley Head L (1966) [] Galleys printed on verso only (Glouchester Road Bookshop 3/92) $600.

049c: THE COMEDIANS The Bodley Head L (1966) [1] Published in January 1966. Two dustwrappers noted, one has ads for two other Greene books on back dustwrapper flap, the other has a 23 line quote by Greene concerning his visits to Haiti. Priority unknown (Ward Arrington, Grove Antiques) $25/100

049d: THE COMEDIANS The Viking Press NY
(1966) [1]   "Published in January 1966" on
copyright page $15/60

050a: VICTORIAN DETECTIVE FICTION *A
Catalogue...* The Bodley Head L (1966) [2] 25 cc
for Presentation. Greene and Dorothy Glover's
collection with preface by Greene $1,000/1,250

050b: VICTORIAN DETECTIVE FICTION *A
Catalogue...*   The Bodley Head L (1966) [2] 475
sgd no cc $500/750

051a: MAY WE BORROW YOUR HUSBAND?
And Other Comedies of the Sexual Life The Bodley
Head L (1967) [2] 500 sgd no cc. Issued in a clear
acetate dustwrapper and slipcase $250/350

051b: MAY WE BORROW YOUR HUSBAND?
And Other Comedies of the Sexual Life The Bodley
Head L (1967) [1] $15/60

051c: MAY WE BORROW YOUR HUSBAND?
And Other Comedies of the Sexual Life The Viking
Press NY (1967) [1] (Publisher has no printing
quantity information) $10/40

052a: COLLECTED ESSAYS The Bodley Head L
(1969) [1] $25/100

052b: COLLECTED ESSAYS   The Viking Press
NY (1969) [1] 4,000 cc $25/75

053a: SHAKESPEARE - PREISE 1968 UND 1969
Stiftung Hamburg 1969 [] Wraps. Bilingual text of
Greene's speech accepting prize (Ian McKelvie #60) $200.

054a: TRAVELS WITH MY AUNT The Bodley
Head L (1969) [] Galleys printed on recto only $600.

054b: TRAVELS WITH MY AUNT The Bodley
Head L (1969) [1] (Published November 1969) $15/60

054c: TRAVELS WITH MY AUNT The Bodley Head   Toronto 1969 [] UK sheets bound with a Canadian title page and UK dustwrapper priced in Canadian dollars. Precedes US? (Alphabet Books) $15/60

054d: TRAVELS WITH MY AUNT   The Viking Press   NY (1970) [] Uncorrected proof in yellow wraps (Waiting for Godot 2/91) $125.

054e: TRAVELS WITH MY AUNT   The Viking Press   NY (1970) [1] 50,000 cc $15/50

055a: MR. VISCONTI...*An Extract From Travels With My Aunt*   Bodley Head   L (1969) [] 300 cc. Wraps. Illustrated by Edward Ardizzone. Privately distributed by author and publisher for Christmas 1969 $450.

056a: TRIPLE PURSUIT *A Graham Greene Omnibus* NY (1971) [] (Words Etc. 10/90) $10/40

057a: A SORT OF LIFE   The Bodley Head   L (1971) [1] 1,000 cc. P.177:4 has "Sir John Barrie" vs. "J.M. Barrie." (Gloucester Road Bookshop #2) $100/125

057b: A SORT OF LIFE   The Bodley Head   L (1971) [1] Second issue with "J.M. Barrie" $15/50

057c: A SORT OF LIFE   Simon & Schuster   NY (1971) [1] $10/40

058a: COLLECTED STORIES   The Bodley Head   L (1972) [1] Volume 8 of the Collected Edition with significant changes to one story and 3 previously uncollected stories $25/75

058b: COLLECTED STORIES   The Viking Press NY (1973) [1] 7,500 cc $25/75

059a: THE PLEASURE DOME   Secker & Warburg L (1972) [1] $25/75

059b: GRAHAM GREENE ON FILM Simon and
Schuster NY (1972) [1] $15/50

060a: THE VIRTUE OF DISLOYALTY Privately
Printed (Bodley Head) L (1972) [] 300 cc. Wraps.
Privately distributed by author and publisher in
November 1972 (ref.c) $500.

061a: THE HONORARY CONSUL The Bodley
Head L (1973) [] Galleys printed on rectos only
(Gloucester Road Bookshop 3/92) $600.

061b: THE HONORARY CONSUL The Bodley
Head L (1973) [1] $15/60

061c: THE HONORARY CONSUL Simon &
Schuster   NY (1973) [1] Uncorrected proof in
yellow wraps with textual differences (Steven
Temple) $150.

061d: THE HONORARY CONSUL Simon &
Schuster NY (1973) [1] 9 1/2" tall in flint gray
cloth with gold lettering on spine (Wobbe A59b) $10/40

061e: THE HONORARY CONSUL Simon &
Schuster NY (1973) [1] Variant: 9 3/16" tall in
midnight blue cloth with red lettering (ref.b). This
latter state (which is also thinner and has matte
finished dustwrapper vs. glossy) seems much
scarcer to us as we have only seen one copy of this
and probably 100 copies of the other $50/75

062a: THE PORTABLE GRAHAM GREENE
Viking NY (1973) [1] Edited by Philip Stratford.
Contains enlarged *The Heart of the Matter* and
several essays collected for the first time. Pictorial
boards. Issued without dustwrapper $60.

062b: THE PORTABLE GRAHAM GREENE
Viking NY (1973) [1] Wraps $30.

063a: LORD ROCHESTER'S MONKEY Bodley
Head L (1974) [1] $15/60

063b: LORD ROCHESTER'S MONKEY Viking
Press NY (1974) [1] 15,000 cc $10/40

064a: AN IMPOSSIBLE WOMAN *The Memories
of Dottoressa Moor of Capri* The Bodley Head L
1975 [] Uncorrected Proof in pictorial wraps (David
Rees 11/94) $150.

064b: AN IMPOSSIBLE WOMAN *The Memories
of Dottoressa Moor of Capri* The Bodley Head L
(1975) [1] $10/40

064c: AN IMPOSSIBLE WOMAN *The Memories
of Dottoressa Moor of Capri* The Viking Press NY
(1976) [1] $15/60

   Note: there was a specially bound 1/2 leather
   binding by the publisher for the author
   catalogued by Gloucester Road Bookshop 3/89

064d: AN IMPOSSIBLE WOMAN *The Memories
of Dottoressa Moor of Capri* Bodley Head/Clarke
Irwin Toronto (1978) [] $10/40

065a: SHADES OF GREENE: THE TELEVISED
STORIES Bodley/Heinemann L (1975) [] Issued
without dustwrapper (ref.b) $50.

066a: THE RETURN OF A.J. RAFFLES *An
Edwardian Comedy* The Bodley Head L (1975) [2]
250 sgd no cc. (80 copies reserved for author's use -
Wm. Reese Co.) Issued in dustwrapper $350/400

066b: THE RETURN OF A.J. RAFFLES *An
Edwardian Comedy* The Bodley Head L (1975) [1]
Wraps $35.

066c: THE RETURN OF A.J. RAFFLES *An
Edwardian Comedy* Simon and Schuster NY
(1976) [3] $10/40

067a: A WEDDING AMONG THE OWLS   The
Bodley Head   L 1977 [2] 250 cc.   Wraps in
dustwrapper $400/600

068a: THE HUMAN FACTOR The Bodley Head
L (1978) [1] Publisher's device (figurehead) on title
page $35/75

068b: THE HUMAN FACTOR The Bodley Head
L (1978) [1] Publisher's initials "BH" on title page
(Jos. the Provider) $10/50

068c: THE HUMAN FACTOR   Simon and
Schuster NY   (1978) [3] Uncorrected proof in
yellow wraps $100.

068d: THE HUMAN FACTOR   Simon and
Schuster NY (1978) [3] $10/40

068e: THE HUMAN FACTOR   Franklin Library
Franklin Center (1978) [1] 064a, b&d were
published March 1978. Date of this edition
unknown but copyright copy received 4/14/78.
Bound in full leather (ref.b) $50.

069a: DR. FISCHER OF GENEVA *or The Bomb
Party* Bodley Head   L (1980) [1] (Ref.b.) First
issue with "leave alone" on p.9:4 (Nigel Williams
9/94) $10/40

069b: DOCTOR FISCHER OF GENEVA *or The
Bomb Party* Simon & Schuster NY (1980) [3]
Uncorrected proof in yellow wraps (ref.b) $75.

069c: DOCTOR FISCHER OF GENEVA *or The
Bomb Party* Simon & Schuster NY (1980) [2] 500
sgd no cc. Issued without dustwrapper in slipcase
(ref.b) $200/250

069d: DOCTOR FISCHER OF GENEVA *or The
Bomb Party* Simon & Schuster NY (1980) [3]
(ref.b) $10/30

070a: HOW FATHER QUIXOTE BECAME A
MONSIGNOR Sylvester & Orphanos LA 1980 [2]
4 sgd cc. Printed name of recipient. Issued in
acetate dustwrapper (ref.b) $600.

070b: HOW FATHER QUIXOTE BECAME A
MONSIGNOR Sylvester & Orphanos LA 1980 [2]
26 sgd ltr cc. Issued in acetate dustwrapper (ref.b) $400.

070c: HOW FATHER QUIXOTE BECAME A
MONSIGNOR Sylvester & Orphanos LA 1980 [2]
300 sgd no cc. Issued in acetate dustwrapper (ref.b) $250.

071a: WAYS OF ESCAPE Dennys (T 1980) [2] 53
sgd no cc. Leather bound, in slipcase (R.A. Gekosk) $600/750

071b: WAYS OF ESCAPE Dennys (T 1980) [2] 97
sgd no cc in slipcase. Green cloth (R.A. Gekoski).
Not clear which numbers were used in each issue $350/400

071c: WAYS OF ESCAPE Dennys (T 1980) [0]
Toronto edition precedes U.K. (ref.b) $15/60

071d: WAYS OF ESCAPE Bodley Head L (1980)
[1] (Ref.b) $15/50

071e: WAYS OF ESCAPE Simon & Schuster NY
(1981) [3] Uncorrected proof in yellow wraps
(ref.b) $100.

071f: WAYS OF ESCAPE Simon & Schuster NY
(1981) [3] 54,000 cc. (Published January 1981) $10/35

072a: THE GREAT JOWETT Bodley Head L
(1981) [2] 525 sgd no cc (ref.b). Issued in acetate
dustwrapper $100/250

072b: THE GREAT JOWETT   Bodley Head L
(1981) [1]   (Ref.b) (We have never seen this
catalogued and we get a lot of catalogs) $25/100

073a: MONSIGNOR QUIXOTE Dennys (T 1982)
[1] Toronto edition precedes U.K. (ref.b) $15/50

073b: MONSIGNOR QUIXOTE Bodley Head L
(1982) [1] (Ref.b) $10/40

073c: MONSIGNOR QUIXOTE   Simon &
Schuster NY (1982) [3] Uncorrected proof in
yellow wraps $100.

073d: MONSIGNOR QUIXOTE   Simon &
Schuster NY (1982) [2] 250 sgd no cc. Issued in
slipcase (Evlen Books) $200/250

073e: MONSIGNOR QUIXOTE   Simon and
Schuster NY (1982) [3] (Ref.b) $10/35

074a: J'ACCUSE: THE DARK SIDE OF NICE
Dennys (Montreal 1982) [0] Plain white wraps.
Issued in dustwrapper. French and English text.
"Les Editions (*Lem E'ac*)" on cover $50.

074b: J'ACCUSE: THE DARK SIDE OF NICE
Bodley Head L (1982) [1] Plain wraps and printed
dustwrapper (ref.c). (Beasley Books had a copy
priced in dollars, assume for distribution in U.S. or
Canada) $20/50

075a: ONE NOVEMBER DAY IN 1980... Bodley
Head   (L) no date   [2] 225 cc.   Wraps in
dustwrapper. Extracts from *This Other Man.* Issued
for private distribution (Dalian Books) $300.

076a: A QUICK LOOK BEHIND, FOOTNOTES
TO AN AUTOBIOGRAPHY   Sylvester &
Orphanos LA 1983 [2] 4 sgd cc. "Presentation
Copy." Recipient's name printed. Issued in slipcase
(Peter Selley 12/90) $500.

076b: A QUICK LOOK BEHIND, FOOTNOTES
TO AN AUTOBIOGRAPHY   Sylvester &
Orphanos LA 1983 [2] 26 sgd ltr cc. (Assume
issued in slipcase) $350.

076c: A QUICK LOOK BEHIND, FOOTNOTES
TO AN AUTOBIOGRAPHY Sylvester & Orphanos

LA 1983 [2] 300 sgd no cc. Issued in white cloth slipcase (Heritage Bookshop 10/90) $250.

077a: THE OTHER MAN Bodley Head L (1983) [] Uncorrected proof in yellow wraps (Dalian Books) $100.

077b: THE OTHER MAN Bodley Head L (1983) [1] Greene's conversations with Marie-Francoise Allain (ref.b). (Preceded by a French edition in 1981) $10/40

077c: THE OTHER MAN Simon & Schuster NY (1983) [3] 6,500 cc (ref.b) $10/40

078a: YES AND NO and FOR WHOM THE BELL CHIMES Bodley Head L (1983) [2] 750 sgd no cc (ref.b) $200.

078b: YES AND NO and FOR WHOM THE BELL CHIMES Bodley Head L (1983) [1] (Ref.b) $15/50

078c: YES AND NO *A Play in One Act* Eurographica Helsinki 1984 [2] 350 sgd no cc. Wraps. (Also 12 additional copies for the author) $350.

078d: YES AND NO *A Play in One Act* Eurographica Helsinki 1984 [] 2,000 cc. Wraps in dustwrapper. Text in English and Finnish $20/40

079a: GETTING TO KNOW THE GENERAL Bodley Head   L (1984) [1]   (Ref.b.) (Toronto edition reportedly preceded but since it was printed in Great Britain, we have placed it second) $10/40

079b: GETTING TO KNOW THE GENERAL Dennys (T 1984) [0] "Printed in Great Britain" $10/40

079c: GETTING TO KNOW THE GENERAL Simon & Schuster NY 1984 [3] Uncorrected proof in yellow wraps $75.

079d: GETTING TO KNOW THE GENERAL
Simon & Schuster NY 1984 [3] 34,200 cc $10/35

080a: THE MONSTER OF CAPRI   Eurographica
Helsinki 1985 [2] 500 sgd no cc. Issue in linen
dustwrapper (ref.c) $350/450

081a: THE TENTH MAN   (*The Mail* {Sunday} L
1985) [] Two thin volumes in wraps. Issued as
supplements on March 3rd and 10th $100.

081b: THE TENTH MAN   Dennys (T 1985) [1] No
dustwrapper price on the early copies $10/40

081c: THE TENTH MAN   Bodley Head   L   (1985)
[] Uncorrected proof in yellow wraps $75.

081d: THE TENTH MAN   Bodley Head   L   (1985)
[1] $10/40

081e: THE TENTH MAN   Simon & Schuster   NY
(1985) [3] Uncorrected proof in yellow wraps $60.

081f: THE TENTH MAN   Simon & Schuster   NY
(1985) [3]   Approximately 40,000 cc.   Introduction
and revised text of previously unpublished work $10/35

082a: GRAHAM GREENE COUNTRY   Pavilion
L (1986) [] Illustrated by Paul Hogarth $20/50

083a: THE CAPTAIN AND THE ENEMY   Dennys
(T 1988) []   Uncorrected proof in light blue wraps.
(Published September 1988 at $19.75) (Steven
Temple 9/91) $75.

083b: THE CAPTAIN AND THE ENEMY   Dennys
(T 1988) [] (Bev Chaney) $10/35

083c: THE CAPTAIN AND THE ENEMY
Reinhardt L 1988 [] (Hartley Moorhouse) $10/35

083d: THE CAPTAIN AND THE ENEMY Viking
NY 1988 [0] "Unrevised and unpublished proofs" in
blue printed wraps $60.

083e: THE CAPTAIN AND THE ENEMY Viking
NY 1988 [3] 40,000 cc (PW). Also states "First
American editon published in 1988" on copyright
page $10/30

084a: REFLECTIONS ON TRAVELS WITH MY
AUNT Firsts & Co. NY 1989 [2] 250 sgd no cc. In
flexible paper covered boards. Issued without
dustwrapper or slipcase $250.

085a: DEAR DAVID, DEAR GRAHAM Alembic
Press Oxford 1989 [2] 50 no cc. specially bound in
quarter leather in cloth slipcase $250.

085b: DEAR DAVID, DEAR GRAHAM Alembic
Press Oxford 1989 [2] 200 no cc (Words Etc. 9/89) $150.

086a: WHY THE EPIGRAPH? Nonesuch Press L
(1989) [2] 950 sgd no cc in acetate dustwrapper $175.

086b: WHY THE EPIGRAPH? Nonesuch Press L
(1989) [] Trade without limitation page (David Rees
5/92) $60.

087a: YOURS ETC. LETTERS TO THE PRESS
1945-1989 Reinhardt Books/Viking L/NY (1989)
[] $10/40

087b: YOURS ETC. LETTERS TO THE PRESS
1945-1989 Lester & Orpen Dennys T 1989 []
Simultaneously issued with the UK publication $10/40

088a: A WEED AMONG THE FLOWERS
Sylvester & Orphanos LA 1990 [2] 4 sgd cc. Each
with printed name of recipient. Miniature book with
preface by Stephen Spender, signed by both $500.

088b: A WEED AMONG THE FLOWERS
Sylvester & Orphanos LA 1990 [2] 26 sgd ltr cc $300.

088c: A WEED AMONG THE FLOWERS
Sylvester & Orphanos LA 1990 [2] 300 sgd no cc $250.

089a: THE LAST WORD *and Other Stories*
Reinhardt and Viking L 1990 [] $10/35

089b: THE LAST WORD *and Other Stories* Lester
& Orpen Dennys   (T 1990) [1] Simultaneously
issued with U.K. edition $10/35

089c: THE LAST WORD *and Other Stories*
Viking NY (1991) [] (Published February 1991 at
$18.95) $5/25

090a: REFLECTIONS Lester & Orpen Dennys (T
1990) [1] Simultaneously issued with U.K. edition $5/30

090b: REFLECTIONS Reinhardt L (1990) []
(Also seen with U.S. sticker pasted over U.K. price
on flap) $5/30

091a: CONVERSATIONS WITH GRAHAM
GREENE University Press of Mississippi Jackson
1992 [] (Published February 1992 at $32) $20/40

091b: CONVERSATIONS WITH GRAHAM
GREENE University Press of Mississippi Jackson
1992 [] Wraps. (Published February 1992 at $14.95) $20.

092a: A WORLD OF MY OWN Reinhardt L
1992 [] $5/25

093a: A DREAM DIARY Viking NY (1994) []
Uncorrected proof in gray wraps $50.

093b: A DREAM DIARY Viking NY (1994) [] $5/25

094a: THE GRAHAM GREENE FILM READER
Applause NY 1994 [] Uncorrected Proof in
yellow printed wraps (Waverly Books 12/94) $40.

094b: THE GRAHAM GREENE FILM READER
Applause NY 1994 [] $5/25

DAVIS GRUBB
(1919 - 1980)

Grubb was born in 1919 in Moundsville, West Virginia, a small town on the Ohio River where generations of his family had lived for 200 years.

001a: THE NIGHT OF THE HUNTER Harper (NY 1953) [2] 1,000 sgd cc. Trade edition with tipped-in page. Noted in dustwrapper with advance reviews on back and the regular trade dustwrapper as well as a plain glassine dustwrapper (Herb Yellin 3/90). Also with printed note about special edition tipped-in. Also dustwrapper verso devoted to promotional text (Beasley Books 5/91) $100/200

001b: THE NIGHT OF THE HUNTER Harper (NY 1953) [1] $35/175

001c: THE NIGHT OF THE HUNTER Hamish Hamilton L (1954) [1] $15/75

002a: A DREAM OF KINGS Scribners NY 1955 [5] $25/125

003a: ICEY AND WALT APPROVE OF PREACHER, JOHN DOESN'T, PEARL DOES (No publisher, place, or date) [2] 250 sgd cc. Broadside with black-and-white illustration by Grubb, signed by Grubb and Lillian Gish. We assume this was tied to movie of *The Night Of The Hunter* which was released in 1955 (Wilder Books #17) $125.

004a: THE WATCHMAN Scribners NY (1961)
[5] $12/60

004b: THE WATCHMAN Michael Joseph L
1962 [] Uncorrected Proof in wraps marked "for
inspection" and showing provisional publication
date as "20/8/62" and a provisional price of "16/"
(Nicholas Pounder 5/95) $75.

004c: THE WATCHMAN M. Joseph L (1962) [] $10/40

005a: THE VOICES OF GLORY Scribners NY
(1962) [5] "A.8.62[H]" $12/60

005b: THE VOICES OF GLORY Michael Joseph
L (1963) [1] $8/40

006a: TWELVE TALES OF SUSPENSE AND
THE SUPERNATURAL Scribners NY (1964) [5]
"A-2.64[V]" $30/150

007a: A TREE FULL OF STARS Mountain State
Press Richwood, W.Va. (1965) [] Presumed issued
without dustwrapper (L.W. Currey 7/91) $100.

007b: A TREE FULL OF STARS Scribners NY
(1965) [5] "A-8.65[V]" $15/75

008a: SHADOW OF MY BROTHER   Holt,
Rinehart & Winston NY (1966) [1] $10/50

008b: SHADOW OF MY BROTHER Hutchinson
L 1966 [] $8/40

009a: THE GOLDEN SICKLE: A TALE   World
NY (1968) [1] $15/75

010a: FOOL'S PARADE World NY (1969) [1] $8/40

010b: FOOL'S PARADE Hodder L 1971 [] $7/35

011a: THE BAREFOOT MAN Simon & Schuster
NY (1971) [1] $7/35

012a: THE SIEGE OF 318: *Thirteen Mystical Stories* Back Fork Books Webster Springs, W.Va. (1978) [0] $12/60

013a: ANCIENT LIGHTS Viking NY 1982 [] Uncorrected proof in yellow wraps $75.

013b: ANCIENT LIGHTS Viking NY 1982 [1] $25/75

013c: ANCIENT LIGHTS Viking NY 1982 [1] Wraps. Issued simultaneously $25.

014a: YOU NEVER BELIEVE ME *and Other Stories* St. Martin's NY (1989) [] (Published August 1989 at $16.95) $5/25

DASHIELL HAMMETT
(1894 - 1961)

Hammett was born on the Eastern Shore of Maryland. He left school at thirteen and his work in various occupations included eight years as a Pinkerton detective (before and after service in the Army). Among the celebrated cases he worked on were those of Nicky Arnstein and "Fatty" Arbuckle, and he won his first promotion by catching a man who had stolen a Ferris wheel (*Twentieth Century Authors*, Haycraft & Kunitz).

Hammett wrote screenplays during the 1930s and 1940s. He became politically active in the late thirties. In 1940 he became the National Chairman of the Committee on Election Rights, a group to promote the political candidacy of Communist Party members. He rejoined the Army in 1942 as a private and was honorably discharged as a sergeant in 1945. He taught mystery writing at the Jefferson School of Social Science from 1946 to 1956 and also served as the president of the New York Civil Rights Congress during this period. He was sentenced to six months in prison in 1951 for criminal contempt of court in connection with a case on the Civil Rights Congress bail fund. After his release his income was attached by the IRS.

Hammett had a heart attack in 1955 and died in January 1961. He is buried at Arlington National Cemetery.

REFERENCES:

(a) Bruccoli & Clark. FIRST PRINTINGS OF AMERICAN AUTHORS. Volume 1. Detroit: Gale Research (1977).

(b) Layman, Richard. DASHIELL HAMMETT A DESCRIPTIVE BIBLIOGRAPHY. (Pittsburgh): University of Pittsburgh, 1979.

(c) Layman, Richard. SHADOW MAN. New York: Harcourt, Brace, Jovanovich (1981).

001a: RED HARVEST Knopf NY/L 1929 [0] $750/5,000

002a: THE DAIN CURSE Knopf NY/L 1929 [0]
"dopped in" for "dropped in" 260:19 (may be in all
copies of the first edition) $750/5,000

002b: THE DAIN CURSE Knopf NY/L 1930 [1]
"First published 1930..." Ref.b A2.1.d states this is
the fourth printing and first English edition, it also
calls for a skull and crossbones on front upper right
hand corner but also noted without this (Nicholas
Pounder 5/90). (Priority unknown) $300/2,000

003a: THE MALTESE FALCON Knopf NY/L
1930 [0]   Haycraft-Queen Cornerstone. (Sold for
$27,000 plus 10% commission at auction in 1992) $1,000/15,000

003b: THE MALTESE FALCON   Knopf L/NY
1930 [0] $600/3,000

003c: THE MALTESE FALCON Modern Library
NY (1934) [1] Adds new introduction by Hammett $30/150

003d: THE MALTESE FALCON   Pocket Books
NY (1944) [1] Wraps in dustwrapper $15/75

003e: THE MALTESE FALCON Arion Press SF
1983 [2] 400 no. cc. Issued in slipcase $500/550

003f: THE MALTESE FALCON North Point Press
San Francisco 1984 [] $10/40

003g: THE MALTESE FALCON Franklin Library
Franklin Center   (1987)   [2] Limited Edition.
Illustrated with stills from the film. Decorated
leather $100.

004a: THE GLASS KEY Knopf L/NY 1931 [0] $500/3,000

004b: THE GLASS KEY Knopf NY/L 1931 [0] $250/2,000

005a: CREEPS BY NIGHT   John Day Company
NY (1931) [0] Selected and introduction by
Hammett $60/300

005b: MODERN TALES OF HORROR   Gollancz
L 1932 [0] New title $60/300

006a: THE THIN MAN   Knopf   NY 1934 [1] No
priority on dustwrapper color. "There are four
dustwrapper variants" (Pepper & Stern 3/92) but
not described. We know of two with and without
front flap blurbs in red and green. Also noted in
"Book-of-the-Month Club" wrap-around band
(Paul Rassam 1/91) $300/2,000

006b: SIX REDBOOK NOVELS   (McCall   NY
1934) [0] Includes *The Thin Man*. Issued without
dustwrapper, from plates from *Redbook* appearance
(Dec. 1933) $125.

006c: THE THIN MAN   Barker L 1934 [1] $200/1,000

007a: SECRET AGENT X-9 (BOOK ONE)
McKay   Ph (1934) [0]   Printed boards (no
dustwrapper). Illustrated by Alex Raymond $1,500.

008a: SECRET AGENT X-9 (BOOK TWO)
McKay   Ph (1934) [0]   Printed boards (no
dustwrapper). Illustrated by Alex Raymond $1,000.

009a: SECRET AGENT X-9   Nostalgia Press, Inc.
NY (1976) [0] Combines all of Book One and Two
and adds new material from newspaper publication
of the comic strip $60.

010a: DASHIELL HAMMETT OMNIBUS   Knopf
NY   1935 [1] "Published August 12, 1935" on
copyright page.   Contains *Red Harvest*, *The Dain
Curse* and *The Maltese Falcon* $30/150

011a: THE COMPLETE DASHIELL HAMMETT
Knopf   NY 1942   [1]   One volume edition.
"Published July 20, 1942" on copyright page. Con-

tains *Red Harvest, The Dain Curse, The Maltese Falcon, The Glass Key* and *The Thin Man* $30/150

012a: $106,000 BLOOD MONEY Lawrence E. Spivak (NY 1943) [0] Wraps. Bestseller Mystery No. B40. "The Big Knockover" and "$106,000 Blood Money" collected as a novel $125.

012b: THE BIG KNOCK-OVER Lawrence E. Spivak (NY 1961) [0] #J36. New title. Later reprint (Nelson Freck 11/90). Also see 025a $25.

013a: THE BATTLE OF THE ALEUTIANS "...29th Engineers..." (Adak AL/SF 1944) [0] Blue wraps. Text by Hammett, captions by Robert Colodny $300.

014a: THE ADVENTURES OF SAM SPADE *and Other Stories* Spivak (NY 1944) [0] Wraps. Introduction by Ellery Queen. Queen's Quorum $175.

014b: THE ADVENTURES OF SAM SPADE *and Other Stories* World Cleveland/NY (1945) [] First cloth bound $35/175

014c: THEY CAN ONLY HANG YOU ONCE Spivak/American Mercury NY (1949) [0] Wraps. New title. "A Mercury Mystery" $40.

015a: THE CONTINENTAL OP Spivak (NY 1945) [0] Medium greenish-blue wraps. Introduction by Ellery Queen. "Bestseller Mystery No. B62" $175.

016a: THE RETURN OF THE CONTINENTAL OP Spivak (NY 1945) [0] Red wraps. Introduction by Ellery Queen. "Jonathan Press Mystery #J17" $150.

017a: HAMMETT HOMICIDES Spivak (NY 1946) [0] Yellow-green wraps. Introduction by Ellery Queen. "Bestseller Mystery No. B81" $150.

018a: DEAD YELLOW WOMEN Spivak (NY 1947) [0] Green wraps. Introduction by Ellery Queen. "Jonathan Press Mystery No. J29". Price of 25¢ on front cover (Mordida Books 6/95) $150.

019a: NIGHTMARE TOWN Spivak NY (1948) [0] Reddish-brown wraps. Introduction by Ellery Queen. "A Mercury Book, No. 120" $125.

020a: THE CREEPING SIAMESE Spivak (NY 1950) [0] Red wraps. Introduction by Ellery Queen. "Jonathan Press Mystery No. J48" $100.

021a: THE DASHIELL HAMMETT OMNIBUS Cassell L (1950) [1] Contains *The Thin Man*, *The Maltese Falcon*, *The Glass Key*, *The Dain Curse*, *Red Harvest* and four short stories $30/150

022a: WOMAN IN THE DARK Spivak (NY 1951) [0] Dark bluish-green wraps. Introduction by Ellery Queen. "Jonathan Press Mystery No. 59" $125.

022b: WOMAN IN THE DARK Knopf NY (1988) [1] Uncorrected proof in green wraps (Waverly Books 11/88). Lime green wraps (Monroe Stahr 12/94) $60.

022c: WOMAN IN THE DARK Knopf NY 1988 [1] (publ 9/88 at $15.95) 25,000 cc (PW). Robert Parker Appreciation $6/30

022d: WOMAN IN THE DARK Headline (L 1988) [1] $6/30

023a: A MAN NAMED THIN *And Other Stories* Ferman (NY 1962) [0] Soft greenish-blue wraps. Edited and with introduction by Ellery Queen. "Mercury Mystery No. 233" $100.

024a: THE NOVELS OF DASHIELL HAMMETT Knopf NY 1965 [1] "Published October 1965" on copyright page $15/60

025a: THE BIG KNOCKOVER   Random House NY (1966) [] Uncorrected proof in spiral bound blue wraps (Waiting For Godot 7/89) $400.

025b: THE BIG KNOCKOVER   Random House NY (1966) [1]   Edited and introduction by Lillian Hellman. Includes first appearance of "Tulip" $25/100

025c: DASHIELL HAMMETT STORY OMNI-BUS   Cassell   L (1966) [1] Edited and with introduction by Lillian Hellman. "F.766" on copyright page $25/75

026a: BOOK REVIEWS WHICH APPEARED IN SATURDAY REVIEW OF LITERATURE   No publisher   Portage, Indiana   1969 [] Brown cloth boards, gold spine lettering; issued without dustwrapper. Not For Sale. Fewer than 30 copies, produced as printing exercise (ref.b) $NVA

027a: THE CONTINENTAL OP   Random House NY (1974) [4] $15/60

027b: THE CONTINENTAL OP   Macmillan   (L 1975) [1] $10/50

027c: THE CONTINENTAL OP   Franklin Library Franklin Center 1984 [2] "Limited Edition" in full leather $75.

028a: THE DIAMOND WAGER   as Samuel Dashiell   No publisher   Portage, Indiana   1977 []About 10 copies. Unbound sheets. Not For Sale. Produced as printing exercise. Originally appeared in October, 1929, issue of *Detective Fiction Weekly* under pseudonym Samuel Dashiell $NVA

029a: THE CRUSADER   D'Ambrosio   Sherman Oaks, CA (1980) [2] 5 sgd no artist's proofs. Signed by the artist. First separate appearance of this story which appeared in August 1923 issue of *The Smart Set* under the name "Mary Jane Hammett." Miniature in slipcase $200.

028b: THE CRUSADER   D'Ambrosio   Sherman
Oaks, CA (1980) [2] 85 sgd no cc. Signed by the
artist $125.

Ernest Hemingway signature

ERNEST HEMINGWAY
(1899 - 1961)

Hemingway started his career as a newspaperman and foreign correspondent in Paris in the 1920s. He was one of the most prominent members of the "lost generation," which he documented in *The Sun Also Rises*, his first major success. He was in Spain in the late 1930s and a correspondent during W.W.II. His style was, and still is, very influential on many modern prose writers. He received a Pulitzer for *The Old Man and the Sea* and a Nobel Prize in 1954.

REFERENCES:

(a) Cohn, Louis Henry. A BIBLIOGRAPHY OF THE WORKS OF ERNEST HEMINGWAY. New York: Random House, 1931. (Used for information through 1930.)

(b) Hanneman, Andre. ERNEST HEMINGWAY, A COMPREHENSIVE BIBLIOGRAPHY. Princeton University Press, Princeton, 1967; and A SUPPLEMENT TO... Princeton: Princeton University Press, 1975. (Used for the balance except where noted.)

(c) Inventory or catalog entries.

(d) Matthew J. Bruccoli and C. E. Frazer Clark, Jr., editors. FIRST PRINTINGS OF AMERICAN AUTHORS. Volume 1. Detroit, Michigan: Gale Research Co. (1977).

(e) THE MARCIA AND JOHN GOIN ERNEST HEMINGWAY COLLECTION. Santa Barbara: Joseph the Provider Books, 1992.

001a: THREE STORIES & TEN POEMS (Contact Paris 1923) [0] 300 cc. Wraps. Issued in a glassine dustwrapper. Also a copy with poems in different sequence than ref.b (Maurice Neville) $20,000.

001b: THREE STORIES & TEN POEMS Bruccoli/Clark Bloomfield Hills (1977) [2] 3,000 cc. In dustwrapper. Facsimile edition (ref.c) $40/100

002a: in our time (sic) Three Mountains Press Paris 1924 [2] 170 no cc. Issued in boards $17,500.

002b: IN OUR TIME: STORIES Boni & Liveright NY 1925 [0] 1,335 cc. New title. Revised and enlarged $1,000/6,000

002c: IN OUR TIME: STORIES Cape L (1926) [1] Textual changes in 2 stories. Green cloth, gold stamped (ref.b); dark blue cloth, spine lettering in white and no blind stamping (Glenn Horowitz #8 and R.A. Gekoski #2, and David Mayou #19). Blue cloth is the remainder binding (Ergo Books 4/92) $600/3,000

002d: IN OUR TIME: STORIES Scribners NY 1930 [0] 3,240 cc. Copyright page must contain publisher's seal (ref.c). Adds new Hemingway material and introduction by Edmund Wilson $300/1,500

002e: in our time (sic): STORIES Bruccoli/Clark Bloomfield Hills (1977) [2] 1,700 cc. Facsimile. Issued in dustwrapper (ref.c) $50/125

003a: THE TORRENTS OF SPRING Scribners NY 1926 [0] 1,250 cc. Publisher's seal on copyright page (ref.d). Bound in dark green cloth. Ref.e noted a copy in black cloth with a dustwrapper clearly printed in 1928 or later, although otherwise exactly the same. $800/4,000

003b: THE TORRENTS OF SPRING Crosby Continental Eds. Paris 1932 [0] Wraps. Large paper edition 7 1/2" x 5 5/8" priced at 125 francs. Some issued with cellophane wrapper asking "Have you read this Hemingway?" Colophon states it was published in December 1931 $400.

003c: THE TORRENTS OF SPRING Crosby Continental Eds. Paris 1932 [0] Wraps. Small paper

edition 6 1/16" x 4 3/4" priced 10 francs. Has open
letter to E.H. by Caresse Crosby $200.

003d: THE TORRENTS OF SPRING   Cape L
(1933) [1] $200/850

004a: TODAY IS FRIDAY (The As Stable Publ.
Englewood, NJ 1926) [2] 300 no cc. Wraps. "260
for sale..."   Pamphlet, issued in printed white
envelope (ref.b); blue envelope (Jos. the Provider
#26) $3,000.

005a: THE SUN ALSO RISES   Scribners   NY
1926 [0] 5,090 cc (5a & 5b). Publisher's seal.
P.181:26 "stoppped" vs "stopped". Dustwrapper
error "In Our Times" vs. "In Our Time" $750/17,500

005b: THE SUN ALSO RISES   Scribners   NY
1926 [0]   P.181:26 corrected.   Second   issue
dustwrapper listing "In Our Time" $300/2,500

005c: FIESTA Cape L (1927) [1] New title $500/5,000

005d: THE SUN ALSO RISES   Franklin Library
Franklin Center 1977 [] Illustrated by Stan Hunter $75.

005e: THE SUN ALSO RISES   Omnigraphics
Detroit   1990   [0] 712 cc. Edited by Matthew
Bruccoli. A facsimile of the manuscript with
thousands   of   unpublished   words   and   an
unpublished introduction explaining   "The Lost
Generation."   2   volumes.   Issued   without
dustwrapper $250.

006a: MEN WITHOUT WOMEN Scribners NY
1927 [0] 7,650 cc (6a, b & c). Earliest state. Book
(printed on 80-pound paper) weighing more than
15.8 oz. and with perfect folio "3" on page 3. Issued
in tan dustwrapper with black lettering, with no
blurbs in the three orange bands across the front.
(There were trial dustwrappers which were printed
on gray paper. Front flap had original $2.00 price

but was otherwise blank. The back flap and rear panel also blank. The trial dustwrapper may well have accompanied a few early copies sent out for review {Ref.e}). $600/3,500

006b: MEN WITHOUT WOMEN Scribners NY 1927 [0] 2,200 of the 7,650 copies that had 128 pages of the text on 70-pound paper resulting in a weight of about 15 ounces $400/3,000

006c: MEN WITHOUT WOMEN Scribners NY 1927 [0] Second printing on 65-pound stock weighing 13 to 14 oz. Dustwrapper has two extracts from reviews on front panel and publisher comments on this book on front flap $150/750

006d: MEN WITHOUT WOMEN Cape L (1928) [1] Slight textual changes $250/1,250

006e: MEN WITHOUT WOMEN World NY (1946) [1] First illustrated edition. Illustrated by John Groth with a note by him on E.H. $15/75

007a: A FAREWELL TO ARMS Scribners NY 1929 [] Wraps. Uncorrected long galley proofs 6"x24" (Pepper & Stern #18) $10,000.

007b: A FAREWELL TO ARMS Scribners (NY 1929) [] Trial Dummy in full brown cloth with gilt lettered leather spine label. ($1,900 at auction in 1994) $3,500.

007c: A FAREWELL TO ARMS Scribners NY 1929 [2] 510 sgd no cc. Boxed. 10 copies "Not For Sale," 500 copies for sale. Issued and signed simultaneously with first regular edition $6,500/7,500

007d: A FAREWELL TO ARMS Scribners NY 1929 [0] 31,050 cc. Copyright page contains publisher's seal. No disclaimer on p.[x] ("None of these characters..."). First printing dustwrapper has blurb on front flap reading "Katharine Barclay" instead of the correct spelling, "Catherine Barkley".

May have also been misspelled on later dustwrappers — $300/1,500

007e: A FAREWELL TO ARMS Scribners NY 1929 [0] Second printing with disclaimer — $50/350

007f: A FAREWELL TO ARMS Cape L (1929) [1] Printed gray wraps. Advance copy. Also noted in buff wraps (Glenn Horowitz 5/94) — $2,000

007g: A FAREWELL TO ARMS Cape L (1929) [1] P.66:28 "seriosu" (ref.d) Also noted with wrap-around band with quote by Arnold Bennett (R.A. Gekoski #7) — $150/750

007h: A FAREWELL TO ARMS Cape L (1929) [1] With error corrected — $50/500

007i: A FAREWELL TO ARMS Scribners NY 1948 [0] Publisher's Dummy in same cloth as published book with 10 leaves on which are pasted the title, chapter heading page, two pages of text and eight of the 29 Rasmusson illustrations (ref.e) — $600.

007j: A FAREWELL TO ARMS Scribners NY 1948 [5] 5,300 cc. New introduction by the author and illustrations by Daniel Rasmusson (issued without dustwrapper in slipcase) — $150/500

007k: A FAREWELL TO ARMS Franklin Library Franklin Center 1975 [2] Limited Edition — $60.

008a: INTRODUCTION TO KIKI OF MONT-PARNASSE Edward W. Titus NY 1929 [0] 25 cc. Wraps. 8 pages with front cover as title. Wire stitched — $4,500.

008b: KIKI'S MEMOIRS Edward W. Titus Paris 1930 [0] 1,000 cc. Stiff paper wraps with wrap-around band. Hemingway introduction. Issued in glassine wrapper and unprinted, cardboard mailing slipcase — $350.

009a: FOUR POEMS (House of Books NY 1930)
[] 12 cc. Unpublished. Galley proofs only (ref.c) $5,000.

010a: ("BASTARD NOTE") (House of Books NY
1931) [2] 93 no. cc. Broadside Facsimile of the
proof of legal disclaimer from *A Farewell to Arms*.
Also an unnumbered copy (Wm. Reese Co. 2/91) $850.

011a: DEATH IN THE AFTERNOON Scribners
NY 1932 [5] 25 cc. Salesman's dummy in black
cloth $6,000.

011b: DEATH IN THE AFTERNOON Scribners
NY 1932 [] Advance copy in plain brown wraps,
sewn unbound sheets including all photographs and
the frontis. In dustwrapper (proof?). Only known
advance proof copy (Thomas A. Goldwasser 10/94) $7,500.

011c: DEATH IN THE AFTERNOON Scribners
NY 1932 [5] 10,300 cc $300/1,750

011d: DEATH IN THE AFTERNOON Cape L
(1932) [] Wraps. Advance proof in green printed
wraps $2,000.

011e: DEATH IN THE AFTERNOON Cape L
(1932) [1] $150/750

012a: GOD REST YOU MERRY GENTLEMEN
House of Books NY 1933 [2] 300 no cc $1,250.

013a: STORIES (TITLE TO BE DETERMINED)
Scribners NY 1933 [] 30 cc. Saleman's dummy in
black cloth and gray dustwrapper with blue lettering $5,000.

013b: WINNER TAKE NOTHING Scribners
NY/L 1933 [5] 20,300 cc. First appearance of 6
of the stories $200/1,000

013c: WINNER TAKE NOTHING Cape L (1934)
[1] $125/650

014a: QUINTANILLA Pierre Matisse Gallery NY (1934) [] Folio sheet folded to make 6 pages with long essay by Hemingway. 6 1/8" x 9 3/4" folded size (Between the Covers 11/90). We had a copy that was 6 1/8" x 9 3/8". Hanneman B16 calls for 3 1/8" x 6 7/8" which apparently is wrong $500.

015a: GREEN HILLS OF AFRICA Scribners NY 1935 [] 30 cc. Salesman's dummy in green cloth. Contains photo and "cast of characters" omitted in the book. Issued in dustwrapper with different type than published version $6,000/7,500

015b: GREEN HILLS OF AFRICA Scribners NY 1935 [5] 10,550 cc. Spine is usually faded or discolored, estimates assume better than usual condition. Normal fading would probably reduce price by half $350/1,250

015c: GREEN HILLS OF AFRICA Cape L (1936) [1] Includes dedicatory letter not in U.S. edition $150/750

016a: TO HAVE AND HAVE NOT Scribners NY 1937 [5] 30 cc. Salesman's dummy with title "To Have and To Have Not". Issued in dustwrapper $5,000/6,000

016b: TO HAVE AND HAVE NOT Scribners NY 1937 [5] 10,130 cc $200/850

016c: TO HAVE AND HAVE NOT Cape L (1937) [1] Top edge stained blue (ref.b); also unstained (Maurice Neville #8) $125/600

017a: THE SPANISH EARTH   J.B. Savage Cleveland 1938 [2] 1,000 no cc (a&b). Pictorial endpapers showing F.A.I. banner estimated at 50 to 100 of the 1,000 copies. Glassine dustwrapper $1,500.

017b: THE SPANISH EARTH   J.B. Savage Cleveland 1938 [2] Second issue has plain endpapers and Hemingway disclaimer on rear pastedown. In glassine dustwrapper $650.

018a: THE FIRST 48 Scribners NY 1938 [5] 30
cc. Salesman's dummy issued in white dustwrapper
marked: "Permanent Jacket in Preparation" $6,0007,500

018b: THE FIFTH COLUMN AND THE FIRST
FORTY-NINE STORIES Scribners NY 1938 [5]
5,350 cc. New title. First appearance of "The Fifth
Column" and 4 uncollected stories $300/1,500

018c: THE FIFTH COLUMN AND THE FIRST
FORTY-NINE STORIES Cape L (1939) [] Proof
in printed green wraps (John De Paovo 12/90) $1,000.

018d: THE FIFTH COLUMN AND THE FIRST
FORTY-NINE STORIES Cape L (1939) [1] Two
bindings, light brown cloth stamped in black (ref.b).
Also stamped in red (ref.d). No known priority $125/600

019a: THE SPANISH WAR Fact L 1938 [0]
Wraps. The July issue of *Fact* magazine with 72 of
98 pages by Hemingway $300.

020a: THE FIFTH COLUMN *A Play in Three Acts*
Scribners NY 1938 [5] 30 cc. Salesman's dummy in
black cloth. Dustwrapper not mentioned in ref.b $5,000.

020b: THE FIFTH COLUMN *A Play in Three Acts*
Scribners NY 1940 [5] 1,174 cc. First separate
edition $600/3,000

020c: THE FIFTH COLUMN Penguin Harmonds-
worth 1966 [] Wraps $50.

020d: THE FIFTH COLUMN Cape L (1968) []
First separate U.K. hardback edition with a preface
comprising only that text from the original 1938
preface referring to the play(ref.e) $25/75

020e: THE FIFTH COLUMN AND FOUR
STORIES OF THE SPANISH CIVIL WAR Chas.
Scribner's Sons NY (1969) [] Uncorrected galley
proof in spiral bound wraps (Wm. Reese Co. 5/89)

Hemingway's name does not appear on either the wrapper or the title page $1,250.

020f: THE FIFTH COLUMN AND FOUR STORIES OF THE SPANISH CIVIL WAR Chas. Scribner's Sons NY (1969) [5] 15,000 cc. Possibly including a second printing before publication (ref.b). 4 stories previously "uncollected." States "A-8.69(C)" on copyright page $30/150

021a: THE GREAT CRUSADE Longmans, Green & Co. NY 1940 [0] Wraps and dustwrapper. Preface by Hemingway to Gustav Regler's book. Published in June or July as a promotional piece for book, which was published in September. Includes title page, picture of author, biography, blank, Hemingway preface vii - xi (xii blank), xiii (contents), (xiv), 3-6 (text). Stapled in dustwrapper of published book (ref.c) $350.

022a: FOR WHOM THE BELL TOLLS Scribners NY 1940 [5] 15 cc. Wraps. Unrevised proofs in brown paper covers for BOMC judges. Last two chapters omitted $7,500.

022b: FOR WHOM THE BELL TOLLS Scribners NY 1940 [5] 30 cc. Salesman's dummy in white dustwrapper with red lettering and statement "Permanent Jacket in Preparation" (ref. e) $5,000/6,000

022c: FOR WHOM THE BELL TOLLS Scribners NY 1940 [] 15 cc. Advance copy. Bound uncut in same cloth as trade edition. 8 5/8" x 5 3/4" vs. 8 1/4" x 5 5/8" for published edition $2,000.

022d: FOR WHOM THE BELL TOLLS Scribners NY 1940 [5] 75,000 cc (d&e). Photographer's name missing from back panel of dustwrapper $75/750

022e: FOR WHOM THE BELL TOLLS Scribners NY 1940 [5] With photographer's name on back panel $75/250

022f: FOR WHOM THE BELL TOLLS Cape L
(1940) [] Uncorrected Proof in printed wraps with
the earlier date of 1940 on copyright page $1,000.

022g: FOR WHOM THE BELL TOLLS Cape L
(1941) [1] (Noted with Book Society wrap-around
band - Maurice Neville #13) $100/500

022h: FOR WHOM THE BELL TOLLS Limited
Editions Club   Princeton University Press
Princeton 1942 [] Uncorrected Proof in plain blue
wraps (ref. e) $500.

022i: FOR WHOM THE BELL TOLLS Limited
Editions Club   Princeton University Press
Princeton 1942 [2] 15 cc for presentation by the
author stating "One of 15 Presentation Copies 'Out
of Series'" $1,500.

022j: FOR WHOM THE BELL TOLLS Limited
Editions Club   Princeton University Press
Princeton 1942 [2] 1,500 cc. Signed by Lynd Ward,
the illustrator. Issued in slipcase $200/300

023a: MEN AT WAR *The Best War Stories of All
Time* Crown NY (1942) [5] 20,500 cc. Edited and
with introduction by Hemingway $60/300

023b: MEN AT WAR *The Best War Stories of All
Time* Crown NY (1955) [] "New Edition Published
1955." Author's introduction edited for this edition $15/75

024a: VOYAGE TO VICTORY *An Eye-Witness
Report of The Battle for a Normandy Beachhead*
(Crowell-Collier NY 1944) [0] Wraps. A
promotional booklet (Printed in July 1944). Mottled
gray paper covers.   Wire-stapled. Yellow
dustwapper printed in red, black and white. $1,250/2,500

025a: THE VIKING PORTABLE HEMINGWAY
Viking Press NY 1944 [1] 20,000 cc. Edited by
Malcolm Cowley (Published September 18, 1944) $50/250

026a: SELECTED SHORT STORIES Editions for Armed Services NY no date [1945] [0] 57,000 cc. Wraps. No. K-9. Believe to have been issued in 1945 .... $150.

027a: THE PORTABLE HEMINGWAY Cape L (1946) [] Proof in printed wraps. Never published under this title (ref.e) .... $300.

027b: THE ESSENTIAL HEMINGWAY Cape L (1947) [1] New title $30/150

028a: ACROSS THE RIVER AND INTO THE TREES Cape L (1950) [1] Wraps. Advance copies in printed wrappers .... $1,000.

028b: ACROSS THE RIVER AND INTO THE TREES Cape L (1950) [1] Precedes American by 3 days $50/250

028c: ACROSS THE RIVER AND INTO THE TREES Scribners NY 1950 [5] Wraps. Unrevised proofs for review .... $1,000.

028d: ACROSS THE RIVER AND INTO THE TREES Scribners NY 1950 [5] 75,000 cc. First issue dustwraper with yellow lettering on spine $40/250

028e: ACROSS THE RIVER AND INTO THE TREES Scribners NY 1950 [5] Second issue of dustwrapper with orange lettering on spine $40/200

028f: ACROSS THE RIVER AND INTO THE TREES Scribners NY 1950 [] 25 cc. Blue cloth, "Advance Copies" run off later from discarded plates with a number of typos .... $200.

029a: SELECTED STORIES (Cape L 1951) [1] First Travelers' Library edition. Contains 19 stories (ref.e) $15/75

030a: THE OLD MAN AND THE SEA *Life Magazine* NY (1952) [] 5,000 cc. Uncorrected galley proofs (entire text). Long, unbound sheets, folded twice. Stamped "Advance Galley Proofs | For Your Personal Reading Only | *Life* Publication Date, Sept. 1" $500.

030b: THE OLD MAN AND THE SEA *Life Magazine* XXXIII (September 1, 1952) [0] Wraps. Preceded book publication by eleven days $75.

030c: THE OLD MAN AND THE SEA Scribners NY 1952 [5] 30 cc. First sets of sheets bound for presentation in black buckram. Pages untrimmed (ref.a). Page edges trimmed (ref.e). Issued in dustwrapper $5,000.

030d: THE OLD MAN AND THE SEA Scribners NY 1952 [5] 50,000 cc. Two lines of production symbols end of text on rear dustwrapper flap (ref.a but never seen). (BOMC dustwrapper has symbols on end of text and their trademark appears on front flap.) Deep blue ink in Hemingway photo changed to olive in later states $150/750

030e: THE OLD MAN AND THE SEA Cape L 1952 [] Uncorrected Proof in printed brown publisher's wraps (Anthony Sillem 10/94) $1,000.

030f: THE OLD MAN AND THE SEA Cape L (1952) [1] First edition dustwrapper not printed on both sides. (Later issue dustwrapper has art on one side and excerpts and reviews on the other) $40/200

030g: THE OLD MAN AND THE SEA Reprint Society London (1953) [] First illustrated edition. 16 drawings by C.F. Tunnicliffe and 18 by Raymond Sheppard $25/125

030h: THE OLD MAN AND THE SEA Scribner's NY (1960) [5] "A-9.60(Q)" on copyright page First U.S. illustrated edition (same illustrations as in 030g) $25/100

030i: THE OLD MAN AND THE SEA   Franklin
Library, Franklin Center, 1975 [] "Limited edition"
in full blue leather $75.

030j: THE OLD MAN AND THE SEA   Limited
Editions Club   NY (1990) [2] 600 sgd no cc.
Illustrated with photogravures by Alfred Eisenstaedt
and signed by him. Full leather in clam shell box.
(There were 30 signed numbred sets of the
photogravures sold separately) $1,000.

031a: THE HEMINGWAY READER   Scribner's
NY 1953 [5] 15,850 cc. First appearance in book
form of "The Fable of the Good Lion." Introduction
and preface by Charles Poore. Errata slip tipped-in
(ref.e) $35/175

032a: THE COLLECTED POEMS   (Pirated
edition. No place or date) [0] Wraps. Number One
of The Library of Living Poetry. 9" x 6". White
paper covers of same weight as pages. Wire stapled.
Printed without permission of the author $100.

032b: THE COLLECTED POEMS (Pirated edition.
No place or date) [0] 5" x 7 1/4".   White paper
covers of same weight as pages with Hemingway
portrait on inside cover and photo on back (Also
noted in heavy lavender printed wraps with order of
poems different, back cover blank -per ref.c) $60.

032c: THE COLLECTED POEMS   (Pirated
edition) S.F. 1960   [] Hemingway portrait across
from title page; back cover blank except for "50
cents" on left upper corner. (Actually published by
Haskell House circa 1967) $40.

032d: THE COLLECTED POEMS Haskell House
NY 1970   [] First hardbound edition. Reprint of
032c. Adds Haskell House imprint on title page.
Issued without dustwrapper (ref.e) $100.

032e: THE SUPPRESSED POEMS OF ERNEST HEMINGWAY (No publisher, place or date) [0] Wraps. Number one of The Library of Living Poets. 6 3/4" x 4 3/4" White margin around photo on back cover. Assume this is same book with new title (Watermark West 5/89) $25.

033a: HEMINGWAY'S FIRST PICTURE STORY (*Colliers Magazine* NY 1954) [0] 16 pp. Offprint $2,000.

034a: TWO CHRISTMAS TALES The Hart Press (Berkeley) 1959 [2] 150 cc. Wraps. Not For Sale. Originally appeared in the *Toronto Star Weekly* 12/22/23 $1,250.

035a: ETCHED PORTRAITS OF E.H. Apiary Press Northampton 1961 [2] 50 sgd no cc. Seven etchings by Carol Heimburg with extract from E.H.'s *Banal Story*. Signed by the artist $750.

036a: THE SNOWS OF KILIMANJARO *and Other Stories* Scribner's NY (1961) [5] Wraps. "A-1.61(C)" on copyright page. Includes "My Old Man". (Reprinted in 1962 with same storie as 37b $100.

036b: THE SNOWS OF KILIMANJARO *and Other Stories* Scribner's NY 1962 [] 4 new stories added and 2 deleted. Green cloth in dustwrapper $50/200

036c: THE SNOWS OF KILIMANJARO Penguin Harmondsworth 1963 [1] Wraps. (Published 2/21/63 at 3/6.) "This selection published...1963" $75.

037a: THE KILLERS *and Other Stories* V. Verlag Ferdinand... (Germany 1966) [] Wraps. Issued as "Sckoninchs Englische Lesebogen" but text is in English. First of this collection (Waiting For Godot) $200.

038a: THE WILD YEARS (Dell NY 1962) [1] 127,673 cc. Wraps. First Edition paperback #3577. Edited by Gene Z. Hanrahan $50.

039a: THREE NOVELS OF ERNEST HEMINGWAY Scribner's NY (1962) [5] "A-5.62[COL] on copyright page. Includes *The Sun Also Rises,* with introduction by Malcolm Cowley; *A Farewell to Arms,* with introduction by Robert Penn Warren; and *The Old Man and the Sea* with introduction by Carlos Baker (ref. e) $50/200

040a: THE SHORT HAPPY LIFE OF FRANCIS MACOMBER Penguin Harmondsworth 1963 [] Wraps $100.

041a: A MOVEABLE FEAST Cape London (1964) [] Advance excerpt issued to promote first UK edition. Wraps. Text on rectos. Precedes all other forms of text (ref.e) $200.

041b: A MOVEABLE FEAST Scribners NY (1964) [] Spiral bound galley proofs in proof of dustwrapper (Pepper & Stern). Also spiral bound in publisher's blue wraps with orange label affixed to front cover. 5½" x 11" (James Cummins 12/94). (Same??) $1250.

041c: A MOVEABLE FEAST Scribners NY (1964) [5] 85,000 cc. "A-3.64[H]" on copyright page $25/100

041d: A MOVABLE FEAST Cape L (1964) [] "Uncorrected proof" in green decorated wraps with title as "Movable". (Laid into a proof dustwrapper {ref.e}) $400.

041e: A MOVEABLE FEAST Jonathan Cape L (1964) [1] Noted with both white and brown endpapers but it looks more like pale rose-brown speckled with white. Priority unknown $15/75

042a: *Excerpts From* BY-LINE: ERNEST HEMINGWAY *Selected Articles and Dispatches of ...* Scribners NY (1967) [] Wraps. Stapled promotional pamphlet, eight pages $300.

042b: BY-LINE: ERNEST HEMINGWAY *Selected Articles and Dispatches of* .... (Scribner's NY 1967) [] Uncorrected Proof in spiral-bound blue wraps (James Cummins 12/94) $500.

042c: BY-LINE: ERNEST HEMINGWAY: *Selected Articles and Dispatches of...* Scribners NY (1967) [5] "A-3.67[V]" on copyright page. Edited by William White $25/100

042d: BY-LINE: ERNEST HEMINGWAY *Selected Articles and Dispatches of...* Collins L 1968 [1] $25/75

043a: TWO STORIES Grafisk Forlag Copenhagen (1967) [] Pictorial Wraps. Prints *Fifty Grand* and *The Undefeated* in English (ref.e) $40.

044a: THE UNDEFEATED Higher School Publishing House Moscow 1968 [] Wraps. First separate edition. English text (Ian McKelvie 2/90) $75.

THE FIFTH COLUMN AND FOUR STORIES OF THE SPANISH CIVIL WAR see 020e

045a: THE ONLY NICE PEOPLE IN CANADA | *Les Seuls Gens Bien Du Canada* Privately Printed Toronto (1969) [2] 500 cc. Two folio broadsides, each fold once, one in English and one in French. Letter to Sylvia Beach dated 11/6/23 $100.

046a: ERNEST HEMINGWAY, CUB RE-PORTER *Kansas City Star Stories* University of Pittsburgh Press (Pittsburgh 1970) [2] 200 sgd no cc. Issued in special binding. Edited by Matthew J. Bruccoli (signed by editor) $125.

046b: ERNEST HEMINGWAY, CUB RE-PORTER *Kansas City Star Stories* University of Pittsburgh Press (Pittsburgh 1970) [0] Edited by Matthew J. Bruccoli $15/60

047a: ISLANDS IN THE STREAM (Scribners NY 1970) [0] Wraps. Page galleys distributed in advance (ref.c)
$1,000.

047b: ISLANDS IN THE STREAM (Scribners NY 1970) [] Uncorrected proofs in tall spiral bound blue wraps (Pepper & Stern 7/88)
$650.

047c: ISLANDS IN THE STREAM Scribners NY (1970) [5] 75,000 cc "A-9.70(V)" on copyright page
$15/75

047d: ISLANDS IN THE STREAM Collins L 1970 [] Publisher's press kit containing poster, sign, release, letter, and promotional booklet
$150.

047e: ISLANDS IN THE STREAM Collins L 1970 [] Uncorrected proof in printed blue wraps (Jos. the Provider #23). Also long spiral bound sheets in blue wraps (John De Padva 12/91)
$500.

047f: ISLANDS IN THE STREAM Collins L 1970 [] Advance Reading copy in plain wraps laid in dustwrapper (ref.e)
$250.

047g: ISLANDS IN THE STREAM Collins L 1970 [1] (Noted with wrap-around band: "The only Hemingway novel you can't have read." Also blurb by Mary Hemingway
$12/60

048a: WILL YOU LET THESE KIDDIES MISS SANTA CLAUS? (Bruccoli & Clark Bloomfield Hills 1970) [2] 125 no cc. Orange wrappers (ref.c)
$250.

049a: THE CHRISTMAS GIFT Ka' Bunsha Tokyo 1970 [] (American Dust Co. 4/93)
$100.

050a: ERNEST HEMINGWAY'S APPRENTICE-SHIP *Oak Park, 1916-1917* (Bruccoli Clark | Micro.Ed. Wash., DC 1971) [2] 200 sgd no cc in special binding. Edited and signed by Matthew J. Bruccoli (ref.b)
$125.

050b: ERNEST HEMINGWAY'S APPRENTICE-
SHIP *Oak Park, 1916-1917* (Bruccoli Clark/Micro.
Ed. Wash., DC 1971) [0] In dustwrapper (ref.e) $15/60

051a: THE NICK ADAMS STORIES Scribners
NY 1972 [] Galley Sheets ring bound in plain
wraps with publisher's label. Printed on rectos only,
with five sheets (preface and table of contents) laid
in (ref.e) $600.

051b: THE NICK ADAMS STORIES Scribners
NY (1972) [5] 25,000 cc. "A-4.72(V)" on copyright
page. Eight previously unpublished pieces $20/100

052a: WE ARE PLEASED TO OFFER AN
ERNEST HEMINGWAY LETTER... Gotham NY
(1973) [2] 100 no. cc. Single sheet folded once.
Reproduces letter from Cuba in 1948 to W.G.
Rogers regarding Gertrude Stein $175.

053a: FABLE *(A Devine Gesture)* (Oliphant Press
NY 1973) [] Twin long folio sheets. "Proof of
December 14, 1973" (Wilder Books 6/93) $300.

053b: A DIVINE GESTURE Aloe Editions (NY)
1974 [2] 250 no cc. Stiff wraps. First complete book
edition $150.

054a: THE ENDURING HEMINGWAY (Scribners
NY 1974) [] Spiral bound plain wraps with printed
labels. 2 volumes. "Miss Mary's Lion" appears in
book form for the first time (Reese 6/89) $250.

054b: THE ENDURING HEMINGWAY Scribners
NY (1974) [] $15/75

055a: THE FIRST FORTY NINE STORIES
Franklin Library Franklin Center 1977 [] Full
leather (Watermark West 5/89) $75.

056a: KEEPSAKE FOR THE FRIENDS OF
MARGUERITE COHN University of Virginia
Charlottesville 1977 [2] 150 cc. Wraps. Prints two

pages of a Hemingway letter and an early photo
(Waiting For Godot #2) $100.

057a: HOKUM: A PLAY Sans Souci Wellesley
Hills (1978) [2] 73 no cc. Issued hors-commerce.
White buckram in dustwrapper and slipcase. (There
were three copies of uncorrected galley proofs
noted, one was offered for $850 by In Our Time
2/90) $150/250

057b: HOKUM: A PLAY Sans Souci Wellesley
Hills (1978) [2] 26 sgd ltr cc. Written with Morris
McNeil, signed by publisher (Jos. the Provider #25).
Brown buckram in dustwrapper and slipcase $300/400

057c: HOKUM: A PLAY Sans Souci Wellesley
Hills (1978) [2] 200 no cc (ref.c). Brown buckram
in dustwrapper and slipcase $150/250

058a: 88 POEMS Harcourt, Brace... NY (1979) []
Uncorrected proofs in printed blue wraps (ref.c) $250.

058b: 88 POEMS Harcourt, Brace... NY (1979) [4]
Dustwrapper entitled "87 POEMS" (Phoenix
Bookshop #200) $15/200

058c: 88 POEMS Harcourt, Brace... NY/SD (1979)
[] Edited by Nicholas Gerogiannis (ref.c) $15/60

059a: THE FAITHFUL BULL Hamish Hamilton
L (1980) [2] 100 sgd no cc (a&b). Pictorial boards.
Illustrated, signed and numbered by Michael
Foreman on the title page. In slipcase. There was a
separate signed and numbered illustration laid in,
which was numbered as if there were 100 copies but
reportedly only 25 were actually pulled (James
Jaffe) $750.

059b: THE FAITHFUL BULL Hamish Hamilton
L (1980) [2] Pictorial boards. Illustrated, signed
and numbered on title page. In slipcase but without
the separate signed and numbered illustration $350.

059c: THE FAITHFUL BULL   Hamish Hamilton
L (1980) [1] Issued without dustwrapper in slipcase $35/75

059d: THE FAITHFUL BULL   Hamish Hamilton
L 1980 [1] Wraps $35.

060a: E.H.: SELECTED LETTERS, 1917-1961
Scribner's   NY (1981) [] Wraps.   Uncorrected
proofs. Numerous differences from published
version (Jos. the Provider #20) $400.

060b: E.H.: SELECTED LETTERS, 1917-1961
Scribner's NY (1981) [2] 500 sgd no cc. Edited
and signed by Carlos Baker. Issued in glassine
dustwrapper and slipcase (ref.c) $175/250

060c: E.H.: SELECTED LETTERS, 1917-1961
Scribner's NY (1981) [3] (ref.c) $10/50

060d: E.H.: SELECTED LETTERS, 1917-1961
Granada L (1981) [1] "Publ by...1981" $8/40

061a: ERNEST HEMINGWAY ON WRITING
Scribner's   NY (1984) [3] Edited by Larry W.
Phillips $20/60

062a: THE DANGEROUS SUMMER   Scribner's
NY   (1985) [] Wraps.   "Uncorrected Proof" in
yellow (ochre?) wraps.   Introduction by James
Michener $250.

062b: THE DANGEROUS SUMMER   Scribner's
NY (1985) [3] 60,000 cc (PW). (Published June
24, 1985 at $17.95) $10/50

062c: THE DANGEROUS SUMMER   Hamilton
Hamish L (1985) [] Advance copies in blue printed
wraps (Dalian Books) $100.

062d: THE DANGEROUS SUMMER   Hamilton
Hamish L (1985) [1] $10/50

063a: DATELINE: TORONTO *The Complete Toronto Star Dispatches 1920-1924* Scribner's NY (1985) [3] Edited by William White $10/40

064a: ALONG WITH YOUTH: HEMINGWAY THE EARLY YEARS Oxford NY/Oxford 1985 [3] Book by Peter Griffin. Includes previously unpublished short stories and letters. (Published October 3, 1985 at $17.95) $10/40

065a: SHORT STORIES Folio Society L 1986 [] Issued without dustwrapper in slipcase. Selected and introduced by David Hughes; illustrated by Ian Becil $40/60

066a: THE GARDEN OF EDEN Scribner's NY 1986 [] Uncorrected Proofs from corrected typescript with all additions and deletions reproduced. One of a small number submitted to a book club (so stamped) (ref.e) $200.

066b: THE GARDEN OF EDEN Scribner's NY 1986 [] Uncorrected proof "copyright to come" in off-white wraps. Reportedly the publisher restricted distribution of this proof and requested copies be returned so that, although recent, they are not common (Ken Lopez 4/90). "A particularly prohibitive note is emblazoned on the front wrapper about the restrictive nature of these proofs, the small number prepared, and the registration and numbering of each copy sent out to reviewers" (William Reese Co. 4/95) $200.

066c: THE GARDEN OF EDEN Scribner's NY 1986 [1] 100,000 cc (PW). (Published May 1986 at $18.95) $7/35

066d: THE GARDEN OF EDEN Hamish Hamilton L (1986) [] Uncorrected proofs in pink wraps (Dalian Books) $75.

066e: THE GARDEN OF EDEN Hamish Hamilton L (1986) [] $8/40

067a: THE COMPLETE SHORT STORIES OF ERNEST HEMINGWAY Scribner's NY 1986 [] Two volumes. Uncorrected proof in printed wraps. Foreword by John, Patrick and Gregory Hemingway reproduced from fair copy typescript. Stamped "Submission | Book of The Month Club Inc." on front covers. (Pepper & Stern 10/90) $250.

067b: THE COMPLETE SHORT STORIES Scribner's NY 1987 [] Uncorrected proofs. Printed wraps. Foreword signed "John, Patrick, and Gregory Hemingway." (ref.e) $125.

067c: THE COMPLETE SHORT STORIES Scribner's NY 1987 [] 50,000 cc (PW). (Published December 2, 1987 at $19.95.) Includes seven stories "never before published" $10/30

068a: CONVERSATIONS WITH ERNEST HEMINGWAY University of Mississippi Jackson (1986) [3] Edited by Matthew Bruccoli $25/50

068b: CONVERSATIONS WITH ERNEST HEMINGWAY University of Mississippi Jackson (1986) [3] Wraps $25.

069a: CHRISTMAS ON THE ROOF OF THE WORLD *A Celebration in The Swiss Alps* Redpath Minneapolis (1987) [] Pictorial wraps. First separate edition. Issued in publisher's plastic sleeve with mailing envelope and card $30.

070a: HEMINGWAY'S SPAIN Chronicle Books S.F. (1989) [3] Written by Barnaby Conrad with excerpts from Hemingway's work as captions for photographs by Loomis Dean. (Published October 1989 at $29.95) $10/40

070b: HEMINGWAY'S SPAIN Chronicle Books S.F. (1989) [3] Wraps. (Published at $18.95) $20.

071a: MARLIN (Big Fish Books SF 1992) [] 1,000 cc. First separate appearance. Illustrated with

photographs by Robert Herrero Sotolongo. First
published in *Holiday* magazine. (Published at $35) $10/40

(signature)

CHESTER HIMES
(1909 - 1984)

Himes was born in Jefferson City, Missouri, and attended Ohio State for two years in the 1920s. He worked for the Writers Project (WPA) in Ohio and served seven years in prison for armed robbery. He left the United States in 1953, and all of his Harlem crime stories (except the last, _Blind Man with a Pistol_), were originally published in French and then translated for American paperback distribution.

REFERENCES:

(a) Private collection, inventory, dealer catalogs

(b) Reilly, John M. TWENTIETH-CENTURY CRIME AND MYSTERY WRITERS. Second Edition. New York: St. Martin's Press (1985).

001a: IF HE HOLLERS LET HIM GO Doubleday
GC 1945 [1] $100/500

001b: IF HE HOLLERS LET HIM GO Falcon
Press (L 1947) [1] Black cloth with gold lettering
on spine $50/200

002a: LONELY CRUSADE Knopf NY 1947 [1] $50/250

002b: LONELY CRUSADE Falcon Press (L
1950) [] $15/75

003a: CAST THE FIRST STONE Coward
McCann NY (1952) [0] $40/200

003b: CAST THE FIRST STONE   Longmans   T
1953 [] $15/75

004a: THE THIRD GENERATION   World   NY
(1954) [1] $40/200

005a: THE PRIMITIVE   Signet/NAL   NY (1956)
[1] Wraps. 169,000 cc. Signet Paperback Original
#1264 $100.

005b: THE END OF THE PRIMITIVE   Allison &
Busby   L 1990 [] New title. First complete edition
in English. 005a was expurgated (Ming Books 7/93) $60.

006a: FOR LOVE OF IMABELL   Fawcett
Greenwich   (1957)   [1]   Wraps.   "Gold   Medal
Original" #717. Priced: 25¢. (Published as *A Rage
In Harlem* by Avon in 1965 {ref.b}) $100.

006b: A RAGE IN HARLEM   Panther   L 1969 []
Wraps $40.

006c: A RAGE IN HARLEM   Allison & Busby   L
(1985) [1] First hardback edition $15/45

007a: THE REAL COOL KILLERS   Avon   NY
(1959) [0] Wraps. "Avon Original" T-328 $75.

007b: THE REAL COOL KILLERS   Panther   L
1969 [] $40.

007c: THE REAL COOL KILLERS   Allison &
Busby   L (1985) [1] First hardback edition $15/45

008a: THE CRAZY KILL   Avon   NY (1959) [0]
Wraps. "Paperback Original" T-357 $75.

008b: THE CRAZY KILL   Panther   L 1968 []
Wraps in dustwrapper (Iain Sinclair) $25/75

008c: THE CRAZY KILL   Allison & Busby   L
(1984) [] First hardback $15/50

009a: ALL SHOT UP Avon NY (1960) [0] Wraps.
"Avon Original" T-434 $75.

009b: ALL SHOT UP Panther L 1969 [] Wraps $35.

010a: THE BIG GOLD DREAM Avon NY (1960)
[] Wraps.   Note: Between The Covers had a
Berkeley edition (NY 1960). Priority unknown $75.

010b: THE BIG GOLD DREAM Panther L 1968
[] $35.

011a: PINKTOES Olympia Press Paris (1961) [1]
Wraps. "Printed in July 1961" on back page $150.

011b: PINKTOES Putnam NY (1965) [0] Note:
Susan Heller/Pages for Sages had copy with two
dustwrappers: (1) title deep burgundy, author in
brown-red; (2) title in light lavender, author in gray.
(Priority unknown) $25/100

011c: PINKTOES Barker L 1965 [] $10/50

012a: COTTON COMES TO HARLEM   Putnam
NY (1965) [1] $50/250

012b: COTTON COMES TO HARLEM Muller L
(1966) [] (Heritage Bookshop 9/92) $25/75

013a: THE HEAT'S ON Putnam NY (1966) [0]
(Published as *Come Back Charleston Blue* by
Berkley, NY 1970 {ref.b}) $30/150

013b: THE HEAT'S ON Muller L 1966 [] $25/75

013c: THE HEAT'S ON   Allison & Busby L
(1986) [1] $5/25

014a: RUN MAN RUN Putnam NY (1966) [0]
(First published in Paris under title *Dare Dare*.)
Two bindings noted: red and orange, distinctly
different. Priority unknown $30/150

014b: RUN MAN RUN Muller L 1967 [] $25/75

015a: BLIND MAN WITH A PISTOL   Morrow NY 1969 [0] (Published as *Hot Day, Hot Night* by Dell, NY 1979 {ref.b}) $30/150

015b: BLIND MAN WITH A PISTOL Hodder L 1969 [] $25/75

015c: BLIND MAN WITH A PISTOL   Allison & Busby L (1986) [1] $5/25

016a: THE QUALITY OF HURT Doubleday GC 1972 [1] Autobiography. Volume 1 with tipped-in page signed by author (Evlen Books #1) $100/175

016b: THE QUALITY OF HURT Doubleday GC 1972 [1] $25/100

016c: THE QUALITY OF HURT Michael Joseph L (1973) [1] $15/60

017a: BLACK ON BLACK Doubleday GC 1973 [1] $30/150

017b: BLACK ON BLACK M. Joseph L (1975) [] (Maurice Neville 11/88) $15/60

018a: MY LIFE OF ABSURDITY Doubleday GC 1976 [1] Autobiography. Volume II. (Published November 26, 1976 at $9.95) $25/75

019a: A CASE OF RAPE   Targ Editions NY (1980) [2] 350 sgd no cc.   Issued in glassine dustwrapper. (Originally published in French, *Un Affaire de Viol*) $100.

019b: A CASE OF RAPE   Howard University Washington 1984 [0] $10/30

020a: THE COLLECTED STORIES OF CHESTER HIMES Allison & Busby L 1990 [] Precedes the U.S. edition $15/45

020b: THE COLLECTED STORIES OF
CHESTER HIMES Thunder Mountain Press (NY
1991) [] Uncorrected Proof in light brown wraps
(Waverly Books 9/91) $50.

020c: THE COLLECTED STORIES OF
CHESTER HIMES Thunder Mountain Press (NY
1991) [] Cloth. (Published May 1991 at $ 21.95) $5/25

020d: THE COLLECTED STORIES OF
CHESTER HIMES Thunder Mountain Press (NY
1991) [] Wraps. (Published May 1991 at $12.95) $10.

THE END OF THE PRIMITIVE see 005b

021a: PLAN B   University Press of Mississippi
Jackson 1993 [] (Published September, 1993 at
$20.) (Published in French in Paris in 1986 {Joseph
the Provider 5/92}) $

022a: CONVERSATION WITH CHESTER
HIMES University Press of Mississippi Jackson
1995 [] (To be published in November 1995 in
cloth) $

022b: CONVERSATION WITH CHESTER
HIMES University Press of Mississippi Jackson
1995 [] (To be published in November 1995 in
wraps) $

Langston Hughes (signature)

LANGSTON HUGHES
(1902 - 1967)

James Langston Hughes was born in Joplin, Missouri, but was raised by his grandmother in Lawrence, Kansas, until the age of twelve when he went to live with his mother. He attended high school in Cleveland, Ohio. After graduation he stayed with his father on his ranch in Mexico and then attended Columbia University for a year. From 1922 to 1925 he worked as a seaman visiting Africa and Holland; and as a waiter, cook and doorman in Paris and Italy. He returned to the states in 1925 and was working in the dining room of the Wardman Park Hotel in Washington when he was "discovered" by Vachel Lindsay. His writing was largely concerned with depicting Negro life in America.

At the time of his death in 1967, Hughes was the most translated of all living American poets.

REFERENCES:

(a) Dickinson, Donald C. A BIBLIOGRAPHY OF LANGSTON HUGHES. Second Edition Revised. Hamden, Ct.: Archon Books, 1972.

(b) Bruccoli, Matthew J., Editor. FIRST PRINTINGS AMERICAN AUTHORS. Volume 3. Detroit: Gale Research Co. (1978).

(c) The Glenn Carrington Collection (at Howard University, Washington, D.C.) compiled by Karen L. Jefferson and Brigitte M. Rouson, June, 1977.

Reference (a) supplied the titles and quantities for the Knopf titles but did not indicate whether the place or date was on the title page or how to identify the first editions. Reference (b) includes about

80 sheet music entries, which we did not include herein. We have seen very few offered for sale but would assume a range of $15 to $150 depending on age and condition. Reference (c) contained a few items not mentioned in reference (a).

001a: THE WEARY BLUES Knopf NY 1926 [0] 1,500 cc (a & b). First issue dustwrapper without blurb for 002a (Joseph The Provider 7/89) $500/3,000

001b: THE WEARY BLUES Knopf NY 1926 [0] Second issue dustwrapper with blurb for 002a (Joseph The Provider 7/89) $500/2,000

001c: THE WEARY BLUES Knopf NY 1931 [] "Special Edition" with introduction by Carl Van Vechten $50/250

002a: FINE CLOTHES TO THE JEW Knopf NY 1927 [0] 1,546 cc. Green and yellow polygons and red lines vs. pastel striped paper (Thomas Goldwasser 10/92). Dustwrapper seen with "second printing" at foot of rear flap but there was only one printing of the book (perhaps refers to a book that was advertised there??) $300/1,750

003a: FOUR NEGRO POETS Simon & Schuster NY   no date [1927] [0] Wraps. Also includes McKay, Toomer and Cullen $250.

004a: NOT WITHOUT LAUGHTER Knopf NY 1930 [0] 2,500 cc $200/1,000

004b: NOT WITHOUT LAUGHTER Allen & Unwin L 1930 [] $100/400

005a: FOUR LINCOLN UNIVERSITY POETS Lincoln University 1930 [0] Wraps. Edited by Hughes $175.

006a: DEAR LOVELY DEATH Troutbeck Press Amenia, NY 1931 [2] 100 sgd cc. Frontis by Amy

Spingarn, printed by Dard Hunter. Orange printed
boards, cloth back (Serendipity Books) $1,750.

007a: THE NEGRO MOTHER *and Other Dramatic
Recitations* Golden Stair Press (NY 1931) [2] 17
sgd no cc. Bound in Roma paper for presentation
(ref.b) $2,500.

007b: THE NEGRO MOTHER *and Other
Dramatic Recitations* Golden Stair Press (NY
1931) [0] Wraps $1,000.

008a: THE NEGRO MOTHER Golden Stair Press
NY (1931) [] Golden Stair Broadside No. 1 (ref.b) $250.

009a: THE BLACK CLOWN Golden Stair Press
NY (1931) [] Golden Stair Broadside No. 2 (ref.b) $250.

010a: BROKE Golden Stair Press NY (1931) []
Golden Stair Broadside No. 3 (ref.b) $250.

011a: THE BIG-TIMER Golden Stair Press NY
(1931) [] Golden Stair Broadside No. 4 (ref.b) $250.

012a: DARK YOUTH OF THE U.S.A. Golden
Stair Press NY (1931) [] Golden Stair Broadside
No. 5 (ref.b) $250.

013a: BARREL HOUSE: NORTHERN CITY
Trout Beck Press No place or date [1932] []
Broadside poem 8" x 15" (Argosy - Cat. 732). Ref.b
lists date as 1930 $200.

014a: THE DREAM KEEPER *and Other Poems*
Knopf NY 1932 [1] 500 cc $250/1,000

015a: SCOTTSBORO LIMITED *Four Poems and
A Play in Verse* Golden Stair Press NY 1932 [2]
30 cc sgd by Hughes and Prentiss Taylor, the
illustrator $2,000.

015b: SCOTTSBORO LIMITED Golden Stair
Press NY 1932 [0] Wraps $600.

016a: POPO AND FIFINA Macmillan NY 1932 [1] 4,000 cc. "Published August, 1932" on copyright page. Written with Arna Bontemps (ref.b) $250/750

017a: A NEGRO LOOKS AT SOVIET CENTRAL ASIA Co-operative Publishing Society of Foreign Workers in the U.S.S.R. Moscow, Leningrad 1934 [0] 1,500 cc. Wraps (ref.b) $500.

018a: THE WAYS OF WHITE FOLKS Knopf NY 1934 [1] 2,500 cc $250/750

018b: THE WAYS OF WHITE FOLKS Allen & Unwin L 1934 [] $100/400

019a: AUGUST 19th A POEM FOR CLARENCE NORRIS Communist Party Birmingham (1934) [0] Broadside $300.

020a: A NEW SONG International Workers Order NY 1938 [0] Wraps. Introduction by Michael Gold $350.

021a: THE BIG SEA Knopf NY 1940 [1] 3,200 cc $150/600

021b: THE BIG SEA Hutchinson L 1940 [] $100/300

022a: THE NEGRO SPEAKS OF RIVERS (No publisher, place or date [1941]) [] Illustrated broadside. First separate printing. Issued in mailing envelope (ref.b) $200.

023a: GOOD-BYE CHRIST (No publisher) Pasadena November, 1940 [0] Broadside (9" x 5 3/8"). First separate printing of an attack on Hughes who was reading in Pasadena (Wm Reese Co. 9/90) $200.

024a: SHAKESPEARE IN HARLEM Knopf NY 1942 [1] 3,300 cc. Illustrated by McKnight Kauffer $125/500

025a: MY AMERICA (Milwaukee Interracial Federation 1943?) [0] Single sheet printed on both sides (ref.b) $175.

026a: FREEDOM'S PLOW   Musette Publishers NY 1943 [0] Wraps. Light blue ink with "Buy United States War Bonds and Stamps" device on verso of rear wrap $250.

027a: JIM CROW'S LAST STAND   Negro Publication Society of America (no place [Atlanta]) (1943) [0] Wraps. Race and Culture Series No. 2. First issue with "Belt" upside down on contents page (Serendipity Books) $300.

027b: JIM CROW'S LAST STAND   Negro Publication Society of America (no place [Atlanta]) 1943 [0] Wraps. "Belt" corrected $150.

028a: LAMENT FOR DARK PEOPLE *and Other Poems* (No publisher) (Netherlands) 1944 [2] 50 no. cc. Wraps (ref.b) $600.

028b: LAMENT FOR DARK PEOPLE *and Other Poems* No publisher (Netherlands) 1944 [0] 250 cc. Wraps $350.

029a: BALLAD OF THE SEVEN SONGS American Negro Press Association (No publisher, place or date [circa mid 1940s]) [0] Legal size, mimeographed one side only, 3 pages (Cather & Brown) $250.

030a: MASTERS OF THE DEW   Reynal & Hitchcock NY (1947) [0] Jacques Roumain's book translated by Hughes and Mercer Cook $100/450

031a: FIELDS OF WONDER Knopf NY 1947 [1] 2,500 cc $75/350

031b: FIELDS OF WONDER   L 1947 [] (Catalogued by Peter Ellis 12/89 but no publisher indicated, not in ref.a,b or c) $50/250

032a: STREET SCENE Chappell NY (1948) [0] Wraps. Two-act musical with lyrics by Hughes (ref.b) $175.

033a: CUBA LIBRE *Poems* by Nicolas Guillen Anderson & Richie LA 1948 [2] 500 cc. Translated by Hughes and Ben Carruthers. Assume issued without dustwrapper $300.

034a: IN HENRY'S BACKYARD (No publisher, place or date) [] 8 1/2" x 14" printed sheet laid in a copy of the book by this name written by B. R. & G. Weltfish, NY (1948) (Joseph Dermont) $150.

035a: TROUBLED ISLAND Leeds Music Corp NY 1949 [0] Wraps. Opera by Wm. Grant Still with libretto by Hughes. Verso of title page states "World premiere Thursday, March 31st 1949..." (ref.b) $350.

036a: ONE WAY TICKET Knopf NY 1949 [1] 3,500 cc. Illustrated by Jacob Lawrence $60/300

036b: ONE WAY TICKET L 1949 [] (Catalogued by Peter Ellis 12/89, but no publisher indicated, not in ref.a, b or c) $40/200

037a: THREE STUDENTS LOOK AT LINCOLN IN 1929 *A Survey of the College of Lincoln University by Three Members of Professor Labaree's Class in Sociology* (No publisher or place [assume Lincoln University]) "Reprinted with permission...April 1950" [0] Mimeographed sheets $250.

038a: THE POETRY OF THE NEGRO 1746-1949 Doubleday GC 1949 [1] Edited by Hughes and Arna Bontemps $40/200

039a: EMPEROR OF HAITI *An Historical Drama* (Author, no place or date [circa 1949]) [] Mimeographed sheets, plastic-like cover. Derived from Hughes libretto for *Troubled Island* (Between The Covers 10/90) $1,000.

040a: SIMPLE SPEAKS HIS MIND Simon & Schuster (NY 1950) [0] $60/300

040b: SIMPLE SPEAKS HIS MIND   Simon &
Schuster (NY 1950) [0] Wraps $75.

040c: SIMPLE SPEAKS HIS MIND   Gollancz L
1951 [0] $40/200

041a: GYPSY BALLADS (Beloit Poetry Journal
Beloit 1951) [0] Wraps.   Hughes translation of
Lorca's work comprises entire fall issue $125.

042a: MONTAGE OF A DREAM DEFERRED
Henry Holt NY (1951) [1] $100/400

043a: LAUGHING TO KEEP FROM CRYING
Henry Holt NY (1952) [1] $50/250

043b: LAUGHING TO KEEP FROM CRYING L
1952 [] (Catalogued by Peter Ellis 12/89 but no
publisher indicated, not in ref.a, b or c) $30/150

044a: FIRST BOOK OF NEGROES   Franklin
Watts   NY 1952 [1] "First   Printing" on
acknowledgments page (ref.b) $50/250

044b: FIRST BOOK OF NEGROES   Bailey &
Swinfen L 1956 [] $30/150

045a: SIMPLE TAKES A WIFE Simon & Schuster
(NY)   1953 [1] Paper boards issued without
dustwrapper $200.

045b: SIMPLE TAKES A WIFE Gollancz L 1954
[0] $30/150

046a: FAMOUS AMERICAN NEGROES Dodd,
Mead NY 1954 [0] $50/250

047a: LINCOLN UNIVERSITY POETS   Fine
Edition Press NY 1954 [1] Edited by Hughes and
others. Dustwrapper assumed $50/200

048a: FIRST BOOK OF RHYTHMS   Franklin
Watts NY (1954) [1] $50/250

048b: FIRST BOOK OF RHYTHMS Bailey & Swinfen L 1956 [] $30/150

048c: FIRST BOOK OF RHYTHMS Edmund Ward L (1964) [1] "First published in Great Britain by Edmund Ward...1964" $15/50

049a: FIRST BOOK OF JAZZ Franklin Watts NY (1955) [1] "First Printing" facing title page $50/250

049b: FIRST BOOK OF JAZZ Bailey L 1957 [] $30/150

050a: FAMOUS NEGRO MUSIC MAKERS Dodd, Mead NY 1955 [0] $50/250

051a: THE SWEET FLYPAPER OF LIFE Simon & Schuster (NY 1955) [1] 2,920 cc. (Schuster's library- Thomas Goldwasser Books 10/92) $50/200

051b: THE SWEET FLYPAPER OF LIFE Simon & Schuster (NY 1955) [1] Wraps. 22,000 cc. (Schuster's library- Thomas Goldwasser Books 10/92) $75.

052a: I WONDER AS I WANDER *An Autobiograhical Journey* Rinehart NY (1956) [5] $50/250

053a: A PICTORIAL HISTORY OF THE NEGRO IN AMERICA Crown NY (1956) [0] Written with Milton Melzer. Later printings noted on dustwrapper, but books themselves are no different $50/200

053b: A PICTORIAL HISTORY OF THE NEGRO IN AMERICA Crown NY (1963) [0] "New Revised Edition" $25/100

053c: A PICTORIAL HISTORY OF BLACK AMERICANS Crown NY (1973) [0] New title. Fourth revised edition. Adds C. Eric Lincoln as co-author $25/50

054a: FIRST BOOK OF THE WEST INDIES Franklin Watts NY (1956) [1] $40/200

054b: FIRST BOOK OF THE WEST INDIES
Bailey & Swinfen L 1956 [] — $30/150

054c: FIRST BOOK OF THE CARIBBEAN Ward
(no place) 1965 [] (ref. b) — $12/60

055a: SELECTED POEMS OF GABRIELA
MISTRAL Indiana University Press Bloomington
(1957) [0] Translated by Hughes — $25/125

056a: SIMPLE STAKES A CLAIM Rinehart NY
(1957) [5] — $50/200

056b: SIMPLE STAKES A CLAIM Gollancz L
1958 [0] — $25/100

057a: FAMOUS NEGRO HEROES OF AMERICA
Dodd, Mead NY 1958 [0] — $40/200

058a: THE BOOK OF NEGRO FOLKLORE
Dodd, Mead NY 1958 [0] Edited by Hughes and
Arna Bontemps — $40/200

059a: TAMBOURINES TO GLORY John Day
NY (1958) [0] — $40/200

059b: TAMBOURINES TO GLORY Gollancz L
1959 [0] — $25/100

060a: LANGSTON HUGHES READER Braziller
NY 1958 [1] — $25/75

061a: SELECTED POEMS OF LANGSTON
HUGHES Knopf NY 1959 [1] 5,650 cc.
Illustrated by McKnight Kauffer — $30/150

062a: REMARKS BY LANGSTON HUGHES IN
ACCEPTANCE OF 45TH SPRINGARN MEDAL
AT NAACP 51ST ANNUAL CONVENTION. (No
publisher or place 1960) [] Single sheet printed on
both sides — $150.

063a: SIMPLY HEAVENLY   Dramatist Play Service (NY 1959) [0] Wraps. Front cover: "Books and Lyrics by..." vs. "Book" $125.

064a: AN AFRICAN TREASURY *Articles | Essays | Stories | Poems by Black Africans* Crown   NY (1960) [0] Selected by Hughes. Plain white endpapers (H.E. Turlington) $25/75

064b: AN AFRICAN TREASURY *Articles | Essays | Stories | Poems by Black Africans* Crown   NY (1960) [0] Map endpapers. $3.50 price. Leaves 8 1/4" x 5 1/2" (Beasley Books) $20/60

064c: AN AFRICAN TREASURY *Articles | Essays | Stories | Poems by Black Africans* Gollancz   L 1961 [] $15/50

065a: THE FIRST BOOK OF AFRICA   Franklin Watts NY (1960) [1] (Ref.b) $50/200

065b: THE FIRST BOOK OF AFRICA   Mayflower L 1961 [] $25/125

065c: THE FIRST BOOK OF AFRICA   Franklin Watts NY (1964) [3] Revised edition $25/75

066a: ASK YOUR MAMA Knopf NY 1961 [1] $25/125

067a: MOTHER AND CHILD *A Theatre Vignette* American Place Theatre NY   (1961) [0] Wraps. Mimeographed sheets in folder. 30 copies for production use (Joseph The Provider, and ref.b) $250.

068a: THE BALLAD OF THE BROWN KING Sam Fox NY 1961 [] Written with Margaret Bond (ref.b) $200.

069a: THE BEST OF SIMPLE Hill & Wang NY (1961) [0] $35/125

069b: THE BEST OF SIMPLE Hill & Wang NY (1961) [0] Wraps $50.

070a: FIGHT FOR FREEDOM Norton NY (1962) [0] (Note: The Berkley edition is a reprint) $25/100

071a: FIVE PLAYS BY LANGSTON HUGHES Indiana University Press Bloomington (1963) [0] Edited and introduction by Webster Smolley $25/100

072a: POEMS FROM BLACK AFRICA University of Indiana Press Bloomington (1963) [0] Edited by Hughes $25/100

073a: SOMETHING IN COMMON *and Other Stories* Hill & Wang NY (1963) [1] Wraps. "First American Century Series Edition For 1963" $60.

073b: SOMETHING IN COMMON... Hill & Wang NY (1963) [1] $25/100

074a: NEW NEGRO POETS USA University of Indiana Bloomington (1964) [0] Edited by Hughes, foreword by Gwendolyn Brooks $30/150

075a: SIMPLE'S UNCLE SAM Hill & Wang NY (1965) [1] (Published October 18, 1965 at $3.95 - Review slip) $30/150

075b: SIMPLE'S UNCLE SAM Hill & Wang NY (1965) [1] Wraps $60.

075c: SIMPLE'S UNCLE SAM Gollancz L 1965 [0] (Not in ref.a, b or c) $20/100

076a: BOOK OF NEGRO HUMOR Dodd Mead NY (1966) [0] $30/150

077a: THE CIVIL RIGHTS CALENDAR 1965 Carver Federal Savings & Loan Association (NY 1965) [0] Wraps and envelope. Historical facts selected and text by Hughes (ref.b) $75.

078a: A 1966 CALENDAR OF INVENTIONS AND DISCOVERIES Carver Federal Savings & Loan Association. (NY 1966) [0] Wraps and enve-

lope. Historical facts selected and text by Hughes
(ref.b) — $75.

079a: EMPEROR HAILE SALASSIE ON
LIBERATION DAY MAY 5, 1966 No publisher or
place 1966 [0] Folio (ref.b) — $125.

080a: THE BACKLASH BLUES Broadside Press
Detroit 1967 [0] Small broadside on stiff blue card
(ref.b) — $60.

081a: BLACK MAGIC *A Pictorial History of The
Negro In American Entertainment* Prentice Hall
Englewood Cliffs (1967) [] Long galley sheets
printed on one side only and stapled (Ken Lopez) — $450.

081b: BLACK MAGIC *A Pictorial History of The
Negro In American Entertainment* Prentice Hall
Englewood Cliffs (1967) [0] Written with Milton
Melzer — $75/250

082a: THE BEST SHORT STORIES BY NEGRO
WRITERS Little Brown B (1967) [1] Edited and
introduction by Hughes — $25/125

083a: THE PANTHER AND THE LASH Knopf
NY No date [0] Advance uncorrected proof on long
galley sheets. Spiral bound in light blue unprinted
wraps "Published July 1965 at $4.00" — $350.

083b: THE PANTHER AND THE LASH Knopf
NY 1967 [1] — $30/150

083c: THE PANTHER AND THE LASH Knopf
NY 1967 [1] Wraps — $50.

084a: IS LOVE Unicorn Press no place [Santa
Barbara] no date [1967] [2] 325 cc and a few
overrun copies. Broadside poem. Issued as part of
Unicorn Folio Series 1, no. 3, July 1967 (H.E.
Turlington 10/95) — $50.

085a: PAIR IN ONE   Unicorn Press   no place [Santa Barbara] no date [1968] [2] 350 cc and a few overrun copies. Broadside poem. Issued as part of Unicorn Folio Series 2, no. 2, September 1968 (H.E. Turlington 10/95) $50.

086a: BLACK MISERY   P.S. Erikson NY (1969) 0[1] $25/75

087a: THE INNOCENT   (Publisher?)   Santa Barbara   (1969)   [] Broadside (Sylvester & Orphanos 3/94) $75.

088a: DON'T YOU TURN BACK   Knopf NY (1969) [0] Selected by Lee Bennett Hopkins, introduction by Arna Bontemps $15/75

089a: GOOD   MORNING   REVOLUTION Lawrence Hill & Co. Westport, NY (1973) [3] Also states first edition.   Uncollected social protest writings edited by Faith Berry $20/60

089b: GOOD   MORNING   REVOLUTION Lawrence Hill & Co. Westport, NY (1973) [3] Wraps $25.

090a: ARNA BONTEMPS-LANGSTON HUGHES LETTERS 1925-1967 Dodd, Mead NY (1980) [3] Edited by Charles H. Nichols $12/60

091a: LANGSTON HUGHES IN THE HISPANIC WORLD AND HAITI   Archon Books (Hamden, Ct.) 1977   [] Edited by Edward J. Mullen. Appears most of these would be first book appearances $8/40

092a: DREAM   BOOGIE   *Poems   on   the Underground* No publisher L 1979 [0] Broadside poem 11x 24" $75

093a: LANGSTON HUGHES: *Laughing to Keep From Crying and 25 Jesse Simple Stories* Franklin Library Franklin Center 1981 [2] Limited Edition $65.

094a: LET AMERICA BE AMERICA AGAIN
Black Oak Books Berkeley 1990 [2] 200 cc.
Broadside (Waiting For Godot Books 7/90) $45.

095a: MULE BONE: *A Comedy Of Negro Life*
Harper Perennial NY (1991) [] Written with Zora
Neale Hurston. Includes the original Hurston short
story *The Bone Of Contention*, on which the play
was based, together with letters from Hurston and
Hughes. Published primarily as a paperback, this
hardbound issue was done in a very small edition
with most copies going primarily to libraries. Not
issued in dustwrapper (Joseph The Provider Books
5/95) $150

095b: MULE BONE: *A Comedy Of Negro Life*
Harper Perennial NY (1991) Wraps. Written with
Zora Neale Hurston (Joseph The Provider Books
5/95) $25.

096a: THE RETURN OF SIMPLE Farrar, Straus &
Giroux/Hill & Wang NY 1994 [1] Over half of
the stories have never before appeared in book form
(Published July 1994 at $20.00). (Waverly Books
12/94) $10/30

097a: THE SWEET AND SOUR ANIMAL BOOK
Knopf NY 1994 [] Illustrated by students of the
Harlem School of the Arts (Published October
1994 at $15.95) $

098a: THE COLLECTED POEMS OF
LANGSTON HUGHES Knopf NY 1994 []
Uncorrected Proof in green printed wraps. (James S.
Jaffe 1/95) $75.

098b: THE COLLECTED POEMS OF
LANGSTON HUGHES Knopf NY 1994 [1] 860
poems edited by Arnold Rampersad and David
Rossell. (Published November 1994 at $ 30.00) $

Robinson Jeffers.

ROBINSON JEFFERS
(1887 - 1962)

Jeffers was born in Pittsburgh, Pennsylvania. He was the son of a minister and was educated in the classics from early childhood. He received an B.A. and studied for three years at the College of Medicine (U.S.C.) and for one year in Forestry at the University of Washington. Thereafter, he decided to be a poet, and a legacy left him by a cousin allowed him the independence to follow this path.

The following price guide does not include estimates for books with editions of 30 copies or less if there are no recent records. These books would probably retail for $2,000 and up.

REFERENCES:

(a) Alberts, S.S. A BIBLIOGRAPHY OF THE WORKS OF ROBINSON JEFFERS. Rye, NY: Cultural History Research, Inc., 1966.

(b) Bruccoli, Matthew J., Editor. FIRST PRINTINGS OF AMERICAN AUTHORS. Volume 3. Detroit: Gale Research (1978).

(c) Bradley, Van Allen. THE BOOK COLLECTOR'S HAND-BOOK OF VALUES 1982-1983 New York: G.P. Putnam (1982).

(d) The Robinson Jeffers Collection at the University of Houston, compiled by Rodgers and Meador, 1975.

001a: FLAGONS AND APPLES Grafton L.A.
1912 [0] 500 cc. Written as John Robinson Jeffers $1,500.

001b: FLAGONS AND APPLES (Cayucos Books
no place 1970) [1] "Re-issued by..." (ref.b) $15/50

002a: CALIFORNIANS Macmillan NY 1916 [1]
Advance copies marked with perforated stamp on

title page. "Published October 1916." 1,200 copies in total (with 002b) $350/1,000

002b: CALIFORNIANS Macmillan NY 1916 [1] "Published October 1916". 1,200 copies in total (with 002a) $250/850

002c: CALIFORNIANS Cayucos Books (no place) 1971 [2] 50 sgd no cc. Issued without dustwrapper (ref.b). Signed by William Everson $300.

002d: CALIFORNIANS Cayucos Books (no place) 1971 [0] 450 no cc. Issued without dustwrapper (ref.b) $125.

003a: TAMAR *and Other Poems* Peter Boyle NY (1924) [0] 500 cc. Issued with gray unmarked dustwrapper. Also in plain tan dustwrapper (Waverly Auction #46) $500/750

004a: ROAN STALLION TAMAR *and Other Poems* Boni & Liveright NY 1925 [0] 3,500 cc. Wraps. Prospectus for book $125.

004b: ROAN STALLION TAMAR *and Other Poems* Boni & Liveright NY 1925 [0] 1,200 cc. Dustwrappers of later printings marked with the number of printing (also true of other B&L trade dustwrappers below) $150/600

004c: ROAN STALLION TAMAR *and Other Poems* Boni & Liveright NY 1925 [2] 12 sgd no cc. Blue or red binding, printed after trade edition $1,750.

004d: ROAN STALLION TAMAR *and Other Poems* Hogarth L 1928 [0] 440 cc of which 130 were pulped (Howard Woolmer 167). Issued with dustwrapper. Sheets printed in US, with title and copyright page printed by Hogarth $150/600

004e: ROAN STALLION TAMAR *and Other Poems* Modern Library NY (1935) [1] Adds an introduction by Jeffers and 15 poems not in Boni &

Liveright edition (ref.b). Issued in various colors of cloth $25/125

004f: ROAN STALLION TAMAR *and Other Poems* Yolla Bolly Press Covelo 1990 [2] Illustrated by Karin Wikstrom. 60 deluxe copies signed by illustrator. Issued with extra print and commentary by Tim Hunt. Priced at $850 pre-publication and $950 post-publication $1,000.

004g: ROAN STALLION TAMAR *and Other Poems* Yolla Bolly Press Covelo 1990 [2] 75 no cc. Illustrated by Karin Wikstrom. Bound in full sage-gray pigskin suede. Issued without extra print or commentary. Published at $625 (Joseph The Provider 1/95) $650.

005a: LIGHTS AND SHADOWS FROM THE LANTERN (Gelber & Lilienthals Bookshop S.F. 1926) [0] 250 copies (Maurice Neville). Wraps. Promotional pamphlet for the shop (Vol. 1, No. 7) featuring Jeffers' *All The Corn in One Barn* on the cover. $100.

006a: THE WOMEN AT POINT SUR Boni & Liveright NY 1927 [0] 2,200 cc. Ref.a states "Woman" vs. "Women" on half-title page (ref.a typo?). Book Peddler reports copy with "Women" on half title. (Second and third printings are so marked on copyright page) $60/300

006b: THE WOMEN AT POINT SUR Boni & Liveright NY (1927) [2] 265 sgd no cc. Large paper. 250 copies for sale. Published 2 months after trade edition. Issued in glassine wrapper and slipcase. (15 copies marked "Presentation" Maurice Neville 7/89) $400/500

006c: THE WOMEN AT POINT SUR Blue Oak Press (Auburn 1975) [0] Adds an afterword by Bill Hotchkiss and illustrations by Nancy Olson (ref.b). Assume issued in dustwrapper $15/50

006d: THE WOMEN AT POINT SUR *and other Poems* Liveright NY 1977 [3] Wraps. New title. 4 corrections and adds 5 poems. Afterword by Tim Hunt

$30.

007a: POEMS Book Club of California S.F. 1928 [2] Approximately 10 sgd (marked as printer's) copies. Specially bound in half (red) morocco in slipcase

$1,750/2,000

007b: POEMS Book Club of California S.F. 1928 [2] 310 sgd no cc. Printed by Grabhorn Press. Issued in unmarked slipcase (copies also signed by Ansel Adams would be priced higher)

$1,250/1,350

008a: AN ARTIST John S. Mayfield (Austin 1928) [2] 96 cc. Wraps. Colophon states 96 copies but Alberts states that printer's records show 200 copies were printed

$850.

009a: CAWDOR *and Other Poems* Liveright NY 1928 [2] 375 sgd no cc with 350 copies for sale. Issued in glassine dustwrapper in slipcase

$350/450

009b: CAWDOR *and Other Poems* Liveright NY 1928 [0] 1,900 cc

$50/250

009c: CAWDOR *and Other Poems* Hogarth Press L 1929 [0] 520 cc printed but 270 pulped later. "Hogarth Living Poet, First Series, No. 12". Orange paper boards. Issued without dustwrapper (Howard Woolmer, *A Checklist of the Hogarth Press*)

$350.

009d: CAWDOR Yolla Bolly Press (Covelo 1983) [2] 225 sgd no cc. Signed by James Houston (afterword) and Mark Livingston (illustrator). (Additional 15 copies "Not For Sale.") First separate edition

$400.

010a: ROBINSON JEFFERS Carmelite Carmel by the Sea 1928 [0] 1,350 cc. Wraps. Supplement to the Carmelite

$250.

011a: DEAR JUDAS *and Other Poems* Liveright
NY 1929 [0] 3,000 cc $50/250

011b: DEAR JUDAS *and Other Poems* Liveright
NY 1929 [2]   25 sgd ltr cc. Issued in slipcase.
(Published 2 weeks after trade edition) $1,400/1,500

011c: DEAR JUDAS *and Other Poems* Liveright
NY 1929 [2] 350 sgd no cc. Issued in slipcase.
(Published 2 weeks after trade edition) $350/450

011d: DEAR JUDAS *and Other Poems* Hogarth
Press L 1930 [0] 236 cc (64 copies pulped of 300
printed). Issued without dustwrapper $350.

011e: DEAR JUDAS *and Other Poems* Liveright
NY 1977 [3] With 6 corrections. Includes afterword
and textual notes by Robert J. Brophy. Issued in
library binding of laminated boards (Steven Temple
#23 7/88) $15/45

012a: STARS Flame Press (Pasadena) 1930 [2] 6
cc (80 copies stated on p.8 but on recto a tipped-in
errata slip states "It was a great BLUNDER to use
an "a" for an "i" in "incredible" * far greater to have
but 72 of 80 copies survive the printing."
Reportedly all but 6 copies were then destroyed.)
Issued in black boards without dustwrapper $1,500.

012b: STARS Flame Press (Pasadena) 1930 [2]
110 no cc. Wraps. (Second edition. Issued in blue
wraps) $850.

013a: APOLOGY FOR BAD DREAMS   Ward
Ritchie Paris 1930 [2] 30 no cc. Wraps $1,250.

013b: APOLOGY FOR BAD DREAMS   James
Linden S.F. 1986 [2] 50 no cc. With photographs
by Michael Mundy. Issued in cloth clamshell
portfolio (Transition #7) $450.

014a: WINTER SUNDOWN (H. Taylor S.F.
1930) [0] Broadside. Note: Jeffers gave Taylor

permission to reprint this poem in an anthology. The anthology was never published but Taylor made several copies on heavy white paper. 2 copies known (ref.a) $1,500.

015a: DESCENT TO THE DEAD Random House NY (1931) [2] 50 sgd cc, each marked as "review copy". Issued without dustwrapper in unmarked slipcase $650/750

015b: DESCENT TO THE DEAD Random House NY (1931) [2] 500 sgd no cc. Issued without dustwrapper in slipcase $350/450

016a: THURSO'S LANDING *and Other Poems* Liveright NY (1932) [2] 200 sgd no cc. Nos. 1-185 for sale (there were also 6 out-of-series copies). Issued in cellophane dustwrapper and slipcase $500/600

016b: THURSO'S LANDING *and Other Poems* Liveright NY (1932) [0] 2,570 cc $50/250

017a: GIVE YOUR HEART TO THE HAWKS *and Other Poems* Random House NY 1933 [2] 200 sgd no cc. Nos. 1-185 for sale. Issued in slipcase $450/550

017b: GIVE YOUR HEART TO THE HAWKS *and Other Poems* Random House NY 1933 [0] $40/200

018a: RETURN: AN UNPUBLISHED POEM Grabhorn Press S.F. 1934 [2] 3 cc. On vellum, specially bound in morocco $1,750.

018b: RETURN: AN UNPUBLISHED POEM Grabhorn Press S.F. 1934 [2] 250 no cc. Issued in wraps $350.

019a: ROCK AND HAWK (Frederic Prokosch no place) 1934 [2] 20 cc. Wraps. Reportedly more than 20 were actually printed $400.

020a: GEORGE STERLING   Book Club of
Southern California S.F. 1935 [] 500 cc. Wraps.
Sterling letter to Albert Bender with one page essay
on Sterling by Jeffers (Joseph the Provider 12/92) $75.

021a: SOLSTICE *and Other Poems*   Random
House   NY   1935 [2] 320 sgd cc.   Printed by
Grabhorn   Press.   Issued   in   unprinted   gray
dustwrapper $400/500

021b: SOLSTICE *and Other Poems*   Random
House NY 1935 [0] $40/200

022a: THE BEAKS OF EAGLES AN UNPUB-
LISHED POEM   Privately printed   S.F. 1936 [0]
135 cc.   Wraps. Printed by Grabhorn Press for
Albert M. Bender $600.

023a: FOUR POEMS AND A FRAGMENT (S.S.
Alberts Yonkers 1935) [0] Wraps. (Catalogued for
$5,500 - Serendipity Cat. #40) $NVA

024a: HOPE IS NOT FOR THE WISE AN UN-
PUBLISHED POEM   Quercus   Press   San Mateo
(1937) [2] 24 no cc. Wraps. For private distribution
(There may also be unnumbered copies) $1,750.

025a: A POEM (Quercus Press San Mateo) 1937
[2] 5 cc. Printed for "Una and Robinson Jeffers."
Issued in folio $3,000.

025b: A POEM (Quercus Press San Mateo) 1937
[2] 10 cc. "Printed in an edition of ten copies and
the type distributed." Issued in folio $2,000.

026a: SUCH COUNSELS YOU GAVE TO ME
Random House NY (1937) [2] 300 sgd no cc.
Illustrated by Fritz Eichenburg.   Issued without
dustwrapper in slipcase. (Ref.c states that it was
issued in dustwrapper but we have not seen one) $400/500

026b: SUCH COUNSELS YOU GAVE TO ME
Random House NY (1937) [0] $35/175

027a: THE SELECTED POETRY OF ROBIN-
SON JEFFERS Random House NY (1938) [1] $50/250

028a: THE HOUSE DOG'S GRAVE - HAIG'S
GRAVE (Quercus Press San Mateo 1939) [2] 30
no cc. Includes an original photograph by Horace
Lyon. Bound in morocco $2,500.

029a: TWO CONSOLATIONS   (Quercus Press
San Mateo) 1940 [2] 250 cc of which 200 copies
were for sale. Also noted in variant green paper
binding. The Library of Congress deposit copy was
in this binding. (Robert Dagg 3/95) $500.

030a: THE CONDOR (Quercus Press San Mateo)
1940 [0] 12 cc. Wraps $1,500.

031a: BE ANGRY AT THE SUN Random House
NY (1941) [2] 100 sgd no cc. Issued in slipcase $900/1,000

031b: BE ANGRY AT THE SUN Random House
NY (1941) [1] $35/175

032a: MEDEA *Freely Adapted from The Medea of
Euripides* Random House NY (1946) [1] Pp.99-
100 integral, word "least" lacking p.99:21 $75/200

032b: MEDEA *Freely Adapted from The Medea of
Euripides* Random House NY (1946) [1] Word
"least" present p.99:21 $25/125

032c: MEDEA *Freely Adapted from The Medea of
Euripides* Random House NY (1946) [1] English
issue with labels on title page and dustwrapper flap
(Glenn Horowitz) $25/125

032d: MEDEA *Freely Adapted from The Medea of
Euripides* French NY (1948) [0] Wraps. First
assumed to have $1.00 on front flap $40.

033a: NATURAL MUSIC Book Club of Calif.
(SF) 1947 [2] 25 cc. Wraps (on parchment-like
paper, french fold). Folio #12 $500.

033b: NATURAL MUSIC   Book Club of Calif. (SF) 1947 [0]   750 cc.   Printed by Quercus Press. Folio #12 — $125.

034a: THE DOUBLE AXE *and Other Poems* Random House NY (1948) [1] With tipped-in page signed by Jeffers (ref.c) — $900/1,000

034b: THE DOUBLE AXE *and Other Poems* Random House NY (1948) [1] — $30/150

034c: THE DOUBLE AXE *and Other Poems* Liveright NY 1977 [3]   2 corrections. Adds 11 poems — $10/40

035a: POETRY GONGORISM AND A THOU-SAND YEARS   Ward Ritchie (LA) 1949 [2] 200 cc. Boards. Issued without dustwrapper — $350.

035b: POETRY GONGORISM AND A THOU-SAND YEARS   Folcroft (no place) 1970 [2] 150 cc. Photo offset reprint — $40.

036a: MEDITATION ON SAVIORS (Hermes SF 1951) [2] 5 cc — $1,500.

037a: HUNGERFIELD *And Other Poems* Privately Printed (SF) 1952 [0]   30 cc.   Printed by Grabhorn Press — $3,500.

038a: (Untitled...honors Theodore Max Lilienthal) (Grabhorn SF 1953) [0] 30 cc — $3,000.

039a: HUNGERFIELD *And Other Poems* Random House NY (1954) [1] — $30/150

040a: VISITS TO IRELAND   Ward Ritchie   LA 1954 [2] 300 cc. Written by Una Jeffers, foreword by Jeffers. Issued without dustwrapper in slipcase (ref.c) — $350/400

041a: THE LOVING SHEPHERDESS   Random House NY 1956 [2] 115 cc signed by Jeffers and

Jean Kellogg. Boxed (some with extra suite of
plates may be priced higher) $1,350/1,500

042a: THEMES IN MY POEMS   Book Club of
Calif.   SF 1956 [2] 350 cc.   Plain brown
dustwrapper (ref.c) $300/350

043a: THE OCEAN'S TRIBUTE Grabhorn Press
for Ted Lilienthal and Carroll Harris (no place)
1958 [0] "In honor of the awarding of the 1958
Fellowship of the Academy of American Poets to
Robinson Jeffers..." Folio $175.

044a: FIRST BOOK (*My First Publication*) (Book
Club of California San Francisco 1961) [] Sewn
pictorial wraps. Edited and introduced by James
Hart. First separate edition (Waiting For Godot
Books 2/95) $75.

045a: AVE VALE ROBINSON JEFFERS
(Grabhorn SF 1962) [2] 250 cc. Wraps. First
appearance of "The Epic Stars" $250.

046a: THE BEGINNING & THE END *and Other
Poems* Random House NY (1963) [1] $15/75

047a: TO THE STONE-CUTTERS Cody's Books
(Berkeley) 1964 [0] Broadside which also included
a Dylan Thomas Poem $150.

048a: A LETTER FROM ROBINSON JEFFERS
Whitnah & Filpott (no place) 1964 [0] 250 cc.
Broadside $150.

049a: SELECTED POEMS Vintage NY (1965) [0]
Wraps. "V-295" $50.

050a: NOT MAN APART Sierra Club SF (1965)
[0] Jeffers' poems and Ansel Adams' photos $50/125

051a: RHYTHM AND RHYME (Peters Gate Press
Monterey 1966) [2] 500 no cc. Small card in
mailing envelope $60.

052a: THE SELECTED LETTERS OF
ROBINSON JEFFERS 1897-1962 John Hopkins
Baltimore (1968) [0] Edited by Ann N. Ridgeway $15/60

053a: HOW BEAUTIFUL IT IS (Moe's Books
Berkeley 1969) [] Broadside (ref.d) $40.

054a: CAWDOR A LONG POEM MEDEA
AFTER EURIPIDES New Directions (NY 1970)
[0] Wraps. "NDP 293" $30.

055a: JEFFERS' COUNTRY - THE SEED PLOTS
OF ROBINSON JEFFERS' POETRY Scrimshaw
Press (SF) 1971 [2] 500 cc. Jeffers' poems and
Horace Lyon's photos $50/100

055b: JEFFERS' COUNTRY - THE SEED PLOTS
OF ROBINSON JEFFERS' POETRY Scrimshaw
Press (SF) 1971 [2] 3500 cc. Wraps $50.

056a: STILL THE MIND SMILES AT ITS OWN
REBELLIONS... Druid Press Berkeley (1972) [2]
50 sgd no cc. Broadside signed by illustrator,
Robert Baldock $175.

056b: STILL THE MIND SMILES AT ITS OWN
REBELLIONS... Druid Press Berkeley (1972) [2]
200 cc. Broadside $60.

057a: THE ALPINE CHRIST *and Other Poems*
Cayucos Books no place 1973 [2] 250 no. cc.
Signed by William Everson. Issued in acetate
dustwrapper $250.

057b: THE ALPINE CHRIST *and Other Poems*
Cayucos Books no place 1974 [0] Issued in plain
white dustwrapper (Transition #4) $50/75

058a: CASSANDRA No publisher or place (1973)
[2] 100 sgd no cc. Broadside by James Kirwan with
Jeffers' poem. Signed by Kirwan $125.

059a: TRAGEDY HAS OBLIGATIONS Lime Kiln Press (SC) 1973 [2] 200 no. cc. Signed by William Everson and Allison Clough — $350.

060a: THE JOURNEY Pomegranite Sausalito 1974 [0] 3 broadsides by James Kirwan with Jeffers' poems — $75.

061a: BRIDES OF THE SOUTH WIND POEMS 1917-1922 Cayucos Bks no place 1974 [2] 285 sgd no cc. Signed by William Everson — $200.

062a: "SHINE, PERISHING REPUBLIC" Lime Kiln Press Santa Cruz 1974 [2] 100 cc. Single sheet. 17"x13". For Gleeson Library Association (Waiting For Godot) — $75.

063a: GRANITE & CYPRESS *Rubbings from The Rock Poems Gathered from His Stone Mason Years* Lime Kiln Press SC 1975 [2] 100 sgd no cc. Signed by William Everson. Issued in cypress wood slipcase with granite inset — $5,000.

064a: THE DESERT Dawson's Book Shop LA 1976 [1] Wraps — $60.

065a: GEORGE STERLING'S DEATH (Poltroon) SF (1976) [0] 75 cc. Wraps. Folio — $100.

066a: IN THIS WILD WATER *The Suppressed Poems of Robinson Jeffers* Ward Ritchie Pasadena (1976) [1] Edited by James Sheel — $15/60

067a: HEADLANDS Friends of Earth SF (1976) [2] 800 sgd cc. Edited by David Brower. Photos by Richard Kauffman, with Jeffers' poems. Signed by Brower and Kauffman — $150/200

068a: RENATE PONSOLD | ROBERT MOTHERWELL: APROPOS ROBINSON JEFFERS California State University Long Beach 1981 [2] 1,500 cc. Wraps — $40.

069a: WHAT ODD EXPEDIENTS *and Other Poems* Archon Books (Hamden, Ct) 1981 []
Edited by Robert I. Scott. 30 poems, 16 previously unpublished · $12/60

070a: CURB SCIENCE? Quintessence Publ. Amador City 1982 [2] 200 no cc. 11"x8.5" broadside (Chloe's Books) · $40.

071a: THE LAST CONSERVATIVE Quintessence Publ. Amador City 1982 [2] 100 no cc. 27"x17" Folded once. First printing of this poem (Chloe's Books) · $75.

072a: ROBINSON JEFFERS: A PORTRAIT Carolyn and James Robertson (Yolla Bolly Press Covelo 1983) [2] 280 sgd no cc, by Jeffers' family and signed by his son, Garth. Issued in glassine dustwrapper. (260 copies for sale.) Includes previously unpublished photographs · $300.

073a: UNA AND ROBINSON JEFFERS *Two Early Letters to Hazel Pinkham* Occidental College LA 1983 [2] 150 cc. Issued in wraps (Pepper & Stern) · $75.

074a: HAWK TOWER Quintessence Publ. Amador City 1985 [2] 100 no cc signed by the artist. 20"x13.5" broadside · $75.

075a: FROM THE PURSE-SEINE No publisher Amador City no date [1985?] [] Broadside, 14"x10" (Chloe's Books) · $40.

076a: INSCRIPTION / FOR A GRAVE STONE (No publisher [Quintessence?] Amador City no date [1985?]) [] Broadside, 12"x9" inches (Chloe's Books) · $40.

077a: THE REMEMBRANCE (No publisher [Quintessence?] Amador City no date [1985?]) [] 11"x8.5" broadside (Chloe's Books) · $40.

078a: ROBINSON JEFFERS & RELIGION (Peter R. Koch SF 1986) [] 125 cc. Folio leaf folded to 4 pages. Introduction by Robert J. Brophy (George Houle) $60.

079a: ROCK AND HAWK Random House NY (1987) [] Selection of shorter poems edited by Robert Hass (Chloe's Books) $8/40

080a: POINT LOBOS Wolf Editions Oakland 1987 [2] 25 no. subscriber's cc. Unbound folio pages laid in publisher's cloth portfolio. 15 poems by Jeffers with introduction by Wm. Everson. Illustrated with 15 original photos by Wolf Von Dem Bussche (Jos. The Provider 4/90) $2,000.

081a: WHERE SHALL I TAKE YOU TO *The Love Letters of Una and Robinson Jeffers* Yolla Bolly Press Covelo, CA 1987 [2] 25 sgd no cc. Signed by Garth Jeffers. Issued in full leather and slipcase $750/850

081b: WHERE SHALL I TAKE YOU TO *The Love Letters of Una and Robinson Jeffers* Yolla Bolly Press Covelo, CA 1987 [2] 225 no cc. Issued in slipcase. Edited by Robert Kafka with foreword by Garth Jeffers $275/325

082a: TO CELEBRATE THE CENTENARY OF THE BIRTH OF ROBINSON JEFFERS AND BLANCHE MATTHIAS (Quintessence Amador City 1987) [2] 100 sgd no cc. 20"x13.5" broadside illustrated with drawing of Tor House and explaination of Blanche's contribution to its construction. (Chloe's Books 10/90) $45.

083a: SELECTED POEMS: *The Centenary Edition* Carcanet Manchester 1987 [] Wraps. Edited and introduced by Colin Falck. No hardbound edition (Ian McKelvie 11/91) $40.

084a: SONGS & HEROES Arundel Press L.A. 1988 [2] 50 Deluxe copies on Gutenberg paper. 22

previously unpublished poems from Jeffers' early years (Chloe's Books 9/89) $300.

084b: SONGS & HEROES Arundel Press L.A. 1988 [2] 200 no. cc (Chloe's Books 9/89) $200.

085a: THE COLLECTED POETRY OF ROBINSON JEFFERS Volume I, 1920-1928 Stanford University Press Stanford 1988 [] Edited by Tim Hunt. (Published at $60.) $15/60

086a: THE COLLECTED POETRY OF ROBINSON JEFFERS Vol II Stanford University Press Stanford 1989 [] Edited by Tim Hunt (Published at $60) $15/60

087a: A BOOK OF GAELIC AIRS FOR UNA'S MELODEON Book Club of California S.F. 1989 [2] 500 cc. Gaelic songs by Una Jeffers with illustrations by Robinson $100/200

088a: THE INSCRIPTIONS AT TOR HOUSE AND HAWK TOWER Imprenta Glorias L.A. (1989) [2] 50 cc. Foreword by Ward Ritchie and signed by him and Gloria Stuart, the printer. In clamshell box (Argosy Books 5/90) $450/500

089a: FIRE ON THE HILLS Quintessence Amador City (no date) [2] 10 cc. 8.5" x 11" broadside (Chloe's Books 10/90) $60.

090a: NOVA Quintessence Amador City 1990 [2] 20 sgd cc. Signed by printers. 22.5" x 9.8" broadside (Chloe's Books 10/90) $60.

091a: SELF-CRITICISM IN FEBRUARY Quintessence Amador City 1990 [2] 20 sgd cc. Signed by printers. Broadside (Chloe's Books has cataloged this as 22.5" x 11.5" and as 19" x 11.5"??) $60

092a: THE COLLECTED POETRY OF ROBINSON JEFFERS Volume III Stanford Uni-

versity Press Stanford 1991 [] (Joseph The
Provider 12/94) $15/60

093a: LOVE THE WILD SWAN Quintessence
Press Amador City 1991 [2] 50 cc. Broadside
(Chloe's Books cataloged this as 15" x 21½" and
22.5 x 14.5"??) $50.

094a: GRAY WEATHER Quintessence Press
Amador City 1991 [2] 37 cc. Broadside (Chloe's
Books 5/91) $50.

095a: THE INHUMANIST Quintessence Amador
City 1991 [2] 65 cc. 22.5" x 14.5" broadside
(Chloe's Books 5/91) $50.

096a: SHIVA Quintessence Press Amador City
(no date [1991?]) [2] 50 letterpress cc. 22" x 14.5"
(Chloe's Books 5/91) $50.

097a: ...NOT MAN APART... Doug Tompkins no
place 1992 [] Wraps. First separate printing. Issued
as a New Year's greeting for the "Deep Ecology"
movement. Two stiff printed sheets. One, on light
stock paper prints the text of the poem; the other,
on very heavy stock paper, prints a message about
the "Deep Ecology" movement. Hinged at top
(Waiting For Godot 2/95) $75.

098a: THE HOUSE THAT JEFFERS BUILT
Yolla Bolly Press Covelo, CA 1993 [2] 175 sgd
no cc. Signed by Garth Jeffers. 2 vols. *The Building
of Tor House* by Donnan Jeffers (unsigned) and
Memories of Tor House by Garth Jeffers (signed).
Issued in matching slipcases. (Assume no Robinson
Jeffers content) $175/250

Jack Kerouac (signature)

JACK KEROUAC
(1922-1969)

Jean Louis Kerouac was born in Lowell, Massachusetts, to French Canadian immigrants. He was a very good football player in high school and as a result he was sent to Horace Mann Prep School to gain weight and improve scholastically before going on to college at Columbia. His college athletic career, however, was short as he was injured in the first game and sidelined for the season. The next year he dropped out and wrote and wandered, eventually to find himself the "King of the Beats," the central figure in a group which included Burroughs, Ginsberg, Corso, Holmes, et al.

Many critics have been less than kind to Kerouac's work, but there is little doubt that his place in literary history is secure; and that interest in his work has not decreased over the years.

REFERENCES:

(a) Charters, Ann. A BIBLIOGRAPHY OF WORKS BY JACK KEROUAC 1939-1975. Revised Edition. New York: Phoenix Bookshop, 1975.

(b) Morrow, Bradford, Bookseller. CATALOGUE FIVE *The Walter Reuben Collection of Jack Kerouac.* Santa Barbara: (no date [1979]).

(c) Bruccoli, Matthew J., Editor. FIRST PRINTINGS OF AMERICAN AUTHORS. Volume 1. Detroit: Gale Research (1977).

(d) Dealer catalogs or inventory.

(e) Anstee, Rod. JACK KEROUAC, THE BOOTLEG ERA *An Annotated List.* Sudbury, Massachusetts: Water Row Press, 1994.

Reference (a) is a very good bibliography. However, no copyright page information was included thus the first edition identification codes included herein were derived from reference (c) or other sources.

Pacific Red Car Press reported that each of their press runs were only 100 copies.

001a: THE TOWN & THE CITY Harcourt, Brace NY (1950) [1] "Advance Review" copy in salmon colored wraps $1,000.

001b: THE TOWN & THE CITY Harcourt, Brace NY (1950) [1] 15,000 cc printed (10,500 bound). Author's name given as John Kerouac $150/750

001c: THE TOWN & THE CITY Eyre & Spottiswoode L (1951) [] Author's name given as John Kerouac $60/300

002a: ON THE ROAD Viking Press NY 1957 [1] 7,500 cc in total (a&b). Issued with additional white dustwrapper with printed blurb: "This is a copy of the first edition" (ref.b) $400/4,000

002b: ON THE ROAD Viking Press NY 1957 [1] $400/2,500

002c: ON THE ROAD Andre Deutsch (L 1958) [] 3,000 cc. Author's photo on dustwrapper rear flap (ref.b). Ref.a states photo on front flap. Len Deighton designed dustwrapper $150/750

002d: ON THE ROAD Andre Deutsch (L 1958) [] Second issue dustwrapper with author's photo on front flap $150/500

002e: ON THE ROAD   Signet/(New American Library NY 1958) [0] Wraps $35.

003a: RIVER OF RED WINE   (No publisher or place) (1958) [0] Wraps. Introduction by Kerouac to Jack Micheline's book $100.

004a: THE SUBTERRANEANS Grove Press Inc.
NY (1958) [2] 100 no cc. Bound in half cloth $750.

004b: THE SUBTERRANEANS Grove Press Inc.
NY (1958) [1] States published in 3 editions: an
Evergreen Book (E-99), a hardback edition and a
specially bound limited edition of 100 copies. This
is the estimated price for hardback in dustwrapper $300/1,250

004c: THE SUBTERRANEANS Grove Press Inc.
NY (1958) [1] Wraps. First issue with printing all
in white on cover (Alphabet Books) $75.

004d: THE SUBTERRANEANS Grove Press Inc.
NY (1958) [1] Wraps. Second issue with printing
in blue and white and publishers address changed
on rear cover and title page (Alphabet Books). (Ken
Lopez has seen this second issue both with first
edition stated and unstated. Therefore, the colors for
this issue give credence to this being the second
issue) $45.

004e: THE SUBTERRANEANS Avon Publications NY (1959) [0] Wraps. "Avon T-302". New
preface by Henry Miller and statement by Kenneth
Rexroth on p.1 (later printings numbered "T-340
and "T-390") $35.

004f: THE SUBTERRANEANS Avon Book
Division NY (1959) [0] Wraps. First Canadian
edition similar to 004e except the words "Printed in
Canada" bottom copyright page (ref.b) $35.

004g: THE SUBTERRANEANS Andre Deutsch (L
1960) [] 5,000 cc. First state in red paper-covered
boards (ref.b vs. red cloth in ref.a). Variants in blue
and green covers (ref.a). (Variant in black cloth-
Dalian Books 12/94) $50/200

005a: THE DHARMA BUMS Viking Press NY
1958 [1] 13,000 cc $75/400

005b: THE DHARMA BUMS Andre Deutsch (L 1959) [1] 4,000 cc. First printing incorrectly states "First Published 1950" and usually covered with label with correction. Red, blue or black binding, priority unknown $50/200

006a: DOCTOR SAX Grove Press NY 1959 [] Uncorrected Proof in plain white wraps with handwritten title, etc., on cover and stamped "Uncorrected Page Proof" in red (Ken Lopez 9/92) $2,500.

006b: DOCTOR SAX Grove Press NY (1959) [2] 4 sgd no cc (numbered 1-4). Beige linen cloth, brown cloth on spine, spine lettered in gold $4,000.

006c: DOCTOR SAX Grove Press NY (1959) [2] 26 sgd ltr cc (lettered A-Z). Beige linen with brown cloth on spine, spine letter in gold $2,500.

006d: DOCTOR SAX Grove Press NY (1959) [1] Gray cloth lettered in gold on spine. States "Published in three editions..." (500 copies - Vagabond 8/89) $200/1,000

006e: DOCTOR SAX Grove Press NY (1959) [1] Wraps. "Evergreen Original E-160". Spine lettering measures 6 7/16" (long) or 5 1/16", priority unknown. Also noted with lettering on spine 7/16" high in dark red and light red and 9/16" high in light red. No known priority or relation between height and length of the lettering (Second Life Books 12/90) $60.

006f: DOCTOR SAX Evergreen L 1961 [] Wraps ref.b $40.

006g: DOCTOR SAX Andre Deutsch (L 1977) [1] "First published 1977 by..." (Ref.a states Andre Deutsch L 1974 is first) ("1977" catalogued by Dalian Books, Waiting For Godot, and Fine Book Co. as first British hardback) $50/250

007a: 4 HAIKUS (untitled) (No publisher or place 1959) [0] Wraps. 1 leaf unpaged. 6"x9" stiff gray wraps imprinted "Grecort Review" in black ("few" copies issued) — $250.

008a: MAGGIE CASSIDY Avon Book Division NY (1959) [0] Wraps. Avon G1035. Two page spread for title page with the author's name on left and title etc. on right. Introduction by Henry Miller — $100.

008b: MAGGIE CASSIDY Avon Book Division NY (1959) [0] Wraps. Title page on one leaf. Later printing per ref.a. — $30.

008c: MAGGIE CASSIDY Avon Book Division NY (1959) [] Wraps. First Canadian edition. The words "Printed in Canada" at bottom of copyright page (ref.b) — $50.

008d: MAGGIE CASSIDY "A Panther Book" No. 1092 (L 1960) [] Wraps. Maggie pictured on cover as blond in long black stockings — $75.

008e: MAGGIE CASSIDY "A Panther Book" No. 1092 (L 1960) [] Wraps. Second issue: Maggie pictured on cover as redhead in blue jeans — $50.

008f: MAGGIE CASSIDY "An Avon Book" NY (1968) [] Wraps. Deletes Henry Miller introduction. Cover different from 008a, b & c — $15.

008g: MAGGIE CASSIDY Andre Deutsch (L 1974) [1] First hardback edition — $50/250

009a: MEXICO CITY BLUES Grove Press NY (1959) [2] 4 sgd cc. Beige paper with brown cloth on spine, spine lettering in gold — $4,000.

009b: MEXICO CITY BLUES Grove Press NY (1959) [2] 26 sgd ltr cc (lettered A-Z). Beige paper with brown cloth on spine. Spine lettered in gold. Issued in acetate dustwrapper — $2,500.

009c: MEXICO CITY BLUES Grove Press NY (1959) [1] Gray cloth lettered in gold on spine. States "Published in three editions..." Ref.a has white dustwrapper printed in red green and black. Also noted as white printed in black only (Waiting For Godot 4/90) $200/1,000

009d: MEXICO CITY BLUES Grove Press NY (1959) [] Wraps. Evergreen Original E-184 $75.

010a: THE AMERICANS Grove Press NY (1960) [0] Introduction by Kerouac, photographs by Robert Frank. Ref.a mentions Grove reissued the book in both hardback and paperback with new material, but gives no details. $250/750

010b: THE AMERICANS Grossman Publ NY 1969 [1] "Revised and Enlarged Edition 1969" $75/250

011a: EXCERPTS FROM VISIONS OF CODY (New Directions NY 1959) [2] 750 sgd no cc. Acetate dustwrapper. There are an additional 55 out-of-series copies. (One copy, marked "B", sent out for review {Ken Lopez 4/91}) $1,000.

012a: HYMN - GOD PRAY FOR ME Pax NY 1959 [0] 11" x 17" broadside folded in quarters issued as Pax No. 10 by *Jubilee Magazine*. Glossy white paper printed in black $250.

012b: HYMN - GOD PRAY FOR ME (No publisher) NY 1969 [0] Piracy broadside measuring 8 1/2" x 11" folded in quarters $60.

012c: HYMN - GOD PRAY FOR ME Yes! Press (Portland, OR 1971) [2] 325 cc (approximately 20 out-of-series copies). 9" x 11" on cocoa-brown text-weight paper $75.

012d: HYMN - GOD PRAY FOR ME Calaban (Montclair 1985) [2] 150 no cc. Wraps (Water Row Books) $75.

013a: THE SCRIPTURE OF THE GOLDEN
ETERNITY Totem Press NY (1960) [0] Wraps.
First printing in white wraps printed in purple
(three variant sizes - priority unknown) $200.

013b: THE SCRIPTURE OF THE GOLDEN
ETERNITY Totem Press NY (1960) [0] Wraps.
Second printing in white wraps printed in red $60.

013c: THE SCRIPTURE OF THE GOLDEN
ETERNITY Totem Press NY (1960) [0] Third
printing is in white wrapper printed in black $40.

013d: THE SCRIPTURE OF THE GOLDEN
ETERNITY Centaur Press L (no date [1960?]) [0]
Pasted over title page of first American edition(?) is
rectangle of white paper printed in black reading
"Centaur Press Ltd. 9 St. Anne's Close..." $150.

013e: THE SCRIPTURE OF THE GOLDEN
ETERNITY Corinth Books NY 1970 [0] Wraps $25.

014a: TRISTESSA   Avon Book Division   NY
(1960) [0] Wraps. Avon T-429 $75.

014b: TRISTESSA Avon Book Division NY 1960
[0] Same as 014a but "Printed in Canada" on
copyright page (Water Row Books) $50.

014c: TRISTESSA World Distributors L (1963)
[0] Wraps. Incorrectly states "Originally published
in Great Britain by Andre Deutsch..." No. 1235 in
Consul Books Series. Also see item 23b. $75.

015a: LONESOME TRAVELER   McGraw-Hill
NY/T/L (1960) [] Uncorrected galley proofs in
string-tied covers with label on front (Skyline
Books catalogued copy for $3,500) $NVA

015b: LONESOME TRAVELER   McGraw-Hill
NY/T/L (1960) [1] Illustrations and dustwrapper by
Larry Rivers $50/250

015c: LONESOME TRAVELLER Andre Deutsch (L 1962) [1] Very dark brown boards lettered in gilt on spine. These were made up first to fill Boots Libraries' order (First issue {Robt Temple}). Did not include six pages of Larry Rivers' drawings   50/150

015d: LONESOME TRAVELLER Andre Deutsch (L 1962) [1] 4,000 cc. William Gichel photo of author on front of dustwrapper incorrectly attributed to "William Belcher" on flap - existence of corrected dustwrapper's unknown. Bound in light red textured boards - not red cloth as stated by ref.a $25/100

016a: RIMBAUD (City Lights Books SF 1960) [0] 2,000 cc. Broadside on yellow paper printed in black and folded in fifths $150.

016b: RIMBAUD (City Lights Books SF 1960) [0] 2,000 cc. Broadside. Second printing. Printed on yellow paper in red ink $60.

017a: BOOK OF DREAMS City Lights Books (SF 1961) [] 5,000 cc. White paperwraps printed in blue (second through fifth printing in black on white paperwraps) $175.

017b: BOOK OF DREAMS Mandarin Books L 1961 [] $50/250

018a: PULL MY DAISY Grove Press NY (1961) [1] Wraps. Evergreen Original E-294 $175.

018b: PULL MY DAISY Evergreen Books Ltd. L 1961 [] Wraps $100.

018c: PULL MY DAISY Pacific Red Car Publ. (L 1984) [2] 100 cc. Wraps (ref.c) $50.

019a: NOSFERATU (DRACULA) New York Film Society Winter 1960-61 [0] Single folded sheet making 4 pages with notes by Kerouac (B16 in ref.a) $300.

020a: BIG SUR   Farrar, Straus & Cudahy   NY (1962) [1] $40/200

020b: BIG SUR   Andre Deutsch (L 1963) [1] Bound in blue or black cloth. Priority unknown $30/150

021a: POEM   (*Jubilee Magazine* no place [NY] 1962) [0] Unfolded broadside measuring 12 3/4" x 18 1/2". "I demand that the Human race..." Pax no. 17 $250.

022a: AN INTERVIEW WITH JACK KEROUAC (Farrar NY 1963) [] Wraps. A two-page release in which Kerouac answers questions about *Visions of Gerard* (B28 in ref.a) $200.

023a: VISIONS OF GERARD   Farrar, Straus & Co. NY (1963) [1] $35/175

023b: VISIONS OF GERARD AND TRISTESSA Andre Deutsch (L 1964) [] 3,500 cc. New title $30/150

023c: VISIONS OF GERARD   Mayflower-Dell (no place 1966) [] Wraps. Dell Book no. 9349. First separate British edition $40.

024a: DESOLATION ANGELS   Coward-McCann, Inc. NY (1965) [] Uncorrected proof, spiral bound in plain wraps (Wm. Reese Co. 5/89) $750.

024b: DESOLATION ANGELS   Coward-McCann, Inc. NY (1965) [0] $50/250

024c: DESOLATION ANGELS   Andre Deutsch (L 1966) [] 4,000 cc $30/150

025a: SATORI IN PARIS   Grove Press NY (1966) [1] $35/175

025b: SATORI IN PARIS   Grove Press NY (1966) [] Wraps. Evergreen Black Cat Book BC-135 $30.

025c: SATORI IN PARIS Andre Deutsch (L 1967)
[1] Price clipped as issued by publisher (Water Row
Books 8/91) $25/100

026a: A PUN FOR AL GELPI (Lowell House
Printers Cambridge, Mass 1966) [2] 100 cc. 6"x 9"
unfolded broadside (ref.a). Actually 6" x 19" (Ken
Lopez 2/91). (Lame Duck Books offered a signed
copy for $3,500 and suggested all 100 copies were
signed) $NVA

027a: AN IMAGINARY PORTRAIT OF
ULYSSES GRANT | EDGAR ALLEN POE
(Portents Brooklyn 1967) [2] 10 sgd no cc. Signed
by Hugo Weber. Broadside, 9 1/2" x 13 1/4".
Unfolded, printed in black on heavy orange paper $450.

027b: AN IMAGINARY PORTRAIT OF
ULYSSES GRANT | EDGAR ALLEN POE
(Portents Brooklyn 1967) [] 190 cc $250.

028a: SOMEDAY YOU'LL BE LYING (Kryia
Press Pleasant Valley 1967) [2] 100 no cc. 12" x
17" broadside. (Beasley Books catalogued one
dated 1967. Ref.a states 1968) $350.

028b: SOMEDAY YOU'LL BE LYING Kyria
Press Pleasant Valley 1968   [2] 26 ltr cc.
Broadside poem illustrated with an original
woodcut (Skyline Books 4/95) $500.

029a: VANITY OF DULUZ *An Adventurous
Education, 1935-46* Coward-McCann NY (1968)
[0] Noted in black and purple only, without usual
blue and yellow as well (Beasley Books) $30/150

029b: VANITY OF DULUZ *An Adventurous
Education, 1935-46* Andre Deutsch (L 1969) []
Bound in green boards per ref.b, correcting ref.a
which calls for cloth. First issue dustwrapper priced
in shillings (Alphabet Books 10/89) $25/125

029c: VANITY OF DULUZ *An Adventurous Education, 1935-46* Andre Deutsch (L 1969) [] Second issue dustwrapper priced in pounds (Alphabet Books 10/89) $25/100

030a: A LAST HAIKU (Portents NY 1969) [0] 10" x 14" broadside issued at a "Memoriam" after author's death $125.

031a: SCATTERED POEMS City Lights Books (SF 1971) [0] 3,000 cc. Wraps. Pocket Poets Series No. 28 $75.

032a: PIC Grove Press, Inc. NY (1971) [1] Wraps. Grove Press Zebra Book Z-1090-Z (reissued in 1973 as Black Cat B-366) $50.

032b: THE SUBTERRANEANS | PIC | TWO NOVELS Andre Deutsch (L 1973) [0] Part of Uniform Edition $25/100

032c: PIC Quartet Books L (1974) [1] Wraps. "Published by ... 1974." First separate U.K. edition $30.

033a: NOT LONG AGO JOY ABOUNDED AT CHRISTMAS (Oliphant Press NY 1972) [] Approximately 195 cc. Wraps. Ref.b calls for mailing envelope $125.

034a: UNCOLLECTED WRITINGS (No publisher) NY 1971 [] Xeroxed pages (approximately 2" thick) in clasp-bound wraps. There is a dispute regarding this item. All agree that David Stivender produced it. We were told by Robert Wilson (Phoenix Bookshop) that there were 12 copies printed in 1971 and 12 copies of a revised and enlarged edition in 1972. The copies were given to friends, none were sold. Jeff Weinberg reports that only 4 copies were done by Stivender and that then Berrigan made 4 copies and sold them to Wilson and that Arthur Knight was also making copies and selling them for $100. We have seen a copy with "1971 - Revised and Enlarged 1972" on it, but Weinberg says that there never was a revised edition and that this was, in fact, the only edition, they just added the statement on the title page. We were later told by Marshall Clements that he and Stivender prepared this item, "we simply typed the 'Revised and Enlarged 1972' part onto the original 1971 title page, which David had signed and dated in 1971. There probably were not 12 copies in total." $600.

035a: VISIONS OF CODY   McGraw-Hill   NY (1973) [] Wraps. Perfect bound uncorrected galleys in blue wraps (ref.a). Also plain wraps with cloth-taped spine and trial dustwrapper. Printed on rectos only (Pharos 4/91) $1,500.

035b: VISIONS OF CODY McGraw-Hill   NY/ St.Louis/S.F. (1973) [1] Issued in both white and buff dustwrappers (Jeffrey H. Weinberg). White is reportedly a remainder dustwrapper $25/125

035c: VISIONS OF CODY   Andre Deutsch   (L 1973) [1] On front dustwrapper flap: "Never before published in its entirety" $25/100

036a: OLD ANGEL MIDNIGHT   Booklegger Albion (L 1973) [] Pirated English edition $50.

036b: OLD ANGEL MIDNIGHT Unicorn Book-shop Dyfed Wales 1976 [0] Wraps $50.

036c: OLD ANGEL MIDNIGHT   Midnight Press (no place 1985) [] Wraps $30.

036d: OLD ANGEL MIDNIGHT Water Row Press (no place [MA] 1992 [] 6 cc. Uncorrected Galley Proof in plain white spiral-bound wraps. 8 ½ x 11".   This proof is for a 1993 limited edition hardback (Boiled Hippo Books 12/94) $150.

036e: OLD ANGEL MIDNIGHT Grey Fox Press SF 1993 [2] 10 sgd ltr cc. Signed by Ann Charters and Michael McClure (prefaces). First complete edition $200.

036f: OLD ANGEL MIDNIGHT Grey Fox Press SF 1993 [2] 50 sgd no cc. Issued without dustwrapper or slipcase. Signed by Michael McClure and Ann Charters (prefaces) (Boiled Hippo Books 12/94) $125.

036g: OLD ANGEL MIDNIGHT Grey Fox Press SF 1993 [] Wraps. First complete trade edition (Water Row 11/94) $15.

037a: TWO EARLY STORIES Aloe Editions (no place) 1973 [2] 175 no. cc. Wraps. (Printed in NY but publisher is in London) $150.

037b: TWO EARLY STORIES Pacific Red Car (no place [L] 1984) [0] 100 cc. Wraps (ref.c) $40.

038a: TRIP TRAP Grey Fox Press Bolinas 1973 [] Wraps. Written with Albert Saiso and Lew Welch $60.

039a: HOME AT CHRISTMAS (Marshall Clements... NY 1973) [] Approximately 197 cc (Phoenix Bookshop #200). Wraps. Ref.b calls for a mailing envelope $125.

039b: HOME AT CHRISTMAS (cover title) (Pacific Red Car L 1984) [0] Wraps. Approximately 100 copies $40.

040a: BELIEF AND TECHNIQUE FOR MODERN PROSE Cowell Press (no place) 1974 [2] 50 cc. Broadside (Skyline Books 3/91) $175.

040b: BELIEF & TECHNIQUE FOR MODERN PROSE (Santa Cruz H.S. Adult Printing Class 1976) [] Broadside less than 50 cc (Serendipity Books) $75.

040c: BELIEF & TECHNIQUE FOR MODERN PROSE Evergreen (no place) 1976 [] (Ken Lopez 4/92) $75.

041a: WOMAN *Unspeakable Visions of the Individual* (UVI) (Arthur & Kit Knight California, Pa) 1976 [] 500 cc. Previously unpublished poem on postcard (green, pink and cream variants) $25.

042a: JUNK   UVI (California, Pa.) 1976 [0] 500 cc Previously unpublished poem on postcard (blue and pink variants) $25.

043a: THREE   UVI (California, Pa.) 1976 [0] 1,500 cc. Previously unpublished poem on postcard $20.

044a: HEAVEN AND OTHER POEMS Grey Fox Press Bolinas (1977) [] Wraps $35.

045a: TAKE CARE OF MY GHOST, GHOST Ghost Press (Berkeley?) 1977 [2] 200 cc. Wraps. Suppressed by Stella Kerouac $175.

046a: NEAL IN COURT   UVI   California, PA (1977) [] Folio broadside of previously unpublished poem with portrait of Kerouac by Carolyn Cassidy $60.

047a: THREE BY JACK KEROUAC (UVI   Ca. 1978) [0] Postcard $20.

048a: LOWELL WAS THE KINGDOM OF THE WORLD A Bunch of Students Press Lowell 1978 [] Broadside. 8" x 10" $35.

049a: UNE VEILLE DE NOEL (UVI 1980) [0] 100 cc. Wraps (ref.e) $50.

050a: FOUR CHORUS POEMS   (Corubolo & Castiglione Verona 1981) [2] 60 sgd cc in wraps. Signed by Enrico Baj (Bromer Booksellers 6/92) $250.

051a: JACK KEROUAC 1922-1969 No publisher (London?) 1982 [0] Broadside (ref.e #24). Also a xeroxed booklet (Lowell circa 1989) produced, as required, for people taking a tour of Kerouac's Lowell sites conducted by Roger Brunelle and Reginald Ouellette (ref.e #44) $40.

052a: SAN FRANCISCO BLUES Beat Books (no place 1983) [0] 500cc. Wraps. Text based on transcription of tape recorded reading by Kerouac; substantial section of original text inadvertently omitted (ref.e) $50.

052b: SAN FRANCISCO BLUES Pacific Red Car (L 1990) [] 500 cc in wraps with Elliot Erwitt photo of Kerouac on cover (ref.e)

053a: DEAR CAROLYN; LETTERS TO CAROLYN CASSIDY (UVI no place? 1983) [0] Wraps. 1,000 cc (Jeffrey H. Weinberg) $50.

054a: HOME AT CHRISTMAS (No publisher) L (no date [1984]) [0] Wraps (ref.d) $50.

055a: TWO EARLY STORIES Pacific Red Car (no place [London]) 1984 [0] 100 cc. Wraps (ref.e) $60.

056a: TWO STORIES FROM JACK KEROUAC (cover title) (Pacific Red Car Publ. no place [L]) 1984 [2] 100 cc. Wraps (ref.e) $60.

057a: THE GREAT WESTERN BUS RIDE Pacific Red Car Publ. (L 1984) [2] 100 cc. Wraps (ref.c) $60.

058a: AWAKENING FROM A DREAM OF ROBERT FOURNIER (Bus Press L 1985) [0] Approximately 100 cc. Wraps. (Ref.e) $60.

059a: LAST WORDS Zeta (L 1985) [0] 500 cc. Wraps. Collected essays (ref.c) $60.

060a: THE VISION OF THE HOODED WHITE ANGELS Pacific Red Car (L 1985) [0] 100 cc. Wraps (ref.c) $60.

061a: RONNIE ON THE MOUND No publisher, place or date (circa 1985) [0] Wraps. "Apparently mailed to the correspondents of a Vancouver-based Kerouac fan (club)..." (ref.e) $60.

062a: CELINE AND OTHER TALES Pacific Red Car (L) 1985 [0] 100 cc. Wraps. First book publication of various magazine and journal items $50.

063a: AMERICAN HAIKUS Caliban Press Montclair (1986) [2] 125 no. cc. Wraps. Previously unpublished poems (Chloe's Books) $50.

064a: THE MEXICAN GIRL (Pacific Red Car L 1987) [0] 100 cc. Wraps. First separate appearance of selection from *On The Road* (Water Row Books) $50.

065a: THE NORTHPORT HAIKUS Beat Scene Press Coventry, England 1989 [2] 125 cc. Stapled wraps (Water Row 9/89) $25.

066a: JACK KEROUAC: I HAD A SLOUCH HAT TOO ONE TIME (Toledo Poets Center [Toledo] 1989) [0] 11" x 30" poster (ref.e) $40.

067a: JACK KEROUAC : SAFE IN HEAVEN DEAD Hanuman Madras/ NY 1990 [0] Small wraps. 4" x 2 5/8". Issued in dustwrapper. Collection of interviews $10.

068a: VISIONS OF AMERICA Water Row Press Sudbury, MA 1991 [2] 250 no cc. Broadside printed and designed by Barry Sternlieb in the format of a multi-colored print with this previously unpublished Kerouac text, as well as an unpublished drawing by Kerouac as background. Approximately 10 x 14 inches, the broadside is contained in a hardcover case, bound in deluxe cloth. The text is a portion of one of Kerouac's travel notebooks circa April, 1952 dealing with his journey across Arizona with Neal Cassidy and Carolyn Cassidy $125.

069a: POMES ALL SIZES City Lights SF (1992)
[] Wraps. Pocket Poets Series No. 48. An
unpublished collection of poetry with an
introduction by Allen Ginsberg. Kerouac's name
missing from spine on first edition (Water Row
Books 4/93) $25.

070a: GOOD BLOND & OTHERS Grey Fox Press
SF 1993 [2] 10 sgd ltr cc. Issued in cloth without
dustwrapper. 44 uncollected shorter works
(magazine appearances and scattered writings).
Preface by Robert Creely, signed by him (Water
Row Books 11/94) $200.

070b: GOOD BLOND & OTHERS Grey Fox Press
SF 1993 [2] 50 sgd no cc. Issued in cloth without
dustwrapper. Preface by Robert Creely, signed by
him $125.

070c: GOOD BLONDE & OTHERS Grey Fox
Press SF 1993 [] Wraps $10.

071a: TANGIER POEM Literary Renaissance/
White Field Press Louisville 1993 [] Poster
approximately 13"x30". Features Kerouac's 1957
poem from *Pomes All Sizes* (Water Row Books
11/94) $25.

OLD ANGEL MIDNIGHT see 036e & f

072a: THE HISTORY OF BOP (Caliban Press
Montclair/Canton 1993) [2] 200 cc in stiff
paperwraps. Issued in handmade paper covers
(Water Row Books 11/94) $75.

073a: SELECTED LETTERS 1940-1956 Viking
NY 1994 [] (Vagabond Books 12/94) $10/30

074a: THE PORTABLE JACK KEROUAC Viking
no place (1995) [] Uncorrected Proof in dark
brown printed wraps (Waverly Books 4/95) $100.

074b: THE PORTABLE JACK KEROUAC Viking
(NY 1995) [1] $5/25

KEN KESEY

Kesey was born in Colorado in 1935. He received a B.A. from the University of Oregon in 1957 and attended Stanford as a Woodrow Wilson Fellow.

After college, Kesey worked in a mental hospital and turned the experience into his most famous work, *One Flew Over The Cuckoo's Nest*. His further adventures with the "Merry Pranksters" were the subject of Tom Wolfe's *The Electric Kool-Aid Acid Test*.

He lives in Oregon and has a motion picture company, Intrepid Trips, and publishes *Spit In The Ocean* magazine.

REFERENCES:

(a) Bruccoli & Clark. FIRST PRINTINGS OF AMERICAN AUTHORS. Volume 1. Detroit: Gale Research (1977).

(b) Inventory or catalog entries.

001a: ONE FLEW OVER THE CUCKOO'S NEST
Viking NY (1962) [1] Text revised in later editions
(Ken Lopez #24) $350/1,500

001b: ONE FLEW OVER THE CUCKOO'S NEST
Methuen L (1962) [1] Actually 1963 per ref.a $50/250

001c: ONE FLEW OVER THE CUCKOO'S
NEST: *A Play in Two Acts* Samuel French NY
(1974) [0] Yellow wraps printed in black. Price:
$2.00. Dale Wasserman's play of Kesey's work $60.

002a: SOMETIMES A GREAT NOTION Viking NY (1964) [] Wraps. Uncorrected proofs in two spiral bound volumes (Joseph The Provider) $750.

002b: SOMETIMES A GREAT NOTION Viking NY (1964) [1] 11,371 cc. First issue has publisher's logo (Viking ship) on half-title (before title page {Serendipity Books}). Ken Lopez had a copy with logo on second half-title (after title page - before text). Lopez identifies a first printing/issue, dustwrapper with photographer's name as Hank Krangler, changed to Hank Kranzler on second printing/issue. It would seem to us that the logo on second half title would be a mistake as publisher's do not normally put their logos on that half title. This issue is certainly much scarcer than the issue with the logo on first half title (we have never had one, at least, that we remember). However, Lopez's copy with logo on second half title was in the second issue dustwrapper, which would indicate it was later. Of course, the dustwrapper might have been switched. Oh well, so much for definitive bibliographical information. (Published 7/27/64 at $7.50) $50/250

002c: SOMETIMES A GREAT NOTION Methuen L (1966) [1] $30/150

003a: KESEY'S GARAGE SALE Viking / Intrepid Trips NY (1973) [1] Edited and contribution by Kesey $35/125

003b: KESEY'S GARAGE SALE Viking / Intrepid Trips NY (1973) [1] Wraps $50.

004a: "WHOLE EARTH CATALOG, March 1971" [] Wraps. Supplement edited by Kesey and Paul Krassner $75.

005a: KESEY Northwest Review Books Eugene, OR (1977) [1] Edited by Michael Strelow and staff. Introductions by Malcolm Cowley and John Clark

Pratt. Includes drawings and photos by Kesey as well as facsimile manuscript pages and much unpublished material (Water Row 7/88) $40/150

005b: KESEY Northwest Review Books Eugene, OR (1977) [1] Wraps $50.

006a: THE DAY AFTER SUPERMAN DIED Lord John Press Northridge 1980 [2] 50 sgd no cc. Deluxe copies issued without dustwrapper or slipcase (ref.b) $250.

006b: THE DAY AFTER SUPERMAN DIED Lord John Press Northridge 1980 [2] 300 sgd no cc. Issued without dustwrapper or slipcase (ref.b) $125.

007a: LAST GO ROUND Taylor Pleasant Hill, NY 1984 [] Original screenplay. 111 copied pages, punch-bound in binder with label. Unpublished (Joseph The Provider 5/92) $750.

008a: DEMON BOX Viking [NY 1986] [0] Wraps. "Unrevised and Unpublished Proofs" in light green printed wraps (ref.b). States: "Published August 18, 1986 at $17.95" $125.

008b: DEMON BOX Viking (NY 1986) [1] 39,730 cc. Although proof stated that the price would be $17.95 it actually was published at $18.95 $10/40

008c: DEMON BOX Methuen L (1986) [] $10/40

009a: STILL KESEY No publisher NY 1986 [] Wraps. Program for a Kesey performance promoting *Demon Box*. Contains songs and poems by Kesey? (Ken Lopez #30) $35.

010a: CAVERNS Penguin (NY 1990) [3] Wraps. 30,000 cc (PW). Also states "First published in Penguin Books 1990". Written with "O.U. Levon," introduction by Kesey who also "edited" this class project by 13 students at the University of Oregon. (Published January 1990 at $8.95) $35.

011a: THE FURTHER INQUIRY Viking [NY] 1990) [] Uncorrected proof in salmon colored wraps laid in proof dustwrapper (Ken Lopez 7/91). Orange wraps (Bev Chaney, Jr. 1/95) $60.

011b: THE FURTHER INQUIRY Viking NY 1990 [] 8-page excerpt in wraps and proof dustwrapper (Watermark West 11/90) $40.

011c: THE FURTHER INQUIRY Viking (NY 1990) [3] 50,000 cc (PW). Also states "First Published in 1990 By Viking..." (Published at $24.95) $7/35

011d: FOR FURTHER INQUIRY Viking (NY 1990) [1] Wraps $20.

012a: LITTLE TRICKER THE SQUIRREL MEETS BIG DOUBLE THE BEAR Viking (NY 1990) [3] Also states "First Published in 1990..." First separate edition; illustrated by Barry Moser $6/30

013a: THE SEA LION Viking [NY] (1991) [0] Uncorrected Proof in blue printed wraps $50.

013b: THE SEA LION Viking [NY] (1991) [0] Advance Reading copy in bluewraps. 48 pp. of text only. This may be duplicate of 013a? $50.

013c: THE SEA LION Viking (NY 1991) [] $6/30

014a: CAN YOU PASS THE ACID TEST? (No publisher, place or date) [2] 350 sgd no cc. Poster 19" x 24" (Water Row Books 4/93) $75.

015a: SAILOR SONG Viking (no place 1991) [] Xeroxed sheets $75.

015b: SAILOR SONG Viking [NY] (1992) [0] Advance Uncorrected Proof in stiff pictorial wraps. "Coming from Viking August 1992" on back cover (ref.b). In dustwrapper? (Monroe Stahr Books 7/92). $50.

015c: SAILOR SONG Viking (NY 1992) [2] 100 sgd no cc. Issued in dustwrapper without slipcase (William Reese Co. 9/95) $100/150

015d: SAILOR SONG   Viking   NY 1992 [] 100,000 cc (PW).   (Published August 1992 at $23.00) $5/20

016a: "WAYNE ALTENHOFFEN STOOD UP WITH A BLACK LEDGER..." Black Oak Books Berkeley 1992 [] Broadside. 6½" x 12¾". Excerpt from *Sailor Song.* Issued on the occasion of the author's reading at Black Oak Books. Printed by Okeanos Press (Ken Lopez 3/95) $60.

017a: LAST GO ROUND *A Dime Western* Viking [NY] (1994) [0] Advance uncorrected proof in pictorial glossy pictorial wraps. Written with Ken Babbs. Also see 007a $40.

017b: LAST GO ROUND *A Dime Western* Viking NY 1994 [2] 200 sgd no cc. Issued in dustwrapper without slipcase. Written with Ken Babbs. Signed by Kesey and Babbs (Water Row Books 11/94) $50/100

017c: LAST GO ROUND *A Dime Western* Viking NY 1994 [] 50,000 cc. Written with Ken Babbs. (Published July 1994 at $20.95) $

STEPHEN KING

Stephen King was born in 1947 in Portland, Maine. He had a short career as a high school English teacher before becoming a one-man industry in supernatural horror fiction.

Bibliographical assistance provided by Lloyd W. Currey, John Knott, and Otto Penzler (Mysterious Press). Unless otherwise stated, reference (a) was used through Entry 22 and reference (b) thereafter.

REFERENCES:

(a) Underwood, Tim and Miller, Chuck. FEAR ITSELF. San Francisco/Columbia, Pa.: Underwood-Miller, 1982.

(b) Inventory, dealer catalogs, or private collections.

(c) BRITISH BOOKS IN PRINT 1983. London: Whitaker & Sons (1983).

001a: CARRIE Doubleday GC 1974 [1] Wraps. "Special Edition Not For Sale." White wraps printed in black, "To be published April 1974" (ref.b). (James Strand in Barry Levin Books catalog of 12/90 reported two issues: first issue with "050" in gutter of page 199; second issue with "P6". Our understanding is that the special edition was printed in the 50th week of 1973, thus the "050" (on all the special edition copies we are aware of). The trade has the code "P6" {sixth week in 1974}. It doesn't seem to us that Doubleday would have printed more special editions at the same time as the trade but Strand's finding seems to indicate they did.) $950.

001b: CARRIE   Doubleday   GC   1974   [1]   30,000 cc $150/750

001c: CARRIE   New English Library   (L   1974)   [1] 1,000   cc.   "First   NEL   hardback   edition   1974" (ref.b). Quantity furnished verbally by publisher's representative $175/850

002a: SALEM'S LOT   Doubleday   GC   1975   [] Uncorrected Proof in tall, thin, green printed wraps $3,000.

002b: SALEM'S LOT   Doubleday   GC   1975   [1] 20,000 cc (b, c & d). First issue dustwrapper priced at $8.95, refers to "Father Cody" in dustwraper write-up (Lloyd Currey). (Although at least one dealer has stated he sold "Cody" in unclipped dustwrapper with $7.95 price??) $200/2,000

002c: SALEM'S LOT   Doubleday   GC   1975   [1] Second issue: dustwrapper price clipped and $7.95 added. "Father Cody" in dustwrapper write-up (Lloyd Currey) $250/1,250

002d: SALEM'S LOT   Doubleday   GC   1975   [1] Third   issue: $7.95   and   "Cody"   changed   to "Callahan" on dustwrapper write-up (Lloyd Currey) $150/600

002e: SALEM'S LOT   New English Library   (L 1976) [1] $100/500

003a: THE SHINING   Doubleday   GC 1977 [1] Uncorrected proof in blue printed wraps with black cloth spine (L.W. Currey) $2,000.

003b: THE SHINING   Doubleday   GC   1977   [1] 25,000 cc. Dustwrapper price: $8.95 $60/300

003c: THE SHINING   New English Library   (L 1977) [1] (Ref.b) $60/300

004a: RAGE   Signet   (NY 1977) [3] 75,000 cc (estimated). Wraps. Also states "First printing, September 1977." Written as Richard Bachman. Number W 7645 (ref.b) $125.

004b: RAGE   New English Library   (L 1983) [1] Wraps. "First... Feb 1983" (ref.b) $50.

005a: NIGHT SHIFT   Doubleday   GC   1978 [1] 12,000 cc. Dustwrapper price: "N. S. |$8.95" $150/750

005b: NIGHT SHIFT   New English Library   (L 1978) [1] (Ref.b) $100/400

006a: THE STAND   Doubleday   GC   1978 [1] 70,000 cc. Dustwrapper price: $12.95. (Firsts have been seen in later dustwrappers priced $18.95) $50/250

006b: THE STAND   New English Library   (L 1979) [1] (Ref.b) $60/300

THE STAND | *The Complete and Uncut Edition* see 057a.

007a: THE DEAD ZONE   Viking NY   (1979) [1] 50,000 cc. (Published August 16, 1979 at $11.95) $25/125

007b: THE DEAD ZONE   MacDonald & Jane's   L (1979) [1] (Ref.b) $35/175

008a: THE LONG WALK   Signet   (NY 1979) [3] Wraps. Also states "First Printing, July 1979." Written as Richard Bachman. Number J 8754 (ref.b) $100.

008b: THE LONG WALK   New English Library (L 1980) [] Wraps (Lloyd W. Currey 11/88) $50.

009a: FIRESTARTER   Phantasia   Huntington Woods   1980 [2] 725 sgd no cc. Issued in dustwrapper and slipcase. Signed and dated on 3

days: 6th, 7th & 8th of July per ref.a. Also signed on the 5th (ref.b)
$300/600

009b: FIRESTARTER Phantasia Huntington Woods 1980 [2] 26 sgd ltr cc. Issued without dustwrapper or slipcase. All dated July 8, 1980
$7,500.

009c: FIRESTARTER Viking NY (1980) [] Uncorrected proof in orange wraps (Waiting for Godot)
$500.

009d: FIRESTARTER Viking NY (1980) [1] 100,000 cc
$20/100

009e: FIRESTARTER MacDonald L (1980) [1] 600 cc. Wraps. Proof copy with no copyright information (back panel stated the quantities) (ref.b)
$400.

009f: FIRESTARTER MacDonald L (1980) [1] 10,000 cc (ref.b)
$35/150

010a: THE MONKEY *Gallery Magazine* (NY) 1980 [0] Wraps. Included in November issue
$50.

011a: ROADWORK New American Library (NY 1981) [3] Wraps. Written as Richard Bachman. Signet paperback, also states "First Printing, March 1981." Number E9668
$100.

011b: ROADWORK New English Library (L 1983) [1] Wraps (ref.b)
$50.

012a: DANSE MACABRE Everest NY 1981 [] Uncorrected Proof in orange wraps (Waverly Books 4/94)
$350.

012b: DANSE MACABRE Everest NY (1981) [2] 15 sgd ltr cc. Issued without dustwrapper in black slipcase
$2,500/2,750

012c: DANSE MACABRE Everest NY (1981) [2] 250 sgd no cc. Issued in glassine dustwrapper in black slipcase
$750/850

012d: DANSE MACABRE Everest NY (1981)
[1] About 35 cc. Issued without limitation leaf or
frontispiece.   Given as gifts by publisher (L.W.
Currey 9/90). Issued without dustwraper in slipcase
(Captain's Bookshelf 9/91) $750.

012e: DANSE MACABRE Everest NY (1981) [0]
Copy noted with review slip dated 20 April 1981.
Code on copyright page is "RRD281" $25/100

012f: DANSE MACABRE MacDonald L 1981 [] $15/75

012g: DANSE MACABRE MacDonald L 1981 []
Wraps (ref.c) $25.

013a: STEPHEN   KING   *4 Early Novels*
Heinemann/Octopus   NY 1981 [1] Includes first
four books (ref.b) $15/50

014a: CUJO Viking NY (1981) [] Folded and
gathered signatures, unbound, preceded bound
proofs (Bev Chaney) $350.

014b: CUJO Viking NY 1981 [] Uncorrected
Proof in gray wraps (Bert Babcock 2/91) $250.

014c: CUJO Viking NY (1981) [1] 150,000 cc.
(Published September 8, 1981 at $13.95) $15/60

014d: CUJO Mysterious Press NY (1981) [2] 26
sgd ltr cc. "Not For Sale" (Otto Penzler). In acetate
dustwrapper and slipcase $1,000/1,250

014e: CUJO Mysterious Press NY (1981) [2] 750
sgd no cc. Issued without dustwrapper in slipcase $300/400

014f: CUJO MacDonald L (1982) [1] $15/75

015a: JAUNT *Gallery Magazine* (NY) 1981 []
Wraps. Included in December issue $50.

016a: CREEPSHOW New American Library NY (1982) [3] Wraps. Based on movie script. "First printing, July 1982"$40.

017a: DIFFERENT SEASONS Viking NY (1982) [1] Wraps. "Unrevised and unpublished proof" in gray-brown wraps (ref.b)$250.

017b: DIFFERENT SEASONS Viking NY (1982) [1] 200,000 cc. (Published April 27, 1982 at $16.95)$15/60

017c: DIFFERENT SEASONS Macdonald & Co. L (1982) [1] (Ref.b)$15/75

018a: THE DARK TOWER: THE GUNSLINGER Donald Grant (West Kingston 1982) [2] 26 sgd ltr cc. Issued in dustwrapper and slipcase. Actually, there were 35 lettered copies (L. W. Currey 7/94)$2,500/2,750

018b: THE DARK TOWER: THE GUNSLINGER Donald Grant (West Kingston 1982) [2] 12 "Publisher's Copies" signed by King and artist Michael Whelan. Issued in dustwrapper and cloth slipcase (L.W. Currey)$2,500/2,750

018c: THE DARK TOWER: THE GUNSLINGER Donald Grant West Kingston (1982) [2] 500 sgd no cc. Issued in dustwrapper and slipcase$1,250/1,500

018d: THE DARK TOWER: THE GUNSLINGER Donald Grant West Kingston (1982) [1] 10,000 cc. There were some defective copies but these were replaced to make up the total of 10,000 copies according to the publisher. Note: dustwrapper also lists limited edition price$100/500

018e: THE DARK TOWER: THE GUNSLINGER Donald Grant West Kingston (1984) [] 10,000 cc. Second printing indicated; dustwrapper does not list limited edition$50/200

018f: THE DARK TOWER: THE GUNSLINGER New American Library NY 1988 [] 1,500,000 cc

(PW). Wraps. (Published September 1988 at
$10.95) $15.

018g: THE DARK TOWER: THE GUNSLINGER
Sphere Books Ltd. (L 1988) [1] [] Wraps. "First
Published by Sphere Books Ltd 1988" $20.

019a: THE RUNNING MAN Signet (NY 1982)
[3] Wraps. Also states "First printing, May 1982".
Written as Richard Bachman. Number AE 1508 $75.

019b: THE RUNNING MAN New English Library
(L 1983) [1] Wraps (ref.b) $40.

020a: WHISPERS Stuart Schif Birmingham 1982
[2] 26 sgd ltr cc. King issue of *Whispers Magazine*
bound in cloth without dustwrapper (ref.b). Includes
Before the Play and *It Grows on You* $400.

020b: WHISPERS Stuart Schif Birmingham 1982
[2] 350 sgd no cc. Issued without dustwrapper
(ref.b) $250.

020c: WHISPERS Stuart Schif Birmingham 1982
[0] Wraps $40.

021a: FEAR ITSELF Underwood-Miller SF/
Columbia, PA 1982 [2] 250 sgd cc. Horror fiction
of King with a foreword and signed by King and
other contributors $250/300

021b: FEAR ITSELF Underwood-Miller SF/
Columbia, PA 1982 [1] 4,775 cc $15/75

021c: FEAR ITSELF New American Lib/Plume
NY 1984 [] Adds additional chapter and updated
bibliography $15.

021d: FEAR ITSELF Pan L 1990 [] Wraps $15.

022a: THE PLANT Philtrum Press Bangor 1982
[2] 26 sgd ltr cc. Issued in sewn wraps (L.W.
Currey) $3,500.

022b: THE PLANT Philtrum Pr Bangor 1982 [2] 200 no cc. Wraps. Published November 1982 for holiday greeting (L.W. Currey). Also see items 031 and 039 $750.

023a: THE RAFT *Gallery Magazine* (NY) 1982 [0] Wraps. Included in November issue $50.

024a: RITA HAYWORTH AND SHAWSHANK REDEMPTION Thorndike Press Thorndike, ME 1982 (John W. Knott Jr.) [] Pictorial boards without dustwrapper. First separate printing of a story from *Different Seasons*. Large print edition. Publisher would not disclose quantity printed, but our impression is that there were probably only 1,000 copies many of which did not sell, and those that did were sold to libraries, which would account for its scarcity $450.

025a: CHRISTINE Donald Grant W. Kingston (1983) [2] 26 sgd ltr cc. Issued in dustwrapper (*American Book Prices Current* 1994) $1,000/1,250

025b: CHRISTINE Donald Grant W. Kingston (1983) [2] 1,000 sgd no cc. Issued in dustwrapper and slipcase. (Also, about 20 copies marked "Publisher's Copy" on the limitation page where the copy number would normally go {Barry R. Levin 12/94}) $350/450

025c: CHRISTINE Viking NY (1983) [1] Wraps. "Unrevised and unpublished proofs..." in yellow wraps $200.

025d: CHRISTINE Viking NY (1983) [1] 270,000 cc. (Published April 29, 1983 at $16.95) $15/60

025e: CHRISTINE Hodder & Stoughton L (1983) [1] Wraps. "Uncorrected Proof" in trial dustwrapper (Anthony F. Smith) $150/250

025f: CHRISTINE Hodder & Stoughton L (1983) [1] 12,000 cc $15/75

026a: BLACK MAGIC & MUSIC (Bangor Historical Society Bangor 1983) [0] Wraps. 8-page **program** distributed at meeting where King spoke. There were only a few hundred copies (L.W. Currey). Includes biographical page and photo plus ads. (There is also a **pamphlet** which is only about King, his talk and photos) $250.

027a: PET SEMATARY Doubleday GC 1983 [1] Pictorial wraps. "Uncorrected Galley". Corrections throughout and not typeset. Reportedly only 30 to 50 copies (L.W. Currey) $450.

027b: PET SEMATARY Doubleday GC 1983 [1] Wraps. "Uncorrected Galley". No corrections, typeset, same size as trade $175.

027c: PET SEMATARY Doubleday GC 1983 [1] 250,000 cc (ref.b). First issue dustwrapper: text at bottom of rear panel has "1982" as date of *Caretakers* by Tabitha King (Barry R. Levin 9/93) $10/75

027d: PET SEMATARY Doubleday GC 1983 [1] Second issue dustwrapper: date of *Caretakers* changed to "1983" $10/50

027e: PET SEMATARY Hodder & Stoughton L (1983) [1] 15,000 cc $15/75

028a: FRANKENSTEIN Dodd, Mead NY (1983) [2] 26 sgd ltr cc. Shelley's story with King introduction and signed by him $500/600

028b: FRANKENSTEIN Dodd, Mead NY (1983) [2] 500 sgd no cc. Issued in tissue dustwrapper in slipcase. Shelley's story with King introduction and signed by him $200/300

028c: FRANKENSTEIN Dodd, Mead NY (1983) [1] Shelley's story with King introduction $10/40

029a: CYCLE OF THE WEREWOLF Enchant-
ment (Westland 1983) [2] 8 sgd no cc. Publisher's
copies in dustwrapper and slipcase $850/1,000

029b: CYCLE OF THE WEREWOLF Enchantment (Westland 1983) [2] 100 no cc (numbered 1
to 100) signed by King and artist with artist signed
sketch laid in. In dustwrapper and slipcase $850/1,000

029c: CYCLE OF THE WEREWOLF Enchantment (Westland 1983) [2] 250 no cc (numbered 101
to 350) signed by King and artist. (The laid in
signed artist sketch that was in 029b is not
included.) Issued in dustwrapper and slipcase. $250/350

029d: CYCLE OF THE WEREWOLF (Portfolio)
Enchantment (Westland 1983) [2] 20 numbered
publisher copies. Portfolio includes 12 full-color
and 12 black-and-white illustrations. Also includes
1,500 word essay by King on Wrightson. Signed by
King and Wrightson. Also five signed and
numbered "printers" copies (L.W. Currey 9/95) $400.

029e: CYCLE OF THE WEREWOLF (Portfolio)
Enchantment (Westland 1983) [2] 350 sgd no cc.
Portfolio includes 12 full-color and 12 black-and-
white illustrations. Also includes 1,500 word essay
by King on Wrightson. Signed by King and
Wrightson (Anthony F. Smith) $300.

029f: CYCLE OF THE WEREWOLF Enchantment (Westland 1983) [0] 7,500 cc (Anthony F.
Smith) $30/150

029g: CYCLE OF THE WEREWOLF New
American Library/Signet (NY 1985) [3] Wraps $30.

029h: CYCLE OF THE WEREWOLF New
English Library (L 1985) [] Wraps (Maurice
Neville) $30.

030a: GRANDE ILLUSIONS Image Pittsburgh 1983 [1] Wraps. Written by Tom Savin, introduction by King. "First printing, January 1983" $75.

030b: BIZARRO Harmony Books NY (1983) [3] Wraps. New title. Reprint which also states "First Edition" $20.

031a: THE PLANT Philtrum Press Bangor 1983 [2] 26 sgd ltr cc. issued in sewn wraps (L.W. Currey) $3,000.

031b: THE PLANT Philtrum Press Bangor 1983 [2] 200 no. cc. Wraps. Issued for Holiday Greeting. Different than item 022a (Otto Penzler) $750.

032a: (OMNIBUS) Heineman L 1983 [] Collects *Carrie, Salem's Lot,* and *The Shining* (Nicholas Burrows 9/91) $10/40

033a: THINNER New American Library NY (1984) [3] Wraps. "Special ABA Edition Uncorrected Advance Proofs." Written as Richard Bachman $125.

033b: THINNER New American Library NY (1984) [3] 26,000 cc. Written as Richard Bachman (quantity from Publisher's Weekly 3/22/85 although proof {033a} stated 50,000 copies to be printed) $25/100

033c: THINNER New English Library (L 1984 1985?) [1] 15,000 cc. Noted with yellow wrap-around band printed in black, "Stephen King writing as Richard Bachman" $25/100

034a: THE TALISMAN Viking (Middlesex 1984) [1] Written with Peter Straub. (Published September 17, 1984) $15/60

034b: THE TALISMAN Viking/Putnam (NY 1984) [1] Wraps. Written with Peter Straub. "Unrevised and unpublished proofs" in yellow wraps. Also a copy in pink wraps with preliminary pages hand-numbered (pages were not numbered in yellow proof) (Pepper & Stern) — $200.

034c: THE TALISMAN Viking/Putnam (NY 1984) [1] (Published November 1984) — $10/35

034d: THE TALISMAN Donald Grant W. Kingston 1984 [2] 1,200 sgd no cc. 2 volumes. "Special Illustrated Edition" (colored plates) issued without dustwrapper in slipcase (ref.b). There are also 5 "artists" copies signed by authors and the other artists (Elliot Shorter), 70 numbered copies (Anthony Smith #10), and an unknown number designated "Publisher's Copy" signed by King and Straub (Barry R. Levin 12/94) — $500/600

034e: THE TALISMAN Donald Grant W. Kingston 1984 [1] 10,000 cc. Two volumes. Issued without dustwrapper in slipcase — $60/125

035a: THE BREATHING METHOD Chivers Press Bath (England) (1984) [1] "First printing in Great Britain 1982... 1984" First separate printing of a story from *Different Seasons*. Large print edition in pictorial boards without dustwrapper (ref.b) — $350.

036a: THE EYES OF THE DRAGON Philtrum Press Bangor 1984 [2] 250 sgd cc numbered in red, reserved for private distribution. Issued without dustwrapper in slipcase. Also 10 copies signed by the illustrator (Kenneth R. Linkhauser) and numbered again on verso (Barry R. Levin 9/94) — $1,600.

036b: THE EYES OF THE DRAGON Philtrum Press Bangor 1984 [2] 1,000 sgd cc numbered in black (1 through 1,000), issued without dustwrapper in slipcase (ref.b) — $550/650

036c: THE EYES OF THE DRAGON Viking (NY 1987) [0] "Unrevised and unpublished proofs" in olive-green printed wraps — $150.

036d: THE EYES OF THE DRAGON Viking (NY 1987) [1] 400,000 cc (although 1,000,000 cc announced in PW). (Published February 2, 1987 at $18.95) $7/35

036e: THE EYES OF THE DRAGON Macdonald (L 1987) [1] $10/50

037a: SKELETON CREW Putnam NY (1985) [3] Wraps. Uncorrected proof in yellow wraps $150.

037b: SKELETON CREW Putnam NY (1985) [3] 500,000 cc (quantity per *Publisher's Weekly* but don't believe that it was that high). (Published June 21, 1985 at 18.95) $7/35

037c: SKELETON CREW Macdonald L 1985 [] Uncorrected Proof in white card covers printed in gray and black with publication date of 6/20/85 $125.

037d: SKELETON CREW Macdonald L 1985 [] Advance Reading Copy in wraps. Includes 7 of the 22 stories (Bert Babcock 5/91) $125.

037e: SKELETON CREW MacDonald (L and Sydney 1985) [1] $10/50

037f: SKELETON CREW Scream Press Santa Cruz 1985 [2] 52 sgd doubled ltr cc. Bound in full leather with zipper around edges (Pepper & Stern 3/89). "...produced from first state sheets of which 52 were lettered and seventeen were distributed to the author, artist and designer... marked "S/P Presentation Copy" and signed by King, artist J. K. Potter and publisher Jeff Conner (Lloyd W. Currey 5/95) $2,000.

037g: SKELETON CREW Scream Press Santa Cruz 1985 [2] "Presentation" copies (Barry R. Levin 6/91, Lloyd W. Currey 5/95) $NVA

037h: SKELETON CREW Scream Press Santa Cruz 1985 [2] 1,000 sgd no cc. Issued in dustwrapper and slipcase. Signed by King and J.K. Potter (artist). One story not in Putnam edition $250/350

038a: THE BACHMAN BOOKS *Four Early Stories* New American Library NY (1985) [3] 200 cc. Uncorrected proof in orange wraps. Introduction by King $150.

038b: THE BACHMAN BOOKS *Four Early Stories* New American Library NY (1985) [3] 15,000 cc. Also states "First Plume Pr..." Noted in dustwrapper which omits "The Bachman Books" on front panel (Bert Babcock) $25/100

038c: THE BACHMAN BOOKS *Four Early Stories* New American Library NY (1985) [3] 350,000 cc. Wraps. Also states "First Plume Pr...October 1985" $30.

038d: THE BACHMAN BOOKS *Four Early Stories* New English Library (L 1986) [1] 2,000 cc (publisher's representative) $25/125

039a: THE PLANT (Part III)   Philtrum Press Bangor 1985 [2] 26 sgd ltr cc.   Issued in sewn wraps (Fine Book Co.) $2,500.

039b: THE PLANT (Part III)   Philtrum Press Bangor 1985 [2] 200 sgd no cc $750.

040a: SILVER BULLET   New American Lib/Signet (NY 1985) [] Stiff pictorial wraps. Includes *Cycle of the Werewolf*, screenplay for *Silver Bullet* and new foreword by King $35.

041a: ES (IT) Edition Phantasia (Germany 1986) [2] 250 no cc in bordello-red velvet slipcase. Page edges stained bright red $500/600

041b: IT Viking (no place or date [NY 1986]) [0] Approximately 200 cc. "Uncorrected page proofs" in red printed wraps. $150.

041c: IT Viking NY 1986 [1] 800,000 cc (PW).
(Published September 1986 at $22.95) $10/40

041d: IT   Hodder & Stoughton   L (1986) [0]
"Presentation page proofs" in red wraps printed in
white and orange $125.

041e: IT Hodder & Stoughton L (1986) [0] 30,000
cc (publisher's representative) $15/75

042a: NEBEL (THE MIST)   Edition Phantasia
(Linkenheim 1986) [2] 30 no cc (Roman numerals).
Issued in dustwrapper and slipcase. First separate
edition. Distribution reportedly stopped by King's
foreign agents, and only about 100 copies of this
and the next item are extant (L.W. Currey). Also 2
copies with" Presentation Copy" in English on
limitation page (Barry R. Levin 6/91) $2,000.

042b: NEBEL (THE MIST)   Edition Phantasia
(Linkenheim 1986) [] "500" no cc (see note above).
Issued in dustwrapper and slipcase (L.W. Currey) $600/750

043a: MISERY   Viking   (NY 1987) [0] "Uncor-
rected Proofs" in red printed wraps $150.

043b: MISERY Viking (NY 1987) [1] 1,000,000
cc (PW). (Published June 8, 1987 at $19.95) $10/40

043c: MISERY Hodder & Stoughton L 1987 []
Uncorrected proof in blue printed wraps (Robert
Gavora 12/94) $150.

043d: MISERY Hodder & Stoughton L (1987) $10/50

044a: THE TOMMYKNOCKERS Putnam NY
(1987) [3] "Uncorrected Proof" in pictorial wraps $100.

044b: THE TOMMYKNOCKERS Putnam NY
(1987) [3] King's "Permissions to come" at foot of
copyright page (Castlerock 2/88 called for this and

King's name in red on front of dustwrapper, but we've seen the "Permissions to come" on book club editions so, unsure of this point. Barry R. Levin {7/90} reports that Frank Halpern noted pp.257-258 on a stub on "Permissions to come" state) $10/40

044c: THE TOMMYKNOCKERS Putnam NY (1987) [3] King's name in gold foil on dustwrapper and "Permissions to come" deleted. (Published November 1987 at $19.95) $10/30

044d: THE TOMMYKNOCKERS Hodder & Stoughton L (1988) [] (Maurice Neville) $15/60

045a: THE DARK TOWER II: THE DRAWING OF THE THREE (West Kingston R.I. 1987) [2] About 50 cc marked "Author's Copy" on limitation leaf (L.W. Currey 1/93). Also 5 no cc presented to the artist Phil Hale (S.M. Mossberg 10/94). Also seen with "Publisher's Copy" signed by King and Phil Hale (Barry R. Levin 9/93) $1,500.

045b: THE DARK TOWER II: THE DRAWING OF THE THREE Donald Grant (West Kingston, R.I. 1987) [2] 850 sgd no cc. Issued in dustwrapper and slipcase $350/450

045c: THE DARK TOWER II: THE DRAWING OF THE THREE Donald Grant (West Kingston, R.I. 1987) [1] 30,000 cc $25/100

045d: THE DARK TOWER II: THE DRAWING OF THE THREE New American Library NY (1989) [3] Uncorrected Proof in orange wraps (Fine Books Co. 1/94) $75.

045e: THE DARK TOWER II: THE DRAWING OF THE THREE New American Library NY (1989) [3] Special Reading Copy "Not for Resale". Also states "First Plume Printing, March, 1989" $50.

045f: THE DARK TOWER II: THE DRAWING OF THE THREE New American Library NY 1989

[3] Wraps.　Also states "First Plume Printing, March, 1989"　$25.

046a: STEPHEN KING GOES TO HOLLYWOOD New American Library　NY 1987 [] Wraps. Illustrated guide to King's movies and an interview　$30.

047a: THE IDEAL, GENUINE MAN　By Don Robertson Philtrum Press　Bangor 1987 [2] 500 sgd no cc. Issued in dustwrapper without slipcase. Introduction by King, signed by both　$60/125

047b: THE IDEAL, GENUINE MAN By Don Robertson Philtrum Press　Bangor 1987 [1] 2,200 cc　$10/40

048a: THE DOCTOR'S CASE　Carroll & Graf NY 1987 [] Wraps. Separate advance uncorrected proof of story published in *The New Adventures of Sherlock Holmes* not included in proof for later book. Only separate edition (Beasley Books 3/89)　$300.

049a: BARE BONES *Conversations in Terror with Stephen King* Underwood-Miller　LA/Columbia 1988　[] 6 cc (Underwood-Miller Catalog 8/90). Edited by Tim Underwood and Chuck Miller. Uncorrected proof in tan wraps　$200.

049b: BARE BONES *Conversations in Terror with Stephen King* Underwood-Miller　LA/Columbia 1988 [2] 52 ltr cc. Issued in red leather without dustwrapper in slipcase　$125/175

049c: BARE BONES *Conversations in Terror with Stephen King* Underwood-Miller　LA/Columbia 1988 [2] 100 cc stamped "Presentation Copy". Issued without dustwrapper in slipcase　$75/125

049d: BARE BONES *Conversations in Terror with Stephen King* Underwood-Miller　LA/Columbia 1988 [2] 1,000 no. cc　$35/75

049e: BARE BONES *Conversations in Terror with Stephen King* McGraw Hill NY (1988) [] (L.W. Currey)

$10/25

049f: BARE BONES *Conversations in Terror with Stephen King* New English Library L 1989 [] Wraps

$35.

050a: MY PRETTY PONY (Whitney Museum NY 1988) [2] 250 sgd cc (not numbered {S. M. Mossberg}), 150 copies for sale at $2,200. Stainless steel with a digital watch inset. Nine (9) lithographs by Barbara Kruger and previously unpublished story by King (64 pages). Signed by both. "First state of the box has red leather label with silver lettering on the spine. The second state omits the spine label." (Barry R. Levin 6/92)

$2,500.

050b: MY PRETTY PONY (Knopf NY 1989) [1] 15,000 cc (all allowed by King). "First Trade Edition" on last page. Issued without dustwrapper in slipcase. (Published October 1989 at $50.)

$50/100

050c: MY PRETTY PONY Franklin L 1989? [] Issued without dustwrapper (Cold Tonnage Books 8/91)

$30.

051a: NIGHTMARES IN THE SKY Viking (NY no date [1988]) [0] Uncorrected proof in plain white wraps and dustwrapper. Contains sample text by King and photos (Gargoyles) by f-stop Fitzgerald

$75.

051b: NIGHTMARES IN THE SKY Viking NY 1988 [] 250,000 (PW). (Published October 1988 at $24.95)

$10/40

051c: NIGHTMARES IN THE SKY Publisher? L 1988 []

$10/40

052a: DOLAN'S CADILLAC Lord John Press Northridge, CA 1988 [0] 100 cc. Proof copies in dark blue wraps and in gray-green wraps (priority unknown, assume issued simultaneously)

$150.

052b: DOLAN'S CADILLAC   Lord John Press
Northridge, CA 1988 [2] 26 sgd ltr cc. Issued in
slipcase $1,000/1,250

052c: DOLAN'S CADILLAC   Lord John Press
Northridge, CA 1988 [2] 100 sgd no cc "For
Presentation." Issued with leather spine and marbled
boards (Cadillac on endpaper). (Note: slipcases
were added to the copies sold later, initially they
were not intended) $750/800

052d: DOLAN'S CADILLAC   Lord John Press
Northridge, CA 1988 [2] 100 sgd cc "For
Presentation." Issued in cloth with Cadillac on
boards and endpapers $500.

052e: DOLAN'S CADILLAC   Lord John Press
Northridge, CA 1988 [2] 250 sgd no cc. Issued
with leather spine, marbled boards and light gray
endpapers (see note on 052c) $500.

052f: DOLAN'S CADILLAC   Lord John Press
Northridge, CA 1988 [2] 1,000 sgd no cc. Issued
in cloth with black endpapers $300.

053a: LETTERS FROM HELL   Lord John Press
Northridge 1988 [2] 500 sgd no cc. Broadside $125.

054a: THE DARK HALF Hodder & Stoughton L
1989 [] "Presentation Proof Copy" in illustrated
wraps (Barry Levin 12/89) $200.

054b: THE DARK HALF Hodder & Stoughton L
1989 [] 55,000 cc (estimated) (Cold Tonnage Books
3/90). Precedes U.S. edition. (Published October 12,
1989) $15/60

054c: THE DARK HALF Viking (NY 1989) [0]
Uncorrected proof in printed white wraps. Some
were in proof dustwrapper without text on flaps $100/200

054d: THE DARK HALF   Viking (NY 1989) []
1,500,000 cc.   (Published November 1989 at
$21.95) $7/35

055a: FEAST OF FEAR *Conversations with
Stephen King*   Underwood-Miller   San Rafael/
Lancaster 1989 [2] 50 no cc "For Private Use." In
dustwrapper and slipcase (L.W. Currey 11/89) $125/200

055b: FEAST OF FEAR *Conversations With
Stephen King*   Underwood-Miller   San Rafael/
Lancaster 1989 [2] 550 no cc $100.

056a: INTRODUCTION TO *THE COLLECTOR*
BY JOHN FOWLES   Book-of-the-Month Club
Camp Hill, PA   1989   [] Wraps.   Small 12-page
separate pamphlet introducing the BOMC's issue of
The Collector included only with this edition $50.

057a: THE STAND   *The Complete and Uncut
Edition* (Doubleday NY 1990) [] Reportedly 200
cc. Uncorrected proofs in white wraps. (Barry R.
Levin cataloged a copy in proof dustwrapper at
$600 {7/90}) $150.

057b: THE STAND   *The Complete and Uncut
Edition* (Doubleday NY 1990) [2] 52 sgd ltr cc in
red silk lined ebony box with engraved plate. $1,750/2,000

057c: THE STAND   *The Complete and Uncut
Edition* (Doubleday NY 1990) [2] 1,250 sgd no cc.
Signed by King and Bernie Wrightson, the
illustrator. Full leather with raised bands in red silk
lined ebony box with engraved plate.(Published at
$325.) (First state label in metallic gold never
issued. 25 plates only?? {Fine Books Co. 1/94}) $1,000/1,250

057d: THE STAND   *The Complete and Uncut
Edition* (Doubleday NY 1990) [1] "May 1990" on
copyright page. Over 500 pages, setting changed to
1990. Contains new beginning and ending, 12
illustrations by Wrightson, and a new preface by
King $7/35

057e: THE STAND *The Complete and Uncut Edition* Hodder & Stoughton L 1990 [] Advance Readers Sample. 66 pages in wraps (Barry R. Levin 7/90) $150.

057f: THE STAND *The Complete and Uncut Edition* (Hodder & Stoughton/Doubleday L 1990) [0] 50,000 cc. (There is some question as to whether this precedes the U.S. edition. Available in April in London {Cold Tonnage Books 8/90}) $10/40

058a: FOUR PAST MIDNIGHT Viking NY 1990 [] Uncorrected Proof in blue printed wraps (Michael Thompson 12/91) $200.

058b: FOUR PAST MIDNIGHT Viking NY (1990) [] Uncorrected proofs in glossy pictorial wraps and dustwrapper $100/200

058c: FOUR PAST MIDNIGHT Viking NY (1990) [] 1,500,000 cc. First issue has gold embossed "S.K." on front cover. Second has "S.K." blind stamped (Barry R. Levin). (Published September 1990 at $22.95) $6/30

058d: FOUR PAST MIDNIGHT Macdonald L (1990) [1] Proof in printed blue wraps and dust-wrapper priced at £4.95 $75/150

058e: FOUR PAST MIDNIGHT Macdonald L (1990) [1] Dustwrapper priced at £4.99 (Barry R. Levin 12/90) $10/40

059a: *"The work of horror really is a dance..."* Oreanos Press SF 1990 [] Broadside. 13½" x 7½" (7 x 14½" Ken Lopez 3/95). First separate appearance. Originally published in *Danse Macabre* $50.

060a: SLEEPWALKERS Creative Artists Agency (no place or date [circa 1990]) [] 116 page original screenplay. Punch bound in agency wraps (Joseph the Provider Books 1/91) $150.

061a: TWICE THE POWER Hodder & Stoughton (Kent   1991) [] Wraps. "Presentation Proof". Includes *Needful Things* and a story from *Four Past Midnight* (Barry R. Levin 11/91) $150.

061b: TWICE THE POWER Hodder & Stoughton L 1991 [] Proof in printed wraps. Prints the text of *Needful Things* and *Secret Window, Secret Garden*, the first proof of the forthcoming novels and the second part of the forthcoming paperback *Four Past Midnight*; unpublished in this form (Ferret Fantasy 11/94) $350.

062a: NEEDFUL THINGS Viking (NY 1991) [0] 795 cc (publisher's records). Uncorrected Proof in white pictorial wraps (Robert Gavora Bookseller 11/94) $75.

062b: NEEDFUL THINGS Viking NY 1991 [0] (Robert Gavora Bookseller 6/95) $6/30

063a: THE DARK TOWER III: THE WASTE-LAND Donald Grant Hampton Falls (1991) [] Advance Review Copy in white printed wraps. (With 12 4-color plates in envelope {Robert Gavora Bookseller 11/91}). (With 13 plates {Barry R. Levin 12/91}) $200.

063b: THE DARK TOWER III: THE WASTE-LAND Donald Grant Hampton Falls (1991) [2] 1,200 sgd no cc. Issued in dustwrapper and slipcase $300/400

063c: THE DARK TOWER III: THE WASTE-LAND Donald Grant Hampton Falls (1991) [2] "Publisher's Copy", signed limited (number??) (Barry R. Levin 9/93) $NVA

063d: THE DARK TOWER III: THE WASTE-LAND Donald Grant Hampton Falls 1991 [] (Robert Gavora 6/95) $10/50

063e: THE DARK TOWER III: THE WASTE-LAND Plume NY 1992 [] Uncorrected Proof in blue printed wraps. (Michael Thompson 12/91) $50.

063f: THE DARK TOWER III: THE WASTELAND Plume NY (1992) [] 1,500,000 cc (PW). Wraps. (Published January 1992 at $15.00) $15.

064a: THE SHAPE UNDER THE SHEET: *The Complete Stephen King Encyclopedia* Popular Culture (place?) 1991? [] 800-page compendium and concordance by Stephen J. Spignesi $100.

065a: GERALD'S GAME Hodder & Stoughton L (1991) [] (Precedes U.S. edition {Barry R. Levin 6/92}). (Simultaneous {Robert Gavora 9/92}) $10/50

065b: GERALD'S GAME Hodder & Stoughton L 1992 [] $7/35

065c: GERALD'S GAME Viking (no place 1992) [0] Uncorrected Proof in tan wraps $75.

065d: GERALD'S GAME Viking NY 1992 [] 2,000 cc. Issued without dustwrapper in cardboard slipcase. **Printed message** from King on front endpaper. Special ABA issue offered to attendees of the 1992 ABA fair in Anaheim, CA $125.

065e: GERALD'S GAME Viking NY 1992 [3] 1,500,000 cc (PW). Also states "First Published in 1992 By Viking..." (Published July 1992 at $23.50) $5/25

066a: GRAVEN IMAGES Grove Press NY 1992 [] Wraps. Proof (excerpt?) with only King introduction and a few pictures and captions $60.

066b: GRAVEN IMAGES Grove Press NY 1992 [0] 9" x 12" wraps. 500 full-color and 100 black-and-white illustrations by Ronald V. Burst. King introduction. (Published October 1992 at $50) $25/50

067a: SELECTED FROM CARRIE   Literacy Volunteers of New York   NY 1992 [] Decorated wraps. 64 pages $30.

068a: DOLORES CLAIBORNE Viking [NY] (1992) [0] Uncorrected Proof in off-white (cream) wraps $75.

068b: DOLORES CLAIBORNE Viking (NY 1992) [] 1,500,000 cc (PW). (Published December 1992 at $23.50) $5/25

068c: DOLORES CLAIBORNE Viking NY 1993 [] First U.S. Edition but with U.K. price (£14.99), "For export only" (Nicholas and Helen Burrows 1/95) $5/40

068d: DOLORES CLAIBORNE   Hodder & Stoughton L (1992) [1] 2,000 cc (estimated). "First Published in Great Britain 1992". "Special Limited Christmas Edition". Issued without dustwrapper in slipcase with label on front of slipcase. Book has label on half-title with facsimile of King's signature $125.

068e: DOLORES CLAIBORNE   Hodder & Stoughton L (1993) [] Uncorrected Proof in pictorial wraps.   "Hodder & Stoughton export edition 1992..first printed in Great Britain 1993" (David Rees 2/93) $75.

068f: DOLORES CLAIBORNE   Hodder & Stoughton L (1993) [1] $7/35

069a: NIGHTMARES AND DREAMSCAPES Viking (no place 1993) [0] "Unrevised and Unpublished Proofs" in off-white wraps $75.

069b: NIGHTMARES AND DREAMSCAPES Viking (no place or date) [0] Promotional Excerpt in pictorial wraps. 16 pp. with the story *Suffer the Little Children* $40.

069c: NIGHTMARES AND DREAMSCAPES Viking (NY 1993) [3] 1,500,000 cc (PW). Also states "First published in 1993 ..." (Published September 1993 a $27.50) | $5/25

069d: NIGHTMARES AND DREAMSCAPES Hodder & Stoughton L 1993 [] Proof in glossy wraps (Nicholas and Helen Burrows 4/95) | $75.

069e: NIGHTMARES AND DREAMSCAPES Hodder & Stoughton L 1993 [2] 2,000 cc (estimated). Special Limited Christmas Edition, with facsimile signature on half-title. Issued without dustwrapper in slipcase (Robert Gavora 6/95) | $125/150

069f: NIGHTMARES AND DREAMSCAPES Hodder & Stoughton L 1993 [] First issue: dustwrapper priced £15.99 and "The House on Maple Street" on p.448 (Andy Richards {UK} 8/94) | $10/50

069g: NIGHTMARES AND DREAMSCAPES Hodder & Stoughton L 1993 [] Second issue: dustwrapper priced £16.99 and "The House on Maple Street" on p.433 (Andy Richards {UK} 8/94) | $6/30

070a: INSOMNIA Mark Ziesing Books Shingle Town, CA 1994 [2] 1,250 sgd no cc. Issued in tray case. Illustrated by Phil Hale | $150/200

070b: INSOMNIA Mark Ziesing Books Shingle Town, CA 1994 [2] 3,750 cc. Gift Edition. Preceded the red & white trade edition by two months. Issued in dustwrapper and slipcase (Robert Gavora 11/94) | $25/75

070c: INSOMNIA Viking (no place 1994) [] Uncorrected Proof in white wrappers printed in red (Waiting For Godot Books 2/95) | $75.

070d: INSOMNIA Viking NY 1994 [] 1,500,000 cc (PW). (Published October 1994 at $27.95) | $5/25

070e: INSOMNIA Hodder & Stoughton L 1994 [2] 200 sgd no cc (numbered bookplate, signed by King and affixed to half-title). Deluxe leather-bound edition. Issued without dustwrapper (John W. Knott, Jr. 1/95) $350.

070f: INSOMNIA Hodder & Stoughton L 1994 [] Gift Edition with facsimile signature. Issued in slipcase (Andy's Books 12/94) $100.

070g: INSOMNIA Hodder & Stoughton L 1994 [] (Andy's Books 12/94) $8/40

071a: ROSE MADDER Hodder & Stoughton L 1995 [2] 250 no. cc with bookplate signed by King, specially bound in red leather with matching slipcase (Cold Tonnage Books 9/95) $250./300

071b: ROSE MADDER Hodder & Stoughton L 1995 [] Published at £16.99 (Cold Tonnage Books 9/95) $

071c: ROSE MADDER Viking (NY 1995) [] Uncorrected proof in rose-colored printed wraps (Waverly Books 6/95) $75.

071d: ROSE MADDER Viking (NY 1995) [3]

ELMORE LEONARD

Leonard was born in New Orleans in 1925. He graduated from the University of Detroit and worked as a free lance writer and with various advertising companies before turning to writing full-time in 1967.

Contemporary Authors mentioned that Leonard planned to use a pseudonym of Emmett Long, but we did not find any books under this name. A book entitled *3:10 to Yuma* was listed as one of his in the front of *Glitz* but Leonard told us that there was no book published under that title although it was a Columbia Picture in 1957. *Hombre* was selected as one of the 25 best westerns of all time by the Western Writers of America in 1977.

Leonard has written a number of screen plays, including *La Brava*, *Desperados*, and *Street Life*.

Quantities provided by publishers' representatives.

REFERENCES:

(a) Reilly, John M., Editor. TWENTIETH-CENTURY CRIME AND MYSTERY WRITERS. Second Edition. New York: St. Martin's Press (1985).

(b) Oberschmidt, Louise and Hemlock, Allen. *Unofficial Elmore Leonard Checklist*. (Else Fine Books, Box 43, Dearborn, MI 48121.)

(c) Inventory and dealer catalogs.

001a: THE BOUNTY HUNTERS   Houghton Mifflin Boston 1954 [0] 3,500 cc $300/1,500

001b: THE BOUNTY HUNTERS   Houghton Mifflin in association with Ballantine NY 1954 [0] Wraps. Issued simultaneously with hardback (No.54 35¢) $125.

001c: THE BOUNTY HUNTERS Hale London 1956 [] $125/600

002a: THE LAW AT RANDADO   Houghton Mifflin Boston 1955 [0] 3,500 cc $200/1,000

002b: THE LAW AT RANDADO Dell NY (1956) [] Wraps. No.863 at 35¢ price (Alphabet Books) $100.

002c: THE LAW AT RANDADO Hale London 1957 [] $100/500

003a: ESCAPE FROM FIVE SHADOWS Houghton Mifflin Boston 1956 [0] 4,000 cc $200/1,000

003b: ESCAPE FROM FIVE SHADOWS Hale London 1957 [] $100/500

004a: THE TALL T Avon NY 1957 [] Wraps. Actually includes three stories by three authors. Leonard's *The Tall T* is the first book appearance of a magazine story (Mordida Books 12/94) $75.

005a: LAST STAND AT SABER RIVER   Dell NY 1959 [1] Wraps. "Dell First Edition" A184. "First Printing April 1959" on copyright page. Priced at 25¢ (35¢ ??) $100.

005b: LAWLESS RIVER Hale London 1959 [] New title $100/400

005c: STAND ON THE SABER Corgi London 1960 [] Wraps. New title $25.

006a: HOMBRE Ballantine (NY 1961) [0] Wraps. "A Paperback Original" #526K priced 35¢ $150.

006b: HOMBRE Hale L 1961 [] $125/600

006c: HOMBRE Thorndike Press Thorndike, Maine (1986) [] First U.S. hardback. Issued without dustwrapper $100.

006d: HOMBRE Armchair Detective Library NY 1989 [2] 26 sgd ltr cc. Issued without dustwrapper in slipcase (ref.c) $175/200

006e: HOMBRE Armchair Detective Library NY 1989 [2] 100 sgd no cc. Issued without dustwrapper in slipcase (ref.c) $75/125

006f: HOMBRE Armchair Detective Library NY 1989 [] Trade edition. Issued without dustwrapper (ref.c) $40.

007a: THE BIG BOUNCE Fawcett Greenwich (1969) [0] Wraps. #R2079. Priced at 60¢ $100.

007b: THE BIG BOUNCE Hale London 1969 [] $35/150

007c: THE BIG BOUNCE Armchair Detective (NY 1989) [2] 26 sgd ltr cc. New introduction by Leonard. Issued without dustwrapper in slipcase $200/250

007d: THE BIG BOUNCE Armchair Detective (NY 1989) [2] 100 sgd no cc. Issued without dustwrapper in slipcase $75/125

007e: THE BIG BOUNCE Armchair Detective NY (1989) [3] Also states "First Armchair Detective Edition: March 1989". Issued without dustwrapper. Published at $18.95 $30.

008a: THE MOONSHINE WAR Doubleday GC 1969 [1] $125/500

008b: THE MOONSHINE WAR Hale London 1970 [] $40/200

009a: VALDEZ IS COMING Hale London (1969) [1] Black cloth (or simulated cloth) stamped in silver on spine. Price on dustwrapper: "18 | - net" $100/400

009b: VALDEZ IS COMING Fawcett Gold Medal (NY 1970) [1] Wraps. "Printed in U.S.A. October 1970" No.R2328. Priced at 60¢ (there are also copies priced at 75¢, which we assume are later printings, with same cover art and copyright information) .... $85.

010a: FORTY LASHES LESS ONE Bantam NY (1972) [1] Wraps. "Published April 1972" on copyright page. No. S6928. Priced at 75¢ .... $60.

010b: FORTY LASHES LESS ONE Thorndike Press Thorndike, Maine [1989 (Waverly Books)] [] Issued without dustwrapper. First hardback edition .... $75.

011a: FIFTY-TWO PICK-UP Delacorte NY (1974) [1] $50/250

011b: FIFTY-TWO PICK-UP Secker & Warburg London (1974) [1] $25/125

012a: MR. MAJESTYK Dell (NY 1974) [1] Wraps. "First Printing June 1974" on copyright page. No.5887. Priced at $1.25 .... $50.

013a: SWAG Delacorte NY (1976) [1] $30/150

013b: RYAN'S RULES Dell NY 1978 [] Wraps. New title. No.18393. Priced at $1.50 .... $35.

014a: THE HUNTED Dell (NY 1977) [1] Wraps. "First printing Sept 1977" on copyright page. No.13425. Priced at $1.75 .... $50.

014b: THE HUNTED Secker & Warburg London 1978 [] $40/200

014c: THE HUNTED Mysterious Press NY (1986) [3] Wraps. Uncorrected proof in yellow-orange printed wraps. Also states "First...Printing: April 1986" $75.

014d: THE HUNTED Mysterious Press NY (1986) [3] $10/50

015a: UNKNOWN MAN: NO. 89 Delacorte NY 1977 [1] 5,000 cc $75/350

015b: UNKNOWN MAN: NO. 89 Secker & Warburg London (1977) [1] Blue cloth $25/125

015c: UNKNOWN MAN: NO. 89 Penzler NY (1993) [2] 26 sgd ltr cc $150/200

015d: UNKNOWN MAN: NO. 89 Penzler NY (1993)   [2] 100 sgd no cc. Issued without dustwrapper in slipcase (ref.c) $50/75

015e: UNKNOWN MAN: NO. 89 Penzler NY (1993) [3] Trade issued without dustwrapper $25.

016a: THE SWITCH Bantam NY (1978) [0] Wraps. "June 1978." #11885 4. Priced at $1.95 $60.

016b: THE SWITCH Secker & Warburg London (1979) [1] Black cloth $50/250

017a: GUNSIGHTS Bantam NY (1979) [0] Wraps. "August 1979." No. 12888. Priced at $1.50 $50.

017b: GUNSIGHTS Thorndike Press NY 1988 [] Issued without dustwrapper in pictorial laminated boards. First hardback edition (ref.c) $75.

018a: CITY PRIMEVAL *High Noon in Detroit* Arbor House NY 1980 [3] $15/75

018b: CITY PRIMEVAL *High Noon in Detroit* W.H. Allen London 1981 [1] 1,500 cc $25/100

019a: GOLD COAST Bantam NY (1980) [3] Wraps. "December 1980." No. 13321. Priced at $2.25 $50.

019b: GOLD COAST W.H. Allen London 1982 [1] 1,250 cc (some pulped per publisher) $50/250

020a: SPLIT IMAGES Arbor House NY (1981) [3] $10/50

020b: SPLIT IMAGES W.H. Allen L (1983) [0] 1,300 cc $25/100

021a: CAT CHASER Arbor House NY (1982) [3] $10/50

021b: CAT CHASER Viking (Harmondsworth 1986) [] $10/50

022a: STICK Arbor House NY (1983) [3] Wraps. "Advance Readers Copy Not for Sale" $50.

022b: STICK Arbor House NY (1983) [3] $7/35

022c: STICK Allen Lane (L 1984) [1] "Published in Great Britain...1984" on copyright page $8/40

023a: LA BRAVA Arbor House NY (1983) [3] Uncorrected proof in orange wraps $50.

023b: LA BRAVA Arbor House NY (1983) [3] $6/30

023c: LA BRAVA Viking (L/Harmondsworth 1984) [1] Noted with "Publication set for Oct. 25, 1984" on review slip $7/35

023d: LA BRAVA Mirisch Corp. Universal City 1986 [] 119-page screenplay in printed wraps (Pepper & Stern 7/91) $175.

024a: THE ELMORE LEONARD READER Avon NY 1983 [0] Salmon wraps. Collects excerpts from *Stick, Split Images, Cat Chaser, City Primeval, Fifty-two Pick-up* and *Unknown Man: No. 89* (Alphabet Books 5/92) $15.

024b: AVON PRESENTS ELMORE LEONARD Avon NY 1984 [] (Cardinal Books 3/93) $15.

025a: GLITZ Mysterious Press NY (1985) [2] 26 sgd ltr cc. Issued without dustwrapper in slipcase $200/250

025b: GLITZ Mysterious Press NY (1985) [2] 500 sgd no cc. Issued without dustwrapper in slipcase $50/75

025c: GLITZ Arbor House NY (1985) [3] Advance Reading Copy. Black wraps with white lettering and Snoopy reading *Glitz* on back $40.

025d: GLITZ Arbor House NY (1985) [3] 75,000 cc. (Published February 1985 at $14.95) $6/30

025e: GLITZ Viking (L/Harmondsworth 1985) [1] $7/35

026a: DUTCH TREAT Arbor House NY (1985) [3] Uncorrected proof in orange-brown wraps. Issued without introduction $60.

026b: DUTCH TREAT Mysterious Press NY 1985 [2] 26 sgd ltr cc. Introduction by George Will. Issued without dustwrapper in slipcase $150/200

026c: DUTCH TREAT Mysterious Press NY 1985 [2] 350 sgd no cc. Issued without dustwrapper in slipcase $75/100

026d: DUTCH TREAT Arbor House NY (1985) [3] Includes *The Hunted, Mr. Majestyk* and *Swag*. (This is the first U.S. hardcover edition of first two titles.) (Published November 22, 1985 at $17.95) $7/35

026e: DUTCH TREAT Viking L 1985 [] $8/40

027a: DOUBLE DUTCH TREAT Arbor House NY (1986) [] Uncorrected proof in white wraps. Excluding Greene's introduction which is laid-in (H.E. Turlington) $75.

027b: DOUBLE DUTCH TREAT Arbor House NY (1986) [3] 50,000 cc (PW). (Published April 1986 at $17.95.) Introduction by Graham Greene $6/30

028a: BANDITS Arbor House NY (1987) [2] 60 sgd no cc. Xerox of manuscript laid in box covered in gold foil with oversize dustwrapper art glued on top. For ABA Board Members (Bookfinders 12/89) $150.

028b: BANDITS Arbor House NY (1987) [] Advance reading copy in glossy pictorial wraps $35.

028c: BANDITS Arbor House NY (1987) [3] 250,000 cc (PW). (Published in January 1987 at $17.95) $5/25

028d: BANDITS Mysterious Press NY 1987 [2] 26 sgd ltr cc. Issued in slipcase $125/175

028e: BANDITS Mysterious Press NY 1987 [2] 300 sgd no cc. Issued in slipcase $75/100

028f: BANDITS Viking (L 1987) [] $6/30

029a: TOUCH Arbor House NY (1987) [3] Uncorrected proof in pale blue wraps. Also noted in proof dustwrapper (Monroe Stahr Books 8/93) $50.

029b: TOUCH Arbor House NY (1987) [3] 100,000 cc (PW). (Published September 21, 1987 at $17.95) $5/25

029c: TOUCH Viking L 1988 [] $6/30

030a: FREAKY DEAKY Arbor House/Wm. Morrow NY (1988) [3] 150,000 cc (PW). (Announced to be published May 1988 at $17.95 but came out at $18.95.) Following errors noted: "hadanything" p.26:2, "usuallyin" p.40:9, "at" vs. "ate" p.186:12 and "name sof" vs. "names of" p.238:14-15 (Jeff Klaess) - all copies? $6/30

030b: FREAKY DEAKY Viking L 1988 [] $7/35

031a: KILLSHOT Arbor House/Wm. Morrow NY (1989) [0] Uncorrected proofs in yellow wraps $50.

031b: KILLSHOT Arbor House/Wm. Morrow NY (1989) [3] 150,000 cc (PW). Also states first edition. (Published April 1989 at $18.95) $6/30

031c: KILLSHOT Viking L 1989 [] $7/35

032a: ERNESTO PALMER GOT THE NAME CHILI Black Oak Books (Berkeley) 1989 [] Broadside. 20.5" x 15.5". Also noted as 13" x 15.5". Also noted as 13" x 8" printed in two colors (Chloe's Books 9/95) $30.

033a: GET SHORTY Delacorte (NY 1990) [] Advance reading copy in decorated wraps. First issue without ABA printing notice (Waverly Books 9/90) $75.

033b: GET SHORTY Delacorte (NY 1990) [] Advance reading copy in decorated wraps. Second issue with ABA printing notice (Waverly Books 9/90) $40.

033c: GET SHORTY Delacorte (NY 1990) [3] Large print edition published simultaneously. (Published at $18.95.) Issued without dustwrapper $25.

033d: GET SHORTY Viking L 1990 [] $6/30

034a: MAXIMUM BOB Delacorte NY (1991) [] Uncorrected Proof in yellow wraps $50.

034b: MAXIMUM BOB Delacorte NY (1991)
[2] 200 sgd no cc. Issued without dustwrapper in
slipcase $75/125

034c: MAXIMUM BOB Delacorte NY (1991) []
(Published August 1991 at $20) $5/25

034d: MAXIMUM BOB Viking L 1991 [] $6/30

035a: NOTEBOOKS Lord John Press Northridge
1991 [2] 50 sgd no cc. Issued without dustwrapper $150.

035b: NOTEBOOKS Lord John Press Northridge
1991   [2] 300 sgd no cc.   Issued without
dustwrapper $75.

035c: NOTEBOOKS Lord John Press Northridge
1991 [] 1,550 cc. Issued without dustwrapper $30.

036a: RUM PUNCH Delacorte (NY 1992) []
Uncorrected Proof in mauve wraps (Waverly Books
6/92) $50.

036b: RUM PUNCH Delacorte (NY 1992) [3]
Also states "August 1992" on copyright page.
(Published August 1992 at $21.00) $5/25

036c: RUM PUNCH Ultramarine Hastings-on-
Hudson, NY 1992 [2] 26 sgd no cc. Issued in full
leather $400.

036d: RUM PUNCH Ultramarine Hastings-on-
Hudson, NY 1992 [2] 100 sgd no cc. Issued in
quarter leather and marbled boards without
dustwrapper $200.

037a: MAXIMUM LEONARD   Dell/Delacorte
(NY 1993) [] Glossy wraps. Advance excerpts
from four Leonard novels including *Pronto*. Issued
for promotion (Between The Covers 5/95) $15.

038a: PRONTO Delacorte NY 1993 [] Advance
Reading Copy in pictorial wraps $40.

038b: PRONTO Delacorte NY 1993 [] (Published
October 1993 at $21.95) $5/25

039a: THE ELMORE LEONARD SAMPLER Dell
NY 1993 [] Wraps. Excerpts from *Pronto, Rum
Punch, Maximum Bob* and *Get Shorty*. Issued for
promotion $15.

040a: RIDING THE RAP Delacorte (NY 1995) []
Advance Reading Copy from uncorrected proof, in
gold and red printed wraps (Waverly Books 4/95) $50.

040b: RIDING THE RAP Delacorte (NY 1995)
[3] Trade edition $

John McPhee

JOHN McPHEE

McPhee was born in Princeton, New Jersey, in 1931. He graduated from Princeton and spent a year at Cambridge University. He is a staff writer for the _New Yorker_, while continuing to live in Princeton and teach writing at the University.

We wish to thank Michael Juliar for providing much of the bibliographic information contained herein.

001a: A SENSE OF WHERE YOU ARE   Farrar NY (1965) [1] $100/400

001b: A SENSE OF WHERE YOU ARE   Farrar NY (1978) [] "Second Edition, 1978" on copyright page. Very short "Author's Note" added $10/40

002a: THE HEADMASTER Farrar NY (1966) [1] $25/125

003a: ORANGES Farrar Straus NY (1967) [1] $20/100

003b: ORANGES Heinemann L (1967) [0] $15/75

004a: THE PINE BARRENS Farrar NY (1968) [1] $40/200

004b: THE PINE BARRENS Farrar NY 1981 [1] Photographs by Bill Curtsinger. "First of the Special Edition" $25/75

005a: A ROOMFUL OF HOVINGS _and Other Profiles_ Farrar NY (1968) [1] $30/150

006a: LEVELS OF THE GAME Farrar NY (1969) [0] "Uncorrected Proof" in tall peach wraps. Spiral bound $200.

006b: LEVELS OF THE GAME Farrar NY (1969) [1] $15/75

006c: LEVELS OF THE GAME   MacDonald   L
(1970) [1] $12/60

007a: THE CROFTER AND THE LAIRD   Farrar
NY 1970 [] Uncorrected Proof in tall spiral-bound
wraps (Ken Lopez Books '93) $300.

007b: THE CROFTER AND THE LAIRD   Farrar
NY (1970) [1] $30/150

007c: THE CROFTER AND THE LAIRD   Angus
L (1972) [1] $20/100

007d: THE CROFTER AND THE LAIRD Newton
Abbot Country Book Club   L 1973 [] (Ian
McKelvie 6/88) $15/75

008a: ENCOUNTERS WITH THE ARCHDRUID
Farrar NY 1971 [] Uncorrected Proof in ring-
bound galley sheets (Ken Lopez 1993) $250.

008b: ENCOUNTERS WITH THE ARCHDRUID
Farrar NY (1971) [1] $25/125

009a: WIMBLEDON *A Celebration* Viking NY
(1972) [1] $25/100

009b: WIMBLEDON *A Celebration*   Hamish
Hamilton L 1972 [] Copy also noted with Viking
on spine of book and dustwrapper but London title
page (advance?) $25/100

010a: THE DELTOID PUMPKIN SEED   Farrar
NY (1973) [1] $10/50

011a: THE CURVE OF BINDING ENERGY
Farrar NY (1973) [1] Wraps. Uncorrected Proof in
tall yellow wraps $250.

011b: THE CURVE OF BINDING ENERGY
Farrar NY (1974) [1] $25/125

012a: PIECES OF THE FRAME   Farrar   NY (1975) [0] "Uncorrected Proof" in tall blue printed wraps $250.

012b: PIECES OF THE FRAME   Farrar   NY (1975) [1] $25/125

013a: THE SURVIVAL OF THE BARK CANOE Farrar NY 1975 [] Uncorrected Proof in tall, aqua-colored wraps $400.

013b: THE SURVIVAL OF THE BARK CANOE Farrar NY (1975) [1] $40/200

014a: THE JOHN McPHEE READER Farrar NY (1976) [0] "Uncorrected First Proof" in red printed wraps $125.

014b: THE JOHN McPHEE READER Farrar NY (1976) [1] $15/60

014c: THE JOHN McPHEE READER Farrar NY (1976)   [] Wraps. Issued simultaneously with hardcover. (Ken Lopez 3/95) $25.

015a: COMING INTO THE COUNTRY   Farrar NY (1977) [1] "Uncorrected Page Proof" in light blue printed wraps $125.

015b: COMING INTO THE COUNTRY   Farrar NY (1977) [1] $12/60

015c: COMING INTO THE COUNTRY Hamish Hamilton L (1978) [] $12/60

016a: GIVING GOOD WEIGHT   Farrar   NY (1979) [1] Wraps. "Uncorrected Page Proofs" in gray printed wraps $125.

016b: GIVING GOOD WEIGHT   Farrar   NY (1979) [1] Advance reading copy in wraps used for dustwrapper $50.

016c: GIVING GOOD WEIGHT   Farrar   NY
(1979) [1] $7/35

017a: BASIN AND RANGE   Farrar   NY   (1981)
[0] "Uncorrected Proof" in tall green printed wraps $100.

017b: BASIN AND RANGE   Farrar   NY   (1981)
[0] (There were a large number that were
remaindered with mark) $50/100

017c: BASIN AND RANGE   Promontory Press
(NY 1985) [0] Photos by Galen Rowell, Text by
McPhee. Quarto cloth boards $30/75

018a: ALASKA - IMAGES OF THE COUNTRY
Sierra Club Book SF (1981) [2] 500 sgd no cc.
Issued without dustwrapper in slipcase $300/400

018b: ALASKA - IMAGES OF THE COUNTRY
Sierra Club Book SF (1981) [3] Photos by Galen
Rowell, text by McPhee from *Coming Into The
Country*. (Published October 15, 1981 at $37.50) $25/75

019a: THE FAIR OF SAN GENNARO   Press-22
Portland (1981) [2] 50 sgd no cc (Roman numerals).
Issued in slipcase $300/350

019b: THE FAIR OF SAN GENNARO   Press-22
Portland (1981) [2] 200 sgd no cc $175.

020a: RIDING THE BOOM EXTENSION
Metacom Press Worcester 1983 [2] 4 hardbound
trial copies signed by Mc Phee and marked "Trial"
on the colophon page. (Joseph the Provider 1/95
cataloged copy in full blue cloth with marbled
endpapers and dustwrapper) $400.

020b: RIDING THE BOOM EXTENSION
Metacom Press Worcester 1983 [2] 26 sgd ltr cc.
Cloth spine, marbled boards, in dustwrapper.
(Published October 1983. Not For Sale.) $250/350

020c: RIDING THE BOOM EXTENSION
Metacom Press Worcester 1983 [2] 150 sgd no cc.
Wraps. (Published October 1988 at $32.50) $150.

021a: IN SUSPECT TERRAIN Farrar NY (1983)
[1] "Unrevised, Uncorrected Proofs".   Large
signatures in dustwrapper of published edition $100.

021b: IN SUSPECT TERRAIN Farrar NY (1983)
[1] $8/40

022a: ANNALS OF A FORMER WORLD Farrar
NY (1983) [2] 450 sgd no cc. Contains *Basin &
Range* and *In Suspect Terrain*.   Issued without
dustwrappers in two separate volumes in slipcase
(both volumes are signed and numbered) $100/150

022b: ANNALS OF A FORMER WORLD Farrar
NY (1983) [] Wraps. 2 volumes in slipcase.
Contains *Basin & Range* and *In Suspect Terrain* $35.

023a: LA PLACE DE LA CONCORDE SUISSE
Farrar NY (1984) [1] Uncorrected Proof in dark
green printed wraps $75.

023b: LA PLACE DE LA CONCORDE SUISSE
Farrar NY (1984) [2] 200 sgd no cc.   Issued
without dustwrapper in slipcase $100/150

023c: LA PLACE DE LA CONCORDE SUISSE
Farrar NY (1984) [1] $7/35

023d: LA PLACE DE LA CONCORDE SUISSE
(Faber & Faber L 1985) [] (Noted in a copy of *In
The Highlands* {027a} a mention of *The Swiss
Army* in wraps by Faber & Faber. New title for
paperback edition? We've never seen) $7/35

024a: TABLE OF CONTENTS Farrar NY (1985)
[1] Wraps. "Uncorrected Page Proofs" in orange
printed wraps $75.

024b: TABLE OF CONTENTS Farrar NY (1985)
[2] 150 sgd no cc. Issued without dustwrapper in
slipcase $125/175

024c: TABLE OF CONTENTS Farrar NY (1985)
[1] (A collection of 8 pieces previously published in
The New Yorker.) (Published October 7, 1985 at
$15.95) $7/35

025a: RISING FROM THE PLAINS   Farrar NY
1986 [] Uncorrected proof in tan wraps $75.

025b: RISING FROM THE PLAINS   Farrar NY
1986 [1] 30,000 cc (PW). (Published October 6,
1986 at $15.95) $6/30

026a: IN THE HIGHLANDS   Faber & Faber L
(1986) [1] Wraps. Contains *The Crofter and the
Laird* and three essays from *Pieces of the Frame.*
No hardback $100.

027a: HEIRS OF GENERAL PRACTICE   Farrar
NY (1986) [] Wraps. First separate publication of an
essay in *Table of Contents* (Ken Lopez 10/89) $100.

028a: OUTCROPPINGS   Peregrine Smith Books
Salt Lake City (1988) [3]   Also states "First
Edition". Selections from McPhee and photographs
by Tom Till. Edited by Christopher Merrill.
dustwrapper flap corner reads: "$29.95 FFT until
until December 31, 1988." When clipped reads:
"$34.95" (Published August 1988 at $34.95) $20/60

029a: THE CONTROL OF NATURE Farrar NY
(1989) [] Uncorrected proof in green wraps (Bev
Chaney 8/89) $75.

029b: THE CONTROL OF NATURE Farrar NY
(1989) [1] 40,000 cc. (Published June 1989 at
$15.95) $6/30

030a: PRINCETON Council of the Humanities
(Princeton University Press) Princeton, NJ [1989])
[] [8] page stapled pamphlet $150.

031a: LOOKING FOR A SHIP Farrar NY 1990
[] Uncorrected Proof in blue wraps (Bev Chaney,
Jr. 6/91) $60.

031b: LOOKING FOR A SHIP Farrar NY (1990)
[1] 75,000 cc (PW). (Published September 1990 at
$17.95) $5/25

032a: ASSEMBLING CALIFORNIA Farrar Straus
& Giroux NY 1993 [] Uncorrected Proof in red
wraps $60.

032b: ASSEMBLING CALIFORNIA Farrar Straus
& Giroux NY (1993) [1] (Published February
1993 at $ 20.00). Front and rear endpapers have
time charts (variant has time chart on rear endpaper
only, front endpaper blank) $5/25

033a: THE RANSOM OF RUSSIAN ART Farrar,
Straus & Giroux NY (1994) [] Uncorrected Proof
in red wraps (Ken Lopez 5/95) $60.

033b: THE RANSOM OF RUSSIAN ART Farrar,
Straus & Giroux NY (1994) [] (Bev Chaney, Jr.
1/95) $5/25

Thomas Merton (signature)

THOMAS MERTON
(1915-1968)

Thomas Merton was born in France. His father was a New Zealand painter, his mother an American Quaker. The family moved frequently and lived in America during Merton's early years. Merton attended schools in England and moved to America at the age of 21. He received his B.A. and M.A. from Columbia and was reportedly influenced by the example of Gerard Manley Hopkins in his final decision to convert to Catholicism in 1938. In 1941 he joined the Trappist Monastery of Gethsemani in Kentucky and was assigned the name Father Louis. For the rest of his life, he devoted himself to contemplation and writing on religious topics as well as supporting the civil rights, anti-Vietnam and anti-nuclear movements.

We have tried over the years to include most of the offprints and small mimeographed editions of Merton's writings, but they are so voluminous that we are sure, even with 173 items, many are still missing.

REFERENCES:

(a) Dell'Isola, Frank. THOMAS MERTON: A BIBLIOGRAPHY. (Ohio): The Kent State University Press (1975).

(b) Breit, Marquita. THOMAS MERTON: A BIBLIOGRAPHY, Metuchen: Scarecrow Press, 1974. The entries from this source were not listed in either ref.a or c.

(c) Breit, Marquita E. and Daggy, Robert E. THOMAS MERTON: A COMPREHENSIVE BIBLIOGRAPHY. New Edition. New York: Garland Publishing, 1986.

(d) Private collections, inventory or catalog entries.

We would like to thank Robert Briden, Larry Dean, Robert Hershoff, Janette Cantrell and Robert Daggy (indirectly); and New Directions for the first printing quantities.

001a: THIRTY POEMS New Directions   Norfolk (1944) [0] $100/400

001b: THIRTY POEMS New Directions   Norfolk (1944) [0] Wraps in dustwrapper $40/100

002a: THE KINGDOM OF JESUS... Kennedy NY (1946) [0] By St. John Eudes, translated anonymously by Merton as "A Trappist Father" $125/350

003a: A MAN IN THE DIVIDED SEA   (New Directions   NY 1946) [0]   (Second edition is in printed boards replicating the dustwrapper, without colophon statement and with ads as late as 1950 {Wm. Reese Co. 2/91}) $50/150

004a: THE SOUL OF THE APOSTOLATE Gethsemani   (Trappist 1946) [0] By DOM J-B Chautard, translated anonymously by Merton -"A Monk." In black leather without dustwrapper $350.

004b: THE SOUL OF THE APOSTOLATE Image GC (1961) [1] Wraps.   Translation attributed to Merton with his introduction $30.

005a: FIGURES FOR AN APOCALYPSE   New Directions Norfolk (1948) [0] Copyright 1947, but actually published in March 1948 $50/150

006a: GUIDE TO CISTERCIAN LIFE   Gethsemani Trappist (1948) [0] Wraps $250.

007a: CISTERCIAN CONTEMPLATIVES Gethsemani   Trappist (1948) [2] 10,000 cc.   Written anonymously by Merton. Issued without dustwrapper $150.

007b: CISTERCIAN CONTEMPLATIVES Gethsemani Trappist (1948) [0] Wraps $40.

008a: THE SPIRIT OF SIMPLICITY... Gethsemani Trappist 1948 [0] By St. Bernard, translated

anonymously by Merton as "A Cistercian Monk."
Issued without dustwrapper $125.

009a: EXILE ENDS IN GLORY... Bruce
Milwaukee (1948) [0] First printing has comment
on back of dustwrapper "His a talent for beyond."
No comment on later printings $50/150

009b: EXILE ENDS IN GLORY... Clonmore &
Reynolds Dublin (1951) [1] Ref.d $25/100

010a: THE SEVEN STOREY MOUNTAIN
Harcourt NY (1948) [1] Off-white cloth with black
lettering. (Small number issued per publisher). We
have identified a first issue/state dustwrapper with
caption on one of the pictures on back "Author
second from left." This version on the three copies
(in white) that we have handled or seen The first
issue/state dustwrapper has all flap corners clipped.
A bogus facsimile of the first edition is in
circulation. It is in white cloth with glossy second
state/issue dustwrapper without price on flap. The
true first measures (holding the book closed) 35cm
wide 208cm tall (facsimile measures 33cm and
210cm). [Note: the photographer's name "Daniel
Frances Connell" is not under the bottom
photograph on rear panel on either the first or
second issue dustwrapper, but is on the facsimile
dustwrapper] $800/1,750

010b: THE SEVEN STOREY MOUNTAIN
Harcourt NY (1948) [1] Black cloth lettered in
gold. 6,000 copies in both bindings (ref.a) but
publisher's record indicates 10,000 copies. Picture
cropped on rear panel of dustwrapper and captioned
"Author on the left." We have seen this change on
two copies of first edition and never seen it on the
white cloth edition. Therefore, we assume this is a
legitimate second issue/state dustwrapper and not a
second printing (all later printings have "Author on
left"). Also the last paragraph on back dustwrapper
flap mentions Catholic Press Association Award for
1948, which is not on later printing dustwrappers. $150/750

010c: ELECTED SILENCE Hollis & Carter (L 1949) [1] (ref.c) New title. Foreword by Evelyn Waugh who edited the book extensively — $75/250

010d: THE SEVEN STOREY MOUNTAIN Sheldon Press L (1975) [1] "Published in Great Britain in 1975" on copyright page. First unedited U.K. edition — $10/40

011a: WHAT IS CONTEMPLATION St. Mary's College Holy Cross 1948 [0] Wraps — $175.

011b: WHAT IS CONTEMPLATION Burns & Oates L (1950) [1] Wraps — $75.

012a: SEEDS OF CONTEMPLATION New Directions (Norfolk, Conn. 1949) [2] 100 sgd cc. Issued in brown slipcase — $1,250/1,500

012b: SEEDS OF CONTEMPLATION New Directions (Norfolk, Conn. 1949) [0] — $50/250

012c: SEEDS OF CONTEMPLATION New Directions (Norfolk, Conn. 1949) [1] "Seventh printing/First Revised Edition" on copyright page. (Also noted as revised edition without any statement?) — $10/50

013a: GETHSEMANI MAGNIFICAT Gethsemani Trappist 1949 [0] Written anonymously by Merton. Issued in boards without dustwrapper — $250.

014a: THE WATERS OF SILOE Harcourt NY (1949) [1] — $25/75

014b: THE WATERS OF SILENCE Brun L (1950) [2] 5 cc. New title. Deluxe edition in black leather. Issued without dustwrapper or box. No. I-V for presentation. Evelyn Waugh foreword — $1,000.

014c: THE WATERS OF SILENCE Brun L (1950) [2] 120 no. cc. Deluxe edition in black leather. Issued without dustwrapper or box. Evelyn

Waugh foreword. Total limitation and number are on copyright page. In addition, on the verso of the first half title it states: "Editions Deluxe Limited/The Collector's Book Club/...fifty copies, numbered 1 to 50, are available to members ..." $500.

014d: THE WATERS OF SILENCE Hollis & Carter L (1950) [1] Noted with wrap-around band (Ergo Books 12/90) $25/75

014e: THE WATERS OF SILOE Garden City GC (1951) [0] Textual changes (see Dell'Isola A11b) $8/40

015a: THE TEARS OF THE BLIND LIONS New Directions (NY 1949) [0] 5,097 cc (assume a&b) $25/100

015b: THE TEARS OF THE BLIND LIONS New Directions (NY 1949) [0] Wraps in dustwrapper and mailing envelope $35/75

016a: MONASTIC ORIENTATION Gethsemani Trappist 1950 [] Wraps (ref.b) $150.

017a: WHAT ARE THESE WOUNDS? Bruce Milwaukee (1950) [0] $15/60

017b: WHAT ARE THESE WOUNDS? Clonmore & Reynolds Dublin no date [] $15/60

018a: SELECTED POEMS OF THOMAS MERTON Hollis & Carter L 1950 [1] From first three books $25/100

019a: A BALANCED LIFE OF PRAYER (Gethsemani Trappist 1951) [0] Wraps $125.

020a: THE ASCENT TO TRUTH Harcourt NY (1951) [1] $25/75

020b: THE ASCENT TO TRUTH Hollis & Carter L (1951) [1] Blue cloth (ref.d) $15/60

020c: THE ASCENT TO TRUTH   Clonmore & Reynolds Dublin (1951) [1] $15/60

020d: LA MONTEE VERS LA LUMIERE [THE ASCENT TO TRUTH]   Editions Albin   Paris (1958) [2] 10 cc numbered "I" to "X". Issued in black simulated leather without dustwrapper. Revised from American edition $NVA

020e: LA MONTEE VERS LA LUMIERE [THE ASCENT TO TRUTH]   Editions Albin   Paris (1958) [2] 300 no cc. Issued in black simulated leather without dustwrapper $400.

021a: DEVOTIONS IN HONOR OF ST. JOHN OF THE CROSS   (Gethsemani   Trappist 1953) [0] Wraps $125.

022a: THE SIGN OF JONAS Harcourt NY (1953) [1] $25/75

022b: THE SIGN OF JONAS Hollis & Carter L (1953) [1] (Ref.c.) (Also noted with wrap-around band with Evelyn Waugh blurb) $15/60

023a: BREAD IN THE WILDERNESS   New Directions (NY 1953) [0] 2,000 cc. Running head on p.24 inverted, p.30:25 and p.30:26 are repeated. Latin cross on front cover $50/150

023b: BREAD IN THE WILDERNESS Hollis & Carter L (1954) [1] $25/75

023c: BREAD IN THE WILDERNESS   New Directions (NY 1960) [0] 1,970 cc. Reprint of 023a. Smaller size, without cross on cover $15/35

024a: THE LAST OF THE FATHERS... Harcourt NY (1954) [1] $15/60

024b: THE LAST OF THE FATHERS... Hollis & Carter L (1954) [1] $10/40

024c: THE LAST OF THE FATHERS   Catholic Book Club L (1954) [] (Ken Lopez 3/95) $10/30

025a: NO MAN IS AN ISLAND   Harcourt NY (1955) [1] $15/60

025b: NO MAN IS AN ISLAND   Hollis & Carter L 1955 [1] $10/50

026a: THE TOWER OF BABEL (Jubilee NY no date [1955?]) [0] An offprint. 16 pages in pictorial cover, priced 25¢ on back (ref.d) $200.

026b: THE TOWER OF BABEL (New Directions Norfolk 1957) [2] 250 sgd no cc. Issued in slipcase $1,000/1,250

027a: THE LIVING BREAD   Farrar, Straus & Cudahy NY (1956) [1] $15/60

027b: THE LIVING BREAD   Burns & Oates L (1956) [1] (Ref.d) $10/40

028a: PRAYING THE PSALMS Liturgical Press Collegeville (1956) [0] Wraps. Cover noted in very dark green on textured paper, and a medium to light green on flat stock. Priority unknown (ref.d) $100.

028b: THE PSALMS ARE OUR PRAYERS Burns & Oates L 1957 [0] New title. Wraps $60.

029a: SILENCE IN HEAVEN: A BOOK OF MONASTIC LIFE Crowell/ Studio NY 1956 [] Wraps (ref.c) $100.

029b: SILENCE IN HEAVEN: A BOOK OF MONASTIC LIFE Thames & Hudson L 1957 [] Blue cloth in dustwrapper (Dalian Books 2/94) $50/100

030a: MARTHE, MARIE ET LAZARE Brouwer (Paris 1956) [0] Wraps. No English version located by Dell'Isola $100.

031a: NOTES ON SACRED AND PROFANE ART No publisher, place or date (*Jubilee Magazine* 1956) [0] An offprint. Large single sheet folded to make four pages. No pagination. Obviously not the pages from the magazine (ref.d) $250.

032a: BASIC PRINCIPLES OF MONASTIC SPIRITUALITY Gethsemani (Trappist) 1957 [0] Wraps $125.

032b: BASIC PRINCIPLES OF MONASTIC SPIRITUALITY Burns & Oates L (1957) [0] Wraps $100.

033a: FIVE POEMS BY THOMAS MERTON Pax NY 1957 [] Broadside. Pax No.4. 12"x 18" (Wm. Reese Co. 12/92) $125.

034a: THE SILENT LIFE Farrar, Straus NY (1957) [1] $15/60

034b: THE SILENT LIFE Burns & Oates L 1957 [1] Also noted as published by Thames and Hudson, London, 1957 (Dalian Books 5/90) $10/50

035a: THE STRANGE ISLANDS New Directions (Norfolk) 1957 [0] 3,243 cc (bound at three different times in 1957) $25/75

035b: THE STRANGE ISLANDS Hollis & Carter L (1957) [1] (Ref.d) $15/60

036a: MONASTIC PEACE Gethsemani (Trappist 1958) [2] 5,000 cc. Wraps $150.

037a: LIFE AT GETHSEMANI Gethsemani Trappist 1958 [] Photographs by Shirley Burden, Terrell Dickey and the Monk of Gethsemani (ref.b) $125.

038a: THOUGHTS IN SOLITUDE Farrar, Straus NY (1958) [1] $15/60

038b: THOUGHTS IN SOLITUDE Burns & Oates
L (no date [1958?]) [0] Ref.d $10/50

039a: PROMETHEUS / A MEDITATION (King
Library Lexington) 1958 [2] 150 cc. Issued without
dustwrapper $650.

040a: NATIVITY KERYGMA   (Gethsemani
Trappist 1958) [0] Issued without dustwrapper $250.

040b: NATIVITY KERYGMA North Central Publ.
St. Paul 1958 [] (Ref.b. Not in ref.a or c) $150.

041a: THE UNQUIET CONSCIENCE Hammer
Lexington (1958) [2] Limited to 50 cc (Black Sun
Books). 4-page booklet in wraps of Merton's
translation of Bargellini. (Later bound in buckram
with printed paper label (Hammer Varia B3)
(Bromer Booksellers 2/92) $250.

042a: THE   CHRISTMAS   SERMONS   OF
GUERRIC OF IGNY (Gethsemani Trappist 1959)
[0] Issued in tissue dustwrapper $150.

043a: WHAT OUGHT I TO DO? Stamperia +
Lexington 1959 [2] 50 no cc. Merton's translation
from Migne's Latin *Patrology* $600.

044a: THE SECULAR JOURNAL OF THOMAS
MERTON Farrar, Straus NY (1959) [0] $15/60

044b: A SECULAR JOURNAL   Hollis & Carter L
(1959) [0] New title (Ref.c) $15/60

045a: SELECTED POEMS OF THOMAS
MERTON New Directions (NY 1959) [0] Wraps.
From first five books of poetry $35.

045b: SELECTED POEMS OF THOMAS
MERTON ENLARGED EDITION New Directions
(NY 1967) [0] Wraps. Enlarged edition $30.

046a: THE SOLITARY LIFE Stamperia + Lexington 1960 [2] 60 no cc with some copies signed. Number of copies signed undetermined. Signed copies have sold in the $1,200 to $1,500 range

$500.

047a: LITURGICAL FEASTS AND SEASONS Gethsemani Trappist 1960 [] Assume wraps. Two volumes (ref.c)

$200.

048a: THE OX-MOUNTAIN PARABLE OF MENG TZU Stamperia + Lexington 1960 [2] 100 no cc

$600.

049a: FOUR POEMS OF CESAR VALLEJO Pax NY 1960 [] Broadside, folded. Pax No. 11. 7" x 20" (Wm. Reese Co. 12/92)

$75.

050a: SPIRITUAL DIRECTION AND MEDI-TATION Liturgical (Collegeville 1960) [0] Have seen three copies all in undersized dustwrappers (ref.c)

$25/75

050a: SPIRITUAL DIRECTION AND MEDITA-TION Burns & Oates L 1961 []

$20/60

051a: GOD IS MY LIFE Reynal NY 1960 [0] Introduction by Merton, photographs by Shirley Burden

$50/150

052a: DISPUTED QUESTIONS Farrar, Straus NY (1960) [1]

$15/50

052b: DISPUTED QUESTIONS Hollis & Carter L 1961 [0] (Ref.d)

$15/50

053a: THE WISDOM OF THE DESERT New Directions (NY 1960 [1961]) [0] 2,510 cc. Translation by Merton. Copyright date 1960, but actually published in 1961. (5,000 copies printed but only 2,510 bound)

$25/100

053b: THE WISDOM OF THE DESERT   Hollis
and Carter L 1961 [0] (Ref.d) $15/60

054a: THE BEHAVIOR OF TITANS   New
Directions (NY 1961) [0] 3,000 cc $25/100

055a: SELECTIONS ON PRAYER   Gethsemani
Trappist 1961 [] Wraps (ref.b) $125.

056a: THE NEW MAN Farrar, Straus NY (1961)
[0] $15/60

056b: THE NEW MAN   Burns & Oates L (1962)
[1] $10/40

057a: NEW SEEDS OF CONTEMPLATION New
Directions (NY   1962) [0] 7,907 cc.   Bound
between December 1961 and May 1967 $15/50

058a: LORETTO AND GETHSEMANI   Geth-
semani Trappist 1962 [] Wraps (ref.c) $125.

059a: ORIGINAL CHILD BOMB New Directions
(NY 1962) [2] 500 sgd no cc. Issued with plain
cellophane wrapper $500.

059b: ORIGINAL CHILD BOMB   (New Directions NY 1962) [0] 8,000 cc.   Issued without
dustwrapper. (Colophon   states   "Printed   ...
December 1961") $100.

059c: ORIGINAL CHILD BOMB (Unicorn Press
no place or date) [0] Wraps. Looks like same sheets
but "Unicorn Press 0-87775-158-7 $5.00" on back
cover $25.

060a: HAGIA SOPHIA Stamperia + Lexington
1962 [2] 69 no cc. Wraps. Number of copies signed
undetermined. (Price is for unsigned/signed) $500/1,250

060b: HAGIA SOPHIA   (Trappist   Kentucky)
January 1962 [0] Spiral-bound stiff wraps. Seven

mimeographed pages. Prepared by Merton for those who could not afford the limited edition. Included is a 3-paragraph comment by Merton on poem and the other edition (Wm. Reese Co. 9/94) $150.

061a: TWO ARTICLES: ROOT OF WAR / RED OR DEAD (Fellowship Publ. NY 1962) [] Wraps. First separate edition (ref.b) $75.

062a: SELECTIONS FROM THE PROTREPTIKOS BY CLEMENT OF ALEXANDRIA New Directions (NY 1962) [] Wraps. Translated by Merton (Am Here Books 11/94). Issued in dustwrapper (Lame Duck Books 4/95) $50/125

063a: CLEMENT OF ALEXANDRIA Burns & Oatcs L 1962 [2] 750 cc. Wraps (Ian McKelvie) $75.

063b: CLEMENT OF ALEXANDRIA New Directions (NY 1962 [1963]) [0] 3,930 cc. Wraps. Essay and translation by Merton. Colophon shows 1962 but Dell'Isola notes publication February 1963. (Cataloged by one dealer as having a dustwrapper) $50/75

064a: LORETTO AND GETHSEMANI Gethsemani Trappist (1962) [] Wraps (ref.c) $100.

065a: A THOMAS MERTON READER Harcourt NY 1962 [] Uncorrected Galleys in spiral-bound wraps decorated with house logo (Wm. Reese Co. 9/92) $200.

065b: A THOMAS MERTON READER Harcourt NY (1962) [1] $10/50

066a: COLD WAR LETTERS Privately Printed (no place) 1962 [] Unprinted spiral-bound salmon colored wraps. 88 mimeographed pages. 44 letters from Merton to friends and opinion-makers. "Strictly confidential, not for publication" (Wm. Reese Co. 9/94) $2,000.

066b: COLD WAR LETTERS (Trappist 1963) []
Yellow textured wraps, spiral bound. Mimeographed. Second, vastly enlarged edition for private
circulation. 111 letters. (Wm. Reese Co. 9/94) $750.

067a: LIFE AND HOLINESS Chapman & Hall L
1963 [] (Ref.c) $15/60

067b: LIFE AND HOLINESS Herder & Herder
(NY 1963) [0] $15/50

068a: BREAKTHROUGH TO PEACE New
Directions NY 1963 [0] 15,037 cc. Wraps. Edited
and introduction by Merton $40.

069a: THE BLACK REVOLUTION Southern
Christian Leadership Conference Atlanta 1963 []
Wraps (ref.b) $150.

070a: EMBLEMS OF A SEASON OF FURY New
Directions NY (1963) [0] Wraps $40.

071a: EXAMINATION OF CONSCIENCE AND
"CONVERSATIO MORUM" Gethsemani Trappist
1963 [] Wraps (ref.b). (Waiting For Godot
catalogued a coy as 1965, but the magazine
appearance ws in 1963 so the offprint should have
been in 1963) $200.

072a: THE NAME OF THE LORD Gethsemani
Trappist 1963 [] Wraps (ref.b) $200.

073a: PRE-BENEDICTINE MONACHISM
SERIES I Gethsemani Trappist 1963 [] Wraps
(ref.b) $200.

074a: THE SOLITARY LIFE: GUIGO THE
CARTHUSIAN (Stanbrook +) Worcester 1963 [1]
Wraps. A letter as introduction and translated by
Merton. Colophon p.(12) "December 1963" Also
noted stating "Last one hundred copies" $150.

Also see item 134

075a: THE CHRISTIAN AS PEACEMAKER
Fellowship Publications Nyack, NY (1963) []
Wraps $35.

076a: THE EARLY LEGEND - *Six Fragments*
(Trappist) June 1963 [] 11 mimeographed leaves,
stapled (Wm. Reese Co. 9/94). (Published in New
Directions #18 the next year) $200.

077a: ATLAS WATCHES EVERY EVENING
(Trappist) July 1963 [] 7 mimeographed leaves,
stapled. Published the next year in New Directions
#18 (Wm. Reese Co. 9/94) $200.

078a: THE LEGEND OF TUCKER CALIBAN
(Trappist) July 1963 [] 9 mimeographed leaves,
stapled. Published as *The Negro Revolt* in *Jubilee*
Magazine (Wm. Reese Co. 9/94) $200.

079a: COME TO THE MOUNTAIN St. Benedict's
Monastery Snowmass 1964 [] Wraps.
(Subsequently issued as *Cistercian Life*. See 128a) $150.

080a: THE TRAGEDY OF FATHER PERRIN
Gethsemani Trappist 1964 [] Wraps (ref.c) $175.

081a: SEEDS OF DESTRUCTION Farrar, Straus
NY (1964) [1] $15/50

082a: PRE-BENEDICTINE MONACHISM
SERIES II Gethsemani Trappist 1964 [] Wraps
(ref.b) $175.

083a: NOTES BY THE ARTIST FOR AN
EXHIBITION OF HIS DRAWINGS Spalding
College Louisville 1964 [] Wraps (ref.c) $175.

084a: HONEST TO GOD: LETTER TO A
RADICAL ANGLICAN No publisher or place
1964 [] Wraps (ref.b) $150.

085a: VARIETIES OF UNBELIEF- *A Review*
Privately Printed   no place   December 1964 [] 5
mimeographed leaves, stapled. Appeared in the
January 8, 1965 edition of *The Commonweal*
(Waiting For Godot Books 1/93) $200.

086a: VICTOR HAMMER/A RETROSPECTIVE
EXHIBITION/APRIL 4-25, 1965   North Carolina
Museum   Raleigh   1965 [0] Wraps. Catalog 23,
containing a foreword by Merton $100.

087a: GANDHI ON NON-VIOLENCE   New
Directions (NY 1965) [1] 10,059 cc. Wraps. Edited
and introduction by Merton (ref.b) $50.

088a: THE POORER MEANS   Gethsemani
Trappist 1965 [] Wraps (ref. b) $125.

089a: THE WAY OF CHUANG TZU   New
Directions (NY 1965) [1] 5,073 cc in total. 3,021
copies bound in 1965, and 2,052 copies bound in
1967. The latter may have been the paper edition $15/60

089b: THE WAY OF CHUANG TZU   New
Directions (NY 1965) [1] Wraps $30.

090a: FOR A RENEWAL OF EREMITISM IN
THE MONASTIC STATE Gethsemani Trappist
1965 [] Wraps (ref.b) $100.

091a: SEASONS OF CELEBRATION   Farrar,
Straus NY 1965 [] Uncorrected Galleys in spiral-
bound printed wraps (Wm. Reese 9/92) $250.

091b: SEASONS OF CELEBRATION   Farrar,
Straus NY (1965) [1] $15/50

092a: REFLECTIONS ON LOVE: EIGHT
SACRED POEMS Gethsemani Trappist 1966 []
(Ref.b) $125.

093a: REDEEMING THE TIME Burns & Oates L (1966) [1] Wraps. This is an abridged version of *Seeds of Destruction*, deleting a number of sections and adding a new section apparently never published elsewhere (ref.c) $40.

094a: (VIETNAM AND THE AMERICAN CONSCIENCE) New York University NY (1966) [0] Wraps. A program for a Town Hall meeting including Merton's *Nhat Hanh is My Brother* $75.

095a: RAIDS ON THE UNSPEAKABLE New Directions (NY 1966) [0] 5,099 cc. Wraps $40.

096a: MONASTIC LIFE AT GETHSEMANI (Gethsemani Trappist 1966) [0] Wraps $75.

097a: GETHSEMANI / A LIFE OF PRAISE Gethsemani (no place [Trappist]) 1966 [0] $25/75

098a: THE ZEN KOAN Lugano Review Lugano 1966 [0] Offprint in wraps (Wm. Reese Co. 9/93) $200.

099a: CONJECTURES OF A GUILTY BY-STANDER Doubleday GC 1966 [1] $15/60

099b: CONJECTURES OF A GUILTY BYSTANDER Burns & Oates L (1968) [] Issued in dustwrapper (Bev Chaney, Jr. 1/95) $15/50

099c: CONJECTURES OF A GUILTY BY-STANDER Burns & Oates L (1968) [] Wraps (ref.c) $25.

100a: A FOREWORD TO MARCEL AND BUDDHA (Gethsemani) January 1967 [] Mimeographed sheets stapled. Published in *The Journal of Religious Thought* 1967-1968 as a foreword to Sally Donnelly's essay *Marcel and Buddha: A Metaphysics of Enlightenment* $200.

101a: A NEW CHRISTIAN CONSCIOUSNESS?
(Privately Printed no place) February 1967 [] 11
pages stapled (Waiting For Godot 7/90) $300.

102a: A PRAYER OF CASSIODORUS   Stanbrook Abbey Press (Worcester) 1967 [0] Preface
and translation by Merton.   White cloth issued
without dustwrapper $125.

102b: A PRAYER OF CASSIODORUS   Stanbrook Abbey Press   (Worcester) 1967 [0] Wraps
(James S. Jaffe Rare Books) $50.

103a: CHRIST IN THE DESERT   Monastery of
Christ... Abiquiu, N.M. 1967 [] Wraps (ref.c) $150.

104a: MYSTICS AND ZEN MASTERS   Farrar,
Straus NY 1967 [] Uncorrected Proof in spiral-
bound printed wraps (Wm. Reese 9/92) $250.

104b: MYSTICS AND ZEN MASTERS Farrar,
Straus NY (1967) [1] $15/50

105a: A CAROL (Unicorn Press Santa Barbara
1967) [] Uncorrected Proof. There are two states of
the proof of this broadside, which was published as
part of Unicorn Folio Series One, December 1967.
In its published form the broadside was folded to
make four pages with the title on the first page,
reproduction of a Merton drawing on the second,
the poem facing the drawing on the third, and the
fourth page blank. The first state of the proofs has
only the title and the poem (H.E. Turlington 5/95) $150.

105b: A CAROL (Unicorn Press Santa Barbara
1967) [] Uncorrected Proof. Second state of proof
with Merton's drawing, and with title placed
differently than in first state (H.E. Turlington 5/95) $100.

105c: A CAROL 1967   (Unicorn Press   Santa
Barbara 1967) [2] 325 cc. Broadside. 11" x 12½".
Originally issued in Unicorn Folio Series One. 300
copies (H. E. Turlington 5/95) $75.

106a: BLESSED ARE THE MEEK... Catholic Peace Fellowship Nyack, NY 1967 [] Wraps. 12 pages $75.

107a: THE PLAGUE Seabury NY (1968) [0] Wraps. Introduction and commentary by Merton on Camus' book $40.

108a: CABLES TO THE ACE New Directions (NY 1968) [1] 1,725 cc $25/75

108b: CABLES TO THE ACE New Directions (NY 1968) [1] 5,095 cc. Wraps $30.

109a: FAITH AND VIOLENCE University of Notre Dame Press 1968 [0] Wraps $75.

110a: LANDSCAPE, PROPHET AND WILD-DOG Black Bird Press Syracuse 1968 [2] 25 sgd no cc. Poems by Merton, etchings by Don Cortese, all of which are numbered and signed or initialed by Cortese (not signed by Merton) $650.

111a: ZEN AND THE BIRDS OF APPETITE New Directions (NY 1968) [0] 2,067 cc $25/75

111b: ZEN AND THE BIRDS OF APPETITE New Directions (NY 1968) [0] 4,019 cc. Wraps $30.

112a: FOUR FREEDOM SONGS G.I.A Publ. Chicago 1968 [] Words by Merton. Assume issued in wraps $75.

113a: THE TRUE SOLITUDE Hallmark (NY 1969) [0] Gift book. Selections from the writings of Merton $10/40

114a: MY ARGUMENT WITH THE GESTAPO Doubleday GC 1969 [1] Actually written while at Columbia in the 1930s (ref.c) $15/60

115a: THE CLIMATE OF MONASTIC PRAYER
Cistercian Publ. Spencer, Mass. 1969 [] Wraps
(ref.c) $10/50

115b: THE CLIMATE OF MONASTIC PRAYER
Irish University Press Shannon 1969 [] Irish
sheets. Cloth in dustwrapper $15/75

115c: CONTEMPLATIVE PRAYER Herder &
Herder (NY 1969) [0] New title. Ref.a shows
spine lettered in violet. Also noted with spine
lettered in blue (Steven Temple) $10/50

116a: THE GEOGRAPHY OF LOGRAIRE New
Directions (NY 1969) [0] 2,068 cc $25/75

116b: THE GEOGRAPHY OF LOGRAIRE New
Directions NY 1969 [0] 6,059 cc. Wraps $30.

117a: COME TO THE MOUNTAIN St. Benedict's
Cistercian Monastery Snowfall, Colorado no date
[] Stiff wraps. 68 pages of text by Merton, 35
photos. Circa 1969. (By The Way Books 7/93) $75.

118a: ST. MAEDOC Unicorn (Santa Barbara)
1970   [] Uncorrected Proof of this broadside,
published as Unicorn Broadsheet 7. Various
publisher's directions, initial title letter taped on,
one correction to text (H.E. Turlington 5/95) $150.

118b: ST. MAEDOC FRAGMENT OF AN IKON
Unicorn no place 1970 [0] New title. 11"x14"
broadside (Waiting For Godot 10/89) $75.

118c: ST. MAEDOC Unicorn Press (Greensboro)
1981 [0] Folded broadside in stiff wraps (the
original was issued unfolded) $40.

119a: A HIDDEN WHOLENESS: THE VISUAL
WORLD OF THOMAS MERTON Houghton
Mifflin B 1970 [] Uncorrected Proof spiral-bound
in stiff wraps with proofs of photos laid in (Bev
Chaney Jr. 2/91) $175.

119b: A HIDDEN WHOLENESS: THE VISUAL WORLD OF THOMAS MERTON   Houghton Mifflin B 1970 [1] Photos by Merton, text by John Howard Griffin $25/75

119c: A HIDDEN WHOLENESS: THE VISUAL WORLD OF THOMAS MERTON Norman Berg Publ.   Dunwoody   1977 [] Wraps. Photos by Merton. Less than 1,000 copies. $50.

120a: EARLY POEMS/1940-1942   (Anvil Press Lexington 1971) [2] 150 cc. Beige boards lettered in black on spine, text printed in black and red (also wraps version?) Issued in dustwrapper (By the Way Books 7/93) $400/500

121a: OPENING THE BIBLE Liturgical College-ville (1971) [0] Published 1971 per ref.a, but copyright date 1970. Dustwrapper shorter than book $15/50

121b: OPENING THE BIBLE Liturgical College-ville (1971) [0] Wraps $30.

121c: OPENING THE BIBLE Allen and Unwin L 1972 [] (ref.c) $15/50

122a: CONTEMPLATION IN A WORLD OF ACTION Doubleday GC 1971 [1] $15/60

123a: THOMAS MERTON ON PEACE McCall NY (1969 [1971]) [0] (Last copyright date is 1969 but actually published in 1971) $15/60

124a: THE THOMAS MERTON STUDIES CENTER Unicorn Press Santa Barbara 1971 [] 500 cc.   Merton, John Howard Griffin, Msgr. Horrigan.   Issued without dustwrapper (Bromer Booksellers 2/92) $100.

124b: THE THOMAS MERTON STUDIES CENTER Unicorn Press Santa Barbara 1971 [] 1,000 cc. Wraps (H.E. Turlington 5/95) $35.

125a: THE JAGUAR AND THE MOON Unicorn Greensboro 1971 [] 100 cc. Wraps (H.E. Turlington 5/95). Ref.b&c state "1974" and it probably is but we assume it was copyright 1971 by Pablo Antonio Cuadra with translation by Merton $75.

125b: THE JAGUAR AND THE MOON Unicorn Greensboro 1971 [] 500 cc in boards (H.E. Turlington 5/95) $75.

126a: PASTERNAK / MERTON: SIX LETTERS University of Kentucky Lexington 1973 [2] 150 no cc $400.

127a: THE ASIAN JOURNAL OF THOMAS MERTON New Directions (NY 1973) [0] 10,046 cc $15/60

127b: THE ASIAN JOURNAL OF THOMAS MERTON Sheldon Press L (1974) [1] $15/50

127c: THE ASIAN JOURNAL OF THOMAS MERTON New Directions (NY 1975) [0] Wraps $25.

128a: CISTERCIAN LIFE Cistercian Book Service Spencer, Ma. 1974 [0] Reprint of item 079a per ref.b, but includes 1969 material at rear (Declaration of the General Charter of 1969 on Cistercian life). It appears to have been issued by various abbeys which put their own cover and title page on it. We have seen copies with Merton as author; and copies that were obviously the same book without any credit to Merton $35.

129a: HE IS RISEN Argus Niles, Il. (1975) [3] Wraps (ref.d). (U.K. issued with "£1" sticker over price $50.

130a: SPIRITUAL DIRECTION AND MEDITATION AND WHAT IS CONTEM-PLATION? Anthony Clarke Wheathampstead, England 1975 [] (By The Way Books 7/93.) Also see 050 $40.

131a: ISHI MEANS MAN   Unicorn Press Greensboro (1976) [0] Issued without dustwrapper (ref.b) $60.

131b: ISHI MEANS MAN   Unicorn Press Greensboro (1976) [0] Wraps (ref.b) $30.

132a: THE POWER AND MEANING OF LOVE (Sheldon Press   L 1976) [] This is an abridged version of *Disputed Questions* (ref.c) $10/30

133a: THOMAS MERTON ON ZEN   Sheldon Press L 1976 [] (Ref.c) $15/60

134a: ON THE SOLITARY LIFE Banyan Pawlet 1977 [2] 240 no cc. By Guigo with translation by Merton (ref.d). Large thin paperwraps, issued in an envelope with title printed on front $175.

135a: THE MONASTIC JOURNEY Sheldon Press L 1977 [] (Ref. c) $15/60

135b: THE MONASTIC JOURNEY Sheed, Andrews Kansas City (1977) [1] (Ref.c) $10/40

136a: THE COLLECTED POEMS OF THOMAS MERTON New Directions NY 1977 [] 1,225 cc (ref.c). First printing had incomplete index (only went to "W") corrected in second printing. Assume second printing would be stated but not sure $25/75

136b: THE COLLECTED POEMS OF THOMAS MERTON Sheldon Press L (1978) [1] (Ref.c) $15/40

137a: THE THOMAS MERTON 1979 AP-POINTMENT CALENDAR   Sheed, Andrews Kansas City 1978 [0] Calendar/drawings (ref. d) $25.

138a: A CATCH OF ANTI-LETTERS   Sheed, Andrews Kansas City (1978) [0] With Robert Lax (ref.b) $10/50

139a: THE THOMAS MERTON 1980 AP-
POINTMENT CALENDAR Andrews Kansas City
1979 [0] calendar/drawings (ref.d) $25.

140a: LOVE AND LIVING Farrar, Straus NY
(1979) [] Uncorrected Proof in yellow wraps
(Bromer Booksellers 9/90) $75.

140b: LOVE AND LIVING Farrar, Straus NY
(1979) [] (Ref.c) $10/50

141a: THE THOMAS MERTON 1981 AP-
POINTMENT CALENDAR Andrews.. 1981 [0]
Calendar/photographs (ref.d) $25.

142a: GEOGRAPHY OF HOLINESS Pilgrim
Press NY (1980) [0] (Ref.d) $15/60

143a: THOMAS MERTON ON ST. BERNARD
Cistercian Kalamazoo 1980 [0] $15/60

143b: THOMAS MERTON ON ST. BERNARD
Cistercian Kalamazoo 1980 [] Wraps $25.

143c: THOMAS MERTON ON ST. BERNARD
Mowbray L 1980 [] $10/40

143d: THOMAS MERTON ON ST. BERNARD
Mowbray L 1980 [] Wraps $20.

144a: THE NONVIOLENT ALTERNATIVE
Farrar, Straus NY 1980 [] New title. Revised
edition of item 123a *Thomas Merton on Peace*
(ref.c) $10/40

145a: INTRODUCTIONS EAST & WEST: *The
Foreign Prefaces* Unicorn Greensboro (1981) [0]
The foreign prefaces of Merton edited by Robert E.
Daggy (ref.d) $20/60

145b: INTRODUCTIONS EAST & WEST: *The
Foreign Prefaces* Unicorn Greensboro (1981) []
Wraps (ref.d) $30.

146a: THE LITERARY ESSAYS OF THOMAS MERTON New Directions (NY 1981) [1] Edited by Brother Patrick Hart (ref.c) $12/60

146b: THE LITERARY ESSAYS OF THOMAS MERTON New Directions (NY 1985) [1] Wraps (ref.c) $25.

147a: WOODS, SHORE, DESERT: A NOTE-BOOK Museum of New Mexico Press Santa Fe (1982 [1983]) [0] Copyright 1982 but actually published 1983. Photography by Merton. Published price: $14.95 (ref.c) $25/50

147b: WOODS, SHORE, DESERT: A NOTE-BOOK Museum of New Mexico Press Santa Fe (1982 [1983]) [0] Wraps. Copyright 1982, actually published in 1983. Published price: $6.95 (ref.c) $25.

148a: BLAZE OF RECOGNITION: THROUGH THE YEAR WITH THOMAS MERTON: DAILY MEDITATIONS Doubleday GC 1983 [1] (ref.d) $10/40

149a: THE INNER EXPERIENCE (Abbey of Gethsemani Trappist, KY 1983/84) [0] Wraps. Offprints from *Cistercian Studies*. We have seen two: II SOCIETY AND THE INNER SELF (No.2 1983) and V INFUSED CONTEMPLATION (No.1 1984). So, there are at least five of them (ref.d) $75 (each)

150a: THE HIDDEN GROUND OF LOVE Farrar, Straus NY (1985) [1] Selected and edited by Wm. H. Shannon (ref.c) $10/40

151a: ST. AELRED OF RIEVAULX AND THE CISTERCIANS (I) Cistercian Studies no place 1985 [] Wraps. 12-page offprint (Waiting For Godot Books 9/92) $75.

151b: ST. AELRED OF RIEVAULX AND THE CISTERCIANS (II) Cistercian Studies no place 1985 [] Wraps. 13-page offprint (Waiting For Godot Books 9/92) $75.

152a: EIGHTEEN POEMS New Directions (NY 1985) [2] 250 cc. Issued without dustwrapper in slipcase. Printed at Yolla Bolly Press (ref.d) $200/250

153a: KEEPING A SPIRITUAL JOURNAL WITH THOMAS MERTON Doubleday GC NY 1987 [1] Pictorial boards in slipcase. Quotations from Merton in a personal book of days. Selected and edited by Naomi Burton Stone with photos by Catherine Hopkins $50/75

154a: THE ALASKAN JOURNAL OF THOMAS MERTON Turkey Press Isla Vista (1988) [2] 140 no cc. Bound in linen over boards. Issued without dustwrapper in a slipcase with a photo taken by Merton mounted on one side (ref.d) $225.

154b: THE ALASKAN JOURNAL OF THOMAS MERTON New Directions (NY 1989) [0] (Published March 1989 at $19.95) $10/35

154c: THE ALASKAN JOURNAL OF THOMAS MERTON New Directions NY 1989 [0] Wraps. (Published March 1989 at $9.95) $20.

155a: A VOW OF CONVERSATION: JOURNAL 1964-65 Farrar, Straus NY (1988) [1] Uncorrected proof in green wraps (Bev Chaney) $60.

155b: A VOW OF CONVERSATION: JOURNAL 1964-65 Farrar, Straus NY (1988) [1] Edited by Naomi Burton Stone. (Published July 1988 at $17.95 {copy in hand} but announced at $16.95) (PW) $6/30

156a: ENCOUNTER - THOMAS MERTON & D. T. SUZUKI Larkspur Press (Monterey, KY) 1988 [2] 60 no cc. Issued with marbled paper boards and a white buckram spine. (Published at $135.) (Also 4 sets of page press proofs, two pages to a leaf printed on rectos only {Henry Turlington 1/90}) $175.

156b: ENCOUNTER - THOMAS MERTON & D. T. SUZUKI Larkspur Press (Monterey, KY) 1988 [2] 1,000 no cc. Issued in flint gray cloth with a white printed dustwrapper. (Published at $37.50) — $25/75

157a: THOMAS MERTON IN ALASKA New Directions NY (1988) [] The Alaskan conferences, journals and letters (Bev Chaney Jr. 9/91) — $6/30

157b: THOMAS MERTON IN ALASKA New Directions NY (1988) [] Wraps (Bev Chaney Jr. 9/91 — $10.

158a: THE ROAD TO JOY: *The Letters of Thomas Merton to New and Old Friends* Farrar Straus & Giroux NY (1989) [] Uncorrected Proof in printed green wraps (Bev Chaney, Jr. 1/95) — $50.

158b: THE ROAD TO JOY: *The Letters of Thomas Merton to New and Old Friends* Farrar NY 1989 [] Selected and edited by Robert E. Daggy. (Published August 1989 at $29.95) — $6/30

159a: AN EASTER ANTHOLOGY Owensboro Museum of Fine Arts KY 1989 [] Wraps (Bev Chaney Jr. 9/89) — $40.

160a: MONK'S POND University Press of Kentucky Louisville (1989) [0] Wraps. Republication of Merton's magazine, all 4 issues with introduction by Robt. E. Daggy. Includes Patrick Hart, Jack Kerouac, Wendell Berry and Louis Zukofsky (Bev Chaney 9/89) — $50.

161a: LETTERS FROM TOM Fort Hill Press Scarsdale no date [1989] [2] 500 no cc. Pictorial stiff wraps. Thomas Merton to W.H. Ferry 1961-1968 (Bev Chaney Jr.) — $40.

162a: PREVIEW OF THE ASIAN JOURNEY Crossroad NY (1989) [0] Conversations with Merton in Santa Barbara in 1968, transcribed and edited by Walter Capps — $6/30

163a: DIALOGUE ABOUT THE HIDDEN GOD
Dim Gray Bar Press (NY) 1989 [2] 100 cc. Merton's
translation of Nicholas of Cusa's work. Issued
without dustwrapper. (Published at $80) $100.

164a: HONOURABLE READER: *Reflections On
My Work* Crossroad Publications NY 1989 []
Revised and expanded version of *Introduction East
and West* $35.

165a: THOMAS MERTON: THE POET AND THE
CONTEMPLATIVE LIFE   Columbia University
NY 1990 [0] Wraps. An exhibition compiled by
Patrick T. Lawlor, with a foreword by Kenneth A.
Lohf $25.

166a: THE SCHOOL OF CHARITY Farrar, Straus
NY (1990) [] Uncorrected proof in green wraps $50.

166b: THE SCHOOL OF CHARITY Farrar &
Straus NY (1990) [] The letters of Merton on
religious renewal and spiritual charity. (Published
November 1990 at $24.95) $6/30

167a: FATHER LOUIE Timkin Publ. (NY 1991)
[2] 25 sgd ltr cc (Roman numerals). Photos of
Merton by Ralph Eugene Meatyard, edited by Barry
Magid, with an essay by Guy Davenport (includes
some correspondence). Book signed by Guy
Davenport with 52 original photographs in a
clamshell case $5,000.

167b: FATHER LOUIE Timkin Publ. (NY 1991)
[2] 100 sgd no cc. Signed by Davenport with
original print tipped-in. Issued in box $200/250

167c: FATHER LOUIE Timkin Publ. (NY 1991)
[0] (Published June 1991 at $ 40.00) $20/40

167d: FATHER LOUIE Timkin Publ. (NY 1991)
[0] Wraps. (Published at $19.95) $25.

168a: "One of the Greatest Tragedies of Our Time..." (first line) Black Oak Books Berkeley 1991 [2] 500 cc. 8" x 15.4" broadside (Chloe's Books 5/91) $25.

169a: THE SPRINGS OF CONTEMPLATION Farrar, Straus & Giroux NY (1992) [] Uncorrected Proof in printed red wraps. (Bev Chaney, Jr. 5/92) $40.

170a: THE SPRINGS OF CONTEMPLATION Farrar, Straus & Giroux NY (1992) [] $10/30

171a: THE COURAGE FOR TRUTH: *The Letters of Thomas Merton to Writers* Farrar, Straus & Giroux NY 1993 [] Uncorrected Proof in gray wraps. Edited by Christine M. Bochen. Fourth in the series $35.

171b: THE COURAGE FOR TRUTH: *The Letters of Thomas Merton to Writers* Farrar, Straus & Giroux NY (1993) [] (Published August 1993 at $30.00) $6/30

172a: WITNESS TO FREEDOM *The Letters of Thomas Merton In Times of Crisis* Farrar, Straus & Giroux NY 1994 [] Uncorrected Proof in cream wraps (Bev Chaney, Jr. 10/94) $35.

172b: WITNESS TO FREEDOM: *The Letters of Thomas Merton In Times of Crisis* Farrar, Straus & Giroux NY (1994) [] Concluding volume in five volume series (Bev Chaney, Jr. 1/95) $25

0173a: THE HARMONIES OF EXCESS White Fields Press/Literary Renaissance (Louisville) 1995 [] 11" x 20" poster. Poem illustrated with a photograph of Merton (Chloe's Books 8/95) $25.

TONI MORRISON

Morrison was born in 1931 in Lorain, Ohio. She received her undergraduate degree from Howard University and her masters from Cornell. She taught at Texas Southern University and at Howard. In 1965 she joined Random House as senior editor. Morrison was awarded the Nobel Prize in literature in 1993.

001a: THE BLUEST EYE   Holt Rinehart   NY (1970) [1]   Noted in two different dustwrappers: one with "1070" at bottom of front flap; the other without these numbers.   There are no other differences. $250/1,750

001b: THE BLUEST EYE   Chatto & Windus   L 1979 [0] Scarce in unclipped dustwrapper $40/200

002a: SULA   Knopf   NY   1974   [1] Uncorrected proof in light blue wraps $600.

002b: SULA   Knopf   NY   1974   [1] (Published January 1974 at $5.95) $150/750

002c: SULA   Allen Lane   L (1974) [] (Joseph A. Dermont 3/95.) There was also a Chatto & Windus reprint in 1980 (Waiting For Godot 2/92) $25/100

003a: SONG OF SOLOMON Knopf NY 1977 [1] Uncorrected proof in light tan wraps. Typeset but page numbers written in. Also noted in gray wraps (Chapel Hill Rare Books 5/92) $450.

003b: SONG OF SOLOMON Knopf NY 1977 [1] $50/250

003c: SONG OF SOLOMON Chatto & Windus L 1978 [0] Also noted in price clipped dustwrapper with £8.95 sticker added $15/60

004a: THE HARLEM BOOK OF THE DEAD Morgan & Morgan Dobbs Ferry, NY (1978) [0] Written by James Van Der Zee, Owen Dodson and Camille Billops. Foreword by Morrison $150/500

005a: TAR BABY Knopf NY 1981 [] Uncorrected Proof in light blue wraps $200.

005b: TAR BABY Knopf NY 1981 [1] $15/75

005c: TAR BABY Franklin Library Franklin, PA 1981 [2] "Limited Edition." Full leather. Reportedly precedes trade edition. Includes special preface by Morrison. Assume signed $150.

005d: TAR BABY Chatto & Windus L 1981 [] Uncorrected Proof in salmon colored wraps $150.

005e: TAR BABY Chatto & Windus L 1981 [0] "Published by Chatto & Windus" on copyright page. Noted with dustwrapper price at £6.95 with sticker for £8.95 over it $10/50

006a: A BRIEF VIGNETTE FROM TAR BABY Bookslinger Editions no place 1982 [2] 90 sgd no cc. Broadside published on the occasion of the author reading at the Walker Art Center in March 1982 (Ulysses Bookshop 3/92) $250.

007a: BELOVED Knopf NY 1987 [] Wraps. Spiral-bound typescript in two volumes for use of Book-of-Month Club staff (Pepper & Stern List 7) $350.

007b: BELOVED Knopf NY 1987 [] Uncorrected proof in blue wraps (apparently two versions-one slightly taller with different typeface, but have not seen) $200.

007c: BELOVED Knopf NY 1987 [1] 100,000 cc (PW) $15/75

007d: BELOVED Chatto & Windus L (1987) [] $10/50

008a: RACE-ING JUSTICE EN-GENDERING POWER Pantheon NY 1992 [] Uncorrected Proof in blue wraps. Also noted in green wraps (Waverly Books 8/95) $100.

008b: RACE-ING JUSTICE EN-GENDERING POWER Pantheon NY 1992 [] Wraps. Morrison edited this paperback original (Waverly Books List 12/94) $30.

009a: PLAYING IN THE DARK: *Whiteness and the Literary Imagination* Harvard Cambridge 1992 [] Uncorrected Proof in yellow wraps $150.

009b: PLAYING IN THE DARK: *Whitness and the Literary Imagination* Harvard University Press Cambridge 1992 [3] (Published May 1992 at $14.95.) (Between The Covers 3/95) $15/75

010a: JAZZ Knopf NY 1992 [] Wraps. Uncorrected Proof in buff wraps (color also described as tan {Bev Chaney, Jr. 6/94}; and cream wraps {Waverly Books 6/92}) $100.

010b: JAZZ Franklin Library Franklin Center 1992 [2] "Limited Edition." Signed. Full leather $150.

010c: JAZZ Knopf NY 1992 [1] 175,000 cc (PW). (Published April 1992 at $21.00) $8/40

010d: JAZZ Chatto & Windus L 1992 [] $7/35

011a: CONVERSATIONS WITH TONI MORRISON University Press of Mississippi Jackson 1994 [] Cloth. Edited by Danille R. Taylor-Guthrie. (Published at $37.50) $20/50

011b: CONVERSATIONS   WITH   TONI
MORRISON   University Press of Mississippi
Jackson 1994 [] Wraps. (Published at $14.95) $25.

012a: LECTURE   AND   SPEECH   OF
ACCEPTANCE, UPON THE AWARD OF THE
NOBEL PRIZE FOR LITERATURE... Knopf NY
1994 []   Issued without dustwrapper (Books etc.
11/94) $50.

TIM O'BRIEN

O'Brien was born in Austin, Minnesota, in 1946. He did some graduate work at Harvard and then served in the Army during Vietnam, an experience which influenced his first three books. His third book, *Going After Cacciato*, won the National Book Award for 1978.

001a: IF I DIE IN THE COMBAT ZONE Delacorte NY (1973) [1] $150/750

001b: IF I DIE IN THE COMBAT ZONE Calder & Boyers L (1973) [1] $25/125

002a: NORTHERN LIGHTS Delacorte (NY 1975) [1] 5,000 cc. (Published August 20, 1975 at $8.95) $75/300

002b: NORTHERN LIGHTS Marion Boyers L (1976) [1] "Originally published in Great Britain in 1976 by..." Black cloth. Reportedly only 900 copies (Nicholas Burrows 1/90). Pages 171-172 on a cancel stub (Alphabet Bookshop 8/92). Not a state we've seen $25/125

003a: GOING AFTER CACCIATO Delacorte NY (1978) [1] National Book Award Winner for 1979 $30/150

003b: GOING AFTER CACCIATO Jonathan Cape L 1978 [1] $15/75

004a: SPEAKING OF COURAGE Neville Santa Barbara 1980 [] Long Galley Proofs, one of five sets (Ken Lopez 11/91) $300.

004b: SPEAKING OF COURAGE Neville Santa Barbara 1980 [2] 26 sgd ltr cc. Full leather without dustwrapper or slipcase. A chapter that was excised from *Going After Cacciato* and later appeared in *The Things They Carried* $400.

004c: SPEAKING OF COURAGE Neville Santa Barbara 1980 [2] 300 sgd no cc. Issued without dustwrapper or slipcase. (Cataloged by Ken Lopez as 350 copies) $150.

004d: SPEAKING OF COURAGE Granta [L date??] [] Offprint in wraps with an Author's Note explaining the story's conception. Possibly 50 copies (Ken Lopez 8/95) $150.

005a: "A Soviet SS-13 whizzed right over the house..." Toothpaste Press (West Branch, Iowa) 1980 [2] 150 sgd no cc. Broadside with advance excerpt from the novel *The Nuclear Age* $75.

005b: "A Soviet SS-13 whizzed right over the house..." Toothpaste Press (West Branch, Iowa) 1980 [] Broadside (not signed or numbered) (Am Here Books 5/92) $50.

006a: THE NUCLEAR AGE Press 22 Portland (1981) [] Proof copy of the limited edition comprising an excerpt from O'Brien's work-in-progress, later published with the same title. The proof resembles the wrappered issue, but is unnumbered and stamped "Proof Set/May 5 1981" on the front fly leaf and the colophon (Ken Lopez 5/95) $250.

006b: THE NUCLEAR AGE Press 22 Portland (1981) [2] 26 sgd ltr cc. Hardbound. (Poetry) (Euclid Books). Assume issued without dustwrapper or slipcase $400.

006c: THE NUCLEAR AGE Press 22 Portland (1981) [2] 125 sgd no cc. Issued in wraps and dustwrapper. (Poetry) $75/125

007a: THE NUCLEAR AGE Knopf NY 1985 [1]
Uncorrected proof in light brown wraps. (Novel) $125.

007b: THE NUCLEAR AGE Knopf NY 1985 [1]
(Published October 10, 1985 at $16.95.) (Novel) $10/40

007c: THE NUCLEAR AGE Collins L 1986 []
(Novel) $10/40

008a: *"How to Tell a True War Story"* Minnesota
Center for Book Arts   no place   1987   [2] 150 no
cc. Broadside.   10½" x 11". Excerpt from *The
Things They Carried.* (Ken Lopez 7/91) $75.

008b: *"How to Tell a True War Story"* Black Oak
Books Berkeley 1990 [] Broadside. 8" x 12 3/4"
(Waiting For Godot Books 10/90) $50.

008c: *"How to Tell A True War Story"* Black
Oak/Okeanos Berkeley 1992 [] Broadside. 8" x
13" (Ken Lopez 12/94) $50.

009a: THE THINGS THEY CARRIED Franklin
Library Franklin Center 1990 [2] Signed "Limited
Edition" in full leather with special introduction by
the author $75.

009b: THE THINGS THEY CARRIED Houghton
Mifflin   B 1990 [] Two stories excerpted from
forthcoming book in decorated stapled wraps
(Monroe Stahr 3/90) $40.

009c: THE THINGS THEY CARRIED Houghton
Mifflin   B 1990 [3] (Published March, 1990 at
$19.59) $7/35

009d: THE THINGS THEY CARRIED Collins L
1990 [] $8/40

010a: STYLE   Logan Elm Press/Ohio State
University   no place   1993   [2] 250 sgd cc.
Broadside. 12" x 18". Excerpts from *The Things
They Carried.* Illustrated by Jack Shiffman $100.

011a: IN THE LAKE OF THE WOODS Houghton
Mifflin/Seymour Lawrence   B   1994 [] Wraps.
Advance Reading Copy in glossy pictorial wraps
(Orpheus Books 11/94) $60.

011b: IN THE LAKE OF THE WOODS Houghton
Mifflin B/NY 1994 [] Uncorrected page proof in
clear plastic cover over bound 8½" x 11" sheets.
Issued after the Advance Reading Copy and
incorporating a substantial number of textual
changes the author made after the advance reading
copy had been printed. Thus this is the first
appearance of the final version of the text. (Ken
Lopez 5/95) $150.

011c: IN THE LAKE OF THE WOODS Houghton
Mifflin/Seymour Lawrence   B   1994 [] Advance
excerpt in printed stiff wraps.   40 pages   (Bev
Chaney, Jr. 10/94) $35.

011d: IN THE LAKE OF THE WOODS Houghton
Mifflin/Seymour Lawrence B 1994 [] 75,000 cc
(PW). (Published October 1994 at $21.95) $6/30

011e: IN THE LAKE OF THE WOODS Flamingo
L 1995 [] Wraps $25.

ffi Orwell –

GEORGE ORWELL
(1903 - 1950)

E·A·Blair·

E.A. BLAIR

Orwell was born Eric Arthur Blair in Motihari, Bengal. His father was a Sub-Deputy Opium Agent (dealing in the legal opium trade between India and China); his mother was the daughter of a wealthy French teak merchant in Burma.

The year after his birth, his mother took him to England to live. He attended Eton and then went to Burma in 1922, where he served as an assistant superintendent of police. In 1927, while on leave in England Orwell decided not to return to Burma, but instead tramped around England and France, which gave him the material for his first book.

In 1936, Orwell went to Spain, originally to work as a freelance war correspondent, but ended up volunteering for the militia. He was wounded and eventually escaped to France and then back to England. Rejected by the Army on medical grounds, he volunteered for the Home Guard in London, where he stayed throughout World War II, working as talks producer for the BBC and literary editor of *The Tribune*.

In 1945, *Animal Farm* brought Orwell his first monetary success which allowed him to drop most of his journalistic work and concentrate on essays and his next novel, *1984*. He moved with his adopted son Richard (his wife Eileen having died in 1945) to Jura, a Scottish island, to work, but his health failed rapidly and he

was almost an invalid by the end of 1947. Orwell managed to
finish *1984* (he typed the final draft himself) but was soon in the
sanitarium where he would die in 1950.

The information herein on first printing quantities is based on Alan
C. Smith's *Catalog 2*, which in turn references *Notes Toward a
Bibliography* by I.R. Willison (1952 thesis) and a checklist
published in *Bulletin of Bibliography* (Volume 23, Nos. 5 and 10,
Volume 24, No. 8) by Zoltan G. Zeke, William White, M. Jeanifer
McDowell, I.R. Willison and Ian Angus; and information from
Harcourt which showed total hardcover sales.

001a: DOWN AND OUT IN PARIS AND
LONDON   Gollancz L (1932) [] Wraps.   An
advance copy issued in December 1932 $7,500.

001b: DOWN AND OUT IN PARIS AND
LONDON Gollancz L 1933 [0] 1,500 cc. (January
1933) $500/3,500

001c: DOWN AND OUT IN PARIS AND
LONDON   Gollancz L 1933 [] Second printing
(stated). 500 cc. (January 1933) $100/450

001d: DOWN AND OUT IN PARIS AND
LONDON   Gollancz   L 1933 [] Third Printing
(stated). 1,000 cc. (February 1933) $75/250

001e: DOWN AND OUT IN PARIS AND
LONDON Harper & Bros. NY 1933 [1] 1,750 cc $300/1,500

001f: DOWN AND OUT IN PARIS AND
LONDON Secker & Warburg L 1986 [] Volume
one of *The Complete Works* edited by Peter
Davison. Restores censored material and adds
Orwell's modifications and notes used in the 1935
French translation $15/60

002a: BURMESE DAYS Harper & Bros. NY 1934
[1] 2,000 cc $250/1,250

002b: BURMESE DAYS   Gollancz   L 1935 []
2,500 cc $300/1,500

003a: A CLERGYMAN'S DAUGHTER   Gollancz
L 1935 [0] 1,500 cc $350/1,750

003b: A CLERGYMAN'S DAUGHTER   Harper
NY 1936 [] 500 cc. English sheets $250/1,250

003c: A CLERGYMAN'S DAUGHTER   Harper
NY 1936 [] 500 cc. U.S. sheets. Although James
Jaffe, who had an extensive collection of Orwell,
does not believe Harper ever printed any copies $200/1,000

003d: A CLERGYMAN'S DAUGHTER Harcourt
Brace NY (1960) [0] $25/125

004a: KEEP THE ASPIDISTRA FLYING   Gol-
lancz L 1936 [] 3,000 cc. 484 copies of this edition
used in 1942 reissue $350/2,000

004b: KEEP THE ASPIDISTRA FLYING   Harcourt Brace   NY (1956) [1] 8,863 cc (total
hardcover sales), first may have been only 1,500
copies $25/100

005a: THE ROAD TO WIGAN PIER Gollancz L
1937 [0] 1,000 cc $300/1,500

005b: THE ROAD TO WIGAN PIER Gollancz L
1937 [0] 38,000 cc. Limp oil cloth covers. Left
Book Club edition $125.

005c: THE ROAD TO WIGAN PIER Gollancz L
1937 [] Limp oil-cloth covers. First half of text as
supplementary offering for May 1937. 32 plates,
chapters 1 to 7 only (1,750 copies {David Mayou}) $600.

005d: THE ROAD TO WIGAN PIER Gollancz L
1937 [] Uncorrected Proof labled "Second Proof"
and stamped "Uncorrected" with Gollancz's fore-

word excised so assume it was made up as a proof
for the American edition (R.A. Gekoski 4/92) $750.

005e: THE ROAD TO WIGAN PIER Harcourt
Brace NY (1958) [1] 4,106 total hardcover sales.
First may have been 3,500 copies. (Published July
30, 1958) $25/125

006a: HOMAGE TO CATALONIA Secker &
Warburg L 1938 [1] 1,500 cc $300/2,000

006b: HOMAGE TO CATALONIA Harcourt
Brace NY (1952) [1] 7,517 cc (total hardcover
sales). (Published May 15, 1952) $25/125

007a: COMING UP FOR AIR Gollancz L 1939
[0] 2,000 cc $350/2,000

007b: COMING UP FOR AIR Harcourt Brace NY
(1950) [0] 8,753 cc (total hardcover sales).
(Published January 19, 1950) $25/75

008a: INSIDE THE WHALE Gollancz L 1940 []
1,000 cc $300/1,500

009a: THE LION AND THE UNICORN Secker &
Warburg L 1940 [] Uncorrected Proof in blue
wraps. (Pepper & Stern 5/92) $750.

009b: THE LION AND THE UNICORN Secker &
Warburg L 1941 [1] 7,500 cc $50/250

010a: THE BETRAYAL OF THE LEFT Gollancz
L 1941 [1] 500 cc. Limp cloth covers. Left Book
Club edition. Written with Victor Gollancz, John
Strachey and others $350.

010b: THE BETRAYAL OF THE LEFT Gollancz
L 1941 [1] 1,300 cc. Public Edition $125/500

011a: VICTORY OR VESTED INTEREST?
Routledge L 1942 [] 6,100 cc (a & b). Written with
G.D.H. Cole and others $100/300

011b: VICTORY OR VESTED INTEREST? Routledge L 1942 [] Labour Book Service Edition. Issued without dustwrapper $150.

012a: TALKING TO INDIA Allen & Unwin L (1943) [1]   A selection of English language broadcasts to India. Edited and introduction by Orwell. Includes E.M. Forster, Orwell, Cyril Connolly, et al. Red cloth stamped in white on spine $75/300

013a: ANIMAL FARM Secker & Warburg L 1945 [1] 4,500 cc. (Also noted in dustwrapper with "Searchlight Books each 2s net" and picture of train engine on rear of dustwrapper) $300/1,500

013b: ANIMAL FARM   Harcourt Brace   NY (1946) [1] Advance copies in printed gray wraps $450.

013c: ANIMAL FARM   Harcourt Brace   NY (1946) [1] 50,000 cc. Black cloth. Also noted in secondary binding in blue-green cloth $40/200

013d: ANIMAL FARM Harcourt Brace NY (1954) [0] First illustrated U.S. edition. Illustrated by Joy Batchelor and John Halas. (Published September 9, 1954 at $2.95.) (U.S. precedes??) $30/150

013e: ANIMAL FARM Secker & Warburg L 1954 [] First illustrated edition $30/150

013f: ANIMAL FARM *A Fable in Two Acts* French NY (1954) [0] Wraps. Adapted by Nelson Bond $35.

014a: CRITICAL ESSAYS Secker & Warburg L 1946 [1] 3,000 cc $50/250

014b: DICKENS, DALI AND OTHERS Reynal & Hitchcock NY 1946 [] Uncorrected Proof in maroon-cloth-backed tan card covers with publisher's label on front. New title (Blackwell's Rare Books 6/94) $500.

014c: DICKENS, DALI AND OTHERS Reynal &
Hitchcock NY (1946) [0] 5,000 cc
$35/175

015a: JAMES BURNHAM AND THE MANA-
GERIAL REVOLUTION (Socialist Book Centre L
1946) [0] "First published in Polemic 3 under the
title *Second Thoughts on James Burnham*"
$750.

015b: JAMES BURNHAM AND THE MANA-
GERIAL REVOLUTION Young Socialist League
Berkeley   no date   (cover) [] 8 1/2" x 11"
mimeographed sheets in stapled wraps. Introduction
by James Robertson dated January 29, 1955
(Waiting For Godot 11/89)
$650.

016a: LOVE OF LIFE AND OTHER STORIES
Paul Elek L 1946 [0] Introduction to Jack London's
book by Orwell
$35/175

017a: THE ENGLISH PEOPLE Collins L 1947
[0] 26,000 cc
$25/75

017b: THE ENGLISH PEOPLE Haskell House
NY 1974 [] Reprint of Collins' edition
$10/40

018a: POLITICS AND THE ENGLISH LAN-
GUAGE Paul A. Bennett (Evansville) 1947 [0]
Wraps. First separate edition of essay that appeared
in *The New Republic* and *Horizon* (London)
$250.

019a: BRITISH PAMPHLETEERS Volume 1
Wingate L 1948 [1] Edited by Orwell with
Reginald Reynolds. Introduction by Orwell. There
was also a volume 2 in 1951 but Orwell was not
involved
$25/100

020a: NINETEEN EIGHTY-FOUR Secker &
Warburg L 1949 [1] 25,500 cc (a&b). Red
dustwrapper seems to be preferred (priority
uncertain). Both noted in Book Society wrap-around
bands. A publisher's employee stated the ratio of
green to red (or maroon) was about 2 to 1 (Cobby-

dale Books   9/94), although this ratio has been
estimated much higher, up to 20 to 1 $300/3,000

020b: NINETEEN EIGHTY-FOUR   Secker &
Warburg L 1949 [1] Green dustwrapper $300/1,500

020c: NINETEEN EIGHTY-FOUR Harcourt Brace
NY (1949) [1] 20,000 cc (c&d). Red dustwrapper
also preferred on U.S. edition (prority uncertain) but
Book-of-the-Month Club issue was blue and
perhaps that is why blue is considered later
(published June 13, 1949) $50/300

020d: NINETEEN EIGHTY-FOUR   Harcourt
Brace NY (1949) [1] Blue dustwrapper $50/150

020e: NINETEEN EIGHTY-FOUR   S.J. Reginald
Saunders Toronto 1949 [1] First Canadian stated.
Dustwrapper priced $3.00. All copies noted have a
Book-of-the-Month Club dot on lower right corner
of back cover $15/75

020f: NINETEEN EIGHTY-FOUR Dramatic Publ.
Chicago 1963 [] Wraps. First play edition. Adapted
by Robert Owens $40.

020g: 1984 | *Facsimile of the Extant Manuscript*
Secker & Warburg/M & S Press London/Weston,
Mass. 1984 [2] 55 no cc in full leather by Gray
Parrot. Issued in clam shell box (Trupenny Books
5/91) $650/750

020h: 1984 | *Facsimile of the Extant Manuscript*
Secker & Warburg/M & S Press London/Weston,
Mass, 1984 [] Issued in dustwrapper and slipcase.
Edited by Peter Davison $25/75

020i: 1984 | *Facsimile of the Extant Manuscript*
Harcourt, Brace   S.D. (1984) [1]   Issued in
dustwrapper and slipcase $20/60

021a: SHOOTING AN ELEPHANT   Secker &
Warburg L (1950) [1] 7,500 cc $35/175

021b: SHOOTING AN ELEPHANT   Harcourt Brace NY (1950) [1] 4,000 cc. (Published October 26, 1950) $25/125

022a: SUCH, SUCH WERE THE JOYS Harcourt Brace NY (1953) [1] Title essay not included in English edition. 5,617 copies total hardcover sales. First may have been 4,000 copies. (Published February 26, 1953) $25/125

022b: ENGLAND YOUR ENGLAND Secker & Warburg L 1953 [1] New title. Deletes "Such, Such Were the Joys" and adds two pieces from *The Road To Wigan Pier* $25/125

023a: A COLLECTION OF ESSAYS Doubleday GC 1954 [] Wraps. Doubleday Anchor Books A29 $40.

023b: SELECTED ESSAYS   Penguin Books (Harmondsworth 1957) [1] New title. Wraps. Penguin Books 1185 $40.

024a: THE ORWELL READER Harcourt Brace NY (1956) [1] Edited by Richard Rovere $15/60

025a: SELECTED WRITINGS Heinemann L (1958) [1] Edited by George Bott $15/60

026a: COLLECTED ESSAYS Mercury Books L 1961 [] Wraps $35.

026b: COLLECTED ESSAYS Heinemann L (1966) [] Wraps. (Mercury Books #17) $25.

027a: DECLINE OF THE ENGLISH MURDER, AND OTHER ESSAYS   Penguin Books (Harmondsworth 1965) [1] Wraps $60.

028a: THE COLLECTED ESSAYS, JOURNA-LISM AND LETTERS OF GEORGE ORWELL Secker & Warburg L (1968) [0] 4 volumes. Edited by Sonia Orwell and Ian Angus $75/250

028b: THE COLLECTED ESSAYS, JOURNA-
LISM AND LETTERS OF GEORGE ORWELL
Harcourt, Brace & World NY (1968) [1] About
10,500 copies total hardcover sales. (Published
October 23, 1968) $60/125

029a: HOP PICKING: GEORGE ORWELL IN
KENT Bridge Books (Wateringbury 1970) [2] 300
no. cc. First separate publication of an essay in
Collected Essays $60.

030a: SIX NOVELS Secker & Warburg L 1976
[] First thus $10/40

031a: TEN "ANIMAL FARM" LETTERS TO HIS
AGENT LEONARD MOORE   Frederic Brewer
Press Bloomington (1984) [2] 200 no. cc. Edited by
Michael Sheldon. Published for the Friends of Lilly
Library $35/75

032a: THE WAR COMMENTARIES Duckworth /
BBC (L 1985) [2] 250 sgd no cc. 2 volumes
signed by William J. West, editor $100.

032b: THE WAR COMMENTARIES Duckworth /
BBC (L 1985) [] $10/40

032c: THE WAR COMMENTARIES   Pantheon
NY 1985 [] Uncorrected Proof in red wraps. (Bev
Chaney, Jr. 6/91) $50.

032d: THE WAR COMMENTARIES   Pantheon
NY (1985) [1] Edited and introduction by W.J.
West $10/40

033a: THE LOST WRITINGS Arbor House NY
(1985) [3]   Advance sheets in proof dustwrapper
(Beasley Books 6/89). Also, bound signatures of
English edition without the title/copyright pages;
laid-in U.S.dustwrapper (Ampersand Books 7/92)
Same? $40/60

033b: THE LOST WRITINGS   Arbor House   NY
(1985) [3] $10/30

Cynthia Ozick [signature]

CYNTHIA OZICK

Ozick was born in 1928 in New York City. She graduated from New York University and received a Masters from Ohio State in 1951. She has taught at various universities and writing workshops since 1965, including New York University, Indiana University, and City University of New York.

001a: TRUST New American Library NY 1966
[] Tall, thin galley proofs in ring-bound wraps
(Joseph the Provider Books 1/91) $500.

001b: TRUST New American Library NY (1966)
[] Wraps. Uncorrected proofs. Spiral bound in two
volumes (Joseph The Provider) $300.

001c: TRUST New American Library (NY 1966)
[1] $50/250

001d: TRUST MacGibbon & Kee (L 1966) [1] $25/125

002a: THE PAGAN RABBI _and Other Stories_
Knopf NY 1971 [1] $15/75

002b: THE PAGAN RABBI _and Other Stories_
Secker & Warburg L (1972) [1] $10/40

003a: DARK SOLILOQUY Seabury NY (1975)
[0] Poems of Gertrude Kolman with foreword by
Ozick $10/40

004a: BLOODSHED AND THREE NOVELLAS
Knopf NY 1976 [1] $10/40

004b: BLOODSHED AND THREE NOVELLAS
Secker & Warburg L 1976 [] $10/40

005a: LEVITATION *Five Fictions* Knopf NY 1981 [1] Uncorrected proof in light blue wraps. Contains story "The Laughter of Akiva" which did not appear in published book (Waverly Books) — $100.

005b: LEVITATION *Five Fictions* Knopf NY 1981 [1] Wraps. Proof copy substituting "Putter Messer and Xanthippe" for "The Laughter..." — $60.

005c: LEVITATION *Five Fictions* Knopf NY 1981 [1] — $6/30

005d: LEVITATION Secker & Warburg L (1982) [] — $6/30

006a: ART & ARDOR Knopf NY 1983 [] Uncorrected proof in red wraps (Waiting For Godot) — $60.

006b: ART & ARDOR Knopf NY 1983 [1] — $6/30

007a: THE CANNIBAL GALAXY Knopf NY 1983 [1] Uncorrected proof in white or cream printed wraps — $60.

007b: THE CANNIBAL GALAXY Knopf NY 1983 [1] 12,500 cc — $6/30

007c: THE CANNIBAL GALAXY Secker & Warburg L 1984 [] — $6/30

008a: THE MESSIAH OF STOCKHOLM Knopf NY 1987 [1] — $5/25

008b: THE MESSIAH OF STOCKHOLM Deutsch L 1987 [] — $5/25

009a: METAPHOR & MEMORY Knopf NY 1989 [] Uncorrected proof in salmon-colored wraps (Waverly Books 3/89) — $50.

009b: METAPHOR & MEMORY Knopf NY 1989 [1] (Published April 12, 1989 at $19.95) — $5/25

010a: THE SHAWL *A Story and A Novella* Knopf
NY 1989 [] Uncorrected Proof in cream (tan)
wraps $40.

010b: THE SHAWL *A Story and A Novella* Knopf
NY 1989 [1] (Published September 9, 1989 at
$12.95) $5/25

010c: THE SHAWL *A Story and A Novella*
Jonathan Cape L 1991 [] Wraps in dustwrapper
(Chris Coupland 9/91) $6/30

011a: INK AND INKLING *Mark Podwal, Master
of True Line* Mount Holyoke College Art Museum
South Hadley, Mass. 1990 [] Wraps. 40-page
illustrated exhibition catalog (Turtle Island
Booksellers 9/91) $30.

012a: EPODES *First Poems* Logan Elm Press
Columbus, Ohio 1991 [2] 26 sgd ltr cc with an
extra suite of prints. Published at $3,000. 47 poems
and introduction by Ozick with four multi-colored
prints by Sidney Chafetz $NVA

012b: EPODES *First Poems* Logan Elm Press
Columbus, Ohio (1991) [2] 124 sgd no cc. Also
signed by illustrator Sidney Chafetz $75.

013a: WHAT HENRY JAMES KNEW *and Other
Essays on Writers* Jonathan Cape L 1993 [] (Ian
McKelvie 2/95.) We do not know of an American
edition $6/30

ROBERT B. PARKER

Robert Parker was born in Springfield, Massachusetts. He worked as a technical and advertising writer at various companies from 1957 to 1962. Thereafter, he was an instructor in English at Boston University, Massachusetts State College and Northeastern University. He received his Ph.D. from Boston University in 1970.

Parker's character, Spenser, has a good sense of humor, jogs, lifts weights and is a gourmet cook, albeit with gourmand leanings. The television series based on Parker's detective was popular though short lived. He has also written a number of film scripts which have been cataloged between $150 and $400.

Entries are based primarily on past or present inventory, except for first three entries which were listed in *Contemporary Authors*. In a letter to us, Parker verified that he did not write *Mature Advertising*, which was also listed under his name.

001a: THE PERSONAL RESPONSE TO LITERATURE   Houghton Mifflin B 1970 []
Written with Peter L. Sandberg $30/150

002a: THE PRINCE AND THE KING: SHAKESPEARE'S MACHIAVELLIAN CYCLE
Revue Des Langues   Vivantes 1972 [] Stapled wraps. Offprint of Parker's thesis (Herb Yellin) $125.

003a: ORDER AND DIVERSITY *The Craft of Prose*   Wiley NY 1973 [] Written with John R. Marsh $25/125

004a: SPORTS ILLUSTRATED WEIGHT TRAINING   Lippincott   Philadelphia 1974 [] Pictorial boards without dustwrapper $100.

005a: THE GODWULF MANUSCRIPT Houghton Mifflin B 1974 [1] 7,500 cc. Portion appeared in January 1974 issue of *Argosy*, not October 1973 as stated on copyright page (Robert A. Hittel) $75/350

005b: THE GODWULF MANUSCRIPT Deutsch (London 1974) [1] $30/150

006a: GOD SAVE THE CHILD Houghton Mifflin B 1974 [1] 7,500 cc $75/350

006b: GOD SAVE THE CHILD Deutsch (London 1975) [1] $25/125

007a: THE VIOLENT HERO University Microfilm Ann Arbor 1974 [] Photocopied and bound in buckram, as issued (Pepper & Stern 6/91) $75.

008a: MORTAL STAKES Houghton Mifflin B 1975 [1] 10,000 cc $50/250

008b: MORTAL STAKES Deutsch (L 1976) [1] Issued without front endpaper (Peter Jolliffe) $25/100

009a: PROMISED LAND Houghton Mifflin B 1976 [1] 12,500 cc. Winner of the Edgar Allan Poe Award for best novel of 1976 $25/125

009b: PROMISED LAND Deutsch (L 1977) [1] $12/60

010a: THREE WEEKS IN SPRING Houghton Mifflin B 1978 [3] Written with his wife Joan Parker $15/75

010b: THREE WEEKS IN SPRING Deutsch (London 1978) [1] $10/50

011a: THE JUDAS GOAT Houghton Mifflin B 1978 [3] 15,000 cc $20/100

011b: THE JUDAS GOAT Deutsch (London 1982)
[1] $10/50

012a: WILDERNESS   Delacorte (NY 1979) [1]
"Uncorrected proof" in printed gray wraps and in
beige wraps (Waverly 5/88) $150.

012b: WILDERNESS   Delacorte (NY 1979) [1]
15,000 cc $12/60

012c: WILDERNESS Deutsch (London 1980) [1] $10/40

013a: LOOKING FOR RACHEL WALLACE
Delacorte (NY 1980) [1] 10,000 cc $20/100

013b: LOOKING FOR RACHEL WALLACE
Deutsch (London 1980) [1] $12/60

014a: EARLY AUTUMN Delacorte (NY 1981) [1]
27,500 cc. Includes 15,000 for Playboy Book Club
but do not believe that they were marked in any way $10/50

015a: A SAVAGE PLACE   Delacorte (NY 1981)
[1] "Advance Uncorrected Proof" in printed light
red wraps $150.

015b: A SAVAGE PLACE   Delacorte (NY 1981)
[1] 15,000 cc $10/50

015c: A SAVAGE PLACE   Piatkus (Essex 1982)
[1] 1,750 cc $12/60

016a: CEREMONY   Delacorte (NY 1982) [1]
"Uncorrected Proof" in printed blue wraps $125.

016b: CEREMONY   Delacorte (NY 1982) [1]
15,000 cc $10/40

016c: CEREMONY Piatkus (L 1982) [1] 1,750 cc $12/60

017a: SURROGATE Lord John Press Northridge
1982 [2] 50 sgd no cc. Deluxe edition $275/350

017b: SURROGATE Lord John Press Northridge 1982 [2] 300 sgd no cc. Issued in dustwrapper without slipcase $125/200

018a: THE WIDENING GYRE Delacorte (NY 1983) [1] 20,000 cc $10/40

019a: A SPENSERIAN SONNET Lord John Press Northridge 1983 [2] 26 sgd ltr cc. Broadside $125.

019b: A SPENSERIAN SONNET Lord John Press Northridge 1983 [2] 100 sgd no cc. Broadside $75.

020a: LOVE AND GLORY Delacorte (NY 1983) [] "Uncorrected Proof" in tall rose/brown wraps. Also described as salmon wraps (Bev Chaney, Jr. 9/91) $75.

020b: LOVE AND GLORY Delacorte (NY 1983) [1] 15,000 cc $10/50

021a: THE PRIVATE EYE IN HAMMETT AND CHANDLER Lord John Press Northridge 1984 [2] 50 sgd no cc. Marbled boards and red leather spine (this is an edited version of his Doctoral Dissertation). Note: Copies may be available at University Microfilms (Armchair Detective - Summer 1985) $200.

021b: THE PRIVATE EYE IN HAMMETT AND CHANDLER Lord John Press Northridge 1984 [2] 300 sgd no cc. Issued without dustwrapper $125.

022a: VALEDICTION Delacorte (NY 1984) [1] 40,000 cc $10/40

022b: VALEDICTION Severn House (L 1986) [] $8/40

023a: BACKFIRE Santa Teresa Press Santa Barbara 1984 [] "Proof" stamped on front cover of wraps $50.

023b: BACKFIRE   Santa Teresa Press   Santa Barbara 1984 [2] 26 sgd ltr cc.   Issued without dustwrapper in slipcase $300/350

023c: BACKFIRE   Santa Teresa Press   Santa Barbara 1984 [2] 100 sgd no cc.   Chandler screenplay with Parker introduction. Issued without dustwrapper or slipcase $175.

023d: BACKFIRE   Santa Teresa Press   Santa Barbara 1984 [2] 200 sgd no cc. Wraps $75.

024a: A CATSKILL EAGLE Delacorte (NY 1985) [2] 500 sgd no cc. "Uncorrected Proof" in blue printed wraps with signed bookplate on inside cover. A few copies were numbered one of "400" in error $100.

024b: A CATSKILL EAGLE Delacorte (NY 1985) [1] 60,000 cc (PW) $10/40

024c: A CATSKILL EAGLE   Viking (Middlesex 1986) [1] $7/35

025a: RAYMOND CHANDLER'S UNKNOWN THRILLER... Mysterious Press NY 1985 [] Wraps. Introduction to the screenplay of *Playback*. Special edition to register copyright (Pepper & Stern estimated at 30 copies) $125.

025b: RAYMOND CHANDLER'S UNKNOWN THRILLER... Mysterious Press NY 1985 [2] 26 sgd ltr cc. Issued in slipcase $200/250

025c: RAYMOND CHANDLER'S UNKNOWN THRILLER... Mysterious Press NY 1985 [2] 250 sgd no cc. Issued in slipcase $75/125

025d: RAYMOND CHANDLER'S UNKNOWN THRILLER... Mysterious Press NY 1985 [0] $7/35

025e: RAYMOND CHANDLER'S UNKNOWN THRILLER.... Harrap L 1985 [1] $7/35

026a: PARKER ON WRITING Lord John Press Northridge 1985 [2] 75 sgd no cc. Deluxe edition with leather spine. Issued without dustwrapper $150.

026b: PARKER ON WRITING Lord John Press Northridge 1985 [2] 300 sgd no cc. Issued in cloth without dustwrapper $100.

027a: TAMING A SEA-HORSE Delacorte (NY 1986) [2] 500 sgd no cc. "Uncorrected Page Proof" in sea-green wraps with signed/numbered label on inside cover $75.

027b: TAMING A SEA-HORSE Delacorte (NY 1986) [1] (Published June 6, 1986 at $15.95) $6/30

027c: TAMING A SEA-HORSE Viking (Harmondsworth 1987) [1] $6/30

028a: SOME CELTICS Lord John Press (Northridge) 1986 [2] 26 sgd ltr cc. Broadside. Illustrated by Joseph Pastor $175.

028b: SOME CELTICS Lord John Press (Northridge) 1986 [2] 100 sgd no cc. Broadside. Illustrated by Joseph Pastor $100.

029a: PALE KINGS AND PRINCES Delacorte NY (1987) [2] 500 sgd no cc. Uncorrected proof in red wraps with signed/numbered label on inside cover $75.

029b: PALE KINGS AND PRINCES Delacorte NY (1987) [2] 225 sgd no cc. Issued without dustwrapper in slipcase $75/125

029c: PALE KINGS AND PRINCES Delacorte NY (1987) [1] 125,000 cc (PW). (Published June 5, 1987 at $15.95.) (The large print edition may have been issued simultaneously, ISBN number is on copyright page of this edition) $6/30

029d: PALE KINGS AND PRINCES Viking (L 1988) [] $6/30

030a: A CRIMSON JOY Delacorte (NY 1988) [2] 500 sgd no cc. Uncorrected proof in red wraps with signed/numbered label on inside cover $75.

030b: A CRIMSON JOY Delacorte (NY 1988) [2] 250 sgd no cc. Issued without dustwrapper in slipcase $75/125

030c: A CRIMSON JOY Delacorte (NY 1988) [3] "June 1988" also stated. (Published July 1988 at $16.95) (The large print edition apparently issued simultaneously at $17.95) $6/30

031a: SPENSER'S BOSTON Japan 1988 [] Photographs of the four seasons with text by Parker (Herb Yellin 3/90) $50/100

031b: SPENSER'S BOSTON Penzler NY (1994) [] (Buckingham Books 3/95) $20/40

032a: WOMEN IN THE DARK Knopf NY 1988 [1] 25,000 cc (PW). First hardbound edition of Hammett's book with "An Appreciation" by Parker. (Published September 1988 at $15.95) $6/30

033a: PLAYMATES Putnam NY (1989) [3] Advance Reading Copy in pictorial wraps $40.

033b: PLAYMATES Putnam NY (1989) [2] 250 sgd no cc. Issued without dustwrapper in slipcase $75/125

033c: PLAYMATES Putnam NY (1989) [3] 122,000 cc (PW). (Published May 1989 at $17.95) $5/25

033d: PLAYMATES Viking L 1990 [] $6/30

034a: THE EARLY SPENSER... Delacorte NY 1989 [] First three Spenser novels. (Published June 1989 at $13.95) $5/20

035a: POODLE SPRINGS Putnam NY (1989) [3]
2,852 cc. Advance Reading Copy in pictorial wraps
(given away at ABA). Parker completes a Raymond
Chandler novel. $40.

035b: POODLE SPRINGS Putnam NY (1989) [3]
150,000 cc. (Published September 1989 at $18.95) $5/25

035c: POODLE SPRINGS MacDonald L 1990 []
Uncorrected Proof in pictorial wraps (David Rees
5/91) $50.

035d: POODLE SPRINGS MacDonald (L 1990)
[2] 250 sgd no cc. Signed on plate on half-title.
Issued without dustwrapper in slipcase $50/100

035e: POODLE SPRINGS MacDonald (L 1990)
[1] $6/30

036a: STARDUST Putnam NY 1990 [] Uncor-
rected proof in yellow wraps $60.

036b: STARDUST Putnam NY 1990 [2] 200 sgd
no cc. Issued without dustwrapper in slipcase $75/125

036c: STARDUST   Putnam   NY 1990 [3]
(Published June 1990 at $18.95) $5/25

036d: STARDUST Viking L 1991 [] $6/30

037a: A YEAR AT THE RACES Viking NY
1990 [3] Also states " First published in 1990 by..."
Written with Joan H. Parker. Photographs by
William Strode $20/50

038a: PERCHANCE TO DREAM Putnam NY
1991 [] Uncorrected Proof in gray wraps $50.

038b: PERCHANCE TO DREAM. Putnam NY
1991 [] (Published January 1991 at $18.95) $5/25

038c: PERCHANCE TO DREAM MacDonald L
1991 [] $6/30

039a: PASTIME Putnam NY 1991 [] Uncorrected
Proof in pictorial decorated wraps $40.

039b: PASTIME Putnam NY 1991 [] Special
ABA Convention edition in dustwrapper   (Bud
Schweska 6/95) $20/40

039c: PASTIME Putnam NY 1991 [2] 150 sgd
no cc. Issued without dustwrapper in slipcase $75/125

039d: PASTIME Putnam NY 1991 [] (Published
July 1991 at $19.95) $5/20

040a: DOUBLE DEUCE Putnam NY 1992 []
Uncorrected Proof in dark yellow (gold) wraps $40.

040b: DOUBLE DEUCE Putnam NY 1992 []
Prepublication copy used for promotion at the ABA
convention in special ABA dustwrapper (Robert
Gavora 1/95) $15/30

040c: DOUBLE DEUCE Putnam NY (1992) [2]
135 sgd no cc.   Issued without dustwrapper in
slipcase $75/125

040d: DOUBLE DEUCE Putnam NY 1992 []
Signed on tipped-in page (Waverly Books 9/92) $25/40

040e: DOUBLE DEUCE Putnam NY 1992 []
(Published July 1, 1992 at $19.95) $5/20

041a: PAPER DOLL   Putnam   NY   1993   []
Uncorrected Proof in red wraps $40.

041b: PAPER DOLL Putnam NY (1993) [2] 135
sgd no cc. Issued without dustwrapper in slipcase $75/125

041c: PAPER DOLL Putnam NY 1993 [] Wraps.
Signed. Special ABA Convention edition $40.

041d: PAPER DOLL Putnam NY 1993 [3] $5/20

042a: WALKING SHADOW Putnam NY 1994 []
Uncorrected Proof in printed red wraps $40.

042b: WALKING SHADOW Putnam NY (1994)
[2] 100 sgd no cc. Issued without dustwrapper in
slipcase $100/150

042c: WALKING SHADOW Putnam NY 1994 []
First edition book in special ABA Convention
dustwrapper (Robert Gavora 10/94) $5/35

042d: WALKING SHADOW Putnam NY 1994
[] (Published June 1994 at $19.95) $5/20

043a: ALL OUR YESTERDAYS Delacorte NY
1994   [] Advance Reading Copy in wraps
(Vagabond Books 4/95) $25.

043b: ALL OUR YESTERDAYS Delacorte NY
(1994) [] (Else Fine Books 10/94) $5/20

043c: ALL OUR YESTERDAYS Publisher?? L
1994 [] (Michael Johnson 6/95) $5/20

044a: THIN AIR Putnam NY 1995 [] Advance
Presentation Edition in pictorial printed wraps.
Signed by Parker on front end paper (Waverly
Books 4/95). (Also noted as signed on special leaf) $50.

044b: THIN AIR Putnam NY 1995 [2] 75 sgd no
cc. Issued without dustwrapper in slipcase $100/150

044c: THIN AIR Putnam NY 1995 [3] $5/20

David Plante (signature)

DAVID PLANTE

Plante was born in Providence, Rhode Island in 1940. He received a B.A. from Boston College and taught in Massachusetts before becoming a full-time writer. He has lived in England since 1966.

REFERENCES:

(a) Bixby, George. "David Plante: A Bibliographical Checklist" in AMERICAN BOOK COLLECTOR. Volume 5, No. 6. November-December 1984.

(b) Inventory.

001a: THE GHOST OF HENRY JAMES MacDonald L (1970) [1] No errata slip	$30/150
001b: THE GHOST OF HENRY JAMES MacDonald L (1970) [1] Errata slip tipped in, correcting errors on pages 8, 113 and 133	$25/125
001c: THE GHOST OF HENRY JAMES Gambit B 1970 [1]	$25/100
002a: SLIDES MacDonald L (1971) [1]	$15/75
002b: SLIDES Gambit B 1971 [1]	$12/60
003a: RELATIVES Jonathan Cape L (1972) [1]	$15/75
003b: RELATIVES Avon/Equinox (NY 1974) [1] Wraps	$25.
004a: THE DARKNESS OF THE BODY Jonathan Cape L (1974) [1] David Hockney dustwrapper	$15/75

005a: FIGURES IN BRIGHT AIR   Gollancz   L
1976 [0] David Hockney dustwrapper $12/60

006a: THE FAMILY   Gollancz   L 1978 [0]
(Published April 1978) $10/50

006b: THE FAMILY Farrar Straus NY (1978) [1] $10/40

007a: WAR Wooley Dale Press L 1980 [2] 300
no cc. 24 pages in labeled wraps. A television play
originally laid into *Cipher* No. III   (Ian McKelvie
2/92) $60.

008a: THE COUNTRY   Gollancz   L 1981 [0]
(Published March 1981) $10/50

008b: THE COUNTRY Atheneum   NY 1981 [1]
5,000 cc. (Published September 23, 1981 at $9.95) $6/30

009a: THE WOODS   Gollancz   L 1982 [0]
(Published January 28, 1982 at £7.95) $10/50

009b: THE WOODS Atheneum NY 1982 []
Uncorrected Proof in green wraps $30.

009c: THE WOODS Atheneum NY 1982 [1] $6/30

010a: DIFFICULT WOMEN Gollancz L 1983 [0]
(Published January 1983) $10/40

010b: DIFFICULT WOMEN Atheneum NY 1983
[] Uncorrected Proof in beige wraps $30.

010c: DIFFICULT WOMEN Atheneum NY 1983
[1] 7,500 cc $6/30

011a: THE FRANCOEUR NOVELS Dutton NY
(1983) [3] Wraps.   Contains *The Family*, *The
Country* and *The Woods* $20.

011b: THE FRANCOEUR FAMILY   Chatto/
Hogarth L (1984) [0] Wraps. New title. (Published
November 1984 at $4.95) $25.

012a: THE FOREIGNER Chatto/Hogarth L (1984) [0] Wraps. "Advance Proof - published: November 1984". Copyright page blank (ref.b) $60.

012b: THE FOREIGNER Chatto/Hogarth L (1984) [1] "Published in 1984" on copyright page $10/50

012c: THE FOREIGNER Atheneum NY 1984 [] Uncorrected Proof in olive wraps $30

012d: THE FOREIGNER Atheneum NY 1984 [1] 7,000 cc. (Published September 27, 1984) $6/30

013a: THE CATHOLIC Chatto & Windus L (1985) [] $10/40

013b: THE CATHOLIC Atheneum NY 1986 [] $6/30

014a: THE NATIVE Chatto & Windus L (1987) [1] $10/40

014b: THE NATIVE Atheneum NY 1988 [] (Published April 1988 at $13.95) $5/25

015a: MY MOTHER'S PEARL NECKLACE Albondocani Press NY 1987 [2] 26 sgd ltr cc. Issued in wraps $125.

015b: MY MOTHER'S PEARL NECKLACE Albondocani Press NY 1987 [2] 150 sgd no cc. Issued in wraps $75.

016a: THE ACCIDENT Ticknor & Fields NY 1991 [] (Published May 1991 at $18.95) $5/25

017a: ANNUNCIATION Ticknor & Fields NY 1994 [] Advance reading copy in wraps (Ken Lopez 8/95) $30.

017b: ANNUNCIATION Ticknor & Fields NY 1994 [] (Published May 1994 at $21.95) $5/20

Thomas Pynchon [signature]

THOMAS PYNCHON

Thomas Pynchon was born in 1937 in Glen Cove, New York. He graduated from Cornell University. He served in the Navy and worked as an editorial writer for Boeing Aircraft at one time. Pynchon is a reclusive writer and there is not much personal information available.

REFERENCES:

(a) Berry, Linda P. "Thomas Pynchon" in FIRST PRINTINGS OF AMERICAN AUTHORS. Volume 1. Detroit: Gale Research (1977).

(b) Monahan, Matthew. "Thomas Pynchon: A Bibliographical Checklist" in the AMERICAN BOOK COLLECTOR. Volume 5, No. 3. May/June 1984.

(c) THOMAS PYNCHON: A Bibliography of Primary and Secondary Materials. (Elmwood Park, Illinois): Dalkey Archive Press (1989).

(d) Inventory.

001a: V. Lippincott Ph (1963) [0] Wraps. Advance reading copy in fawn wrappers (ref.b). (Estimated at 100 copies) $1,000.

001b: V. Lippincott Ph (1963) [0] In first issue dustwrapper without reviews on back $250/1,250

001c: V. Lippincott Ph (1963) [0] In second issue dustwrapper with reviews on back (Wm. Reese Co.) $250/750

001d: V Jonathan Cape L 1963 [] Uncorrected Proof in wraps and trial dustwrapper (Antic Hay Rare Books 5/91) $500/1,000

001e: V. Jonathan Cape L (1963) [1] Presumed first state with top edge stained purple (Robert Dagg Cat. 18 12/94), not mentioned in references $75/350

002a: THE CRYING OF LOT 49 Lippincott Ph (1966) [] Uncorrected proof. Spiral bound in yellow wraps $2,500.

002b: THE CRYING OF LOT 49 Lippincott Ph (1966) [1] $100/400

002c: THE CRYING OF LOT 49 Jonathan Cape L (1967) [1] (Ref.b) $50/200

002d: THE CRYING OF LOT 49 Bantam NY (1967) [0] Wraps. First Canadian edition. "Bantam edition published May 1967," "Printed in Canada" (Alphabet Books) $50.

003a: GRAVITY'S RAINBOW Viking NY (1973) [] Uncorrected proofs sewn and glued into endpapers but not bound (ref.c) $2,500.

003b: GRAVITY'S RAINBOW Viking NY (1973) [] Uncorrected proofs in printed blue wraps with proof or trial dustwrapper $3,000/4,000

003c: GRAVITY'S RAINBOW Viking NY (1973) [1] 4,000 cc. First printing dustwrapper has $15.00 price and "ISBN" printed in white over red on rear panel. National Book Award winner for 1974 $125/650

003d: GRAVITY'S RAINBOW Viking NY (1973) [1] 15,000 cc. Wraps. Simultaneous paperback issue (ref.b) $75.

003e: GRAVITY'S RAINBOW Jonathan Cape L (1973) [1] (Ref.b) $50/250

003f: GRAVITY'S RAINBOW Jonathan Cape L (1973) [] Pictorial wraps (Hartley Moorhouse Books 4/92). Issued simutaneously with cloth-bound issue (Buddenbrooks 3/95) $75.

004a: MORALITY AND MERCY IN VIENNA (Aloes Books L 1976) [0] 1,000 cc. Wraps. Large, double, printer's-register cross in black and sepia between title and author's name on front cover (Robert Temple). Cross above "P" in "Pynchon" (Lepper); above "ie" in "Vienna" (Charles Michaud, *Firsts Magazine* 4/94). First separate edition and not collected in 010a. $75.

004b: MORALITY AND MERCY IN VIENNA (Aloes Books L 1976) [0] 2,000 cc. Second edition in glazed white wraps, lacks cross, title page in black and pale greyish brown. (Actually printed in 1978 -Robert Temple) $50.

004c: MORALITY AND MERCY IN VIENNA (Aloes Books L 1976) [0] 2,000 cc. Issued in unglazed wraps without cross. Title in milk chocolate (actually printed in 1980 -Robert Temple) $35.

> Note: Ref.c described four different issues but no priority was given and identifying them involved differentiating between colors which we're not too good at; and Robt. Temple Books (who is really Peter Allen) always seems so authoritative.

005a: LOW-LANDS (Aloes Books L 1978) [2] 1,500 cc. Glazed wraps, price (60p) on back cover (Robert Temple) $75.

005b: LOW-LANDS (Aloes Books L 1978) [] 2,000 cc. Unglazed wraps (pulp board) without price. (Actually published 1980 according to Robert Temple) $40.

005c: LOW-LANDS (Aloes Books L 1978) [] 1,000 cc. Same as 005a but without price on back cover. (Actually printed in 1982) $25.

006a: THE SECRET INTEGRATION (Aloes Books L 1980) [2] 2,500 cc. Wraps. Publisher and

quantity stated on back cover (ref.b). (3,000 copies
according to Robert Temple) $40.

006b: THE SECRET INTEGRATION (Aloes
Books L 1980) [] Wraps. Without quantity on back
cover (Nicholas Pounder 5/90) $25.

007a: ENTROPY (Trystero Troy Town, England
[1981] [0] Wraps. Although it states 1967 in book
the date is actually 1981. In green wraps with black
stamping (ref.b) $75.

007b: ENTROPY (Trystero Troy Town, England
[1983] [0] Wraps. Second printing in white wraps
with photograph montage on cover (ref.b) $35.

008a: THE SMALL RAIN Aloes Books (L 1982)
[0] Wraps (ref.b). (2,000 copies according to Robert
Temple) $40.

009a: A JOURNEY INTO THE MIND OF WATTS
(Mouldwarp Westminster 1983) [0] Wraps. First
separate printing and not included in 010a (ref.b).
Red wraps with black lettering $75.

009b: A JOURNEY INTO THE MIND OF WATTS
(Mouldwarp Westminster 1983) [0] Illustrated
wraps with photo montage on covers (Charles
Michaud in *Firsts Magazine* 4/94) $30.

010a: SLOW LEARNER Little Brown B (1984) []
Unbound signatures laid in proof dustwrapper, not
more than 10 copies (Glenn Horowitz) $500/1,000

010b: SLOW LEARNER Little Brown B (1984)
[1] 27,500 cc (ref.b). Introduction by Pynchon,
includes *Low-Lands, The Secret Integration,
Entropy, The Small Rain*, and "Under The Rose".
(Published January 1984) $10/40

010c: SLOW LEARNER Little Brown B (1984)
[1] 12,500 cc. Wraps. These were part of the
original run of 40,000 cloth bound copies with the

cloth removed and paper covers attached
(publisher's records) $20.

010d: SLOW LEARNER Jonathan Cape L (1984)
[1] Wraps. Uncorrected Proof in brick-red printed
wraps (ref.c) $125.

010e: SLOW LEARNER Jonathan Cape L (1985)
[1] (Ref.d) $10/40

011a: VINELAND Little Brown B (1990) [3]
125,000 cc. Also states "First Edition". At the
author's request no proof copies were made. About
200 copies of the trade edition were distributed with
promotional sheet laid in (Joseph The Provider
3/90). In spite of the foregoing comment, we have a
feeling there was a proof, as a major reviewer
indicted there had been a major rewrite between the
proof and the published book. (Published February
1990 at $19.95) $10/40

011b: VINELAND Secker & Warburg L (1990)
[1] Published the same day as U.S. edition $10/50

012a: OF A FOND GHOUL: *Being a
Correspondence Between Corlies M. Smith and
Pynchon* Brown Litter Press NY 1990 [2] 50 no
cc in wraps (Antic Rare Books 5/91) $100.

Ayn Rand (signature)

AYN RAND
(1905 - 1982)

Ayn Rand was born as Alisa Rosenbaum in St. Petersburg, Russia, in 1905. She graduated with a major in history from the University of Leningrad in 1926. She then emigrated to the United States and became a naturalized citizen in 1931. Ayn Rand was a screen-writer in the early 1930s and late 1940s. She edited *The Objectivist* from 1962 to 1971 and *The Ayn Rand Letter* thereafter.

Her philosophical credo, objectivism, holds that man is primarily a rational creature whose happiness lies in self-fulfillment. His only responsibility is towards himself ("the virtue of selfishness"); and those individuals who practice this doctrine realize fully the rational element in man's nature.

The pamphlets listed herein were reprinted over time by one or more of the following: The Nathaniel Branden Institute, The Objectivist, The Palo Alto Book Service and/or The Intellectual Activist. ZIP codes started in 1965. The four addresses used, chronologically, were 36 East 36th Street, 120 East 34th Street, 165 East 35th Street and 350 Fifth Avenue. In addition, the titles of other available pamphlets listed in each title may indicate an obvious later printing.

REFERENCE:

(a) Perinn, Vincent. AYN RAND | A FIRST DESCRIPTIVE BIBLIOGRAPHY. (Rockville): Q&B (Quill & Brush, 1990).

(c) Inventory.

001a: WE THE LIVING Macmillan NY 1936 [1] 3,000 cc. "Published April, 1936" on copyright page. (Blue cloth without stamping/lettering is a trial binding and would be worth more) $500/2,500

001b: WE THE LIVING   Cassell L (1936) [1] 3,000 cc. Dark blue cloth (trial binding?) (Heritage Bookshop 11/91) $400/2,000

001c: WE THE LIVING   Random House   NY (1959) [1] 40,000 cc. Re-edited and new foreword by author $30/150

002a: NIGHT OF JANUARY 16th   Longmans, Green and Co. NY (1936) [1] Issued in blue wraps with several different addresses. Priority of addresses unknown, but all copies state "First Edition" and all later printings have a number "2" or "3" through "12" in place of the "First Edition" $600.

002b: NIGHT OF JANUARY 16th   World Publishing Co. NY/Cleveland (1968) [1] 25,000 cc. (estimated). "First Printing 1968" on copyright page. Definitive edition with new introduction by Rand. [Note: we had a copy with sticker on rear panel reading: "Distributed in USA by W.W. Norton..."] $25/100

003a: ANTHEM Cassell L (1938) [1] 3,500 cc (a&b). "6s Net" on spine of dustwrapper, noted with label over price, but the label had fallen off so we're not sure what was on it $500/4,000

003b: ANTHEM Cassell L (1938) [1] Second state of dustwrapper has "Colonial Edition" printed on flap $500/2,500

003c: ANTHEM Pamphleteers LA 1946 [0] Less than 50 copies bound in gilt stamped red morocco for the author's use (Sotheby's NY sale of June 17-18, 1992. Pre-auction estimate was $4000; it was passed). Price estimated for unsigned copy $2,500.

003d: ANTHEM Pamphleteers LA 1946 [0] 2,000 cc. Wraps. Revised edition, new foreword, comprising the entire issue of *The Freeman*, Vol III, No. 1. Stapled cover printed in black $500.

003e: ANTHEM Pamphleteers LA 1946 [0] 1,500 cc. Wraps. Cover printed in red, publisher's address is 725 Venice Boulevard $200.

003f: ANTHEM Phamphleteers LA 1946 [0] 1,500 cc. Wraps. Cover printed in red; publisher's address is 1151 South Broadway. [Note: a 1947 edition with same address exists. States "Second Printing"] $100.

003g: ANTHEM Caxton Caldwell 1953 [0] 50,000 cc. First hardbound edition $50/250

004a: THE FOUNTAIN HEAD Bobbs-Merrill Indianapolis (no date) [] Advance Publisher's Binding Dummy. Bound in golden-brown cloth with stamping as published trade edition. Proof dustwrapper has final design, and the flaps and back panel are blank. The proof text for the flaps is pasted onto the front endpapers, and contains errors that were later corrected. Twenty blank pages bound in. The book measures 5 7/8" x 5"; the published edition is 6" x 8 3/4". The particular copy described was the author's and may be unique. (Pepper & Stern cataloged at $15,000 12/94) $NVA

004b: THE FOUNTAINHEAD Bobbs-Merrill Ind. (1943) [1] 7,500 cc. Red cloth. Dustwrapper is priced at $3.00 with Bobbs-Merrill titles on back $500/2,500

004c: THE FOUNTAINHEAD Bobbs-Merrill Ind. (1943) [1] 12,000 cc (estimated). Green cloth. In dustwrapper which is priced at $3.00 and has photograph of author on back with three critical reviews. First two lines on p.748 inverted (Fine Books Co. 4/94) $300/1,500

004d: THE FOUNTAINHEAD Cassell L (1947)
[1] 5,250 cc (estimated) $200/1,000

004e: THE FOUNTAINHEAD Bobbs-Merrill Ind.
(1968) [1] 100,000 cc. "First Printing 1943 | 25th
Anniversary Edition, 33rd Printing 1968" with new
foreword by the author $25/125

005a: A LETTER FROM AYN RAND... To The
Readers of *The Fountainhead* (Bobbs-Merrill? no
place or date [circa 1945]) [0] Pictorial wraps, 8
pages stapled (Waiting For Godot Books 2/95) $300.

006a: SCREEN GUIDE FOR AMERICANS
Motion Picture Alliance no place (1947) [0] Wraps.
8 page pamphlet. Copyright 1947 $300.

007a: ATLAS SHRUGGED Random House NY
(1957) [1] George Salter dustwrapper. "10/57"
bottom of front dustwrapper flap and the publisher's
name and address bottom of back flap. Also noted
without these marks but perhaps a later dustwrapper
put on a first (Steven Temple Books) $125/600

007b: ATLAS SHRUGGED Random House NY
(1967) [2] 2,000 sgd no cc. Issued in acetate
dustwrapper in slipcase. Tenth Anniversary Edition $1,750/2,000

008a: TEXTBOOK OF AMERICANISM Privately Printed NY 1959 [0] 14-page pamphlet with
no address or price $250.

009a: NOTES ON THE HISTORY OF AMERI-
CAN FREE ENTERPRISE Privately Printed/The
Platen Press NY 1959 [0] 8-page pamphlet with no
address or price $250.

010a: FAITH AND FORCE Privately Printed NY
1960 [0] 16-page pamphlet with no address or price.
(Reprinted by Nathaniel Branden Institute) $250.

011a: FOR THE NEW INTELLECTUAL Random
House NY (1961) [1] 75,000 cc $30/150

012a: THE OBJECTIVIST ETHIC Branden Institute (NY 1961) [0] 20-page pamphlet. Address has postal zone "NY 16." Priced at $1.00 $125.

013a: THE INTELLECTUAL BANKRUPTCY OF OUR AGE Branden Institute (NY 1961) [0] 12-page pamphlet. Address has postal zone "NY 16." Priced at 50¢. (Actually published in 1962) $125.

014a: AMERICA'S PERSECUTED MINORITY: BIG BUSINESS Branden Institute NY (1962) [0] Wraps. First has date on front cover and address with postal zone vs. zipcode $100.

015a: CONSERVATISM: AN OBITUARY Branden Institute (NY 1962) [0] 14-page pamphlet. Address as "NY 16". Priced at 50¢ $100.

016a: HOW NOT TO FIGHT AGAINST SOCIALIZED MEDICINE Branden Institute (NY 1963) [0] Wraps. Address as "NY 16". Priced at 25¢ $100.

016b: THE FORGOTTEN MAN OF SOCIAL-IZED MEDICINE: THE DOCTOR Branden Institute (NY 1964) [0] New title. Reprint adding an essay by Leonard Peikoff $75.

017a: THE GOAL OF MY WRITING Branden Institute (NY 1963) [0] 10-page pamphlet. Address as "NY 16" $100.

018a: THE FASCIST NEW FRONTIER Branden Institute (NY 1963) [0] 14-page pamphlet. Address as "NY 16". Priced at 50¢ $100.

019a: AN ANALYSIS OF "EXTREMISM" AND OF RACISM Branden Institute (NY 1963) [0] 22-page pamphlet. Address as "NY 16" $75.

020a: IS ATLAS SHRUGGING? Branden Institute (NY 1964) [0] Wraps $100.

021a: THE VIRTUE OF SELFISHNESS, A NEW
CONCEPT OF EGOISM New American Library
(NY 1964) [1] 116,000 cc (a&b). Wraps. "Signet
Paperback Original P2602". Also noted with gold
sticker "not available in any other edition." First
state **without** business reply card bound in center $75.

021b: THE VIRTUE OF SELFISHNESS, A NEW
CONCEPT OF EGOISM New American Library
(NY 1964) [1] Wraps. With business reply card
bound in middle $50.

021c: THE VIRTUE OF SELFISHNESS, A NEW
CONCEPT OF EGOISM New American Library
(NY 1964 [1965]) [1] 25,000 cc. Blue cloth.
Actually published in 1965 $30/150

022a: PLAYBOY'S INTERVIEW WITH AYN
RAND Branden Institute (NY 1964 [1965]) [0] 16-
page pamphlet. Address as "NY 16". Priced at 50¢.
Copyright 1964 but actually published January 1965 $75.

023a: THE CASHING-IN: THE STUDENT
REBELLION Branden Institute (NY 1965) [0] 34-
page pamphlet. Address as "NY 10016" $75.

024a: WHAT IS CAPITALISM? Branden Institute
(NY 1965) [0] Wraps. Address as "NY 10016";
although, one copy has been catalogued as "NY 16,
NY" on verso of front wrapper (Wilder Books) $75.

025a: THE OBJECTIVIST NEWSLETTER
Volume 1-4 1962-1965 The Objectivist NY (1967)
[0] 5,000 cc (estimated). Blue cloth. Issued without
dustwrapper. Edited in part by Rand $250.

026a: AYN RAND IN DEFENSE OF
CAPITALISM New American Library NY 1966
[0] Wraps. 2 mimeographed sheets, stapled.
Promotional piece, issued in conjunction with
publication of *Capitalism* (Serendipity Books) $60.

027a: CAPITALISM: THE UNKNOWN IDEAL
New American Library NY (1966) [2] 700 sgd cc.
Green and black cloth issued without dustwrapper
in slipcase which was numbered by author at
bottom. We had a copy with a postcard from Rita
Schugar of NAL laid in, which stated, "Due to
unprecedented demand NAL has agreed to publish a
second printing of 300 copies, identical to the first
edition except it will not be numbered." Available
for shipment November 20. Our copy was a signed
first edition with the number 133 written on bottom
of slipcase $1,250/1,500

027b: CAPITALISM: THE UNKNOWN IDEAL
New American Library NY (1966) [2] 300 sgd cc.
Signed first edition but in unnumbered slipcase
(Bauman Rare Books 4/95) $1,250/1,350

027c: CAPITALISM: THE UNKNOWN IDEAL
New American Library (NY 1966) [1] 100,000 cc $30/150

027d: CAPITALISM: THE UNKNOWN IDEAL
New American Library/Signet (NY 1967) [1]
Wraps. "This edition includes two new articles...
not... in hardcover edition" $60.

028a: THE ROOTS OF WAR The Objectivist (NY
1966) [0] Wraps $100.

029a: INTRODUCTION TO OBJECTIVIST
EPISTEMOLOGY The Objectivist (NY 1967) [0]
Wraps. (Reprints stated) $100.

029b: INTRODUCTION TO OBJECTIVIST
EPISTEMOLOGY New American Library NY
(1979) [3] Wraps. Also states "First Mentor
Printing, April, 1979". Includes an additional essay
by Leonard Peikoff $50.

030a: REQUIEM FOR MAN The Objectivist (NY
1967) [0] Wraps $85.

031a: OF LIVING DEATH The Objectivist (NY 1968) [0] $75.

032a: THE ROMANTIC MANIFESTO: A PHILOSOPHY OF LITERATURE World NY/Cleveland (1969) [1] 25,000 cc (estimated) $25/125

033a: THE CAMPRACHICOS The Objectivist (NY 1970) [0] Wraps $75.

034a: THE NEW LEFT New American Library (NY 1971) [1] 50,000 cc (estimated). Wraps. Signet paperback original $50.

034b: THE NEW LEFT New American Library (NY 1975) [] Wraps. "Revised Edition" with an additional article by the author $35.

035a: THE MORAL FACTOR Palo Alto Book Service Palo Alto (1976) [0] Wraps $60.

036a: GLOBAL BALKANIZATION Palo Alto Book Service Palo Alto (1977) [0] Wraps $50.

037a: CULTURAL UPDATE Palo Alto Book Service Palo Alto (1978) [0] Wraps $50.

038a: THE AYN RAND LETTER Volumes I-IV (1971-1976) Palo Alto Book Service Palo Alto (1979) [1] Large (9"x11"). Blue cloth issued without dustwrapper $125.

039a: PHILOSOPHY: WHO NEEDS IT Bobbs-Merrill Ind/NY (1982) [1] 10,000 cc (estimated). With first two lines of copyright notice stamped $25/100

039b: PHILOSOPHY: WHO NEEDS IT Bobbs Merrill Ind/NY (1982) [1] 50,000 cc. With copyright lines printed $15/60

040a: THE OBJECTIVIST | VOLUMES 5-10 | 1966-1971 Palo Alto Book Service Palo Alto

(1982) [1] Blue-green cloth issued without dustwrapper $125.

041a: THE EARLY AYN RAND New American Library NY 1984 [3] Also states "First Printing, August 1984" on copyright page $15/60

042a: THE AYN RAND LEXICON | OBJEC-TIVISM FROM A-Z New American Library NY 1986 [3] Also states "First Printing, November 1986" on copyright page. (Published at $18.50) $10/40

043a: THE VOICE OF REASON | ESSAYS IN OBJECTIVIST THOUGHT New American Library NY (1989) [3] Also states "First Printing, January 1989" on copyright page. Introduction by Leonard Peikoff. (Published at $19.95) $6/30

044a: LETTERS OF AYN RAND Dutton NY 1995 [] Uncorrected proof in light blue printed wraps (Waverly Books 9/95). Edited by Michael S. Berliner, with introduction by Leonard Peikoff $75.

044b: LETTERS OF AYN RAND Dutton NY 1995 [3] Also states "First Printing, June, 1995" on copyright page $5/25

044c: LETTERS OF AYN RAND Dutton NY 1995 [2] 225 sgd no cc. Signed by Berliner. Issued in clamshell box with facsimile letter and envelope tied to inside cover. (Issued by Paper Tiger Press August 1995 at $150 {$125 pre-publication}) $

LAURA RIDING

Laura Riding was born in New York City in 1901. Her original name was Reichenthal which she legally changed to Riding. She attended Cornell where she met and married Louis Gottschalk, a modern history teacher. She won a prize *The Fugitives* offered for the best unpublished poems with her poem "The Quids." Nancy and Robert Graves were taken with the poem and wrote to invite Riding to visit them. Riding showed up as the Graves were going to Egypt and accompanied them. On their return, Robert left Nancy, and after Laura recovered from her suicide attempt in 1929, they moved to Mallorca. She was a very productive writer and editor for the next ten years until she and Graves went to America in 1939. At that time she met Schuyler Jackson (whom she married in 1941), renounced poetry, and did not publish again until the 1970s.

REFERENCES:

(a) Wexler, Joyce Piell. LAURA RIDING, A BIBLIOGRAPHY. New York/London: Garland Publishing, Inc., 1981.

(b) Woolmer, J. Howard. A CHECKLIST OF THE HOGARTH PRESS 1917-1938. New York: Woolmer-Brotherson, Andes, 1976.

(c) Mason, Ellsworth. "The Robert Graves and Laura Riding Jackson Collection of Ellsworth Mason". Unpublished (Copyright 1976. An annotated list of Mason's collection was acquired by the University of Tulsa in 1976).

(d) Matthews, T.S. UNDER THE INFLUENCE. London: Cassell (1977).

001a: THE CLOSE CHAPLET   Hogarth L 1926
[0] Issued without dustwrapper. Author's name

given as Laura Riding Gottschalk. Number of copies unknown per ref.b. (Published October 1926) $600.

001b: THE CLOSE CHAPLET Adelphi Co. NY (1926) [0] Issued with tissue dustwrapper (ref.c). Author's name given as Laura Riding Gottschalk. English sheets used (Bradford Morrow) $450/500

002a: ANATOLE FRANCE AT HOME by Marcel Le Goff Adelphia Co. NY 1926 [] Issued in dustwrapper. Laura Riding Gottschalk's translation. Author's name misspelled on title page $50/250

003a: VOLTAIRE Hogarth L 1927 [0] Approximately 250 cc (ref.b). Issued without dustwrapper. Author's last name "Gottschalk" cancelled by double rule $500.

004a: A SURVEY OF MODERNIST POETRY Heinemann L 1927 [0] 1,000 cc. Written with Robert Graves $125/400

004b: A SURVEY OF MODERNIST POETRY Doubleday Doran & Co. GC 1928 [0] 500 cc. Written with Robert Graves $125/450

004c: A SURVEY OF MODERNIST POETRY Haskell House (NY) 1969 [] A reprint of the first English edition. (In print) $75.

004d: A SURVEY OF MODERNIST POETRY Folcroft Library Edition (Folcroft, Pa) 1971 [2] 150 cc $50.

004e: A SURVEY OF MODERNIST POETRY Scholarly Press (St.Clair Sh.) 1972 [] A reprint of the first American edition $50.

004f: A SURVEY OF MODERNIST POETRY Norwood Editions (Norwood, Pa) 1976 [] A reprint of first English edition. Also reprinted in 1977 and 1978 $30.

005a: CONTEMPORARIES AND SNOBS Jonathan Cape L (1928) [1] Beige cloth over boards. (Published February 1928) $100/400

005b: CONTEMPORARIES AND SNOBS Doubleday Doran GC 1928 [0] Gray paper over boards, maroon cloth on spine $75/300

005c: CONTEMPORARIES AND SNOBS Scholarly Press (St. Clair Sh.) 1971 [] (Reprint of first American edition?) $40.

006a: ANARCHISM IS NOT ENOUGH Jonathan Cape   L (1928) [1] Blue cloth over boards. (Published May 1928) $75/300

006b: ANARCHISM IS NOT ENOUGH Doubleday Doran GC 1928 [0] Orange paper over boards $60/250

007a: A PAMPHLET AGAINST ANTHOLOGIES Jonathan Cape L (1928) [1] Orange cloth over boards in dustwrapper. Written with Robert Graves. (Published July 1928) $75/350

007b: A PAMPHLET AGAINST ANTHOLOGIES Doubleday Doran GC 1928 [0] Buff paper over boards $75/300

007c: A PAMPHLET AGAINST ANTHOLOGIES AMS Press (NY) 1970 [] Issued without dustwrapper $35.

008a: LOVE AS LOVE, DEATH AS DEATH Seizin Press Hammersmith L 1928 [2] 175 sgd no cc. Beige cloth over boards in tissue dustwrapper (Glenn Horowitz). Issued in plain slipcase (Joseph The Provider Books 5/92). Neither the tissue or slipcase are mentioned in ref.a $500/600

009a: POEMS: A JOKING WORD Jonathan Cape L 1930 [0] Beige cloth over boards. Cream dustwrapper printed in black. (Published July 1930) $75/350

010a: FOUR UNPOSTED LETTERS TO CATHERINE Hours Press Paris (1930) [2] 200 sgd no cc. Issued in tissue dustwrapper (Bradford Morrow). (Published July 1930) $400/450

010b: FOUR UNPOSTED LETTERS TO CATHERINE Persea Books NY 1993 [] Uncorrected Proof in gray wraps (Waiting For Godot Books 9/93) $50.

010c: FOUR UNPOSTED LETTERS TO CATHERINE Persea Books NY (1993) [] $5/25

011a: EXPERTS ARE PUZZLED Jonathan Cape L (1930) [1] Beige cloth over boards, cream dustwrapper printed in black. (Published November 1930) $75/350

012a: THOUGH GENTLY Seizin Press Deya, Majorca 1930 [2] 200 sgd no cc. Issued in glassine dustwrapper (Second Life Books), in glassine and paper dustwrapper (Anacapa Books) $400/500

013a: TWENTY POEMS LESS Hours Press Paris 1930 [2] 200 sgd no cc. Issued in tissue dustwrapper (Bradford Morrow) $500.

014a: THE SEIZIN PRESS Seizin Press Mallorca (1931) [0] Broadside prospectus written with and containing a Robert Graves poem (Anacapa Books) $250.

015a: THE SEIZIN PRESS Seizin Press Deya, Mallorca (1931) [0] Broadside advertising *No Trouble*, *Though Gently* and *To Whom Else?* as already printed and *Laura and Francisca* to be ready in the summer of 1931, written with Robert Graves (Carl Hahn collection) but did not contain a poem by Graves $300.

016a: LAURA AND FRANCISCA Seizin Press Deya, Majorca 1931 [2] 200 sgd no cc. Issued in tissue dustwrapper (Bradford Morrow). (Published November 1931) $400.

017a: NO DECENCY LEFT Jonathan Cape L (1932) [1] Written with Robert Graves under the pseudonym Barbara Rich $400/2,000

018a: THE FIRST LEAF Seizin Press Deya, Majorca 1933 [0] A single sheet folded twice; unbound, tied, uncut $250.

019a: EVERYBODY'S LETTERS Arthur Baker L (1933) [1] Black cloth over boards. Dustwrapper black with light blue lettering. (Published February 1933) $75/350

020a: THE LIFE OF THE DEAD Arthur Baker L no date [1933] [2] 200 sgd no cc. Wraps. Signed by both Riding and the illustrator, John Aldridge $500.

021a: POET: A LYING WORD Arthur Baker L 1933 [1] $125/450

022a: PICTURES (Seizin Press L 1933) [0] Pamphlet with paper cover serving as title page and endpaper $250.

023a: 14A Arthur Barker L (1934) [1] Written with George Ellidge. Blue cloth over boards $150/500

024a: AMERICANS Primavera (LA) 1934 [2] 200 no cc. Issued without dustwrapper. Printed by Ward Ritchie. (Published August 1934) $550.

025a: FOCUS I (No publisher or place) (1935) [0] Wraps. 12-page magazine published by Riding and Graves which includes letters between members of their group $300.

026a: FOCUS II (No publisher or place) (1935) [0] Wraps. 24-pages $250.

027a: THE SECOND LEAF Seizin Press Deya, Majorca 1935 [0] Unbound, tied sheaf. Estimated at less than 100 copies by various dealers $400.

028a: FOCUS III (No publisher or place) 1935 [0]
Wraps. 40 pages $250.

029a: EPILOGUE I (Volume 1) Seizin Press
Deya, Majorca 1935 [0] Periodical issued in book
format. Riding was Editor and Robert Graves was
Associate Editor $300.

030a: FOCUS IV (No publisher or place) 1935 [0]
Wraps. 64 pages $200.

031a: PROGRESS OF STORIES Seizin & Constable L (1935) [1] Green cloth over boards. Buff
dustwrapper printed in red $75/350

031b: PROGRESS OF STORIES Books for Libraries Press (Freeport, NY) 1971 [] Assume issued
without dustwrapper $40.

031c: PROGRESS OF STORIES Dial Press NY
1982 [1] A new enlarged edition with new material
and new preface by Laura (Riding) Jackson $10/40

031d: PROGRESS OF STORIES Carcanet
Manchester 1982 [] $10/40

032a: ALMOST FORGOTTEN GERMANY
Seizin Press / Constable Majorca/London (1936)
[1] Translation of George Schwarz's book by
Riding and Graves $250/1000

033a: THE MOON'S NO FOOL Seizen/Constable
Deya/London 1936 [] Written by Tom Matthews
who states in ref.d (p.147) "...Laura wrote, using me
as a pencil" $50/250

034a: CONVALESCENT CONVERSATIONS
Seizin Press/Constable Majorca/L (1936) []
Uncorrected proof in brown wraps (R.A. Gekoski
1987) $600.

034b: CONVALESCENT   CONVERSATIONS
Seizin Press/Constable Majorca/L (1936) [1] Written by Riding under the pseudonym Madeleine Vara $125/500

035a: EPILOGUE II (Volume II) Seizin Press/
Constable Majorca/L 1936 [1] Periodical printed in
book format. Riding was Editor and Graves was
Associate Editor $250.

036a: EPILOGUE III   (Volume III)   Seizin
Press/Constable   Majorca/L 1937 [1] Periodical
printed in book format. Riding was Editor and
Graves was Associate Editor $200.

037a: A PERSONAL LETTER / WITH A RE-
QUEST FOR REPLY No publisher London
January 1937 [0] 400 cc. Mimeographed sheets
with facsimile signature at end (10 1/4" x 8 1/4")
(Serendipity Books) $750.

038a: A TROJAN ENDING Seizin Press/Constable
Majorca/L (1937) [1] Folding map at rear $75/350

038b: A TROJAN ENDING Random House NY
(1937) [1] Gray cloth over boards $50/200

038c: A TROJAN ENDING Random House NY
(1937) [1] Variant binding in red cloth, front design
in black, spine omits design $25/175

038d: A TROJAN ENDING Carcanet (Manchester
1984) [1] New afterword by Riding $6/30

039a: COLLECTED POEMS Cassell L (1938) [1]
Green cloth over boards. Buff dustwrapper printed
in black and orange $60/300

039b: COLLECTED POEMS Random House NY
(1938) [1] Royal blue cloth over boards. Buff
dustwrapper printed in dark blue and black. English
sheets (Serendipity Books) $75/350

039c: THE POEMS (of Laura Riding) *A New Edition of the 1938 Collection* Carcanet Manchester 1980 [] New title. "With New Prefatory Material and Notes." With errata slip $10/40

039d: THE POEMS OF LAURA RIDING *A New Edition of the 1938 Collection* Persea Books NY 1980 [] With New Prefatory Material and Notes. With errata slip $10/40

040a: THE WORLD AND OURSELVES Chatto & Windus L 1938 [0] Fourth volume of Epilogue Magazine. Edited by Riding $50/250

041a: PRELIMINARY QUESTIONS (Seizin Press L 1938) [0] Broadside published anonymously, inserted in some copies of next item (Serendipity Books) $500.

042a: THE COVENANT OF LITERAL MORALITY Seizin Press (no place) 1938 [0] Paper covers $750.

043a: TO THE ENDORSERS OF THE COVENANT OF LITERAL MORALITY Suffolk February 1939 [0] Approximately 45 cc. Mimeographed sheets (13"x8") signed in type at end (Serendipity Books) $1,200.

044a: THE LEFT HERESY IN LITERATURE AND LIFE by Harry Kemp, Riding and others Methuen L (1939) [1] Orange cloth dustwrapper has black lettering on red and white hammer and sickle. Originally priced "7s6d" (later "8s6d") $60/300

044b: THE LEFT HERESY IN LITERATURE AND LIFE Folcroft Lib. Editions (Folcroft, Pa) 1974 [] Issued without dustwrapper $40.

044c: THE LEFT HERESY IN LITERATURE AND LIFE Norwood Editions (Norwood Pa) 1977 [] Issued without dustwrapper $40.

045a: LIVES OF WIVES   Cassell   L (1939) [1]
Green cloth. Buff dustwrapper printed in black and
sienna $75/350

045b: LIVES OF WIVES   Random House   NY
(1939) [1]   Brown cloth. Buff dustwrapper printed
in black and yellow. English sheets $50/250

046a: SELECTED POEMS: IN FIVE SETS   Faber
and Faber L (1970) [1] 6,000 cc. Wraps. Issued
without endpapers $40.

046b: SELECTED POEMS: IN FIVE SETS   W.W.
Norton   NY (1973) [1] 1,500 cc.   Brown cloth.
Dustwrapper white on brown and blue pattern $10/50

046c: SELECTED POEMS: IN FIVE SETS   W.W.
Norton   NY (1973) [1] 3,000 cc. Wraps. Issued
simultaneously $20.

047a: THE   TELLING   University   of
London/Athlone Press no place 1972 [0] Author's
name given as "Laura (Riding) Jackson." Blue
cloth. White dustwrapper printed in gray and purple $10/50

047b: THE TELLING Harper and Row NY (1973)
[2] 100 sgd cc (ref.a) (200 copies {Serendipity
Books}), Unknown number of copies (Waiting For
Godot Books 2/91) $75/125

047c: THE TELLING Harper & Row NY (1973)
[0] Yellow cloth. Yellow dustwrapper printed in
black and blue. Author's name given as "Laura
(Riding) Jackson" $5/25

048a: FROM THE CHAPTER "TRUTH" IN
RATIONAL MEANING: A NEW FOUNDATION
FOR... Priapus Press (Berkhamsted) 1975 [0] 45 cc.
Wraps. Author's name given as "Laura (Riding)
Jackson". A pamphlet with glossy white paper
covers $100.

049a: IT HAS TAKEN LONG... (Special issue of *Chelsea 35*) (NY 1976) [2] 200 sgd no cc. Wraps. Signed by Laura (Riding) Jackson (Anacapa Books) (Not mentioned in ref.a) $100.

049b: IT HAS TAKEN LONG... (NY 1976) [0] Wraps $25.

THE POEMS OF LAURA RIDING see 039c&d

050a: HOW A POEM COMES TO BE (Lord John Press Northridge 1980) [2] 150 sgd no cc (155 copies issued {Lilly Library card catalog}). Broadside (22"x15") signed "Laura (Riding) Jackson" $75.

051a: DESCRIPTION OF LIFE Targ Editions NY 1980 [] Uncorrected Proof. Only 6 copies per publisher (George Robert Minkoff 4/91) $125

051b: DESCRIPTION OF LIFE Targ Editions (NY) 1980 [2] 350 sgd no cc. Issued with glassine dustwrapper $100.

052a: SOME COMMUNICATIONS OF BROAD REFERENCE Lord John Press Northridge 1983 [2] 26 sgd ltr cc $175.

052b: SOME COMMUNICATIONS OF BROAD REFERENCE Lord John Press Northridge 1983 [2] 125 sgd no cc. Issued without dustwrapper $100.

053a: FIRST AWAKENINGS *The Early Poems of Laura Riding* Persea Books NY (1992) [] Edited by Elizabeth Friedman, Alan J. Clarke and Robert Nye $5/25

054a: THE WORD WOMAN *And Other Related Writings* Persea Books NY (1993) [] Uncorrected Proof in blue wraps (Waiting For Godot Books 2/95) $40.

054b: THE WORD WOMAN *And Other Related Writings* Persea Books NY (1993) [] $5/25

VITA SACKVILLE-WEST
1892-1962

English author Vita Sackville-West, was born at Knole in 1892. She was known primarily as a poet but was also a distinguished biographer, a good novelist, and wrote a number of impressive and readable books on gardening. She was married (at Knole) to Harold Nicolson in 1913, and although she had a number of affairs, remained his wife until her death.

REFERENCES:

(a) Gretton, John R. "V. Sackville-West" in *Antiquarian Book Monthly Review*. December, 1975.

(b) Stevens, Michael. V. SACKVILLE-WEST: A CRITICAL BIOGRAPHY. New York: Scribners (1974). Includes previously unpublished poems.

(c) Woolmer, J. Howard. A CHECKLIST OF THE HOGARTH PRESS 1917-1938. Andes, New York: Woolmer/Brotherson Ltd., 1976.

Ref.a and b provided a basic list of books by the author and ref.c provided quantities for the Hogarth titles. All first edition identification of individual titles were based on information provided by Dr. R. S. Speck and Barry Eigen, from their fine collections, Burton Weiss or books at the Lilly Library (which were noted by Carl Hahn on a visit). We thank them all for taking their time to greatly improve this guide.

001a: CHATTERTON *A Drama in Three Acts* J. Salmon Sevenoaks 1909 [0] Reportedly 100 copies. Title page is cover, no wraps or cloth binding per Nigel Nicolson. But, the evidence supports the fact that several bindings were produced. Serendipity had a copy in dark blue wraps with gold stamping; R.S. Speck (San Francisco) has a copy in dark red wraps; and the Urbana Collection has a copy in dark gray wraps. The printing on the wraps is identical in all cases $5,000.

001b: CHATTERTON *A Drama in Three Acts* J. Salmon Sevenoaks 1909 [0] Two copies have been noted in dark blue boards with gilt lettering (Northwestern University and R.S. Speck). No known dustwrapper $6,500.

002a: AN EASTERN FANTASY No place (Seven Oaks?) no date [1913] [0] Two-page program for a play by VS-W performed at Knole, including text of a prologue by VS-W (one known copy) $1,500.

003a: CONSTANTINOPLE Complete Press L 1915 [0] Wraps $600.

004a: POEMS OF WEST AND EAST John Lane L 1917 [0] Light blue boards with paper labels, cloth spine. Assume dustwrapper exists although none reported $150/750

005a: HERITAGE Collins L (1919) [0] Red cloth blind-stamped on front. Spine printed in black. Dustwrapper gray, printed in red $150/750

005b: HERITAGE Doran NY (1919) [0] Light brown cloth printed on front and spine or with just a paper label on front. Priority unknown. Also noted with title printed on spine and paper label (Barry Eigen) $100/400

006a: ORCHARD AND VINEYARD John Lane L 1921 [0] "To-" on verso of title. Light blue boards with paper labels and cloth spine. Light blue dustwrapper lettered in black. $100/400

> Note: There are also a "few copies ... which I [VS-W] had specially bound" in Italian decorative paper boards (letter of VS-W, owned by Dr. R.S. Speck)

007a: THE DRAGONS IN SHALLOW WATERS Collins L 1921 [0] Red boards lettered in black in pictorial dustwrapper $125/500

007b: THE DRAGONS IN SHALLOW WATERS Putnam NY 1922 [0] Green boards lettered in red in tan dustwrapper $75/350

008a: KNOLE AND THE SACKVILLES Heinemann L 1922 [1] White boards and light tan dustwrapper both illustrated by William Nicholson $150/750

008b: KNOLE AND THE SACKVILLES Doran NY (no date 1924?) [0] Verso states "Printed in England" (The Bookshop 10/89). English sheets. Tipped-in title page. Doran imprint at foot of spine. No publisher's logo on copyright page $125/500

008c: KNOLE AND THE SACKVILLES Lindsay Drummond   L 1947 [] New edition with new preface and previously unpublished photographs $30/150

008d: KNOLE AND THE SACKVILLES Ernest Benn L 1958 [] Wraps. "Fourth Edition". Revised with new foreword by the author $50.

009a: THE HEIR Heinemann L 1922 [2] 50 no cc, numbered 1 to 50. Cloth in dustwrapper. Frontis portrait of Sackville-West by William Strang $450/600

009b: THE HEIR Privately printed (no place or date) [2] 50 no. cc, numbered 51 to 100. Cloth spine, paper boards, assume issued without dustwrapper. Frontis photo of author (ref.b&d) $450.

009c: THE HEIR Heinemann L 1922 [1] Brown cloth printed in gilt on front and spine (Barry Eigen) $100/400

009d: THE HEIR Doran NY 1922 [0] English sheets. Dark tan cloth with orange printing on front and spine; in white dustwrapper (Barry Eigen) $60/300

009e: THE HEIR Richards Press L 1949 [1] Title story only. "First published ... 1922 | Reprinted ... 1949" on copyright page. Green boards lettered in gilt on spine in light tan pictorial dustwrapper $50/200

010a: THE DIARY OF LADY ANNE CLIFFORD Heinemann L 1923 [] Edited and preface by V.S-W. Brown cloth with title in gold on spine (Barry Eigen) $50/200

010b: THE DIARY OF LADY ANNE CLIFFORD Doran NY 1923 [0] English sheets in red boards. No dustwrapper seen but assume there was one $50/200

011a: GREY WETHERS Heinemann L (1923) [1] Gray cloth printed in black. In decorative dustwrapper $100/400

011b: GREY WETHERS Doran NY (1923) [5] Blue boards lettered in black. In decorative dustwrapper. Also noted in blue boards lettered in blue (Barry Eigen) $75/300

012a: CHALLENGE Doran NY (1923) [0] "Printed in Great Britain" on copyright page. Six paragraphs on dustwrapper front. Light green cloth $125/500

012b: CHALLENGE Doran NY (1923) [0] "Printed in USA" on copyright page. Three paragraphs on dustwrapper front plus quote from "The Bookman." Red cloth $100/400

012c: CHALLENGE Collins L 1974 [1] $15/60

013a: SEDUCERS IN ECUADOR   Hogarth   L 1924 [0] 1,500 cc (ref.c). Red and black cloth with label on spine lettered in red. In plain cream-colored dustwrapper printed in red (Barry Eigen) $100/400

013b: SEDUCERS IN ECUADOR   Doran   NY (1925) [5] Red, blue and black decorated boards in matching dustwrapper $50/200

014a: PASSENGER TO TEHERAN   Hogarth   L 1926 [0] 1,640 cc (ref.c). Red and black cloth $150/600

014b: PASSENGER TO TEHERAN   Doran   NY 1927 [0] "Printed in Great Britain" on copyright page. Decorative paper boards with cloth spine and label. Gray dustwrapper lettered in red $100/400

014c: PASSENGER TO TEHERAN   Moyer Bell Mt. Kisko (1990) [1] "This Edition First Published in UK 1990 by Cock Bird Press" $10/40

014d: PASSENGER TO TEHERAN   Moyer Bell Mt. Kisko   (1991)   [1] First printing in US. Introduction by Nigel Nicolson, V. S-W's son $10/30

015a: THE LAND Heinemann L 1926 [2] 125 sgd no cc. Issued without dustwrapper in slipcase $1,000/1,250

015b: THE LAND   Heinemann   L 1926 [1] 1,000 cc. Hawthornden Prize for 1927. Red boards with white/cream label printed in red in pictorial dustwrapper $100/400

015c: THE LAND George H. Doran NY 1927 [0] English sheets in red boards with label on spine and light tan lettered dustwrapper. (Reprinted by Doubleday, Doran   GC {1931} with pictorial dustwrapper of English edition) $50/250

016a: APHRA BEHN Gerald Howe L (1927) [1] Dark blue cloth lettered in gilt on spine in light brown dustwrapper with blue lettering and pattern $40/200

016b: APHRA BEHN Viking NY 1928 [0] Blue boards with yellow label on front and spine. Dustwrapper in light tan, patterned in yellow and lettered in green. (Also seen lettered in blue {Barry Eigen}) $30/150

017a: TWELVE DAYS Hogarth L 1928 [0] 2,025 cc (ref.c) $125/500

017b: TWELVE DAYS Doubleday Doran NY 1928 [0] English sheets $75/350

018a: THE ENGLISH CHARACTER University Press Oxford 1928 [0] 150 cc. 22 pages in gray stiff wraps lettered in black on front $350.

019a: ANDREW MARVELL Faber L 1929 [2] 75 sgd no cc on handmade paper in yellow cloth. Issued in glassine dustwrapper (Ian McKelvie) $600.

019b: ANDREW MARVELL Faber L 1929 [1] Both gray-blue boards and dustwrapper have Rex Whistler drawing $30/150

020a: KING'S DAUGHTER Hogarth L 1929 [0] 1,000 cc. Boards. Issued without dustwrapper with an orange wrap-around band (ref.c) $300/350

020b: KING'S DAUGHTER Doubleday GC 1930 [1] Black boards with labels on spine and front. In orange paper dustwrapper $30/150

021a: THE EDWARDIANS Hogarth (L) 1930 [2] 125 sgd no cc. Issued without dustwrapper $750.

021b: THE EDWARDIANS Hogarth (L) 1930 [0] 3,030 cc (ref.c). (Also seen with "Colonial Edition" printed in red on dustwrapper front) $100/400

021c: THE EDWARDIANS Doubleday Doran GC 1930 [1] (Ref.b) $30/150

022a: ALL PASSION SPENT Hogarth L 1931 [0] 4,040 cc (ref.c) $125/500

022b: ALL PASSION SPENT Doubleday Doran NY 1931 [] Red cloth lettered in black. In black dustwrapper printed in white and gold, with flowers in vases on spine and front $50/200

023a: SELMA LAGERLOF *Her Life and Work* Publisher? L 1931 [2] 130 sgd no cc. Translated by Geo. Timpson, preface by V.S-W. Half-vellum, signed by Lagerlof $250.

023b: SELMA LAGERLOF *Her Life and Work* Publisher? L 1931 [0] Translated by Geo. Timpson, preface by V.S-W. $40/125

023c: SELMA LAGERLOF *Her Life and Work* Publisher? L 1931 [0] Contains "Postlude, 1937" at end (not in 023a or b). Tipped-in sheets so assume same sheets as 023b $25/75

024a: V. SACKVILLE-WEST Ernest Benn (L 1931) [0] Wraps. Title page is cover $100.

024b: V. SACKVILLE-WEST Ernest Benn (L 1931) [0] Simulated cloth wraps. "V. Sackville-West" only words on cover $50.

025a: INVITATION TO CAST OUT CARE Faber L [1931] [2] 200 sgd no cc. Issued without dustwrapper $650.

025b: INVITATION TO CAST OUT CARE Faber L 1931 [0] Wraps $100.

026a: ELEGIES FROM THE CASTLE OF OUINO (Hogarth L 1931) [2] 8 sgd no cc on vellum. Translated by Vita and Edw. Sackville-West from the German of Rainer Maria Rilke (ref.c) ($24,200. at Garden Sale in 1989) $NVA

026b: ELEGIES FROM THE CASTLE OF OUINO
(Hogarth L 1931) [2] 230 sgd no cc in parchment
dustwrapper and slipcase (ref.c) $1,750/2,000

027a: SISSINGHURST Hogarth L 1931 [2] 500
sgd no cc. Issued without dustwrapper (ref.c) $600.

027b: SISSINGHURST Samson Press Warling-
ham 1933 [2] 500 sgd no cc. "Second Edition".
Flexible beige cloth without dustwrapper $300.

027c: SISSINGHURST Hogarth L 1964 [] Re-
issue $20/50

027d: SISSINGHURST National Trust Kent 1972
[0] Wraps $40.

028a: THE DEATH OF NOBLE GODAVARY
Benn L (1932) [1] Wraps $60.

029a: FAMILY HISTORY Hogarth L 1932 [1]
12,170 cc. Orange cloth printed in gold on spine
only (ref.c) $100/400

029b: FAMILY HISTORY Doubleday GC 1932
[1] Red cloth with black lettering and design on
front cover and spine $50/200

030a: THIRTY CLOCKS STRIKE THE HOUR
Doubleday Doran GC 1932 [1] Green cloth printed
in black. (Not published in UK) $50/250

031a: COLLECTED POEMS Hogarth L 1933 [2]
150 sgd no cc. "Volume One" (only volume
published). Orange boards lettered in gilt on spine
in white dustwrapper lettered in black (ref. c) $550/650

031b: COLLECTED POEMS Hogarth L 1933 [1]
3,045 cc (ref.c) $50/250

031c: COLLECTED POEMS Doubleday Doran
GC 1934 [0] No copyright information. "Printed in
England" $40/175

031d: COLLECTED POEMS Doubleday Doran NY 1934 [0] "Printed in the U.S.A." Brown boards with spine label in pink. Dustwrapper lettered in black and decorated in gilt $30/150

032a: THE DARK ISLAND Hogarth L 1934 [1] 10,590 cc. Also noted in dustwrapper with "Colonial Edition" printed on front; and with "Published in Canada | By | Longmans, Green & Company" label on title page. [Note: Unsold copies were rejacketed in 1943 as Number 2 in Hogarth Crown Library Series at 5s] $50/250

032b: THE DARK ISLAND Doubleday Doran GC 1934 [1] Light blue cloth with blue lettering (Barry Eigen) $30/150

033a: HOW DOES YOUR GARDEN GROW? Doubleday Doran & Co. GC 1935 [1] V. S-W wrote chapters 9-12; others by Beverly Nichols, Compton Mackenzie, *et al.* $30/150

034a: SAINT JOAN OF ARC Cobden-Sanderson L (1936) [2] 100 sgd no cc (out of 120 total copies). White buckram; top page edges gilt $450.

034b: SAINT JOAN OF ARC Cobden-Sanderson L (1936) [1] Orange cloth printed in gold. Issued with wrap-around band (Joseph the Provider) $50/250

034c: SAINT JOAN OF ARC Doubleday Doran GC 1936 [1] Red boards in gray dustwrapper lettered in black. Also noted in blue boards and light blue dustwrapper and in blue cloth $30/150

034d: JOAN OF ARC Hogarth L 1937 [1] 5,000 cc. New title. A condensation of 034a $25/125

034e: SAINT JOAN OF ARC M. Joseph L 1948 [1] Revised edition $15/60

035a: MARVELL AND I   Boosey & Co. L 1937
[] Sheet Music. 4 pages. Words by V. S-W, music
by Angelo Barry (Waiting For Godot Books 2/92) $75.

036a: SOME FLOWERS   Cobden Sanderson   L
(1937) [0] Pictorial covers. Not seen with
dustwrapper $125.

037a: PEPITA Hogarth L 1937 [1] 9,950 cc (ref.c).
Orange cloth stamped in gold on spine $40/200

037b: PEPITA Doubleday Doran   GC 1937 [1]
White boards with colored, decorative dustwrapper $25/125

038a: SOLITUDE Hogarth L 1938 [2] 100 sgd no
cc. Issued in dustwrapper $450/550

038b: SOLITUDE   Hogarth L 1938 [1] 3,018 cc
(ref.c). Orange cloth with gold lettering on spine
only, in plain cream-colored dustwrapper with black
lettering $50/250

038c: SOLITUDE Doubleday Doran GC 1939 [0]
English sheets. Blue cloth, crown and author's name
on front cover. In blue-gray dustwrapper with blue
lettering $30/150

039a: COUNTRY NOTES M. Joseph L (1939) [1]
Photographs by Bryan and Norman Westwood.
Wrap-around band on some copies (Peter Jolliffe) $40/200

039b: COUNTRY NOTES Harper NY 1940 [1]
Noted in cream, brown and light green cloths.
Priority unknown $25/125

040a: COUNTRY NOTES IN WARTIME Hogarth
L 1940 [1] Gray boards in pictorial dustwrapper.
Also noted in light blue cloth lettered in red on
spine $30/150

040b: COUNTRY NOTES IN WARTIME
Doubleday Doran NY 1941 [1] Green boards in
pictorial dustwrapper $25/125

041a: ENGLISH COUNTRY HOUSES Collins L 1941 [0] $25/75

042a: SELECTED POEMS Hogarth L (1941) [1] Red boards in green dustwrapper. Also noted in orange boards with pale green lettering on spine only (Barry Eigen) $25/125

043a: GRAND CANYON M. Joseph L (1942) [1] Bleiler (p.173) lists under "Imaginary War." Purple boards. Also noted in yellow Book Society wrap-around band $30/150

043b: GRAND CANYON Doubleday GC 1942 [1] Off-white boards in pictorial dustwrapper $25/125

044a: THE EAGLE AND THE DOVE M. Joseph L (1943) [1] Dark blue cloth lettered in silver on spine only $20/100

044b: THE EAGLE AND THE DOVE Doubleday GC 1944 [1] Red boards with gray lettering on spine in gray lettered dustwrapper $15/60

045a: THE WOMEN'S LAND ARMY M. Joseph L (1944) [1] Red boards with red lettering and gilt device. In pictorial dustwrapper $30/150

046a: ANOTHER WORLD THAN THIS M. Joseph L (1945) [1] Edited by V.S-W and Harold Nicolson. Gray boards lettered and decorated in green and silver. In white dustwrapper decorated in green with black lettering $15/75

047a: TIMOGAD Poetry Society L (1944) [0] Broadsheet. 46-line poem in French $75.

048a: SISSINGHURST CASTLE No publisher, place or date [circa 1945] [0] Four leaves with map of the gardens. In stiff paperwraps. Authorship attested to by VS-W's son. First guide to Sissinghurst. One copy known $500.

049a: THE GARDEN M. Joseph L (1946) [2] 750 sgd no cc. Issued in plain paper dustwrapper $300/350

049b: THE GARDEN M. Joseph L (1946) [1] 15,000 cc. Red boards with silver lettering on spine in decorated red dustwrapper lettered in black. Also noted in brown cloth (Ian McKelvie 8/91) $25/100

049c: THE GARDEN Doubleday GC 1946 [1] Light green boards printed in dark green. In yellow and green dustwrapper lettered in green and white. Also noted in pictorial cloth (Barry Eigen) $15/75

050a: THE OLD CHORISTER TO HIMSELF AS A BOY (Dropmore Press L 1946) [2] 100 sgd no cc. Small folio sheet folded to make 4 pages $350.

051a: THE MARIE CURIE HOSPITAL Tay Press (L 1946) [0] Stiff white wraps lettered on front in black. The title article and most of the other text is by VS-W $200.

052a: THE DEVIL AT WESTEASE Doubleday GC 1947 [1] (*Hubin Crime Fiction*, p.351.) Red boards lettered in black on spine. In red, white and blue decorated dustwrapper. Also noted in cloth (Barry Eigen). No British edition $50/200

053a: NURSERY RHYMES Dropmore Press L 1947 [2] 25 sgd no cc, numbered 1 thru 25. Orange red cloth with vellum/parchment corners and spine. In white dustwrapper with gilt decoration (as on book), lettered in black on spine $1,350/1,500

053b: NURSERY RHYMES Dropmore Press L 1947 [2] 525 no cc (numbered 26 to 550). Blue boards with lettering and decoration as on 053a. In same dustwrapper as 053a. Also noted in blue cloth in white dustwrapper printed in blue (Barry Eigen) $200/300

053c: NURSERY RHYMES M. Joseph L (1950) [1] Drawings by Philippe Jullian. Yellow boards lettered in red. In white dustwrapper lettered and decorated in blue, red and black. Also noted as tan or off-white and lettered and decorated in blue, black, orange and green (Barry Eigen) $25/100

054a: SACKVILLE COLLEGE No publisher East Grinstead no date [published during the 1940s] [0] Four stapled leaves. All significant text by VS-W $150.

055a: KNOLE, KENT The National Trust Kent 1948 [] Assume wraps (ref.a) $75.

055b: KNOLE, KENT The National Trust L (1949 or 1950) [0] Wraps. The date is on the cover. No date inside. It appears to be the type of souvenir shop item that may have had new covers printed up every few years (Peter Jolliffe Cat.34 has this {1950} as the first. Dr. Speck has a copy, essentially the same but dated 1949). The 1950 issue had "Price one shilling and six pence" $60.

056a: IN YOUR GARDEN M. Joseph L (1951) [1] Gray cloth stamped in gold on spine only. In decorated dustwrapper $25/75

057a: WILD AND NATURAL GARDENING *Journal of the Royal Horticultural Society* L 1951 [] Offprint in wraps of Volume LXXVI. Six-page lecture with six pages of photos (Ulysses 3/94) $250.

058a: HIDCOTE MANOR GARDEN The National Trust Kent 1952 [] Guide book. Assume wraps $100.

058b: HIDCOTE MANOR GARDEN (Country Life L 1963) [0] Green wraps $40.

059a: WALTER DE LA MARE AND *"THE TRAVELLER"* Geoffrey Cumberlege/Amen House L 1953 [0] Gray wraps. Warton Lecture January 7, 1953. From the proceedings of the British Academy, Volume 39. 14-page offprint (pages numbered [23]-36) without title page; all information on cover. Priced "3s.6d.net" $75.

060a: THE EASTER PARTY M. Joseph L (1953)
[1] Red boards with gilt lettering on spine. In red
dustwrapper lettered in black and white $25/125

060b: THE EASTER PARTY   Doubleday   GC
1953 [1] Green boards lettered black on red on
spine. In pictorial dustwrapper. Also noted in green
cloth edged in black and lettered in violet or pink $15/75

061a: IN YOUR GARDEN AGAIN M. Joseph L
(1953) [1] Green boards lettered in gilt on spine. In
yellow pictorial dustwrapper $25/125

062a: BERKELEY CASTLE (1955) English Life
Derby no date (1955?) [] Guide book in stiff
decorated wraps. We have not seen this edition. We
recently bought one by this publisher © 1971 but
still assume an earlier one exists $100.

063a: UNION MILL, CRANBROOK No publisher
(L 1955) [] Single sheet folded to make 4 pages. An
appeal to save the mill signed in facsimile by VS-W
(Glenn Horowitz) $200.

064a: MORE FOR YOUR GARDEN M. Joseph L
(1955) [1] Red boards lettered in gilt on spine. In
green dustwrapper decorated and lettered in red and
deep blue $25/125

065a: EVEN MORE FOR YOUR GARDEN M.
Joseph L (1958) [1] Cloth boards printed in gold on
spine. In dustwrapper decorated in green over white
with black lettering $25/100

066a: A JOY OF GARDENING *A Selection for
Americans* Harper NY (1958) [1] Yellow boards
with green cloth spine lettered in gilt. In green
dustwrapper with border and decorations in yellow.
Lettered in black $25/100

067a: DAUGHTER OF FRANCE M. Joseph L
(1959) [1] Red boards lettered in gilt on spine. In
orange dustwrapper decorated and lettered in black $25/100

067b: DAUGHTER OF FRANCE Doubleday GC 1959 [1] Off-white boards lettered on spine in gilt with green devices. In pictorial dustwrapper. Also noted in light gray cloth lettered in gilt with light blue devices $15/75

068a: NO SIGNPOSTS IN THE SEA M. Joseph L (1961) [1] Red boards lettered in gilt on spine. In decorated dustwrapper $15/75

068b: NO SIGNPOSTS IN THE SEA Doubleday GC 1961 [1] Black pictorial boards in gilt and blue on front. In pictorial dustwrapper. Both by Jack Keats $10/50

069a: FACES *Profiles of Dogs* Harvill Press L (1961) [0] Photos by Laelia Goehr. Black boards lettered in gilt on front and spine $50/150

069b: FACES *Profiles of Dogs* Doubleday GC 1962 [] $35/100

070a: ROSES IN THE GARDEN *Journal of the Royal Horticultural Society* L 1961 [] Offprint in wraps of Volume LXXXV. Four color and three black-and-white plates (Ulysses 3/94) $200.

071a: V. SACKVILLE-WEST'S GARDEN BOOK M. Joseph L (1968) [1] Green boards lettered in gilt on spine. In pictorial dustwrapper $25/75

071b: V. SACKVILLE-WEST'S GARDEN BOOK Atheneum NY 1968 [1] 2,000 cc. English sheets in red boards with gilt lettering on front and spine. In same dustwrapper as 071a $25/75

072a: DEAREST ANDREW M. Joseph L 1979 [1] V.S-W's letters to Andrew Reiber, 1951-1962 $10/50

072b: DEAREST ANDREW Scribner's NY (1979) [] $10/35

073a: THE LETTERS OF VITA SACKVILLE-WEST TO VIRGINIA WOOLF Hutchinson L (1984) [1] "Uncorrected Proof" in orange wraps with publication date "22.10.84 - 12.95" $75.

073b: THE LETTERS OF VITA SACKVILLE-WEST TO VIRGINIA WOOLF Hutchinson L (1984) [1] $10/40

073c: THE LETTERS OF VITA SACKVILLE-WEST TO VIRGINIA WOOLF Wm. Morrow NY (1985) [0] Uncorrected bound galleys in gray wraps $60.

073d: THE LETTERS OF VITA SACKVILLE-WEST TO VIRGINIA WOOLF Wm. Morrow NY (1985) [3] $10/40

074a: ORCHARDS: A FRAGMENT FROM *THE LAND* Hermit Press Buxton 1987 [2] 250 no cc. One colored and two black-and-white wood engravings by Anthony Christmas. Issued in patterned boards without dustwrapper (Bertram Rota 3/92) $75.

075a: VITA AND HAROLD Weidenfeld & Nicolson L (1992) [1] Letters of VS-W and Harold Nicolson, edited by Nigel Nicolson $7/35

075b: VITA AND HAROLD Putnam NY 1992 [] (Published July 1992 at $24.95) $6/30

J.D. SALINGER

Salinger was born in New York City in 1919. He was the son of Solomon and Marie Salinger. His father worked for a cheese manufacturer and it was believed (but unconfirmed) that his Irish mother had been an actress in vaudeville. He attended Valley Forge Military Academy in Pennsylvania, New York University, and Columbia University. He served in the Army during WWII. Salinger's first book appearance was in *The Kit Book for Soldiers, Sailors and Marines* with © 1942 on page facing title page (usually seen © 1943). His first book, *The Catcher in the Rye* (1951), received major critical and popular recognition at the time of publication and is now a classic. Salinger has not published a story in 25 years but still finds an audience for his novel and short stories.

In 1986, he successfully challenged Ian Hamilton's unauthorized biography. The court ruled in Salinger's favor and Hamilton had to delete quotations from unpublished letters and material resulting in a complete rewrite of the biography. It was a ruling that will affect biographers and publishers for years to come.

REFERENCES:

(a) Starosciak, Kenneth. J.D. SALINGER A THIRTY YEAR BIBLIOGRAPHY 1938-1968. No publisher [Starosciak], place or date.

(b) Bixby, George. *J.D. Salinger: A Bibliographic Checklist* in AMERICAN BOOK COLLECTOR. Volume 2, Number 3. May/June, 1981.

001a: THE CATCHER IN THE RYE (Little Brown B 1951) [0] 833 cc. Folded publicity broadside sent to booksellers (ref.b) $500.

001b: THE CATCHER IN THE RYE Little Brown B 1951 [1] 10,000 cc. The first issue dustwrapper has a photograph of Salinger on the back panel which was dropped on later printings (ref.b). (We have seen later printings with the photo in a priced dustwrapper which was slightly taller than the first printing). Presumed earliest form of dustwrapper omits Book-of-the-Month Club slug (ref.b). We have never seen a copy without slug at the bottom of rear dustwrapper flap and assume this would be the place it is omitted. (The first Canadian edition was the Book-of-the-Month Club edition printed in Toronto) $500/3,500

001c: THE CATCHER IN THE RYE Hamish Hamilton L (1951) [1] (Ref.b) $100/500

002a: NINE STORIES Little Brown B (1953) [1] 4,995 cc $300/1,500

002b: FOR ESME - WITH LOVE AND SQUA-LOR *And Other Stories* Hamish Hamilton L (1953) [1] (Ref.b) $75/400

003a: FRANNY AND ZOOEY Little Brown B (1961) [1] 25,000 cc $40/200

003b: FRANNY AND ZOOEY Heinemann L (1962) [1] (Ref.b) $20/100

004a: RAISE HIGH THE ROOF BEAM, CARPENTERS, AND SEYMOUR *An Introduction* Little Brown B (1963) [0] Wraps. Uncorrected proof, spiral bound in light green printed wraps (Serendipity Books) $1,750.

004b: RAISE HIGH THE ROOF BEAM, CARPENTERS, AND SEYMOUR *An Introduction* Little Brown B [1963] [1] Copyright dates are 1955 and 1959 but published in 1963. First issue contains no dedication page, estimated at 30 copies (ref.a), at 20 copies (ref.b) 100,000 in total (b, c & d) $500/600

004c: RAISE HIGH THE ROOF BEAM, CARPENTERS, AND SEYMOUR *An Introduction* Little Brown B (1963) [1] Second issue has dedication page before half-title (in front of title page) (ref.a) $125/200

004d: RAISE HIGH THE ROOF BEAM, CARPENTERS, AND SEYMOUR *An Introduction* Little Brown B (1963) [1] Ref.a states third issue has dedication tipped-in after title page (in normal position). Ref.b does not believe there is any priority on copies that have the dedication page tipped-in at various places. We have made separate entries because the presumed third state is much more common than the second. $20/100

004e: RAISE HIGH THE ROOF BEAM, CARPENTERS, AND SEYMOUR *An Introduction* Heinemann L (1963) [1] (Ref.b) Also noted with gold rather than silver stamping on spine (Maurice Neville) $15/75

005a: THE COMPLETE UNCOLLECTED SHORT STORIES OF J.D. SALINGER (No publisher, place or date) [0] Two volumes. Volume 1: cream wrappers, purple stamping, stapled spine. Volume 2: stiff white glossy wraps, purple stamping, perfect bound. No title pages in either volume. Pages not typeset $750.

005b: THE COMPLETE UNCOLLECTED SHORT STORIES OF J.D. SALINGER (No publisher, place or date) [0] Two volumes. Both perfect bound in stiff glossy pictorial wraps. Both contain a title page and are typeset. Volume 1 has a short preface not in 005a.

Supposedly, both issues were successfully suppressed by Salinger's lawyers, although ref.b only notes this on 005a. We had a set of 005b with a note stating the second edition, of about 7,500 copies, was published on August

17 (or 19), 1974. This note was signed by John Greenberg who claimed to have published the piracy. He was on his way out of the country at the time. $450.

006a: J.D. SALINGER | A WRITING LIFE Random House NY (1986) [3] Uncorrected proofs. Yellow printed wraps. Rear cover blank. This biography by Ian Hamilton probably shouldn't be listed but the Salinger collector has so few titles, we thought we'd include this as it does have unpublished letters and papers quoted. Salinger successfully stopped publication of the book. The precedent established by this case will haunt biographers. Supposedly very few copies of these proofs exist, estimated at 65 copies (James S. Jaffe 9/93). $2,500.

007a: IN SEARCH OF J.D. SALINGER *A Writing Life* Random House NY (1988) [3] Uncorrected proof in yellow wraps. By Ian Hamilton. The "legal version" of 006a after Salinger successfully challenged the original in court $200.

007b: IN SEARCH OF J.D. SALINGER *A Writing Life* Random House NY (1988) [3] $7/35

MARY LEE SETTLE

Settle was born in Charleston, West Virginia, in 1918. She served in the Women's Auxiliary Air Force and was associated with the Office of War Information in England during WWII. After winning the National Book Award for *Blood Ties* and enduring the treatment afforded an award winner, she founded the PEN/Faulkner Award in 1980, an award given by a jury of fiction writers who each year honor five American novelists. The winner receives a prize of $15,000. She resides in Charlottesville with her husband W. Tazewell.

We would like to thank Henry Turlington for his help on this guide.

001a: THE LOVE EATERS Heinemann L (1954) [1] $60/300

001b: THE LOVE EATERS Harper NY (1954) [0] $50/250

002a: THE KISS OF KIN Heinemann L (1955) [1] $50/250

002b: THE KISS OF KIN Harper NY (1955) [0]
Code on copyright page "G-E" $40/200

003a: O BEULAH LAND Viking NY 1956 [1]
13,000 cc. Second book in *Beulah Quintet* $25/125

003b: O BEULAH LAND Heinemann L (1956) [1] $15/75

004a: KNOW NOTHING Viking NY 1960 [1]
5,000 cc. Third book in *Beulah Quintet* $25/125

004b: KNOW NOTHING Heinemann L (1961) [1] $12/60

005a: FIGHT NIGHT ON A SWEET SATUR-DAY Viking NY (1964) [1] 6,500 cc $15/75

006a: ALL THE BRAVE PROMISES Delacorte NY (1966) [] Uncorrected proof in ring-bound wraps (H.E. Turlington 7/95) $150.

006b: ALL THE BRAVE PROMISES Delacorte NY (1966) [1] $15/75

006c: ALL THE BRAVE PROMISES Heinemann L (1967) [] $10/50

007a: THE STORY OF FLIGHT Random House NY 1967 [0] $50/125

007b: THE STORY OF FLIGHT Random House NY 1967 [0] Pictorial boards without dustwrapper $75.

008a: THE CLAM SHELL Bodley Head L (1971) [] $12/60

008b: THE CLAM SHELL Delacorte NY (1971) [1] $10/50

009a: THE SCOPES TRIAL F. Watts NY 1972 [] $25/100

010a: PRISONS Putnam NY (1973) [0] First book in *Beulah Quintet* $12/60

010b: THE LONG ROAD TO PARADISE Constable L 1974 [] New title $12/60

011a: BLOOD TIE Houghton Miffilin B 1977 [] Uncorrected Proof in yellow wraps (Tristero 12/94) $75.

011b: BLOOD TIE Houghton Mifflin B 1977 [3] National Book Award for 1978 $10/50

012a: ACCEPTANCE SPEECH: NATIONAL BOOK AWARD (Palaemon Winston-Salem 1978) [2] 26 sgd ltr cc $125.

012b: ACCEPTANCE SPEECH: NATIONAL
BOOK AWARD (Palaemon Winston-Salem 1978)
[2] 100 sgd no cc. Broadside $75.

013a: THE SCAPEGOAT Random House NY
(1980) [] Uncorrected proof in red wraps $60.

013b: THE SCAPEGOAT Random House NY
(1980) [4] Fourth book in the *Beulah Quintet* $7/35

014a: THE KILLING GROUND Farrar NY (1982)
[1] Uncorrected proofs in salmon colored wraps
(Bert Babcock) $50.

014b: THE KILLING GROUND Farrar NY
(1982) [] Advance Reading Copy in printed
(glossy) wraps (Between the Covers 10/91) $35.

014c: THE KILLING GROUND Farrar NY (1982)
[2] 150 sgd no cc. Issued without dustwrapper in
slipcase. The fifth book of the *Beulah Quintet* $60/100

014d: THE KILLING GROUND Farrar NY (1982)
[1] 25,000 cc. (Published June 14, 1982) $7/35

015a: WATER WORLD Dutton NY (1984) [3]
Also states "First Edition" $15/75

016a: CELEBRATION Farrar NY (1986) []
Uncorrected proofs in yellow wraps (Bev Chaney
9/89) $50.

016b: CELEBRATION Franklin Library Franklin
Center 1986 [2] "Limited Signed Edition" in full
leather with 3-page special introduction. About
6,500 cc $50.

016c: CELEBRATION Farrar NY (1986) [0]
(Published September 1989 at $18.95) $6/30

017a: "MAUGHAM" *The Yale Review* (New
Haven) 1987 [] Offprint in staple-bound printed
wraps. Text paginated (428)-439 $60.

018a: THE SEARCH FOR BEULAH LAND *The Story Behind the Beulah Quartet* Scribner's NY (1988) [2] 500 no cc in stapled wraps. Issued with boxed sets of the *Beulah Quintet*, as well as separately. Some copies signed but not called for $60.

019a: CHARLEY BLAND   Farrar   NY 1989 [] Uncorrected proof in blue wraps (Bev Chaney 11/89) $40.

019b: CHARLEY BLAND   Franklin Library Franklin Center 1989 [2] Signed "Limited Edition" in full green leather $50.

019c: CHARLEY BLAND   Farrar   NY 1989 [1] Dustwrapper (back) has "ISBN 0-374-28588-8 0989" Reportedly all withdrawn and destroyed (Jackson Bryer) $5/75

019d: CHARLEY BLAND   Farrar   NY 1989 [1] Dustwrapper (back) has   "ISBN 0-374-12078-1 1089" $5/25

020a: TURKISH REFLECTIONS *A Biography Of A Place* Prentice-Hall NY (1991) [] Introduction by Jan Morris $10/30

021a: OBSESSION   Quill & Brush   (Rockville) 1994 [0] 600 cc. Wraps. "PEN/Faulkner Chapbook Series No. 1" on rear cover.   15 original essays, written by Settle and 14 others for 1993 PEN/Faulkner Gala. (In-print at $15) $

021b: OBSESSION   Quill & Brush   (Rockville) 1994 [2] 200 sgd no cc. Signed by all 15 contributors. Gray cloth in slipcase. Original signed and numbered silk screen by Lou Stovall secured in place on front pastedown with silk ribbons. (In-print at $100) $

021c: OBSESSION   Quill & Brush   (Rockville) 1994 [2] 26 sgd ltr cc. Signed by all 15 contributors.

Issued in full leather in cloth clam shell slipcase with original signed and numbered silk screen by Lou Stovall held in place by ribbons inside the front cover of case. (Published price: $200) $250.

022a: CHOICES   Nan A. Talese / Doubleday NY/L+ (1995) [3] Advance reading copy in wraps (Bert Babcock 6/95) $35.

022b: CHOICES   Nan A. Talese / Doubleday NY/L+ (1995) [3] Also states "First Edition". Published at $24.95

Elizabeth Spencer [signature]

ELIZABETH SPENCER

Elizabeth Spencer was born in Carrollton, Mississippi, in 1921. She received a B.A. from Belhaven College in Jackson, Mississippi, and a M.A. from Vanderbilt University in Nashville, Tennessee, in 1943. She married John Rusher in 1956. She has worked as a reporter and taught at various colleges and universities. Ms. Spencer has received many awards and fellowships, including a Guggenheim. She presently resides in Chapel Hill, North Carolina.

We would like to thank Henry Turlington for his assistance in initial preparation of this guide.

001a: FIRE IN THE MORNING Dodd, Mead NY (1948) [0] $100/500

002a: THIS CROOKED WAY Dodd, Mead NY (1952) [0] $40/200

002b: THIS CROOKED WAY Gollancz L 1953 [1] $25/125

003a: THE VOICE AT THE BACK DOOR McGraw-Hill NY (1956) [0] $20/100

003b: THE VOICE AT THE BACK DOOR Gollancz L 1957 [] $12/60

003c: THE VOICE AT THE BACK DOOR Time NY (1965) [0] Wraps. New introduction by author $15.

004a: THE LIGHT IN THE PIAZZA McGraw-Hill NY (1960) [1] $10/50

004b: THE LIGHT IN THE PIAZZA   Heinemann L (1961) [1] $8/40

005a: KNIGHTS & DRAGONS   McGraw-Hill NY (1965) [1] $10/50

005b: KNIGHTS & DRAGONS   Heinemann   L 1966 [] $10/40

006a: NO PLACE FOR AN ANGEL   McGraw-Hill NY (1967) [1] $10/50

006b: NO PLACE FOR AN ANGEL   Weidenfeld and Nicolson L (1968) [] $8/40

007a: SHIP ISLAND *And Other Stories*   McGraw-Hill   NY (1968) [2] 150 cc with signed and numbered label on front endpaper. Issued for First Editions Limited $50/75

007b: SHIP ISLAND *And Other Stories*   McGraw-Hill NY (1968) [1] $10/40

007c: SHIP   ISLAND   *And   Other   Stories* Weidenfeld and Nicolson L (1969) [] $7/35

008a: THE SNARE   McGraw-Hill   NY (1972) [3] Also states "First Edition" $10/50

009a: THE STORIES OF ELIZABETH SPENCER Doubleday   GC 1981 [1]   Foreword by Eudora Welty $20/60

009b: THE STORIES OF ELIZABETH SPENCER Penguin (Harmondsworth 1983) [] Wraps $25.

010a: MARILEE *Three Stories*   University Press of Mississippi 1981 [2] 300 sgd no cc. Issued in tissue dustwrapper $50.

010b: MARILEE *Three Stories*   University Press of Mississippi 1981 [0] Wraps $15.

011a: THE MULES   Palaemon   Winston-Salem
1982 [2] 26 sgd ltr cc $100.

011b: THE MULES   Palaemon Press   Winston-
Salem 1982 [2] 150 sgd no cc. Wraps $50.

012a: THE SALT LINE Doubleday GC/T 1984 [1]
Uncorrected proof in green wraps (Bert Babcock) $40.

012b: THE SALT LINE Doubleday GC/T 1984
[1] (Published January 27, 1984 at $15.95) $5/25

012c: THE SALT LINE Penguin (Harmondsworth
1985) [] Wraps $10.

013a: JACK OF DIAMONDS Viking NY 1988 []
(Published August 1988 at $15.95) $5/25

014a: THE LEGACY Mud Puppy Press (Chapel
Hill) 1988 [2] 26 sgd ltr cc. White silk with white
leather spine and signed wood cut by Michael
McCurdy (illustrator) laid-in. Issued in black cloth
folding box (Bert Babcock 3/89) $200.

014b: THE LEGACY Mud Puppy Press (Chapel
Hill) 1988 [2] 100 sgd no cc. In illustrated boards
with cloth spine. Issued without dustwrapper $60.

015a: CONVERSATIONS WITH ELIZABETH
SPENCER   University Press of Mississippi
Jackson 1991 [] Edited by Peggy Prenshaw. $15/30

015b: CONVERSATIONS WITH ELIZABETH
SPENCER   University Press of Mississippi
Jackson 1991 [] Wraps $15.

016a: THE NIGHT TRAVELLERS Viking (NY
1991) [0] Unrevised and Unpublished Proofs in
cream colored wraps. ("Beige" wraps {Monroe
Stahr Books 5/95}) $20.

016b: THE NIGHT TRAVELLERS Viking (NY
1991) [] (Published August 1991 at $ 19.95) $5/20

017a: ON THE GULF   University Press of
Mississippi Jackson/L (1991) [2] 26 sgd ltr cc.
Issued without dustwrapper in slipcase. Six stories,
first appearance of one (Nouveau Rare Books
11/94) $125/150

017b: ON THE GULF   University Press of
Mississippi Jackson/L (1991) [2] 50 sgd no cc.
Issued without dustwrapper in slipcase $75/100

017c: ON THE GULF   University Press of
Mississippi Jackson/ L (1991) [3] $5/25

John Steinbeck (signature)

JOHN STEINBECK
(1902-1968)

Steinbeck was born in Salinas, California. He attended Stanford specializing in marine biology, but supported himself for many years as a laborer until the success of *Tortilla Flat*. His range of subject matter was broad. His books *The Grapes of Wrath*, which won a Pulitzer Prize in 1940, *Of Mice and Men* and *East of Eden* are considered classics; and *In Dubious Battle* is still considered one of the best strike novels. He received the Nobel Prize for Literature in 1962.

The Goldstone and Payne bibliography (ref.a) is an excellent one. The first printing quantities included herein that were not in ref.a (about 18 titles) were obtained from Viking Press.

REFERENCES:

(a) Goldstone, Adrian and Payne, John R. JOHN STEINBECK *A Bibliographical Catalogue of the Adrian H. Goldstone Collection*. Austin: Humanities Research Center, The University of Texas (1974).

(b) JOHN STEINBECK *A Collection of Books & Manuscripts Formed by Harry Valentine*. Santa Barbara: Bradford Morrow Bookseller, Ltd. (Catalogue Eight) (1980).

001a: CUP OF GOLD *A Life of Henry Morgan, Buccaneer* McBride NY 1929 [1] 1,537 cc. Top edge stained blue. (Also copies noted with top unstained) $750/7,500

001b: CUP OF GOLD *A Life of Henry Morgan, Buccaneer* Covici Friede NY (1936) [0] 939 cc or less. New front material. Maroon cloth, spine stamped in gilt. Remainder sheets of first edition sheets. In dustwrapper that does not have "Covici Friede" on spine $150/750

001c: CUP OF GOLD *A Life of Henry Morgan, Buccaneer* Covici Friede NY (1936) [0] Blue cloth. Dustwrapper has Covici Friede on spine $60/300

001d: CUP OF GOLD *A Life of Henry Morgan, Buccaneer* Heinemann L/T (1937) [1] Blue cloth, spine stamped in gilt $200/1,250

002a: THE PASTURES OF HEAVEN Brewer, Warren & Putnam NY 1932 [0] 2,500 cc (a,b,c&e). Approximately 650 copies sold. Green cloth, front cover stamped in gilt, top edges stained black. No mention of *Cup of Gold* on dustwrapper $500/5,000

002b: THE PASTURES OF HEAVEN Brewer, Warren & Putnam NY 1932 [0] Approximately 1,000 copies from Brewer sheets. Robert O. Ballou imprint on cloth spine, dustwrapper still has Brewer imprint $250/1,750

002c: THE PASTURES OF HEAVEN Robert O. Ballou NY 1932 [0] Quantity unknown but made up from remaining 850 sets of first sheets. Ballou on book spine and dustwrapper $150/1,250

002d: THE PASTURES OF HEAVEN Phillip Allan L (1933) [1] Green cloth, spine printed in black $150/1,250

002e: THE PASTURES OF HEAVEN Covici Friede NY (no date) [] Balance of first edition sheets not used by Ballou. Published about 1935 $150/750

003a: NOTHING SO MONSTROUS (Pynson Printers NY) 1936 [0] 370 cc for 5 subscribers to use as Christmas gifts. First separate publication. Limitation page has name of subscribers (no numbers). In glassine dustwrapper. According to ref.a "50 copies for Elmer Adler [the printer], 100 for Frederick B. Adams, Jr., 150 for Ben Abramson, 50 for Edwin J. Beinecke, and 20 for Howard Mott. For some reason, unknown at this time, no copies were printed for Mott and copies exist without a name on the presentation page." However, in 1978 Howard Mott found a copy with his name printed on the colophon. The Jonathan Goodwin copy bore no name on the colophon, James Cummins reports (12/94) a copy printed for Hester Barres, and inscribed to "Andy, 1936". Possibly unique. We've had a copy with printed colophon page "at the request of" "The Colophon for...Pierce Butler" and another for "Charles W. Luke". Also noted without an imprint for one of the subscribers, and the space for the recipient blank (William Reese Co. 4/95) $1,500.

003b: NOTHING SO MONSTEROUS Richard West no place 1980 [2] 150 cc issued without dustwrapper $50.

004a: TO A GOD UNKNOWN Ballou NY (1933) [1] 598 cc. Green cloth, stamped in gilt, top edges stained black $300/3,000

004b: TO A GOD UNKNOWN Covici Friede NY (1935) [1] 900 cc. Beige cloth, front wrapper and spine printed in green, top edges green "First published 1933" on cancel title page $200/1,000

004c: TO A GOD UNKNOWN Heinemann L/T (1935) [1] Blue cloth spine stamped in gilt $150/1,250

005a: TORTILLA FLAT (Covici Friede NY 1935) [0] "Uncorrected Galley Proofs" in brown wraps with label on front. Printed on one side only, no title page $5,000.

005b: TORTILLA FLAT Covici Friede NY (1935) [0] Wraps. Approximately 500 cc in printed paper wrappers, sewn and wrapped in the dustwrapper $1,500.

005c: TORTILLA FLAT Covici Friede NY (1935) [0] 4,000 cc. Tan cloth printed in blue, top edges stained blue $300/1,500

005d: TORTILLA FLAT Heinemann L (1935) [0]
Blue cloth stamped in gilt. Also noted with "3/6"
price stamped under "7/6" price on spine of
dustwrapper (Robert Dagg 7/93) $150/1,250

TORTILLA FLAT *A Play in Three Acts* see 010

005e: TORTILLA FLAT Modern Library NY
(1937) [0] New introduction by Steinbeck. Noted in
variant dustwrappers and reinforced buckram
binding (ref.a). No copy stating first edition seen
(Andes, *Modern Library Bibliography*, p.169) $20/100

005f: TORTILLA FLAT Viking Press NY (1935
[but probably 1938]) [] Unrecorded trial binding:
The text of the book from the "Chapter Headings"
(Roman numberal "v") through the end of the book
(p.317) appear to be the same as in the Covici
Friede edition. However, both the title page and
spine of this book bear the Viking Press imprint.
The dustwrapper is identical to the Covici Friede
edition except the spine and lower rear flap have
"Covici Friede" blocked out and "Viking Press"
printed thereon. This book was illustrated by Ruth
Gannett and a dedication page has been added after
the copyright page which reads "To Susan Gregory
of Monterey." The first eight printings of the Covici
Friede editions through 1937 do not contain any
dedication. The 1947 edition illustrated by Peggy
Worthington which was previously thought to be
the first Viking imprint of the book also contained
the dedication to Susan Gregory. The dedication to
her in this early (probably 1938) edition, would lead
to the conclusion that Steinbeck had knowledge of
its publication. Pat Covici moved from the firm of
Covici Friede to Viking Press as Senior Editor in
1938. (Nick Adams & Co. cataloged at $2,000 8/95) $NVA

005g: TORTILLA FLAT Viking Press NY (1947)
[1] With 17 color illustrations by Peggy
Worthington. Beige cloth, with colored pictorial

endpapers. Also variant in green boards without front cover illustration. Black cloth spine printed in gold (James Dourgarian 5/90) $60/250

005h: TORTILLA FLAT   Franklin Library Franklin Center 1977 [2] Illustrated by Herbert Tauss. Imitation leather without dustwrapper. Contains *Tortilla Flat, Of Mice and Men* and *Cannery Row* $75.

006a: IN DUBIOUS BATTLE Covici Friede NY (1936) [2] 99 sgd no cc. In tissue dustwrapper and black slipcase with orange paper label printed in black. (Lettered copies exist but number unknown, "Printer's Copy B" offered by Brad Morrow catalogue 8 and "B" by Joseph the Provider catalog 34 for $5,000) $4,000/5,000

006b: IN DUBIOUS BATTLE Covici Friede NY (1936) [0] Yellow cloth, top edges stained red $250/1,250

006c: IN DUBIOUS BATTLE Heinemann L/T (1936) [1] $150/750

007a: SAINT KATY THE VIRGIN (Covici Friede NY 1936) [2] 199 sgd no cc. Issued in decorated boards, gilt cloth spine printed in red, in glassine dustwrapper. Some copies with slip laid in for *Of Mice and Men*; and some with slip stating "Season's Greetings..." Also an unnumbered copy (Bruce Howard 2/91) $2,500.

008a: OF MICE AND MEN Covici Friede NY (1937) [0] Salesman's dummy. 16 pages of text $5,000.

008b: OF MICE AND MEN Covici Friede NY (1937) [0] 2,500 cc. First issue/printing: p.88 has a bullet between the 8's; "and only moved because the heavy hands were pendula" on p.9:20-21. Printed by J.J. Little and Ives Co. NY $200/1,000

008c: OF MICE AND MEN Covici Friede NY (1937) [0] Second issue/printing with p.9:21 reading "loosely" and bullet on p.88 deleted. Printed by Haddon Craftsmen. "According to Goldstone and Payne the first printing was done by J.J. Little and Ives, and twenty days later the second was printed by the Haddon Craftsmen." Pepper & Stern report a copy "with a corrected page, but was printed by J.J. Little and Ives. Obviously, Goldstone and Payne were incorrect, and those copies printed by the Haddon Craftsmen are even later issues." We would think it would not make sense to change printers on the second, and Haddon probably did the BOMC edition $30/150.

008d: OF MICE AND MEN Heinemann L/T (1937) [1] Blue cloth, spine stamped in gilt, top edges stained blue. Blue dustwrapper printed in black. (Some copies with wrap-around band.) Also a variant with pink top edge and dustwrapper printed in black $100/500

008e: OF MICE AND MEN Limited Editions Club NY 1970 [2] 1,500 cc signed by illustrator (Fletcher Martin). Issued in denim-covered boards with leather spine in brown paper slipcase with blue denim edging $75/125

009a: OF MICE AND MEN *A Play in Three Acts* Covici Friede NY (1937) [1] Salesman's dummy. 16 pages of text $4,000.

009b: OF MICE AND MEN *A Play* Covici Friede NY (1937) [0] Copies in proof dustwrapper that is 10mm taller than trade dustwrapper and has no printing on back flap or rear panel (Joseph the Provider) $200/1,500

009c: OF MICE AND MEN *A Play in Three Acts* Covici Friede NY (1937) [0] Beige cloth, top edges stained blue. (Peter Howard of Serendipity Books stated in a catalog that the first issue dustwrapper has no reviews on back panel. Not mentioned in other references and apparently not the same as 9b.

Paul Garon of Beasley Books says the dustwrapper has reviews of play performance, not of this book, and is the same dustwrapper he had on an advance review copy years ago) \$200/1,000

009d: OF MICE AND MEN *A Play* Dramatist Play Service NY (1937) [0] Wraps. Ref.a lists (1937) but Waiting For Godot listed (1951) or later as first acting edition based on comments in text of that volume \$75.

010a: TORTILLA FLAT *A Play in Three Acts* Covici Friede NY (1937) [] Salesman's dummy in tan cloth and dustwrapper, 8 pages of text. Dramatization by Jack Kirkland. (\$2,400 at auction in 1994) \$2,200/2,400

010b: TORTILLA FLAT *A Play in Three Acts* Covici NY (1937) [] \$50/250

011a: THE RED PONY Covici Friede NY 1937 [2] 52 ltr cc. (Not listed in ref.a but ref.b catalogued copy "H" and Pepper & Stern catalogued copy "CC" and Geo. Robt. Minkoff "QQ"). Ken Lopez (1/92) offered copy "Y" in a slipcase \$2,000/2,250

011b: THE RED PONY Covici Friede NY 1937 [2] 699 sgd no cc. Flexible beige cloth, clear cellophane dustwrapper. Issued in tan slipcase with limitation number on spine \$1,250/1,500

011c: OF MICE AND MEN · THE RED PONY Evergreen Books L 1940 [1] Wraps. "First issued in Evergreen..." \$75.

011d: THE RED PONY Viking Press NY 1945 [1] Coarse beige cloth. Printed by Kipe Offset Process Company. "Illustrated edition first published in 1945." Issued without dustwrapper in blue-gray paperboard slipcase. Assume first state. (Ref.a listed 011e & f as variants) \$75/150

011e: THE RED PONY Viking Press NY 1945 [1]
Variant: fine beige cloth. "Printed by Zeese-
Wilkinson Co" or by "Rogers-Kellogg-Stillson".
Issued without dustwrapper in blue-gray paperboard
slipcase $50/125

011f: THE RED PONY Viking Press NY 1945 [1]
Variant: fine beige glazed cloth. Printed by Rogers-
Kellogg-Stillson. Tan paperboard slipcase $50/125

011g: THE RED PONY Viking Press NY 1945 [1]
Variant: slightly darker beige cloth and without
front cover illustration or blue border (John Payne) $60/125

011h: THE RED PONY Heinemann L (1949) []
Stiff wraps. States "First Published in *The Long
Valley* 1939, Reprinted 1949." "The Book of The
Film" $125.

012a: THEIR BLOOD IS STRONG   Simon J.
Lubin Society of California, Inc.   SF 1938 [0]
Wraps. Title page is cover. Later printings state $1,000.

012b: THEIR BLOOD IS STRONG   Perfection
Form Co. Logan, Iowa (circa. 1970) [0] Wraps.
Two issues noted (priority, if any, unknown): light
brown covers with light brown lettering, 27.1 cm
high; and gray-brown covers with dark brown
lettering, 26.9 cm high (Watermark West 12/94) $25.

013a: THE LONG VALLEY Viking NY 1938 [1]
8,000 cc $100/500

013b: THE LONG VALLEY Heinemann   L/T
(1939) [0] $75/350

013c: 13 GREAT STORIES FROM *The Long
Valley* Avon NY (1943) [0] Wraps. New title $40.

014a: THE GRAPES OF WRATH (Viking NY
1939) [0] Wraps. Offprint of pp.3-16 for booksellers $400.

014b: THE GRAPES OF WRATH Viking NY (1939) [] Salesman's dummy with 9 pages of text (ref.b) (Eight pages of text {Bruce Howard}, 10 pages of text {both Glenn Horowitz and Nick Adams & Co.) Four known copies (Nick Adams & Co.) $5,000.

014c: THE GRAPES OF WRATH Viking NY (1939) [1] Wraps. Advance proof in plain brown cover $7,500.

014d: THE GRAPES OF WRATH Viking NY (1939) [1] 50,000 cc (ref.a) but a Viking representative says records show 19,804 copies actually printed. Dustwrapper states "First Edition" on lower right corner of front flap. Awarded Pulitzer Prize in 1940. It may be of interest to note an inscribed copy was purchased at auction in 1994 for over $11,000 including buyer's premium (reportedly by Denis Tyrrel) $350/2,500

014e: THE GRAPES OF WRATH Macmillan Toronto (1939) [1] Viking book with title page "Toronto | the Macmillan Company of Canada..." Copyright page states "Printed in U.S.A. by Stratford Press..." and "First published in April 1939". Viking dustwrapper with Viking blacked over on spine and "Macmillan" in middle of spine $100/500

014f: THE GRAPES OF WRATH Heinemann L/T (1939) [1] (Also noted with Book Society wrap-around band) $75/350

014g: THE GRAPES OF WRATH Limited Editions Club NY 1940 [2] 1,146 cc sgd by illustrator (Thomas Hart Benton). Two volumes. Issued in glassine dustwrappers and slipcase $900/1,000

015a: JOHN STEINBECK REPLIES (Friends of Democracy NY 1940) [0] Wraps. Unbound, folded-sheet to create 4-page pamphlet (Diane Peterson 2/91) $1,000.

015b: A LETTER WRITTEN... FRIENDS OF DEMOCRACY Overlook Press Stanford, Ct. 1940 [2] 350 cc. New title. Brown paper boards in glassine dustwrapper $600.

016a: THE FORGOTTEN VILLAGE Viking NY 1941 [1] 15,000 cc $50/250

017a: SEA OF CORTEZ Viking NY 1941 [1] Salesman's dummy with 12 pages of text. Blue cloth stamped in silver on front cover only; top edge stained green rather than the orange of the published book (Between the Covers 1/95). Title page and 10 pages of text (Bruce Howard 2/91). The dustwrapper is blank on the flaps and the rear panel. (Lame Duck Books 4/95) $2,500/3,500

017b: SEA OF CORTEZ Viking NY 1941 [1] Review copies in plain brown wraps. Also noted with only first half of text and no appendix (Diane Peterson) $2,500.

017c: SEA OF CORTEZ Viking NY 1941 [1] 7,500 cc. Green cloth, top edges stained orange $150/650

017d: THE LOG FROM THE SEA OF CORTEZ Viking NY 1951 [1] 7,500 cc. New title with narrative portion only and "About Ed Ricketts" by Steinbeck. Maroon cloth (ref.a), also gray-green cloth (Bev Chaney) $100/400

017e: THE LOG FROM THE SEA OF CORTEZ Heinemann L (1958) [1] $50/200

018a: THE MOON IS DOWN (Viking NY 1942) [] Unrevised galley proofs in brown wraps with yellow label (ref.b) $3,500.

018b: THE MOON IS DOWN Viking NY 1942 [2] 700 cc. Sewn and wrapped in dustwrapper. Advance copies for booksellers $600.

018c: THE MOON IS DOWN Viking NY 1942 [1] 65,000 cc (c&d). Without printer's name on copyright page. Large period between "talk" and "this" on p.112:11 — $100/250

018d: THE MOON IS DOWN Viking NY 1942 [1] Printer "Haddon of Kingsport" on copyright page and period deleted on p.112:11. (018c scarcer but priority unknown.) Bound in both blue and red/maroon cloth. (Noted in both rough and smooth textured dustwrappers with "For Defense, Buy U.S. Bonds" on back of the smooth textured; or, "The Men in the Services Need Books" on the rough textured (Diane Peterson 2/91). We had a copy without "Haddon" on copyright page — $15/75

018e: THE MOON IS DOWN Heinemann L/T (1942) [1] Terra cotta cloth (Note: there is a brown cloth variant binding and a copy has been noted with the second up-stroke of the "N" in "Novel" on title page damaged, assume later {Robert Temple #40}) — $25/125

019a: THE MOON IS DOWN *Play in Two Parts* Dramatists Play Service (NY 1942) [0] 1,000 cc. Stiff yellow wraps printed in black. 1,250 sets of sheets printed (250 to Viking). Sheets bulk 12mm and 188mm tall (second edition bulked 8mm and was 186mm tall) — $450.

019b: THE MOON IS DOWN *Play in Two Parts* Viking NY 1942 [] 250 cc. Blue cloth (from Dramatists Play Service sheets) — $350/1,750

019c: THE MOON IS DOWN *Play in Two Parts* English Theatre Guild L (1943) [0] Stiff red wraps printed in black — $100.

019d: THE MOON IS DOWN *Play in Two Parts* Heinemann Melbourne (1944) [] First Australian edition possibly using English sheets, but with the U.S. dustwrapper design (Todd's Books 11/95) $10/50

020a: BOMBS AWAY Viking NY 1942 [1] 20,000 cc. (Note: "Second Printing" on bottom of rear panel of dustwrapper of that printing) $50/250

021a: THE VIKING PORTABLE LIBRARY STEINBECK Viking NY (1943) [0] 26,000 cc. "Published by...Viking...in July 1943" on copyright page. Selected by Pascal Covici $35/125

021b: THE PORTABLE STEINBECK Viking NY (1946) [] Introduction by Lewis Gannett. Revised. Additional chapter and new title. Copyright dates for the book in the biographical notes do not match those printed on the copyright page. Dustwrapper price: $2.00 $25/100

021c: THE PORTABLE STEINBECK Viking NY (1946) [] Copyright dates corrected. Dustwrapper price: $3.00 $20/60

021d: THE PORTABLE STEINBECK Viking NY (1946) [] Wraps. Price: $1.95 $30.

021e: THE STEINBECK OMNIBUS Heinemann M/L/T (1950) [1] New title. Edited by Covici $50/200

022a: HOW EDITH McGILLCUDDY MET RLS The Rowfant Club Cleveland 1943 [2] 152 no cc. Plain green dustwrapper $2,250/2,500

023a: THE STEINBECK POCKET BOOK Blakiston Philadelphia (1943) [1] Stiff, colored pictorial wraps. Distributed by Pocket Books. "First Printing November 1943" $60.

024a: CANNERY ROW Viking NY 1945 [1] Galley proofs in tan wraps with yellow label (ref.b) $3,500.

024b: CANNERY ROW Viking NY 1945 [1] Advance Review Copy in printed blue wraps $750.

024c: CANNERY ROW   Viking   NY 1945 [1]
78,000 cc (c&d). Light buff cloth $125/500

024d: CANNERY ROW Viking   NY 1945 [1]
Second issue in yellow cloth $40/200

024e: CANNERY ROW Heinemann L/T (1945)
[1] Strong orange-yellow cloth (variants in brilliant
orange-yellow or deep orange cloth) $40/200

025a: THE WAYWARD BUS Viking NY 1947
[1] 100,000 cc (a&b). Dark reddish-orange cloth
with gold lettering on front and brown lettering on
spine. Blind-stamped bus showing up lighter than
rest of binding $75/250

025b: THE WAYWARD BUS Viking NY 1947
[1] Variants in brown cloth with bus darker; pink-
brown with bus same shade; and emerald green
cloth with top page edge stained red (John Payne) $20/100

> Note: the Book-of-the-Month Club edition
> (600,000 copies so, you will see a lot of
> them) has a dot on the lower back cover. It
> was printed by H. Wolff, while the first was
> printed by Haddon Craftsman. Additionally,
> we had a copy of the first edition in gray
> cloth stamped in brick red with the bus
> blind-stamped. It was not a book club and
> no one we talked to had ever seen another
> copy so bound.

025c: THE WAYWARD BUS Heinemann L/T
(1947) [0] Coarse red cloth (variants are in purple
cloth or blue cloth - see ref.a) $30/150

026a: VANDERBILT CLINIC (Presbyterian
Hospital NY 1947) [0] Wraps. Photographs by
Victor Keppler $650.

027a: THE PEARL Viking NY 1947 [] Narrow
(4to) uncorrected galleys in plain wraps (Joseph the
Provider) $3,500.

027b: THE PEARL Viking NY 1947 [1] 40,000 cc
(b&c). Dustwrapper has photograph of Steinbeck
looking to his left (toward spine) $50/250

027c: THE PEARL Viking NY 1947 [1]
Dustwrapper has photograph of Steinbeck looking
to his right $50/150

027d: THE PEARL Heinemann M/L/T (1948) [1] $50/150

028a: THE FIRST WATCH (Ward Ritchie Press
L.A.) 1947 [2] 60 no cc. Buff wraps with hand-ties.
In envelope $3,500.

029a: A RUSSIAN JOURNAL Viking NY 1948
[1] 28,000 cc (all five bindings). No priority but
ref.a states the rarest of the five is grayish-green
cloth with light grayish-yellow-brown spine $100/250

029b: A RUSSIAN JOURNAL Viking NY 1948
[1] Light bluish-green cloth and moderately yellow
spine (most common) $50/200

029c: A RUSSIAN JOURNAL Heinemann L/M/T
(1949) [1] $50/200

030a: FOREWORD TO "BETWEEN PACIFIC
TIDES" (Privately Printed Stanford) 1948 [] Wraps.
Estimated at 10 copies in Harvard Library Catalog
and at 25 copies by Cohn in a letter to Hersholt $7,500.

THE STEINBECK OMNIBUS see 021e

031a: ON A CALIFORNIA RANCH *Selected
Stories* Bayerischen Sculbuch Verlag 1950 [0]
Text in English $150.

032a: BURNING BRIGHT Viking NY 1950 [1]
15,000 cc $35/175

032b: BURNING BRIGHT Heinemann M/L/T
(1951) [1] $20/100

033a: EAST OF EDEN Viking NY 1952 [] Unrevised galleys (12 1/2"x7 1/2") in plain brown
wraps. Many textual differences $7,500.

033b: EAST OF EDEN Viking NY 1952 [] Proof
in plain wraps laid in dustwrapper $4,500/5,000

033c: EAST OF EDEN Viking NY 1952 [2] 1,500
sgd cc. 750 copies for private distribution. Issued in
glassine dustwrapper and slipcase $1,500/1,750

033d: EAST OF EDEN Viking NY 1952 [1]
110,000 cc. P.281:38 has "bite" for "bight"
(Agathon Books 2/95) $150/600

033e: EAST OF EDEN Heinemann L (1952) [1] $40/200

033f: CHAPTER THIRTY-FOUR FROM THE
NOVEL *EAST OF EDEN* Privately Printed
(Bronxville) 1952 [2] 125 cc. Limp buff wraps with
tipped-in white chipboard between endpapers and
thread ties) $1,000.

034a: THE SHORT NOVELS OF JOHN
STEINBECK Viking NY 1953 [0] 15,000 cc.
Brick red cloth printed in black, top edge yellow,
front edge untrimmed. Includes *Tortilla Flat*, *The
Red Pony*, *Of Mice and Men*, *The Moon Is Down*,
Cannery Row, and *The Pearl* $25/100

034b: THE SHORT NOVELS OF JOHN
STEINBECK Heinemann M/L/T (1954) [1] $25/100

035a: VIVA ZAPATA! Edizioni Filmcritica (Rome
1953) [0] Wraps $300.

035b: VIVA ZAPATA! Viking/Compass NY
(1975) [1] Wraps $150.

036a: SWEET THURSDAY (Viking NY 1954) []
Wraps. Uncorrected galley proofs in blue paper
cover with label (ref.b) $4,500.

036b: SWEET THURSDAY Viking NY 1954 [1] Wraps. Advance review copy sewn and wrapped in published dustwrapper — 750.

036c: SWEET THURSDAY Viking NY 1954 [1] 60,000 cc. Beige cloth, top edge red. (Book Club not printed in red on title page and without printer's name on copyright page. Also seen with top edge unstained and red dot on back, but title page printed in red and with printer's name on copyright page {Isaiah Thomas Books}). Later issue dustwrapper adds blurbs beneath photo of Steinbeck on rear panel (Steven C. Bernard) — $30/150

036d: SWEET THURSDAY Heinemann M/L/T (1954) [1] — $25/125

037a: PIPE DREAM Viking NY 1956 [1] Text and lyrics of the Rogers and Hammerstein musical based on *Sweet Thursday* — $25/125

038a: POSITANO Ente Provinciale per il Turismo-Salerno (Italy 1954) [0] Wraps. First printing in English with date opposite title page (ref.a mistakenly states "1955"). Printed wraps — $500.

038b: POSITANO Ente Provinciale per il Turismo-Salerno (1959) [0] Wraps. Second printing. Pictorial wraps. Date opposite title page — $150.

039a: JOHN STEINBECK ON MATUSON REVELATIONS... Cameron & Kahn NY 1955 [] 8 1/2"x11" broadside (Pepper & Stern) — $200.

040a: UN AMERICAIN A NEW-YORK ET A PARIS Rene Julliard Paris (1956) [2] 30 no cc. Wraps — $600.

040b: UN AMERICAIN A NEW-YORK ET A PARIS Rene Julliard Paris (1956) [0] Wraps — $400.

041a: A LETTER FROM JOHN STEINBECK TO HIS EDITOR ABOUT *The Short Reign of Pippin IV* Viking NY 1957 [] 8 1/2"x11" broadside $200.

042a: THE SHORT REIGN OF PIPPIN IV (Viking NY 1957) [] Unrevised galley proof in spiral bound in blue wraps $1,750.

042b: THE SHORT REIGN OF PIPPIN IV Viking NY 1957 [1] 40,000 cc $25/125

042c: THE SHORT REIGN OF PIPPIN IV Heinemann M/L/T (1957) [] Uncorrected proof in yellow wraps (Dalian Books) $300.

042d: THE SHORT REIGN OF PIPPIN IV Heinemann M/L/T (1957) [1] Blue cloth. (Variant in red cloth. Also noted in red boards lettered in silver on spine {Michael Thompson}) $15/75

043a: ONCE THERE WAS A WAR Viking NY 1958 [1] 10,000 cc. "Published in 1958 by ..." $40/200

043b: ONCE THERE WAS A WAR Heinemann L/M/T (1959) [1] $15/75

044a: LIKE CAPTURED FIREFLIES J. Wilson McKenney (no place) 1959 [] Broadside (10"x14"). 12 cc handset. Article on teachers originally written for November 1955 *CTA Journal* (James M. Dourgarian) $400.

045a: CHRYSANTHEMUMS AND BREAKFAST Suenska Bokforlaget Bonniers 1959 [] Wraps. First separate publication of excerpts from *The Long Valley*, published in English in Sweden (Fine Books 5/92) $200.

046a: THE WINTER OF OUR DISCONTENT Viking NY 1961 [] Spiral bound uncorrected proofs (Joseph The Provider) $3,000.

046b: THE WINTER OF OUR DISCONTENT Viking NY 1961 [2] 500 cc. Blue pictorial dustwrapper and clear cellophane dustwrapper stamped in red "Limited Edition" (ref.a-A2q). Spine stamped in gilt, top page edge yellow $500/750

046c: THE WINTER OF OUR DISCONTENT Viking NY 1961 [1] 15,000 cc. Bright blue cloth, spine stamped in silver top edge blue. (Also noted with gilt lettering and top edges stained yellow {Books of Savage, Md.}; tan cloth {Nelson Bond}) $25/125

046d: THE WINTER OF OUR DISCONTENT Heinemann L/M/T (1961) [1] Uncorrected proof in gray wraps (ref.b) $500.

046e: THE WINTER OF OUR DISCONTENT Heinemann L/M/T (1961) [1] $15/75

047a: MOLLY MORGAN Dramatic Publishing Co. Chicago (1961) [] Wraps. A play in 3 acts. A dramatization by Reginald Lawrence from *The Pastures of Heaven*. Noted in gray-olive and yellow wraps (later issue: slip pasted on copyright page $40.

048a: TRAVELS WITH CHARLEY IN SEARCH OF AMERICA (Viking NY 1962) [1] Unrevised galley proofs in pink wraps and spiral binder (ref.b). Also noted with revised text on leaf 155 pasted in. (Unrevised still accessible.) (Wm. Reese Co.) $3,500.

048b: TRAVELS WITH CHARLEY IN SEARCH OF AMERICA Viking NY (1962) [1] 31,000 cc. Book measures 6" x 8 5/8". (Book Club has small brown square on back cover.) We had a variant that also had a dustwrapper priced at $4.95 and "Published in 1962 by..." on copyright page. But this variant had "Winner of the 1962 Nobel Prize for Literature" on front of dustwrapper and measured 5 3/4" x 8 1/2" and was 1-inch thick (slightly smaller than normal first) $35/175

048c: TRAVELS WITH CHARLEY IN SEARCH OF AMERICA   Heinemann L/M/T (1962) [1] Advance uncorrected proof in green printed wraps $400.

048d: TRAVELS WITH CHARLEY IN SEARCH OF AMERICA Heinemann L/M/T (1962) [1] $25/125

049a: THE PREPARED TEXT OF JOHN STEINBECK'S NOBEL PRIZE ACCEPTANCE SPEECH (December 10, 1962) Viking NY (no date) []   Folio mimeographed sheets printed on rectos only, 4 pages, stapled.   Steinbeck's acceptance speech, differing slightly in punctuation from the published version. This issue has a long, four-paragraph "Biographical and Bibliographical Note" about John Steinbeck not printed in the final published version. This almost certainly precedes the published version and presumably was produced for in-house use and distribution due to inquiries immediately following Steinbeck's Nobel Prize speech given that the published version would have taken some weeks or months to prepare. (Waiting For Godot 2/95) $750.

049b: SPEECH ACCEPTING THE NOBEL PRIZE FOR LITERATURE Viking NY 1962 [2] 3,200 cc. New title. Plain white or cream wraps in printed buff dustwrapper. "For Friends..." $125.

050a: A LETTER FROM JOHN STEINBECK EXPLAINING WHY HE COULD NOT WRITE AN INTRO... (Random House NY 1964) [0] Orange wraps. Separate publication of "introduction" for Ted Patrick's *The Thinking Dog's Man* $1,000.

051a: JOHN EMERY Privately Printed NY (1964) [2] 200 cc. Includes two eulogies (at Emery's Funeral) delivered by Steinbeck and Zachary Scott. Red decorated cloth with leather spine, issued without dustwrapper $750.

052a: A LETTER FROM JOHN STEINBECK
Roxburghe & Zamorano Clubs (S.F.) 1964 [2] 150
cc. Off-white paper wraps. Not for sale. Letter to
one of Steinbeck's teachers at Stanford, written in
the 1920s $500.

053a: AMERICA AND AMERICANS Viking NY
(1966) [] Uncorrected proofs in loose sheets
punched at left, string tied with printed cover sheet
and typed label. Sectional titles are present as typed
slip taped in proper position (Wm. Reese Co. 5/89) $2,500.

053b: AMERICA AND AMERICANS Viking NY
(1966) [1] Half-blue and half-green cloth, spine
reading top to bottom $50/150

053c: AMERICA AND AMERICANS Viking NY
(1966) [1] Spine reading bottom to top $25/75

053d: AMERICA AND AMERICANS   Heine-
mann L (1966) [1] $25/100

054a: JOURNAL OF A NOVEL Viking NY
(1969) [2] 600 cc. "This first edition...is limited to
600 copies." Issued in glassine dustwrapper and
slipcase $200/300

054b: JOURNAL OF A NOVEL Viking NY
(1969) [1] 20,000 cc $15/75

054c: JOURNAL OF A NOVEL Heinemann L
(1970) [1] $10/50

055a: JOHN STEINBECK HIS LANGUAGE
(Grace Hoper Press) Aptos, Ca. 1970 [2] 150 cc.
Cream wraps with deckled edges (A. Covici in
Diane Peterson 2/91). Introduction by James Hart $300.

055b: JOHN STEINBECK HIS LANGUAGE
(Grace Hoper Press) Aptos, Ca. 1970 [] Second
issue in white wraps and trimmed edges $150.

056a: STEINBECK COLLECTION Heron Books
L (1971) [] 16 titles in 13 vols. Illustrated by 10
artists. Gilt decorations on simulated leather
bindings (Authors Of The West 2/91) $250.

057a: STEINBECK A LIFE IN LETTERS Viking
NY (1975) [2] 1,000 no cc. Edited by Elaine
Steinbeck and Robt Wallsten. Includes facsimile of
letter not in trade edition. Issued in slipcase (ref.b) $75/125

057b: STEINBECK A LIFE IN LETTERS Viking
NY (1975) [1] 25,000 cc (ref.b) $15/50

057c: STEINBECK A LIFE IN LETTERS
Heinemann L (1975) [1] (Ref.b) $10/50

058a: THE ACTS OF KING ARTHUR AND HIS
NOBLE KNIGHTS Farrar Straus NY (1976) []
"Uncorrected proof" in printed gray wraps. Textual
differences from published version (ref.b) $600.

058b: THE ACTS OF KING ARTHUR AND HIS
NOBLE KNIGHTS Farrar Straus NY (1976) [1] $15/75

058c: THE ACTS OF KING ARTHUR AND HIS
NOBLE KNIGHTS Heinemann L (1976) [] (ref.b) $15/75

059a: THE COLLECTED POEMS OF AMNESIA
GLASSCOCK Manroot SF 1976 [2] 250 no cc.
Wraps. Title page attributes to Steinbeck but
actually by his wife Carol. First published
pseudonymously in the Monterey Beacon in 1935.
Glassine paper dustwrapper $100.

060a: LOVE POEMS TO GWYN CONGER
STEINBECK (No publisher) Austin 1978 []
Unpublished typescript. 28 love poems with mock-
up of the title page prepared for publication for
members of Steinbeck family but never published
(Macdonnell Rare Books 12/90) $250.

061a: LETTERS TO ELIZABETH Book Club of
California SF 1978 [2] 500 cc. Edited by Florian J.

Shasky and Susan Riggs (ref.b). Issued in
dustwrapper $150/250

062a: FLIGHT Tale Blazer 1979 [] Wraps. First
separate edition $25.

062b: FLIGHT Yolla Bolly Press Covelo, CA
1984 [2] 250 sgd no cc. Afterword by Wallace
Stegner and illustrated by Karin Wikstrum (signed
by them). Issued in slipcase $500/600

063a: THE CHRYSANTHEMUMS Tale Blazer
1979 [] Wraps $25.

064a: A LETTER OF INSPIRATION (Charles and
Ingrid Sacks no place) 1980 [] 100 cc. 4-page
Christmas greeting from the Sacks' reprinting a
Steinbeck letter to the inmates of Connecticut State
Prison in 1938. First separate edition (Diane
Peterson 2/91) $100.

065a: YOUR ONLY WEAPON IS YOUR WORK
(Steinbeck Research Center San Jose 1985) [2] 50
sgd no cc. Signed by editor (we assume). Letter
from Steinbeck to Dennis Murphy. Edited by
Robert DeMott $60.

065b: YOUR ONLY WEAPON IS YOUR WORK
(Steinbeck Research Center San Jose 1985) [2] 450
no cc. Wraps $40.

066a: HOW MR. HOGAN ROBBED A BANK
(Tales For Travellers Napa, Ca. 1986) [0] Single
sheet, map folded to 24 pages. First separate
appearance $25.

067a: CONVERSATIONS WITH JOHN STEIN-
BECK University Press of Mississippi Jacksonville
1988 [] Edited by Thomas Fensch $20/50

067b: CONVERSATIONS WITH JOHN STEIN-
BECK University Press of Mississippi Jacksonville
1988 [] Wraps $25.

068a: THE HARVEST GYPSIES *On the Road to "THE GRAPES OF WRATH"* Heyday Berkeley 1988 [] Wraps only (Chloe's Books). Illustrated with photographs by Dorothy Lange, et al. (Published November 1988 at $7.95) $30.

069a: JOHN STEINBECK ON WRITING Ball State University/Steinbeck Society Muncie, Indiana 1988 [] Stapled wraps. 56 pages. Edited by Tetsumaro Hayashi $25.

070a: WORKING DAYS *The Journals of THE GRAPES OF WRATH* Viking NY 1989 [0] Edited by Robert DeMott. Uncorrected proofs in light blue wraps $75.

070b: WORKING DAYS *The Journals of THE GRAPES OF WRATH* Viking NY 1989 [3] Also states "First Published in 1989..." on copyright page. (Published April 1989 at $18.95) $6/30

071a: BREAKFAST Anchor Acorn Press Petaluma 1990 [2] ?? signed no cc. Wraps. Illustrated and signed by Colleen Dwire Weaver (Dourgarian Book 11/92) $100.

072a: ZAPATA *A Narrative* Yolla Bolly Press (Covelo 1991) [2] 40 sgd (by illustrator) no cc. Illustrated by Karin Wikstrom with an extra signed print. A supplemental text and 7 illustrations colored by hand. This filmscript by Steinbeck has never been published before. (Published at $1,750.) [Note: there were also 27 copies, signed by the artist, in a "portfolio version" reserved for publisher and priced at $1,650 (Joseph The Provider 1/95)] $1,750.

072b: ZAPATA *A Narrative* Yolla Bolly Press Covelo (1991) [2] 190 sgd (by the artist) no cc. "Slipcased Version" bound in buckram. The 187-page text consists of Steinbeck's original biographical narrative of Zapata together with his introduction. Illustrated with 18 woodcuts by Karin

Wikstrom, 7 of which are full-page illustrations, hand printed on German paper and tipped-in. (Published at $650) $650.

072c: ZAPATA *The Little Tiger*   William Heinemann L (1991) [0] First British edition and first trade edition preceded by the Yolla Bolly limited editions 1991. States "First published in US of A 1991" but no statement of UK. Previously unpublished commentary and script for the film (Waverly Books 1/95) $60.

073a: NOVELS AND STORIES, 1932-1937 Library of America (NY 1994) [] Unbound signatures sent out for review prior to publication in lieu of bound proofs or galleys (Ken Lopez 12/94) $75.

073b: NOVELS AND STORIES, 1932-1937 Library of America (NY 1994) [] $10/40

ROBERT STONE

Stone was born in Brooklyn in 1937 (or thereabouts). His first book was considered the finest first novel by an American writer in 1968 by voters for the William Faulkner Award. *Dog Soldier* shared the 1975 National Book Award with Thomas Williams (*The Hair of Harold Roux*).

REFERENCES:

(a) Lopez, Ken, and Chaney, Bev, Jr. ROBERT STONE: A Bibliography, 1960-1992. Hadley, Massachusetts: Numinous Press, 1992.

001a: CHILDREN OF LIGHT Houghton Mifflin B [1966] [] 57 cc. Tall spiral bound proofs. Original title $1,500.

001b: A HALL OF MIRRORS Houghton Mifflin B 1967 [1] 5,000 cc. New title. All copies seen have pages 67-70 tipped in (Bev Chaney). First dustwrapper has Stone holding a coffee cup in photo on back panel (American Dust Co.) not mentioned in ref.a $100/500

001c: A HALL OF MIRRORS Bodley Head L (1968) [1] Reportedly, 1,000 cc $50/250

002a: DOG SOLDIERS Houghton Mifflin B 1974 [1] "Uncorrected Proof" in orange wraps with title page reproduced on front cover $400.

002b: DOG SOLDIERS Houghton Mifflin B 1974
[1] "Uncorrected Proof" in brown wraps with
publisher's letter on front cover $250.

002c: DOG SOLDIERS Houghton Mifflin B 1974
[] Advance reading copy in wraps (Monroe Stahr
5/93) $150.

002d: DOG SOLDIERS Houghton Mifflin B 1974
[1] 5,000 cc (ref.a), 12,000 cc (given to us by
publisher) $30/150

002e: DOG SOLDIERS (Secker & Warburg L
1975) [1] 2,500 cc. "Published in 1975" on
copyright page. Houghton Mifflin printed sheets for
this edition (with its second printing) and for the
Book-of-the-Month Club edition and there is at
least one copy of the English sheets in a Houghton
Mifflin Book Club casing with blindstamp and in
US dustwrapper. Also noted in UK dustwrapper $25/100

003a: A FLAG FOR SUNRISE Knopf NY 1981
[1] "Uncorrected Proof" in tall yellow printed
wraps. "To be published 11/9/81 - 65,000 cc".
Noted in two sizes: 10 1/4" tall and 10 5/8" tall $150.

003b: A FLAG FOR SUNRISE Knopf NY 1981
[1] 65,387 cc $10/50

003c: A FLAG FOR SUNRISE Secker & Warburg
L (1981) [1] Copyright information on next leaf not
on back of title page $15/75

004a: CHILDREN OF LIGHT Deutsch (L 1986)
[] Uncorrected Proof in blue wraps $250.

004b: CHILDREN OF LIGHT Deutsch (L 1986)
[1] 4,500 cc. "First Published in Great Britain By
..." (no date in statement) on copyright page.
Preceded US edition by one week $25/125

004c: CHILDREN OF LIGHT Knopf NY 1986 []
Uncorrected proof in yellow wraps $125.

004d: CHILDREN OF LIGHT   Knopf NY 1986
[1] 39,603 cc. (Published March 1986 at $17.95) $8/40

005a: IMAGES OF WAR | A VIETNAM PRO-
FILE   Addison-Weslet B (1986) [3] Photos by
Julene Fischer, text by Stone.   Issued with
dustwrapper (stores) and without dustwrapper
(subscription) $25/50

006a: SONG OF NAPALM Little Brown B (1988)
[1] Written by Bruce Welgl. Introduction by Stone $10/50

007a: DEEDS OF WAR Thames & Hudson NY
(1989) [1] Vietnam photographs by James
Nachtwey with introduction by Stone $10/50

008a: DAY OF THE LOCUST *A New Introduction*
(Book-of-the-Month Club   no place 1989) [0]
Stapled wraps. Seven-page introduction distributed
with this new edition of Nathaniel West's book $75.

009a: OUTERBRIDGE REACH Ticknor & Fields
NY 1992 [] Advance uncorrected proofs in glossy
pictorial wraps. Reportedly, about 700 copies.
Differs from published book $75.

009a: OUTERBRIDGE REACH Franklin Library
Franklin Center 1992 [2] 3,300 sgd cc in full
leather $200.

009c: OUTERBRIDGE REACH Ticknor & Fields
NY 1992 [2] 300 sgd no cc. Issued in slipcase
without dustwrapper $75/150

009d: OUTERBRIDGE REACH Ticknor & Fields
NY 1992 [3] 52,500 cc. (Published March 1992 at
$21.95) $6/30

009e: OUTERBRIDGE REACH Deutsch (L
1992) [] 3,000 cc $10/50

010a: *"Carefully, he examined his imagined positions ..."* Black Oak Books Berkeley 1992 [] Broadside. 6 1/2" x 13 1/2" (Bev Chaney Jr. 10/94) $40.

011a: HELPING Dim Gray Bar Press NY 1993 [2] 100 sgd no cc. Issued in slipcase. (Published at $200)   200.

REX STOUT

Rex (Todhunter) Stout was born in 1886 in Noblesville, Indiana. He was a precocious child and had read the bible at five and all of Shakespeare by twelve. Stout graduated from high school at sixteen. He attended the University of Kansas but decided college had nothing to teach him. His first writing money ($12) was earned in 1917 for a poem he wrote for *Smart Set*. They apparently never printed it. He served as a Yeoman on Roosevelt's yacht during a stint in the U.S. Navy. He was president of Vanguard Press between 1925 and 1928. In 1959 he won the Mystery Writers of America Grand Master Award.

The bibliography, *Rex Stout: An Annotated Primary and Secondary Bibliography* (edited by Guy M. Townsend, et al, Garland Publishing, New York/ London, 1980), was used for the titles, publishers and dates; but as it did not contain any detailed information on title page and copyright page content, or quantities, it served only as a starting point for this guide.

Although many of the Viking editions were not seen ([]), as far as we know all of the Viking first editions would state "Published in 19--", "Published by Viking in 19--", or, "First Published by Viking in 19--" and later printings would be noted.

The price estimates for the British editions are really "estimates" based on comparable first U.S. prices. Very few have been catalogued. The reason may be that there is little interest on the part of Stout collectors in these editions.

We would like to thank Greg Brumfield for his assistance in preparing this guide.

001a: HOW LIKE A GOD Vanguard NY 1929 [0]
Copies also noted with "Discussion Copy" stamped

on front endpaper and dustwrapper. Used for Vanguard promotional program $250/1,500

001b: HOW LIKE A GOD Morley and Mitchell Kennerley L 1931 [] $150/750

002a: SEED ON THE WIND Vanguard NY 1930 [0] $200/1,000

002b: SEED ON THE WIND Morley and Mitchell Kennerley L 1931 [] $75/400

003a: GOLDEN REMEDY Vanguard NY 1931 [0] (A contract with Morley & Kennerley exists for a British edition but it is not believed to have been published) $100/500

004a: FOREST FIRE Farrar & Rinehart NY (1933) [5] $150/750

004b: FOREST FIRE Faber & Faber L 1934 [] (Black-Bird Books) $75/350

005a: THE PRESIDENT VANISHES Farrar & Rinehart NY 1934 [5] Published anonymously $150/750

006a: FER-DE-LANCE Farrar & Rinehart NY (1934) [5] Haycraft-Queen Cornerstone $600/6,000

006b: FER-DE-LANCE Cassell L 1935 [] $150/1,500

007a: THE LEAGUE OF FRIGHTENED MEN Farrar & Rinehart NY (1935) [5] Haycraft-Queen Cornerstone (added by Queen) $500/5,000

007b: THE LEAGUE OF FRIGHTENED MEN Cassell L 1935 [] $125/1,250

008a: O CARELESS LOVE Farrar & Rinehart NY 1935 [5] $100/600

009a: THE RUBBER BAND Farrar & Rinehart NY (1936) [5] $400/4,000

009b: THE RUBBER BAND Cassell L 1938 [] $125/1,250

009c: TO KILL AGAIN Curl NY 1960 [1] Wraps.
New title. No. 136 $50.

010a: THE RED BOX   Farrar & Rinehart   NY
(1937) [5] $350/3,500

010b: THE RED BOX Cassell L 1937 [] $100/1,000

011a: THE HAND IN THE GLOVE   Farrar &
Rinehart NY (1937) [5] $300/3,000

011b: CRIME ON HER HANDS Collins L 1939 []
New title $100/1,000

011c: THE HAND IN THE GLOVE Hogarth L
1984 [] With introduction by Mort Cadogan and
Patricia Craig $10/40

012a: TOO MANY COOKS   Farrar & Rinehart
NY (1938) [5] $300/3,000

012b: TOO MANY COOKS *American Magazine*
no place 1938 [0] Gold box with printed endpaper
as title page and 36 cards laid in as follows:
"Important" note from Nero Wolfe, "Menu," 34
individual recipe cards. In dustwrapper with rear
flap attached between box and cover $2,000.

012c: TOO MANY COOKS Collins L 1938 [] $75/750

013a: MR. CINDERELLA Farrar & Rinehart NY
(1938) [5] $100/600

013b: MR. CINDERELLA Faber & Faber L (1939)
[] 2,000 cc $50/300

014a: SOME BURIED CAESAR   Farrar &
Rinehart   NY (1939) [5] Condensed version
appeared in *The American Magazine* as "The Red
Bull" $250/2,500

014b: SOME BURIED CAESAR Collins L 1939
[] $60/600

014c: THE RED BULL Dell NY 1945 [] Wraps.
New title $50.

015a: MOUNTAIN CAT Farrar & Rinehart NY
(1939) [5] $100/600

015b: MOUNTAIN CAT Collins L 1940 [] $50/250

016a: DOUBLE FOR DEATH Farrar & Rinehart
NY (1939) [5] $100/600

016b: DOUBLE FOR DEATH Collins L 1940 [] $50/300

017a: OVER MY DEAD BODY Farrar & Rinehart
NY (1940) [5] $200/2,000

017b: OVER MY DEAD BODY Collins L 1940 [] $50/300

018a: WHERE THERE'S A WILL   Farrar &
Rinehart NY (1940) [5] Red cloth printed in black
on spine and front cover $150/1,500

018b: WHERE THERE'S A WILL Collins L 1941
[] $50/250

019a: THE BROKEN VASE   Farrar & Rinehart
NY (1941) [5] $60/600

019b: THE BROKEN VASE Collins L 1942 [] $40/200

020a: ALPHABET HICKS Farrar & Rinehart NY
(1941) [5] $100/600

020b: ALPHABET HICKS Collins L 1942 [] $40/200

020c: THE SOUND OF MURDER Pyramid NY
1965 [] Wraps. New title $40.

021a: BLACK ORCHIDS Farrar & Rinehart NY
(1942) [5] Red cloth printed in black $125/1,250

021b: BLACK ORCHIDS Collins L 1943 [] $50/250

022a: THE   ILLUSTRIOUS   DUNDERHEADS
Knopf NY 1942 [1] Edited by Stout who said it
was actually compiled by Laura Z. Hobson $20/100

023a: WRITERS' WAR BOARD REPORTING
No publisher or place 1943 [] 3 pages, measuring
14 x 8½", stapled together at upper left corner.
Bulletin #1, dated April 13, 1943. Apparently a
flyer sent to an unknown number of writers listing
the board's current projects (The Fine Books Co.
1/95) $400.

024a: NOT QUITE DEAD ENOUGH   Farrar &
Rinehart NY (1944) [5] Brick-red cloth printed in
black. Published price: $2.00 $100/750

024a: THE NERO WOLFE OMNIBUS   World
Cleveland 1944 [] $25/125

025a: RUE MORGUE NO. 1 Creative Age NY
(1946) [0] Edited by Stout and Louis Greenfield $25/125

026a: THE SILENT SPEAKER Viking NY 1946
[1] 25,000 cc. Green cloth with yellow lettering and
red line. (Published October 21, 1946 at $2.50) $60/500

026b: THE SILENT SPEAKER Collins L 1947 [] $30/150

027a: TOO MANY WOMEN Viking NY 1947 [1]
18,000 cc. (Published October 20, 1947 at $2.50) $50/400

027b: TOO MANY WOMEN Collins L 1948 [] $25/125

028a: AND BE A VILLAIN Viking NY 1948 [1]
15,000 cc. Gray cloth printed in red and green.
(Book club dustwrapper is blank on back flap.)
(Published September 27, 1948 at $2.50) $40/250

028b: MORE DEATHS THAN ONE Collins L
1949 [] New title $25/125

029a: THE SECOND CONFESSION Viking NY 1949 [] Wraps. Advance copy bound in dustwrapper (Else Fine Books) $750.

029b: THE SECOND CONFESSION Viking NY 1949 [1] 14,500 cc. Dark greenish cloth printed in yellow. (Published September 6, 1949 at $2.50) $50/300

029c: THE SECOND CONFESSION Collins L 1950 [] $20/100

030a: TROUBLE IN TRIPLICATE Viking NY 1949 [1] 10,000 cc. Yellow cloth printed in red. First book appearances of three novelettes: *Before I Die; Help Wanted, Male;* and *Instead of Evidence.* (Published February 11, 1949 at $2.50) $40/250

030b: TROUBLE IN TRIPLICATE Collins L (1949) [] $20/100

031a: THREE DOORS TO DEATH Viking NY 1950 [1] Green cloth printed in black. First book appearances of three novelettes: *Man Alive, Omit Flowers,* and *Door to Death* $40/250

031b: THREE DOORS TO DEATH Collins L 1950 [] $15/75

032a: IN THE BEST FAMILIES Viking NY 1950 [1] 15,000 cc. Yellow cloth printed in purple. (Published September 29, 1950 at $2.50) $50/300

032b: EVEN IN THE BEST FAMILIES Collins L 1951 [] New title $15/75

033a: CURTAINS FOR THREE Viking NY 1951 [1] 8,500 cc. Gray cloth printed in red and black. First book appearances of three novelettes: *The Gun With Wings, Bullet For One,* and *Disguise For Murder.* (Published February 23, 1951 at $2.50) $40/250

033b: CURTAINS FOR THREE Collins L 1951 [] $15/75

034a: DOOR TO DEATH   Dell   NY   [1951]   [0]
Wraps.   Priced   10¢.   First   separate   edition.
(Copyright 1949) $75.

035a: MURDER BY BOOK   Viking   NY 1951 [1]
14,000 cc. Yellow boards printed in red. (Published
October 12, 1951 at $2.50) $40/250

035b: MURDER BY BOOK Collins L 1952 [] $15/75

036a: TRIPLE JEOPARDY   Viking   NY 1952 [1]
Yellow cloth printed in black. Dustwrapper price:
$2.50. First book appearances of three novelettes:
Home To Roost, *The Cop Killer* and *The Squirt and
the Monkey* $40/200

036b: TRIPLE JEOPARDY Collins L 1952 [] $15/75

037a: PRISONER'S BASE Viking NY 1952 [1]
14,500 cc. Green cloth printed in black on spine and
front cover. (Published October 24, 1952 at $2.50) $30/200

037b: OUT GOES SHE   Collins   L 1953 [] New
title $15/75

038a: THE GOLDEN SPIDERS Viking NY 1953
[1] 12,500 cc. Greenish-gray cloth spine printed in
yellow and patterned boards. (Published October
10, 1953 at $2.50) $30/200

038b: THE GOLDEN SPIDERS Collins L 1954 [] $12/60

039a: THREE MEN OUT   Viking   NY 1954 [1]
Red cloth stamped in black on spine and front
cover. Dustwrappper price: $2.50 $30/175

039b: THREE MEN OUT Collins L 1955 [] $12/60

040a: THE BLACK MOUNTAIN Viking NY
1954 [1] 14,000 cc. Black cloth printed in gold.
(Published October 14, 1954 at $2.75) $35/175

040b: THE BLACK MOUNTAIN Collins L 1955
[] $10/50

041a: FULL HOUSE *A Nero Wolfe Omnibus*
Viking   NY 1955 [1]   7,000 cc. Green boards
printed in red. Includes *The League of Frightened
Men, And be a Villian* and three novelettes: *The
Gun With Wings, Bullet for One* and *Disguise for
Murder*. (Published June 16, 1955 at $3.50) $30/150

042a: BEFORE MIDNIGHT Viking NY 1955 [1]
12,500 cc. Light blue cloth with darker blue
lettering. (Published October 27, 1955 at $2.75) $35/175

042b: BEFORE MIDNIGHT Collins L 1956 [] $10/50

043a: MIGHT AS WELL BE DEAD Viking NY
1956 [1]   12,650 cc. Yellow cloth spine and blue
boards. (Published October 26, 1956 at $2.75) $35/175

043b: MIGHT AS WELL BE DEAD Collins L
1957 [] $10/50

044a: EAT, DRINK, AND BE BURIED Viking
NY 1956 [1] 5,000 cc. Edited by Stout. (Published
October 18, 1956 at $3.50) $30/150

044b: FOR TOMORROW WE DIE MacDonald L
1958 [] New title Three stories deleted $15/75

045a: THREE WITNESSES Viking NY 1956 [1]
Blue-gray cloth with gold lettering. Dustwrapper
price: $2.75. First book appearances of three
novelettes: *The Next Witness, When a Man Murders*
and *Die Like a Dog* $30/150

045b: THREE WITNESSES Collins L 1956 [] $10/50

046a: THREE FOR THE CHAIR Viking NY 1957
[1] Yellow cloth printed in black and blue. First
book appearances of three novelettes: *Too Many
Detectives, A Window for Death* and *Immune to
Murder* $40/200

046b: THREE FOR THE CHAIR Collins L 1958
[] $10/50

047a: IF DEATH EVER SLEPT Viking NY 1957
[1] 12,500 cc. Gray-blue cloth printed in blue; top
edge yellow $25/125

047b: IF DEATH EVER SLEPT Collins L 1958 [] $8/40

048a: ALL ACES Viking NY 1958 [1] Dark red
cloth printed in black. Dustwrapper price: $3.95.
Includes *Some Buried Caesar, Too Many Women*
and three novelettes originally published in *Trouble
in Triplicate* $25/125

049a: AND FOUR TO GO Viking NY 1958 [1]
8,900 cc. Blue cloth printed in red; top page edges
stained red. First book appearances of four
novelettes: *Christmas Party, Easter Parade, Fourth
of July Picnic* and *Murder Is No Joke*. (Published
July 2, 1958 at $2.95 {ref.a showed 2/14/58}) $35/175

049b: CRIME AND AGAIN Collins L 1959 []
New title $12/60

050a: CHAMPAGNE FOR ONE Viking (NY
1958) [0] Final galley proof sheets with publisher's
label (Boston Book Co 1993) $400.

050b: CHAMPAGNE FOR ONE Viking NY 1958
[1] 11,500 cc. Black cloth printed in lavender.
(Published November 24, 1958 at $2.95) $20/125

050c: CHAMPAGNE FOR ONE Collins L 1959 [] $8/40

051a: PLOT IT YOURSELF Viking NY 1959 [1]
10,500 cc. Light green cloth lettered in red on spine
with design on cover. (Published October 30, 1959
at $2.95). $40/200

051b: MURDER IN STYLE Collins L 1960 []
New title $12/60

052a: THREE AT WOLFE'S DOOR Viking NY 1960 [1] Orange cloth stamped in brown; top edge olive. Dustwrapper price: $2.95. First book appearances of three novelettes: *Poison a la Carte, Method Three for Murder* and *The Rodeo Murder* $40/200

052b: THREE AT WOLFE'S DOOR Collins L 1960 [] $10/40

053a: TOO MANY CLIENTS Viking NY 1960 [1] 11,500 cc. Yellow cloth lettered in red on spine; publisher's logo on front. (Published October 28, 1960 at $2.95) $25/125

053b: TOO MANY CLIENTS Collins L 1961 [] $8/40

054a: FIVE OF A KIND Viking NY 1961 [1] Gray cloth (paper?) stamped in dark green. Dustwrapper price: $3.95. Includes *The Rubber Band, In the Best of Families* and three novelettes: *Door to Death, Man Alive* and *Omit Flowers* $25/100

055a: THE FINAL DEDUCTION Viking NY 1961 [1] Red cloth stamped in blue on spine and front cover $20/100

055b: THE FINAL DEDUCTION Collins L 1962 [] $8/40

056a: HOMICIDE TRINITY Viking NY (1962) [1] 9,000 cc. Blue cloth with pink lettering on spine; front blind stamped. Includes the first book appearances of three novelettes: *Eeny Meeny Murder Mo, Death of a Demon* and *Counterfeit for Murder*. (Published April 26, 1962 at $2.95) $30/150

056b: HOMICIDE TRINITY Collins L 1963 [] $10/50

057a: GAMBIT Viking NY (1962) [1] 11,000 cc. Blue cloth stamped in red. (Published October 12, 1962 at $3.50) $25/125

057b: GAMBIT Collins L (1963) [1] $8/40

058a: THE MOTHER HUNT Viking NY (1963)
[1] Gray cloth with pink and blue lettering and
design on spine. Dustwrapper price: $3.50 $20/100

058b: THE MOTHER HUNT Collins L 1964 [] $8/40

059a: TRIO FOR BLUNT INSTRUMENTS Viking
NY (1964) [1] Bright orange cloth lettered on spine
and front in blue and black; top edge black.
Dustwrapper price: $3.50   Includes first book
appearances of three novelettes: *Kill Now, Pay
Later; Murder is Corny;* and *Blood Will Tell* $20/100

059b: TRIO FOR BLUNT INSTRUMENTS
Collins L 1965 [] $8/40

060a: A RIGHT TO DIE Viking NY (1964) [1]
12,000 cc. Blue cloth spine and blue boards lettered
in black on spine and front. (Published October 22,
1964 at $3.50). $20/100

060b: A RIGHT TO DIE Collins L 1965 [] $8/40

061a: ROYAL FLUSH Viking NY (1965) [1]
Light gray cloth stamped in blue on front and spine;
top edge stained dark blue. Dustwrapper price:
$3.95. Includes *Fer-de-Lance* and *Murder by the
Book* and three novelettes: *The Next Witness, When
a Man Murders* and *Die Like a Dog* $25/125

062a: THE DOORBELL RANG Viking NY
(1965) [1] 12,000 cc. Black cloth spine lettered in
red and silver, red patterned boards. Dustwrapper
price: $3.50. (Published October 22, 1964 but
released in 1965) $15/75

062b: THE DOORBELL RANG Collins L (1966)
[1] $8/40

063a: DEATH OF A DOXY Viking NY (1966)
[1] Gray cloth spine with blue lettering $15/75

063b: DEATH OF A DOXY Collins L 1967 [] $7/35

064a: THE FATHER HUNT Viking NY (1968) [1] 17,000 cc. Black cloth spine lettered in white, red boards. Black endpapers. Dustwrapper price: $3.75. (Published May 28, 1968 at $4.50) $15/75

064b: THE FATHER HUNT Collins L 1969 [] $8/40

065a: KINGS FULL OF ACES Viking NY (1969) [1] Red cloth printed in black on spine. Dustwrapper price: $4.50. Includes *Plot it Yourself* and *Too Many Cooks* and three novelettes published in *Triple Jeopardy* $25/125

066a: DEATH OF A DUDE Viking NY (1969) [1] 15,000 cc. Black cloth spine and blue boards. (Published August 20, 1969 at $4.50) $15/75

066b: DEATH OF A DUDE Collins L (1970) [1] $8/40

067a: THREE ACES *A Nero Wolfe Omnibus* Viking NY (1971) [1] Includes *Too Many Clients*, *Might As Well Be Dead*, and *The Final Deduction* $20/100

068a: THREE TRUMPS Viking NY (1973) [1] 3,500 cc. Dark green cloth with gold lettering on spine. Includes *The Black Mountain, If Death Ever Slept* and *Before Midnight*. (Published April 6, 1973 at $6.95) $25/125

069a: PLEASE PASS THE GUILT Viking NY (1973) [1] 15,000 cc. Bright red cloth spine stamped in gilt, black boards and black endpapers. Dustwrapper price: $5.95. "0973" at bottom of front flap. (Published September 24, 1973 at $5.95) $12/60

069b: PLEASE PASS THE GUILT Collins L 1974 [] $7/35

070a: THE NERO WOLFE COOK BOOK Viking NY (1973) [1] 2,500 cc. Green cloth. Stout and others $25/125

070b: THE NERO WOLFE COOK BOOK Penguin (Harmondsworth) 1981 [] Wraps $40.

071a: BAD FOR BUSINESS Hamish Hamilton L 1973 [] First separate edition (was included in *The Second Mystery Book* in 1940) $10/50

071a: TRIPLE DECK *A Nero Wolfe Omnibus* Viking NY (1974) [1] 5,000 cc. Black cloth stamped in gold on spine and dark blue endpapers. Dustwrapper has "0774" at bottom of front flap. Includes *And Be a Villian, The Second Confession* and *In the Best of Families*. (Published May 27, 1974 at $8.95 {ref.a shows 4/5/74}. $12/60

072a: A FAMILY AFFAIR Viking NY (1975) [1] Black cloth spine stamped in silver and blue on spine; blue boards. Dustwrapper price: $5.95. "0975" at bottom of front flap $10/40

072b: A FAMILY AFFAIR Collins L (1976) [1] Proof in red wraps $60.

072c: A FAMILY AFFAIR Collins L (1976) [1] $7/35

073a: THE FIRST REX STOUT OMNIBUS Penguin L 1976 [] $35.

074a: JUSTICE ENDS AT HOME *And Other Stories* Viking NY (1977) [0] Unrevised Proof in dark orange wraps with publication date as 5/77 $50.

074b: JUSTICE ENDS AT HOME *And Other Stories* Viking NY (1977) [1] 14,000 cc. Black cloth spine and dark gray boards. Edited by John McAleer (Published August 25, 1977 at $8.95) $8/40

075a: CORSAGE James Rock Bloomington 1977 [2] 26 ltr cc. Edited by Michael Bourne $450/650

075c: CORSAGE James Rock Bloomington 1977 [2] 250 no. cc $200/350

075d: CORSAGE James Rock Bloomington 1977
[2] 1,500 cc. Wraps $100.

076a: ROYAL DECREE *Conversations With Rex
Stout* Pontes Press Ashton 1983 [2] 1000 sgd no
cc in wraps. Conversations with John McAleer and
signed by him $35.

077a: DEATH TIMES THREE Bantam NY 1985
[] Wraps. Collects *Bitter End, Frame-Up for
Murder* and *Assault on a Brownstone* (Mordida
Books 6/95) $35.

078a: UNDER THE ANDES Penzler NY (1985)
[1] $10/40

078b: UNDER THE ANDES Queen's Council
Pontes Press Ashton, MD 1987 [2] 500 sgd no cc.
Wraps. Signed by John McAleer (Cardinal Books
10/95) $25.

**For those who must have everything, the follow-
ing books by Robert Goldsborough continue Rex
Stout's Nero Wolfe:**

MURDER IN E MINOR Bantam Books NY
(1986) [3] Also states "A Bantam Book | April
1986"

DEATH ON DEADLINE Bantam Books NY
(1987) [3] Also states "A Bantam Book | May
1987"

THE BLOODIED IVY Bantam Books NY (1988)
[3] Also states "A Bantam Book | August 1988"

THE LAST COINCIDENCE Bantam Books NY
(1989) [3] Also states "A Bantam Book |
December 1989"

FADE TO BLACK Bantam Books NY (1990)
[3] Also states "A Bantam Book | November 1990"

SILVER SPIRE   Bantam Books   NY   (1992)   [3]
Also states " A Bantam Book | November 1992"

THE MISSING CHAPTER   Bantam Books   NY
(1994)   [3] Also states "A Bantam Book | January
1994"

ALEXANDER THEROUX

Theroux was born in 1939, the older brother of best-selling author Paul Theroux. He spent some time as a novice in a Trappist monastery before earning a Ph.D. at the University of Virginia (with a dissertation on Beckett). He has taught at Harvard and M.I.T. Known for his ornate style, Dr. Theroux has written essays, short stories, poetry, plays, children's books, and three novels.

We would like to thank Steven Moore for his assistance in the preparation of this guide.

001a: THREE WOGS   Gambit   B   1972   []
"Uncorrected Galley Proofs" in dark orange wraps $600.

001b: THREE WOGS   Gambit B 1972 [1] First
issue dustwrapper: sepia-toned photo and rear flap
text reading, "Trappist monaster in Kentucky"
(Lame Duck Books 9/91) $40/200

001c: THREE WOGS   Chatto & Windus/Wildwood
House (L 1973) [1] $30/150

001d: THREE WOGS Chatto & Windus/Wildwood
House (L 1973) [] Wraps. Wildwood House issued
paper editions simultaneously $40.

001e: THREE WOGS Godine B (1975 [1974]})
[0] Wraps. Contains essay, *Theroux Metaphrastes,*
not in hardcover editions $35.

002a: THEROUX METAPHRASTES (Godine B
1975) [0] Wraps $60.

003a: THE SCHINOCEPHALIC WAIF   Godine
(B 1975) [1] $25/75

004a: THE GREAT WHEADLE TRAGEDY
Godine (B 1975) [1] $20/60

005a: MASTER SNICKUP'S CLOAK Paper Tiger
(Limpsfield, Surrey Sept. 1979) [1] 20,000 cc total
for UK and US editions. Published in September $25/100

005b: MASTER SNICKUP'S CLOAK Harper &
Row   NY   (1979)   [1] Pictorial boards in
dustwrapper. (Also issued in a library binding.)
Noted in dustwrappers with two different prices,
$7.95 and "$7.89" (Waiting For Godot 2/95. {We
assume the library binding is the one priced at
$7.89}). Published in October $25/75

006a: DARCONVILLE'S CAT Doubleday GC
1981 [1] 5,000 cc (a&b). With signed tipped in leaf
(Boston Book Annex 12/88) $50/125

006b: DARCONVILLE'S CAT Doubleday GC
1981 [1] Reportedly the first issue has black
endpapers but we have not seen a copy without
black endpapers $20/100

006c: DARCONVILLE'S CAT Hamish Hamilton
L (1983) [0] US edition with HH's stamp on title
page. Also noted with HH sticker on title page (Ian
McKelvie 5/90) $12/60

007a: THE LANGUAGE OF SAMUEL BECKETT
University of Virginia (Charlottesville) 1968 []
Actually produced in 1981. An authorized facsimile
of the author's doctoral dissertation (Carol Cohen
11/91) $50.

008a: A CHRISTMAS FABLE (Privately printed)
December 1983 [2] 50 no cc $200.

009a: AN ADULTERY Simon & Schuster NY
1987 [] Galley sheets, double spaced, xeroxed with
black cloth spine $125.

009b: AN ADULTERY Simon & Schuster NY
(1987) [] Uncorrected proof in printed green wraps.
Also, blue-gray wraps (Lame Duck Books 9/90);
and blue-green wraps (Lame Duck Books 4/95) $75.

009c: AN ADULTERY Simon & Schuster NY
(1987) [3] Also states "First Edition" $10/50

009d: AN ADULTERY Hamish Hamilton L
(1988) [1] Uncorrected proof in white wraps $75.

009e: AN ADULTERY Hamish Hamilton L
(1988) [1] $10/50

010a: THE LOLLIPOP TROLLOPS *And Other
Poems* Dalkey Archive (Normal, IL 1992) [2] 9
sgd cc (signed by A.T. and Edward Gorey).
Uncorrected proof in red wraps (Boston Book Co.
7/92) $300.

010b: THE LOLLIPOP TROLLOPS *And Other
Poems* Dalkey Archive Press (Normal, IL 1992) []
Uncorrected proof in illustrated red wraps. One of a
small number produced by the author, himself
(Lame Duck Books 12/94) $100.

010c: THE LOLLIPOP TROLLOPS *And Other
Poems* Dalkey Archive Press (Normal, IL 1992)
[2] 100 sgd no cc of which 50 copies were for sale
and 50 copies were hors commerce. Issued in
dustwrapper without slipcase $150/200

010d: THE LOLLIPOP TROLLOPS *And Other
Poems* Dalky Archive Press (Normal, IL 1992) [1]
340 cc. Cloth binding and dustwrapper $25/75

010e: THE LOLLIPOP TROLLOPS *And Other
Poems* Dalkey Archive Press (Normal, IL 1992)
[1] Wraps (Versetility Books 1/95) $20.

011a: HISTORY IS MADE AT NIGHT *And Other
Poems* Aralia Press (West Chester) 1992 [2] 150

cc. Red cloth with printed spine label, issued without dustwrapper. A selection of poems published in *Lollipop Trollops*, originally intended to precede that volume, but due to the exigencies of the letterpress actually published later (James S. Jaffe 11/94) $125.

012a: THE PRIMARY COLORS Henry Holt NY (1994) [] Uncorrected proof in maroon wraps (Waiting For Godot Books 2/95) $60.

012b: THE PRIMARY COLORS Henry Holt NY 1994 [] (Published April 1994 at $17.95) $5/20

013a: WATERGRAPHS Base Canard Boston (1994) [2] 15 sgd Roman numeraled copies. Deluxe issue bound in quarter leather without dustwrapper or slipcase (Lame Duck Books 12/94) $400.

013b: WATERGRAPHS Base Canard Boston (1994) [2] 100 sgd no cc. Bound in linen, issued without dustwrapper or slipcase. (Waiting For Godot says total edition is 116 copies) $125.

PAUL THEROUX

Theroux was born in Medford, Massachusetts, in 1941. He received a B.A. in English from Amherst and taught in Milawi, Uganda, and Singapore before turning to writing full time.

The following bibliographical details are based on "Paul Theroux: A Bibliographical Checklist" compiled by Bev Chaney in the *American Book Collector*, January/February 1983, and updates furnished by Mr. Chaney. The printing quantities were provided by Houghton Mifflin. The *American Book Collector* issue that contains the checklist, which provides more specific information (than this guide) are still available from Mr. Chaney, 73 Croton Avenue, Ossining, New York 10562.

001a: WALDO Houghton Mifflin B 1967 [1] 4,000 cc. Indeterminate number of dustwrappers printed in red vs. white, priority unknown. Also noted in apparent proof state of dustwrapper ¼" taller than published version (Waiting For Godot Books 3/95) $50/250

001b: WALDO Bodley Head L (1968) [1] $40/200

002a: FONG AND THE INDIANS Houghton Mifflin B 1968 [1] 3,500 cc $40/200

002b: FONG AND THE INDIANS Hamilton L (1976) [1] Introduction not in U.S. edition. Binding stamped in both silver and gold, priority unknown but silver noted in clipped dw with new price pasted on, so perhaps later. Also noted with white letters (Hartley Moorhouse); and red cloth with white letters and lacking Hamilton insignia on spine (Maurice Neville) $20/100

003a: GIRLS AT PLAY Houghton Mifflin B 1969
[1] 4,000 cc $30/150

003b: GIRLS AT PLAY Bodley Head L (1969)
[1] $50/250

004a: MURDER IN MOUNT HOLLY Alan Ross
(L 1969) [0] $300/1,500

005a: JUNGLE LOVERS Houghton Mifflin B
1971 [1] 4,500 cc $25/125

005b: JUNGLE LOVERS Bodley Head L (1971)
[1] $25/125

006a: SINNING WITH ANNIE Houghton Mifflin
B 1972 [] Uncorrected Proof in red wraps (Lame
Duck Books 11/94) $350.

006b: SINNING WITH ANNIE Houghton Mifflin
B 1972 [1] 3,500 cc $40/200

006c: SINNING WITH ANNIE Hamilton L
(1975) [1] $40/200

007a: V.S. NAIPAUL: AN INTRODUCTION...
Deutsch (L 1972) [1] $250/1,250

007b: V.S. NAIPAUL: AN INTRODUCTION...
Heinemann Educational Books L 1972 [] Wraps
(David Mayou 6/89) $75.

007c: V.S. NAIPAUL: AN INTRODUCTION...
Africana Press no place or date [] Reportedly
1,000 cc printed in U.S. (not seen) $100/450

007d: V.S. NAIPAUL Holmes/Meier NY 1972 []
Listed in the *Cumulative Book Index* (not seen) $75.

008a: SAINT JACK Houghton Mifflin B 1973 [1]
7,500 cc $20/100

008b: SAINT JACK Bodley Head L (1973) [1] $30/150

009a: THE BLACK HOUSE Houghton Mifflin B 1974 [1] "Uncorrected Proofs" in olive tan wraps (Published September 3, 1974) $200.

009b: THE BLACK HOUSE Houghton Mifflin B 1974 [1] 10,000 cc. Top edges stained brown on some copies, priority unknown $15/75

009c: THE BLACK HOUSE Hamilton L (1974) [1] $15/75

010a: THE GREAT RAILWAY BAZAAR Houghton Mifflin B 1975 [3] 7,500 cc. Binding with "By Rail Through Asia" on spine on all copies of first printing (Bev Chaney, Jr.) $25/125

010b: THE GREAT RAILWAY BAZAAR Hamilton L (1975) [1] Reportedly only 1,000 cc (Nicholas Burrows 1/90) $40/200

011a: THE FAMILY ARSENAL Hamilton L (1976) [1] $15/75

011b: THE FAMILY ARSENAL Houghton Mifflin B 1976 [3] 30,000 cc. Dustwrapper has "0876" on front flap. (Book-of-the-Month Club edition dustwrapper does not have this number. The BOMC book is exactly the same except for square blind stamped on back) $12/60

012a: THE CONSUL'S FILE Hamilton L (1977) [] Uncorrected proofs in yellow wraps (Dalian Books 6/90) $150.

012b: THE CONSUL'S FILE Hamilton L (1977) [1] $15/75

012c: THE CONSUL'S FILE Houghton Mifflin B 1977 [3] 20,000 cc $12/60

013a: PICTURE PALACE Hamilton L (1978) [1] $12/60

013b: PICTURE PALACE   Franklin Library Franklin, Pa. 1978 [2] 8,001 sgd cc. In full leather with introduction by author. Reportedly the true first, but we assume first U.S. $60.

013c: PICTURE PALACE   Houghton Mifflin B 1978 [3] 40,000 cc (c&d). Also states "First Trade Edition." Dustwrapper has silver lettering and black background $12/60

013d: PICTURE PALACE   Houghton Mifflin B 1978 [3] Dustwrapper has black lettering and silver background $10/50

014a: A CHRISTMAS CARD   Houghton Mifflin B 1978 [3] 12,000 cc $15/75

014b: A CHRISTMAS CARD (Weekly Reader B 1978) [] Pictorial boards $30.

014c: A CHRISTMAS CARD Hamilton L (1978) [1] $12/60

015a: THE   OLD   PATAGONIAN   EXPRESS Houghton Mifflin B 1979 [] Uncorrected Proof in green wraps (Bev Chaney, Jr. 6/91) $125.

015b: THE   OLD   PATAGONIAN   EXPRESS Houghton Mifflin B 1979 [3] 60,000 cc $10/50

015c: THE   OLD   PATAGONIAN   EXPRESS Hamilton L (1979) [1] $15/75

016a: Announcement for LONDON SNOW Bev Chaney Croton-on-Hudson, NY 1979 [] Folded and gathered sheets, only two sets pulled   (Bev Chaney 6/91) $150.

016b: Announcement for LONDON SNOW   Bev Chaney Croton-on-Hudson, NY 1979 [2] 100 sgd cc. Folded card $125.

016c: LONDON SNOW   M. Russell (Salisbury 1979) [2] 450 sgd no cc. Glassine dustwrapper. Signed by Theroux and John Lawrence (illustrator). 300 copies for U.S., 150 copies for England $150.

016d: LONDON SNOW Houghton Mifflin B 1980 [] Uncorrected proofs in blue wraps (Bev Chaney, Jr.) $100.

016e: LONDON SNOW Houghton Mifflin B 1980 [3] 9,000 cc $12/60

016f: LONDON SNOW Hamilton L (1980) [1] $12/60

017a: WORLD'S END+ Houghton Mifflin B 1980 [] Uncorrected proofs in green wraps $100.

017b: WORLD'S END+ Houghton Mifflin B 1980 [3] Copy in proof dustwrapper with blank flaps (Waiting For Godot 6/89) $10/75

017c: WORLD'S END+ Houghton Mifflin B 1980 [3] 20,000 cc $10/50

017d: WORLD'S END+   Hamilton   L (1980) [] Uncorrected proofs in green wraps $125.

017e: WORLD'S END+ Hamilton L (1980) [1] $10/50

018a: THE MOSQUITO COAST Hamilton L (1981) [1] $15/75

018b: THE MOSQUITO COAST   Houghton Mifflin B 1981 [3] Wraps. "Advance Reading Copy" in pictorial wraps used for dustwrapper. Approximately 350 copies $75.

018c: THE MOSQUITO COAST   Houghton Mifflin B 1982 [2] 350 sgd no cc. Issued without dustwrapper in slipcase $75/125

018d: THE MOSQUITO COAST   Houghton Mifflin B 1982 [3] 40,000 cc $8/40

018e: THE MOSQUITO COAST Saul Zaentz Co. L (no date [circa 1980s]) [] Film script by Theroux. In window wraps. Not used (Words Etc. 9/89) $200.

019a: THE TURN OF THE YEARS M. Russell (Salisbury 1982) [2] 150 sgd no cc. Theroux's introduction in V.S. Pritchett's book. Signed by both. Issued with tissue dustwrapper $175.

019b: THE TURN OF THE YEARS Random House NY (1982) [2] 500 sgd cc. Issued without dustwrapper in slipcase. Signed only by Pritchett $50/75

020a: THE LONDON EMBASSY Hamilton L (1982) [1] $12/60

020b: THE LONDON EMBASSY Houghton Mifflin B 1983 [] Uncorrected proof in white wraps (Bev Chaney, Jr. 9/89) $100.

020c: THE LONDON EMBASSY Houghton Mifflin B 1983 [3] 22,000 cc. The story "Volunteer Speaker" omitted in U.S. edition $8/40

021a: SAILING THROUGH CHINA M. Russell (Salisbury 1983) [2] 150 sgd no cc. Signed by Theroux and Patrick Procktor (illustrator). Issued in tissue dustwrapper. Reportedly 400 copies in total including U.S. numbered "--/400." [Note: we had a copy numbered "4" and signed by Theroux, then numbered "254" and signed by Proctor] $150.

021b: SAILING THROUGH CHINA M. Russell (Salisbury 1983) [1] "September" stated but actually October $8/40

021c: SAILING THROUGH CHINA Houghton Mifflin B 1984 [2] States 250(?) sgd no cc. 150 copies for U.K. and 250 copies for U.S. but numbered "-/400" [see note in 021a]. Issued in dustwrapper $125/150

021d: SAILING THROUGH CHINA Houghton
Mifflin B 1984 [3] 15,000 cc $10/50

022a: THE KINGDOM BY THE SEA Hamilton L
(1983) [1] $7/35

022b: THE KINGDOM BY THE SEA Houghton
Mifflin B 1983 [] Uncorrected proof in green wraps
(Bev Chaney, Jr. 9/89) $75.

022c: THE KINGDOM BY THE SEA Houghton
Mifflin B 1983 [2] 250 sgd no cc. Issued without
dustwrapper in slipcase $75/125

022d: THE KINGDOM BY THE SEA Houghton
Mifflin B 1983 [3] Signed on tipped in sheet $50/75

022e: THE KINGDOM BY THE SEA Houghton
Mifflin B 1983 [3] 75,000 cc $7/35

023a: DR. SLAUGHTER Hamilton L (1984) []
Uncorrected Proof in printed wraps. The dedication
page reads "Dedication to Come"   (Thomas A.
Goldwasser 5/95) $75.

023b: DR. SLAUGHTER Hamilton L (1984) [1] $8/40

023c: HALF MOON STREET Houghton Mifflin
B 1984 [] New title. Uncorrected proof in gray
wraps with second novel entitled "Buried Alive" vs.
"Doctor DeMarr" (Bev Chaney, Jr. 9/89) $75.

023d: HALF MOON STREET Houghton Mifflin
B 1984 [3] 50,000 cc. Contains two novellas not in
English edition. In trial dustwrapper with flaps and
rear blank (Bert Babcock) $8/75

023e: HALF MOON STREET Houghton Mifflin
B 1984 [3] In regular dustwrapper $8/40

024a: SUNRISE WITH SEAMONSTERS *Travels
and Discoveries* Houghton Mifflin B 1985 [3] Un-

corrected proof in tall printed lime-green wraps
(Waverly Books) | $60.

024b: SUNRISE WITH SEAMONSTERS *Travels
and Discoveries* Houghton Mifflin B 1985 [3] | $6/30

024c: SUNRISE WITH SEAMONSTERS *Travels
and Discoveries* Hamilton L (1985) [1] | $8/40

025a: PATAGONIA REVISITED M. Russell
(Salisbury 1985) [2] 250 sgd no cc. Written with
Bruce Chatwin and signed by both. Issued in tissue
dustwrapper | $250.

025b: PATAGONIA REVISITED M. Russell
(Salisbury 1985) [1] 3,000 cc | $10/50

025c: PATAGONIA REVISITED Houghton
Mifflin B 1986 [1] | $8/40

026a: THE IMPERIAL WAY Houghton Mifflin B
1985 [1] (Published November 19, 1985 at $19.95) | $8/40

026b: THE IMPERIAL WAY Hamilton L 1985
[1] | $8/40

027a: THE SHORTEST DAY OF THE YEAR *A
Christmas Fantasy* Sixth Chamber Press
(Leamington Spa 1986) [2] 26 sgd ltr cc. Issued in
quarter leather without dustwrapper in slipcase | $300/350

027b: THE SHORTEST DAY OF THE YEAR *A
Christmas Fantasy* Sixth Chamber Press
(Leamington Spa 1986) [2] 175 sgd no. cc. In cloth.
Issued without dustwrapper | $225.

028a: O-ZONE Franklin Press Franklin Center
1986 [2] "Limited Signed Edition" in full leather
with special message | $75.

028b: O-ZONE Putnam NY (1986) [3] Uncor-
rected Proof in yellow wraps | $50.

028c: O-ZONE Putnam NY (1986) [3] 65,000 cc.
Also states "First Putnam Edition". (Published
September 20, 1986 at $19.95) $6/30

028d: O-ZONE Hamish Hamilton L (1986) []
Advance uncorrected proof in blue printed wraps $50.

028e: O-ZONE Hamish Hamilton L (1986) [1] $7/35

029a: THE WHITE MAN'S BURDEN Hamish
Hamilton L (1987) [1] $10/50

030a: RIDING THE IRON ROOSTER | BY
TRAIN THROUGH CHINA Hamish Hamilton L
(1988) [] $10/50

030b: RIDING THE IRON ROOSTER | BY
TRAIN THROUGH CHINA Putnam NY 1988 []
Advance reading copy in pictorial wraps $50.

030c: RIDING THE IRON ROOSTER | BY
TRAIN THROUGH CHINA Putnam NY 1988 []
70,000 cc. (Published May 1988 at $21.95) $7/35

031a: MY SECRET HISTORY Hamish Hamilton
L (1989) [2] 150 sgd no cc. Specially bound for
London Limited Editions. In glassine dustwrapper $150.

031b: MY SECRET HISTORY Hamish Hamilton
L (1989) [3] Also states "First Published in Great
Britain 1989 by..." on copyright page $8/40

031c: MY SECRET HISTORY Putnam NY
(1989) [3] Uncorrected proof in white or pale gray
wraps (Ken Lopez 10/89) $50.

031d: MY SECRET HISTORY Putnam NY
(1989) [3] 7,500 cc. (Published June 1989 at
$21.95) $7/35

032a: CHICAGO LOOP Hamish Hamilton L 1990
[] Uncorrected proof in green and white patterned
wraps (Bev Chaney, Jr. 3/90) $60.

032b: CHICAGO LOOP Hamish Hamilton London no date [] Printed wraps. Sample booklet issued in conjunction with W. H. Smith to promote the novel in their shops. The first chapter of the book is reproduced in full (Andrew Hayes 6/95) $20.

032c: CHICAGO LOOP Hamish Hamilton L 1990 [] $7/35

032d: CHICAGO LOOP Random House NY (1991) [] Uncorrected Proof in blue pictorial wraps (Bev Chaney, Jr. 9/91). Also noted in blue-gray coated wraps $40.

032e: CHICAGO LOOP Random House NY (1991) [1] Signed on tipped in sheet $5/50

032f: CHICAGO LOOP Random House NY (1991) [1] (Published March 1991 at $20.00) $5/25

033a: DR. DE MARR Hutchinson (L 1990) [1] Illustrated by Marshall Arisman $10/50

034a: TO THE ENDS OF THE EARTH Random House NY (1991) [] Advance Uncorrected Proof in glossy decorated wraps (Waiting For Godot 2/92). Contains large excerpts from six of his travel books $40.

034b: TO THE ENDS OF THE EARTH Random House NY (1991) [] $5/25

035a: THE HAPPY ISLES OF OCEANIA: *Paddling The Pacific* Putnam NY 1992 [] Uncorrected Proof in blue wraps (Bev Chaney, Jr. 6/92) $40.

035b: THE HAPPY ISLES OF OCEANIA: *Paddling The Pacific* Putnam NY 1992 [] (Published June 1992 at $24.95) $5/25

035c: THE HAPPY ISLES OF OCEANIA *Paddling The Pacific* Hamish Hamilton L (1992)

[] Uncorrected Proof in glossy pictorial wraps (Bev Chaney, Jr. 1/95) $50.

035d: THE HAPPY ISLES OF OCEANIA Hamish Hamilton L (1992) [] $6/30

036a: NOWHERE IS A PLACE *Travels in Patagonia* Sierra Club Books SF (1992) [] 15,000 cc (PW). Written with Bruce Chatwin; photos by Jeff Gnass. Adds 100 photos to *Patagonia Revisited* (1985) and an introduction by Theroux which is a memorial to Chatwin. (Published October 1992 at $25.00) (Bev Chaney, Jr. 1/95) $25/50

037a: MILLROY THE MAGICIAN   Hamish Hamilton L (1993) [] Uncorrected Proof in glossy wraps $50.

037b: MILLROY THE MAGICIAN   Hamish Hamilton L (1993) [] (Waiting For Godot 2/95) $6/30

037c: MILLROY THE MAGICIAN   Random House NY (1994) [] (Published January 1994 at $24.00) $5/25

038a: THE PILLARS OF HERCULES *A Grand Tour of The Mediterranean* Putnam NY 1995 [] (Published October 1995 at $27.50) $

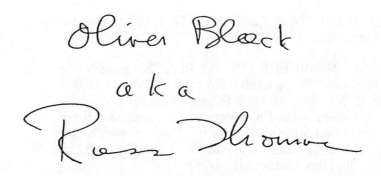

ROSS THOMAS
(1926-1995)

Thomas was born in Oklahoma City in 1926. He graduated from the University of Oklahoma, served during WWII and worked in public relations and consulting through 1966 (the last five years with the U.S. Government).

The following is based on dealer catalogs, private collections, or inventory holdings.

We would like to thank William Holland for bibliographical assistance.

001a: THE COLD WAR SWAP Morrow NY 1966
[0]   Winner of the Edgar Award for Best First
Novel $150/750

001b: SPY IN THE VODKA Hodder & Stoughton
(L 1967) [1] $75/350

002a: THE SEERSUCKER WHIPSAW   Morrow
NY 1967 [0] $100/450

002b: THE SEERSUCKER WHIPSAW Hodder &
Stoughton L 1968 [] $40/200

003a: CAST A YELLOW SHADOW Morrow NY
1967 [0] $50/250

003b: CAST A YELLOW SHADOW Hodder &
Stoughton (L 1968) [1] $25/125

004a: THE SINGAPORE WINK Morrow NY
1969 [0] (Published January 30, 1969 at $5.95) $60/300

004b: THE SINGAPORE WINK Hodder &
Stoughton L 1969 [] $30/150

005a: WARRIORS FOR THE POOR *The Story of
Vista* Morrow NY 1969 [0] Written with William
Cook $30/150

006a: THE BRASS GO-BETWEEN Morrow NY
1969 [0] Written as Oliver Bleeck. "Sociey" p.208:3
(Jeff Klaess), all copies? $60/300

006b: THE BRASS GO-BETWEEN Hodder &
Stoughton (L 1970) [1] Written as Oliver Bleeck $25/125

007a: THE FOOLS IN TOWN ARE ON OUR
SIDE Hodder & Stoughton (L 1970) [] $35/175

007b: THE FOOLS IN TOWN ARE ON OUR
SIDE   Morrow NY 1971 [0]   First issue
dustwrapper with review on back of *The Singapore
Wink* $30/150

007c: THE FOOLS IN TOWN ARE ON OUR
SIDE Morrow NY 1971 [0] Second issue
dustwrapper with reviews of this book (Else Fine
Books 3/93) $30/100

008a: PROTOCOL FOR A KIDNAPPING
Morrow NY 1971 [0] Written as Oliver Bleeck.
First state in red and tan boards (Dunn & Powell
11/92) $40/200

008b: PROTOCOL FOR A KIDNAPPING Hodder
& Stoughton L (1971) [] Written as Oliver Bleeck $25/100

009a: THE BACKUP MEN Morrow NY 1971 [0] $30/150

009b: THE BACKUP MEN   Hodder & Stoughton
L (1971) [] $25/75

010a: THE PROCANE CHRONICLE   Morrow
NY 1972 [0] Written as Oliver Bleeck $40/200

010b: THE THIEF WHO PAINTED SUNLIGHT
Hodder & Stoughton L (1972) [] New title. Written
as Oliver Bleeck $25/125

011a: THE PORKCHOPPERS Morrow NY 1972
[0] Uncorrected Proof in orange printed wraps
(Waiting For Godot Book 2/91) $300.

011b: THE PORKCHOPPERS Morrow NY 1972
[0] $35/175

011c: THE PORKCHOPPERS   Hamish Hamilton
L (1974) [1] $25/75

012a: IF YOU CAN'T BE GOOD Morrow NY
1973 [0] $25/125

012b: IF YOU CAN'T BE GOOD   Hamish
Hamilton L (1974) [1] $25/75

013a: THE HIGHBINDERS Morrow NY 1974 [3]
Written as Oliver Bleeck $30/150

013b: THE HIGHBINDERS Hamish Hamilton L
(1974) [1] Written as Oliver Bleeck $25/75

014a: THE MONEY HARVEST   Morrow   NY
1975 [] Uncorrected Proof in light brown wraps
(Waverly Books 1/92) $150.

014b: THE MONEY HARVEST   Morrow   NY
1975 [3] $25/125

014c: THE MONEY HARVEST Hamish Hamilton
L (1975) [1] $25/75

015a: NO QUESTIONS ASKED   Morrow   NY 1976 [3] Written as Oliver Bleeck $40/200

015b: NO QUESTIONS ASKED Hamish Hamilton L 1976 [] Written as Oliver Bleeck $25/75

016a: YELLOW-DOG CONTRACT Morrow NY 1977 [3] $20/100

016b: YELLOW-DOG CONTRACT   Hamish Hamilton L (1977) [] $15/60

017a: CHINAMAN'S CHANCE Simon & Schuster NY (1978) [3] $20/100

017b: CHINAMAN'S CHANCE Hamish Hamilton L (1978) [1] $15/60

018a: THE EIGHTH DWARF Simon & Schuster NY (1979) [3] $12/60

018b: THE EIGHTH DWARF Hamish Hamilton L (1979) [1] $10/50

019a: THE MORDIDA MAN   Simon & Schuster NY 1981 [3] $12/60

019b: THE MORDIDA MAN Hamish Hamilton L (1981) [1] $10/50

020a: MISSIONARY STEW   Simon & Schuster NY (1983) [] Uncorrected Proof in yellow wraps $75.

020b: MISSIONARY STEW   Simon & Schuster NY (1983) [3] 14,400 cc $10/40

020c: MISSIONARY STEW Hamish Hamilton L (1984) [1] $10/40

021a: BRIARPATCH   Simon & Schuster   NY (1984) [3] Wraps. "Advance Uncorrected Proof" in yellow printed wraps $100.

021b: BRIARPATCH Simon & Schuster NY
(1984) [3] 25,600 cc. Winner of the Edgar Prize for
1985 $10/40

021c: BRIARPATCH Hamish Hamilton L (1985)
[1] $10/40

022a: OUR FAIR CITY Universal Studio
Universal City 1984 [] Wraps. Shooting script for
an episode of the television show *Simon and Simon*
(Pepper & Stern) $125.

023a: OUT ON THE RIM Mysterious Press NY
(1987) [] 150 cc. Uncorrected bound manuscript in
salmon colored printed wraps (Alphabet Books
11/91). Also noted in pink wraps (Beasley Books
8/93) $100.

023b: OUT ON THE RIM Mysterious Press NY
(1987) [3] 3,000 cc. Also states "First Printing
October 1987." Advance Review copy in pictorial
wraps. One dealer listed as "500 copies," but our
experience with books handed out at the ABA
(which this was) is that the publishers do 2,500 to
3,000 copies $40.

023c: OUT ON THE RIM Mysterious Press NY
(1987) [3] 100,000 cc (PW). (Published October 2,
1987 at $17.95) $7/35

023d: OUT ON THE RIM Century Hutchinson L
1988 [] $7/35

024a: BROWN PAPER AND SOME STRING
California Mystery ... Conference San Rafael, CA
1987 [0] Wraps. 2 leaves folded to make 8 pages.
Not sewn or stapled. 400 copies (Fine Books Co.
1/89) $50.

025a: THE FOURTH DURANGO Mysterious
Press NY 1989 [2] 500 sgd no cc. Advance
reading copy with signed plate on inside front
cover. Also noted without signed plate $50.

025b: THE FOURTH DURANGO Mysterious Press NY 1989 [3] Also states "First printing..." P.44 last line "Gear" for "Bear" (Jeff Klaess). All copies? (Published September 18, 1989 at $18.95) $6/30

026a: SPIES, THUMBSUCKERS, ETC. Lord John Press Northridge (1989) [2] 50 sgd no cc. Deluxe edition $200.

026b: SPIES, THUMBSUCKERS, ETC. Lord John Press Northridge (1989) [2] 300 sgd no cc $75.

027a: TWILIGHT AT MAC'S PLACE Mysterious Press NY (1990) [] Uncorrected Proof in beige wraps $75.

027b: TWILIGHT AT MAC'S PLACE Mysterious Press NY (1990) [2] 100 sgd no cc. Issued without dustwrapper in slipcase $75/150

027c: TWILIGHT AT MAC'S PLACE Mysterious Press NY (1990) [3] Also states "First Printing: November 1990" on copyright page $6/30

028a: VOODOO, LTD Mysterious Press NY (1992) [] Advance Reading Copy in pictorial wraps $40.

028b: VOODOO, LTD Mysterious Press NY (1992) [3] Also states "First Printing: October 1992." (Published October 1992 at $19.95) $5/25

029a: AH, TREACHERY! Mysterious Press NY 1994 [] Advance reading copy in pictorial wraps (Waverly Books 12/94) $40.

029b: AH, TREACHERY! Mysterious Press NY 1994 [] (Published November 1994 at $21.95) $

Anne Tyler [signature]

ANNE TYLER

Anne Tyler was born in Minneapolis in 1941. She received her B.A. from Duke and attended Columbia University. She has lived in Baltimore for most of her writing career and has written principally of that city or small Southern towns. She was awarded the Pulitzer Prize for *Breathing Lessons*.

We wish to acknowledge Alfred A. Knopf, Inc., for their co-operation in supplying the quantities printed for their titles.

001a: IF MORNING EVER COMES Knopf NY 1964 [1] 4,000 cc. Dustwrapper price is "$4.95" and has "10/64" on front flap. (Published October 19, 1964.) (Note: there is a later printing dustwrapper that has "10/64" but is priced "$5.95" on front flap and mentions *The Tin Can Tree* and *A Slipping-down Life* on back flap.) $300/1,500

001b: IF MORNING EVER COMES Chatto & Windus L 1965 [0] Front dustwrapper flap has "that" for "than" in quote (James Jaffe 11/84. All copies?) $150/600

002a: THE TIN CAN TREE Knopf NY 1965 [1] Number of copies unknown, estimated at 7,500. (Published January 16, 1965) $200/1,000

002b: THE TIN CAN TREE Macmillan L 1966 [1] $75/300

003a: A SLIPPING-DOWN LIFE Knopf NY 1970 [1] 8,484 cc. (Published March 11, 1970) $75/300

003b: A SLIPPING-DOWN LIFE Severn House (L 1983) [1] "First U.K. Hardcover Edition" $15/75

004a: THE CLOCK WINDER Knopf NY 1972 [1]
7,423 cc. (Published April 24, 1972) ... $200/1,000

004b: THE CLOCK WINDER Chatto & Windus
L 1973 [0] "Published by Chatto & Windus" on
copyright page ... $75/300

005a: CELESTIAL NAVIGATION Knopf NY
1974 [1] 10,273 cc. (Published March 27, 1974) ... $50/250

005b: CELESTIAL NAVIGATION Chatto &
Windus L 1975 [] (Published March 1975) ... $25/125

006a: SEARCHING FOR CALEB Knopf NY
1976 [1] 10,000 cc. (Published January 8, 1976) ... $60/300

006b: SEARCHING FOR CALEB Chatto &
Windus L 1976 [0] (Published May 1976) ... $25/125

007a: EARTHLY POSSESSIONS Knopf NY
1977 [1] 12,500 cc. Noted in two dustwrappers,
glossy stock and course non-glossy paper, priority
unknown (Waiting For Godot). (Published May 25,
1977) ... $50/250

007b: EARTHLY POSSESSIONS Chatto &
Windus L 1977 [0] (Published October 1977) ... $20/100

008a: MORGAN'S PASSING Knopf NY 1980 []
Uncorrected proof in salmon colored wraps
(Waverly Books 6/90) ... $250.

008b: MORGAN'S PASSING Knopf NY 1980 [1]
12,500 cc. (Published March 21, 1980) ... $20/100

008c: MORGAN'S PASSING Chatto & Windus L
1980 [] Folded and gathered sheets of U.S. edition
in proof U.K. dustwrapper (Ken Lopez 2/90) ... $75/150

008d: MORGAN'S PASSING Chatto & Windus L
1980 [0] (Published October 1980) ... $15/75

009a: A VISIT WITH EUDORA WELTY
Pressworks Chicago (1980) [0] Wraps. Reportedly
only 100 copies $200.

010a: DINNER AT THE HOMESICK RES-
TAURANT Knopf NY 1982 [] Uncorrected proofs
in off-white or cream, colored wraps. Also noted in
tan wraps (Jason Smith 9/94) $175.

010b: DINNER AT THE HOMESICK RES-
TAURANT Knopf NY 1982 [1] 20,000 cc.
(Published March 25, 1982 at $13.50) $15/85

010c: DINNER AT THE HOMESICK RES-
TAURANT Chatto & Windus L 1982 [0]
(Published September 1982) $12/60

011a: BEST AMERICAN SHORT STORIES
Houghton Mifflin B 1983 [ ] 6,000 cc. Edited by
Tyler $15/75

011b: BEST AMERICAN SHORT STORIES
Houghton Mifflin B 1983 [] 14,000 cc. Wraps $25.

012a: THE ACCIDENTAL TOURIST Knopf NY
1985 [] Uncorrected proof in cream wraps, first
state (Ken Lopez) $175.

012b: THE ACCIDENTAL TOURIST Knopf NY
1985 [] Uncorrected proof in red wraps, second
issue (Ken Lopez) $125.

012c: THE ACCIDENTAL TOURIST Knopf NY
1985 [1] With signed tipped in page. Reportedly
850 copies (Bev Chaney 11/90); about 700 copies
(Ken Lopez 3/92) $125/150

012d: THE ACCIDENTAL TOURIST Knopf NY
1985 [1] 75,000 cc. (Published September 11, 1985
at $16.95) $12/60

012e: THE ACCIDENTAL TOURIST Chatto &
Windus/ Hogarth L (1985) [] Uncorrected proof in

reddish brown on white wraps printed in black. Photo offset of typescript in oversize "Proof Only" dustwrapper priced £9.95, although proof had probable price at £8.95 (Steven Temple 6/92) $75/150

012f: THE ACCIDENTAL TOURIST Chatto & Windus L (1985) [1] "Published in 1985 by ..." $12/60

013a: BREATHING LESSONS Knopf NY 1988 [] Spiral bound sheets submitted to Book-of-the-Month Club prior to proof. Bound in card stock cover (Ken Lopez 6/89) $300.

013b: BREATHING LESSONS Knopf NY 1988 [] Uncorrected proof in gray wraps (Waverly 11/88) $100.

013c: BREATHING LESSONS Knopf NY 1988 [] Uncorrected proof, signed on tipped in sheet (Bookfinders 9/92). Issued in publisher's folding cardboard box (Gordon Beckhorn 10/94) $125/150

013d: BREATHING LESSONS Franklin Library Franklin Center 1988 [2] "Signed Limited Edition" with special message and illustrated. Estimated at 3,000 cc (Ken Lopez 10/92) which would seem low to us $125.

013e: BREATHING LESSONS Knopf NY 1988 [1] 175,000 cc (PW) (proof stated there would be 150,000 copies). Awarded the Pulitzer Prize. (Published September 1988 at $18.95) $8/40

013f: BREATHING LESSONS Chatto & Windus L (1989) [ ] $8/40

014a: FOUR COMPLETE NOVELS Avenel NY 1990 [] Collects *Dinner At The Homesick Restaurant, If Morning Ever Comes, Morgan's Passing,* and *The Tin Can Tree* (Revere Books 2/93) $25/50

015a: SAINT MAYBE Knopf NY 1991 [] Uncorrected Proof in cream colored wraps. Also noted in buff colored wraps. Same? (Monroe Stahr Books 5/95) $100.

015b: SAINT MAYBE Franklin Library Franklin Center 1991 [2] Sgd ltd edition in full leather, with special introduction by Tyler. Perhaps as "few" as 7,500 cc (Waiting For Godot Books 2/95) $100.

015c: SAINT MAYBE Knopf NY 1991 [1] 500 copies estimated (Ken Lopez 1/92). Signed on tipped in leaf $50/75

015d: SAINT MAYBE Knopf NY 1991 [1] 250,000 cc (PW). (Published September 1991 at $22.00) $6/30

015e: SAINT MAYBE Chatto & Windus L 1991 [] $7/35

016a: A NEW COLLECTION Wing Books NY (1991) []   First collected edition of *Accidental Tourist*, *Breathing Lessons* and *Searching for Caleb* (Revere Books 8/93) $15/30

017a: YOUR PLACE IS EMPTY Wm. Ewert Concord 1992 [2] 40 sgd no cc. Handbound in boards; glassine dustwrapper $350.

017b: YOUR PLACE IS EMPTY Wm. Ewert Concord 1992 [2] 60 sgd no cc in plain white wraps and stiff blue dustwrapper with title stamped in gold. (Published at $135) $150/200

018a: TUMBLE TOWER Orchard Books NY (1993) [1] Illustrated by Mitra Modarressi, the author's daughter $6/30

019a: LADDER OF YEARS Knopf NY 1995 [] Uncorrected Proof in pale yellow printed wraps (Waverly Books 4/95) $100.

019b: LADDER OF YEARS Knopf NY 1995 []
Advance Reading Copy in pictorial wraps. "This
edition reproduces what was to have been dust
jacket art but which has since been changed" (Ken
Lopez 4/95) $60.

019c: LADDER OF YEARS Knopf NY 1995 [1]
Signed tipped in leaf (in trade edition) $50/75

019d: LADDER OF YEARS Knopf NY 1995 [1]
300,000 cc (Waverly Books 4/95). (Published May
1995 at $24.00) $5/25

019e: LADDER OF YEARS Chatto & Windus L
1995 [] $7/35

ALICE WALKER

Alice Walker was born in 1944 in Georgia. She graduated from Sarah Lawrence College in 1965 and taught at Jackson State, Wellesley and the University of Massachusetts, among others. She won a Pulitzer Prize for her book *The Color Purple*.

REFERENCES:

(a) FIRST PRINTINGS OF AMERICAN AUTHORS. Volume 2. Detroit: Gale Research Co. (1978). (Used through item 007a unless otherwise noted.)

(b) Inventory, private collections, and/or dealer catalogs. (Used for balance of entries.)

001a: ONCE Harcourt, Brace & World NY (1968) [1] $200/1,000

001b: ONCE Women's Press L 1986 [] Wraps $60.

002a: THE THIRD LIFE OF GRANGE COPE-LAND Harcourt NY (1970) [1] (Published August 5, 1970 at $5.95) $75/350

002b: THE THIRD LIFE OF GRANGE COPE-LAND (Women's Press L 1985) [] (Nicholas and Helen Burrows 1/95) $10/50

003a: FIVE POEMS Broadside Press Detroit 1972 [] 500 cc. One leaf folded to make four pages (ref.b) $75.

004a: REVOLUTIONARY PETUNIAS Harcourt NY (1973) [1] $100/500

004b: REVOLUTIONARY PETUNIAS Harcourt NY (1973) [1] Wraps. Simutaneous issue $60.

004c: REVOLUTIONARY PETUNIAS Women's Press (L 1984) [] Wraps $40.

005a: IN LOVE & TROUBLE *Stories for Black Women* Harcourt NY (1973) [4] $100/500

005b: IN LOVE & TROUBLE *Stories for Black Women* Women's Press (L 1984) [] $10/40

006a: LANGSTON HUGHES, AMERICAN POET Crowell NY (1974) [3] "1" on copyright page. Pictorial boards in dustwrapper $250/850

006b: LANGSTON HUGHES, AMERICAN POET Crowell NY (1974) [3] Red cloth in dustwrapper. "1" on copyright page (ref.b) $250/850

006c: LANGSTON HUGHES, AMERICAN POET Crowell NY (1974) [3] Wraps. "1" on copyright page (ref.b) $100.

007a: MERIDIAN Harcourt NY (1976) [4] (Published at $7.95, later $12.95) $60/300

007b: MERIDIAN Deutsch (L 1976) [1] $25/125

008a: ZORA NEALE HURSTON *A Literary Biography* University of Illinois Urbana (1977) [0] Written by Robert Hemenway with foreword by Alice Walker $25/75

009a: GOOD NIGHT WILLIE LEE.... Dial NY (1979) [] Uncorrected Proof in yellow wraps with black spine strip. Estimated at 15 copies (Bev Chaney, Jr. 9/91) $950.

009b: GOOD NIGHT WILLIE LEE... Dial NY (1979) [1] $100/450

009c: GOOD NIGHT WILLIE LEE... Dial NY (1979) [1] Wraps. Simutaneous issue $75.

009d: GOOD NIGHT WILLIE LEE... Women's Press (L 1987) [1] Wraps $35.

010a: I LOVE MYSELF WHEN I AM LAUGHING Feminist Press NY 1979 [] Wraps. A Zora Neale Hurston Reader edited by Walker $50.

011a: YOU CAN'T KEEP A GOOD WOMAN DOWN Harcourt NY (1981) [4] $60/300

012a: THE COLOR PURPLE Harcourt NY (1982) [] Uncorrected proof in blue wraps $1,500.

012b: THE COLOR PURPLE Harcourt NY (1982) [4] 10,000 cc. Winner of the Pulitzer Prize for 1983. First printing dustwrapper has one address on rear flap, later printings have two (Joel Sattler) $150/750

012c: THE COLOR PURPLE Harcourt NY (1982) [4] Wraps. Issued simultaneously (Steven Bernard 3/90) $60.

012d: THE COLOR PURPLE Women's Press (L 1983) [] Wraps (Bert Babcock) $40.

012e: WATCH FOR ME IN THE SUNSET or THE COLOR PURPLE Warner Burbank 1984 [] 98-page draft of screenplay in wraps (Pepper & Stern 7/91) $150.

012f: THE COLOR PURPLE (Women's Press L 1986) [1] "This hardcover edition published 1986" on copyright page $15/75

012g: THE COLOR PURPLE Harcourt San Diego 1992 [] 10th Anniversary edition with a new preface $10/40

013a: IN SEARCH OF OUR MOTHERS' GARDENS   Harcourt Brace   NY (1983) [] Uncorrected proof in blue wraps $125.

013b: IN SEARCH OF OUR MOTHERS' GARDENS Harcourt Brace NY (1983) [4] $15/75

013c: IN SEARCH OF OUR MOTHERS' GARDENS Women's Press (L 1984) [1] $10/50

014a: ON SIGHT Walker Art Center | Tooth Paste Press Minn. 1983 [2] 90 sgd no cc. Broadside $250.

015a: "While love is unfashionable..." (first line) Moe's Books (Berkeley) 1984 [0] Broadside issued as a New Year's Greeting $75.

016a: HORSES MAKE A LANDSCAPE LOOK MORE BEAUTIFUL Harcourt Brace San Diego (1984) [3] Uncorrected page proof in blue printed wraps $150.

016b: HORSES MAKE A LANDSCAPE LOOK MORE BEAUTIFUL Harcourt Brace San Diego (1984) [3] Also states "First Edition ABCDE" $15/75

016c: HORSES MAKE A LANDSCAPE LOOK MORE BEAUTIFUL Women's Press (L 1985) [1] Wraps $35.

017a: TO HELL WITH DYING Harcourt Brace San Diego (1988) [] Advance copy. Unbound signatures laid into dustwrapper (Ken Lopez 5/95) $200.

017b: TO HELL WITH DYING Harcourt Brace San Diego (1988) [3] Illustrated by Catherine Deeter. Two states of dustwrapper noted: one with a price of $13.95, and the other without a price. (Published April 1988 at $13.95) $12/60

018a: LIVING BY THE WORD: *Selected Writings 1973-1987* Harcourt Brace San Diego (1988) [3]

Advance copy consisting of folded and gathered sheets in dustwrapper (Alice Robbins 7/92) $125.

018b: LIVING BY THE WORD: *Selected Writings 1973-1987* Harcourt Brace San Diego (1988) [3] Also states "First Edition ABCDE" on copyright page. Uncorrected proof in blue printed wraps $100.

018c: LIVING BY THE WORD: *Selected Writings 1973-1987* Harcourt Brace San Diego (1988) [3] Also states "First Edition ABCDE" on copyright page. (Published May 1988 at $15.95) $7/35

019a: FROM ALICE WALKER Black Oak Books Berkeley 1988 [] Illustrated Broadside, 8½ x 14". An extract from *Living by the Word* (Waverly Books 2/95) $60.

020a: THE TEMPLE OF MY FAMILIAR Harcourt Brace San Diego (1989) [] Advance reading copy in pictorial wraps with erratum sheet restoring missing line from p.375 (Bert Babcock 6/89) $75.

020b: THE TEMPLE OF MY FAMILIAR Harcourt Brace San Diego (1989) [2] 500 sgd no cc. Issued without dustwrapper in slipcase $100/150

020c: THE TEMPLE OF MY FAMILIAR Harcourt Brace San Diego (1989) [3] Also states "First Edition" on copyright page. (Published May 1989 at $19.95) $7/35

020d: THE TEMPLE OF MY FAMILIAR (Women's Press L 1989) [1] $7/35

021a: THIS IS MY CENTURY *New & Collected Poems* University of Georgia Athens 1989 [] (Bev Chaney 9/89) $10/50

022a: HER BLUE BODY EVERYTHING WE KNOW *Earthling Poems 1965-1990 Complete*

Harcourt Brace San Diego (1991) [] Uncorrected Proof in blue wraps $100.

022b: HER BLUE BODY EVERYTHING WE KNOW *Earthling Poems 1965-1990 Complete* Harcourt Brace San Diego (1991) [2] 111 sgd no cc. Issued in slipcase $300/350

022c: HER BLUE BODY EVERYTHING WE KNOW *Earthling Poems 1965-1990 Complete* Harcourt Brace San Diego (1991) [3] Also states "First Edition" on copyright page. (Published April 1991 at $22.95) $6/30

023a: FINDING THE GREEN STONE Harcourt Brace San Diego (1991) [] Proof consisting of unbound sheets laid into a finished dustwrapper (Waverly Books 1/92) $75/125

023b: FINDING THE GREEN STONE Harcourt Brace San Diego (1991) [3] Also states "First Edition" on copyright page. Illustrated by Catherine Deeter $6/30

024a: PETUNIAS (Cowell Press no place 1991) [] Wraps. Excerpt from *You Can't Keep A Good Woman Down*. Reportedly, only four copies made (Ken Lopez 12/91) $400.

025a: POSSESSING THE SECRET OF JOY Harcourt Brace San Diego (1992) [] Photocopied sheets of the *edited* manuscript, 8½ x 11". Cover note by Deborah Warren, Director of Sales at HBJ, indicating that this state precedes the bound galleys by four weeks. Numerous changes evident in Walker's hand, including her responses to a copy editor's questions and marks (in one case she notes that she has *deliberately* run two words together, *etc.*). Pages 178-179 of the sheets are a note "To the Reader" and are present in two quite different states, one of which reproduces numerous holographic changes and comments of Walker's. (Ken Lopez 5/95) $150.

025b: POSSESSING THE SECRET OF JOY
Harcourt Brace   San Diego   1992   [] Wraps.
Uncorrected Proof in yellow wraps (gold wraps
{Waverly Books 6/92}; pumpkin wraps {Gordon
Beckhorn 10/93}) $125.

025c: POSSESSING THE SECRET OF JOY
Harcourt Brace San Diego 1992 [2] 250 sgd no cc $150/200

025d: POSSESSING THE SECRET OF JOY
Harcourt Brace   San Diego (1992) []   (Published
June 1992 at $19.95) $5/25

025e: POSSESSING THE SECRET OF JOY
Jonathan Cape   L   (1992)   [1] Proof in glossy
pictorial wraps $60.

025f: POSSESSING THE SECRET OF JOY
Jonathan Cape L (1992) [1] (Alice Robbins 11/94) $7/35

026a: EVERYDAY   USE,   FOR   YOUR
GRANDMAMA   Perfection Learning Center
Logan, Iowa 1992 [] First separate appearance $20.

027a: WARRIOR MARKS *Female Genital
Mutilation And The Sexual Binding Of Women*
Harcourt Brace   San Diego   1993   [] Written with
Pratibha Parmar. (Published November 1993 at
$24.95) $5/25

028a: EVERYDAY USE Rutgers University Press
New Brunswick, NJ 1994 [] (Published at $30) $

028b. EVERYDAY USE Rutgers University Press
New Brunswick, NJ 1994 [] Wraps. (Simultaneous
issue. Published at $8) $

Robt Penn Warren

ROBERT PENN WARREN
(1905-1989)

Warren was born in Guthrie, Kentucky. He graduated from Vanderbilt, received a Masters degree from the University of California, Berkeley, and attended Yale and Oxford, the latter as a Rhodes Scholar. He was a member of both the "Fugitives" and the "Agrarians" and was the co-founding editor of *The Fugitive* in the 1920s and founding editor of *Southern Review* (1935-42), magazines which were major influences.

He taught at numerous universities, and received many awards, including three Pulitzer Prizes, two for poetry and one for fiction. Warren is considered by many to be one of the best poets of this century, although much more acclaim seems to be given to his novels, critical studies and social comment. He was the first American Poet Laureate.

(a) Grimshaw, James A., Jr. ROBERT PENN WARREN *A Descriptive Bibliography 1922-1979*. Charlottesville: University Press of Virginia (1981).

(b) Huff, Mary Nance. ROBERT PENN WARREN *A Bibliography*. New York: David Lewis, 1968.

(c) Dealer catalog entries, inventory or *Books-In-Print*.

001a: JOHN BROWN *The Making of A Martyr* Payson & Clarke Ltd. NY 1929 [0] Approximately 500 cc $300/1,500

002a: THIRTY-SIX POEMS Alcestis Press NY 1935 [2] 20 sgd no cc (numbers "I" to "XX"). Wraps. Printed on Duca Di Dudena paper. Clear wax paper dustwrapper $2,500.

002b: THIRTY-SIX POEMS   Alcestis Press   NY 1935   [2] 135 sgd no cc (numbered "1" to "135"). Wraps. Printed on Strathmore permanent all-rag paper. Clear wax paper dustwrapper. (Also 10 "out-of-series" copies for review) $1,750.

003a: AN   APPROACH   TO   LITERATURE Louisana State University   Baton Rouge 1936 [0] Analyses and discussions by Cleanth Brooks, John Purser and Warren (textbook) $75/300

003b: NOTES   ON   AN   APPROACH   TO LITERATURE Prentice Hall NJ 1965 [] New title. 32 pages in stapled wraps (Waiting For Godot 6/80) $60.

004a: A SOUTHERN HARVEST *Short Stories By Southern Writers*   Houghton Mifflin   B 1937 [0] 2,500 cc. Edited by Warren $60/300

005a: UNDERSTANDING POETRY   Lousiana State University/Holt NY (1938) [0] With Cleanth Brooks $75/250

006a: NIGHT RIDER Houghton Mifflin   B 1939 [0] 5,000 cc. Gray cloth with maroon lettering on front and spine $150/750

006b: NIGHT RIDER   Eyre & Spottiswoode   L (1940) [1] $60/300

007a: ELEVEN POEMS ON THE SAME THEME New Directions Norfolk, Conn. (1942) [0] Gray boards and dustwrapper $60/300

007b: ELEVEN POEMS ON THE SAME THEME New Directions   Norfolk, Conn. (1942) [0] Wraps in dustwrapper $25/100

008a: UNDERSTANDING FICTION   Louisana State University/Crofts Baton Rouge/NY   (1943) [0] With Cleanth Brooks. Textbook. No dustwrapper noted in ref.a but reportedly issued in glassine dustwrapper. (Published January 1943) $150.

009a: STATEMENT OF ASHBY WYNDHAM
University Press   Sewanee, Tennessee   1943   []
Offprint from *Sewanee Review*   (H.E. Turlington
10/90) $300.

010a: AT HEAVEN'S GATE Harcourt, Brace NY
(1943) [1] 5,000 cc. Light blue cloth (assumed first
binding). (Published August 1943) $75/400

010b: AT HEAVEN'S GATE Harcourt, Brace NY
(1943) [1] Green cloth $50/300

010c: AT HEAVEN'S GATE Eyre & Spottiswoode
L (1946) [1] $40/200

011a: SELECTED POEMS 1923-1943   Harcourt,
Brace NY (1944) [1] 1,500 cc $75/350

011b: SELECTED POEMS 1923-1943   The Fortune Press L (1952) [0] (Ref.a shows 1952, ref.b
had 1951. We had a copy listing *All The King's
Men* but not *The Circus In The Attic*, so it may have
been done as early as 1946) $50/250

012a: ALL THE KING'S MEN Harcourt, Brace
NY (1946) [1] 15,000 cc. Dark red (maroon) cloth,
spine lettered in gilt. Pulitzer Prize for Fiction in
1947. Dustwrapper back panel has "What Sinclair
Lewis says ..." Later dustwrappers moved Lewis's
statement to the back flap, and had six other reviews
on back panel under heading "First Reviews of *All
The King's Men*" $300/1,500

012b: ALL THE KING'S MEN   Eyre & Spottiswoode L (1948) [1] Omits Cass Mastern story
and makes other revisions. Dustwrapper in blue and
white $60/300

012c: ALL THE KING'S MEN   Eyre & Spottiswoode L (1948) [1] In red dustwrapper with
English reviews (Maurice Neville) $60/250

012d: ALL THE KING'S MEN   Modern Library
NY (1953) [1] 7,500 cc. New introduction by
Warren $15/75

012e: ALL THE KING'S MEN Time NY (1963)
[0] 65,000 cc. Wraps. New introduction by Warren.
One "x" on last page $35.

012f: ALL THE KING'S MEN Franklin Library
Franklin Ctr 1977 [2] "Signed Limited Edition" in
full leather with Special Message. (First Franklin
signed book) $125.

012g: ALL THE KING'S MEN Limited Editions
Club (NY 1989) [2] 600 sgd no cc, in two volumes.
Signed by Warren and the artist, Hank O'Neal
(photogravures). New introduction by the author.
Issued in slipcase $800/1,000

013a: BLACKBERRY WINTER   Cummington
Press (Cummington MA) 1946 [2] 50 sgd no cc
(numbered in small Roman numerals 1-50). In clear
wax paper and plain white (unprinted) dustwrapper.
Signed by author and illustrator (Wightman
Williams) $2,250/2,500

013b: BLACKBERRY WINTER   Cummington
Press (Cummington MA) 1946 [2] 280 no. cc
(numbered 1-280). Issued in clear wax paper
dustwrapper and plain white paper dustwrapper
(unprinted) $1,000/1,250

014a: U.S. LIBRARY OF CONGRESS QUAR-
TERLY JOURNAL...   Library of Congress
Washington, DC 1945 [0] Wraps. Current acqui-
sitions for 1944-1945. Edited by Warren $75.

015a: THE RIME OF THE ANCIENT MARINER
Reynal & Hitchcock NY (1946) [0] Illustrated by
Alexander Calder. Includes "A Poem of Pure
Imagination." (58 pages) $40/250

016a: THE CIRCUS IN THE ATTIC   Harcourt, Brace NY (1947) [1] 3,500 cc $60/300

016b: THE CIRCUS IN THE ATTIC   Eyre & Spottiswoode L (1952) [1] $35/175

017a: MODERN RHETORIC Harcourt NY (1949) [1] 9,294 cc. The first has an "A" on copyright page. Written with Cleanth Brooks. No dustwrapper noted $100.

018a: FUNDAMENTALS OF GOOD WRITING Harcourt NY (1950) [1] With Cleanth Brooks $50/200

018b: FUNDAMENTALS OF GOOD WRITING Dennis Dobson L 1952 [] (Alphabet Books 3/89) $15/75

019a: WORLD ENOUGH AND TIME   Random House NY (1950) [2] Unknown quantity. Special limited edition for booksellers. Issued in clear plastic wrap. Numbered, but no total limitation stated $100/125

019b: WORLD ENOUGH AND TIME   Random House NY (1950) [1] 37,000 cc. (Published June 20, 1950) $15/75

019c: WORLD ENOUGH AND TIME   Random House   NY [1950] [2] 1,000 sgd cc. "Kentucky Edition." No publication date but Ref.a notes copies signed in October 1950. Assume issued after trade edition. Issued in dustwrapper (Waiting For Godot 11/89) $200/250

019d: WORLD ENOUGH AND TIME   Eyre & Spottiswoode L 1951 [0] $15/75

020a: WILLIAM FAULKNER AND HIS SOUTH University of Virginia (Charlottesville) 1951 [0] 15 pages (8 stapled mimeographed sheets) (Henry Turlington 11/88). Lecture only partially reprinted in *Selected Essays*. (Also noted as 4 mimeo sheets?) $350.

021a: BROTHER TO DRAGONS... Random
House (NY 1953) [1] 4,975 cc $20/100

021b: BROTHER TO DRAGONS... Eyre &
Spottiswoode (L no date) [0] (Published in 1954) $15/75

021c: BROTHER TO DRAGONS... Random
House NY (1967) [] Unrevised proof in red wraps,
with label on front wrapper, of the revised edition
(H.E. Turlington 10/95) $75.

021d: BROTHER TO DRAGONS... Random
House NY (1967) [] Trade of revised edition $5/25

022a: AN ANTHOLOGY OF STORIES...
Louisana State University Baton Rouge (1953) [0]
2,923 cc. Edited by Warren and Cleanth Brooks $50/150

023a: SHORT STORY MASTERPIECES Dell
NY (1954) [] 357,933 cc. Wraps. Edited by Warren
and Albert Erskine. "First Edition" No. F16 $50.

024a: BAND OF ANGELS Random House NY
(1955) [1] 25,000 cc $15/75

024b: BAND OF ANGELS Secker & Warburg L
1956 [0] $12/60

025a: SIX CENTURIES OF GREAT POETRY
Dell First Edition (NY 1955) [] 200,000 cc. Wraps.
Edited by Warren and Albert Erskine. No. FE69 $40.

026a: SEGREGATION... Random House NY
(1956) [1] 4,500 cc $20/100

026b: SEGREGATION... Eyre & Spottiswoode L
1957 [1] $15/75

027a: TO A LITTLE GIRL... (Jane Doggett no
place 1956) [0] Approximately 175 cc. Issued
without dustwrapper $2,500.

028a: A NEW SOUTHERN HARVEST *An Anthology* Bantam Books NY (1957) [] Wraps. Edited by Warren and Albert Erskine. No. F1556 $40.

029a: PROMISES *Poems 1954-1956* Random House NY (1957) [1] Pulitzer Prize for Poetry in 1958 and the National Book Award for Poetry. (Some copies seen with National Book Award sticker on front of dustwrapper) $20/100

029b: PROMISES Poems *1954-1956* Eyre & Spottiswoode L 1959 [1] (Wrap-around band noting prizes on some copies would be worth more) $15/75

030a: SELECTED ESSAYS Random House NY (1958) [1] 4,000 cc $20/100

030b: SELECTED ESSAYS Eyre & Spottiswoode L (1964) [1] $15/75

031a: REMEMBER THE ALAMO! Random House NY (1958) [1] Ref.a calls for a price of $1.80 and illustrations in black and white only, but we have never seen a copy conforming to this description. We have had two copies, both stating "First Printing," illustrations in white, black and golden-brown, and priced "195/195" on front dustwrapper:

> 1) Blue-green cloth. 2 pages of ads at rear of book for 85 Landmark Books and 38 World Landmark Books and on dustwrapper verso. (We assume this is the first issue)

> 2) Light green cloth. No ads at rear of book. List of 98 Landmark Books and 50 World Landmark Books on verso of dustwrapper. This copy adds "Jacket illustration by Taylor Oughton" to rear dustwrapper flap. (We assume this is a later issue)

There was also a library edition published in October 1958 at $1.95 (ref.a) $50/250

032a: HOW TEXAS WON HER FREEDOM... San Jacinto Museum.. Texas 1959 [0] 512 cc. Green paper covered boards, green cloth spine. No dustwrapper noted in ref.a — $450.

032b: HOW TEXAS WON HER FREEDOM... San Jacinto Museum.. Texas 1959 [0] 2,147 cc. Wraps — $300.

033a: THE CAVE Random House NY (1959) [1] 25,000 cc — $10/50

033b: THE CAVE Eyre & Spottiswoode L 1959 [1] — $10/50

034a: THE GODS OF MOUNT OLYMPUS Random House NY (1959) [1] — $50/250

034b: THE GODS OF MOUNT OLYMPUS Frederick Muller Ltd. L (1962) [1] 5,000 cc — $25/125

035a: ALL THE KING'S MEN *A Play* Random House NY (1960) [1] 4,000 cc — $20/100

035b: ALL THE KING'S MEN Dramatist Play Services (NY 1960) [0] Wraps. Script edition with 10 titles advertised on p.67; 7 titles on p.68; and 10 titles on back cover (H.E. Turlington 2/92) — $75.

036a: YOU, EMPERORS, AND OTHERS... Random House NY (1960) [1] 4,000 cc — $30/150

037a: THE SCOPE OF FICTION Appleton NY (1960) [] 5,000 cc. With Cleanth Brooks. No dustwrapper located (ref.a), issued without dustwrapper (L & T Respess 1/95) — $75.

038a: THE LEGACY OF THE CIVIL WAR... Random House NY (1961) [1] 10,000 cc — $20/100

039a: WILDERNESS *A Tale of The Civil War* Random House NY (1961) [1] 28,350 cc — $12/60

039b: WILDERNESS   Eyre & Spottiswoode   L (1962) [] Advance Proofs in green wraps (George Robert Minkoff 4/93) $150.

039c: WILDERNESS   Eyre & Spottiswoode   L (1962) [1] "This edition published 1962" on copyright page $12/60

040a: SELECTED POEMS by Denis Devlin   Holt NY (1963) [0]   2,500 cc. Edited by Warren and Allen Tate $15/75

041a: FLOOD *A Romance of Our Time*   Random House NY (1964) [1] Signed on special tipped in page (Joseph The Provider) $100/125

041b: FLOOD *A Romance of Our Time*   Random House NY (1964) [1] 35,000 cc $12/60

041c: FLOOD   Collins   L 1964 [] Uncorrected proof in blue wraps and dustwrapper $100/200

041d: FLOOD   Collins   L 1964 [0]   8,000 cc $10/50

042a: WHO SPEAKS FOR THE NEGRO? Random House NY (1965) [1] 10,000 cc $15/75

043a: A PLEA IN MITIGATION...   Wesleyan College   Macon, GA 1966 [0]   400-500 cc (a&b). Wraps. First issue with "abstation" for "abstraction" p.5:2 $250.

043b: A PLEA IN MITIGATION...   Wesleyan College   Macon, GA 1966 [0]   Second issue, corrected $175.

044a: SELECTED POEMS *New and Old 1923-1966*   Random House NY (1966) [] Uncorrected proof in ring-bound wraps (H.E. Turlington 10/90) $300.

044b: SELECTED POEMS *New and Old 1923-1966* Random House NY (1966) [2]   250 sgd no cc. Issued in dustwrapper and slipcase $200/250

044c: SELECTED POEMS *New and Old   1923-1966* Random House NY (1966) [1] 5,300 cc $15/75

045a: FAULKNER *A Collection of Critical Essays* Prentice-Hall Englewood Clfs (1966) [0] $25/100

045b: FAULKNER *A Collection of Critical Essays* Prentice-Hall Englewood Clfs (1966) [0] Wraps $40.

046a: MODERN POETRY AND THE END OF AN ERA (publisher?) Macon (1966) [] Stiff wraps (Phoenix Bookshop 5/88) $150.

047a: INCARNATIONS *Poems 1966 - 1968* Random House NY (1968) [] Uncorrected proof in ring-bound wraps (H.E. Turlington 7/93) $300.

047b: INCARNATIONS *Poems 1966 - 1968* Random House NY (1968) [2] 250 sgd no cc. Issued in dustwrapper and slipcase $175/225

047c: INCARNATIONS *Poems 1966 - 1968* Random House NY (1968) [1] 5,000 cc $15/75

047d: INCARNATIONS *Poems 1966 - 1968* W.H. Allen L 1970 [1] $12/60

048a: AUDUBON *A Vision* Random House NY (1969) [] Uncorrected proof in ring-bound wraps (H.E. Turlington 3/93) $300.

048b: AUDUBON *A Vision* Random House NY (1969) [2] 300 sgd no cc. Issued in dustwrapper and slipcase $150/200

048c: AUDUBON *A Vision* Random House NY (1969) [1] 6,300 cc $12/60

049a: MAN IN MOONLIGHT No publisher or place 1969 [] Broadside. First day of issue of stamp commemerating the lunar landing (H.E. Turlington 10/90) $100.

050a: SELECTED POEMS OF HERMAN MELVILLE Random House NY (1970) [1] 4,000 cc. Edited, 85-page introduction, and notes by Warren $15/75

051a: JOHN GREENLEAF WHITTIER'S POETRY University of Minnesota Minneapolis (1971) [0] 2,500 cc (3,000 copies published, 500 copies recently discarded). 60 pages by Warren $10/35

051b: JOHN GREENLEAF WHITTIER'S POETRY University of Minnesota Minneapolis (1971) [0] 3,500 cc. Wraps $15.

052a: HOMAGE TO THEODORE DREISER... Random House NY (1971) [1] 5,000 cc $15/75

053a: MEET ME IN THE GREEN GLEN Random House NY (1971) [2] 300 sgd no cc. Issued in acetate dustwrapper and slipcase $100/150

053b: MEET ME IN THE GREEN GLEN Random House NY (1971) [1] 25,300 cc $12/60

053c: MEET ME IN THE GREEN GLEN Secker & Warburg L (1972) [1] $10/50

054a: HAWTHORNE WAS RELEVENT No publisher or place (1972) [] Stapled offprint from *National Hawthorne Journal* (H.E. Turlington) $125.

055a: OR ELSE *Poem / Poems 1968-1974* Random House NY (1974) [0] "Uncorrected First Proof" in tall red wraps. No copyright information (Pharos 2/89) $200.

055b: OR ELSE *Poem / Poems 1968-1974* Random House NY (1974) [2] 300 sgd no cc. Issued without dustwrapper in slipcase $75/125

055c: OR ELSE *Poem / Poems 1968-1974* Random House NY (1974) [1] 6,500 cc $10/50

056a: DEMOCRACY AND POETRY   Harvard
University Press   Cambridge Mass./L 1975 [0]
4,500 cc $12/60

057a: SELECTED POEMS 1923-1975   Random
House NY (1976) [2] 250 sgd no cc. Issued without
dustwrapper in slipcase $125/175

057b: SELECTED POEMS 1923-1975   Random
House NY (1976) [1] 6,000 cc $12/60

057c: SELECTED POEMS 1923-1975   Random
House NY (1976) [1] 4,000 cc. Wraps $20.

057d: SELECTED POEMS 1923-1975 Secker &
Warburg L (1976) [1] $10/50

057e: SELECTED POEMS 1923-1975 Franklin
Library Franklin Center 1976 [2] "Limited First
Edition." Issued without dustwrapper in brownish
red leather. No published date furnished (ref. a).
(Published in 1981 {Ken Lopez 3/92}) $60.

058a: DREAM OF A DREAM G.K. Hall B (1976)
[] Previously unpublished poem issued as a
Christmas greeting. Single sheet folded to make 4
pages (Waiting For Godot) $125.

059a: A CONVERSATION WITH ROBERT
PENN WARREN   WNET/13   NY 1976 []
Mimeographed sheet of transcript of Bill Moyer's
show, stapled (Waiting For Godot 10/89) $75.

060a: REBUKE OF THE ROCKS   Colorado
College 1976 [2] 150 sgd no cc. 24"x18" broadside.
First separate edition (Geo. Robert Minkoff) $175.

061a: A PLACE TO COME TO Secker & Warburg L (1977) [1] (Published February 1977.
Month earlier than U.S. {ref.a}) $15/75

061b: A PLACE TO COME TO   Random House
NY (1977) [] "Uncorrected First Proof" in red wraps
(Pharos 4/90) $150.

061c: A PLACE TO COME TO   Random House
NY (1977) [2]   350 sgd no cc.   Issued without
dustwrapper in slipcase. (Published March 1977) $75/125

061d: A PLACE TO COME TO   Random House
NY (1977) [1] 50,000 cc. (Published March 1977) $8/40

062a: NOW AND THEN POEMS   1976-1978
Random House NY (1978) [] Uncorrected proof
in red wraps $150.

062b: NOW AND THEN POEMS 1976-1978
Random House NY (1978) [2]   200 sgd no cc.
Issued without dustwrapper in slipcase $100/150

062c: NOW AND THEN POEMS 1976-1978
Random House NY (1978) [1] 5,000 cc. Pulitzer
Prize for Poetry in 1979 $12/60

062d: NOW AND THEN POEMS 1976-1978
Random House NY (1978) [1] Simultaneous issue
in wraps $20.

063a: OLD FLAME Palaemon Press no place 1978
[2] 26 sgd ltr cc. 16"x9" broadside with original
woodcut by Robert Dance. (Also 5 proof copies
{Lovett & Lovett}) $200.

063b: OLD FLAME Palaemon Press no place 1978
[2] 100 sgd no cc. Broadside $125.

064a: FOR AARON COPELAND Palaemon Press
(Winston-Salem 1978) [2] 28 sgd no cc (I-XXVIII).
Reserved for authors. Broadsides by Warren, James
Dickey and Reynolds Price. Laid in quarter cloth
folio $450.

064b: FOR AARON COPELAND Palaemon Press
(Winston-Salem 1978) [2] 50 sgd no cc $350.

065a: KATHERINE ANNE PORTER... Prentice-Hall Englewood Clfs. (1979) [] Edited and 34 pages by Warren $12/60

065b: KATHERINE ANNE PORTER... Prentice-Hall Englewood Clfs. (1979) [] Wraps $20.

066a: TWO POEMS Palaemon Press Ltd (no place 1979) [2] 30 sgd no cc (numbered I-XXX). Marbled paper boards $250.

066b: TWO POEMS Palaemon Press Ltd (no place 1979) [2] 200 sgd no cc (numbered 1-200). Issued without dustwrapper? $125.

067a: JEFFERSON DAVIS GETS HIS CITI-ZENSHIP BACK   Kentucky University Press (Lexington 1980) [0] (Ref.c) $10/50

068a: BEING HERE *Poetry 1977-1980* Random House NY (1980) [] Uncorrected proof in red wraps (H.E. Turlington 10/90) $150.

068b: BEING HERE *Poetry 1977-1980* Random House NY (1980) [2] 250 sgd no cc. Issued in slipcase (ref.c) $100/150

068c: BEING HERE *Poetry 1977-1980* Random House NY (1980) [1] (Ref.c) $8/40

068d: BEING HERE *Poetry 1977-1980* Random House NY (1980) [1] Simultaneous issue in wraps $20.

068e: BEING HERE *Poetry 1977-1980* Secker & Warburg L (1980) [] U.S. sheets (H.E. Turlington 10/90) $12/60

069a: HAVE YOU EVER EATEN STARS? Random House NY (1980) [] Uncorrected proof in red wraps of *Rumor Verified* (H. E. Turlington 10/90) $200.

069b: RUMOR VERIFIED *Poems 1979-1980* Random House NY (1981) [2] 250 sgd no cc. New title. Issued in slipcase (ref.c) $100/150

069c: RUMOR VERIFIED *Poems 1979-1980* Random House NY (1981) [1] (Ref.c) $8/40

069d: RUMOR VERIFIED *Poems 1979-1980* Random House NY (1981) [] Simultaneous issue in wraps $20.

069e: RUMOR VERIFIED *Poems 1979-1980* Secker & Warburg L (1982) [] U.S. sheets $12/60

070a: PROPHECY (Palaemon Press Lexington?) 1980 [2] 45 no cc. Broadside (Henry Turlington 4/90) $125.

071a: ROBERT PENN WARREN TALKING *Interviews 1950-1978* Random House NY (1980) [] Uncorrected Proof in red wraps (H.E. Turlington 10/90) $100.

071b: ROBERT PENN WARREN TALKING *Interviews 1950-1978* Random House NY (1980) [] Edited by Floyd Watkins and John Hiers $15/40

072a: CYCLE King Library Press (Lexington) 1980 [] Broadside. Proof copy on proofing paper (H.E. Turlington 10/90) $250.

072b: CYCLE King Library Press (Lexington) 1980 [] Broadside on white deckle-edged paper $200.

072c: CYCLE King Library Press (Lexington) 1980 [] Broadside on brown unwatermarked paper $125.

073a: BALLAD OF A SWEET DREAM OF PEACE... Pressworks Dallas (1980) [2] 26 sgd ltr cc. In glassine dustwrapper, with score laid in. Illustrated by Bill Komodore. Music by Alexei Haieff $300.

073b: BALLAD OF A SWEET DREAM OF
PEACE... Pressworks Dallas (1980) [2] 350 sgd no
cc. (This was remaindered and the three illus-
trations and the score may be missing -check) $125.

074a: TELL ME A STORY   (University of
Kentucky Lexington) 1980 [] Souvenir of October
28, 1980 reception honoring Warren during the
University's 75th Birthday Symposium. Broadside
with Jill Krementz photo on other side $125.

074b: TELL ME A STORY   Coffee House Press
(Lexington) 1987 [2] 500 cc. Broadside to honor
him as Poet Laureate (Watermark West 7/88) $75.

074c: TELL ME A STORY   NEA/Library of
Congress Washington 1987 [2] 500 sgd no cc.
Broadside (H.E. Turlington 10/90) $125.

RUMOR VERIFIED See 069b-e

075a: LOVE *Four Versions*   Palaemon Press
(Winston-Salem 1981) [2] 26 sgd ltr cc. Issued
without dustwrapper (ref.c) $250.

075b: LOVE *Four Versions*   Palaemon Press
(Winston-Salem 1981) [2] 174 sgd no cc. Issued
without dustwrapper. (Only about 100 copies
printed {Bert Babcock}) $150.

076a: MOUNTAIN MYSTERY   Palaemon Press
(Winston-Salem 1981) [2] 26 sgd ltr cc. Broadside
No. 22 (ref.c) $175.

076b: MOUNTAIN MYSTERY   Palaemon Press
(Winston-Salem 1981) [2] 100 sgd no cc. Broadside
No. 22 (ref.c) $125.

077a: CHIEF JOSEPH OF THE NEZ PERCE
Georgia Review (no place 1982) [] Wraps. A
Georgia Review offprint in printed white wraps
(ref.c) $150.

077b: CHIEF JOSEPH OF THE NEZ PERCE
Random House NY (1983) [] Uncorrected proof in
red wraps (Chapel Hill Rare Books 5/88) $75.

077c: CHIEF JOSEPH OF THE NEZ PERCE
Palaemon Press (Winston-Salem 1982) [2] 5 sgd ltr
cc. Issued in red quarter leather (Joseph Dermont
5/88) $1,500.

077d: CHIEF JOSEPH OF THE NEZ PERCE
Palaemon Press (Winston-Salem 1982) [2] 7 sgd no
cc. Issued in red quarter leather $750.

077e: CHIEF JOSEPH OF THE NEZ PERCE
Palaemon Press (Winston-Salem 1982) [2] 7 sgd ltr
cc. Issued in quarter leather (same as 073c?
Reportedly a different issue. Note: Randy
Weinstein catalogued a copy in black quarter leather
{out-of-series} not lettered but Stuart Wright, the
publisher, stated there were none in black??) $NVA

077f: CHIEF JOSEPH OF THE NEZ PERCE
Random House NY (1983) [2] 250 sgd no cc.
Issued without dustwrapper in slipcase (ref.c) $125/175

077g: CHIEF JOSEPH OF THE NEZ PERCE
Random House NY (1983) [1] (Ref.c) $6/30

077h: CHIEF JOSEPH OF THE NEZ PERCE
Random House NY (1983) [1] Wraps $20.

077i: CHIEF JOSEPH OF THE NEZ PERCE
Secker & Warburg L (1983) [] $8/40

078a: THE FLOWER Palaemon Press (Winston-
Salem 1983) [2] 3 sgd cc. Printed for Rosanna
Warren for private circulation (Joseph Dermont
{not seen}) $NVA

079a: LITTLE GIRL WAKES EARLY Palaemon
Press (Winston-Salem 1984) [2] ? sgd no cc. Broadside. 9"x12 1/2" $100.

080a: SNOWFALL (Parchment Gallery) no place (1984) [2] 80 sgd no cc. Broadside poem. (H.T.Turlington reports it was never distributed) $125.

081a: FROM ROBERT PENN WARREN Stuart Wright Winstom-Salem 1984 [2] 5 sgd no cc. Wraps. Off-print from *Eudora Welty: A Tribute* in printed card covers (Bert Babcock) $300.

082a: NEW AND SELECTED POEMS 1923-1985 Random House NY (1985) [] Uncorrected proof in beige wraps (Waverly 10/89) $75.

082b: NEW AND SELECTED POEMS 1923-1985 Random House NY (1985) [2] 350 sgd no cc. Slipcase (ref.c) $75/125

082c: NEW AND SELECTED POEMS 1923-1985 Franklin Library Franklin Center 1985 [2] "Signed Limited Edition" in full leather $75.

082d: NEW AND SELECTED POEMS 1923-1985 Random House NY (1985) [1] $7/35

082e: NEW AND SELECTED POEMS 1923-1985 Random House NY (1985) [] Wraps. Simultaneous issue $15.

082f: NEW AND SELECTED POEMS Eurographica Helsinki 1986 [2] 350 sgd no cc in printed wraps (James Jaffe 1/91) $125.

083a: POEMS Privately Printed (Winston-Salem 1985) [2] 15 cc in boards with leather spine. Selected by Rosanna Warren (H.E. Turlington 10/90) $750.

084a: "MASTS AT DAWN" Library of Congress Washington, D.C. 1986 [] Broadside. 10"x 13" $35.

085a: A ROBERT PENN WARREN READER Random House NY (1987) [4] Edited by Albert Erskine $6/30

086a: THE ESSENTIAL MELVILLE   Ecco Press
NY (1987) [] (Between The Covers 8/90) $8/40

087a: SIX POEMS BY ROBERT PENN WARREN
Tamazunchale Press Newton, Iowa 1987 [2] 250
no. cc. Miniature book issued without dustwrapper
or slipcase $75.

088a: LITTLE BOY AND LOST SHOE   No
publisher, place or date   [] Signed 17"x 22"
broadside headed "The Nation's Poet."   Assume
published by Library of Congress, Washington
1987 (Waiting For Godot Books 5/91) $125.

089a: PORTRAIT OF A FATHER   University
Press of Kentucky (Lexington 1988) [0] $6/30

090a: NEW AND SELECTED ESSAYS   Random
House NY (1989) [] Uncorrected proof in yellow
wraps $60.

090b: NEW AND SELECTED ESSAYS   Random
House NY (1989) [2] 350 sgd no cc. Issued without
dustwrapper in slipcase $50/100

090c: NEW AND SELECTED ESSAYS   Random
House NY (1989) [] $5/25

091a: TALKING   WITH   ROBERT   PENN
WARREN   University of Georgia Press   Athens,
GA 1990 [] $10/40

Evelyn Waugh [signature]

EVELYN WAUGH
(1903-1966)

Waugh was born in Hampstead, England. He attended Hertford College. He was a schoolmaster at three different small schools from 1925 to 1927, which he explained was a job to the educated as "domestic service was to the uneducated classes." "It is no use pretending I was involved in any way in education. -I enjoyed it very much...I left when I was expelled... for drunkenness..." He then intended to become a cabinet-maker but his future parents-in-law did not approve of carpentry as a career and writing seemed the next most suitable occupation.

He converted to Catholicism in 1930 and many of his later books have a strong Catholic background.

He is considered by many to be one of the more gifted of the writers of the first half of this century; and although such books as *Brideshead Revisited* and *The Loved One* may be his most popular titles, he seemed, in interviews, to consider his *Sword of Honour* trilogy as one of his most important works.

Ref.a included a checklist which included the first "book." Ref.b & c included the titles, publishers and dates, but no descriptive information and only passing mention of a few of the limited editions. Ref.d does not include printing quantities (Little Brown Co. was kind enough to provide these); and is not always clear on how the individual first editions are identified, otherwise it is a very good reference.

It should be noted that although not itemized herein, Chapman & Hall when reissuing Waugh's first four novels made up twelve (12) large paper copies of each on handmade paper and these have been on the market, usually inscribed, for $2,500. to $8,500. In addition, Waugh substantially revised two Thomas Merton Books for English publication, *Elected Silence* in 1949 (*The Seven Storey Mountain*) and *Waters of Silence* (*Siloe*) in 1950.

We would like to thank Edmund A. Hennessy of Carpinteria, California for providing some helpful bibliographical information for this guide.

REFERENCES:

(a) Stopp, Frederick J. EVELYN WAUGH *Portrait of Artist.* London: Chapman & Hall Ltd. (1958).

(b) Davis, Robert M., et al. EVELYN WAUGH *A Checklist of Primary & Secondary Material.* Troy, New York: Whitston Publishing Co., 1972. Out-of-print.

(c) Davis, Robert M. A CATALOGUE OF THE EVELYN WAUGH COLLECTION AT THE HUMANITIES RESEARCH CENTER. Austin: University of Texas; and Troy, New York: Whitston Publishing Co., 1981. In print at $25.00.

(d) Davis, Robert M. et al. A BIBLIOGRAPHY OF EVELYN WAUGH. Troy, New York: Whitston Publishing Co., 1986.

001a: THE WORLD TO COME: A POEM IN THREE CANTOS Privately printed 1916 [] $7,500.

002a: P.R.B. *An Essay on The Pre-Raphaelite Brotherhood 1847 - 1854* Privately Printed by Alastair Graham L 1926 [] 50 cc. Half-cloth $5,000.

002b: P.R.B. *An Essay on The Pre-Raphaelite Brotherhood 1847 - 1854* Dalrymple Press (Kent 1982) [2] 475 no. cc. Introduction by Christopher Sykes. In acetate dustwrapper (Wm. Reese Co.) $200.

003a: ROSSETTI *His Life and Works* Duckworth L 1928 [] Anthony Powell was an editor at Duckworth at the time and was instrumental in obtaining the contract for Waugh. First issue? with gilt lettering (I.D. Edrich). First issue with gilt on spine (Dalian Books 9/92) $500/2,500

003b: ROSSETTI *His Life and Works* Dodd, Mead NY 1928 [0] From the English sheets $250/1,250

004a: DECLINE AND FALL Chapman and Hall L 1928 [1] Reportedly fewer than 2,000 copies. Published 9/18/28. "Originally publ... September 1928" on copyright page. Pages 168 and 169 have "Martin Gaythorn-Brodie" and "Kevin Saunderson" respectively $500/3,500

004b: DECLINE AND FALL Chapman and Hall L 1928 [1] Second issue with pages 168 and 169 with "The Hon. Miles Malpractice" and "Lord Parakeet" respectively $300/3,000

004c: DECLINE AND FALL Doubleday, Doran GC 1929 [1] $300/1,500

004d: DECLINE AND FALL Farrar & Rinehart NY 1929 [5] Doubleday remainder sheets with Farrar title page tipped in $200/1,000

004e: DECLINE AND FALL Chapman and Hall L (1962) [] "This Edition, Reset, 1962" on copyright page. Revised edition with New Preface by Waugh $20/100

004f: DECLINE AND FALL Franklin Library Franklin, PA 1979 [2] "Limited Edition" in full leather $75.

005a: VILE BODIES Chapman and Hall (L) 1930 [1] (Published January 17, 1930) $250/1,250

005b: VILE BODIES J. Cape & Harrison Smith NY (1930) [1] $250/1,000

005c: VILE BODIES Farrar Rinehart NY 1930 [] $150/750

005d: VILE BODIES *A Play* Chapman & Hall L 1931 [] Wraps. Adapted by H. Dennis Bradley $150.

005e: VILE BODIES Chapman & Hall L 1965 [] Revised Edition. "This Edition, Reset, 1965" on copyright page $15/75

006a: LABELS   *A   Mediterranean   Journal*
Duckworth   (L)   1930 [2] 110 sgd no cc. With a
page of author's holograph manuscript tipped in $2,000.

006b: LABELS   *A   Mediterranean   Journal*
Duckworth   L 1930 [1]   Also noted with a Book
Society sticker on front panel (Joseph The Provider
Books 9/90) $200/1,000

006c: A BACHELOR ABROAD   Cape & Smith
NY (1930) [1] New title. "First published in
America, 1930" on copyright page $150/750

006d: A BACHELOR ABROAD   Farrar &
Rinehart NY 1930 [5] $100/400

007a: REMOTE PEOPLE Duckworth L (1931)
[1] First issue with gilt lettering on spine (Dalian
Books 6/89) $500/2,000

007b: THEY WERE STILL DANCING   Cape &
Smith NY (1932) [] New title $175/750

007c: THEY WERE STILL DANCING Farrar &
Rinehart NY (1932) [5] Noted with bottom edge
trimmed and untrimmed $125/450

008a: BLACK MISCHIEF   Chapman & Hall   L
(1932) [2] 250 sgd no cc. Issued in dustwrapper
(Joseph the Provider) $1,250/1,750

008b: BLACK MISCHIEF   Chapman & Hall   L
(1932) [1] Black cloth with variant noted in gray-
blue cloth. Also noted with Book Society wrap-
around band (Serendipity Books) $150/750

008c: BLACK MISCHIEF   Farrar & Rinehart NY
(1934) [5] $100/500

009a: AN OPEN LETTER TO HIS EMINENCE
THE CARDINAL ARCHBISHOP OF WEST-
MINSTER Chapman & Hall (L 1933) [] Proof in
wraps. Waugh indicated there were 5 copies $7,500.

010a: NINETY-TWO DAYS Duckworth L 1934
[] First issue reportedly with gilt lettering on spine,
later spine lettering in black (I.D. Edrich) $350/1,750

010b: NINETY-TWO DAYS   Farrar & Rinehart
NY (1934) [5] $150/750

011a: A HANDFUL OF DUST Chapman & Hall
L (1934) [1] Uncorrected proofs in plain brown
wraps $2,000.

011b: A HANDFUL OF DUST Chapman & Hall
L (1934) [1] Noted in Book Society wrap-around
band (James S. Jaffe) $350/3,000

011c: A HANDFUL OF DUST Farrar & Rinehart
NY (1934) [5] $150/750

012a: EDMUND CAMPION, JESUIT AND
MARTYR Longmans L (1935) [2] 50 no. cc. For
Private Distribution. Issued in red buckram (Glenn
Horowitz 10/88) $2,500.

012b: EDMUND CAMPION, JESUIT AND
MARTYR Longmans L (1935) [1] $125/500

012c: EDMUND CAMPION, JESUIT AND
MARTYR Sheed & Ward NY (1935) [0] "Printed
in Great Britain, 1935" on copyright page $75/350

012d: EDMUND CAMPION, JESUIT AND
MARTYR Little Brown B 1946 [1] Revised with
new introduction. "First Edition published June
1946" on copyright page. Later changed to
"Published June 1946" (ref.d) $20/100

012e: EDMUND CAMPION, JESUIT AND
MARTYR Longmans L 1947 [] $15/75

013a: MR. LOVEDAY'S LITTLE OUTING *And
Other Sad Stories* Chapman & Hall L (1936) [1]
First issue binding: red and black cloth stamped in

gilt. Second issue binding: red cloth stamped in black (Glenn Horowitz 3/91). Also noted in Book Society wrap-around band $200/1,000

013b: MR. LOVEDAY'S LITTLE OUTING *And Other Sad Stories* Little Brown B 1936 [2] 750 cc. "Published October, 1936" - "...750 copies of which 700 copies are for sale" $150/750

014a: WAUGH IN ABYSSINIA Longmans Green L (1936) [1] First issue has pages 163 and 164 not cancelled (Words Etc. 11/89) and dustwrapper front flap not pasted over (R.A. Gekoski). (Steven Temple Books says plain top edge is later but does not describe first state of top edge) $400/2,000

014b: WAUGH IN ABYSSINIA Longmans Green L (1936) [1] Pages 163 and 164 cancelled and front dustwrapper flap has new flap pasted over the original blurb which Waugh felt gave the impression he admired the Italian Fascists $150/750

015a: SCOOP, A NOVEL ABOUT JOURNAL-ISM Chapman & Hall L (1938) [] Uncorrected proof in plain brown wraps with printed white label on front cover (Glenn Horowitz 10/ 88) $2,000.

015b: SCOOP, A NOVEL ABOUT JOURNAL-ISM Chapman & Hall L (1938) [1] First issue with "s" in "as" in last line of p.88 and "Daily Beast" logo in black letters on front cover of dustwrapper. Reportedly, only 100 copies or so, but it doesn't seem so scarce. $250/1,000

015c: SCOOP, A NOVEL ABOUT JOURNAL-ISM Chapman & Hall L (1938) [1] Without "s" in "as" on p.88 and without "Daily Beast" on dustwrapper $150/750

015d: SCOOP, A NOVEL ABOUT JOURNAL-ISM Little Brown B 1938 [] Uncorrected galley proofs (8"x19") in wraps. Printed four columns to the page on one side only (Pepper & Stern 6/90) $1,500.

015e: SCOOP, A NOVEL ABOUT JOURNAL-ISM Little Brown B 1938 [1] 5,010 cc. Also states "Published July 1938" on copyright page $100/450

016a: ROBBERY UNDER LAW, THE MEXI-CAN OBJECT LESSON Chapman & Hall L (1939) [1] $250/1,250

016b: MEXICO *An Object Lesson* Little Brown B 1939 [1] 1,500 cc. New title. Also states "Published September 1939" on copyright page $150/600

016c: ROBBERY UNDER LAW: THE MEXI-CAN OBJECT LESSON Catholic Book Club L (1940) [1] "This edition 1940" $15/75

017a: PUT OUT MORE FLAGS Chapman & Hall L (1942) [] Uncorrected proof in plain brown wraps with a number of textual differences (Glenn Horowitz 10/88) $1,500.

017b: PUT OUT MORE FLAGS Chapman & Hall L (1942) [1] $150/750

017c: PUT OUT MORE FLAGS Little Brown B (1942) [1] 4,054 cc. Also states "Published May 1942" $75/400

018a: WORK SUSPENDED Chapman & Hall L (1942) [2] 25 cc. "This is one of twenty-five Special Press copies..." (Library of Congress). Full leather "For Presentation" (I.D. Edrich 7/87) $1,000.

018b: WORK SUSPENDED Chapman & Hall L 1942 [2] 500 cc. "This edition is limited to 500 copies" $150/600

018c: WORK SUSPENDED *and Other Stories Written Before the Second World War* Chapman & Hall L 1948 [0] Part of Uniform Edition $15/75

019a: BRIDESHEAD REVISITED Chapman & Hall L 1945 [0] 50 cc. Wraps. Special issue (ref.d) $6,000.

019b: BRIDESHEAD REVISITED   Chapman &
Hall L 1945 [0] Catalogue number on verso of title
page (ref.d). Variant dustwrapper printed in pale
green/gray on thin paper stock, printed on both sides
(David Mayou 5/89) $200/1,000

019c: BRIDESHEAD REVISITED   Little Brown
B 1945 [2] 600 cc. "Published September 1945" $175/850

019d: BRIDESHEAD REVISITED   Little Brown
B 1946 [1] 25,000 cc. "First edition after ... 600
copies" - "Published January 1946". Blue cloth.
(The Book-of-the-month Club {BOMC} is usually
in red cloth although there are also gray, maroon-
brown, yellow-brown and orange cloths which are
assumed to be book club issues. The BOMC title
page is dated **1945** but does not have the statement
on edition on verso.) The regular first edition
dustwrapper does not have "Printed in U.S.A." at
bottom of rear flap. (If the BOMC dustwrapper
were clipped where the price should appear on the
front flap, it would be difficult to distinguish except
for the wording on back flap.) The first dustwrapper
has much deeper blues, but hard to tell unless one
had both in hand $60/250

019e: BRIDESHEAD REVISITED   Chapman &
Hall L 1960 [1] Revised with new preface. "This
edition, reset, 1960" on copyright page $15/75

020a: WHEN THE GOING WAS GOOD
Duckworth L 1946 [2] 20 no cc on handmade paper
for presentation by the author (Glenn Horowitz
10/88) $3,000.

020b: WHEN THE GOING WAS GOOD
Duckworth L 1946 [0] Abridged versions of *Vile
Bodies*, *Labels*, *Ninety-Two Days*, and *Mr.
Loveday's little Outing* $40/200

020c: WHEN THE GOING WAS GOOD   Little
Brown B 1947 [1] 7,500 cc $30/125

021a: SCOTT-KING'S MODERN EUROPE
Chapman & Hall L 1947 [] Uncorrected proof in
plain brown wraps (Thomas Goldwasser Books
2/91)

$500.

021b: SCOTT-KING'S MODERN EUROPE
Chapman & Hall L 1947 [0]

$20/100

021c: SCOTT-KING'S MODERN EUROPE Little
Brown B 1949 [1] 10,081 cc. Also states
"Published February 1949" on copyright page

$15/75

022a: WINE IN PEACE AND WAR Saccone and
Speed Ltd L no date [1948] (per Publisher's letter)
[2] 100 sgd no cc. Decorations by Rex Whistler

$1,000.

022b: WINE IN PEACE AND WAR Saccone and
Speed Ltd L no date [1948] (per Publisher's letter)
[0] Issued in plain brown dustwrapper. Also noted
in "original" tissue wrapper (Old New York
Bookshop)

$250/350

023a: THE LOVED ONE Little Brown B 1948 [1]
20,000 cc. Also states "Published June 1948" on
copyright page. Precedes U.K. edition (ref. d).
Essentially the *Horizon Magazine*, February 1948,
text

$20/100

023b: THE LOVED ONE Chapman & Hall (L
1948) [2] 250 sgd no cc. Signed by Waugh and
illustrator Stuart Boyle. Text based on Waugh
revision of the *Horizon Magazine* appearance. In
glassine dustwrapper (Glenn Horowitz)

$1,250.

023c: THE LOVED ONE Chapman & Hall (L
1948) [0]

$50/250

023d: THE LOVED ONE Chapman & Hall L
1965 [1] "This Edition Reset, 1965" on copyright
page. Adds new preface by Waugh

$12/60

24a: A SELECTION FROM THE OCCAS-IONAL SERMONS OF THE RT. REV. MGR KNOX Dropmore Press L 1949 [2] 50 sgd no cc (signed by Rev. Knox). Selected and edited by Waugh. Issued in dustwrapper and slipcase. $1,000/1,250

024b: A SELECTION FROM THE OCCAS-IONAL SERMONS OF THE RT. REV. MGR KNOX Dropmore Press L 1949 [2] 500 cc. Issued in dustwrapper and slipcase (Black Sun Books 12/94) $250/350

025a: HELENA Chapman & Hall L 1950 [] 50 to 100 large paper copies on handmade paper in white buckram (Glenn Horowitz 10/88). (Inscribed copies have been cataloged for $2,700 and $3,600) $1,750.

025b: HELENA Chapman & Hall L 1950 [0] Also noted in wrap-around band (Book Treasury 6/90) $30/150

025c: HELENA Little Brown B 1950 [1] 15,000 cc. Also states "Published October 1950" on copyright page $15/75

025d: THE HEART'S OWN REASONS Publisher?? (NY) no date [1951] [] New title. Single Leaf measuring 12½"x 8". A review of Graham Green's novel *The End of the Affair* (David Mayou 12/94) $400.

026a: THE HOLY PLACES Queen Anne Press L 1952 [2] 50 sgd no cc. Bound in red niger morocco. Signed by Waugh and Reynolds Stone, the illustrator. Issued in dustwrapper (Glenn Horowitz 10/88). Waugh was not happy with this edition and a number of corrections/changes were made in the 1953 edition $1,200/1,500

026b: THE HOLY PLACES Queen Anne Press L 1952 [2] 900 no cc. Bound in red buckram and numbered 51-950. Issued in plain gray dustwrapper $250/300

026c: THE HOLY PLACES   Queen Anne Press British Book Center L/ NY 1953 [2] 50 sgd no cc. Contains a number of corrections/changes over the 1952 edition $1,000/1,250

026d: THE HOLY PLACES   Queene Anne Press/ British Book Center L/NY 1953 [2] 12 no cc. On handmade paper in full red morocco. Issued in pale gray dustwrapper (Glenn Horowitz 3/91) $2,000.

026e: THE HOLY PLACES   Queen Anne Press British Book Center L/ NY 1953 [2] 950 no cc. Two minor corrections in text $200/300

027a: MEN AT ARMS Chapman & Hall L 1952 [] Uncorrected proof in unprinted white wraps and dustwrapper (Glenn Horowitz 10/88) $1,000/1,250

027b: MEN AT ARMS   Chapman & Hall L 1952 [0] First volume in War Trilogy "Sword of Honour" $50/250

027c: MEN AT ARMS Little Brown B (1952) [1] 7,605 cc $20/100

028a: LOVE AMONG THE RUINS Chapman & Hall   L 1953 [2] 350 sgd no cc. Glassine dustwrapper with printed paper flaps (Glenn Horowitz) $450/600

028b: LOVE AMONG THE RUINS Chapman & Hall L 1953 [] Uncorrected proofs for trade issue based on 028a (Glenn Horowitz 10/88) $450.

028c: LOVE AMONG THE RUINS Chapman & Hall L 1953 [0] $30/150

029a: TACTICAL EXERCISE Little Brown B (1954) [1] 7,500 cc. Not published separately in England $30/150

030a: OFFICERS AND GENTLEMEN Chapman & Hall L 1955 [0] Second volume in War Trilogy "Sword of Honour" $30/150

030b: OFFICERS AND GENTLEMEN   Little
Brown B (1955) [1] 12,000 cc $15/75

031a: THE ORDEAL OF GILBERT PINFOLD
Chapman & Hall L 1957 [] Uncorrected proofs in
white wraps (Glenn Horowitz 10/88) $400.

031b: THE ORDEAL OF GILBERT PINFOLD
Chapman & Hall L 1957 [] Large paper copies in
red buckram for friends of the author (David Mayou
3/89). Estimated at 50 to 100 copies (Glenn
Horowitz 10/88) $1,750.

031c: THE ORDEAL OF GILBERT PINFOLD
Chapman & Hall L 1957 [0] $25/125

031d: THE ORDEAL OF GILBERT PINFOLD
Little Brown B (1957) [1] Dustwrapper clipped
and "$3.75" stamped to left of clip. Assumed first
issue of dustwrapper. Most copies have "$3.75"
printed on flap and it is assumed the first
dustwrapers had a mistake and were clipped. There
are over 200 editorial changes in this edition versus
the British edition (Paul Doyle and Alan Clodd in
the Evelyn Waugh Newsletter Winter 1969) $25/125

031e: THE ORDEAL OF GILBERT PINFOLD
Little Brown B (1957) [1] Dustwrapper priced
"$3.75" and unclipped $15/75

032a: THE WORLD OF EVELYN WAUGH Little
Brown B (1958) [1] 7,951 cc. Edited by Charles J.
Rolo $25/125

033a: THE LIFE OF RIGHT REVEREND
RONALD KNOX Chapman & Hall L (1959) []
Uncorrected proof in unprinted red wraps with label
on front (Glenn Horowitz) $350.

033b: THE LIFE OF RIGHT REVEREND
RONALD KNOX Chapman & Hall L (1959) [2]

29 cc. Specially bound for presentation (R.A. Gekoski). (Inscribed copies have been cataloged for $3,000 and $5,000) $2,000.

033c: THE LIFE OF RIGHT REVEREND RONALD KNOX Chapman & Hall L 1959 [0] "Ronald Knox Memorial Prize" slip tipped in before p.13, not in U.S. edition $25/100

033d: MONSIGNOR RONALD KNOX... Little Brown B (1959) [1] 5,447 cc. New title $15/75

034a: TOURIST IN AFRICA Chapman & Hall L 1960 [0] $15/75

034b: TOURIST IN AFRICA Little Brown B (1960) [1] 6,500 cc $12/60

035a: UNCONDITIONAL SURRENDER Chapman & Hall L 1961 [0] Uncorrected proof in printed grAy wraps with a number of textual differences (Glenn Horowitz 10/88) $350.

035b: UNCONDITIONAL SURRENDER Chapman & Hall L 1961 [1] Third volume of the War Trilogy "Sword of Honour" $20/100

035c: THE END OF THE BATTLE Little Brown B (1961) [1] 10,000 cc. New title $15/75

036a: THE SAME AGAIN PLEASE *A Layman's Hope of the Vatican Council* (National Review NY 1962) [0] An off-print. One leaf folded to make 4 pages (Glenn Horowitz 10/ 88) $400.

037a: BASIL SEAL RIDES AGAIN Chapman & Hall L 1963 [2] 750 sgd no cc. Issued in glassine dustwrapper $600.

037b: BASIL SEAL RIDES AGAIN Little Brown B (1963) [2] 1,000 sgd no cc. Blue buckram and acetate dustwrapper $450.

038a: A LITTLE LEARNING   Chapman & Hall
(L) 1964 [0] $15/75

038b: A LITTLE LEARNING   Little Brown   B
(1964) [1] 15,000 cc $10/50

039a: FIZZ, BUBBLY, POP   Steller Press   Barnet
1964   [] Offprint in wraps. From *Wine and Road*
Magazine September 1964 (Any Amount of Books
6/94) $100.

040a: A SWORD OF HONOUR   Chapman & Hall
L 1965 [1] Contains the war trilogy with "Author's
Note" and "Recensions" by Waugh to tie into a
single story $30/150

040b: A SWORD OF HONOR   Little Brown   B   no
date [1966]   [1] 7,500 cc. Last copyright date is
1961 $25/100

040c: A SWORD OF HONOUR   Folio Society   L
1990   [] 3 volumes. Issued without dustwrapper in
slipcase. Illustrated by John Lawrence $50/75

041a: THE DIARIES OF EVELYN WAUGH
Weidenfeld & Nicolson L (1976) [] Uncorrected
proof in drab wraps (I.D. Edrich 1/93) $125.

041b: THE DIARIES OF EVELYN WAUGH
Weidenfeld & Nicolson L (1976) [0] Edited by
Michael Davie $12/60

041c: THE DIARIES OF EVELYN WAUGH
Little Brown B (1976) [1] 15,650 cc $10/40

042a: A LITTLE ORDER Eyre Methuen (L 1977)
[] Uncorrected proof in two sections bound in plain
green wraps, plus five sections unbound   (I.D.
Edrich 1/93) $150.

042b: A LITTLE ORDER Eyre Methuen (L 1977)
[1] Selection of journalism edited by Donat
Gallagher $10/50

042c: A LITTLE ORDER Little Brown B no date [1980] [1] 6,000 cc. Last copyright date is 1977 $10/40

043a: THE LETTERS OF EVELYN WAUGH Weidenfeld & Nicolson L 1980 [] Edited by Mark Amory $10/50

043b: THE LETTERS OF EVELYN WAUGH Ticknor & Fields NH/NY (1980) [3] Also states "First published in USA..." on copyright page $10/40

044a: CHARLES RYDER'S SCHOOLDAYS *And Other Stories* Little Brown B (1982) [1] 2,414 cc $35/150

044b: CHARLES RYDER'S SCHOOLDAYS *And Other Stories* Little Brown B (1982) [1] Wraps $40.

045a: THE ESSAYS, ARTICLES AND REVIEWS OF EVELYN WAUGH Methuen (L 1983) [1] $10/50

045b: THE ESSAYS, ARTICLES AND REVIEWS OF EVELYN WAUGH Little Brown B (1984) [1] 1,800 cc. Edited by Donat Gallagher $10/40

046a: EVELYN WAUGH, APPRENTICE Pilgrim Books Norman 1985 [] Edited by Robert Murray Davis. Included some first book appearances (ref.d) $7/35

047a: WAUGH ON WOMEN Publisher?? NY 1985 [] Edited by Jacqueline McDonnell (Words Etc. 11/89) $10/40

048a: MR. WU AND MRS STITCH *The Letters of Evelyn Waugh and Diana Cooper* Hodder & Stoughton L 1991 [] Edited by Artemis Cooper $10/40

048b: THE LETTERS OF EVELYN WAUGH AND DIANA COOPER Tichnor & Fields NY 1992 [] New title. Uncorrected proof in blue wraps (Waiting For Godot Books 9/94) $50.

048c: THE LETTERS OF EVELYN WAUGH
AND DIANA COOPER   Tichnor & Fields NY
1992 [] $7/35

Colin Wilson [signature]

COLIN WILSON

Wilson was born in Leicester in 1931. He served in the Royal Air Force and worked at various jobs in Paris, Strasbourg, and London, including magazine work on the "Paris Review" and "Merlin." He has been a full-time writer since 1954 as well as a visiting lecturer or professor at a number of colleges in England, Germany and the United States. He considers himself a writer of ideas in the tradition of Shaw, Wells or Sartre and a part of European rather than English literary tradition; and part of the "new existentialism" which is in fundamental disagreement with the pessimistic tradition of Heidegger, Jaspers, Sartre and Camus.

He is obviously prolific and has no plans to slow up. The prices for his first editions are relatively inexpensive at this point.

The basic list of Wilson's books was based on ref.a. This bibliography, however, was not particularly informative, except for title, publisher, date, chronology and whether cloth or wraps. It did not include any information on how to identify first editions, tell you whether or not the date was on the title page, the cloth color, the quantity printed or the exact date published. First edition identification points for the English editions were supplied by George Nozicka, and we thank him for his assistance; and from the Library of Congress stacks, or inventory, for the American editions. Printing quantities, such as they are, were furnished by the publishers.

(a) Stanley, Colin. THE WORK OF COLIN WILSON. San Bernardino: The Borgo Press, 1989.

(b) Drost, Jerome. "Colin Wilson | Checklist of American Editions... 1956-1982" in the _Bulletin of Bibliography._ Volume 44, No. 1, March 1987.

001a: THE OUTSIDER Gollancz L 1956 [0] Blue cloth $50/250

001b: THE OUTSIDER Houghton Mifflin B 1956 [1] 12,000 cc. According to the publisher, the first printing has the date on the title page. There are at least three variants that state "First American Edition" but do not have a date on the title page. We assume these are later printings or Book Club editions. Throughout this century Houghton Mifflin removed the date from the title page after the first printing but never made any other changes, so perhaps they forgot to change the copyright page on later printing(s). The only copy we have had with a review slip was in brown cloth, stamped in silver and black and with a black triangle on back cover. The date was on the title page. We assume this is the true first $30/150

002a: RELIGION AND THE REBEL Gollancz L 1957 [0] Blue cloth. *The Outsider*-Book 2. Variant in gray cloth $25/125

002b: RELIGION AND THE REBEL Houghton Mifflin B 1957 [1] 10,000 cc. Blue cloth $15/75

003a: THE AGE OF DEFEAT Gollancz L 1959 [0] *The Outsider*-Book 3 $20/100

003b: THE STATURE OF MAN Houghton Mifflin B 1959 [1] 6,000 cc. New title. Black cloth $15/75

004a: RITUAL IN THE DARK Gollancz L 1960 [] Advance copy in wraps with 1959 date (Maurice Neville 11/88) $150.

004b: RITUAL IN THE DARK Gollancz L 1960 [0] Red cloth. Copies in wrap-around bands have been catalogued $20/100

004c: RITUAL IN THE DARK Houghton Mifflin B 1960 [1] Black cloth $15/75

004d: RITUAL IN THE DARK *A Screenplay*
Pequod Productions   NY 1967 [] Written with
Stephen Geller. Assume wraps (ref.b) $75.

005a: ADRIFT IN SOHO Gollancz L 1961 [0]
Red cloth $25/125

005b: ADRIFT IN SOHO Houghton Mifflin B
1961 [1] 5,000 cc. Green cloth $15/75

006a: ENCYCLOPEDIA OF MURDER Barker L
(1961) [] Written with Patricia Pitman $20/100

006b: ENCYCLOPEDIA OF MURDER Putnam
NY (1962) [1] Black cloth $15/75

007a: THE STRENGTH TO DREAM Gollancz L
1962 [0] Blue cloth. *The Outsider*-Book 4. Also
noted in green cloth $25/125

007b: THE STRENGTH TO DREAM Houghton
Mifflin B 1962 [1] 4,000 cc. Yellow cloth $15/75

008a: MAN WITHOUT A SHADOW Barker L
(1963) [0] Black cloth $25/125

008b: THE SEX DIARY OF GERARD SORME
Dial NY 1963 [0] New title. Brown boards $20/100

009a: ORIGINS OF THE SEXUAL IMPULSE
Barker   L (1963) [0] Blue-green cloth. *The
Outsider*-Book 5 $20/100

009b: ORIGINS OF THE SEXUAL IMPULSE
Putnam NY (1963) [0] $15/75

010a: THE WORLD OF VIOLENCE Gollancz L
1963 [0] Red paper covered boards $15/75

010b: THE VIOLENT WORLD OF HUGH
GREEN Houghton Mifflin B 1963 [1] 4,000 cc.
New title $20/100

011a: BRANDY OF THE DAMNED Barker L (1964) [1] Brown cloth spine and beige cloth $25/125

011b: CHORDS AND DISCORDS... Crown NY (1966) [] New title. Adds a new chapter on American music $15/75

011c: COLIN WILSON ON MUSIC Pan L 1967 [1] Wraps. New title. Adds a new chapter on American music $35.

012a: NECESSARY DOUBT Barker L 1964 [] $15/75

012b: NECESSARY DOUBT Trident NY 1964 [0] $12/60

013a: RASPUTIN AND THE FALL OF THE ROMANOVS Barker L (1964) [0] Boards $20/100

013b: RASPUTIN AND THE FALL OF THE ROMANOVS Citadel Press Secaucus 1964 [] (Ref.b) $15/75

013c: RASPUTIN AND THE FALL OF THE ROMANOVS Farrar Straus NY (1964) [1] Blue cloth spine. Black boards $15/75

014a: BEYOND THE OUTSIDER Barker L 1965 [] *The Outsider*-Book 6 $20/100

014b: BEYOND THE OUTSIDER Houghton Mifflin B 1965 [1] 5,000 cc. Tan cloth $15/75

015a: EAGLE AND EARWIG Barker L (1965) [1] $15/75

016a: THE GLASS CAGE Barker L (1966) [0] Black cover $15/75

016b: THE GLASS CAGE Random House NY (1967) [1] Blue boards and dark blue cloth spine $12/60

017a: INTRODUCTION TO THE NEW EXIS-
TENTIALISM Hutchinson L (1966) [1] $20/100

017b: INTRODUCTION TO THE NEW EXIS-
TENTIALISM Houghton Mifflin B 1967 [] $15/75

017c: INTRODUCTION TO THE NEW EXIS-
TENTIALISM Houghton Mifflin B 1967 []
Wraps. Simultaneous issue $25.

017d: INTRODUCTION TO THE NEW EXIS-
TENTIALISM Wildwood House L (1980) []
Wraps. New preface by Wilson $20.

018a: SEX AND THE INTELLIGENT TEEN-
AGER Arrow (L) 1966 [1] Wraps $40.

018b: SEX AND THE INTELLIGENT TEEN-
AGER Pyramid Books NY (1968) [] Wraps $40.

019a: THE MIND PARASITES Barker L 1967 [0]
Black cloth $15/75

019b: THE MIND PARASITES Arkham House
SC 1967 [2] 3,045 cc $15/75

020a: AN INTRODUCTION TO JAMES
DROUGHT (*Los Angeles Times* L.A. 1967) [0]
Wraps. Off-print from Times *Calendar Magazine*.
25 pages (ref.b) $75.

021a: BERNARD SHAW: A REASSESSMENT
Hutchinson L (1969) [1] Dark red boards $12/60

021b: BERNARD SHAW: A REASSESSMENT
Atheneum NY 1969 [1] $10/50

022a: A CASEBOOK OF MURDER Frewin L
1969 [0] $20/100

022b: A CASEBOOK OF MURDER Cowles NY
no date [1970] [1] $12/60

023a: THE PHILOSOPHER'S STONE Barker L
(1969) [0] Dark brown boards $15/75

023b: THE PHILOSOPHER'S STONE Crown NY
(1971) [1] $15/75

024a: POETRY AND MYSTICISM   City Lights
SF (1969) [] Wraps $40.

024b: POETRY AND MYSTICISM Hutchinson L
1970 [1] Dark red boards. An expanded version of
024a $15/75

024c: POETRY AND MYSTICISM   City Lights
S.F. (1986) [0] Wraps. First U.S. of 024b $15.

025a: VOYAGE TO A BEGINNING Crown NY
(1969) [0] Blue cloth with black letters. Precedes
U.K. (ref.a) Includes five chapters not included in
the U.K. edition $8/40

025b: VOYAGE TO A BEGINNING Woolf L
1969 [2] 200 sgd no cc (L.J. Sklaroff 4/86, although
Peter Jolliffe and Words Etc. both catalogued it as
one of 300 copies) $60/100

025c: VOYAGE TO A BEGINNING Woolf L
1969 [0] Red cloth $8/40

026a: THE GOD OF THE LABYRINTH Hart-
Davis (L 1970) [1] Dark red boards $15/75

026b: THE HEDONISTS New Amer. Library NY
1971 [] New title. Wraps. 110,000 cc $40.

026c: THE GOD OF THE LABYRINTH Wingbow
Press Berkeley 1982 [] Wraps. Reprint with new
title $15.

027a: THE KILLER New English Library (L 1970)
[1] $15/75

027b: LINGARD Crown (NY 1970) [0] New title $12/60

028a: STRINDBERG Calder L 1970 [] $10/50

028b: STRINDBERG Random House NY (1972)
[4] Black cloth spine and red-orange boards $10/40

029a: THE STRANGE GENIUS OF DAVID
LINDSAY Barker L (1970) [] Written with E.H.
Visiak and J.B. Pick $15/75

030a: THE BLACK ROOM Weidenfeld (L 1971)
[0] $15/75

030b: THE BLACK ROOM Pyramid Books NY
1975 [] Wraps $20.

031a: THE OCCULT *A History*   Hodder &
Stoughton L 1971 [] Uncorrected proofs in gray
wraps (Dalian Books 6/89) $150.

031b: THE OCCULT *A History*   Hodder &
Stoughton L 1971 [] $15/75

031c: THE OCCULT: *A History*   Random House
NY (1971) [] $12/60

032a: L'AMOUR: THE WAYS OF LOVE Crown
NY (1972) [] Sex manual $15/75

033a: NEW PATHWAYS IN PSYCHOLOGY
Gollancz L 1972 [0] $12/60

033b: NEW PATHWAYS IN PSYCHOLOGY
Taplinger NY 1972 [] $10/50

034a: ORDER OF ASSASSINS   Hart-Davis L
(1972) [1] $15/75

035a: STRANGE POWERS Latimer (L 1973) [1]
Dark red/maroon boards $10/50

035b: STRANGE POWERS Random House NY
(1975) [1] $10/40

036a: TREE BY TOLKIEN (Covent Garden Press L 1973) [2] 100 sgd no cc $175/250

036b: TREE BY TOLKIEN (Covent Garden Press L 1973) [2] 500 cc. Olive cloth $25/100

036c: TREE BY TOLKIEN Capra Press SB 1974 [2] 200 sgd no cc. Issued without dustwrapper $100.

036d: TREE BY TOLKIEN Capra Press SB 1974 [] Wraps $25.

037a: A BOOK OF BOOZE Gollancz L 1974 [0] Dark red boards. Also maroon cloth (Dalian Books 9/92) (probably the same) $10/50

038a: HERMAN HESSE Village Press (L 1974) [1] Wraps $40.

039a: HESSE, REICH, BORGES (Leaves of Grass Pa. 1974) [] Wraps $40.

040a: JORGE LUIS BORGES Village Press (L 1974) [1] Wraps $50.

041a: KEN RUSSELL *Director in Search of A Hero* Intergroup Publ. L 1974 [] Wraps $50.

042a: THE RETURN OF LLOIGOR Village Press (L 1974) [1] Wraps. "This separate and revised edition published in 1974..." $50.

043a: THE SCHOOLGIRL MURDER CASE Hart-Davis L (1974) [1] $12/60

043b: THE SCHOOLGIRL MURDER CASE Crown NY (1974) [0] $10/50

044a: WILLIAM REICH Village Press (L 1974) [1] Wraps $40.

045a: THE CRAFT OF THE NOVEL Gollancz L 1975 [0] $12/60

046a: MYSTERIOUS POWERS Aldus L 1975 [] $15/75

046b: MYSTERIOUS POWERS   Danbury Press NY 1975 [] (Ref.a) $12/60

046c: THEY   HAD   STRANGE   POWER Doubleday NY 1975 [] New title $10/40

047a: THE UNEXPLAINED Lost Pleiade Press Lake Oswego 1975 [] A drastically abridged version of *The Occult*, edited by Robert Durand and Roberta Dyer $10/50

048a: ENIGMAS AND MYSTERIES Aldus L 1976 [] $15/75

048b: ENIGMAS AND MYSTERIES   Danbury Press NY 1976 [] (Ref. a) $10/50

048c: ENIGMAS AND MYSTERIES Doubleday NY 1976 [] $10/40

049a: THE GELLER PHENOMENON Aldus L (1976) [1] Black boards $15/75

049b: THE GELLER PHENOMENON   Danbury Press no place [NY per ref.a] (1976) [0] "First Published by Aldus in U.K. in 1976" on copyright page. Wilson's name not on cover. Pictorial paper-cover boards without dustwrapper. This is the first U.S. edition though not stated by publisher $50.

050a: THE SPACE VAMPIRES Random House NY (1976) [4] Ref.a shows U.K. first but L.W. Currey (11/88) and Dalian Books (4/90) stated U.S. preceded by six months $15/75

050b: THE SPACE VAMPIRES   Hart-Davis MacGibbon L (1976) [1] Black boards $12/60

050c: LIFE FORCE Warner NY 1976 [] Wraps. New title $10.

051a: MEN OF MYSTERY   W.H. Allen   L   1977
[0] Edited by Wilson $12/60

051b: DARK DIMENSIONS *A Celebration of the
Occult* Everest NY (1977) [1] New title $10/50

052a: MYSTERIES *An Investigation into .. Occult,
..Paranormal   &   ..Supernatural*   Hodder   &
Stoughton L (1978) [1] $12/60

052b: MYSTERIES *An Investigation into .. Occult,
..Paranormal &...Supernatural* Putnam NY (1978)
[0] $10/50

053a: MYSTERIES OF THE MIND   Aldus Books
L 1978 [] Basically a combination of *Mysterious
Powers* by Wilson and *Minds Without Boundaries*
by Stuart Holroyd with some changes in the
illustrations $12/60

054a: SCIENCE   FICTION   AS   EXIS-
TENTIALISM   Bran's Head Press (Middlesex
1978) [0] Wraps $30.

054b: SCIENCE   FICTION   AS   EXIS-
TENTIALISM *A Personal View* Borgo Press San
Bernardino 1989 [] Slightly revised $10/50

054c: SCIENCE   FICTION   AS   EXIS-
TENTIALISM *A Personal View* Borgo Press San
Bernardino 1989 [] Wraps $15.

055a: THE HAUNTED MAN *The Strange Genius...*
Borgo Press San Bernardino 1979 [2] 12 sgd ltr cc.
Expanded version of the essay in 029a. In imitation
red leather and xeroxed dustwrapper (tacky) $150/250

055b: THE HAUNTED MAN *The Strange Genius..*
Borgo Press San Bernardino 1979 [2] 50 sgd no cc $100/150

055c: THE HAUNTED MAN *The Strange Genius..*
Borgo Press   San Bernardino 1979 [] Library
binding $40.

055d: THE HAUNTED MAN *The Strange Genius..*
Borgo Press San Bernardino 1979 [] Wraps $15.

056a: FRANKENSTEIN'S CASTLE   Ashgrove
Press (Kent 1981) [] Wraps $35.

056b: FRANKENSTEIN'S CASTLE   Ashgrove
Press (Kent 1981) [1] Blue cloth $12/60

057a: STARSEEKERS Hodder & Stoughton   L
1980 [1] Blue boards $12/60

057b: STARSEEKERS Doubleday GC 1980 [1] $10/40

058a: THE WAR AGAINST SLEEP   Aquarian
Press L 1980 [] $15/60

058b: THE WAR AGAINST SLEEP Aquarian
Press L 1980 [] Wraps $20.

059a: ANTI-SARTRE, WITH AN ESSAY ON
CAMUS   Borgo Press San Bernardino 1981 [2]
15 sgd ltr cc in imitation beige leather (Vagabond
Books) $200.

059b: ANTI-SARTRE, WITH AN ESSAY ON
CAMUS   Borgo Press San Bernardino 1981 [2]
50 sgd no cc (Ulysses Bookshop 7/95) $150.

059c: ANTI-SARTRE, WITH AN ESSAY ON
CAMUS Borgo Press San Bernardino (1981) [] $10/50

059d: ANTI-SARTRE, WITH AN ESSAY ON
CAMUS Borgo Press San Bernardino (1981) []
Wraps $15.

060a: THE DIRECTORY OF POSSIBILITIES
Webb & Bower Exeter 1981 [] Edited by Wilson
and John Grant $12/60

060b: THE DIRECTORY OF POSSIBILITIES
Rutledge Press NY 1981 [] $10/40

061a: POLTERGEIST New English Library L 1981 [] $12/60

061b: POLTERGEIST Putnam NY (1982) [0] $10/40

062a: THE QUEST FOR WILHELM REICH Granada L 1981 [1] Gray boards $10/50

062b: THE QUEST FOR WILHELM REICH Anchor/Doubleday GC 1981 [1] White boards with red cloth spine $10/40

063a: WITCHES Dragon's World L 1981 [] $10/50

064a: ACCESS TO INNER WORLDS Hutchinson L 1983 [] $10/40

064b: ACCESS TO INNER WORLDS Hutchinson L 1983 [] Wraps $15.

065a: ENCYCLOPEDIA OF MODERN MURDER Barker L 1983 [] Written with D. Seaman $12/60

065b: ENCYCLOPEDIA OF MODERN MURDER Putnam NY 1984 [] $10/40

065c: ENCYCLOPEDIA OF MODERN MURDER Putnam NY 1984 [] Wraps $15.

066a: A CRIMINAL HISTORY OF MANKIND Granada L (1984) [1] $10/50

066b: A CRIMINAL HISTORY OF MANKIND Putnam NY 1984 [] $10/40

067a: THE JANUS MURDER CASE Granada L (1984) [1] Simulated red cloth $12/60

068a: LORD OF UNDERWORLD *Jung and the Twentieth Century* Agrarian Press Wellingborough (1984) [1] Black cloth $10/50

069a: THE PSYCHIC DETECTIVES... Pan Books
L 1984 [] Wraps $35.

069b: THE PSYCHIC DETECTIVES... Mercury
House S.F. 1985 [] $10/40

070a: AFTERLIFE... Harrap L 1985 [] $10/50

070b: AFTERLIFE... Dolphin/Doubleday GC
1987 [] $10/40

070c: AFTERLIFE... Dolphin/Doubleday GC
1987 [] Wraps $15.

071a: THE BICAMERAL CRITIC Ashgrove Press
Bath 1985 [] Wraps $30.

071b: THE BICAMERAL CRITIC Salem House
Salem (1985) [] Wraps (Antic Hay 10/91) $25.

072a: THE ESSENTIAL COLIN WILSON Harrap
L 1985 [] $10/50

072b: THE ESSENTIAL COLIN WILSON
Celestial Arts Berkeley 1986 [] Wraps $15.

073a: THE PERSONALITY SURGEON New
English Library (Kent 1985) [1] $10/40

073b: THE PERSONALITY SURGEON *A Novel*
Mercury House S.F. (1986) [0] (Published August
4, 1986 at $17.95) $7/35

074a: RUDOLF STEINER... The Aquarian Press
Wellingborough 1985 [] Wraps $50.

075a: G.I. GURDJIEFF... The Aquarian Press
Wellingborough 1986 [] Wraps $50.

075b: G.I. GURDJIEFF... Borgo Press San
Bernardino 1986 [] $10/40

076a: THE LAUREL & HARDY THEORY OF CONSCIOUSNESS Robert Briggs Assoc. Mill Valley 1986 [] Wraps $40.

076b: THE LAUREL & HARDY THEORY OF CONSCIOUSNESS Publisher? SF 1979 [] 12 page essay (Ulysses Bookshop 3/94) $40.

077a: SCANDAL! *An Encyclopaedia* Weidenfeld & Nicolson L (1986) [0] Edited by Wilson and Donald Seaman $10/40

077b: SCANDAL! Stein & Day NY 1986 [] $7/35

077c: AN ENCYCLOPEDIA OF SCANDAL Grafton L 1987 [] Wraps. New title $10.

078a: AN ESSAY ON THE NEW EXISTENTIALISM Paupers' Press Nottingham 1986 [] Wraps $15.

078b: AN ESSAY ON THE NEW EXISTENTIALISM Borgo Press San Bernardino 1988 [] $10/40

078c: AN ESSAY ON THE NEW EXISTENTIALISM Paupers' Press Nottingham 1990 [2] 100 no cc (on book plate). Issued in laminated hardcover without dustwrapper. The "Fourth Impression" $40.

079a: THE BOOK OF GREAT MYSTERIES Robinson Publ. L 1986 [] Wraps. Edited by Wilson and Dr. Christopher Guans $15.

080a: MARX REFUTED... Ashgrove Press Bath 1987 [] Edited by Wilson and Ronald Duncan $10/40

080b: MARX REFUTED... Ashgrove Press Bath 1987 [] Wraps $15.

081a: ALEISTER CROWLEY *The Nature of the Beast* Aquarian Press Wellingborough 1987 [] Wraps

$20.

081b: ALEISTER CROWLEY *The Nature of the Beast* Borgo Press San Bernardino 1989 []

$10/40

082a: THE ENCYCLOPEDIA OF UNSOLVED MYSTERIES Harrap L 1987 [] With Damon Wilson

$10/40

082b: THE ENCYCLOPEDIA OF UNSOLVED MYSTERIES Contemporary Books Chicago 1988 []

$10/40

083a: JACK THE RIPPER... Bantam Press L/NY 1987 [] With Robin Odell

$10/40

084a: THE MUSICIAN AS OUTSIDER Paupers' Press (Nottingham 1987) [1] Wraps

$15.

084b: THE MUSICIAN AS OUTSIDER Borgo Press San Bernardino 1989 []

$10/40

084c: THE MUSICAN AS OUTSIDER Paupers' Press (Nottingham 1990) [2] 100 no cc (on book plate). Issued in laminated hardcover without dustwrapper. The "Second Impression"

$30.

085a: SPIDER WORLD *The Tower* Grafton L 1987 []

$10/50

085b: SPIDER WORLD *The Tower* Grafton L 1987 [] Wraps

$15.

Note: Ace Books NY issued *Spider World: The Desert* 1988, *Spider World: The Tower* 1989, and *Spider World: The Fortress* 1989 in three paperbacks. Each comprising one third of 085a

086a: SPIDER WORLD *The Delta* Grafton L 1987 []

$10/50

086b: SPIDER WORLD *The Delta* Grafton L 1987 [] Wraps $15.

087a: AUTOBIOGRAPHICAL IMPRESSIONS Paupers' Press (Nottingham 1988) [2] 100 no cc (on book plate). Issued in laminated hardback without dustwrapper $75.

087b: AUTOBIOGRAPHICAL REFLECTIONS Paupers' Press (Nottingham 1988) [1] New title. Wraps $15.

088a: THE MAMMOTH BOOK OF TRUE CRIME Robinson Publ. L 1988 [] Wraps. Edited by Howard F. Dossor $20.

089a: THE MISFITS... Grafton L 1988 [] $10/40

089b: THE MISFITS... Carroll & Graf NY 1989 [] $10/40

090a: THE MAGICIAN FROM SIBERIA Robert Hale L 1988 [] $10/40

091a: BEYOND THE OCCULT Bantam Press L/NY 1988 [] $10/40

092a: EXISTENTIALLY SPEAKING... Borgo Press San Bernardino 1989 [] $10/40

092b: EXISTENTIALLY SPEAKING... Borgo Press San Bernardino 1989 [] Wraps $15.

093a: THE DECLINE AND FALL OF LEFTISM Paupers' Press (Nottingham 1989) [2] 100 no cc (on book plate). Issued in laminated hardcover without dustwrapper $75.

093b: THE DECLINE AND FALL OF LEFTISM Paupers' Press (Nottingham 1989) [1] Wraps $15.

094a: THE UNTETHERED MIND Ashgrove Press Bath 1989 [] Edited by Howard F. Dossor $10/40

095a: WRITTEN IN BLOOD... Equation L 1989
[] $10/40

096a: THE SERIAL KILLERS Allen L 1990 []
Written with Donald Seaman $10/40

096b: THE SERIAL KILLERS Allen L 1990 []
Wraps $15.

097a: THE GOTHIC CATHEDRAL *The Archi-
tecture of the Great Church 1130-1530* Thames &
Hudson L 1990 [] $10/40

098a: MUSIC, NATURE AND THE ROMANTIC
OUTSIDER Paupers' Press (Nottingham 1990)
[2] 100 no cc (on bookplate). Issued in laminated
hardcover without dustwrapper $75.

098b: MUSIC, NATURE AND THE ROMANTIC
OUTSIDER Paupers' Press (Nottingham 1990)
[1] Wraps $15.

099a: MARRIAGE AND LONDON Paupers'
Press (Nottingham 1991) [2] 100 no cc (on book
plate). Issued in laminated hardcover without
dustwrapper. Being chapters 7 and 8 of *Voyage to a
Begining* which were not in the U.K. edition (only
the U.S.) $60.

099b: MARRIAGE AND LONDON Paupers'
Press (Nottingham 1991) [0] Wraps $15.

100a: THE MAGICIAN HarperCollins (L 1992)
[] Third of *Spider World* series (L.W. Currey 8/92) $10/40

100b: THE MAGICIAN Grafton NY 1992 [] Third
of *Spider World* series $10/40

101a: SEX, AMERICA AND OTHER INSIGHTS
Paupers' Press (Nottingham 1992) [2] 100 no cc
(on book plate). Issued in laminated hardcover
without dustwrapper. Being chapters 13, 14, and 15

of *Voyages to a Begining* (U.S. edition) with a new
postscript $60.

101b: SEX, AMERICA AND OTHER INSIGHTS
Paupers' Press (Nottingham 1992) [0] Wraps $15.

E I mund wilson (signature)

EDMUND WILSON
(1895-1972)

Wilson was considered by many as the leading man of letters in America. He was concerned with both literary and social themes. He wrote as an historian, poet, novelist, playwright, editor and short story writer. His critical writings on Dos Passos, Hemingway, Fitzgerald and Faulkner attracted public interest to their work. When writing *To the Finland Station* he learned Russian and when he wrote *The Scrolls from the Dead Sea* he learned to read Hebrew. He covered a multitude of subjects and expressed his views in a prose style noted for clarity and precision.

REFERENCES:

(a) Ramsey, Richard David. EDMUND WILSON *A Bibliography.* New York: David Lewis (1971). (Primarily a checklist with no first edition identification or quantities.)

(b) Bruccoli, Matthew J. F. SCOTT FITZGERALD *A Descriptive Bibliography.* Pittsburgh: University of Pittsburgh Press, 1972.

001a: THE EVIL EYE *A Comedy in Two Acts* Triangle Club Princeton 1915 [0] Wraps. Written with F. Scott Fitzgerald $1,750.

002a: THE UNDERTAKER'S GARLAND Knopf NY 1922 [2] 50 cc for "Bookseller Friends". Issued without dustwrapper $250.

002b: THE UNDERTAKER'S GARLAND Knopf NY 1922 [1] "Published September 1922" on copyright page. Written with John Peale Bishop $100/350

003a: DISCORDANT ENCOUNTERS *Plays and Dialogues* A & C Boni NY 1926 [0] $200/1,000

004a: I THOUGHT OF DAISY Scribners NY 1928 [] Salesman's dummy in blue cloth. 8 pages of text (Boston Book Annex) $1,000.

004b: I THOUGHT OF DAISY Scribners NY 1929 [0] $100/450

004c: I THOUGHT OF DAISY W. H. Allen L 1929 [] (We do not know if this exists as we've never seen it) $NVA

004d: I THOUGHT OF DAISY W.H. Allen L [1952] [0] $20/100

004e: I THOUGHT OF DAISY Farrar, Straus & Giroux NY 1953 [0] Reissue with new foreword $25/125

004f: I THOUGHT OF DAISY Ballantine NY 1953 [] Wraps. Issued simultaneously with Farrar hardback $30.

004g: GALAHAD and I THOUGHT OF DAISY Farrar Straus & Giroux NY (1967) [0] First book appearance of *Galahad*. Both revised. New introduction $15/75

005a: POETS, FAREWELL Scribners NY 1929 [0] $125/500

006a: AXEL'S CASTLE Scribners NY 1931 [5] $150/750

007a: THE AMERICAN JITTERS Scribners NY 1932 [5] $150/750

007b: DEVIL TAKE THE HINDMOST Scribner L 1932 [] New title $150/750

008a: TRAVELS IN TWO DEMOCRACIES Harcourt Brace NY (1936) [1] $60/300

009a: THIS ROOM AND THIS GIN AND THESE SANDWICHES: Three Plays New Republic NY 1937 [0] Wraps $300.

010a: THE TRIPLE THINKERS *Ten Essays on Literature* Harcourt Brace NY (1938) [1] Noted in dark green cloth with gold lettering and top edge yellow; and in medium brown cloth with white lettering and top edge unstained. Priority unknown but latter seems cheaper and may have been a remainder binding $60/300

010b: THE TRIPLE THINKERS *Ten Essays on Literature* Oxford L 1939 [] $40/200

010c: THE TRIPLE THINKERS *Twelve Essays...* Revised and Enlarged Lehman L (1952) [1] "First published in this edition in 1952" on copyright page $12/60

011a: WILSON'S CHRISTMAS STOCKING *Fun for Young and Old* No publisher (NY no date [circa 1930's]) [] Red printed wraps (Bromer Booksellers 10/92) $200.

012a: TO THE FINLAND STATION Harcourt Brace NY (1940) [1] $60/300

012b: TO THE FINLAND STATION Secker & Warburg L no date [1941] [0] U.S. sheets $40/150

012c: TO THE FINLAND STATION Anchor Books GC 1953 [] Wraps. No. A6. Substitutes "Summary as of 1940" (essay) for "Appendices" $35.

012d: TO THE FINLAND STATION Farrar, Straus & Giroux NY (1972) [1] New introduction $10/40

013a: THE BOYS IN THE BACK ROOM Colt Press SF 1941 [2] 100 sgd no cc. Issued in acetate dustwrapper $750.

013b: THE BOYS IN THE BACK ROOM Colt Press SF 1941 [2] 1,500 cc $50/250

014a: THE WOUND AND THE BOW Houghton
Mifflin B 1941 [0] $40/200

014b: THE WOUND AND THE BOW Secker and
Warburg L 1942 [] $25/125

014c: THE WOUND AND THE BOW Oxford
University Press NY 1947 [0] "New printing with
corrections, 1947" $15/75

015a: NOTE-BOOKS OF NIGHT Colt Press SF
1942 [2] ?? sgd cc. Reportedly 100 copies were to
be issued but only 10 or so were ever issued. These
were in decorated floral boards with cloth spine
(Chas. Seluzicki 10/89) and dustwrapper (Thomas
Goldwasser Books 6/92) $1,250/2,000

015b: NOTE-BOOKS OF NIGHT Colt Press SF
1942 [2] 21 sgd cc. In the 1970's Andrew Hoyem
acquired the Grabhorn Press inventory which
included 21 sets of the sheets which he bound up in
blue paper boards with a black leather spine
stamped in gold (Glenn Horowitz 10/88) $750.

015c: NOTE-BOOKS OF NIGHT Colt Press SF
1942 [0] Inner tissue and outer dustwrapper
(Bradford Morrow) $60/300

015d: NOTE-BOOKS OF NIGHT Secker and
Warburg L 1945 [1] $25/100

016a: MEMOIRS OF HECATE COUNTY
Doubleday GC 1945 [] Uncorrected Proof in plain
brown wraps (tall sheets from galleys) (Ken Lopez
2/95) $500.

016b: MEMOIRS OF HECATE COUNTY
Doubleday GC 1946 [1] $35/175

016c: MEMOIRS OF HECATE COUNTY W. H.
Allen L (1952) [0] Revised and corrected (Peter
Jolliffe) but not so noted in ref.a. Dustwrapper
priced "12/6 net" and "(in U.S.A. $4.00)" $15/75

016d: MEMOIRS OF HECATE COUNTY L. C. Page NY (1959) [0] Reissue with changes (new copyright) $8/40

017a: EUROPE WITHOUT BAEDEKER Doubleday GC 1947 [1] $25/125

017b: EUROPE WITHOUT BAEDEKER Secker and Warburg L 1948 [1] $15/75

017c: EUROPE WITHOUT BAEDEKER ...*Together With Notes...1963-1964* Farrar, Straus & Giroux NY 1966 [1] "First revised edition, 1966" $10/40

017d: EUROPE WITHOUT BAEDEKER ...*Together With Notes...1963-1964* Rupert Hart-Davis L 1967 [] $10/40

018a: THE LITTLE BLUE LIGHT *A Play* Farrar, Straus & Co. NY (1950) [0] $20/100

018b: THE LITTLE BLUE LIGHT *A Play* Gollancz L 1951 [] $12/60

019a: CLASSICS AND COMMERCIALS Farrar Straus NY (1950) [5] $15/75

019b: CLASSICS AND COMMERCIALS W. H. Allen L 1951 [] $15/75

020a: THE WHITE SAND (Thomas Todd {printer} B 1950) [0] 12 cc. Wraps. 10 page pamphlet $450.

021a: THREE RELIQUES OF ANCIENT WESTERN POETRY COLLECTED BY... (Thomas Todd {printer} B 1951) [0] Wraps. 13 page pamphlet in red wraps $150.

021b: THREE RELIQUES OF ANCIENT WESTERN POETRY COLLECTED BY... No publisher CA 1960 [] Wraps $75.

021c: THREE RELIQUES OF ANCIENT WESTERN POETRY COLLECTED BY... (Gotham Book Mart NY 1964) [] Green wraps $50.

022a: THE SHORES OF LIGHT Farrar, Straus & Young NY (1952) [0] $15/75

022b: THE SHORES OF LIGHT W. H. Allen L 1952 [] $10/50

023a: WILSON'S CHRISTMAS STOCKING... (Thomas Todd {printer} B 1953) [] Red printed wraps. $100 $150.

024a: FIVE PLAYS W. H. Allen L 1954 [0] British precedes U.S. $20/100

024b: FIVE PLAYS Farrar Straus & Young NY 1954 [0] English sheets $15/75

025a: EIGHT ESSAYS Anchor Books GC 1954 [1] Wraps. Number A 37 $40.

026a: THE SCROLLS FROM THE DEAD SEA Oxford University Press NY 1955 [0] $15/75

026b: THE SCROLLS FROM THE DEAD SEA W. H. Allen L 1955 [0] $12/60

026c: THE SCROLLS FROM THE DEAD SEA Collins L 1957 [] Wraps. Slightly "amplified and revised". Also see 041 $30.

027a: A CHRISTMAS DELIRIUM (Thomas Todd B) 1955 [0] Wraps $150.

028a: RED, BLACK, BLOND AND OLIVE... Oxford Univeristy Press NY 1956 [0] $15/75

028b: RED, BLACK, BLOND AND OLIVE... W. H. Allen L 1956 [] $10/50

029a: A LITERARY CHRONICLE: 1920-1950 Anchor Books GC 1956 [0] Wraps. Number A 85 (Library of Congress copy does not state first, but may be reprint) $35.

029b: A LITERARY CHRONICLE: 1920-1950 Peter Smith Gloucester 1961 [] $15/75

030a: A PIECE OF MY MIND Farrar Straus & Cudahy NY (1956) [1] $10/50

030b: A PIECE OF MY MIND W. H. Allen L 1957 [0] $10/40

031a: THE AMERICAN EARTHQUAKE Anchor Books GC 1958 [1] Assume wraps $50.

031b: THE AMERICAN EARTHQUAKE Doubleday NY 1964 [] $15/60

031c: THE AMERICAN EARTHQUAKE Peter Smith Gloucester 1964 [] Rebound issue of the Anchor Books edition $10/50

032a: "Legend and Symbol in *Dr. Zhivago*" [Encounter NY 1959] [] An off-print, undated, but appeared in June issue. 14 pages of text in wraps $75.

033a: APOLOGIES TO THE IROQUOIS Farrar, Straus & Cudahy NY (1960) [0] Brick red cloth lettered in gold on spine] $10/50

033b: APOLOGIES TO THE IROQUOIS W.H. Allen L 1960 [] $10/40

034a: NIGHT THOUGHTS Farrar, Straus & Cudahy NY (1961) [1] $10/50

034b: NIGHT THOUGHTS W.H. Allen L 1962 [0] $10/40

035a: PATRIOTIC GORE Oxford University Press NY 1962 [0] $10/50

035b: PATRIOTIC GORE Oxford University Press NY 1962 [] Wraps. Galaxy Book No. 160 $25.

035c: PATRIOTIC GORE Andre Deutsch L 1962 [] $10/40

036a: THE COLD WAR AND THE INCOME TAX Farrar Straus NY (1963) [] Uncorrected proofs in loose sheet punched at left and string tied into stiff boards (Wm. Reese Co. 7/89) $200.

036b: THE COLD WAR AND THE INCOME TAX Farrar Straus NY (1963) [1] $10/50

036c: THE COLD WAR AND THE INCOME TAX W. H. Allen L 1964 [1] Black cloth lettered in gold on spine $10/40

037a: O CANADA Farrar Straus & Giroux NY (1965) [1] $10/50

037b: O CANADA Hart-Davis L 1967 [1] $10/40

038a: THE BIT BETWEEN MY TEETH Farrar Straus & Giroux NY (1965) [1] $10/50

038b: THE BIT BETWEEN MY TEETH W. H. Allen L 1966 [] $8/40

039a: HOLIDAY GREETINGS 1966 (Thomas Todd {printer} B 1966) [] $125.

040a: A PRELUDE Farrar, Straus & Giroux NY (1967) [] Uncorrected proofs in spiral bound plain wraps (Wm. Reese Co. 7/89) $150.

040b: A PRELUDE Farrar, Straus & Giroux NY (1967) [1] $10/40

040c: A PRELUDE W. H. Allen L 1967 [0] $7/35

041a: THE FRUITS OF THE MLA (NY *Review* NY 1968) [1] Stapled wraps. "First Printing, December 1968." Priced $1.00 $60.

042a: THE DUKE OF PALERMO... Farrar, Straus & Giroux NY (1969) [0] $10/50

042b: THE DUKE OF PALERMO... W.H. Allen L (1969) [] 500 cc. American sheets $15/75

043a: THE DEAD SEA SCROLLS 1947-1969 Oxford Univ. Press NY 1969 [] $12/60

043b: THE DEAD SEA SCROLLS 1947-1969 W.H. Allen L 1969 [] $10/50

044a: HOLIDAY GREETINGS AND DESOLATING LYRICS (Privately Printed no place) 1970 [] Stapled gray printed wraps, 8pp. (Waiting For Godot Books 9/92) $100.

045a: UPSTATE *Records and Recollections of Northern New York* Farrar, Straus & Giroux NY (1971) [1] $10/40

046a: A WINDOW ON RUSSIA Farrar, Straus & Giroux NY (1972) [1] $10/40

046b: A WINDOW ON RUSSIA Macmillan L (1972) [] (Dalian 4/90) $7/35

047a: THE DEVILS AND CANON BARHAM Farrar NY (1973) [1] $10/40

047b: THE DEVILS AND CANON BARHAM Macmillan L 1973 [] $7/35

048a: THE RATS OF RUTLAND GRANGE Gotham Book Mart (NY 1974) [2] 26 sgd ltr cc. Illustrated by Edward Gorey. Issued without dustwrapper in slipcase $700/750

048b: THE RATS OF RUTLAND GRANGE
Gotham Book Mart (NY 1974) [2] 100 sgd no cc.
Issued without dustwrapper in slipcase $300/350

048c: THE RATS OF RUTLAND GRANGE
Gotham Book Mart (NY 1974) [2] 1,000 cc in
wraps $75.

049a: THE TWENTIES Farrar NY (1975) [1] $10/40

049b: THE TWENTIES (Macmillan L 1975) [] $7/35

050a: CORRECTIONS AND COMMENTS
University of Iowa Iowa City (1976) [2] 175 cc $125.

051a: LETTERS ON POLITICIANS 1912-1972
Farrar Straus & Giroux NY (1977) [] Uncorrected
proof. Two volumes in wraps (Paul Rassam 10/95) $75.

051b: LETTERS ON LITERATURE AND
POLITICS Farrar, Straus & Giroux NY (1977) [1]
New title. Edited by Elena Wilson $10/40

052a: ISRAEL AND THE DEAD SEA SCROLLS
Farrar NY 1978 [] $10/50

053a: THE NABOKOV-WILSON LETTERS 1940-
1971 Harper NY (1979) [3] 15,000 cc. Also states
"First Edition". Edited by Simon Karlinsky $12/60

053b: THE NABOKOV-WILSON LETTERS
Weidenfeld & Nicolson L (1980) [1] $10/50

054a: THE THIRTIES Farrar Straus & Giroux NY
(1980) [1] $7/35

055a: THE FORTIES Farrar Straus & Giroux NY
(1983) [] Uncorrected Proof in orange wraps $75.

055b: THE FORTIES Farrar Straus & Giroux NY
(1983) [1] $7/35

056a: THE PORTABLE EDMUND WILSON
Viking NY (1983) [1] $8/40

057a: THE FIFTIES Farrar Straus & Giroux NY
(1986) [] Edited by Leon Edel $7/35

058a: THE SIXTIES *The Last Journal 1960-1972*
Farrar Straus & Giroux NY 1993 [] Uncorrected
proof in gray wraps $75.

058b: THE SIXTIES *The Last Journal 1960-1972*
Farrar Straus & Giroux NY 1993 [] $5/25

BOOKS EDITED OR
CONTAINING INTRODUCTIONS
BY EDMUND WILSON

059a: IN OUR TIME Scribners NY 1930 [0]
3,240 cc. Seal on copyright page. New Hemingway
material with introduction by Wilson $300/1,500

060a: THE LAST TYCOON Scribners NY 1941
[5] An unfinished novel by F. Scott Fitzgerald
(ref.b) $100/600

060b: THE LAST TYCOON Grey Walls Press L
(1949) [1] (Ref. b) $30/150

061a: THE SHOCK OF RECOGNITION
Doubleday Doran NY 1943 [1] $30/150

061b: THE SHOCK OF RECOGNITION Farrar
Straus & Cudahy NY (1955) [1] "Second edition"
with additions and corrections $12/60

061c: THE SHOCK OF RECOGNITION W.H.
Allen L 1956 [] Second edition with additions and
corrections $10/40

062a: THE CRACK-UP ... by F. Scott Fitzgerald
New Directions (NY 1945) [0] 2,520 cc. Title page

in red and black, later printings are in black only
(ref.b) $40/200

062b: THE CRACK-UP ... by F. Scott Fitzgerald
Falcon Press L (1947) [] First English is a later
printing by New Directions with label on page 2
(ref.b) $40/150

063a: THE COLLECTED ESSAYS OF JOHN
PEALE BISHOP Scribners NY 1948 [5] $25/75

064a: PEASANTS AND OTHER STORIES by
Anton Chekhov   Anchor Books   GC 1956 []
Assume wraps $35.

065a: NOVELS OF A.C. SWINBURNE   Farrar,
Straus   NY (1962) [1] 36 page introduction by
Wilson $15/60

P. G. Wodehouse (signature)

P.G. WODEHOUSE
1881-1975

P.G. Wodehouse was born in Guildford, Surrey, England and attended Dulwich College. Belloc called him "the best living writer of English" but his popularity extended beyond the English speaking countries as his works have been translated into over 20 languages. He is one of the most widely collected of English or American authors. He felt he had "built up a nice little conservative business..but I realize that I am not one of the swells who have messages and significance and all that kind of thing." Wodehouse wrote more than 90 books, collaborated on more than 30 plays and musical comedies and wrote more than 20 film scripts. Productive to the end, it is noted in reference.a, page xliii, that "after a good morning's work on latest novel, dies in hospital".

The APG **does not** include prices for books with dustwrappers before 1920 and you are on your own in pricing any copies you may find. We used No Value Assigned (NVA) on the American editions from English sheets up to 1923 because we could find no record of any titles being catalogued recently and assume there were only a few hundred of each. This means one could assume that these issues should retail for the same price or less than the comparable English edition (which is normal practice) or assume these issues are so scarce that they should be worth many times what the English editions are worth.

It should be noted that Jenkins in many or most cases left the "First Published..." notice on later printings and therefore the ads or cloth color are necessary for identification. Walter White, a true Wodehouse devotee - who has passed on to join Plum in that great fairway in the sky, provided the number of titles in the ads for the Autographed Editions on later Jenkins books, which identifies first printing dustwrappers. There is some difference between reference a and b on cloth versus boards on the later Jenkins' books. After 1951 it appears Jenkins used a simulated cloth paper over boards which probably caused the confusion.

In addition, we would like to acknowledge the assistance of William Cagle, the Librarian at the Lilly Library, Indiana University, who took his time to check the Methuen archives at Lilly and provided first printing quantities on the titles published by Methuen; and Simon & Schuster and Little, Brown for providing the first printing quantities on their respective titles. Reference A indicates that until 1915 the first printings did not exceed 2,000 copies. We would also like to thank John Graham for sharing with us the extensive records that he has kept on the recent sales of Wodehouse books.

Because the dustwrappers on any of the books prior to 1920 are scarce and in some instances rare, see Reference A for descriptions of these dustwrappers.

Wodehouse wrote the lyrics for 170 songs. Those published as sheet music would range in value from $40 to $150. Those published in boards or cloth would be priced higher.

REFERENCES:

(a) McIlvaine, Eileen et al. P.G. WODEHOUSE *A Comprehensive Bibliography and Checklist*. New York: James H. Heineman, Inc. (1990).

(b) Jasen, David A. A BIBLIOGRAPHY AND READER'S GUIDE TO THE FIRST EDITIONS OF P.G. WODEHOUSE. Second Edition. (London): Greenhill Books (1986).

(c) Private Collections, inventory or dealer catalogs.

001a: THE POTHUNTERS Adam & Charles Black L 1902 [0] Royal blue cloth silver lettering on spine with silver loving cup on front cover and spine. No advertisements. $4,000.

001b: THE POTHUNTERS Macmillan NY 1902 [0] From English sheets $NVA

001c: THE POTHUNTERS   Adam & Charles Black   L 1902 [0] First sheets reissued (approximately 1909) in gray-blue pictorial cloth (runners) 8 pages advertisements ending with *Mike* $850.

002a: A PREFECT'S UNCLE   Adam & Charles Black L 1903 [0] Red cloth lettered and decorated in gold, black, lavender and pink. No advertisements $3,000.

002b: A PREFECT'S UNCLE   Macmillan NY 1903 [0] From the English sheets $NVA

003a: TALES OF ST. AUSTIN'S Adam & Charles Black L 1903 [0] Light red pictorial cloth with frontis and 11 illustrations by Whitwell, Pocock and Skinner $3,500.

003b: TALES OF ST. AUSTIN'S Adam & Charles Black L 1903 [0] Reissued in light red cloth with gold and black lettered on spine or in olive-green pictorial cloth $850.

004a: THE GOLD BAT Adam & Charles Black L 1904 [0] Dark red pictorial cloth with frontis and 7 illustrations by Whitwell. Advertisements for first three Wodehouse books at back. Bulks 1 1/4" $1,750.

004b: THE GOLD BAT Adam & Charles Black L 1904 [0] Bulks 1 3/8" with 8 page catalog. Ads would indicate this was issued in 1909, as *Mike* is mentioned $650.

004c: THE GOLD BAT Macmillan NY 1923 [0] Presumedly from the English sheets of 1923 English reprint $NVA

005a: WILLIAM TELL TOLD AGAIN Adam & Charles Black L 1904 [0] Off-white cloth lettered in gilt on spine and front cover, top edge gilt, publisher's monogram on title page. Two-pages of ads $1,500.

005b: WILLIAM TELL TOLD AGAIN   Adam & Charles Black L 1904 [0] Same as 005a but with 12-page advertising insert which includes *The White Feather* (1907) $850.

005c: WILLIAM TELL TOLD AGAIN Macmillan NY 1904 [0] From the English sheets $NVA

005d: WILLIAM TELL TOLD AGAIN   Adam & Charles Black L 1904 [0] Tan or light brown pictorial cloth,top edge gilt, gilt on spine only . Same 2-page advertisements as in 005a. Gilt on cover $600.

005e: WILLIAM TELL TOLD AGAIN   Adam & Charles Black L no date [0] Variant state in buff boards with black lettering (R.A. Gekowski), without date on title page and publisher's address on title page (ref.a) $400.

006a: THE HEAD OF KAY'S   Adam & Charles Black   L 1905 [0] Dark red pictorial cloth with frontis and 7 illustrations by Whitwell. No advertisements $3,000.

006b: THE HEAD OF KAY'S   Adam & Charles Black   L 1905 [0] With 8 pages of ads including this book as latest $750.

006c: THE HEAD OF KAY'S   Adam & Charles Black   L 1905 [0] Same as 006b but 8-pages of ads have *Mike* as latest $350.

006d: THE HEAD OF KAY'S   Macmillan   NY 1922 [0] Presumedly from the English sheets of later edition $NVA

007a: LOVE AMONG THE CHICKENS   George Newnes Ltd. L (1906) [0] Tan pictorial cloth with frontis and 3 illustrations by H.M. Brock $6,000.

007b: LOVE AMONG THE CHICKENS   George Newnes Ltd.   L (1906) [0] Same as 007a but "August 1906" on copyright page — $1,000.

007c: LOVE AMONG THE CHICKENS   Circle Publishing Co. NY 1909 [0]   Some copies have page tipped in after half-title "This Advance Copy No. --" which seems more common than the regular issue (6 copies of this catalogued in recent years vs. one of other) — $1,000.

007d: LOVE AMONG THE CHICKENS   Herbert Jenkins   L 1921 [0] List on half-title verso ends with *Indiscretions of Archie*. "Entirely rewritten.." on title page — $350/1,750

008a: THE WHITE FEATHER   Adam and Chas. Black   L 1907 [0] Light brown cloth frontis and 11 illustrations by Townend. No advertisements at end of the book — $3,000.

008b: THE WHITE FEATHER   Adam and Chas. Black   L 1907 [0] Same as 008a but with 8-pages of ads including *Mike* (1909) — $1,000.

008c: THE WHITE FEATHER   Macmillan   NY 1922 [] Presumedly from the English sheets of later edition — $NVA

009a: NOT GEORGE WASHINGTON (written with H. Westbrook)   Cassell & Co.   L 1907 [0] Eight small circles under title on cover and "Cassell & Company" on spine and "9-1907" between p.96-97 — $4,500.

009b: NOT GEORGE WASHINGTON (written with H. Westbrook)   Cassell & Co.   L 1907 [0] Same as 009a but publisher's name on spine reads "Cassell" only. No number on pp.96-97 — $2,000.

009c: NOT GEORGE WASHINGTON (written with H. Westbrook)   Cassell & Co.   L 1907 [0] Same as 009a but seven small circles on cover — $1,250.

009d: NOT GEORGE WASHINGTON (written with H. Westbrook) Continuum NY (1980) [] Edited by Jasen — $10/50

010a: THE GLOBE BY THE WAY BOOK Globe Publ. Co. L (1908) [0] Vermillion pictorial wraps (one of, or the scarcest title, only 2 known copies in private hands {ref.c}) — $10,000.

010b: THE GLOBE BY THE WAY BOOK James Heineman and Sceptre Press Bristol 1985 [2] 500 no cc. Wraps in slipcase (David Mayou) — $250.

011a: THE SWOOP Alston Rivers Ltd. L 1909 [0] Ref.a calls for white pictorial wraps, ref.b for orange pictorial wraps — $5,000.

011b: THE SWOOP James H. Heineman L 1993 [2] 400 cc in wraps — $40.

012a: MIKE Adam & Chas. Black L 1909 [0] Olive-green cloth, frontis and 11 illustrations by T.M.R. Whitwell — $4,000.

012b: MIKE Macmillan NY 1910 [] From the English sheets — $NVA

012c: ENTER PSMITH Adam & Chas. Black L (1935) [1] New title. "Published Spring 1935..." Blue-green cloth lettered in red — $150/750

012d: ENTER PSMITH Macmillan NY (1935) [0] From the English sheets in orange cloth, black letters on spine only (ref.c) — $150/600

012e: ENTER PSMITH Macmillan NY 1935 [0] With "Printed in U.S." on copyright page (ref.c) — $150/600

012f: MIKE AT WRYKYN Herbert Jenkins L (1953) [1] New title. Part one of *Mike* slightly revised. Red cloth lettered in black — $40/200

012g: MIKE AND PSMITH Herbert Jenkins L 1953 [] New title. Last part of *Mike* under new title $35/175

012h: MIKE AT WRYKYN Meredith Press NY no date [1969] [1] Copyright "1953" "First U.S. edition" on copyright page. (Published in 1969 - date appears on lower corner of front dustwrapper flap) $20/100

012i: MIKE AND PSMITH Meredith Press NY no date [1969] [1] Last part of *Mike* under new title $40/200

013a: THE INTRUSION OF JIMMY W.J. Watt & Co. NY (1910) [1] "Published May" on copyright page. Bound in black, lettered in gold with circular color portrait pasted on $500.

013b: A GENTLEMAN OF LEISURE Alston Rivers Ltd. L 1910 [0] New title. Royal blue cloth lettered in gold. Minor changes in the text $1,750.

014a: PSMITH IN THE CITY Adam & Charles Black L 1910 [0] Blue cloth. Frontis and 11 illustrations by Whitwell $1,750.

014b: PSMITH IN THE CITY Macmillan NY 1910 [0] From the English sheets $NVA

015a: THE PRINCE AND BETTY W.J. Watt and Company NY (1912) [1] "Published January" on copyright page. (Reissued with "Popular Edition" stamped on at bottom of spine {ref.b}) $400.

015b: THE PRINCE AND BETTY Mills & Boon Ltd. L (1912) [1] "Published 1912" on copyright page. Bound in red cloth. Substantially different story than 015a $2,750.

015c: PSMITH JOURNALIST Adam & Charles Black L 1915 [0] New title. Revised. Two states of spine stamping-"A.C. Black" and "Black" (Jos. The Provider). Two states of dustwrapper noted: with "Black" 1/8" high; and, "Black" 3/16" (with priority

unknown {Charles Gould}). Also substantially
different story than either 015a or b $1,750.

015d: PSMITH JOURNALIST Macmillan NY
1915 [0] From the English sheets $NVA

016a: THE LITTLE NUGGET Methuen & Co. L
(1913) [1] 1,500 cc (publisher's records). Bound in
red cloth. Two sets of advertisements dated May
and Autumn 1913. 1,500 copies includes 150 in
Colonial cloth and 150 in wraps $1,500.

016b: THE LITTLE NUGGET W. J. Watt & Co.
NY (1914) [1] "Published January" beneath
copyright notice $500.

017a: THE MAN UPSTAIRS Methuen & Co. L
(1914) [1] 1,500 cc (publisher's records). Brown
cloth with advertisements dated 25/10/13. 1,500
copies includes 150 Colonial cloth, 150 Colonial
wraps $2,000.

018a: SOMETHING NEW D. Appleton & Co. NY
1915 [5] Reprinted by Dodd Mead in 1930 $750.

018b: SOMETHING FRESH Methuen & Co. L
(1915) [1] 1,510 cc (publisher's records), includes
250 in Colonial cloth and 200 in Colonial wraps.
New title. Revised. Slightly different from 018a $1,750.

019a: UNEASY MONEY D. Appleton & Co. NY
1916 [5] $750.

019b: UNEASY MONEY Methuen & Co. L
(1917) [1] 1,500 cc (publisher's records). Differs
slightly from the U.S. edition $2,250.

020a: PICCADILLY JIM Dodd Mead & Co. NY
1917 [0] Frontis and 7 illustrations by May Wilson
Preston. Yellow cloth with black lettering $750.

020b: PICCADILLY JIM Herbert Jenkins Limited
L (1918) [0] 5000cc (publisher's records). Minor

changes in text. Mustard cloth, black letters. Quantity noted on second edition (Ergo Books 12/90) $1,250.

021a: THE MAN WITH TWO LEFT FEET Methuen & Co. L (1917) [1] 1,405 cc (publisher's records). 1,500 copies but only 1,405 were bound includes 125 in Colonial cloth and 125 in Colonial wraps $2,500.

021b: THE MAN WITH TWO LEFT FEET A.L. Burt Company NY 1933 [1] Burt is a reprint house but this is the first American edition with 3 stories not in the English edition (ref.a&b). It does state "First Edition" and there was a second printing which is the same but lacks "First Edition" $350/1250

022a: MY MAN JEEVES George Newnes, Limited L (1919) [0] "Printed by Butler and Tanner.." on p.251. Later "Hazell Watson..." $1,500.

023a: THEIR MUTUAL CHILD Boni & Liveright NY 1919 [0] (In 1924, Geo. H. Doran is supposed to have published a reprint of this title as *White Hope* but no known copies {ref.a}) $1,250.

023b: THE COMING OF BILL Herbert Jenkins L (1920) [0] New title. Red cloth, black letters $850.

023c: THE COMING OF BILL Herbert Jenkins L (1920) [0] Green cloth stamped in black with floral design on front cover (Waiting For Godot) $750.

024a: A DAMSEL IN DISTRESS George H. Doran NY (1919) [0] $600.

024b: A DAMSEL IN DISTRESS Herbert Jenkins L (1919) [0] Minor changes in text, deep red cloth, black letters $1,000.

025a: THE LITTLE WARRIOR George H. Doran NY (1920) [0] (Published at $2.00) $400/2,000

025b: JILL THE RECKLESS Herbert Jenkins L (1921) [0] New title. 6 titles on half-title verso begins *Picadilly Jim* ends *Indiscretion of Archie.* Printed by Mayflower Press. Advertisements on pp.315-320. (Published at 7s6d) $400/2,000

026a: INDISCRETIONS OF ARCHIE Herbert Jenkins L 1921 [0] 6 titles on half-title verso ends with *Jill the Reckless* light-blue cloth, blue letters. P.31:12 "friend potatoes" for "fried potatoes." (Published at 7s6d) $500/3000

026b: INDISCRETIONS OF ARCHIE George H. Doran NY (1921) [0] P.31:12 "friend potatoes" for "fried potatoes." No publisher's device on copyright page. Pages 304-308 are blank. Light brown cloth with dark green lettering and decorations. 5 1/4" x 7 5/8" x 1 1/4". (Published at $1.75.) Ref.a notes that this was the last Doran title to be published without the publisher's device on copyright page $300/1,500

026c: INDISCRETIONS OF ARCHIE George H. Doran NY (1921) [0] Same as 026b but tan cover with green lettering and decorations. 5 1/8" x 7 5/8" x 1 3/8". Pp. 304-314 blank. Also noted in light brown cloth (yellowish brown "Poupon" mustard cloth. 5 1/2" x 7 1/2" x 1 3/8" {Charles E. Gould 3/92}) $150/750

027a: THE GOLDEN MOTH: *A Musical Play of Adventure in Three Acts* No publisher L 1921 [] Book by PGW and Fred Thompson; lyrics by PGW. Special presentation copy bound in full blue morocco. Five known copies (David Mayou 11/91) $1,500.

028a: THE CLICKING OF CUTHBERT Herbert Jenkins L 1922 [0] 8 titles on half-title verso beginning with *Piccadilly Jim* and ending with *The Girl on the Boat*. Priced "3/6 net" on front flap (ref.b incorrectly calls for "7s6d"). Sage-green pictorial cloth. (Second printing was also issued in 1922 but in sage-green pebbled cloth) $250/1,500

028b: GOLF WITHOUT TEARS George H. Doran NY (1924) [5] New title. 8 titles opposite title page ending with *A Damsel in Distress*. Ref.a notes that text rewritten to "convert English scenes to American ones." (Published at $2.50) $250/1,750

028c: THE CLICKING OF CUTHBERT Redpath Press (Minneapolis) 1986 [0] Wraps. First separate edition. Issued in envelope (ref.c) $25.

029a: THREE MEN AND A MAID George H. Doran NY (1922) [5] 4 titles (beginning with *Three Men and a Maid* and ending with *A Damsel in Distress* on verso of half-title. (Published April 26, 1922 at $1.75) $300/1,500

029b: THE GIRL ON THE BOAT Herbert Jenkins L 1922 [0] New title. 8 titles on half-title verso beginning with *Piccadilly Jim* and ending with *The Clicking of Cuthbert*. Ads on pp313-320. (Published at 7s6d) $400/2,000

030a: THE ADVENTURES OF SALLY Herbert Jenkins L 1923 [0] 9 titles on half-title verso beginning with *Piccadilly Jim* and ending with *The Girl on the Boat*. Ads on pp.313-321. (Actually published in 1922 at 7s6d) $350/1,750

030b: MOSTLY SALLY George H. Doran NY (1923) [5] New title. 5 titles on verso of half-title ending with *A Damsel in Distress*. (Published at $2) $250/1,500

031a: THE INIMITABLE JEEVES Herbert Jenkins L 1923 [0] 10 titles listed on half-title verso ending with *The Clicking of Cuthbert*. (Published at 3s6d) $250/1,750

031b: JEEVES George H. Doran NY (1923) [5] New title. (Published at $2) $250/1,750

032a: LEAVE IT TO PSMITH Herbert Jenkins L 1924 [0] 11 titles on half-title verso beginning with

Adventures of Sally and ending with *Love Among the Chickens*. Green cloth with dark green lettering. (Published at 7s6d.) (Red-orange cloth variant {Limestone Hills 10/91}) $250/1,750

032b: LEAVE IT TO PSMITH   George H. Doran NY (1924) [5] (Published at $2) $150/750

033a: UKRIDGE Herbert Jenkins L 1924 [0] 13 titles on half-title verso beginning *A Damsel in Distress* and ending with *Leave it to Psmith*. (Published at 7s6d per ref.a, which states the dustwrapper had "3'6 Net" on spine on green label? David Mayou believes 3'6 is right as the *English Catalogue of Books* for 1924 lists this price.) (Note: the "Popular Edition" (on copyright page) dustwrapper is priced at 3s6d. Both came out in June of 1924) $150/1,750

033b: HE RATHER ENJOYED IT   George H. Doran NY (1926) [5] New title. (Published at $2) $150/850

034a: BILL THE CONQUEROR Methuen & Co. L (1924) [1] 10,109 cc (publisher's records) (includes 2,000 Colonial cloth, 850 Colonial wraps and 520 for Goodchild (Canada or Australia??). Advertisements inserted are dated "924" (9/24) on last page. (Published at 7s6d.) $250/1,500

034b: BILL THE CONQUEROR George H. Doran NY (1925) [5] (Published at $2) $150/650

035a: CARRY ON JEEVES Herbert Jenkins L 1925 [0] 13 titles on half-title verso ending with *The Coming of Bill*. (Published at 3s6d) $175/1,000

035b: CARRY ON JEEVES George H. Doran NY (1927) [5] (Published at $2) $125/1,000

036a: SAM THE SUDDEN   Methuen & Co. L (1925) [1] 20,020 copies (publisher's records) (includes 2,500 Colonial cloth, 1,000 Colonial wraps, 1,300 for Goodchild, 590 used on the "3/6" priced "Cheap" or "Popular Edition" edition). (Published October 15, 1925 at 7s6d.) Ads inserted (there are two states noted with "825" and "1125" bottom of p.8 at the bottom of ads, assume "825" precedes {ref.c}). $200/1,250

036b: SAM IN THE SUBURBS George H. Doran NY (1925) [5] (Published at $2) $125/600

037a: THE HEART OF A GOOF Herbert Jenkins L 1926 [0] 14 titles on half-title verso ending with *The Coming of Bill*. P.315-18 advertisements. (Published at 7s6d) $200/1,500

037b: DIVOTS George H. Doran NY (1927) [5] New title. (Published at $2.50) $175/850

038a: THE PLAY'S THE THING Brentano's NY 1927   [] First separate appearance of PGW's adaptation of Ferenc Molnar's work. (Published at $2) $75/350

039a: THE SMALL BACHELOR Methuen & Co. L (1927) [1]   20,000 cc (publisher's records) (includes 2,500 Colonial cloth, 1,000 Colonial wraps, 1,300 McClelland and 590 used in "3/6" edition). Blue cloth (variants also noted in orange and tan cloths). 8 pages of ads inserted at rear with "327" last page of advertisements (ref.c). $250/1,500

039b: THE SMALL BACHELOR George H. Doran   NY (1927) [5] (Published at $2.) Dustwrapper front flap lists 10 titles beginning with *Harmer John* and ending *Pearl Hunger* and back flap list 10 titles beginning *Young Anarchy* and ending *Ironical Tales*. (Copy catalogued with "different listings of other books on both flaps" {Nigel Williams 2/94 at £425}, we assume this was a later dustwrapper) $125/750

039c: THE SMALL BACHELOR McClelland & Stewart Toronto [1927] [] 1,300 cc. English sheets $100/500

040a: MEET MR. MULLINER Herbert Jenkins L (1927) [1] Advertisements on p.313-320. (Published at 7s6d) $150/1,250

040b: MEET MR. MULLINER Doubleday, Doran & Co. GC 1928 [1] (Published at $2) $150/750

041a: MONEY FOR NOTHING Herbert Jenkins L (1928) [1] Advertisements on p.313-320. (Published at 7s6d) $200/1,000

041b: MONEY FOR NOTHING Doubleday Doran GC 1928 [1] (Published at $2) $100/600

042a: MR. MULLINER SPEAKING Herbert Jenkins L (1929) [1] 18 titles on half-title verso. Orange cloth, black letters. (Published at 7s6d.) Rear flap of dustwrapper lists 11 books by Wyndham Martin (10 books by Martin {Nigel Williams 8/93}) $200/1,000

042b: MR. MULLINER SPEAKING Doubleday Doran GC 1930 [1] (Published at $2) $100/600

043a: FISH PREFERRED Doubleday Doran GC 1929 [1] (Published July 1, 1929 at $2) $100/600

043b: SUMMER LIGHTNING Herbert Jenkins L (1929) [1] New title. (Published July 19, 1929 at 7s6d.) $150/750

044a: VERY GOOD JEEVES Doubleday Doran GC 1930 [1] (Published at $1) $150/750

044b: VERY GOOD JEEVES Herbert Jenkins L (1930) [1] (Published at 7s6d). Adds new preface $200/1,000

045a: BIG MONEY Doubleday Doran GC 1931 [1] (Published at $2) $100/450

045b: BIG MONEY Herbert Jenkins L (1931) [1] (Published at 7s6d) $175/1,000

045c: BIG MONEY   McClelland & Stewart
Toronto [1931] [] $60/300

046a: JEEVES OMNIBUS Herbert Jenkins L 1931
[] $250/1,250

047a: IF I WERE YOU   Doubleday Doran   GC
1931 [1] Orange cloth spine with red-brown
lettering. (Published at $2.) Dustwrapper usually
faded, at least somewhat; unfaded would be more $150/750

047b: IF I WERE YOU Herbert Jenkins L (1931)
[1] (Published at 3s6d) $200/1,750

048a: LOUDER AND FUNNIER Faber & Faber L
(1932) [] Uncorrected proof in plain wraps (Pepper
& Stern 2/92) $1,500.

048b: LOUDER AND FUNNIER Faber and Faber
L (1932) [1] Whistler dustwrapper. First issue-
golden-yellow with gold lettering on spine (ref.a)
but notes that both David Jasen and Charles Gould
do not agree. They call for blue-green letters; while
Barry Phelps calls for silver metallic lettering which
often turns blue-green. The copy in the British
Library has gold lettering. (Published at 3s6d) $250/1,750

049a: DOCTOR SALLY Methuen & Co. L (1932)
[1] 10,046 cc (publisher's records). Blue cloth,
black letters. Advertisements inserted at rear with
"232" on last page of ads (ref.c). Ref.a notes "it is
possible that first issue does not have an advertising
supplement." (Published at 3s6d) $200/1,500

050a: NOTHING BUT WODEHOUSE Doubleday,
Doran GC 1932 [1] (Published at $2.39) $50/250

051a: HOT WATER Herbert Jenkirs L (1932) [1]
8 pages of advertisements inserted at rear.
(Published at 7s6d. However, advance review copy
had "2'6 net" on spine but listed price of Hot Water
correctly at "7/6") $175/1,250

051b: HOT WATER Doubleday Doran GC 1932
[1] (Published at $2) $100/650

052a: MULLINER NIGHTS Herbert Jenkins L
(1933) [1] 8 pages of advertisements inserted at
rear. (Published at 7s6d) $150/950

052b: MULLINER NIGHTS Doubleday Doran
GC 1933 [1] (Published at $2) $100/500

052c: MULLINER NIGHTS McClelland &
Stewart T 1933 [] $50/250

053a: THE GREAT SERMON HANDICAP
Hodder and Stoughton L (1933) [0] Red paper
(imitation leather) cover in dustwrapper ("Little
Books of Laughter"). 3" x 4 3/4". (Published at 9s) $250/1,500

053b: THE GREAT SERMON HANDICAP St.
Hugh's Press L no date [1949] [] Green brittle
cover $40/200

053c: THE GREAT SERMON HANDICAP
Heineman NY 1983 [2] 500 cc in wraps $50.

054a: HEAVY WEATHER Little Brown & Co.
Boston 1933 [1] 12,000 cc (publisher's records).
"Published July 1933" on copyright page.
(Published at $2) $75/600

054b: HEAVY WEATHER Herbert Jenkins L
(1933) [1] (Published at 7s6d) $150/1,000

054c: HEAVY WEATHER McClelland & Stewart
T 1933 [] $50/250

055a: CANDLE-LIGHT Samuel French NY/LA/L
(1934) [ ] Wraps. Siegfried Geyer's work adapted
by PGW. Advertisements at rear begin with
Berkeley Square and end with *Farmer's Wife.*
(Published at $2) $100.

056a: P.G. WODEHOUSE (METHUEN'S LIBRARY OF HUMOUR) Methuen L (1934) [1] $30/150

057a: THANK YOU, JEEVES Herbert Jenkins L 1934 [1]   8 pages of advertisements at rear. (Published at 7s6d.) $250/1,000

057b: THANK YOU, JEEVES Little Brown & Co. Boston 1934 [1] 12,000 cc (publisher's records). "Published April 1934" on copyright page. (Published at $2) $100/500

058a: RIGHT HO, JEEVES Herbert Jenkins L 1934 [0] 8 pages of advertisements at rear. Stone gray cloth with red lettering. (Published at 7s6d) $250/1,250

058b: BRINKLEY MANOR Little Brown & Co. Boston 1934 [1] 12,000 cc (publisher's records). New title. "Published October 1934" on copyright page. (Published at $2) $60/400

058c: RIGHT HO, JEEVES McClelland & Stewart (T) 1933 [] $50/250

059a: BLANDINGS CASTLE Herbert Jenkins L (1935) [1] 8 pages of advertisements at rear. (Published at 7s6d). Torquoise cloth, reissued in blue and in orange cloth $200/1,250

059b: BLANDINGS CASTLE Doubleday Doran GC 1935 [1] Green cloth, reissued in orange cloth (first edition still on copyright page) $75/500

ENTER PSMITH see item 012

060a: MULLINER OMNIBUS Herbert Jenkins L 1935 [] $75/400

060b: MULLINER OMNIBUS Taplinger/Arnold Lent NY (1974) [1] $25/125

061a: THE LUCK OF THE BODKINS Herbert Jenkins L (1935) [1] "First printing 1935" on copyright page. Red cloth (variant is in orange cloth and has "First printing 1935" on copyright page). 8 pages of advertisements at rear. (Published at 7s6d) $100/600

061b: THE LUCK OF THE BODKINS   Little Brown & Co.   Boston 1936 [1] 12,000 cc (publisher's records). "Published January 1936" on copyright page. (Published at $2). (Text differs somewhat from the UK edition) $50/250

061c: THE LUCK OF THE BODKINS McClelland & Stewart T 1935 [] $40/200

062a: YOUNG MEN IN SPATS Herbert Jenkins L (1936) [1] Blue-green cloth. 29 titles on front flap of dustwrapper beginning with *Heavy Weather* at 2/6 net and ending with *Jeeves Omnibus* at 7/6 net. Back flap lists 19 titles by Wyndham Martyn ending with *Spies of Peace* at 7/6 net. Variant in orange cloth (Charles Gould) $150/850

062b: YOUNG MEN IN SPATS Doubleday Doran GC 1936 [1] Nine stories from English edition plus three others $100/600

062c: YOUNG MAN IN SPATS   McClelland & Stewart T 1936 [] $50/250

063a: LAUGHING GAS Herbert Jenkins L (1936) [1] 8 pages of advertisements at rear. Purple-red cloth, black letters. (Variant bindings in maroon and in stone-gray cloth {Barry Phelps}, orange boards {Nigel Williams 11/94}. (Published at 7s6d) $150/1,000

063b: LAUGHING GAS Doubleday Doran GC 1936 [1] (Published at $2) $75/500

064a: LORD EMSWORTH AND OTHERS Herbert Jenkins L (1937) [1] 8 pages of advertisements at rear. Bright red cloth with black letters (variant in gray boards with red letters). (Published at 7s6d) $175/1,250

065a: CRIME WAVE AT BLANDINGS Doubleday Doran GC 1937 [1] (Published at $2) $60/300

066a: SUMMER MOONSHINE Doubleday Doran GC 1937 [1] $75/400

066b: SUMMER MOONSHINE Herbert Jenkins L (1938) [1] 8 pages of advertisements at rear. Red cloth, black letters. (Published at 7s6d) $100/650

067a: THE CODE OF THE WOOSTERS Doubleday Doran GC 1938 [1] (Published at $2) $75/450

067b: THE CODE OF THE WOOSTERS Herbert Jenkins L (1938) [1] Green cloth lettered in black. Three variants noted: stone-gray cloth with red lettering, orange cloth with black lettering, and turquoise cloth. (Published at 7s6d) $150/850

068a: THE WEEK-END WODEHOUSE Doubleday, Doran NY 1939 [1] $40/200

068b: WEEK-END WODEHOUSE Herbert Jenkins L (1939) [0] Adds introduction by Hilaire Belloc $60/300

069a: UNCLE FRED IN THE SPRINGTIME Doubleday Doran NY 1939 [1] (Published at $2) $50/350

069b: UNCLE FRED IN THE SPRINGTIME Herbert Jenkins L (1939) [1] Dark red cloth. List of Works of PGW at rear. Reissued both in orange cloth and in turquoise, still stating "First printing 1939" but with different "advertisements at rear. (Published at 7s6d) $100/850

069c: UNCLE FRED IN SPRINGTIME McClelland & Stewart T 1939 [] $40/200

070a: EGGS BEANS AND CRUMPETS Herbert Jenkins L (1940) [1] 3 pages of advertisements for PGW books at rear. (Published at 7s6d). $150/1,000

070b: EGGS BEANS AND CRUMPETS
Doubleday Doran NY 1940 [1] (Published at $2) $50/300

071a: WODEHOUSE ON GOLF Doubleday Doran
NY 1940 [1] (Published at $2.50) $75/400

072a: QUICK SERVICE Herbert Jenkins L (1940)
[1]   Dark red cloth, gold lettering. 3 pages of
advertisements at rear. Front dustwrapper flap lists
18 PGW titles and rear flap lists 22. (Published at
7s6d.) (Variants still stating "First printing 1940"
were noted in orange covers with black lettering;
and turquoise with red lettering but both have 4
pages of advertisements at rear. Variant
dustwrapper noted (Nigel Williams 11/94) in which
the information on the flaps is correct but reversed
(the books which should be listed on the front flap
are on the rear flap and vice versa) $75/450

072b: QUICK SERVICE Doubleday Doran GC
1940 [1] First issue dustwrapper has 5 titles
beginning *John Brown's Cousin* and ending *The
Bright Pavilions* on rear panel. (Published at $2) $35/250

072c: QUICK SERVICE Doubleday Doran GC
1940 [1] Second issue dustwrapper with 6 titles
beginning with *Up at the Villa* and ending with
Oliver Wiswell on rear panel $35/175

072d: QUICK SERVICE Longman Green T
(1941) [1] $30/150

073a: MONEY IN THE BANK Doubleday Doran
GC 1942 [1] (Published at $2) $50/350

073b: MONEY IN THE BANK Herbert Jenkins
St. James (1946) [1] Orange cloth, black letters
printed by Wyman & Sons Ltd. First issue
dustwrapper by Frank Ford $50/350

074a: JOY IN THE MORNING Doubleday & Co.
GC 1946 [1] (Published at $2) $40/200

074b: JOY IN THE MORNING Herbert Jenkins L
(1947) [1] (Published at 8s6d) $40/250

075a: FULL MOON   Doubleday & Co. GC 1947
[1] (Published at $2) $35/175

075b: FULL MOON Herbert Jenkins L (1947) [1]
Printed by Wyman & Sons Ltd. (Published at 8s6d) $35/175

076a: SPRING FEVER Doubleday & Co. GC 1948
[1] (Published at $2.44.) Published simultaneously
with U.K. edition $30/150

076b: SPRING FEVER Herbert Jenkins L (1948)
[1] (Published at 8s6d.) Published simultaneously
with U.S. edition $35/175

077a: UNCLE DYNAMITE   Herbert Jenkins L
(1948) [1] Orange-red cloth. Reissued in orange-
yellow cloth for the Cheap Edition $60/300

077b: UNCLE DYNAMITE Didier NY (1948) [0]
(Published at $2.95.) First issue dustwrapper has
advertisements for other Didier books on back flap
in lieu of reviews of this book (ref.c) $60/300

077c: UNCLE DYNAMITE Didier NY (1948) [0]
In second issue dustwrapper with reviews of this
book $60/200

078a: THE MATING SEASON Herbert Jenkins L
(1949) [1] Orange cloth, black letters. (Published at
8s6d.) Reissued in orange-yellow cloth for the
Cheap Edition $50/250

078b: THE MATING SEASON Didier NY (1949)
[0] (Published at $2.95) $40/200

079a: THE BEST OF P.G. WODEHOUSE Pocket
Books NY (1949) [1] Wraps. Edited by Scott
Meredith $75.

080a: NOTHING SERIOUS Herbert Jenkins L
(1950) [1] Light orange (almost yellow orange)
cloth. (Published at 8s6d.) Reissued in bright orange
cloth for the Cheap Edition $50/250

080b: NOTHING SERIOUS Doubleday & Co. GC
1951 [1] (Published at $2.50) $30/150

081a: THE OLD RELIABLE Herbert Jenkins L
(1951) [1] (Published at 9s6d) $50/250

081b: THE OLD RELIABLE Doubleday & Co.
GC 1951 [1] (Published at $2.75) $30/150

082a: THE BEST OF MODERN HUMOR Medill
McBride NY (1951) [0] Edited by PGW and Scott
Meredith with general introduction by PGW $25/125

083a: BARMY IN WONDERLAND   Herbert
Jenkins L (1952) [1] (Published at 9s6d.) $40/200

083b: ANGEL CAKE Doubleday & Co. GC 1952
[1] New title. (Published at $2.75) $30/150

084a: PIGS HAVE WINGS Doubleday & Co. GC
1952 [1] (Published at $2.75) $30/150

084b: PIGS HAVE WINGS Herbert Jenkins L
(1952) [1] (Published at 9s6d) $40/225

085a: THE WEEK-END BOOK OF HUMOR Ives
Washburn NY (1952) [0] Selected by PGW and
Scott Meredith, general introduction by PGW $25/125

085b: THE WEEK-END BOOK OF HUMOUR
Herbert Jenkins L (1954) [1] $25/125

086a: RING FOR JEEVES Herbert Jenkins L
(1953) [1] (Published at 9s6d.) $50/250

086b: THE RETURN OF JEEVES Simon and
Schuster NY 1954 [1] 6,000 cc (publisher's re-

cords). New title. (Text revised from English edition) | $50/200

MIKE AT WRYKYN and MIKE and PSMITH see item 12

087a: BRING ON THE GIRLS   Simon and Schuster   NY 1953 [1] 10,000 cc (publisher's records). (Published at $3.95) | $25/125

087b: BRING ON THE GIRLS Herbert Jenkins L (1954) [1] Revised and different photographs. Ref.a notes that the text rewritten "to emphasize London productions." (Published at 16s) | $35/175

088a: PERFORMING FLEA   Herbert Jenkins L (1953) [1] (Published at 12s6d.) (Second printing dustwrapper is identical to first) | $45/225

088b: AUTHOR! AUTHOR! Simon and Schuster NY 1962 [1] New title. (Published at $4.50) | $30/150

088c: PERFORMING FLEA Penguin (L 1961) [1] Wraps. Expanded to include complete texts of Berlin Broadcasts (first book publication) | $40.

089a: JEEVES AND THE FEUDAL SPIRIT Herbert Jenkins L (1954) [1] (Published at 9s6d.) (Cheap Edition was printed in 1957 at 6s) | $40/200

089b: BERTIE WOOSTER SEES IT THROUGH Simon and Schuster   NY 1955 [1] 9,000 cc (publisher's records). New title. Tannish-ivory cloth spine and gray-green boards. Variant in Gray-blue cloth spine and boards. Contains a four page dedication not in U.K. edition (ref.c). | $35/175

090a: FRENCH LEAVE Herbert Jenkins L (1956) [1] "First Published 1955" on copyright page but actually January 20, 1956. (Published at 10s6d.) Cheap Edition not published until 1958 at 6s. | $25/125

090b: FRENCH LEAVE Simon and Schuster NY 1959 [1] 10,000 cc (publisher's records). (Published at $3.50) $20/100

091a: AMERICA I LIKE YOU Simon and Schuster NY 1956 [1] Illustrated by Marc Simon. (Published at $3.50) $30/150

091b: OVER SEVENTY Herbert Jenkins L (1957) [1] New title. (Published at 16s) $30/150

092a: SOMETHING FISHY Herbert Jenkins L (1957) [1] Red cloth, black letters, dustwrapper advertisement for Autographed Editions lists 11 titles on first dustwrapper (ref.c). Also noted in purplish binding (Charles E. Gould 10/90), described as maroon-ochre paper-covered boards (Barry Phelps) $25/125

092b: THE BUTLER DID IT Simon and Schuster NY 1957 [1] 7,500 cc (publisher's records). New title. (Published at $3.50) $35/125

093a: COCKTAIL TIME Herbert Jenkins L (1958) [1] (Published at 12s6d.) Bright red cloth. Variants in blue cover with gold letters and in white cover with black lettering on spine. Another variant in blue boards lettered in black (Nigel Williams 11/94; not in ref-a). White boards (ref. b) $30/150

093b: COCKTAIL TIME Simon and Schuster NY 1958 [1] 8,000 cc (publisher's records). (Published at $3.50) $25/125

094a: SELECTED STORIES OF P.G. WODEHOUSE Modern Library (NY 1958) [0] Stated first not seen (George Andes' *A Descriptive Bibliography of The Modern Library...* 1989) $20/100

095a: A FEW QUICK ONES Simon and Schuster NY 1959 [1] 7,500 cc (publisher's records). (Published at $3.50) $30/150

095b: A FEW QUICK ONES Herbert Jenkins L (1959) [1]   Red cloth. Priced at 12/6 net. Dustwrapper lists 20 titles beginning with *Hot Water* and ending *If I Were You*. Contains one story not in U.S. edition (*A Tithe for Charity*). Later issue/printing dustwrappers are priced lower. Book reissued several times: black boards with gold lettering, yellow cover with black lettering, dark blue cover with black lettering and dark blue cover with gold lettering. Contains one story not in U.S. edition $35/175

096a: THE MOST OF P.G. WODEHOUSE Simon & Schuster NY 1960 [1] 1,000 cc signed "Best wishes P.G. Wodehouse" for Kroch and Brentano's First Edition Circle (Barry Phelps biography of Wodehouse, p.195, although, we could find no record of one being cataloged in the last six years which seems unlikely) $NVA

096b: THE MOST OF P.G. WODEHOUSE Simon & Schuster NY 1960 [1] $25/100

097a: HOW RIGHT YOU ARE JEEVES Simon and Schuster NY 1960 [1] 10,000 cc (publisher's records). (Published at $3.50) $25/125

097b: JEEVES IN THE OFFING Herbert Jenkins L (1960) [1] New title. (Published at 13s6d.) First issue: half-title for *A Few Quick Ones*. Red cloth, gold lettering. Dustwrapper laminated $40/200

097c: JEEVES IN THE OFFING Herbert Jenkins L (1960) [1] (Published at 13s6d.) Second issue: half-title corrected. Variant in gold cover with black lettering (dustwrapper lacks lamination) $25/125

098a: THE ICE IN THE BEDROOM Simon and Schuster   NY 1961 [1] 8,000 cc (publisher's records). (Published at $3.75) $25/125

098b: ICE IN THE BEDROOM Herbert Jenkins L (1961) [1] Bright red buckram with gold lettering.

First dustwrapper has "Wodehouse" in yellow, publisher's name in black on back panel. (Reissue is in red buckram with black lettering, dustwrapper Wodehouse in white with publisher's name in blue $25/125

099a: SERVICE WITH A SMILE   Simon and Schuster   NY 1961 [1] 8,750 cc (publisher's records, ref. a states 10,000 cc). (Published at $3.75) $20/100

099b: SERVICE WITH A SMILE Herbert Jenkins L (1962) [1] Red buckram with gold lettering. Variant in red buckram with black lettering. Dustwrapper has 28 titles in list of Autograph Editions. Published at 13s6d. (Reissued in blue boards with gold lettering, dustwrapper has 41 titles in list of Autograph Editions) $20/100

AUTHOR AUTHOR see item 082b

100a: STIFF UPPER LIP, JEEVES   Simon and Schuster   NY 1963 [1] 8,500 cc (publisher's records). (Published at $3.95) $25/125

100b: STIFF UPPER LIP, JEEVES   Herbert Jenkins   L (1963) [1] Red buckram with gold lettering. 32 titles in Autograph Edition beginning with *Hot Water* and ending *Ukridge*. (Reissued in blue boards with black lettering, light gray boards with black lettering, and beige boards with black lettering $25/125

101a: BIFFEN'S MILLIONS Simon and Schuster NY 1964 [1] 9,000 cc (a&b. Publisher's records). Bright yellow buckram. Author's first initials given as "P.J." on spine. (Published at $4.50) $40/100

101b: BIFFEN'S MILLIONS Simon and Schuster NY 1964 [1] Spine corrected to "P.G." (less common per John Graham) $12/60

101c: FROZEN ASSETS Herbert Jenkins L (1964) [1] New title. Pink-red boards, gold letters. Dustwrapper lists 36 titles. No reviews on front flap $25/125

102a: THE BRINKMANSHIP OF GALAHAD THREEPWOOD Simon & Schuster NY (1965) [1] 9,000 cc (publisher's records). (Published at $4.50) $25/100

102b: GALAHAD AT BLANDINGS Herbert Jenkins L (1965) [1] New title. (Published at 16s). Dustwrapper lists 38 titles on back panel $30/150

103a: PLUM PIE Herbert Jenkins L (1966) [1] (Published at 25s) $25/125

103b: PLUM PIE Simon & Schuster NY (1967) [1] 8,500 cc (publisher's records). (Published at $4.95) $20/100

104a: THE PURLOINED PAPERWEIGHT Simon & Schuster NY (1967) [1] 10,000 cc (publisher's records). (Published at $4.50) $20/100

104b: COMPANY FOR HENRY Herbert Jenkins L (1967) [1] New title. (Published at 21s.) Rust colored cloth with white lettering. Variant in black boards with goldlettering (Charles Gould 10/94) $20/100

105a: THE WORLD OF JEEVES Herbert Jenkins L 1967 [] $25/100

105b: THE WORLD OF JEEVES Harper NY (1988) [0] Perennial Library $25/75

106a: DO BUTLERS BURGLE BANKS? Simon & Schuster NY (1968) [1] 11,000 cc (publisher's records, ref. a states 10,000 cc). (Published at $4.50) $15/75

106b: DO BUTLERS BURGLE BANKS? Herbert Jenkins L (1968) [1] (Published at 21s.) Green buckram with silver letters $15/75

MIKE AT WRYKYN see item 012e

107a: A PELICAN AT BLANDINGS Herbert Jenkins L (1969) [1] (Published at 25s) Black cloth, silver letters $20/100

107b: NO NUDES IS GOOD NUDES Simon & Schuster NY (1970) [1] 10,000 cc (publisher's records). New title. (Published at $4.95) $15/75

108a: THE GIRL IN BLUE Barrie & Jenkins L (1970) [1] (Published at 26s) $25/125

108b: THE GIRL IN BLUE Simon & Schuster NY (1971) [1] 11,000 cc (publisher's records). (Published at $5.95) $15/75

109a: MUCH OBLIGED, JEEVES Barrie & Jenkins L (1971) [1] (Published at £1.60) $30/150

109b: JEEVES AND THE TIE THAT BINDS Simon & Schuster NY (1971) [1] 15,000 cc (publisher's records). New title. (Published at $5.) Ref.a notes that PGW's editor at S&S "gave the American editions its title and rewrote the last page to reconcile the change" $15/75

110a: PEARLS, GIRLS AND MONTY BODKIN Barrie & Jenkins L (1972) [1] (Published at £2.20) $20/100

110b: THE PLOT THAT THICKENED Simon & Schuster NY (1973) [3] 15,000 cc (publisher's records). New title. (Published at $6.95) $15/75

111a: THE WORLD OF MR. MULLINER Barrie & Jenkins L 1972 [] $25/100

111b: THE WORLD OF MR. MULLINER Taplinger NY (1974) [1] $25/75

112a: THE GOLF OMNIBUS Barrie & Jenkins L 1973 [] $25/125

112b: THE GOLF OMNIBUS Simon & Schuster NY 1974 [] $25/100

113a: BACHELORS ANONYMOUS Barrie & Jenkins L (1973) [1] (Published at £1.95) $15/75

113b: BACHELORS ANONYMOUS   Simon &
Schuster   NY (1974) [3] 16,000 cc (publisher's
records). (Published at $6.95) $12/60

114a: THE WORLD OF PSMITH   Barrie &
Jenkins L (1974) [1] (Published at £3.50) $25/100

115a: AUNTS AREN'T GENTLEMEN   Barrie &
Jenkins   L (1974) [1] (Published at £2.25.)
Dustwrapper has brown lettering on spine. Variant
with silver lettering on spine (Charles Gould) $20/100

115b: THE CATNAPPERS Simon & Schuster NY
(1974) [0] 15,000 cc (publisher's records). New
title. (Published at $6.95) $12/60

116a: SON OF BITCH Grossman NY 1974 [1]
"Unleashed by P.G. Wodehouse". Introduction and
only text by P.G.W. Photographs by Elliott Erwitt $25/75

116b: SON OF BITCH   Grossman NY 1974 [1]
Wraps $35.

117a: QUEST Alan Salisbury Somerset 1975 [0]
Unlettered blue wraps $NVA

118a: THE WORLD OF UKRIDGE   Barrie &
Jenkins (L 1975) [1] $25/75

119a: THE UNCOLLECTED WODEHOUSE
Continuum Press L 1976 [] $25/100

119b: THE UNCOLLECTED WODEHOUSE
Seabury Press NY (1976) [0] $15/75

120a: THE WORLD OF BLANDINGS   Barrie &
Jenkins L (1976) [1] $15/75

121a: JEEVES, JEEVES, JEEVES   Avon (NY
1976) [1] First combined edition $15/75

122a: SUNSET AT BLANDINGS   Chatto and
Windus L (1977) [0] (Published at £3.95) $15/75

122b: SUNSET AT BLANDINGS   Simon & Schuster   NY (1977) [3] 13,000 cc (publisher's records) $10/50

123a: VINTAGE WODEHOUSE Barrie & Jenkins (L no date [1978]) [1] Edited by Richard Usborne. Copyright dates are 1977 but actually published in 1978 $12/60

124a: THE WORLD OF MR. MULLINER Barrie & Jenkins L (1978) [] First thus with some new material $15/60

125a: THE SWOOP *And Other Stories* Seabury NY 1979 [0] $20/100

NOT GEORGE WASHINGTON see item 009

126a: THE EIGHTEEN-CARAT KID *And Other Stories* Continuum NY (1980) [0] Edited by David A. Jasen $10/50

127a: LIFE AT BLANDINGS Penguin (L 1981) [1] Wraps. First combined edition $20.

128a: WODEHOUSE   ON   WODEHOUSE Hutchinson L (1980) [1] Contains *Something Fresh, Summer Lightning* and *Heavy Weather* $12/60

129a: WODEHOUSE ON CRIME   Ticknor and Fields NH/NY 1981 [ ] Uncorrected Proof in gray wraps (Bev Chaney, Jr. 9/91) $60.

129b: WODEHOUSE ON CRIME   Ticknor and Fields New Haven/NY 1981 [3] Edited by D.R. Benson. Foreword by isaac Asimov $10/50

130a: LIFE WITH JEEVES Penguin (Middlesex 1981) [1] "This collection published 1981..." $12/60

131a: SOME GEMS No place 1982 [2] 100 cc. Tan stitched wraps (George Houle) $150.

132a: TALES FROM THE DRONES CLUB
Hutchison L (1982) []　　　　　　　　　　　　　　$15/75

133a: FIVE COMPLETE NOVELS Avenel Books
NY (1983) [1] "This 1983 edition is published..."　$12/60

134a: FOUR PLAYS Methuen L 1983 [1]　　　　$15/75

134b: FOUR PLAYS Methuen L 1983 [] Wraps　　$25.

135a: THE WORLD OF UNCLE FRED
Hutchinson L (1983) [1]　　　　　　　　　　　　$15/75

136a: FORE! Ticknor & Fields New Haven/NY
1983 [3] Uncorrected proof in light green wraps.
"Published October 14, 1983"　　　　　　　　　　$75.

136b: FORE! Ticknor & Fields New Haven/NY
1983 [3]　　　　　　　　　　　　　　　　　　　$10/50

136c: FORE! Ticknor & Fields New Haven/NY
1983 [] Wraps　　　　　　　　　　　　　　　　$15.

137a: WODEHOUSE NUGGETS Hutchison L
(1983) [1] Selected by Richard Usborne　　　　　$12/60

137b: WODEHOUSE NUGGETS Heineman NY
(1983) [1] 500 cc. UK sheets with new title page　$10/50

138a: THE WORLD OF THE WODEHOUSE
CLERGY Hutchinson L (1984) [1]　　　　　　　$15/75

139a: SIR AGRAVAINE Blandford Press
Poole/Dorset (1984) [1] First published as part of
The Man Upstairs in 1914. First separate edition　$12/60

140a: SHORT STORIES Folio Society L 1983 [0]
Edited and introduction by Christopher Falkus.
Issued without dustwrapper in plain, unlettered
slipcase　　　　　　　　　　　　　　　　　　$25/60

141a: THE HOLLYWOOD OMNIBUS Hutchinson L (1985) [1] "First published in this collection..." on copyright page $15/75

142a: A WODEHOUSE BESTIARY Ticknor & Fields NY 1985 [] Uncorrected proof in green wraps $75.

142b: A WODEHOUSE BESTIARY Ticknor & Fields NY 1985 [0] $10/50

143a: THE POTHUNTERS AND OTHER SCHOOL STORIES Penguin (L 1986) [1] Wraps $35.

144a: THE GOLD BAT AND OTHER STORIES Penguin (L 1986) [0] Wraps $30.

145a: UNCLE FRED FLITS BY Tales For Travellers NAPA 1987 [0] Map fold to 22 pp., plus covers $25.

146a: THE PARROT + Hutchinson L 1988 [] Introduction by Auberon Waugh. Illustrated by David Langdon $10/50

147a: YOURS, PLUM *The Letters of P. G. Wodehouse* Hutchinson L 1990 [] Uncorrected Proof in pictorial wraps (David Rees 6/95) $60.

147b: YOURS, PLUM *The Letters of P.G. Wodehouse* Hutchinson L 1990 [] Edited by Frances Donaldson $10/40

148a: PRINTER'S ERROR Wodehouse Society (Half Moon Bay) 1990 [2] 250 cc in wraps (Waiting For Godot 6/94) $50.

149a: A MAN OF MEANS Porpoise Books L. 1991 [2] 200 no cc. Written with C.H. Bovill. (Published at £50.) (Nigel Williams 11/94) $150.

150a: PLUM'S PEACHES International Polygonics, Ltd. NY 1991 [] (Charles E. Gould 10/94) $10/50

151a: PLUM STONES *The Hidden P.G. Wodehouse* 1993-1995 Galahad Books L [2] 16 sgd ltr cc (A-P) signed by Tony Ring who wrote all the introductions). "Omnibus Edition" 12 vols. bound in one. In full leather. (Published at £395) $750.

151b: PLUM STONES *The Hidden P. G. Wodehouse 1993-1995* Galahad Books L [2] 234 no cc. (numbered 17-250). The twelve volumes include 25 stories which have never appeared in book form in England (published at £10 each): $300.

(a) Book 1. *Wodehouse, Detective Writer* 1993
(b) Book 2. *Unrepublished Reggie Pepper* 1993
(c) Book 3. *Theatrical Stories* 1994
(d) Book 4. *Keggs, The Butler* 1994
(e) Book 5. *First Impressions; Mature Reflections* 1994
(f) Book 6. *There But For The Grace Of God Goes Baxter* 1994
(g) Book 7. *Self-Deritives Par Excellence* 1994
(h) Book 8. *Bertie's Friends* 1994
(i) Book 9. *"In That Shpae, Rotten"* 1995
(j) Book 10. *Ethics And Eugenics* 1995
(k) Book 11. *Wrykyn Havoc* 1995
(l) Book 12. *First Draft* 1995

REFERENCED DEALERS

REFERENCED DEALERS

Charles Agvent, RD 2, Box 377A, Mertztown, PA 19539

Allen and Patricia Ahearn, see Quill & Brush

Aldredge Book Shop, 2909 #1A Maple Ave., Dallas, TX 75201

Alphabet Bookshop, 145 Main Street West, Port Colborne, Ontario L3K-3V3, Canada

Am Here Books, P.O. Box 574, Philo, CA 95466

American Dust Co., 47 Park Ct., Staten Island, NY 10301

The Americanist, 1525 Shenkel Rd., Pottstown, PA 19464

Ampersand Books, P.O. 674 Cooper Station, New York, NY 10276

Anacapa Books, 3090 Claremont Ave., Berkeley, CA 94705

Anchor & Dolphin, 30 Franklin St., Newport, RI 02840

Annex Books, 1083 Bathurst Street, Toronto, Ontario M5R-3G8, Canada

Hugh Anson-Cartwright, 229 College St., Toronto, Ontario M5T-1R4, Canada

Antic Hay Rare Books, P.O. Box 2185, Asbury Park, NJ 07712

Antipodean Books Maps & Prints, P.O. Box 189, Cold Spring, NY 10516

Any Amount of Books, 62 Charing Cross Road, London WC2H-0BB, United Kingdom

Archer's Used and Rare Books, 104 South Lincoln St., Kent, OH 44240

Argosy Book Store, 116 East 59th St., New York, NY 10022

Artis Books, P.O. Box 822, 210 North Second Ave., Alpena, MI 49707

The Arundel Press, 8380 Beverly Blvd., Los Angeles, CA 90048

Ash Rare Books, 25 Royal Exchange, Threadneedle Street, London EC3V-3LP, United Kingdom

The Associates, P.O. Box 4747, Falls Church, VA 22044

Attic Books, P.O. Box 611136, Port Huron, MI 48061

Authors of the West, 191 Dogwood Dr., Dundee, OR 97115

Bert Babcock, 9 East Derry Rd., P.O. Box 1140, Derry, NH 03038

The Backlist, P.O. Box 791, Doylestown, PA 18901

Bartleby's Books, P.O. Box 15400, Chevy Chase, MD 20825

Bay Side Books, P.O. Box 57, Soquel, CA 95073

Beasley Books, 1533 West Oakdale, Chicago, IL 60657

Gordon Beckhorn, 497 Warburton Ave., Hastings-on-Hudson, NY 10706

Bell, Book & Radmall, 4 Cecil Court, London WC2N-4HE, United Kingdom

Steven C. Bernard, 15011 Plainfield La., Darnestown, MD 20874

Between the Covers, 132 Kings Highway East, Haddonfield, NJ 08033

Biblioctopus, 2142 Century Park Ln., Century City, LA 90067

Bishop of Books, 328 Market St., P.O. Box 579, Steubenville, OH 43952

Black Sun Books, 157 East 57th St., New York, NY 10022

Black-Bird Books, 24 Grampton Gardens, London NW2-1JG, United Kingdom

Blackwell's Rare Books, 38 Holywell Street, Oxford OX1-3SW, United Kingdom

Adam Blakeney, 4/10 Charles Street, London W1X-7BH, United Kingdom

Bolerium Books, 2141 Mission #300, San Francisco, CA 94110

Nelson Bond, 4724 Easthill Dr., Sugarloaf Farms, Roanoak, VA 24018

Book Barn, 41 West Main St., Niantic, CT 06357

The Book Block, 8 Loughlin Ave., Cos Cob, CT 06807

Book Harbor, 201 N. Harbor Blvd., Fullerton, CA 92632

The Book Shelf, 1308 Sussex La., Newport Beach, CA 92660

The Book Treasury, P.O. Box 20033, Long Beach, CA 90801

Bookdales, 406 West 65th St., Richfield, MN 55423

Books & Autographs, 287 Goodwin Rd., Eliot, ME 03903

Books West Southwest, 2452 North Campbell Ave., Tucson, AZ 85719

The Bookshop, 400 West Franklin St., Chapel Hill, NC 27516

Boston Book Company & Book Annex, 705 Centre Ave., Jamaica Plain, MA 02130

Bowie & Company, 314 First Ave. South, Seattle, WN 98104

Marilyn Braiterman, 20 Whitfield Rd., Baltimore, MD 21210

The Brick Row Bookshop, 49 Geary St., Suite 235, San Francisco, CA 94108

Bromer Booksellers, 607 Boylston St., Boston, MA 02116

Buckingham Books, 8058 Stone Bridge Rd., Greencastle, PA 17225

Brian & Margaret Buckley, 11 Convent Close, Kenilworth CV8-2FQ, United Kingdom

Buddenbrooks, 31 Newbury St., Suite 201, Boston, MA 02116

Burke's Book Store, 1719 Poplar Ave., Memphis, TN 38104

Nicholas and Helen Burrows, 136 Engadine Street, London SW18-5DT, United Kingdom

By the Way Books, P.O. Box 1759, Grass Valley, CA 95945

Caliban Book Shop, 416 South Craig St., Pittsburgh, PA 15213

The Captain's Book Shelf, P.O. Box 2258, Asheville, NC 28802-2258

Cardinal Books, 4010 NE 136th St., Vancouver, WA 98686

Bev Chaney, Jr., 73 Croton Ave., Ossining, NY 10562

Chapel Hill Rare Books, P.O. Box 456, Carrboro, NC 27510

Chloe's Books, P.O. Box 2249, Loomis, CA 95650

Clearwater Books, 19 Matlock Road, Ferndown, Wimborne, Dorset BH22- 8QT, United Kingdom

Clover Hill Books, P.O. Box 6278, Charlottesville, VA 22906

Cobbydale Books, 13 Aireville Drive, Silsden, Yorkshire BD20 0H4 United Kingdom

Conundrum, 679 Mayfield Ave., Stanford, CT 94305

Cornstalk Bookshop, P.O. Box 336, Glebe, New South Wales, 2037 Australia

Country Lane Books, P.O. Box 47, Collinsville, CT 06022

N.A. Cournoyer Books, 1194 Bank Street, Ottawa, Ontario K1S-3Y1, Canada

William Cowan Books, Ards Cottage, Connel, Argyle, PA37 JPT, Scotland, United Kingdom

Cultured Oyster Books, P.O. Box 404 Planetarium Station, New York, NY 10024-0404

James Cummins, 699 Madison Ave., New York, NY 10021

L.W. Currey, P.O. Box 187 (Water St.), Elizabethtown, NY 12932

G. Curwen Books, 1 West 67th St. #710, New York, NY 10023

Robert Dagg, 49 Geary Street, Suite 225, San Francisco, CA 94108

William & Victoria Dailey, 8216 Melrose Ave., P.O. Box 69160, Los Angeles, CA 90069

Dalian Books, 81 Albion Drive, London Fields, London E8-4LT, United Kingdom

Tom Davidson, 37-3 Avenue L, Brooklyn, NY 11210

Decline and Fall, P.O. Box 659, Stevens Point, WI 54481

Joseph A. Dermont, 13 Arthur St., P.O. Box 654, Onset, MA 02558

Detering Book Gallery, 2311 Bissonnet, Houston, TX 77005

Dinkytown Antiquarian Bookstore, 1316 SE 4th St., Minneapolis, MN 55414

John Dinsmore & Associates, 1037 Castleton Way South, Lexington, KY 40517

Thomas Dorn, P.O. Box 2585, Decatur, GA 30031-2585

James M. Dourgarian, 1595-A Third Ave., Walnut Creek, CA 94596

Duga's Books, 610 Aldama Ct., Ocoee, FL 32761

Dunn and Powell, The Hideaway, Bar Harbor, ME 04609-1714

I.D. Edrich, 17 Selsdon Road, Wanstead, London E11-2QF, United Kingdom

Francis Edwards, The Old Cinema, Castle Street, Hay-on-Wye, via Herford HR2-5DF United Kingdom

Else Fine Books, P.O. Box 43, Dearborn, MI 48121

William English, 48 Galway House, Radnor St., London EC1V-3SL, United Kingdom

Ergo Books, 46 Lisburne Road, London NW3-2NR, United Kingdom

Euclid Books, 227 Euclid St., Santa Monica, CA 90402

Ferret Fantasy, 27 Beechcroft Road, Upper Tooting, London SW19-7BX, United Kingdom

The Fine Books Co., 781 E. Snell Rd., Rochester, MI 48306

First Folio, 1206 Brentwood, Paris, TX 38242-3804

First Impressions, P.O. Box 889, Orland Park, IL 60462

Fuller & Saunders, 3238 P St., NW, Washington, DC 20007

Robert Gavora, 4514 East Burnside St., Portland, OR 97215

R.A. Gekoski, 15a Bloomsbury Square, London WC1A-2LP, United Kingdom

Thomas A. Goldwasser, 126 Post St., Suite 407, San Francisco, CA 94108-4704

Gotham Book Mart, 41 W. 47th Street, New York, NY 10036

William A. Graf, 717 Clark St., Iowa City, IA 52240-5640

Great Northwest Bookstore, 1234 SW Stark St., Portland, OR 97205

Gravesend Books, P.O. Box 235, Pocono Pines, PA 18350

Hawthorn Books, 7 College Park Drive, Westbury-on-Trym, Bristol BS10 -7AN, United Kingdom

Heirloom Bookstore, 4100 Atlanta Hwy., Bogart, GA 30622

Susan Heller, Box 2200-E, Cleveland, OH 44122

Heritage Bookshop, 8540 Melrose Ave., Los Angeles, CA 90069

The Hermitage Bookshop, 290 Filmore St., Denver, CO 80206

Willis E. Herr, 7004 Camino Pachero, San Diego, CA 92111

Historicana, 1200 Edgehill Dr., Burlingame, CA 94010

Richard L. Hoffman, 420 12th St., Apt. F3R, Brooklyn, NY 11215

David Holloway, 7430 Grace St., Springfield, VA 22150

Holloway's Books, P.O. Box 8294, Dallas, TX 75205

David J. Holmes, 230 South Broad St., 3rd Floor, Philadelphia, PA 19102

Glenn Horowitz, 19 E. 76th St., New York, NY 10021

George Houle, 7260 Beverly Blvd., Los Angeles, CA 90036

John Hudak, 184 Columbia Heights #1D, Brooklyn, NY 11201

In Our Time, P.O. Box 390386, Cambridge, MA 02139

Island Books, P.O. Box 19, Old Westbury, NY 11568

James S. Jaffe, 367 W. Lancaster Ave., Haverford, PA 19041

Janus Books, P.O. Box 40787, Tucson, AZ 85717

Jarndyce Antiquarian Books, 46 Great Russell Street, London, WC1B-3PA United Kingdom

Joseph the Provider Books, 10 West Micheltorena, Santa Barbara, CA 93101

The Jumping Frog, 585 Prospect Ave., W. Hartford, CT 06105

Priscilla Juvelis, 1166 Massachusetts Ave., Cambridge, MA 02138

Kenneth Karmiole, P.O. Box 464, Santa Monica, CA 90406

Katonah Book Scout, 75 Meadow La., Katonah, NY 10536

Keane-Egan Books, P.O. Box 529, State College, PA 16804

Key West Island Bookstore, 513 Fleming St., Key West, FL 33040

Gerry Kleier, 322 Manhattan Dr., Vallejo, CA 94591

John W. Knott, Jr., 8453 Early Bud Way, Laurel, MD 20707

Ralph Kristiansen, P.O. Box 524, Kenmore Station, Boston, MA 02215

Kugleman & Bent, P.O. Box 18292, Denver, CO 80218

Lame Duck Books, 90 Moraine St., Jamaica Plain, MA 02130

Larsen Books, Middle Road, Exeter, New South Wales 2579, Australia

James & Mary Laurie, 921 Nicollet Mall, Minneapolis, MN 55402

John Le Bow, 117 langford Rd., P.O. Box 737, Candia, NH 03034

Leaves of Grass, 2433 Whitmore Lake Rd., Ann Arbor, MI 48103

Barry R. Levin, 720 Santa Monica Blvd., Santa Monica, CA 90401

Limestone Hills Book Shop, P.O. Box 1125, Glen Rose, TX 76043

Robert Loren, Link, Booksellers, P.O. Box 511, Las Cruces, NM 88004

Ken Lopez, 51 Huntington Rd., Hadley, MA 01035

Stephen Lupack, 449 Hanover Ave., S. Meriden, CT 06451

MacDonnell Rare Books, 9307 Glendale Dr., Austin, TX 78730

George S. Macmanus Co., 1317 Irving St., Philadelphia, PA 19017

Robert A. Madle, 4406 Bestor Dr., Rockville, MD 20853

Maggs Brothers Ltd, 50 Berkeley Square, London, W1X-6EL United Kingdom

Magnum Opus, P.O. Box 1301, Charlottesville, VA 22902

Main Street Fine Books & Manuscripts, 301 S. Main St., Galena, IL 61036

David Mason, 342 Queen Street West, 2nd floor, Toronto, M5V 2A2 Canada

Bryan Matthews, 742 North Cherokee Ave., Hollywood, CA 90038

David Mayou, 82 Gordon Road, London, W5 2AR, United Kingdom

McClintock Books, P.O. Box 1949, 1454 Sheridan Ave. NE, Warren, OH 44483

R. McLaughlin, 1613 Monterey Dr., Livermore, CA 94550

McGowan Book Company, P.O. Box 16325, Chapel Hill, NC 27516

Ian McKelvie, 45 Hertford Road, London, N2-9BX United Kingdom

Ming Books, 110 Gloucester Avenue, London, NW1-8JA United Kingdom

George Robert Minkoff, 26 Rowe Rd., Alford, MA 01230

Monroe Books, 359 E. Shaw Ave, Suite 102, Fresno, CA 93710

Hartley Moorhouse Books, 10 Ashchurch Terrace, London, W12-9SL, United Kingdom

Mordida Books, P.O. Box 79322, Houston, TX 77279

S.M. Mossberg, 50 Talcott Rd., Rye Brook, NY 10573

Howard S. Mott, 170 South Main St., P.O. Box 309, Sheffield, MA 02157

Mountain Mysteries, P.O. Box 870966, Stone Mountain, GA 30087

J.B. Muns, 1162 Shattuck Avenue, Berkeley, CA 94707

Mysterious Bookshop, 129 W. 56th St., New York, NY 10019

Nineteenth Century Shop, 1047 Hollins St., Baltimore, MD 21223

Nouveau, P.O. Box 12471, 5005 Meadow Oaks Park Dr., Jackson, MS 39211

Oak Knoll Books, 414 Delaware St., New Castle, DE 19720

October Farm, 2609 Branch Rd., Raleigh , NC 27610

John Oliveri, 104 Goldenwood Ct., Cary, NC 27513

David L. O'Neal, 234 Clarenden St., Boston, MA 02116

James F. O'Neil, 160 Commonwealth Ave., #521, Boston, MA 02116

Old New York Book Shop, 1069 Juniper St. NE, Atlanta, GA 30309

The Old Paperphiles, P.O. Box 135, Tiverton, RI 02878

Orpheus Books, 11522 NE 20th St., Bellevue, WN 98004

Palace Collectibles, 15222 Stradbrook, Houston, TX 77062

Pepper & Stern, 355 Boylston St., 2nd floor, Boston, MA 02116

R. & A. Petrilla, P.O. Box 306, Roosevelt, NJ 08555

Pettler & Lieberman, 8033 Sunset Blvd., #977, Los Angeles, CA 90046

Pharos Books, P.O. Box 17, Fair Haven Sta., New Haven, CT 06513

Phoenix Bookshop South, P.O. Box 1018, St. Michaels, MD 21663

James M. Pickard, Pendragon, 21 Grenfell Road, Leicester, LE2-2PA United Kingdom

Philip J. Pirages, P.O. Box 504, 2205 Nut Tree La., Mc Minnville, OR 97128

Polyanthos Books, 600 Park Ave., P.O. Box 343, Huntington, NY 11743

Nicholas Pounder's Bookshop, P.O. Box 451, Kings Cross, New South Wales, 2011 Australia

Providence Bookstore Cafe, 500 Angell St., Providence, RI 02906

Bernard Quaritch, Ltd, 5-8 Lower John Street, Golden Square, London, W1R- 4AU, United Kingdom

Quill & Brush, P.O. Box 5365, Rockville, MD 20848

Randall House, 835 Laguna St., Santa Barbara, CA 93101

Paul Rassam, Flat 5, 18 East Heath Road, London, NW3-1AJ
    United Kingdom

The Reading Lamp, 24032 79th Place W., Edmonds, WA 98026

David Rees, 18A Prentis Road, London, SW16-1QD United
    Kingdom

William Reese Co., 409 Temple St., New Haven, CT 06511

L.& T. Respess Books, P.O. Box 1604, Charlottesville, VA
    22902

Revere Books, P.O. Box 420, Revere, PA 18953

Alice Robbins, 3002 Roundhill Rd., Greensboro, NC 27408

Robert Frost Books, P.O. Box 719, Rensselear, NY 12144

Charlotte Robinson, 4 Morgan House, 127 Longacre, London,
    WC2E-9AA United Kingdom

B&L Rootenberg, P.O. Box 5049, Sherman Oaks, CA 91403

Bertram Rota, 31 Long Acre, Covent Garden, London, WC2E-
    9LT United Kingdom

The Rue Morgue, P.O. Box 4119, 946 Pearl St., Boulder, CO
    80306

Rykken and Scull, P.O. Box 1979, Guerneville, CA 95446

Schoyer's Books, 1404 S. Negley Ave., Pittsburgh, PA 15217

Bud Schweska, P.O. Box 754010, Parkside Station, Forrest Holls,
    NY 11375

Andrew Sclanders, 11 Albany Road, Stroud Green, London, N4-
    4RR United Kingdom

Second Life Books, P.O. Box 242, 55 Quarry Rd., Lanesborough, MA 01237

Second Story Books, 12160 Parklawn Drive, Rockville, MD 20852

Anthony Sellem, 9 Tackleway, Old Town, Hastings, East Sussex, TN34-3DE United Kingdom

Serendipity Books, 1201 University Ave, Berkeley, CA 94702

Sherwood Fine Books, 5911 East Spring St., Suite 402, Long Beach, CA 90808

Skyline Books, P.O. Box T, Forest Knolls, CA 94933

Monroe Stahr Books, 4420 Ventura Canyon Ave., #2, Sherman Oaks, CA 91423

Strand Book Store, 828 Broadway, New York, NY 10003

Sturford Books, Sturford Mead, Corsley, Warminster, Wiltshire, BA12- 7QT United Kingdom

Summer & Stillman, P.O. Box 973, Yarmouth, ME 04096

Raymond M. Sutton, Jr., 430 Main St., P.O. Box 30, Williamsburg, KY 40769

Sylvester & Orphanos, 2484 Cheremoya Ave., P.O. Box 2567, Los Angeles, CA 90078-2567

Tall Stories, 2141 Mission St., Suite 301, San Francisco, CA 94110

Tall Tales, 1551 San Pablo Ave., Oakland, CA 94612

Tamerlane Books, P.O. Box C, Havertown, PA 19083

Taugher Books, 2550 Somerset Dr., Belmont, CA 94002-2926

Robert Temple, 65 Mildway Road, London, N1-4PU United Kingdom

Steven Temple Books, 489 Queen Street West, Toronto, Ontario, M5V-2B4 Canada

Michael R. Thompson, 8312 West Third St., Los Angeles, CA 90048

Michael Thompson, 311 W. Cordova St., Vancouver, British Columbia, V6B- 1E5 Canada

Thorn Books, 624 Moorpark Ave., P.O. Box 1244, Moorpark, CA 93020

TLC Books, 9 N. College Ave., Salem, VA 34153

Henry E. Turlington, P.O. Box 848, Carrboro, NC 27510

Turtle Island Booksellers, 2067 Center St., Berkeley, CA 94704

Tuttle Antiquarian Books, Inc., 26 S. Main St., P.O. Box 541, Rutland, VT 05702

Ulysses Bookshop, 31 & 40 Museum Street, London, WC1A-1LH United Kingdom

Len Unger Rare Books, P.O. Box 5858, Sherman Oaks, CA 91413

Vagabond Books, 2076 Westwood Blvd., Los Angeles, CA 90025

The Veatchs, 20 Veronica Ct., Smithtown, NY 11787

Versetility Books, P.O. Box 1366, Burlington, CT, 06013

Virgo Books, "Little Court", South Wraxall, Bradford-on-Avon, Wilts., BA15 2SE United Kingdom

Waiting for Godot Books, P.O. Box 331, Hadley, MA 01035

Rob Warren, 13 W. 18th St., New York, NY 10011

Water Row Books, P.O. Box 438, Sudbury, MA 01776

Watermark West, 149 N. Broadway, Wichita, KS 67202

Waverley Books, 948 9th St., Santa Monica, CA 90403

Wessel & Lieberman, 121 First Avenue South, Seattle, WA 98104

E. Wharton & Co., 3232 History Dr., Oakton, VA 22124

Wheldon & Wesley, Ltd., Lytton Lodge, Codicote, Hitchin, Herts., SG4-8TE United Kingdom

Jett W. Whitehead, 1412 Center Ave., Bay City, MI 48708

Edna Whiteson, 66 Belmont Avenue, Cockfosters, Herts., EN4-9LA United Kingdom

Wilder Books, P.O. Box 762, Elmhurst, IL 60126

Nigel Williams, 7 Waldeck Grove, London, SE27-0BE United Kingdom

John Windle, 49 Geary St., Suite 233, San Francisco, CA 94108

J. Howard Woolmer, 577 Marienstein Road, Revere, PA 18953

Words Etcetera, Hinton Lodge, Crown Road, Marnhull, Dorset, DT10-1DE United Kingdom

Robert Wright Books, 1083 Bathurst St., Toronto, Ontario, M5R-3G8 Canada

Wrigley-Cross Books, 8001 A SE Powell, Portland, OR 97206

Herb Yellin, 10973 Los Alamos St., Northridge, CA 91326

Yesterday's Books, 25625 Southfield Rd., Suite # 104, Southfield, MI 48075

Yesteryear Book Shop, 3201 Maple Dr., NE, Atlanta, GA 30305

Zeno's, 1955 34th Ave, San Francisco, CA 94116